Roseville Public Library
Roseville, California 95678

W9-AUB-318
.__. 003 10 4817

MAI   c.1
364.1523 EVA
Evans, Stewart P.
The ultimate Jack the Ripper
 companion

OCLC: 45368219

MAR   2001

The Ultimate
JACK THE
RIPPER
COMPANION
An Illustrated Encyclopedia

The Ultimate

JACK THE
RIPPER

COMPANION
An Illustrated Encyclopedia

STEWART P. EVANS &
KEITH SKINNER

CARROLL & GRAF PUBLISHERS, INC
New York

Roseville Public Library
Roseville, California 95678

Carroll & Graf Publishers, Inc.
19 West 21st Street
New York
NY 10010–6805

First published in the UK by Robinson 2000

Copyright © Stewart P. Evans and Keith Skinner 2000

All rights reserved. No part of this publication
may be reproduced in any form or by any means
without the prior permission of the publisher.

ISBN 0–7867–0768–2

Printed and bound in the EU

For
Don Rumbelow

Acknowledgments

The invaluable help of the staff at the Public Record Office, Kew, is gratefully acknowledged, as is that of the Corporation of London Record Office, the London Metropolitan Archives (formerly the Greater London Record Office), the Archive and Museum Departments of the Metropolitan Police, The Royal London Hospital Archives and Museum, City of London Police Museum, British Library Newspaper Library, Richard Davie, Paul Mulveg and Mr J. D. Swanson. Acknowledgment is also made to the Controller of Her Majesty's Stationery Office, via the above offices, and we are also grateful for the permission of Her Majesty Queen Elizabeth II for the use of material from The Royal Archives.

Contents

List of Illustrations

Introduction

The main problem encountered in any serious study of the Whitechapel
Murders and the subject of "Jack the Ripper" is the plethora of myth
and misrepresentation that surrounds the case. Although some of this
obfuscation can be traced back to its contemporary origins, most of it
has gradually developed, feeding on itself over the years in books and
other media so that any new student of the crimes understandably begins
their studies with preconceived ideas, either conscious or subconscious,
on the matter.

The huge volume of primary and secondary source material has, over
the years, been accessed and plundered by various authors. First came the
press reports, then, as they became available, the official records. However, although extensively cited and quoted from, the official papers have
never previously been published at length and until now there has been no
one book that serves as a source of contemporary evidence, objectively
presented in detail and with minimum intrusion from the author. What
has been needed is a survey of all the known facts about the murders, free
of modern commentary and interpretation, that will provide an essential
foundation for further research. This book is a compilation of the major
primary sources, indispensable for any writer or researcher tackling this
enigmatic series of killings.

Something that struck us in our compilation of the material was that
we both experienced a totally new "feel" for the case and the social
conditions of the period. We were also aware of just how much
potentially significant detail it is possible to overlook. In some instances
this reshaped our thinking on and perception of various aspects of the
police investigation. Theories about the murders were expounded at the
time, but these were ideas shaped by the contemporary context in which
they were set. Some of them were very unlikely, others perhaps not so,
but they demonstrate the way in which the great mystery took hold of the
intellects of the time, and they reveal the very human desire to find the
answers to an unsolved series of murders that was, even then, of
international interest. The police were under pressure from Home Office

officials who were demanding results from a force already stretched to its limits. Lack of modern forensic science aids was obviously also a telling factor and even the medical experts could not agree.

The extant police and Home Office records on the murders, held at the Public Record Office at Kew (South-West London) and other archives, are vast and impossible to quote in full, as are the newspaper reports. Therefore a degree of selectivity has been imposed, but not in such a way as to affect the value of the relevant source material available: all the main official reports are included in full, for example. These are supplemented by newspaper accounts to provide the details in missing inquest reports. The main arrests made at the time are mentioned, as are the contemporary or near-contemporary suspects. It is left to the reader to interpret the facts and the evidence accordingly.

Transcribing all the handwritten documents has taken many years and has been a difficult task. The reports are of varying quality. Some are damaged. Some are virtually illegible. Some of the handwriting has proved difficult to identify. Often the original documents contain faint annotated marginalia, impossible to detect or discern when examining the files in their preserved microfilmed state. We have, where possible, attempted to include this important detail, by inspecting the original papers ourselves.

This work presents the full factual history of the Whitechapel Murders of 1888–91, chronologically presented and powerfully told by the people who lived in the shadow of "Jack the Ripper". We hope that it will prove a useful and user-friendly companion.

Stewart P. Evans   Keith Skinner
Cambridgeshire   London
June 2000   June 2000

CHAPTER 1

3 April 1888 – Murder of Emma Smith

The crimes of "Jack the Ripper" are so inextricably interwoven with the Whitechapel Murders that often one is mistaken for the other. The reason for this is that the police files on the so-called Whitechapel Murders began with the murder of Emma Smith on 3/4 April 1888, and did not finish until the murder of Frances Coles on 13 February 1891. In all, eleven murders are included in these files and, in the opinion of the authors, as few as three or as many as six may have been the work of a common hand, that of the criminal now known to history as "Jack the Ripper". A full and true picture cannot be obtained without looking at the whole series of murders and the relevant facts that have survived the passage of time to reach us in the twenty-first century. Herein may lie the vital clue as to the identity of the killer – or it may not. If it is not to be found here, then it is very unlikely that we will ever know the identity of this mysterious killer. Here is the raw material available to the historian and interested reader alike. Here are the known facts.

The first file in the police Whitechapel Murders files was that on the murder of Emma Smith, and it is now missing. This file apparently disappeared from the New Scotland Yard files before they were passed to the Public Record Office. It is therefore fortunate that some of the content of this file remains in the form of notes taken from it by Ian Sharp on behalf of the BBC for their television presentation of the "Jack the Ripper" story in 1973. The murder of Emma Elizabeth Smith is thus recognized as the first of the Whitechapel Murders, and she was the victim of a gang of three unknown street robbers. Many press reports later in the year listed "the murder of an unknown woman in Christmas week 1887" as the first of the murders, but extensive research has failed to find this murder. However, a fellow lodger of Smith's, Margaret Hames, was similarly attacked in the same area on 8 December 1887, and was admitted to the Whitechapel infirmary with chest and face injuries. Records[1] held at the London Metropolitan Archives, reveal that she was not released until two days after Boxing Day 1887.

We begin, therefore, with all that survives from the original police reports on the murder of Emma Smith, first of the Whitechapel Murders.

Emma Elizabeth Smith, 18 George Street, Spitalfields. Son and daughter living in Finsbury Park area. She had lodged at the above address for about eighteen months, paying 4d. per night for her bed. She was in the habit of leaving at about 6 or 7 p.m. and returning at all hours, usually drunk.

On the night of 2nd April, 1888, she was seen talking to a man dressed in dark clothes and white scarf, at 12.15 a.m. [*on the 3rd.*] She returned to her lodgings between 4 and 5 a.m. She had been assaulted and robbed in Osborne Street. London Hospital (near Cocoa factory) Messrs. Taylor Bros. She was attended to by Mr. George Haslip, House Surgeon. She died at 9 a.m. on the 4th. The inquest was held by coroner Wynne Baxter at the Hospital.

The first the police knew of this attack was from the Coroner's Officer who reported in the usual manner on the 6th inst. that the inquest would be held on the 7th inst. Chief Inspector West attended. None of the Pc's in the area had heard or seen anything at all, and the streets were said to be quiet at the time.

The offence had been committed on the pathway opposite No. 10 Brick Lane, about 300 yards from 18 George Street, and half a mile from the London Hospital to which deceased walked. She would have passed a number of Pc's en route but none was informed of the incident or asked to render assistance.

The peritoneum had been penetrated by a blunt instrument thrust up the woman's passage, and peritonitis set in which caused death. She was aged 45 years, 5'2" high, complexion fair, hair light brown, scar on right temple. No description of men.

Edmund Reid

Inspr.

A further report by Chief Inspector West was included:

Her head was bruised, right ear torn, rupture of peritoneum. According to statements made by deceased the motive was robbery.

Deceased could not describe the men who had ill-used her but said there were three of them, and that she was attacked about 1.30 a.m. on the 3rd, while passing Whitechapel Church. *Witnesses* Mary Russell, deputy at 18 George Street, Spitalfields; Annie Lee, lodger (these two escorted her to London Hospital); George Haslip and Margaret Hames (lodger at the above address who was last to see her alive.)

Coroner further expressed his intention of forwarding the particulars of the case to the Public Prosecutor as being one requiring further investigation with respect of the person or persons who committed the crime.

Witnesses stated that they didn't think it necessary to report the circumstances to the police. Whole of police on duty deny all knowledge of the occurrence.

Inspector West

Enquiry to be taken up by Inspector Reid.

The newspapers, however, did carry reports of the inquest and the following appeared in the *Morning Advertiser* of Monday, 9 April 1888, page 7:

THE HORRIBLE MURDER IN WHITECHAPEL

Mr. Wynne Baxter held on Saturday morning, at the London Hospital, an inquiry into the circumstances attending the death of an unfortunate, named Emma Eliza Smith, who was assaulted in the most brutal manner early on Tuesday morning in the neighbourhood of Osborn-street, Whitechapel. – Mary Russell, the deputy-keeper of a common lodging-house in George-street, Spitalfields, stated that the deceased, who had lived eighteen months in the house, left home on Monday evening in her usual health and returned between four and five next morning, suffering from horrible injuries. The woman told witness that she had been shockingly ill-treated by some men and robbed of her money. Her face was bleeding and her ear cut. Witness took her at once to the London Hospital, passing through Osborn-street on the way, near a spot close to a cocoa factory, which Smith pointed out as the place where the outrage had been committed. Smith, who seemed unwilling to go into details, did not describe the men nor give any further account of the occurrence to witness. – Dr. G.H. Hillier, the house surgeon in attendance on Tuesday morning, when the deceased was brought in, said the injuries which the woman had received were horrible. A portion of the right ear was torn, and there was a rupture of the peritoneum and other internal organs, caused by some blunt instrument. The account given of the occurrence, by the unfortunate woman to the doctor, was that about half-past one o'clock on Tuesday morning, when near Whitechapel Church, she crossed over the road to avoid some men, who followed, assaulted her, robbed her of all the money she had, and then committed the outrage. There were two or three men, one of them looking like a youth of about nineteen. The patient died on Wednesday, about nine a.m., of peritonitis. – In reply to questions from the coroner and the jury, the doctor said he had no doubt whatever that death had been caused by the wounds. He had found the other organs generally in a normal condition. The deceased stated that she came from the country, but had not seen any of her friends for ten years. – Another woman subsequently examined as a witness deposed to seeing Smith about a quarter-past twelve on Tuesday morning, near the Burdett-road, talking to a man dressed in dark clothes with a white neckerchief round his neck. She (the witness) had been assaulted a few minutes before seeing Smith, and was getting away from the neighbourhood, where there had been some rough work that night. Two fellows had come up to her, one asking the time and the other striking her on the mouth, and both running away. She did not think the man talking to Smith was one of her assailants. – Mr. John West, chief inspector of police of the H division, said he had no official information of the occurrence. He had questioned the constables on duty in the Whitechapel-road at the time, but none of them had either seen or heard any such disturbance as that indicated in the evidence, nor had seen anyone taken to the hospital. He would make inquiries as to Osborn-street in consequence of what had transpired at the inquest. – The Coroner, in summing up, said that from the medical evidence, which must be true, it was perfectly clear that the poor woman had been murdered, but by whom there was no evidence to show. – After a short consultation, a verdict of "Wilful murder" against some person or persons unknown was returned by the jury.

A similar report was carried in *Lloyds Weekly News* of Sunday, 8 April 1888, on the front page, and is worth citing as it adds important pieces of evidence missed from the previous report:

HORRIBLE MURDER IN WHITECHAPEL

Mr. Wynne Baxter held an inquiry yesterday morning at the London Hospital into the terrible circumstances attending the death of an unfortunate, named Emma E. Smith, who was assaulted in the most brutal manner early on Tuesday morning last in the neighbourhood of Osborn-street, Whitechapel, by several men. The first witness, Mary Russell, the deputy-keeper of a lodging-house in George-street, Spitalfields, deposed to the statement made by the deceased on the way to the London Hospital, to which she was taken between four and five o'clock on Tuesday morning. The deceased told her she had been shockingly maltreated by a number of men and robbed of all the money she had. Her face was bleeding, and her ear was cut. She did not describe the men, but said one was a young man of about 19. She also pointed out where the outrage occurred, as they passed the spot, which was near the cocoa factory (Taylor's). The house-surgeon on duty, Dr. Hellier, described the internal injuries which had been caused, and which must have been inflicted by a blunt instrument. It had even penetrated the peritoneum, producing peritonitis, which was undoubtedly the cause of death, in his opinion. The woman appeared to know what she was about, but she had

probably had some drink. Her statement to the surgeon as to the circumstances was similar to that already given in evidence. He had made a post-
mortem examination, and described the organs as generally normal. He had
no doubt that death was caused by the injuries to the perineum, the abdomen,
and the peritoneum. Great force must have been used. The injuries had set up
peritonitis, which resulted in death on the following day after admission.
Another woman gave evidence that she had last seen Emma Smith between 12
and one on Tuesday morning, talking to a man in a black dress, wearing a
white neckerchief. It was near Farrant-street, Burdett-road. She was hurrying
away from the neighbourhood, as she had herself been struck in the mouth a
few minutes before by some young men. She did not believe that the man
talking to Smith was one of them. The quarter was a fearfully rough one. Just
before Christmas last she had been injured by men under circumstances of a
similar nature, and was a fortnight in the infirmary. – Mr. Chief-inspector
West, H division, said he had made inquiries of all the constables on duty on
the night of the 2nd and 3rd April in the Whitechapel-road, the place
indicated. – The jury returned a verdict of ''Wilful murder against some
person or persons unknown.''

CHAPTER 2

7 August 1888 – Murder of Martha Tabram

The second Whitechapel murder recorded in the police files is that of
Martha Tabram, also known as Turner, on Tuesday, 7 August 1888. *The
Times* of Friday, 10 August 1888, carried the following report:

Yesterday afternoon Mr. G. Collier, Deputy Coroner for the South-Eastern
Division of Middlesex, opened an inquiry at the Working Lads' Institute,
Whitechapel-road, respecting the death of the woman who was found on
Tuesday last, with 39 stabs on her body, at George-yard-buildings, White-
chapel.

Detective-Inspector Reid H Division, watched the case on behalf of
the Criminal Investigation Department.

Alfred George Crow cabdriver, 35, George-yard-buildings, deposed
that he got home at half-past 3 on Tuesday morning. As he was passing the
first-floor landing he saw a body lying on the ground. He took no notice as he
was accustomed to seeing people lying about there. He did not then know
whether the person was alive or dead. He got up at half-past 9, and when he
went down the staircase the body was not there. Witness heard no noise
while he was in bed.

John S. Reeves of 37, George-yard-buildings, a waterside labourer, said
that on Tuesday morning he left home at a quarter to 5 to seek for work.
When he reached the first-floor landing he found the deceased lying on her
back in a pool of blood. He was frightened, and did not examine her, but at
once gave information to the police. He did not know the deceased. The
deceased's clothes were disarranged, as though she had had a struggle with
some one. Witness saw no footmarks on the staircase, nor did he find a knife
or other weapon.

Police-constable Thomas Barrett 226 H, said that the last witness
called his attention to the body of the deceased. He sent for a doctor, who
pronounced life extinct.

Dr. T.R. Killeen of 68, Brick-lane, said that he was called to the
deceased, and found her dead. She had 39 stabs on the body. She had been
dead some three hours. Her age was about 36, and the body was very well

nourished. Witness had since made a post-mortem examination of the body. The left lung was penetrated in five places, and the right lung penetrated in two places. The heart, which was rather fatty, was penetrated in one place, and that would be sufficient to cause death. The liver was healthy, but was penetrated in five places, the spleen was penetrated in two places, and the stomach, which was perfectly healthy, was penetrated in six places. The witness did not think all the wounds were inflicted with the same instrument. The wounds generally might have been inflicted by a knife, but such an instrument could not have inflicted one of the wounds, which went through the chest-bone. His opinion was that one of the wounds was inflicted by some kind of dagger, and that all of them were caused during life.

The CORONER said he was in hopes that the body would be identified, but three women had identified it under three different names. He therefore proposed to leave that question open until the next occasion. The case would be left in the hands of Detective-inspector Reid, who would endeavour to discover the perpetrator of this dreadful murder. It was one of the most dreadful murders any one could imagine. The man must have been a perfect savage to inflict such a number of wounds on a defenceless woman in such a way. The inquiry would be adjourned for a fortnight.

The case was then adjourned.

And so the public was first presented with the basic facts of the first of what was to become a recognized series of murders in the Whitechapel district. It is here that the first of the extant police reports takes up the story in a report, dated 10 August 1888, by Inspector E. Ellisdon, H Division, Metropolitan Police[1]:

METROPOLITAN POLICE

H Division

10th August 1888

I beg to report that at 4.50 a.m. 7th inst. John Reeves of 37 George Yard Buildings, George Yard, Whitechapel, was coming down the stairs of above Buildings to go to work, when he saw a woman lying on the first floor landing. he called P.C. 226H Barrett (on the beat) who found the woman lying in a pool of blood. – there was no blood on the stairs leading to the landing. P.C. sent for Dr. Killeen, 68 Brick Lane, who attended and pronounced life extinct – there being 39 punctured wounds on the body; the police ambulance litter was procured, and the body removed to White-chapel mortuary to await an inquest.

Description, age 37, length 5 ft 3, complexion and hair dark: dress, green skirt, brown petticoat, long black jacket, brown stockings, side-spring boots, black bonnet – all old.

A description was circulated in 116 Infn. 7.8.88 – and the body was photographed same date, but up to the present time it has not been identified.

Two copies of photograph attached.

E. Ellisdon Insp.

T Arnold Supd.

The next relevant report is dated 16 August 1888, and is signed by Inspector Edmund Reid, H Division, Metropolitan Police[2]:

H Division

To the

ASSISTANT COMMISSIONER

CRIMINAL INVESTIGATION DEPARTMENT.

Executed

SUMMARY OF CONTENTS

Further report re murder of a woman in George Yard Buildings 6. 8. 88.

No. 312

3

3rd Special Report

submitted in accordance with P.O. 9th Febry. 1888. The body has been identified by Henry Tabram of 6 River Terrace, East Greenwich, as that of his wife, but she left him some years ago, and has recently been regarded as a prostitute. The witnesses have attended both the Tower and Wellington Barracks, and two men have been identified at each place, but all have been able to give a satisfactory account of themselves on the night of the murder. Enquiries are being continued.

C.H.Cutbush

Supt.

16.8.88

To/AC (CID) [ACB][3].

METROPOLITAN POLICE

H Division

16th day of August 1888

SUBJECT Murder

6. 8. 88

I beg to report that the body of the woman found murdered in George Yard Buildings on 7th inst has been identified by Henry Samuel Tabram of 6 River Terrace, East Greenwich as that of his wife who left him some years ago. She has also been identified by Mrs. Luckhurst of 4 Star Place, Commercial Road, as her lodger Mrs. Tabram but passing by the name of Turner, taking the name of a man with whom she lived until a month ago. Inquiries have also been made and it is found that the deceased resided at 19 George Street, (a Common Lodging House) and passed there in the name of "Emma", since she left Star Place, and was looked upon as a common prostitute, and a friend of Mary Ann Connelly, alias "Pearly Poll", also a prostitute.

On 9th Connelly came to Commercial Street Station, and stated that she, and the deceased were with two soldiers, one a corporal, and the other a private of the Guards from 10 till 11.45 p.m., on Monday 6th, walking about Whitechapel they then separated, she going with the corporal, and the deceased with the private for immoral purposes. She stated that she should know both men again. I then made an arrangement that the whole of the corporals and privates who were on leave on that night should be again paraded, and she promised to attend at the Tower next morning this she failed to do, search was made for her, but she could not be found that day, nor the next. On Sunday P.S. Caunter C.I.D. made inquiry and found her, and on my seeing her, she promised to attend next morning at the Tower.

This she did, but failed to pick out either of the men, afterwards stating that the men had white bands round their caps.

Pc 226H Barrett, who was on duty in George Yard on the night of the murder stated that about 2 am 7th he spoke to a private of the Guards in George Yard, who informed him that he was waiting for his mate who had gone away with a girl. The P.C. stated that he should know the private again. He attended the parade, and picked a private out wearing medals, and afterwards picked out another, stating he was the man and not the first. They were both questioned and beyond all doubt the first was not the man, and the second gave an account of himself, and his time, which on inquiry was found to be correct.

Corporal Benjiman who was granted leave on 6th, and should have returned to the Tower same night did not return till 11.30 pm, Thursday. On his arrival I took charge of his clothing and bayonet, examined them, but found no marks of blood on them. He stated to me that he had been staying with his father Mr Benjiman who keeps the Canbury Hotel, Kingston on Thames. Inquiry was made at Kingston and it was found that the corporal was there all Monday night and left on Tuesday morning.

The authorities at the Tower rendered the police every assistance in parading the men. On 15th I attended Wellington Barracks with Connelly (Pearly Poll) and P.C. Barrett. The Sergeant Major at once paraded the whole of the men consisting of Corporals and Privates who were on leave on the night of 6th and the woman Connelly at once picked out two privates as the men which were with her, & the deceased on the night in question. One named George, wearing three good conduct badges. She called the Corporal and stated that he was the one that she kept with, and the other named Skipper went away with the deceased. On inquiry it was found that George stayed with a woman (supposed to be his wife) at 120 Hammersmith Road. He arrived there at 8 pm 6th and left at 6 am 7th. With regard to Skipper he was in Barracks at 10.5 pm, 6th, which is shown in the book kept for that purpose.

The authorities at Wellington Barracks rendered the Police every assistance, and promised to render further assistance should it be required.

Inquiries are still being made with a view to gain information respecting the murder.

> Edmund Reid
> Inspector
> T Arnold
> Superintendent.

The resumption and close of the inquest was summarized in a further report by Inspector Reid dated 24 August 1888[4], which reads as follows:

H Division

To the   Executive
ASSISTANT COMMISSIONER
CRIMINAL INVESTIGATION DEPARTMENT.
SUMMARY OF CONTENTS.

Report giving result of inquest held on the body of Martha Tabram murdered in George Yard Buildings Whitechapel 7th August 1888.

No. 312
5

5th Special Report submitted in accordance with P.O. 9th February 1888. The inquest was resumed 23rd. inst. when the evidence was completed, and a verdict of wilful murder against some person or persons unknown returned. Enquiries are being continued.

> C.H. Cutbush
> Supt.
> 24.8.88.

To/AC(CID) [ACB].

METROPOLITAN POLICE.
H Division.
24th day of August 1888

SUBJECT Murder
7. 8. 88

I beg to report that Mr. George Collier, deputy Coroner for South East Middlesex resumed the inquiry at the Working Lads' Institute, Whitechapel

Road at 2 pm 23rd instant respecting the death of Martha Tabram, alias Turner, alias Emma, who was found dead in George Yard Buildings, Whitechapel at 4.45 am, 7th inst.

Mr. Henry Samuel Tabram, 6 River Terrace, East Greenwich, attended and identified the deceased as his wife who left him about 13 years ago.

Henry Turner, Victoria Working Men's Home, Commercial Street East, proved living with the deceased about 12 years, until about three weeks prior to her death when he left her.

Mary Bousfield of 4 Star Place, Commercial Road East, proved that the deceased and Turner rented a room at her house for about four months and left in debt about 6 weeks ago without giving any notice.

Ann Morris, sister-in-law of the deceased, residing at 23 Lisbon Street, Cambridge Heath Road, proved seeing her outside the White Swan P.H. Whitechapel Road at 11 pm 6th (Bank Holiday).

Mary Ann Connelly, alias Pearly Poll, stated that she was drinking with the deceased and two soldiers at several public houses in Whitechapel from 10 till 11.45 pm, 6th, when they separated she (Connelly) going up Angel Court with one of the soldiers whom she believed to be a Corporal, and the deceased up George Yard with the other soldier, and she saw nothing more of her until she saw her body in the dead house next day.

The Coroner afterwards addressed the Jury who returned a verdict of "Wilful murder against some person, or persons unknown."

Careful inquiries are still being made with a view to obtain information respecting the case.

Edmund Reid
Inspector
T Arnold Supd.

A further report[5], by Edmund Reid, "L(ocal) Inspector", dated 24 September 1888, furnishes further details of the actions taken by the police in attempting to identify the unknown soldiers who had accompanied Tabram and Connelly on the night of the murder:

METROPOLITAN POLICE
H Division
24th day of September 1888.

SUBJECT Murder in George Yard

Re inspection of Guards at the Tower, and Wellington Barracks.

I beg to report that I attended at the Tower on the 7th ultimo with P.C. 226.H. Barrett the officer who was on duty in George Yard on the night of the murder, and who stated that he saw, and spoke to a guardsman at 2 am in

George Yard on 7th. I saw the Sergeant Major and explained to him my business, he at once conducted the P.C. to the Guardroom where he was shown several prisoners but the P.C. failed to identify any one of them stating as his reason that they were not dressed. I then arranged to have a parade of all the privates and corporals who were on leave on the night of the 6th, at 11 am 8th. On that date I attended with the P.C. and directed him to be careful as to his actions because many eyes were watching him and a great deal depended on his picking out the right man and no other. The P.C. was kept round by the Sergeants Mess until the men were on parade when I directed him to walk along the rank and touch the man he saw in George Yard, if he was there. I with the Officers then walked away and the P.C. passed along the rank from left to right until he reached about the centre when he stepped up to a private wearing medals and touched him. I went and met the P.C. coming towards me when he told me he had picked out the man. I told him to be certain and have another look when he returned to the rank, passed along and picked out a second man about 6 or 7 away from the first. I asked him how he came to pick out two when he replied, the man I saw in George Yard had no medals and the first man I picked out had. I directed him to stand away.

Mrs. Jane Gillbank and her daughter, residing at 23 Catherine Wheel Alley, Aldgate were brought to the Tower by P.Ss Leach and Caunter C.I.D. they having stated that they saw the deceased with a private of the guards on the Sunday before the murder. (At that time the deceased was believed to be a Mrs Withers who was afterwards found alive.) They were sent one at a time along the rank but failed to pick out anyone.

The two men that the P.C. pointed out were then taken to the orderly room, and the others dismissed. On arriving at the orderly room the P.C. stated that he had made a mistake in pointing out the man with medals who was allowed to leave the room at once without his name being taken, and the other gave the name of John Leary. He was asked by me to account for his time on the night of the 6th. He at once stated that he and private Law went on leave in the evening and went to Brixton they stopped there until the Public Houses closed then he (Leary) went to the rear and when he returned he missed Law he looked about for him and not finding him started off to Battersea, and Chelsea, came along past Charing Cross into the Strand, where he met Law about 4.30 am, they both walked along until they got to Billingsgate where they had a drink and came into barracks at 6. Private Law was then sent for, and on his being questioned as to his movements on the night of the 6th he made a statement which agreed in every particular with that which had been made by Private Leary. They were unable to give me the name of any person to whom I could refer. I felt certain in my own mind that P.C. had made a great mistake and I allowed the men to leave the orderly room.

On 9th I was present at the Tower at 11.30 pm when Corporal Benjiman returned. This man had been absent without leave since the 6th. I at once took charge of his clothing and bayonet, and asked him to account for time. He stated that he had been staying with his father Mr. Benjiman, landlord of the Canbury Hotel, Kingston-on-Thames, the whole of the time. On inquiry I found this to be true. I examined his clothing and bayonet but could find no marks of blood on them.

I arranged for another parade of Corporals and Privates at 11 am 10th to enable Mary Ann Connelly alias Pearly Poll to pick out the two men who were in the company of the deceased and herself on the night of the 6th.

On 10th Connelly could not be found, the matter was explained to the Sergeant Major who dismissed the men and promised to have another parade when ever I found "Pearly Poll".

On 12th found Pearly Poll and arranged for a parade at 11 am 13th she attended at the Tower and on looking at the men said, "They are not here, they had white bands round their caps."

I thanked the authorities for the assistance rendered to police and they expressed themselves satisfied with the manner in which I had conducted the inquiry, and promised to give any further assistance should it be required.

On 14th, I arranged for a parade of Corporals and Privates at the Wellington Barracks who were on leave on the night of the 6th.

On 15th I attended with Pearly Poll, when she picked out two privates as the men which were with her and the deceased on the night of the murder. One named George wearing three good conduct badges she called the Corporal and stated that he was the one that remained with her, and the other named Skipper went away with the deceased. On this they were both taken into a room & questioned Skipper stated that he was in barracks at 10 pm 6th, this was proved by the books kept in barracks George stated that he was at 120 Hammersmith Road from 8 pm 6th, till 6 am 7th. This on inquiry was found to be correct. He stayed there with his wife beyond doubt. The authorities at Wellington Barracks rendered every assistance for which I thanked them. They also expressed themselves satisfied with the manner in which the identification had been arranged.

Inquiries were made to find some other person who saw the deceased and Pearly Poll with the privates on the night of the 6th but without success, and Pearly Poll and the P.C. having both picked out the wrong men they could not be trusted again as their evidence would be worthless.

(sgd) Edmund Reid L. Inspector
Jno West Actg Supt

An overall summary[6] of the enquiries made into the murder of Martha Tabram, by Chief Inspector Donald S. Swanson, dated September 1888, is included:

H Division

Murder of Martha Tabram

on 7th August 1888

in George Yard White-

chapel.

Detail of reports in

tabular form for reference.

Ex papers No. 312

METROPOLITAN POLICE

CRIMINAL INVESTIGATION DEPARTMENT,

SCOTLAND YARD,

day of September 1888.

SUBJECT Murder of

Martha Tabram

at 37 George Yard.

Buildings.

I beg to report that the following are the particulars respecting the murder of Martha Tabram:-

450.am7th.Augt.1888, Body of a woman found on landing of George Yard buildings by John Reeves of No37 tenement, in the building as he was leaving to go to work and he reported the fact to P.C. 226H Barrett.

Dr.Keeling [sic] of 68 Brick Lane was called, and examined the body and found thirty nine wounds on body, and neck, and private part with a knife or dagger.

11.$\frac{3}{4}$ pm 6th. Augt. Mrs. Tabram was seen alive by Mary Ann Connolly, alias Pearly Poll, a prostitute, who stated that she and deceased with two soldiers, guards, one of whom was a corporal(?) who was with her, the other a private who was with deceased, had been walking about Whitechapel from 10. to 11$\frac{3}{4}$ pm 6th. At 11.$\frac{3}{4}$ pm deceased and the private went up George Yard together.

2am.7th.Augt. Police Constable 226H. Barrett saw a soldier – a grenadier age 22 to 26. height 5 ft 9 or 10. compl. fair, hair dark small dark brown moustache turned up at ends. with one good conduct badge. no medals. in Wentworth Street; and in reply to the PC he stated he was waiting for a *chum*, who had gone with a girl.

7th.Augt.1888. Inspector Reid took statements from residents of George

Yard Buildings. At 2am 7th.Augt. Mrs Mahoney and her husband passed the spot where body was afterwards found. At 3.30 am Alfred George Crow states he saw something on the landing, but took no notice, and went to bed. Crow is a licensed cab driver. No suspicion is attached to any of residents. The deceased was a stranger to all of them.

It will be observed that from the statement of Mrs Mahoney that the murder took place between 2am and 4.50am 7th. Augt., but as the soldier was last seen with deceased at $11\frac{3}{4}$ pm 6th. two and a quarter hours had elapsed. It is not an uncommon occurrence for tramps and others to sleep on a common stairs in the East End, and I venture to think that the something which the cabman Alfred George Crow saw was the body of Martha Tabram. As close enquiry did not elicit that she had been seen with any one else than a soldier, although from the lapse of time, it is possible she might have been, the following were the steps taken by Police:-

7th Augt.1888. P.C. 226H Barrett was taken to the Tower where he saw some soldiers in the guardroom, but he did not recognise any.

11am8th Augt.1888. The Grenadier Guards who were on leave or absent on night of 6th were paraded and P.C.226H saw them, when he picked out one with medals, and then another both of whom were taken to the orderly room. where the P.C. admitted his mistake in identity in the first, and his name was not taken. The second man, John Leary gave an account of himself on that night, which private Law, to whom he referred, and who was brought into the orderly room corroborated without communicating with Leary, thus clearing Leary.

11.30pm 9th Augt.1888. Corpl. Benjamin returned, having been absent without leave since 6th Augt. His clothing and bayonet were examined, but no marks of blood were on them. He accounted for his time as having stayed with his father at the Canbury Hotel Kingston, which was confirmed on enquiry by police.

11 am 10th Augt. Parade of soldiers at the Tower arranged but the woman Connolly could not be found.

11 am 13th Parade of soldiers at the Tower, Connolly saw them and said, "They are not here they had white bands round their caps"

14th. Arranged for parade of Coldstream Guards, who were on leave or absent on 6th, at Wellington Barracks.

5th. Parade of Coldstream Guards as arranged, when Connolly picked out two one as being the Corporal who was with her, the other as being the one who was with deceased. The one she picked out as the Corporal was a private named George, with two good conduct badges, who stated that he was with his wife at 120 Hammersmith Road from 8 pm 6th to 6 am 7thAugt. Enquiry by police proved this to be correct. The other named Skipper stated that he was in barracks on the night of 6th, and the books shewed that he was in barracks from 10.5 pm 6th. They therefore cleared themselves.

The enquiry was continued amongst persons of deceased's class in the East End, but without any success.

Donald S Swanson

Ch Inspr.

This report has an index written by Chief Inspector Donald Swanson, dated 19 October 1888, listing the steps taken by the police regarding the Tabram murder, and the identity parades held with the Grenadier Guards and the Coldstream Guards respectively. A descriptive form relating to Martha Tabram is also included[7], giving the following details:

Age 35 to 40.
Profession or calling prostitute.
Height 5 feet 3 in.
Hair Dark.
Complexion Dark.
Dress Green skirt, brown petticoat, long black jacket, black bonnet, side-spring boots (all old).

These are the official police reports concerning the murder of Martha Tabram. It will be seen that the investigating officer in charge was the local CID Inspector, Edmund Reid of H Division Metropolitan Police, an officer who was to have a long connection with the case.

The result of the inquest can be found in *The Times* of Friday, 24 August 1888, page 4, column 3:

INQUESTS.

Yesterday afternoon Mr. George Collier, the Deputy Coroner for the South-Eastern Division of Middlesex, resumed his inquiry at the Working Lads' Institute, Whitechapel-road, respecting the death of the woman who was found dead at George-yard-buildings, on the early morning of Tuesday, the 7th inst., with no less than 39 wounds on various parts of her body. The body has been identified as that of MARTHA TABRAN [sic], aged 39 or 40 years, the wife of a foreman packer at a furniture warehouse.

Henry Samuel Tabran [sic], 6, River-terrace, East Greenwich, husband of the deceased woman, said he last saw her alive about 18 months ago, in the Whitechapel-road. They had been separated for 13 years, owing to her drinking habits. She obtained a warrant against him. For some part of the time witness allowed her 12s. a week, but in consequence of her annoyance he stopped this allowance ten years ago, since which time he had made it half-a-crown a week, as he found she was living with a man.

Henry Turner, a carpenter, staying at the Working Men's Home, Commercial-street, Spitalfields, stated that he had been living with the woman Tabran as his wife for about nine years. Two or three weeks previously to this occurrence he ceased to do so. He had left her on two or three occasions in consequence of her drinking habits, but they had come together again. He last saw her alive on Saturday, the 4th inst., in Leadenhall-street. He then gave her 1s. 6d. to get some stock. When she had money she spent it in drink. While living with witness deceased's usual time for coming home was about 11 o'clock. As far as he knew she had no regular companion and he did not know that she walked the streets. As a rule he was, he said, a man of sober habits, and when the deceased was sober they usually got on well together. By Inspector Reid. – At times the deceased had stopped out all night. After those occasions she told him she had been taken in a fit and was removed to the police-station or somewhere else. By the Coroner. – He knew she suffered from fits, but they were brought on by drink.

Mrs. Mary Bousfield, wife of a wood cutter, residing at 4, Star-place, Commercial-road, knew the deceased by the name of Turner. She was formerly a lodger in her house with the man Turner. Deceased would rather have a glass of ale than a cup of tea, but she was not a woman who got continually drunk, and she never brought home any companions with her. She left without giving notice, and owed two weeks' rent.

Mrs. Ann Morris, a widow, of 23, Lisbon-street, E., said she last saw the deceased, who was her sister-in-law, at about 11 o'clock on Bank Holiday night in the Whitechapel-road. She was then about to enter a public house.

Mary Ann Connolly ("Pearly Poll"), who at the suggestion of Inspector Reid was cautioned in the usual manner before being sworn, stated she had been for the last two nights living at a lodging house in Dorset-street, Spitalfields. Witness was a single woman. She had known the woman Tabran for about four or five months. She knew her by the name of Emma. She last saw her alive on Bank Holiday night, when witness was with her about three-quarters of an hour, and they separated at a quarter to 12. Witness was with Tabran and two soldiers – one private and one corporal. She did not know what regiment they belonged to, but they had white bands round their caps. After they separated, Tabran went away with the private, and witness accompanied the corporal up Angel-alley. There was no quarrelling between any of them. Witness had been to the barracks to identify the soldiers, and the two men she picked out were, to the best of her belief, the men she and Tabran were with. The men at the Wellington Barracks were paraded before witness. One of the men picked out by witness turned out not to be a corporal, but he had stripes on his arm. By Inspector Reid. – Witness heard of the murder on the Tuesday. Since the occurrence witness had threatened to drown herself, but she only said it for a lark. She stayed away two days and two nights, and she only said that when asked where she was going. She knew the police were looking after her, but she did not let them know her whereabouts. By a juryman. – The woman Tabran was not drunk. They were, however, drinking at different houses for about an hour and three-quarters. They had ale and rum. Detective-Inspector Reid made a statement of the efforts made by the police to discover the perpetrator of the murder. Several persons had stated that they saw the deceased woman on the previous Sunday with a corporal, but when all the corporals and privates at the Tower and Wellington Barracks were paraded before them they failed to identify the man. The military authorities afforded every facility to the police. ''Pearly Poll'' picked out two men belonging to the Coldstream Guards at the Wellington Barracks. One of those men had three good conduct stripes, and he was proved beyond doubt to have been with his wife from 8 o'clock on the Monday night until 6 o'clock the following morning. The other man was also proved to have been in barracks at five minutes past 10 on Bank Holiday night. The police would be pleased if anyone would give them information of having seen anyone with the deceased on the night of the Bank Holiday. The Coroner having summed up, the jury returned the verdict to the effect that the deceased had been murdered by some person or persons unknown.

CHAPTER 3

31 August 1888 – Murder of Mary Ann Nichols

The murder of Mary Ann Nichols occurred in the early hours of Friday, 31 August 1888. Whether or not either of the two previous murders had been committed by the same hand, which is unlikely, both police and press linked the killing with the previous two, and the idea that a maniac was abroad, killing prostitutes, was born. The police enquiries also revealed the suspect called "Leather Apron", who was quickly made prominent by the sensational press. The reports concerning this murder are enclosed in a file cover[1], as follows:

J Division

To the

ASSISTANT COMMISSIONER
CRIMINAL INVESTIGATION DEPARTMENT.
SUMMARY OF CONTENTS.

Special weekly report re murder of Mary Ann Nichols. at Bucks Row. 31. 8. 88

7.9.88

No. 327

3

3rd. Special Report submitted in accordance with P.O. 9th Febry. 1888. The deceased has been identified as Mary Ann Nichols .a prostitute. who separated from her husband about nine years ago. and has been since 1882 at different periods an inmate of Edmonton, The City of London, Holborn, and Lambeth workhouses. No information to point to the offender can be obtained. A man named "Pizer alias Leather Apron" has been in the habit of ill-using prostitutes in various parts of the Metropolis for some time past, and careful inquiries have been made to trace him, but without success. There is no evidence against him at present. Enquiries are being continued.

W. Davis
Act.Supt.
7.9.88

To/ACC(CID)/ACB   [ ]

A report dated 31 August 1888, by Inspector John Spratling, is the first official summary[2] of the murder of Mary Ann Nichols in Buck's Row, Whitechapel (parentheses indicate portions of document missing).
   The cover [f 241] reads:

C.O. Reference Divisional Reference
Submitted through Executive
J. Division.
Subject Report Re murder of a woman unknown at Bucks Row, Whitechapel 31st inst.

31.1.88.

No. 327

1st Special Report submitted in accordance with P.O. 9th Febry. 1888.
To/A.C.Constbl
To Col P[ ] for information [*missing*]

METROPOLITAN POLICE
J Division.
31st August 1888

P.C. 97J, Neil, reports at 3.45. on 31st inst. he found the dead body of a woman lying on her back with her clothes a little above her knees, with her throat cut from ear to ear on a yard crossing at Bucks Row, Whitechapel. P.C. Neil obtained the assistance of P.C.s 55.H. Smizen [*sic*] and 96J. Thain, the latter called Dr. Llewellyn, No. 152, Whitechapel Road, he arrived quickly and pronounced life to be extinct, apparently but a few minutes, he directed her removed to the mortuary, stating he would make a further examination there, which was done on the ambulance.

   Upon my arrival there and taking a description I found that she had been disembowelled, and at once sent to inform the Dr. of it, l[*atter?*] arrived quickly and on further examination stated that her throat had been cut from left to right, two disti[*nct*] cuts being on left side. The windp[*ipe*] gullet and spinal cord being cut through, a bruise apparently of a th[*umb*] being on right lower jaw, also one o[*n*] left cheek, the abdomen had been [*cut*] open from centre of bottom of ribs a[*long*] right side, under pelvis to left of the stomach, there the wound was jag[*ged*], the omentium [*sic*], or coating of the stomach, was also cut in several places, and tw[*o*] small stabs on private parts, apparently done with a strong bladed knife, supposed to have been done by some le[*ft*] handed person, death being almost instantaneous.

   Description, age about 45, length 5 ft. 2. or 3. compx. dark, hair dark brown (turning grey), eyes brown, bruise on lower right jaw and left cheek, slight laceration of tongue, one tooth deficient front of upper jaw, two on left of lo[wer] do; dress, brown ulster, 7 large brass bu[ttons], (figure of a female riding a horse and [a] man at side thereon), brown linsey fr[ock] grey woollen petticoat, flannel do, white chest flannel, brown stays, white ch[emise], black ribbed woollen stockings, man[s] S.S. boots, cut on uppers, tips on heels, black straw bonnet, trimmed black ve[lvet].

I made enquiries and was informed by Mrs. Emma Green, a widow, New Cottage adjoining, and Mr. Walter Purkis, Essex Wharf, oppisite [sic], also of William Cour[t] Night Watchman to Messrs. Brown & Eagle, Bucks Row, and P.C. 81.G.E.R. Police on [duty] at Wharf near, none of whom heard any scream during the night, or anything to lead them to believe that the murder had been committed there.

The Stations and premises of the East London and District Railways, al[l] the wharves and enclosures in the vicinity have been searched but no trace of any weapon could be found there.

P.C. states he passed through Bucks Row at 3.15 am. and P.S.10.Kirby about the same time, but the woman was not there then and is not known to them.

[sgd] J. Spratling Inspr.
J.Keating Supt.

It has since been ascertained that the dress bears the marks of Lambeth Workhouse and deceased is supposed to have been an inmate of that house. J.Keating Supt.

A further report[3], dated 7 September 1888, by Inspector Joseph Henry Helson, Local Inspector, CID, J (Bethnal Green) Division, casts more light on the murder:

METROPOLITAN POLICE
J Division.
7th day of September 1888

SUBJECT Murder of
M.A. Nichols
at Whitechapel
REFERENCE TO PAPERS
Special report 31.8.88
and 52983
With reference to the subject in the margin, I beg to report that the marks on the clothing led to the identification of the deceased as a woman who had been an inmate of Lambeth Workhouse on several occasions, and that her name was Mary Ann Nichols, it was afterwards ascertained that her husband, William Nichols, was at present residing at 37 Coburg Row, Old Kent Road,

and employed as a machine printer, by Messrs. Purkiss Bacon & Co., Whitefriars St. E.C.

They separated about 9 years since in consequence of her drunken habits. For some time he allowed her 5/- per week, but in 1882, it having come to his knowledge that she was living the life of a prostitute he discontinued the allowance. In consequence of this she became chargeable to the Guardians of the Parish of Lambeth by whom the husband was Summoned to show cause why he should not be ordered to contribute towards her support, and on these facts being proved, the summons was dismissed. They had not spoken to each other since, and the husband has not heard anything of her since. There are no grounds for suspecting him to be the guilty party. Since 1882 she has at different periods been an inmate of Edmonton, The City of London, Holborn and Lambeth Workhouses. She left the latter Institution on the 12th May last to take a situation at Ingleside, Rose Hill Road, Wandsworth, and absconded from there on the 12th of July stealing clothing to the value of £3.10.0. A few days after this she obtained lodgings at 18 Thrawl St. Spitalfields, a common-lodging-house and remained there and at a similar house at 55 Flower and Dean St. close by, until the day before she was found dead. A further examination of the body and clothing, and the result of the Post Mortem Examination, leaves no doubt but that the murder was committed where the body was found, careful search was continued with a view to find any weapon that was used by the murder[er] or murderers (in all probability there was only one) but nothing has been found. Enquiries have also been made from the persons who reside in the locality, watchmen who were employed in adjoining premises, P.C.s on the adjoining beats and in every quarter from which it was thought any useful information might be obtained, but at present not an atom of evidence can be obtained to connect any person with the crime. She was seen walking the Whitechapel Road about 11.p.m. 30th, at 12.30 am 31st she was seen to leave the Frying-pan Public House, Brick Lane, Spitalfields, at 1.20.a.m. 31st she was at the common-lodging, 18 Thrawl St. and at 2.30.a.m. at the corner of Osborne St. and Whitechapel Road, on each occasion she was alone. At 3.45.a.m. or an hour and a quarter later, she is found dead, and no person can be found at present who saw her after 2.30.a.m.

The inquiry has revealed the fact that a man named Jack Pizer, alias Leather Apron, has, for some considerable period been in the habit of ill-using prostitutes in this, and other parts of the Metropolis, and careful search has been, and is continued to be made to find this man in order that his movements may be accounted for on the night in question, although at present there is no evidence whatsoever against him.

The enquiry is being carefully continued, by Inspector Abberline, from

C.O. and myself and every effort used to obtain information that may lead to arrest of the murderer.

J.H.Helson Inspr.
J.Keating Supt.

As early as the end of August a letter was received at the Home Office, from the public sector, to do with concern about the murders. It was thought that the offer of a reward might lead to the detection of the criminal(s).

The file cover[4] concerning this matter is dated 31 August 1888:

[Stamped: – HOME OFFICE 1 SEP.88 DEpt. No.] No. A49301B/1
31 Aug. 1888.   Messrs. L.P.Walter & Son.
REFERENCES, &c.   Forward newspaper extract respecting the recent murders in Whitechapel: & recommends that a reward be offered for the detection of the murderer.

not Pressing
MINUTES.

?Ack: and say that [the practice of offering Rewards for the discovery of criminals has for some time been discontinued; and that so far as the circumstances of the present case have at present been investigated do not disclose any special ground for depart[ure] from the usual custom.
W.P.B.
1.9.88   EWP. 3Sept 88

Wrote Messrs Walter & Son
4 September 1888.

The letter[5] sent by Messrs. Walter & Son, dated 31 August 1888, is enclosed:

A49301B

[Headed paper]
TELEGRAPHIC ADDRESS, "WINTERINE", LONDON, TELEPHONE No.536.
L.&P.WALTER & SON [Stamped:- HOME OFFICE 1 SEP.88 DEPt. No.]
   Manufacturers of   11,12,&13,Church Street
CLOTHING FOR   Spitalfields
   EXPORTATION   LONDON 31/Aug 1888
The Secty of State for
          the HomeDpt
Sir/
   We beg to enclose your report of this fearful murder & to say that such is the state of affairs in this district that we are put to the necessity of having a

night watchman to protect our premises. the only way in our humble opinion to tackle this matter is to offer at once a reward.

Yours Very obediently,

L&PWalter&Son.

This letter is followed by a cutting[6] from the newspaper:

THE [*missing*]

[August 31, 1888.]

HORRIBLE MURDER IN
WHITECHAPEL.

The Central News, says;- Scarcely has the horror and sensation caused by the discovery of the murdered woman in Whitechapel some short time ago had time to abate, than another discovery is made, which; for the brutality exercised on the victim, is even more shocking, and will no doubt create as great a sensation in the vicinity as its predecessor. The affair, up to the present, is enveloped in complete mystery, and the police have as yet no evidence to trace the perpetrators of the horrible deed. The facts are that as Constable John Neil was walking down Bucks-row, Thomas-street, Whitechapel, about a quarter to four o'clock this morning, he discovered a woman, between thirty-five and forty years of age, lying at the side of the street with her throat cut right open from ear to ear, the instrument with which the deed was done tracing the throat from left to right. The wound was about two inches wide, and blood was flowing profusely, in fact, she was discovered to be lying in a pool of blood. She was immediately conveyed to the Whitechapel Mortuary, where it was found that, besides the wound in the throat, the lower part of her person was completely ripped open. The wound extends nearly to her breast, and must have been effected with a large knife. As the corpse of the woman lies in the mortuary it presents a ghastly sight. The victim measures 5ft. 2in. in height. The hands are bruised, and bear evidence of having engaged in a severe struggle. There is the impression of a ring having been worn on one of Deceased's fingers, but there is nothing to show that it had been wrenched from her in a struggle. Some of the front teeth have also been knocked out, and the face is bruised on both cheeks and very much discoloured. Deceased wore a rough brown ulster, with large buttons in front. Her clothes are torn, and cut up in several places, leaving evidence of the ferocity with which the murder was committed. The only way by which the police can prosecute an enquiry at present is by finding someone who can identify the Deceased, and then, if possible, trace those in whose company she was when last seen. In Bucks-row naturally the greatest excitement prevails, and several persons in the neighbourhood state that an affray occurred shortly after midnight, but no screams were heard, nor anything beyond what might have been considered evidence of an ordinary brawl. The woman has not yet been identified. She was wearing workhouse clothes, and it is supposed she came from Lambeth. A night watchman was in the street where the crime was committed. He heard no scream and saw no signs of the scuffle. The body was quite warm when brought to the mortuary at half-past four this morning.

LATEST PARTICULARS.

Immediately on the affair being reported at the Bethnal-green Police-station two inspectors proceeded to the mortuary and examined the clothes, in the hope of being able to discover something likely to lead to her identification. In this they were not successful, as the only articles found on the body were a broken comb and a piece of looking-glass. The wounds, of which there are five, could only have been committed by a dagger or a long sharp knife. The officers engaged in the case are pushing their inquiries in the neighbourhood as to the doings of certain gangs known to frequent these parts, and an opinion is gaining ground amongst them that the murderers are the same who committed the two previous murders near the same spot. It is believed that these gangs, who make their appearance during the early hours of the morning, are in the habit of blackmailing these poor creatures, and where their demands are refused, violence follows. Up till noon Mr. Wynne E. Baxter, the Coroner for the district, had not received any official intimation of the occurrence, but the inquest will most likely be held on Monday morning.

The letter of reply[7] to Messrs. Walter & Son, dated 4 September 1888, from the Home Office is as follows:

A49301   Whitehall
                                   4th September 18[*88*]

Gentlemen,

In reply to your letter of the 31st ultimo, expressing the opinion that a reward should be offered for the detection of the Whitechapel murderer, I am directed by the Secretary of State to inform you that the practice of offering rewards for the discovery of criminals has for some time been discontinued and that so far as the circumstances of the present case have at present been investigated, they do not in his opinion disclose any special ground for departure from the usual custom.

I am,

Gentlemen,

Your odedient Servant,

(sd) E.Leigh Pemberton

Messrs. Walter & Son
11. 12 & 13 Church Street
Spitalfields.

A detailed summary report[8], dated 19 October 1888, relating to the murder of Nichols submitted by Chief Inspector Donald S. Swanson, Criminal Investigation Department, Scotland Yard, reads:

METROPOLITAN POLICE.
CRIMINAL INVESTIGATION DEPARTMENT,
SCOTLAND YARD.
19th day of October 1888

SUBJECT Bucks Row
Murder of Mary Ann Nichols

I beg to report that the following are the particulars relating to the murder of Mary Ann Nichols in possession of police.

3.45 a.m. 31st. Augst. The body of a woman was found lying on the footway in Bucks Row, Whitechapel, by Charles Cross & Robert Paul carmen, on their way to work. They informed P.C. 55H Divn. Mizen in Bakers Row, but before his arrival P.C. 97J Neil on whose beat it was had discovered it. Dr. Llewellyn of 152 Whitechapel Road was sent for, he pronounced life extinct and he describes the wounds as, – throat cut nearly severing head from body, abdomen cut open from centre of bottom of ribs along right side, under pelvis to left of stomach, there the wound was jagged: the coating of the stomach was cut in several places and two small stabs on private parts, which in his opinion may have been done with a strong bladed knife. At first the doctor was of opinion that the wounds were caused by a left handed person but he is now doubtful. 31st Aug. 88 The body was identified by Ellen Holland of 18 Thrawl Street, E. as that of Mary Ann Nichols of the same address, – a common lodging house, – subsequently by the husband, Wm. Nichols of 37 Coburg Road, Old Kent Rd. printers' machinist.

There was no money in pocket of deceased & there was nothing left behind by the murderer.

The results of Police enquiries are as follows:- 2.30 a.m. 31st. Aug. 88 Mrs. Nichols was last seen alive at 2.30 am 31st Aug 1888 in a state of drunkenness at the corner of Osborn Street and Whitechapel Road, by Ellen Holland mentioned above. She was then alone & going in the direction of Bucks Row by Whitechapel Road. An hour and a quarter afterwards the body was found at Bucks Row.

Enquiry was then made at common lodging houses, & the statements of persons taken, but no person was able to say that they had seen her alive more recently than Ellen Holland. The police were unable to learn from any source that any person was seen with her, or with a person supposed to be her after that hour. Coffee stall keepers, prostitutes, the night watchman in Winthorp [sic] Street, – a street parallel to Bucks Row, – as well as the inhabitants of

Bucks Row, were questioned, but they were unable to help the police in the slightest degree. They had not seen the woman, nor had they heard any screams or noise. Enquiry at the common lodging house where Mrs Nichols lived shewed that when she left there at 1.40 <u>am it was for the purpose of getting sufficient money to pay for her bed, – 4d</u> – that she had then no money and she told Ellen Holland at 2.30 a.m. that then she had no money to pay for her bed. Robbery could not therefore be the motive for the murder. Enquiry was made into her history which turns out to be as follows: the deceased through her intemperate habits separated from her husband about 9 years ago and he allowed her 5/- per week till 1882 when it came to his knowledge that she was leading an immoral life and he stopped the allowance. She became chargeable to the Parish of Lambeth and the husband was summoned to shew cause why he should not contribute towards her support, but the summons was dismissed. Since that time the husband has not heard anything of her, and enquiry revealed that she had been leading an irregular life sleeping at common lodging houses and Workhouses for a considerable time previous to her death. The enquiry into her history did not disclose the slightest pretext for a motive on the part of her friends or associates in the common lodging houses.

The absence of the motives which lead to violence and of any scrap of evidence either direct or circumstantial, left the police without the slightest shadow of a trace consequently enquiries were made into the history and accounts given of themselves of persons, respecting whose character & surroundings suspicion was cast in statements made to police.

Amongst such are the three <u>slaughtermen, named Tomkins, Britton and Mumford</u> employed by night at Messrs. Harrison Barber & Coy. premises Winthorp Street. Their statements were taken separately, and without any means of communicating with each other, and they satisfactorily accounted for their time, being corroborated in some portions by the Police on night duty near the premises. Another man named <u>John Piser, better known as "Leather apron"</u> became suspected on account of his alleged levying blackmail on prostitutes and assaulting them if they did not comply with his request, as detailed to police by women in the common lodging houses. On 10th Sept. he was found & his statement taken to the effect that on 31st Augst. he had slept at a common lodging ho: at Holloway Road which was fully corroborated and the date fixed by the proprietor who knows Piser. On 8th Sept. he stayed at 22 Mulberry St. in this he was corroborated by several persons, for the police ascertained that in consequence of suspicions published about him by the press he was in reality afraid to come out.

The case of Annie Chapman took place on 8th Sept. and both enquiries merged into one. The particulars of further enquiries will be found in report of the murder of Annie Chapman.

(sd) Donald S. Swanson
Ch: Inspector

A police descriptive form relating to Mary Ann Nichols is also included, giving her details as follows:

Age	*45*
Profession or calling	*Prostitute*
Hair	*Dark (turning grey)*
Eyes	*Brown*
Face	*Discolouration of face*
Complexion	*Dark*
Marks or peculiarities	*On person a piece of looking glass, a comb, and white handkerchief*
Dress	*Brown ulster, seven large buttons, horse & man standing by side thereon, linsey frock, brown stays, blue ribbed woollen stockings, straw bonnet.*

Note. She was the wife of Wm. Nichols of 37 Coburg Rd. Old Kent Rd. printers machinist.

These reports are the first official papers on the murder of Mary Ann Nichols, further information being contained in some later documents and the contemporary newspaper articles, which also include lengthy reports of the inquest and evidence of the witnesses.

There is an index[9] to the papers on the Nichols murder in the Home Office files:

– Copy –   A49301C/8a
[Stamped:- HOME OFFICE 25 OCT.88 RECd. DEPt.]

	Bucks Row	*No. 2*
	– Murder of Mary Ann Nichols –	
Subject	*Page*	*Remarks*
Hour & date of murder	1	
Wounds on body	1&2	Described by Dr. Llwellyn
Body identified	2	as Mary Ann Nichols, a prostitute
History of deceased	4	
Enquiries by police		
at Common Lod: Hos:	3	
" Coffee stall keepers	3	

" Prostitutes	3	
" Night Watchman	3	in Winthorp [sic] St. nearly
" Slaughtermen	5	parallel to Bucks Row employed
" John Piser	6	by Messrs. Harrison & Barber.
alias		
"Leather Apron"		

As the official inquest papers on Mary Ann Nichols have not been found it is necessary to read the contemporary newspaper reports that are included in the Home Office official papers held at the Public Record Office. In the case of Nichols they are extracted from *The Times*, the first[10] being 3 September 1888, page 12:

THE WHITECHAPEL MURDER.

Up to a late hour last evening the police had obtained no clue to the perpetrator of the latest of the three murders which have so recently taken place in Whitechapel, and there is, it must be acknowledged, after their exhaustive investigation of the facts, no ground for blaming the officers in charge should they fail in unravelling the mystery surrounding the crime. The murder, in the early hours of Friday morning last, of the woman now known as Mary Ann Nicholls [*sic*], has so many points of similarity with the murder of two other women in the same neighbourhood – one Martha Turner, as recently as August 7, and the other less than 12 months previously – that the police admit their belief that the three crimes are the work of one individual. All three women were of the class called "unfortunates," each so very poor, that robbery could have formed no motive for the crime, and each was murdered in such a similar fashion, that doubt as to the crime being the work of one and the same villain almost vanishes, particularly when it is remembered that all three murders were committed within a distance of 300 yards from each other. These facts have led the police to almost abandon the idea of a gang being abroad to wreak vengeance on women of this class for not supplying them with money. Detective-Inspectors Abberline, of the Criminal Investigation Department, and Detective-Inspector Helson, J Division, are both of opinion that only one person, and that a man, had a hand in the latest murder. It is understood that the investigation into the George-yard mystery is proceeding hand-in-hand with that of Buck's-row. It is considered unlikely that the woman could have entered a house, been murdered, and removed to Buck's-row within a period of one hour and a quarter. The woman who last saw her alive, and whose name is Nelly Holland, was a fellow-lodger with the deceased in Thrawl-street, and is positive as to the time being 2.30. Police-constable Neil, 97J, who found the body, reports the time as 3.45. Buck's-row is a secluded place, from having tenements on one side only. The constable has been severely questioned as to his "working" of his "beat" on that night, and states that he was last on the spot where he found the body not more than half an hour previously – that is to say, at 3.15. The beat is a very short one, and quickly walked over would not occupy more than 12 minutes. He neither heard a cry nor saw any one. Moreover, there are three watchmen on duty at night close to the spot, and neither one heard a cry to cause alarm. It is not true, says Constable Neil, who is a man of nearly 20 years' service, that he was called to the body by two men. He came upon it as he walked, and flashing his lantern to examine it, he was answered by the lights from two other constables at either end of the street. These officers had seen no man leaving the spot to attract attention, and the mystery is most complete. The utmost efforts are being used, a number of plain-clothes men being out making inquiries in the neighbourhood, and Sergeants Enright and Godley have interviewed many persons who might, it was thought, assist in giving a clue.

On Saturday afternoon Mr. Wynne E. Baxter, coroner for the South-Eastern Division of Middlesex, opened his enquiry at the Working Lads' Institute, Whitechapel-road, respecting the death of MARY ANN NICHOLS, whose dead body was found on the pavement in Buck's-row, Whitechapel on Friday morning.

Detective-Inspectors Abberline and Helston [*sic*] and Sergeants Enright and Godley watched the case on behalf of the Criminal Investigation Department.

The jury having been sworn and having viewed the body of the dead woman, which was lying in a shell in the Whitechapel Mortuary.

Edward Walker, of 16, Maidswood-road, Camberwell, deposed that he was now of no occupation, but had formerly been a smith. He had seen the body in the mortuary, and to the best of his belief it was that of his daughter, whom he had not seen for two years. He recognized the body by its general appearance and by some of the front teeth being missing. Deceased also had a scar on the forehead which was caused by a fall when she was young. There was a scar on the body of the woman then lying in the mortuary. His daughter's name was Mary Ann Nichols, and she had been married quite 22 years. Her husband's name was William Nichols, a printer's machinist, and he was still alive. They had been living apart for seven or eight years. Deceased was about 42 years of age. The last time witness heard of the deceased was about Easter, when she wrote him a letter. He produced the letter, which was in the handwriting of the deceased. It spoke of a situation she was in, and which, she said, she liked very much. He answered that letter, but had not since heard from the deceased. The last time he saw deceased was in June, 1886, when she was respectably dressed. That was at the funeral of his son, who was burnt to death through the explosion of a paraffin lamp. Some three or four years previous to that the deceased had lived with witness; but he was unable to say what she had since been doing. Deceased was not a particularly sober woman, and that was the reason why they could not agree. He did not think she was "fast" with men, and she was not in the habit of staying out late at night while she was living with him. He had no idea what deceased had been doing since she left him. He did not turn the deceased out of doors. They simply had a few words, and the following morning she left home. The reason deceased parted from her husband was that he went and lived with the woman who nursed his wife during her confinement. Witness knew nothing of his daughter's acquaintances, or what she had been doing for a living. Deceased was not 5ft. 4in. in height. She had five children, the eldest of whom was 21 years of age and the youngest eight or nine. She left her husband when the youngest child was only one or two years of age. The eldest was now lodging with witness. He was unable to say if deceased had recently been living with any one; but some three or four years ago he heard she was living with a man named Drew, who was a house smith by trade and had a shop of his own in York-street, Walworth. Witness believed he was still living there. The husband of the deceased had been summoned for the keep of the children, but the charge was dismissed owing to the fact that she was then living with another man. Deceased was in the Lambeth Workhouse in April last, when she left to go to a situation. Her husband was still living at Coburg-road, Old Kent-road, but witness was not aware if he was acquainted with his wife's death. Witness did not think the deceased had any enemies, as she was too good for that.

Police-constable John Neil 97J, deposed that on Friday morning he was passing down Buck's-row, Whitechapel, and going in the direction of Brady-street, and he did not notice any one about. He had been round the same place some half an hour previous to that and did not see any one. He was walking along the right-hand side of the street when he noticed a figure lying in the street. It was dark at the time, although a street lamp was shining at the end of the row. He walked across and found the deceased lying outside a gateway, her head towards the east. He noticed that the gateway, which was about 9ft. or 10ft. in height and led to some stables, was closed. Houses ran eastward from the gateway, while the Board school was westward of the spot. On the other side of the road was the Essex Wharf. The deceased was lying lengthways, and her left hand touched the gate. With the aid of his lamp he examined the body and saw blood oozing from a wound in the throat. Deceased was lying upon her back with her clothes disarranged. Witness felt her arm, which was quite warm from the joints upwards, while her eyes were wide open. Her bonnet was off her head and was lying by her right side, close

by the left hand. Witness then heard a constable passing Brady-street, and he
called to him. Witness said to him, "Run at once for Dr. Llewellyn." Seeing
another constable in Baker's-row, witness despatched him for the ambulance.
Dr. Llewellyn arrived in a very short time. In the meantime witness had rung
the bell of Essex Wharf and inquired if any disturbance had been heard. He
was told "No." Sergeant Kerby then came, and he knocked. The doctor,
having looked at the woman, said:- "Move the woman to the mortuary; she is
dead. I will make a further examination of her." They then placed deceased
on the ambulance and removed her to the mortuary. Inspector Spratley [*sic*]
came to the mortuary, and while taking a description of deceased lifted up her
clothes and discovered she was disembowelled. That had not been noticed
before. On the deceased was found a piece of comb and a bit of looking-glass,
but no money was found. In the pocket an unmarked white pocket
handkerchief was found. There was a pool of blood where the neck of
deceased was lying in Buck's row. He had not heard any disturbance that
night. The farthest he had been that night was up Baker's-row to the
Whitechapel-road, and was never far away from the spot. The Whitechapel-
road was a busy thoroughfare in the early morning, and he saw a number of
women in that road, apparently on their way home. At that time any one
could have got away. Witness examined the ground while the doctor was
being sent for. (Inspector Spratley [*sic*] observed that he examined the road
after it was daylight.) In answer to a juryman, the witness said he did not see
any trap in the road. He examined the road, but could not see any marks of
wheels. The first persons who arrived on the spot after he discovered the
body were two men who worked at a slaughterhouse opposite [*sic*]. They
stated that they knew nothing of the affair, nor had they heard any screams.
Witness had previously seen the men at work. That would be a quarter past 3,
or half an hour before he found the body.

Mr. Henry Llewellyn, surgeon, of 152, Whitechapel-road, stated that at
4 o'clock on Friday morning he was called by the last witness to Buck's-row.
The officer told him what he was wanted for. On reaching Buck's-row he
found deceased lying flat on her back on the pathway, her legs being extended.
Deceased was quite dead, and she had severe injuries to her throat. Her hands
and wrists were cold, but the lower extremities were quite warm. Witness
examined her chest and felt the heart. It was dark at the time. He should say
the deceased had not been dead more than half an hour. He was certain the
injuries to the neck were not self-inflicted. There was very little blood round
the neck, and there were no marks of any struggle or of blood, as though the
body had been dragged. Witness gave the police directions to take the body to
the mortuary, where he would make another examination. About an hour
afterwards he was sent for by the inspector to see the other injuries he had

discovered on the body. Witness went, and saw that the abdomen was cut very extensively. That morning he had made a post-mortem examination of the body. It was that of a female of about 40 or 45 years. Five of the teeth were missing, and there was a slight laceration of the tongue. There was a bruise running along the lower part of the jaw on the right side of the face. That might have been caused by a blow from a fist or pressure from a thumb. There was a circular bruise on the left side of the face, which also might have been inflicted by the pressure of the fingers. On the left side of the neck, about 1in. below the jaw, there was an incision about 4in. in length, and ran from a point immediately below the ear. On the same side, but an inch below, and commencing about 1in. in front of it, was a circular incision, which terminated at a point about 3in. below the right jaw. That incision completely severed all the tissues down to the vertebrae. The large vessels of the neck on both sides were severed. The incision was about 8in. in length. the cuts must have been caused by a long-bladed knife, moderately sharp, and used with great violence. No blood was found on the breast, either of the body or clothes. There were no injuries about the body until just about the lower part of the abdomen. Two or three inches from the left side was a wound running in a jagged manner. The wound was a very deep one, and the tissues were cut through. There were several incisions running across the abdomen. There were also three or four similar cuts, running downwards, on the right side, all of which had been caused by a knife which had been used violently and downwards. The injuries were from left to right, and might have been done by a left-handed person. All the injuries had been caused by the same instrument.

At this stage Mr. Wynne Baxter adjourned the inquiry until this morning.

The next report[11], respecting the adjourned inquest, appeared in *The Times* of 4 September 1888, page 8:

THE WHITECHAPEL MURDER

Yesterday morning Mr. Wynne E. Baxter, the Coroner for the South-Eastern Division of Middlesex, resumed his inquiry at the Working Lads' Institute, High-street, Whitechapel, respecting the death of MARY ANN NICHOLS, whose dead body was found on the pavement in Buck's-row, Whitechapel, on Friday morning.

Detective-inspector Abberline (Scotland-yard), Inspector Helston [*sic*], and Detective-sergeants P. Enright and Godley watched the case on behalf of the Criminal Investigation Department.

Inspector J. Spratling J Division, was the first witness called. He deposed that at 4.30 on Friday morning he was called to the spot where the body of the deceased was found lying. On getting there he found two constables, one of whom pointed out the exact spot on which he found the body. At that time the blood was being washed away, but he could see some stains in between the stones. He was told that the body had been removed to the mortuary. On going there he found the body was still on the ambulance in the yard. While waiting for the arrival of the keeper of the dead-house he took a description of the deceased, but at that time did not notice any wounds on the body. On the body being put in the mortuary he made a more careful examination, and then discovered the injuries to the abdomen, and at once sent for Dr. Llewellyn. He saw two workhouse men stripping the body.

At this point, in reply to a question, Detective-sergeant P. Enright said he gave instructions that the body should not be touched.

Witness, continuing his evidence, stated he again went to the mortuary and made an examination of the clothing taken off the deceased. The principal parts of the clothing consisted of a reddish ulster, somewhat the worse for wear, a new brown linsey dress, two flannel petticoats, having the marks of the Lambeth Workhouse on them, and a pair of stays. The things were fastened, but witness did not remove them himself, so could not say positively that all the clothing was properly fastened.

The CORONER observed it was such matters as these that threw a most important bearing on the subject. The question of the clothing was a most important one. Later on he directed Constable Thain, 96J, to examine all the premises in the vicinity of the spot where the body was discovered.

Inspector Spratling continuing, said he and Sergeant Godley examined the East London and District Railway embankments and lines, and also the Great Eastern Railway yard, but they were unable to find anything likely to throw any light on the affair. One of Mr. Brown's men wiped up the blood. A constable was on duty at the gate of the Great Eastern Railway yard, which was about 50 yards from the spot where the body was found. He had questioned this constable, but he had not heard anything. Mrs. Green, who also lived opposite the spot, had been seen, and during the night she had not heard anything, although she was up until 4.30 that morning. Mr. Purkis, who also lived close by, stated his wife had been pacing the room that morning, about the time the murder must have been committed, but she had not heard anything. It was 150 yards from the spot where the body was found to Barber's slaughter-yard. That was by walking round the Board school. During the night Constable Neil and another officer were within hearing distance of the spot. He should think deceased had been murdered while wearing her clothes, and did not think she had been dressed after death.

Henry Tomkins, a horse-slaughterer, living at 12, Coventry-street, Bethnal-green, stated he was in the employ of Mr. Barber. Thursday night and Friday morning he spent in the slaughterhouse in Winthrop-street. Witness commenced about his usual time – between 8 and 9 o'clock p.m. On Friday morning he left off work at 20 minutes past 4 and went for a walk. It was their rule to go home when they did so, but they did not do so that morning. A constable told them of the finding of the murdered woman, and they went to look at her. James Mumford, Charles Brittan, and witness worked together. At 12 o'clock witness and Brittan left the slaughterhouse, and returned about 1 o'clock. They did not again leave the slaughterhouse until they heard of the murder. All the gates were open, and witness during the night did not hear any disturbance; the only person who came to the slaughterhouse was the constable. At times women came to the place, but none came that night. Had any one called out "Murder" in Buck's-row he might not have heard it. There were men and women in the Whitechapel-road. Witness and Mumford went and saw the deceased, and then Brittan followed. At that time a doctor and three or four constables were there, and witness remained there until the body was taken away. At night he and his mates generally went out to have a drink. It depended upon what time their work was done when they went home. The constable was at the slaughterhouse at about a quarter past 4, when he called for his cape. It was then that they heard of the murder.

Inspector Helston [*sic*], J Division, deposed that it was a quarter to 7 on Friday morning when he received information of the murder. Having learnt full particulars, he proceeded to the mortuary, where he saw deceased, who had her clothing on. He saw the things removed. The bodice of the dress was buttoned down to the middle and the stays were fastened. There were no bruises on the arms to indicate that a struggle had taken place. The wounds on the abdomen were visible with the stays on, and that proved they could have been inflicted while the stays were on the deceased. he did not examine the spot where the body was found until after the blood had been washed away. Witness was of opinion that the murder was committed at the spot where the body was found. The clothes were very little disarranged, thus showing that the body could not have been carried far.

Constable G. Mizen, 56 H, stated that at a quarter past 4 on Friday morning he was in Hanbury-street, Baker's-row, and a man passing said "You are wanted in Baker's-row." The man, named Cross, stated a woman had been found there. In going to the spot he saw Constable Neil, and by the direction of the latter he went for the ambulance. When Cross spoke to witness he was accompanied by another man, and both of them afterwards went down Hanbury-street. Cross simply said he was wanted by a policeman, and did not say anything about a murder having been committed. He denied that before he went to Buck's-row he continued knocking people up.

George [*sic*] **Cross**, a carman, stated that he left home on Friday morning at 20 minutes past 3, and he arrived at his work, at Broad-street, at 4 o'clock.

Witness walked along Buck's-row, and saw something lying in front of the gateway like a tarpaulin. He then saw it was a woman. A man came along and witness spoke to him. They went and looked at the body. Witness, having felt one of the deceased woman's hands and finding it cold, said "I believe she is dead." The other man, having put his hand over her heart, said "I think she is breathing." He wanted witness to assist in shifting her, but he would not do so. He did not notice any blood, as it was very dark. They went to Baker's-row, saw the last witness, and told him there was a woman lying down in Buck's-row on the broad of her back. Witness also said he believed she was dead or drunk, while the other man stated he believed her to be dead. The constable replied "All right." The other man left witness at the corner of Hanbury-street and turned into Corbett's-court. He appeared to be a carman, and was a stranger to witness. At the time he did not think the woman had been murdered. Witness did not hear any sounds of a vehicle, and believed that had any one left the body after he got into Buck's-row he must have heard him.

William Nichols, a machinist, of Coburg-road, Old Kent-road, stated that the deceased woman was his wife. He had been separated from her for upwards of eight years. The last time he saw her was over three years ago, and he had no idea what she had been doing since that time, nor with whom she had lived. Deceased was much given to drink. They separated several times, and each time he took her back she got drunk, and that was why he had to leave her altogether.

Jane Oram, 18, Thrawl-street, Spitalfields, deposed that deceased had slept at the common lodging-house there for about six weeks. Witness and deceased had occupied the same bed. For eight or ten days she had not been to the lodging-house, but witness saw her on the morning of her death in the Whitechapel-road. Deceased told her she was living where men and women were allowed to sleep, but added that she should come back and live with witness. Witness believed deceased stated she had been living in Flowery Dean-street [*sic*]. Deceased was the worse for drink and refused to stay with witness, although she did all she could to persuade her to do so. Witness did not think she was a fast woman. She was a clean woman, but witness had previously seen her the worse for drink.

Mary Ann Monk stated that she was an inmate of the Lambeth Workhouse. She knew the deceased, who had been an inmate of the union, but that was six or seven years ago.

The CORONER here informed the jury that the police did not propose to offer any further evidence that day, and it would be as well to adjourn the inquiry sufficiently long to give them an opportunity of obtaining further evidence.

The inquiry was accordingly adjourned for a fortnight.

The next extract is from *The Times* dated 18 September 1888, page 12, and relates to the resumed inquest[12] into the murder of Mary Ann Nichols:

THE WHITECHAPEL MURDER.

Yesterday Mr. Wynne E. Baxter, Coroner for the South-Eastern Division of Middlesex, resumed his adjourned inquiry at the Working Lads' Institute, Buck's-row, Whitechapel, respecting the death of Mary Ann Nichols, who was found brutally murdered in Buck's-row, Whitechapel, on the morning of Friday, the 31st ult.

Detective-inspectors Abberline (Scotland-yard) and Helson, and Inspectors Spratling and Chandler watched the case on behalf of the Criminal Investigation Department and Commissioners of Police.

Mr. Llewellyn, surgeon, recalled, said that since the last inquiry he had been to the mortuary and again examined the deceased. She had an old scar on the forehead. No part of the viscera was missing. He had nothing to add to his previous evidence.

Mrs. Emma Green, living at New-cottage, Buck's-row, stated she was a widow, and occupied the cottage next to where the deceased was found. Her daughter and two sons lived with her. Witness went to bed about 11 o'clock on the night of Thursday, August 30, and one of her sons went to bed at 9 o'clock, and the other one at a quarter to 10. Her daughter went to bed when she did, and they occupied the same room. It was a front room on the first floor. Witness did not remember waking up until she heard a knock at the front door about 4 o'clock in the morning. She opened the window and saw three or four constables and two or three other men. She saw the body of deceased lying on the ground, but it was still too dark to clearly distinguish what had happened. Witness heard nothing unusual during the night, and neither her sons or daughter awoke.

By the Jury. – She was a light sleeper, and had a scream been given she would have heard it, though people often went through Buck's-row, and there was often a great noise in it. She did not believe there was any disorderly house in Buck's-row. She knew of no disorderly house in the immediate neighbourhood.

By the CORONER – She saw her son go out, directly the body was removed, with a pail of water to wash the stains of blood away. A constable was with him.

Thomas Ede, a signalman in the employ of the East London Railway Company, said he saw a man on the line on the morning of the 8th.

The CORONER observed that had no reference to this inquiry. The 8th was the morning of the other murder. It was decided to take the witness's evidence.

Witness, continuing, said on Saturday morning, the 8th inst., he was coming down the Cambridge-heath-road, and when just opposite the Foresters' Arms saw a man on the opposite side of the street. His peculiar appearance made witness look at him. He appeared to have a wooden arm, as it was hanging at his side. Witness watched him until he got level with the Foresters' Arms. He then put his hand down, and witness saw about 4in. of the blade of a long knife sticking out of his trousers pocket. Three other men were also looking at him and witness spoke to them. Witness followed him, and as soon as he saw he was followed he quickened his pace. Witness lost sight of him under some railway arches. He was about 5ft. 8in. high, about 35 years of age, with dark moustache and whiskers. He wore a double peak cap, dark brown jacket, and a pair of overalls over a pair of dark trousers. He walked as though he had a stiff knee, and he had a fearful look about the eyes.

By the CORONER. – Witness should say the man was a mechanic. The overalls were perfectly clean. He could not see what kind of a knife it was. He was not a muscular man.

Inspector Helson said they had been unable to trace the man.

Walter Purkiss stated he lived at Essex Wharf, Buck's-row, and was a manager there. His house was in Buck's-row and fronted the street. It was nearly opposite to where the deceased was found. His wife, children, and servant occupied the house with him. Witness and his wife slept in the front portion of the house – the room on the second floor. On the night of the occurrence he went to bed at 11 o'clock or a quarter past 11. Witness awoke at various times during the night and was awake between 1 and 2 o'clock. He did not hear anything until he was called up by the police about 4 o'clock. His wife was awake the greater portion of the night. Neither of them heard a sound during the night, and it was unusually quiet. When the police called him he opened the landing window. He could see the deceased, and there were two or three men there, besides three or four constables. Had there been any quarrelling in the row during the night witness would certainly have heard it.

Patrick Mulshaw, a night porter in the employ of the Whitechapel District Board of Works, living at 3 Rupert-street, Whitechapel, said on the night of this occurrence he was at the back of the Working Lads' Institute in Winthorpe-street [*sic*]. He went on duty about a quarter to 5 in the afternoon, and remained until about five minutes to 6 the next morning, when he was relieved. He was watching some sewage works. He dozed at times during the night, but was not asleep between 3 and 4 o'clock. He did not see any one about during that period, and did not hear any cries for assistance, or any other noise. The slaughterhouse was about 70 yards away from where he was. Another man then passed by, and said, ''Watchman, old man, I believe somebody is murdered down the street.'' Witness then went to Buck's-row, and saw the body of deceased lying on the ground. Three or four policemen and five or six working men were there.

By the CORONER. – If any one had called out for assistance from the spot where the body was he might have heard it. Nothing suspicious occurred during the time he was watching, and he saw no person running away. There was no one about after 11 and 12 o'clock, and the inhabitants of the street appeared to be very orderly persons. He did not often see the police there. During the night he saw two constables, including Constable Neil. He was unable to say what time he saw that officer.

Constable John Phail [sic – Thain], 96J, said he was not brought any closer to Buck's-row in his beat than Brady-street, but he passed the end of it. He passed the end of Buck's-row every 30 minutes. Nothing attracted his attention until about 3.45 a.m., when he was signalled by a brother constable flashing his lamp some way down Buck's-row. Witness went to him, and found Constable Neil standing by the body of the deceased. Neil was by himself. Witness ran for the doctor, and having called Dr. Llewellyn, accompanied him to the spot where deceased was lying. On his return with the doctor, Neil and two workmen were standing by the body. He did not know the workmen. The body was then taken to the mortuary by Sergeant Kerby, Constable Neil, and an officer of the H Division. Witness, acting under orders, waited at the spot for Inspector Spratling. He was present when the spots of blood were washed away. On the spot where the deceased had been lying was a mass of congealed blood. He should say it was about 6in. in diameter, and had run towards the gutter. It appeared to him to be a large quantity of blood.

By the CORONER. – He helped to put the body on the ambulance, and the back appeared to be covered with blood, which, he thought, had run from the neck as far as the waist. He got blood on to his hands. There was also blood on the ground where the deceased's legs had been. Witness afterwards searched Essex Wharf, the Great Eastern Railway, the East London Railway, and the District Railway, as far as Thomas-street, but could find no knife, marks of blood, or anything suspicious. He did not make inquiries at the houses in Buck's-row.

By the Jury. – He did not pass the end of Buck's-row exactly at the end of each half-hour. It was a quarter-past 3 when he was round there before. He did not take his cape to the slaughterhouse, but sent it by a brother constable. When he was sent for the doctor he did not first go to the horse-slaughterers and say that as a murder had been committed he had better fetch his cape. He was not supposed to leave his beat. Shortly before he was called by Constable Neil he saw one or two men going to work in the direction of Whitechapel-road. When he was signalled by Neil he was coming up Brady-street, from the direction of Whitechapel-road.

Robert Baul [*sic* – Paul], a carman of 30, Foster-street, Whitechapel, stated he went to work at Cobbett's-court, Spitalfields. He left home about a quarter to 4 on the Friday morning, and as he was passing up Buck's-row he saw a man standing in the middle of the road. As witness approached him he walked towards the pavement, and witness stepped on to the roadway in order to pass him. He then touched witness on the shoulder, and said, "Come and look at this woman here." Witness went with him, and saw a woman lying right across the gateway. Her clothes were raised almost up to her stomach. Witness felt her hands and face, and they were cold. He knelt down to see if he could hear her breathe, but could not, and he thought she was dead. It was very dark, and he did not notice any blood. They agreed that the best thing they could do would be to tell the first policeman they met. He could not see whether the clothes were torn, and did not feel any other part of her body except the hands and face. They looked to see if there was a constable, but one was not to be seen. While he was pulling the clothes down he touched the breast, and then fancied he felt a slight movement.

By the CORONER. – The morning was rather a chilly one. Witness and the other man walked on together until they met a policeman at the corner of Old Montagu-street, and told him what they had seen. Up to that time not more than four minutes had elapsed from the time he saw the body. He had not met any one before he reached Buck's-row, and did not see any one running away.

Robert Mann, a pauper inmate of the Whitechapel Workhouse, stated he had charge of the mortuary. On the morning in question the police came to the workhouse and told him there was a body at the mortuary. Witness went there about 5 o'clock, and remained there until the body was placed inside the mortuary. He then locked the mortuary door, and went to breakfast. After breakfast witness and Hatfield, another inmate of the workhouse, undressed the body. No police or any one else was present when that was done. Inspector Helson was not there.

By the CORONER. – He had not been told that he must not touch the body. He could not remember Inspector Helson being present, as he was confused. He was sure the clothing was not torn or cut; but could not describe where the blood was. To get off the clothes Hatfield had to cut them down the front.

By the Jury. – The body was undressed in the morning, and was not taken out after it was brought in.

The CORONER said the witness was subject to fits, and his statements were hardly reliable.

James Hatfield said he assisted the last witness in undressing the deceased. Inspector Helson was not there. They first took off the ulster, and put it on the ground. Witness then took the jacket off and put it in the same place. He did not have to cut the dress to get it off, but cut the bands of the two petticoats, and then tore them down with his hands. Deceased was wearing a chemise, and he tore it right down the front. She was not wearing any stays. No one gave them any instructions to strip the body. They did it so as to have the body ready for the doctor. He had heard something about a doctor coming; and he was not aware that any one was present while they were stripping the deceased. Afterwards the police came, and examined the clothing. They found the words "Lambeth Workhouse" on the band of one of the petticoats. Witness cut that portion out by direction of Inspector Helson. That was the first time he had seen Inspector Helson that morning. It was about 6.30 when witness first arrived at the mortuary. Although he had said deceased wore no stays he would not be surprised to find she had stays on.

The Foreman. – Why, you tried the stays on the body of the deceased in my presence at the mortuary, and you said they were short.

Witness admitted his memory was bad.

In answer to the CORONER, Inspector Abberline said they were unable to find the man who passed down Buck's-row while the doctor was examining the body.

Inspector Spratling, J Division, said he had made inquiries at several of the houses in Buck's-row, but not at all of them.

The CORONER. – Then that will have to be done.

Witness further said he had made inquiries at Mrs. Green's, the wharf, at Sneider's Factory, and also at the Great Eastern Wharf, but no one at those places had heard anything unusual during the morning in question. He had seen the Board school keeper, but he had not heard anything. Had the other inhabitants heard a disturbance of any kind they would, no doubt, have communicated with the police. There was a gateman at the Great Eastern Railway, but he was stationed inside the gates, and had not heard anything. There was a watchman employed at Sneider's factory. He distinctly told the mortuary-keeper not to touch the body.

Inspector Helson said he knew of no other evidence.

In answer to a juryman, the officer said the murderer would have no occasion to get on to the Great Eastern Railway, as he could pass along the street.

The Foreman thought that if a substantial reward had been offered by the Home Secretary in the case of the murder in George-yard, these two horrible murders would not have happened. Mr. Matthews thought that rewards got into wrong hands, but if they did, what did it matter so long as the perpetrator was brought to justice?

The CORONER understood there was a regulation that no reward should be offered in the case of the murder of either a rich or a poor person.

The Foreman believed a substantial one would have been offered had a rich person been murdered. He would be glad to give £5 himself for the capture of the murderer.

The inquiry was then adjourned until Saturday.

The report[13] on the adjourned inquest appeared in *The Times* of Monday, 24 September 1888, page 3:

THE WHITECHAPEL MURDERS.

On Saturday, Mr. Wynne E. Baxter, coroner for the South-Eastern Division of Middlesex, resumed his adjourned inquiry at the Working Lads' Institute, Whitechapel-road, respecting the death of Mary Ann Nichols, who was found brutally murdered in Buck's-row, Whitechapel.

William Eade, recalled, stated he had since seen the man whom he saw with the knife near the Foresters'-hall. He had ascertained that his name was Henry James, and that he did not possess a wooden arm.

The CORONER said the man James had been seen, and been proved to be a well-known harmless lunatic. As there was no further evidence forthcoming he would proceed to sum up. Before commencing the few remarks that he proposed to make to the jury, he should, he was sure, be only reflecting their feelings if he first returned his thanks to the committee of the Working Lads' Institute for the use of such a convenient room for the purposes of this inquest. Without their assistance, they would have been compelled to conduct this inquiry in a public house parlour – inconvenient and out of harmony with their functions, for Whitechapel not only did not possess any coroner's court, such as have been erected in St. Luke's, Clerkenwell, the City, and most of the West-end parishes, but it was without any town-hall or vestry-hall, such as were used for inquests at St. George's, Shadwell, Limehouse, and Poplar. To the Working Lads' Institute committee, therefore, he felt they were under obligations deserving of public recognition. The jury would probably have been surprised to find there was no public mortuary in Whitechapel. He had been informed that there was formerly one, but that it was demolished by the Metropolitan Board of Works when making a new street, and that compensation was paid to the local authorities, who have never yet expended it on the object of the trust. Perhaps he had been misinformed, but this he did know, that jury after jury had requested the coroner to draw the attention of the sanitary authorities to the deficiency, and, hitherto, without success. They deemed it essential for the health of the neighbourhood; and surely if mortuaries were found necessary at the West-end, there must be stronger reasons for them here, in the midst of so much squalid crowding. But this inconvenience had been felt in other ways in this inquiry. In the absence of a public mortuary, the police carried the body to the deadhouse belonging to the workhouse infirmary. It was admittedly not ornate in appearance, and was not altogether suited for the purpose to which it had been applied; but they must not forget that such mortuary was a private structure, intended solely for use by the Union authorities, and that its use on other occasions had been allowed only by the courtesy of the guardians, but that only proved the necessity for a public mortuary. Had there been a public mortuary there would also have been a keeper, whose experience would have shown the advisability of the body being attended to only in the presence of the medical witness. He himself trusted now that the attention of the authorities had again been called to this pressing matter, the subject would be taken into serious consideration, and the deficiency supplied. Referring to the facts in the case before him, the Coroner said the deceased had been identified by her father and her husband to have been Mary Ann Nichols, a married woman with five children, and about 42 years of age. She was of intemperate habits, and left her husband eight years ago on account of drink. The husband had not seen her or heard of her for three years. She had evidently formed irregular connexions, but still lived under her father's roof for three or four years, and then either to avoid the restraints of a settled home, or in consequence of her own misconduct, she left her father, who had not seen her for more than two years. She was in the Lambeth Workhouse on several occasions, at Christmas last and again in April. While there last she was fortunate enough to find a lady in Wandsworth willing to take her into her house as a domestic servant, and at the time she wrote her father a letter, which held out some promise of reform; but her fresh start did not appear to have lasted long, for she soon afterwards left her situation in great disgrace. From that time until her death it was pretty clear that she had been living an intemperate, irregular, and vicious life, mostly in the common lodging-houses in that neighbourhood. There was nothing in the evidence as to the movements of the deceased on the day before her death, except a statement by herself that she was living in a common lodginghouse, called the White House, in Flower and Dean-street, Spitalfields; but he believed her movements had been traced by the police, and were not considered to have any connexion with her death. On Friday evening, the 31st of August, she was seen by Mrs. Holland – who knew her well – at the corner of Osborn-street and Whitechapel-road, nearly opposite the parish church. The deceased woman was then much the worse for drink and was staggering against the wall. Her friend endeavoured to persuade her to come home with her, but she declined, and was last seen endeavouring to walk eastward down

Whitechapel. She said she had her lodging money three times that day, but that she had spent it, that she was going about to get some money to pay her lodgings, and she would soon be back. In less than an hour and a quarter after this she was found dead at a spot rather under three-quarters or a mile distant. The deceased was first discovered by a carman on his way to work, who passed down Buck's-row, on the opposite side of the road. Immediately after he had ascertained that the dark object in the gateway was the figure of a woman he heard the approaching footsteps of a man. This proved to be Paul, another carman. Together they went to the woman. The condition of her clothing suggested to them that she had been outraged and had fainted. She was only just dead, if life were really extinct. Paul says he felt a slight movement of her breast, and thought she was breathing. Neither of the carmen appeared to have realized the condition of the woman, and no injuries were noticed by them; but that, no doubt, was accounted for by the early hour of the morning and the darkness of the spot. The carmen reported the circumstances to a constable at the corner of Hanbury-street, 300 yards distant, but although he appeared to have started without delay, he found another constable was already there. In fact, Constable Neil must independently have found the body within a few minutes of the finding of it by the two carmen. The condition in which the body was found appeared to prove conclusively that the deceased was killed on the exact spot in which she was found. There was not a trace of blood anywhere, except at the spot where her neck was lying. That appeared to him sufficient to justify the assumption that the injuries to the throat were inflicted when the woman was on the ground, while the state of her clothing and the absence of any blood about her legs equally proved that the abdominal injuries were inflicted while she was still in the same position. Nor did there appear any grounds for doubt that, if deceased was killed where she was found, she met her death without a cry of any kind. The spot was almost under the windows of Mrs. Green, a light sleeper. It was opposite the bedroom of Mrs. Purkiss, who was awake at the time. Then there were watchmen at various spots within very short distances. Not a sound was heard by any. Nor was there evidence of any struggle. This might have arisen from her intoxication, or from being stunned by a blow. Again, the deceased could not have been killed long before she was found. Constable Neil was positive that he was at the spot half an hour before, and then neither the body was there nor was any one about. Even if Paul were mistaken in the movement of the chest, Neil found her right arm still warm, and even Dr. Llewellyn, who saw the body about a quarter of an hour afterwards, found the body and lower extremities still warm, notwithstanding the loss of blood and abdominal injuries and that those extremities had been uncovered. It seemed astonishing, at first thought, that the culprit should escape detection, for there must surely have been marks of blood about his person. If, however, blood was principally on his hands, the presence of so many slaughter-houses in the neighbourhood would make the frequenters of that spot familiar with blood-stained clothes and hands, and his appearance might in that way have failed to attract attention while he passed from Buck's-row in the twilight into Whitechapel-road and was lost sight of in the morning's market traffic. He himself thought they could not altogether leave unnoticed the fact that the death the jury had been investigating was one of four presenting many points of similarity, all of which had occurred within the space of about five months, and all within a very short distance of the place where they were sitting. All four victims were women of middle age; all were married and had lived apart from their husbands in consequence of intemperate habits, and were at the time of their death leading irregular lives and eking out a miserable and precarious existence in common lodging-houses. In each case there were abdominal as well as other injuries. In each case the injuries were inflicted after midnight, and in places of public resort where it would appear impossible but that almost immediate detection would follow the crime, and in each case the inhuman and dastardly criminals were at large in society. Emma Elizabeth Smith, who received her injuries in Osborn-street on the early morning of Easter Tuesday, the 3d of April, survived in the London Hospital for upwards of 24 hours, and was able to state that she had been followed by some men, robbed and mutilated, and even to describe imperfectly one of them. Martha Tabram was found at 3 a.m. on Tuesday, the 7th of August, on the first-floor landing of George-yard-buildings, with 39 punctured wounds on her body. In addition to these, and the case under the consideration of the jury there was the case of Annie Chapman, still in the hands of another jury. The instruments used in the two earlier cases were dissimilar. In the first it was a blunt instrument, such as a walking-stick; in the second some of the wounds were thought to have been made by a dagger, but in the two recent cases the instruments suggested by the medical witnesses were not so different. Dr. Llewellyn said that the injuries on Nichols could have been produced by a long-bladed instrument moderately sharp. Dr. Phillips was of opinion that those on Chapman were by a very sharp knife, probably with a thin, narrow blade, at least 6 in. to 8 in. in length, probably longer. The similarity of the injuries in the two cases was considerable. There were bruises about the face in both cases, the head was nearly severed from the body in both cases, and those injuries again, had in each case been performed with anatomical knowledge. Dr. Llewellyn seemed to incline to the opinion that the abdominal injuries were inflicted first, and caused instantaneous death; but, if so, it seemed difficult to understand the object of such desperate injuries to the throat, or how it came about there was so little bleeding from the several arteries that the clothing on the upper surface was not stained and the legs not soiled, and there was very much less bleeding from the abdomen than from the neck. Surely it might well be that, as in the case of Chapman, the dreadful wounds to the throat were first inflicted and the abdominal afterwards. That was a matter of some importance when they came to consider what possible motive there could be for all this ferocity. Robbery was out of the question, and there was nothing to suggest jealousy. There could not have been any quarrel, or it would have been heard. The taking of some of the abdominal viscera from the body of Chapman suggested that that may have been the object of her death. Was it not possible that this may also have been the motive in the case they had under consideration? He suggested to the jury as a possibility that these two women might have been murdered by the same man with the same object, and that in the case of Nichols the wretch was disturbed before he had accomplished his object, and, having failed in the open street, he tried again, within a week of his failure, in a more secluded place. If this was correct, the audacity and daring was equal to its maniacal fanaticism and abhorrent wickedness. But that surmise might or might not be correct; the suggested motive might be the wrong one; but one thing was very clear – that the injuries were of such a nature that they could not have been self-inflicted, that no imaginable facts could reduce that to evidence of manslaughter, and that a murder of a most atrocious character had been committed.

The jury, having considered in private, returned a verdict of "Wilful murder against some person or persons unknown." They also thanked the Coroner for the remarks made with reference to the mortuary and for the very able way in which he had conducted the case.

CHAPTER 4

8 September 1888 – Murder of Annie Chapman

The murder of Annie Chapman on the morning of Saturday, 8 September 1888 occurred on the day after the funeral of Mary Ann Nichols. The interval of only just over a week between the two murders obviously caused a sensation: the fears intimated in the press reports of the Nichols murder of a maniacal lone killer at work in the East End streets were apparently confirmed when the details of this horrific new murder became known. Further areas of factual dispute also arose from this killing, notably concerning the items "arranged" on the ground near Chapman's body, items that included, according to legend, two farthings and two rings. The true facts in this regard are shown in the following reports. The first probable sighting of the killer, by the witness Mrs Long, also occurred in this case. The details preserved in the police reports on the Chapman murder are as follows.

The detective and first police officer on the scene of the Chapman murder was Inspector Joseph Chandler of H Division, stationed at Commercial Street. His report[1] on the finding of the body, dated 8 September 1888, follows beginning with the file cover[2].

C.O. REFERENCE. DIVISIONAL REFERENCE.
H302
Submitted through Ex: Bch:
H Division.
Subject Murder of Annie Siffey at 29 Hanbury Street Spitalfields.
No. 334
.1
1st Special Report + submitted in accordance with P.O. 9th Febry. 1888.

WDavis
Actg.Supt
8.9.88

To/AC(CID).

Mr. Williamson.

(vide Actg Supts' report)

I understand Insp. Abberline is taking up this as well as the other murder com

ACB.
8.9.88.

Inspr. Abberline is assisting H in making enquiry into this murder. He was instructed to do so this morning

AFW 8/9/88

Seen ACB

Commercial Street   30o/1
METROPOLITAN POLICE.
H Division.
8th September 1888

I beg to report that at 6.10 a.m. 8th inst. while on duty in Commercial Street, Spitalfields, I received information that a woman had been murdered. I at once proceeded to No. 29 Hanbury Street, and in the back yard found a woman lying on her back, dead, left arm resting on left breast, legs drawn up, abducted small intestines and flap of the abdomen lying on right side, above right shoulder attached by a cord with the rest of the intestines inside the body; two flaps of skin from the lower part of the abdomen lying in a large quantity of blood above the left shoulder; throat cut deeply from left and back in a jagged manner right around throat. I at once sent for Dr. Phillips Div. Surgeon and to the Station for the ambulance and assistance. The Doctor pronounced life extinct and stated the woman had been dead at least two hours. The body was then removed on the Police ambulance to the Whitechapel mortuary.

On examining the yard I found on the back wall of the house (at the head of the body) and about 18 inches from the ground about 6 patches of blood varying in size from a sixpenny piece to a point, and on the wooden pailing [sic] on left of the body near the head patches and smears of blood about 14 inches from the ground.

The woman has been identified by Timothy Donovan "Deputy" Crossinghams Lodging house 35 Dorset Street, Spitalfields, who states he has known her about 16 months, as a prostitute and for past 4 months she had lodged at above house and at 1.45 a.m. 8th inst she was in the kitchen, the worse for liquor and eating potatoes, he Donovan sent to her for the money for her bed, which she said she had not got and asked him to trust her which he declined to do she then left stating that she would not be long gone; he saw no man in her company.

Description, Annie Siffey age 45, length 5 ft, complexion fair, hair (wavy)

dark brown, eyes blue, two teeth deficient in lower jaw, large thick nose; dress black figured jacket, brown bodice, black skirt, lace boots, all old and dirty.

A description of the woman has been circulated by wire to All Stations and a special enquiry called for at Lodging Houses &c to ascertain if any men of a suspicious character or having blood on their clothing entered after 2 am 8th inst.

JL.Chandler Inspr.

Respectfully submitted

Every possible enquiry is being made with a view of tracing the murderer, but up to the present without success. Local Inspector Reid being on his annual leave, the enquiries have been entrusted to Inspector Chandler, and P.Ss Thick & Leach C.I.Dept. I would respectfully suggest that Inspector Abberline, Central, who is well acquainted with H.Division be deputed to take up this enquiry as I believe he is already engaged in the case of the Bucks Row murder which would appear to have been committed by the same person as the one in Hanbury Street.

Jno.West ActgSupt.

It was at this time that enquiries into various suspects brought to police attention began. One of the earliest was Joseph (or Jacob) Isenschmid, aged approximately 38 years, a butcher of 59 Elthorne Road, Holloway. His appearance is first noted in a Metropolitan Police report[3] from Y Division, Holloway, dated 11 September 1888 by Detective Inspector John Styles, commencing with the file cover:

C.O. REFERENCE. DIVISIONAL REFERENCE.
Y 5574

Submitted through H Division
Y Division

Subject Drs Cowan & Crabb
Holloway

This information respects a Joseph Isenschmid a butcher and a lunatic whom they suspect as being connected with the Whitechapel murders.

12.9.88.

To Insp Abberline
JhnWest

12.9.88.　　　ActgSupt

Rec'd by me at 4 pm 12.9.88 at Inquest Sergt. Thick directed to take up the inquiry at once

FGAbberline Inspr.

Seen. ACB 20.9

METROPOLITAN POLICE.

Y Division.

Holloway 11th Sept. 1888

I beg to report that at 10 pm 11th inst Dr Cowan 10 Landseer Road and Dr Crabb of Holloway Road, came to Station and stated that Joseph Isenschmid, a butcher and a lunatic, a lodger at No. 60 Milford Road, and he having left his lodgings on several occasions at various times, it was thought that he might be connected with the recent murders at Whitechapel. In company of Sub Inspr Rose and Sergt Sealey C.I.D. I went to the above address and saw George Tyler occupier who stated that at 11 pm 5th inst he met Isenschmid in Hornsey Road who asked him if he would accommodate him with a lodging, he took him home and he left the house at 1.am 6th returned at 9 pm 6th left again at 1 am 7th returned at 9 pm, left again at 1.am 8th inst returned at 9 pm, left again at 6 am 9th inst returned at 6 pm stayed in house about 30 minutes he then left to go to Tottenham returned at 1 am 10th left again at 2 am returned at 9 pm and left again at 1.am. 11th and has not yet returned. I then proceeded to No. 97 Duncombe Road and saw Mrs. Isenschmid his wife who stated that she had not seen her husband during past two months but he visited the above premises during her absence on 9th inst and took away some clothing she further stated that he was in the habit of carrying large butcher's knives about with him and did not know how he obtained his livelihood. His movements being suspicious I directed P.C. 376. Cracknell to keep observation on the house and to bring Isenschmid to station should he return for enquiries. I also directed observation to be kept on 97 Duncombe Road, Upper Holloway. I respectfully suggest that further enquiries be made by C.I. Department.

No description of man could be obtained sufficient to circulate at present.

Jno Styles DInspr

Submitted through ActSupt "H" a telegram has been forwarded
12/9/88

J.McFadden

ActSupt

The detention of Isenschmid is recorded in an H Division report[4], dated 13 September 1888, by Acting Superintendent John West, commencing with the file cover:

52983

2

METROPOLITAN POLICE.

H Division.

13th September 1888

Correspondence
No 52983

Murder in Hanbury
St. Spitalfields
With reference to the attached I beg to report that no new facts have been brought to the notice of Police. Excepting that a man has been detained at Holloway Station on suspicion, since removed to the Infirmary Fairfield Road, Bow, having been certified as a dangerous lunatic.

Sergeant Thick has examined the man's clothing, but failed to find any trace of blood upon any of it. Enquiries are being made as to the man's whereabouts on the night in question.

This man's name is Joseph Isenschmid, is a butcher by trade but failed in business about 12 months since. His arrest was brought about through information received from Drs Cowan. & Crabb, of Holloway their attention having been called to him by a man named Tyler of 60 Milford Road Holloway who stated that Isenschmid, who was his lodger, had frequently been absent from home at early morning.

The adjourned Inquest on the body of murdered woman was held 12th inst. and further adjourned till 13th. Several witnesses were examined including "Leather Apron".

Enquiries are being made by Inspectors Abberline, Helson & Chandler respecting the various statements made to Police, including that of the Dustman, whom it is alleged, saw a man on the morning of the murder with blood on his clothing.

Jno.West ActgSupt

The next report[5] on the file is from H Division, dated 14 September 1888, by Inspector J.L. Chandler, and relates to a piece of envelope found near the body of Annie Chapman:

C.O. REFERENCE. DIVISIONAL REFERENCE.
4/908

Submitted through H Division
Subject Result of enquiries re envelope found ["on" –*deleted*] near the body of Annie Chapman.

Commercial Street
METROPOLITAN POLICE
H Division

14th September 1888

Murder of
Annie Chapman
I beg to report having made enquiries at the Depot of the 1st Battn. Surrey

Regiment, North Camp, Farnborough, 14th inst, the piece of envelope found near the body of deceased was identified by Capt. Young Actg Adjutant, as bearing the official stamp of the Regiment, and stated that the majority of the men used this paper which they purchased at the canteen. Enquiries were made amongst the men but none could be found who corresponded with anyone living at Spitalfields, or with any person whose address commencing with "2" The pay books were examined and no signature resembled the initials on the envelope. I made further enquiries at the Lynchford Road, Post office, and was informed by the Proprietors Messrs. Summer & Thirkettle, that the letter was posted there also that they had a large quantity of the envelopes & paper in stock, and retailed them to any person.

J.L.Chandler Inspr.

Submitted Jno.West Actg Supt

To Ch Inspr Swanson 3.50 pm.

15.9.88   J.Shore, Supt.

A report[6] on the two murders follows, dated 14 September 1888, from H Division, written by Inspector Abberline:

METROPOLITAN POLICE.

H Division.

14th day of Sept. 1888

SUBJECT re murder
in Whitechapel
REFERENCE TO PAPERS
5 2 9 8 3

Re. Murders in Bucks Row and Hanbury St. 31st Ult & 8th Inst.

I beg to report that the man Stanley who occasionally cohabited with the deceased Annie Chapman and referred to by witnesses at the inquest as the pensioner called at Commercial St. Station this evening and gave a satisfactory account of himself, and will attend the adjourned inquest on 19th Inst. Inquiries have been made at the London Hospital and other places but no useful information has been obtained.

With regard to Commissioner's memorandum of 13th I have submitted special report.

A man named Edward McKenna is now detained at Commercial St. Station for identification supposed same as described in Evening papers & special memo. from C.O. this evening as having been seen at Heath St., and other places with a knife.

F.G.Abberline Inspr.

Jno.West ActgSupt

To Ch Inspr Swanson at
3.50 pm JShoreSupt.

In a report[7] dated 15 September 1888, written at H Division, Commercial Street Police Station, Inspector Chandler gives further information regarding his enquiries into the piece of envelope found near Chapman's body:
The cover states:

$\frac{3}{}$

52983

153   H Division
To the Assistant Commissioner
Criminal Investigation Department
SUMMARY OF CONTENTS
re. murder in Whitechapel 31st Ult. and 8th Inst.
Submitted to A.F. Williamson Esq.
Ch: Constable,
Dond. S. Swanson
ChInsp.
Mr Bruce
Seen ACB.17.9

Commercial Street
METROPOLITAN POLICE.
H Division.
15th September 1888

Reference to Papers
Murder of
Annie Chapman
I beg to report having made enquiries 14th inst. at the depot 1st Battn. Royal Sussex Regiment North Camp Farnborough with reference to the portion of an envelope found near the body of Annie Chapman (and which contained two pills) and was informed by the Adjutant, Capt. Young, that it bore the stamp of the Regt., the fact of its being posted at the Lynchford Road office, shews that the writer, if a soldier posted the letter, himself when out and not in the barracks as usual, enquiries were made amongst the men but none could be found who are in the habit of writing to anyone at Spitalfields, or whose signatures corresponded with the letters on the envelope, that class of paper can be purchased in the canteen and is used by the majority of the men.
    I also made enquiries at the Lynchford Road post Office and was informed by the Post Masters Messrs. Summer and Thirkettle who stated that the letter was posted there but they could not say by whom; also that they had a large quantity of paper and envelopes bearing the Sussex Regimental stamp (identical with the piece found) in stock, that they did them up in small quantities, and retailed them to the public.

I beg to add that at 11 am 15th inst William Stevens a painter, of 35 Dorset Street, Spitalfields, Common Lodging House came to Commercial Street Station, and made the following statement, I know Annie Chapman as a lodger in the same house, I know that on Friday 7th inst the day before the murder she came into the Lodging House and said she had been to the hospital, and intended going into the Infirmary next day. I saw that she had a bottle of medicine, a bottle of lotion and a box with two pills and as she was handling the box it came to pieces, she then took out the pills and picked up a piece of paper from the kitchen floor near the fireplace, and wrapped the pills up in it. I believe the piece of paper with Sussex Regiment thereon to be the same. I do not know of any lodger in the house who has been in the Army.

I beg to add that 35 Dorset Street is a Common Lodging House and frequented by a great many strangers, and it is very probable it may have been dropped there by one of them.

J.L.Chandler Inspr.

I beg to state that to prevent delay Inspr. Chandler at my request proceeded to Farnborough without first obtaining the Commissioners authority. I therefore now beg to ask for that authority.

F.G.Abberline Inspr.

Submitted   Jno.West ActgSupt.

There is a file cover[8] that refers to this retrospective authority sought by Abberline:

C.O. REFERENCE.   DIVISIONAL REFERENCE.

$\frac{3}{52983}$ $\frac{H915}{4}$

168

Submitted through Ch.Constable C.I.D.

H Division

Subject Murder of

Annie Chapman

Applying for Commissioner's covering authority for Inspr. Chandler proceeding to Farnborough to make immediate enquiries in connection with above.

17/9/88.   DSSwanson

ChInspr

MrBruce

ACB for Comr.   ACB 18.9

Acct. for 8s/8d passed

[   ]
12.10.88
Inspr Dillon [?]

On Monday, 17 September 1888, Sergeant William Thick, H Division, submitted a report[9] with reference to the man, Isenschmid, detained at Holloway in connection with the murder:

METROPOLITAN POLICE
H Division.

17th September 1888

SUBJECT Man detained
at Holloway
re murder
REFERENCE TO PAPERS
attached
With reference to attached telegram and report from ''Y'' Division, see also wife's statement attached; re Joseph Isenschmid detained.

I beg to report that I called several times at Mitford Road, Upper Holloway with a view of interviewing Mr. Tyler re the movements of Joseph Isenschmid but failed, and I am also unable to ascertain where he is employed. On calling again yesterday I saw a boy named ''Briggs'' who informed me that Mr. Tyler had removed early that morning, and he did not know where to. The boy was the only person in the house, and stated that several gentlemen had called there for Mr. Tyler during the last few days. He could say no more.

I called on Mrs. Gerlingher, the person referred to in wife's statement, who stated that she did not know the man I referred to and that no person but the regular customers had visited her house a ''Public House''. I have made careful enquiries amongst Germans whom I know in this neighbourhood but failed to find any trace of ''Isenschmid'' having been seen in this neighbourhood.

I called at Fairfield Road Bow Infirmary Asylum where ''Isenschmid'' is still detained. I saw the Medical Superintendent who informed me that ''Isenschmid'' had told him that the girls at Holloway had called him ''Leather Apron'' and that he had said to them in the way of chaff I am ''Leather Apron'' and he supposed they had informed the police. He was a ''butcher'' by trade but had failed in business. He had a few words with his wife and he left her. He was now getting his living by going to the market early in the morning buying sheep's heads; kidneys, and sheep's feet, taking them home to his lodgings, and dressing them then taking them to Restaurants and Coffee Houses in the West End of the town, and selling them, and that was the cause of him being up so early in the morning, and that was the only way open to him to get his livelihood.

The Superintendent would like for police to give instructions what he was to do with Isenschmid. I beg to add that further and careful enquiries are being made with a view of tracing the whereabouts of Mr Tyler, to obtain further particulars from him. Also other persons who are likely to give further details of Isenschmid' movements of dates of the recent murders.

William Thick
P.S.

Submitted;   Jn. West
                              Actg.Supt.

There follows an interesting report[10] by Inspector Abberline, dated 18 September 1888:

METROPOLITAN POLICE.
Criminal Investigation Department,
Scotland Yard,

18th day of Sept. 1888

SUBJECT re murders
in Whitechapel
REFERENCE TO PAPERS
5 2 9 8 3

I beg to report that inquiries have been continued relative to the various matters in connection with the murders including the lunatic who was detained by police at Holloway on 12th Inst., and handed over to the parochial authorities same day. He gives the name of Joseph Isenschmid, and his occupation has been that of a butcher. He is now detained at Bow Infirmary Asylum, Fairfield Road, Bow, and from his description he is believed to be identical with the man seen in the Prince Albert P.H., Brushfield Street, Spitalfields with blood on his hands at 7 a.m. on the morning of the murder of Annie Chapman. [*At this point in the report there are two marginal notations, "Seen, Mr. Williamson has been to see the Dr. at the Infirmary. CW 19.9" and "Identification postponed by order of—WT 20/9".*] Dr. Mickle the Medical Officer of the Institution has been consulted with a view to Isenschmid being seen by Mrs Fiddymont and the other witnesses. The doctor is of opinion this cannot be done at present with safety to his patient. It has been ascertained that this man had been wandering about and away from his home for several weeks past, and when he left his home he took with him two butchers knives. He has been previously confined in an asylum, and is said to be at times very violent. Although at present we are unable to procure any evidence to connect him with the murders he appears to be the most likely person that has come under our notice to have committed the crimes, and every effort will be made to account for his movements on the dates in question.

F.G.Abberline Inspr.
Respectfully submitted
Jno.West ActgSupt.

A further report[11] concerning the detained Isenschmid, dated 19 September 1888 and in the handwriting of Sgt William Thick, follows:

METROPOLITAN POLICE
H Division
19th day of September 1888

SUBJECT Man detained
at Holloway
re murder
REFERENCE TO PAPERS
attached

With reference to attached telegram and report from "Y" Division, re Joseph Isenschmid detained on suspicion of murder.

I beg to report that on 12th inst. I called at the Islington Workhouse and found that Joseph Isenschmid had been removed from there to Fairfield Road, Bow Infirmary Asylum. I then saw Mrs. Isenschmid, his wife at 97 Duncombe Road Upper Holloway who stated that they had been married twenty one years. He is a "Swiss" and was at that time employed as a Journeyman butcher. They then went into business as Pork butchers at 59 Elthorne Road, Upper Holloway, but eventually failed. Her husband then began to get very much depressed and repeatedly stopped away from his home at night and remained away for several days. He has been in Colney Hatch Lunatic Asylum for ten weeks and was discharged from there about the middle of last December and came home supposed to be quite well. He then got employment as Journeyman butcher at a Mr. Marlett's High Street Marylebone and stopped there till Whitsuntide. He then left and has done nothing since to her knowledge. He professed to have had work but did not bring home any money. He has not slept at home for quite two months. About three or four weeks ago he was found in a house in Caledonian Road and was charged. He was taken to Clerkenwell Police Court and remanded for enquiries to be made about him. He was eventually discharged. He then came home again and changed his underclothing and left again. I did not see him again, she then added. I went away into the country to visit my friends last Sunday week, (1st Inst), and returned again on Monday following, (3rd Inst). I was then informed by my daughter that my husband had been home and took his shirts and collars away. Mr. Tyler 60 Mitford Road, Upper Holloway had called during my absence and left a message for me to call on him. I went there on Tuesday morning. I did not see my husband. When he left he had two bone knives and his butchers clothes with him. I don't know what has become of them. I do not think my husband would injure anyone but me. I think he would kill me if he had the chance. He is fond of other women. He used to frequent a Public House kept by a "German" named Gerlinger in Wentworth Street Whitechapel. He is known as the "mad butcher".

This report is unsigned.

On the same date, Wednesday 19 September 1888, Inspector Joseph Henry Helson, J Division, wrote a report[12] with reference to the two murders he was assisting with enquiries into.

The cover reads:

J Division

To the

ASSISTANT COMMISSIONER,
CRIMINAL INVESTIGATION DEPARTMENT
SUMMARY OF CONTENTS

Report re Joseph Isenschmid – detained at Holloway and put in Bow Infirmary Asylum., who is suspected of being the man seen with blood on his hands on the morning of the 8th inst.

19.9.88

METROPOLITAN POLICE
J Division
19th day of September 1888

SUBJECT Murders at
Whitechapel and
Spitalfields
REFERENCE TO PAPERS
5 2 9 8 3
With reference to Joseph Isenschmid detained by Police at Holloway, and sent to the Workhouse as an Insane person, I beg to report that from papers received from Y Division, it is shown that on the 11th inst. Dr Cowan of Landseer Road, and Dr Crabb of Holloway Road, called at Holloway Police

Station, and stated that an insane butcher known by them to have been confined in an Asylum, but recently residing at 97 Duncombe Road, and at 60 Mitford Road, Holloway, was not unlikely to have been the person engaged in committing the recent murders at Whitechapel. In consequence of this information observation was kept at the address given, and in the evening of the 12th inst. Isenschmid was found and conveyed to Holloway Police Station. A telegram was received at 6.35 a.m. 12th inst. at H.D. stating that this man was detained at Holloway and PS Thick, C.I. Dept. H. was as soon as possible, detailed by Inspector Abberline to make enqs. respecting this man, but before he arrived at Holloway the man had been removed to the Workhouse as an insane person, and from the workhouse it was found he had been sent on to the Bow Infirmary Asylum.

The enquiry was continued by the P.S. and on the 18th inst. I went to the Asylum, and saw Dr Mickle, the Resident Medical Officer, and endeavoured to arrange for Isenschmid to be seen at the Institution by Mrs. Fiddymont of the Prince Albert Public House, Brushfield St. and other persons by whom a man was seen in the morning of the 8th inst. at 7. a.m. with blood on his hands, as the description obtained of Isenschmid and that given by the persons referred to makes it very probable that they are identical, but the Doctor was unable to agree to this proposal, as it might prove injurious to the man. He has, at my request, promised that in his conversations with the man daily, he will obtain from him as much information as possible, as to his recent movements, and let me know the result (in confidence) if I call on him from time to time. Also that should he be removed to another Institution, or recover sufficiently to enable him to be discharged to let me know at once. The clothing worn by Isenschmid when arrested is now in possession of the Police, but apparently bears no stains or marks of blood. Enquiries will be continued with a view to find some person or persons to whom he was known, and who may be able to throw some light on his recent movements, but at present no person can be found except his wife, and she has not seen him for two months.

J.H.Helson Insp.
Jno.West ActgSupt.

Submitted

In a lengthy (15-page) Metropolitan Police report[13] from the Criminal Investigation Department, Scotland Yard, dated 19 September 1888, by Inspector Frederick G. Abberline, details of this investigation are given and of the Nichols murder:

C.O. Reference Divisional Reference
Submitted through Executive
J. Division
Subject Report Re Murder of a woman unknown

METROPOLITAN POLICE.
CRIMINAL INVESTIGATION DEPARTMENT,
SCOTLAND YARD,

19th day of Sept. 1888

SUBJECT re. Murder
in Whitechapel
REFERENCE TO PAPERS
5 2 9 8 3

With reference to the subject named in margin.

I beg to report that about 3.40. am 31st Ult. as Charles Cross, "carman" of 22 Doveton Street, Cambridge Road, Bethnal Green was passing through Bucks Row, Whitechapel (on his way to work) he noticed a woman lying on her back on the footway (against some gates leading into a stable yard) he stopped to look at the woman when another carman (also on his way to work) named Robert Paul of 30 Foster St., Bethnal Green came up, and Cross called his attention to the woman, but being dark they did not notice any blood, and passed on with the intention of informing the first constable they met, and on arriving at the corner of Hanbury St. and Old Montague St. they met P.C. 55.H Mizen and acquainted him of what they had seen, and on the Constable proceeding towards the spot he found that P.C. 97J. Neil (who was on the beat) had found the woman, and was calling for assistance. P.C. Neil had turned on his light and discovered that the womans throat was severely cut. P.C. 96J. Thain was also called and sent at once for Dr. Llewellyn of 152 Whitechapel Road, who quickly arrived on the scene and pronounced life extinct and ordered the removal of the body to the mortuary. In the meantime P.C. Mizen had been sent for the ambulance and assistance from Bethnal Green Station, and on Inspr. Spratling and other officers arriving, the body was removed to the mortuary. On arriving there the Inspector made a further examination, and found that the abdomen had also been severely cut in several places exposing the intestines. The Inspector acquainted Dr. Llewellyn who afterwards made a more minute examination and found that the wounds in the abdomen were in themselves sufficient to cause instant death, and he expressed an opinion that they were inflicted before the throat was cut. The body was not then identified On the clothing being carefully examined by Inspr Helson he found some of the underclothing bore the mark of Lambeth Workhouse which led to the body being identified as that of a former inmate named Mary Ann Nichols, and by that means we were able to trace the relatives and complete the identity. It was found she was the wife of William Nichols, of 37 Coburg Street, Old Kent Road, a printer in the employ of Messrs. Perkins, Bacon, & Co. Whitefriars St. City from whom she had been separated about 9 years through her drunken and immoral habits, and that for several years past she had from time to time been an inmate of various workhouses. In May of this year she left Lambeth Work-house and entered the service of Mr. Cowdry, Ingleside, Rose Hill Road, Wandsworth she remained there until the 12th July when she absconded stealing various articles of wearing apparel. A day or two after she became a lodger at 18 Thrawl St. Spitalfields a common lodging-house and slept there and at another common lodging-house 56 Flower and Dean Street up to the night of the murder About 1.40 am. that morning she was seen in the kitchen at 18 Thrawl St. when she informed the Deputy of the lodging-house that she had no money to pay her lodgings She requested that her bed might be kept for her and left stating that she would soon get the money – at this time she was drunk. She was next seen at 2.30. am. at the corner of Osborn St. and Whitechapel Road by Ellen Holland a lodger in the same house who seeing she was very drunk requested her to return with her to the lodging-house. She however refused remarking that she would soon be back and walked away down the Whitechapel Road in the direction of the place where the body was found. There can be no doubt with regard to the time because the White-chapel Church clock chimed 2.30., and Holland called the attention of the deceased to the time. We have been unable to find any person who saw her alive after Holland left her. The distance from Osborn St. to Bucks Row would be about half a mile. Inquiries were made in every conceivable quarter with a view to trace the murderer but not the slightest clue can at present be obtained In the course of our inquiries amongst the numerous women of the same class as the deceased it was ascertained that a feeling of terror existed against a man known as Leather Apron who it appeared have for a considerable time past been levying blackmail and ill-using them if his demands were not complied with although there was no evidence to connect him with the murder. It was however thought desirable to find him and interrogate him as to his movements on the night in question, and with that view searching inquiries were made at all common lodging-houses in various parts of the Metropolis but through the publicity given in the ''Star'' and other newspapers the man was made acquainted with the fact that he was being sought for and it was not until the 10th Inst. that he was discovered when it was found that he had been concealed by his relatives. On his being interrogated he was able however to give such a satisfactory account of his movements as to prove conclusively that the suspicions were groundless.

Suspicion was also attached to three men employed during the night of the murder by Messrs. Barber & Co. ''Horseslaughterers'' Winthorp St. which is about 30 yards from where the body was found. They have however been seen separately and lengthy statements taken from them as to how they spent their time during the night, and the explanations given by them were confirmed by the Police who saw them at work, and no grounds appeared to exist to suspect them of the murders. In the meantime, viz, at 6 am. 8th Inst. the dead and mutilated body of Annie Chapman was found in the yard of 29 Hanbury St., Spitalfields, having been murdered in the same manner, the mutilations being of the same description, but more brutal leaving no doubt that the same person committed both murders. The identification in this case has also been clearly established. She was the widow of a coachman named Chapman who died at Windsor some 18 months since from whom she had been separated several years previously through her drunken habits, and who up to the time of his death made her an allowance of 10/- per week. For some years past she has been a frequenter of common lodging-houses in the neighbourhood of Spitalfields, and for sometime previous to her death had resided at 35 Dorset Street where she was last seen alive at 2 a.m. on the morning of the murder, but not having the money to pay her lodgings left the house remarking she would go and get it, at the time she appeared the worse for drink. From then until her body was found no reliable information can be obtained as to her movements. It was ascertained that for the last two years she has occasionally been visited by a man named Edwd. Stanley, a labourer, who resides at 1 Osborn Place, Whitechapel with that exception she was not known to be acquainted with any particular man. Stanley has been found and interrogated and from his statement it has been clearly established that on the night of 30th Ult. he was on duty with the 2nd Brigade Southern Division Hants Militia at Fort Elson Gosport, and during the night of 7th Inst. he was in bed at his lodgings from midnight until 7 a.m. 8th, an hour after the body was discovered. He is also believed to be a respectable hardworking man, and no suspicion whatever is attached to him. The deceased was in the habit of wearing two brass rings (a wedding and keeper) these were missing when the body was found and the finger bore marks of their having been removed by force. Special inquiries have been made at all places where they may be offered for pledge or for sale by a person believing them to be gold, but nothing has resulted therefrom. Searching inquiries were also made at lodging-houses &c with a view of ascertaining whether any person had been seen to enter with blood on them, with a like result. The inhabitants of the houses adjoining the scenes of the murders have been seen and many called as witnesses before the Coroner, but none of them heard anything to attract their attention on either occasion. No doubt the murders in each case were committed where the bodies were found. Bucks Row is a narrow quiet thoroughfare frequented by prostitutes for immoral purposes at night and no doubt the yard of 29 Hanbury Street has been used for a similar purpose. Several persons have been detained at various stations on suspicion, and there [sic] movements have been inquired into, numerous statements have also been made, and letters received bearing on the subject, but after the most exhaustive inquiries no useful result has been attained. The inquest has been opened on both bodies, and adjourned from time to time, numerous witnesses have been examined, and both stand now adjourned, that on Mary Ann Nichols until 22nd, and on Annie Chapman until today.

Plans have been prepared of the scene of each murder for the information of the Coroner, and are herewith submitted for the information of Commissioner. Inquiries are being continued in every direction in which it is thought information may be obtained, and no effort will be spared to elucidate the mysteries.

I beg to add that the man Isenschmid who was detained at Holloway on 12th Inst, and handed over to the parochial authorities as a lunatic, is identical with the man seen in Prince Albert P.H. Brushfield St. at 7 a.m. on the morning of the murder of Annie Chapman, by Mrs. Fiddymont & other persons. This house is only about 400 yards from the scene of the murder, the man who entered had blood on his hands. Isenschmid has carried on the business of a butcher, but some 12 months ago failed in business. He afterwards became depressed and lost his reason, and was confined in an asylum. He was however liberated about Christmas last as cured, but for some months past he has acted very strangely and for the last six weeks he has been absent from home, and wandering about the streets at all hours. When he left home he had in his possession two large knives that he used in his business. He is now confined in the Bow Infirmary Asylum, Fairfield Road, Bow, and Dr. Mickle has been seen with a view to arrange for Mrs. Fiddymont and other witnesses to see him, but the doctor thinks this cannot be done at present with safety to his patient. As time is of the greatest importance in this case, not only with regard to the question of identity, but also for the purpose of allaying the strong public feeling that exists, I would respectfully suggest that either the Chief Surgeon, or one of the Divl. Surgeons may be requested to see Dr. Mickle the resident medical officer to make if possible some arrangements for the witnesses to see Isenschmid. Ch InsprSwanson.

Plan to A.C. CID.

F.G. Abberline Inspr.

JohnShoreSupt.

An index[14] to the Chapman murder file is included in the Home Office reports. Date-stamped 25 OCT. 88, it lists the contents:

Murder of Annie Chapman

For a complete overview of the whole of the Hanbury Street murder it is necessary to see Chief Inspector Swanson's report[15] of 19 October 1888, to the Home Office:

METROPOLITAN POLICE.
Criminal Investigation Department,
Scotland Yard,
19th day of October 1888

SUBJECT Hanbury Street
Murder of Annie
Chapman.
I beg to report that the following are the facts respecting the murder of Annie Chapman on 8th Sept. at 29 Hanbury Street.

6 a.m. 8th Sept. 1888. The body of a woman was discovered in the back yard of 29 Hanbury St. Spitalfields, by John Davis of that address who immediately informed the police, & Dr. Phillips the Divl. Surgeon was sent for, who stated that in his opinion death had taken place two or three hours. Examination of the body showed that the throat was severed deeply incision jagged. Removed from but attached to body, & placed above right shoulder were a flap of the wall of belly, the whole of the small intestines & attachments. Two other portions of wall of belly & "Pubes" were placed above left shoulder in a large

quantity of blood. Abrasion of head of first phalanx of ring finger, distinct marking of ring or rings, probably the latter:- on proximal phalanx of same finger. The following parts were missing:- part of belly wall including navel; the womb, the upper part of vagina & greater part of bladder. The Dr. gives it as his opinion that the murderer was possessed of anatomical knowledge from the manner of removal of viscera, & that the knife used was not an ordinary knife, but such as a small amputating knife, or a well ground slaughterman's knife, narrow & thin, sharp & blade of six to eight inches in length.

9th Sept. The body was identified as that of Annie Chapman, by John Donovan, 35 Dorset Street, Spitalfields, lodging house keeper, where she had resided & also by her brother Mr. Fontin Smith, 44 Bartholomew Close, E.C.

The results of enquiries were as follows:-

2 a.m. 8th Sept. 1888 She was last seen alive at 2 a.m. 8th Sept. by John Donovan, the deputy of the Common Lodging House, where she resided. At that time she was under the influence of drink, and as she had no money, she left the lodging house to get it, so as to pay for her bed.

4.45 a.m. 8th Sept. John Richardson of 29 Hanbury St. stated that he went out and sat on the steps leading to the back yard, to cut a piece of leather off his boot, but he did not observe the body of the woman.

5.25 a.m. 8th Sept. Albert Cadosch of 27 Hanbury Street, (next door) had occasion to go into the yard at the rear of No. 27, separated only by a wooden fence about 5 feet high, and he heard words pass between some persons apparently at No. 29 Hanbury Street, but the only word he could catch was ''No''. [*Here there is a marginal note* – ''Was the voice of the man that of a foreigner?'']

5.28 a.m. 8th Sept. On Cadosch going back into the yard again he heard a noise as of something falling against the fence on the side next No. 29 Hanbury Street, but he did not take any notice.

5.30 a.m. 8th Sept. Mrs. Long of 32 Church Street stated that she saw a man and woman talking near to No. 29 Hanbury Street. She heard the man say ''Will you'' [*Here there is a marginal note* – ''A foreigner?''] and the woman replied ''Yes'' and passed on. She only saw his back, and would be unable to know him again. She describes him as apparently over 40 years of age. She did not see his face He appeared to be a little taller than the woman and in her opinion looked like a foreigner. She thinks he had a dark coat on, but she could not recognise him again. The woman she positively identified as the deceased.

Then followed the discovery by John Davies as shown on page 1. of this report.

A. The action of Police was as follows. The inhabitants of 29 Hanbury Street were seen and the rooms searched. Their statements were taken as well as the inhabitants of adjoining houses.

B. An immediate and searching enquiry was made at all Common Lodging Houses to ascertain if anyone had entered that morning with blood on his hands face or clothes, or under any suspicious circumstances.

C. A special enquiry to find rings was also made at all pawnbrokers, jewellers, dealers.

D. Enquiry was also made into the antecedents and history of deceased.

E. Several persons, whose antecedents are attached, were detained pending enquiries into their movements covering the dates of 7 & 31st Augst. & 8th Sept.

F. The particulars of other persons seen in different parts of the Metropolis, under what appeared to be suspicious circumstances to the persons giving the information, upon which from the nature of the circumstances no enquiry could be made, were circulated.

G. Enquiries were also made to trace persons suspected, whose address, or particulars respecting them given upon correspondence. These enquiries are being continued.

H. Enquiries were also made to trace three insane students who had attended London Hospital. Result two traced, one gone abroad. [*Here there is a marginal note* – When?]

I. Enquiries were also made amongst women of the same class as deceased, and at public houses in the locality.

Up to the present the combined result of those enquiries did not supply the police with the slightest clue to the murderer. The only indication of the direction to find the murderer lay in the evidence of Dr. Phillips, which was in substance that the individual possessed some skill and anatomical knowledge, and that the instrument with which the injuries were inflicted was probably a small amputating knife, or a well ground butchers knife, narrow and thin, sharp with a blade from six to eight inches long.

If the evidence of Dr. Phillips is correct as to time of death, it is difficult to understand how it was that Richardson did not see the body when he went into the yard at 4.45 a.m. but as his clothes were examined, the house searched and his statement taken in which there was not a shred of evidence, suspicion could not rest upon him, although police specially directed their attention to him. Richardson is a market porter. Again if the evidence of Mrs. Long is correct that she saw the deceased at 5.30 a.m. then the evidence of Dr. Phillips as to probable time of death is incorrect. He was called and saw the body at 6.20 a.m. and he then gives it as his opinion that death occurred about two hours earlier, viz: 4.20 a.m. hence the evidence of Mrs. Long which appeared to be so important to the Coroner, must be looked upon with some amount of doubt, which is to be regretted.

The enquiry into the history of the deceased showed that she was the widow of a coachman named Chapman who died about eighteen months ago, and from whom she had been separated about eight years, on account of her drunken and immoral ways, but her husband had allowed her 10/- per week up to the time of his death. She was then occasionally visited by a man named Stanley, who was known as the pensioner. He came forward, and accounted for his time, and gave evidence before the Coroner. Some pieces of paper were found near the body but they were accounted for as being picked up by the deceased in the Common Lodging home.

Enquiry is still being actively continued in all directions where there is a probable chance of finding a trace, and a further report will be submitted.

A descriptive form relating to Annie Chapman is also included, giving details as follows:

Alias	*Annie Siffey*
Age	*45*
Profession or calling	*Prostitute*
Height	*5 feet*
Hair	*(Wavy) dark brown.*
Eyes	*blue*
Nose	*thick nose*
Mouth	*Two teeth deficient in lower jaw*
Complexion	*Fair*
Marks or Peculiarities	*On person portion of an envelope stamped "Sussex Regiment" dated 23rd Augst. 1888.*
Dress	*Black skirt & jacket, striped petticoat crape bonnet*

CHAPTER 5

September 1888 –
The Chapman Inquest and Police Enquiries

As in the case of Nichols, the inquest report on Chapman is not to be found in any of the official files, and the Home Office files on the murder contain extracts from *The Times* newspaper relevant to this enquiry. The first extract[1] is from *The Times* of Tuesday, 11 September 1888, page 6:

THE INQUEST.

Yesterday morning Mr. Wynne E. Baxter, the Coroner for the North-Eastern Division of Middlesex, who was accompanied by Mr. George Collier, the Deputy Coroner, opened his inquiry in the Alexandra-room of the Working Lads' Institute, Whitechapel-road, respecting the death of Annie Chapman, who was found murdered in the back yard of 29, Hanbury-street, Spitalfields, on Saturday morning.

Detective-inspectors Abberline (Scotland-yard), Helson, and Chandler, and Detective-sergeants Thicke and Leach watched the case on behalf of the Criminal Investigation Department and Commissioners of Police.

The court-room was crowded, and, owing to the number of persons assembled outside the building, the approaches had to be guarded by a number of police-constables.

The jury having been impanelled, proceeded to the mortuary to view the body of the deceased, which was lying in the same shell as that occupied a short time since by the remains of the unfortunate Mary Ann Nichols.

John Davis, a carman, of 29, Hanbury-street, Spitalfields, deposed that he occupied the front room, which was shared by his wife and three sons. About 8 o'clock on Friday night he went to bed, and his sons came in at different times. The last one arrived home about a quarter to 11. Witness was awake from 3 to about 5 o'clock, when he fell off to sleep for about half an hour. He got up about a quarter to 6. Soon afterwards he went across the yard. The front portion of the house faced Hanbury-street. On the ground floor there was a front door, with a passage running through to the back yard. He was certain of the time, because he heard the bell of Spitalfields Church strike. The front door and the one leading into the yard were never locked, and at times were left open at nights. Since he had lived in the house witness had never known the doors to be locked; and when the doors were shut any person could open them and pass into the yard. When he went into the yard on Saturday morning the back door was shut; but he was unable to say whether it was latched. The front door was wide open, and he was not surprised at finding it so, as it was frequently left open all night. Between the yard of 29, Hanbury- street, and the next house there was a fence about 5 ft. high. When witness went down the steps he saw the deceased woman lying flat on her back.

The CORONER here observed that in similar inquiries in the country the police always assisted him by preparing a plan of the locality which happened to be the subject of investigation. He thought the present case was one of sufficient importance for the production of such a plan, and he hoped that in future a plan would be laid before him.

Inspector Chandler told the Coroner a plan would be prepared.

The CORONER replied it might then be too late to be of any service.

Witness, continuing, said the deceased was lying between the steps and the fence, with her head towards the house. He could see that her clothes were disarranged. Witness did not go further into the yard, but at once called two men, who worked for Mr. Bailey, a packing-case maker, of Hanbury-street, whose place was three doors off. These men entered the passage and looked at the woman, but did not go into the yard. He was unable to give the names of these two men, but knew them well by sight. Witness had not since seen the men, who went away to fetch the police. Witness also left the house with them.

In answer to the Coroner, Inspector Chandler said these men were not known to the police.

The CORONER remarked that they would have to be found, either by the police or by his own officer.

Witness further stated that on leaving the house he went direct to the Commercial-street Police-station, and reported what he had seen. Previous to that he had not informed any one living in the house of the discovery. After that he went back to Hanbury-street, but did not enter his house. He had never previously seen the deceased.

In cross-examination, the witness said he was not the first person down that morning, as a man, named Thompson, who also lived in the house, was called about half-past 3. he had never seen women who did not live in the house in the passage since he had lived there, which was only a fortnight. He did not hear any strange noises before getting up on Saturday morning. He did not return to his house until Saturday afternoon.

Amelia Farmer stated that she lived at a common lodginghouse at 30,

Dorset-street, Spitalfields, and had lived there for the past four years. She had identified the body of the deceased in the mortuary, and was sure it was that of Annie Chapman. The deceased formerly lived at Windsor, and was the widow of Frederick Chapman, a veterinary surgeon, who died about 18 months ago. For four years, or more, the deceased had lived apart from her husband, and during that period had principally resided in common lodging-houses in the neighbourhoods of Whitechapel and Spitalfields. About two years since the deceased lived at 30, Dorset-street, and was then living with a man who made iron sieves. She was then receiving an allowance of 10s. a week from her husband. Some 18 months since the payments stopped, and it was then that she found her husband was dead. That fact was also ascertained from a relative of the deceased, who used to live in Oxford-street, White-chapel. The deceased went by the name of Sievey, on account of the man with whom she had cohabited being a sieve maker. This man left her some time ago. During the past week witness had seen the deceased some two or three times. On Monday, in Dorset-street, she complained of feeling unwell. At that time she had a bruise on one of her temples. Witness inquiring how she got it, the deceased told her to look at her breast, which was also bruised. The deceased said, "You know the woman," and she mentioned a name which witness did not remember. Both the deceased and the woman referred to were acquainted with a man called "Harry the Hawker." In giving an account of the bruises, the deceased told witness that on the 1st inst. she went into a publichouse with a young man named Ted Stanley in Commercial-street. "Harry the Hawker" and the other woman were also there. The former, who was drunk, put down a florin, which was picked up by the latter, who replaced it with a penny. Some words passed between the deceased and the woman, and in the evening the latter struck her and inflicted the bruises. Witness again saw the deceased on Tuesday by the side of Spitalfields Church. The deceased again complained of feeling unwell, and said she thought she would go into the casual ward for [a] day or two. She mentioned that she had had nothing to eat or drink that day, not even a cup of tea. Witness gave deceased twopence saying, "Here is twopence to have a cup of tea, but don't have rum." She knew that deceased was given to drinking that spirit. The deceased, who frequently got the worse for drink, used at times to earn money by doing crochet work, and at others by selling flowers. Witness believed she was not very particular what she did to earn a living and at times used to remain out very late at night. She was in the habit of going to Stratford. Witness did not again see the deceased until Friday afternoon, and about 5 o'clock on that day she met her in Dorset-street. The deceased, who was sober, in answer to a question from witness as to whether she was going to Stratford, said she felt too ill to do anything. A few minutes afterwards witness again saw the deceased, who had not moved, and she said, "It's no use my giving way. I must pull myself together and go out and get some money, or I shall have no lodgings." That was the last time witness saw her. She mentioned that she had been an inmate of the casual ward. Deceased was generally an industrial woman, and witness considered her clever. For the last five years she had been living an irregular life, more especially since her husband died. She had two children, and on the death of her husband they were sent away to school. The deceased had a sister and mother, but witness believed they were not on friendly terms.

Timothy Donovan stated he was the deputy of a common lodginghouse at 35, Dorset-street, Spitalfields. He had seen the body in the mortuary, and identified it as that of a woman who had lodged at his place. She had been living there for about four months, but was not there any day last week until Friday. About 7 o'clock that day she came to the lodginghouse and asked him to allow her to go down into the kitchen. He asked where she had been all the week, and she replied, "In the infirmary." He then allowed her to go into the kitchen. She remained there until shortly before 2 o'clock the next morning. When she went out she said, "I have not any money now, but don't let the bed; I will be back soon." At that time there was a vacant bed, and it was the one she generally occupied. She then left the house, but witness did not see which way she turned. She had had enough to drink when he last saw her, but she was well able to walk straight. The deceased generally got the worse for drink on Saturdays, but not on the other days of the week. He told her that she could find money for drink but not for her bed, and she replied that she had only been to the top of the street as far as the Ringers' publichouse. He did not see her with any one that night. On Saturday night deceased used to stay at the lodginghouse with a man of military appearance, and witness had heard he was a pensioner. She had brought other men to the lodginghouse. On the 2d inst. deceased and the pensioner were there together. The deceased paid 8d. a night for her bed. The pensioner was about 45 years of age and about 5 ft. 8 in. in height. At times he had the appearance of a dock labourer and at others the appearance of something better. Witness had never had any trouble with the deceased, who was always very friendly with the other lodgers.

John Evans a night watchman at the lodginghouse, also identified the body of deceased. He saw her leave the house at about a quarter to 2 on Saturday morning. Just before he had asked her whether she had any money for her lodging. She replied that she had not sufficient, and then told the last witness she would not be long before she got it. Witness saw her enter a court called Paternoster-row and walk in the direction of Brushfield-street. Witness should say she was the worse for drink. She told him she had that night been to see one of her sisters who lived at Vauxhall. Before he spoke to her about her lodging money she had been out for a pint of beer. He knew that she had been living a rough life, but only knew one man with whom she associated. That man used to come and see her on Saturdays. He called about half-past 2 on Saturday afternoon to make inquiries about the deceased. He said he had heard of her death. Witness did not know his name or address. After hearing an account of the death of the deceased he went out without saying a word. Witness had never heard any person threaten the deceased, and she had never stated she was afraid of any one. He did not see the deceased leave the lodginghouse with the pensioner on Sunday week. On Thursday the deceased and a woman called Eliza had a fight in the kitchen, during which she got a blow on the chest and a black eye.

The CORONER here intimated that that was as far as he proposed to carry the inquiry at present, and it was adjourned until to-morrow afternoon.

The adjourned inquest resumed on 12 September 1888 and a report[2] of the proceedings appeared in *The Times* of Thursday, 13 September 1888, page 5:

THE ADJOURNED INQUEST.

Yesterday Mr. Wynne E. Baxter, Coroner for the North-Eastern Division of Middlesex, resumed his inquiry at the Working Lads' Institute, Whitechapel-road, respecting the death of Annie Chapman, who was found murdered in the back yard of 29, Hanbury-street, Spitalfields, on Saturday last.

Detective-inspectors Abberline (Scotland-yard) and Helson, J Division, and Sergeant Thicke [sic], H Division, again watched the case on behalf of the Criminal Investigation Department.

Fontaina [sic] Smith stated he had seen the body in the mortuary, and had recognized it as that of Annie Chapman, a widow. Her husband's name was John Chapman, and he had been a coachman at Windsor. The deceased had been separated from him three or four years before his death. She was 47 years of age. Some time ago he met the deceased, who first recognized him. She did not say where she was living, or what she was doing. Witness knew nothing about her associates.

James Kent stated he lived at 20, B Block, King David-lane, Shadwell, and was a packing-case maker, in the employ of Mr. Bailey, 23a, Hanbury-street, Spitalfields. He went to his work at 6 o'clock in the morning. He got to work between 10 minutes and a quarter past 6 on Saturday morning. His employer's gate was open, and he waited for more of the hands to come up. While he was waiting there an elderly man named Davis, who lived two or three doors off, came out of his house and said, "Men, come here." Davis had his belt in his hand. Witness and James Green, who was with witness at the time, went to 29, Hanbury-street, the house where the man came out. They went through the passage, and witness stood at the steps at the back door. He saw a woman lying in the yard by the side of the steps, between them and the partition. Her head was against the house, and the whole of her body was on the ground.

At this stage an officer of police produced a plan of the building and the yard.

Witness, continuing, said the face of the deceased was visible. Her clothes were disarranged, and the apron she was wearing appeared to have been thrown over the clothes. Witness did not go down the steps, and believed no other person entered the yard until the inspector (Chandler) came. He could see that the deceased was dead. She had a handkerchief of some kind round her throat. He could not see any blood, but she was besmeared with blood over the face and hands, as though she had been struggling. He did not notice any other injuries. Her hands were raised and bent, with the palms towards the upper portion of her body, as though she had fought for her throat. There were marks of blood about her legs, but he did not notice any about her clothes. He did not look very particularly about her things, as felt too much frightened. Witness then went to the front of the house, to see whether a constable was coming. He then had some brandy, and afterwards went to the shop and got a piece of canvas to throw over the body. When he returned to the house a mob had assembled. The inspector had arrived, and was in possession of the yard. Witness could not say whether any one went to the body before the inspector came, but he did not think so, as every one appeared too much frightened to go near it. The foreman over witness arrived at the workshop about ten minutes to 6.

James Green, 36, Acton-street, Burdett-road, deposed that he was a packing-case maker in the employ of Mr. Bailey. He got to the workshop about ten minutes past 6 on Saturday morning, and accompanied Kent to the back of 29, Hanbury-street. He looked at the body, and then left the premises with Kent. He did not see any one touch the body, and thought no one went near it. He saw Inspector Chandler arrive, and at that time was on the steps of the landing of his workshop. No one was in the yard when the inspector arrived, but the mob stood at the front door. At that time the body was in the same state as when the witness first saw it.

Amelia Richardson, 29, Hanbury-street, Spitalfields, said she was a widow. She rented half of the house – the ground floor portion, and the workshop and yard. Witness occupied the workshop and carried on business there. She employed her son and a man. They were supposed to begin work at 6 o'clock, but did not do so on Saturday morning. The man did not come until 8 o'clock. He was frequently late. her son lived in John-street, Spitalfields. About 6 o'clock on Saturday morning her grandson, Thomas Richardson, 14 years of age, who lived with her, went down stairs. They heard some one in the passage, and thought the place was on fire. He returned directly afterwards, saying, "Oh, grandmother, there is a woman murdered!" Witness went down immediately, and saw the body of deceased lying in the yard. The police and several others were in the passage, but there was no one in the yard at the time. As she was not properly attired she went back to her room and dressed herself. The police then took possession of the place.

By the CORONER. – She occupied the first-floor front room and her grandson also slept in the same room. They went to bed about half-past 9. She did not sleep through the night, and should say she was awake half of the time. She awoke at 3 o'clock, and only dozed afterwards. She did not hear any noise during the night. Mr. Walker occupied the first-floor back room. He was an old man, and slept there with his son, who was weak minded. The lad was very inoffensive. There were two rooms on the ground floor, and they were occupied by Mrs. Hardyman, who had one son, 16 years of age. He also slept there. Mrs. Hardyman got her living by selling cat's meat, and also used the room for a cat's meat shop. Her son went out selling the meat. Witness occupied the back room for cooking. When witness went to bed, at half-past 9, she locked up that room and took the key with her. It was still locked when she came down in the morning. Mr. John Davis and his wife occupied the third floor front room, together with their three sons. An old woman named Sarah Cox occupied the back room on that floor. Witness kept her out of charity. Mr. Thompson, a carman, his wife, and an adopted little girl, occupied the second floor front room. A few minutes to 4 on Saturday morning witness called Thompson. She heard him leave the house, and before doing so he did not go into the backyard. When he went out he called out "Good morning" to him. Mr. and Mrs. Copsey lived in the second floor back, and were cigar makers. When she went down on Saturday morning all the tenants in the house, except Thompson, were in the house. Witness was not the owner of the house. The front and back doors were always left open, as was the case with all the houses about there, for they were all let out in rooms.

By the jury. – She had property in the place, but was not afraid of the doors being left open. She had never heard of any robberies. About a month ago, at 3 o'clock in the morning, she heard a man on the stairs. She could not hear any one going through the passage, but did not hear any one on Saturday morning. On market mornings there was a great bustle and noise. On that morning she did not hear any cries. If a person had gone through about half-past 3 it might not have attracted her attention, although she would have heard them. People frequently went through into the back yard, and perhaps some who had no business there. She was confident that no one made a noise in going through on Saturday morning, and those who went through must have kept purposely quiet. If she knew it she would not allow any stranger to go through.

Annie Hardyman, 29, Hanbury-street, said she occupied the ground-floor front room. On Friday night she went to bed about half-past 10. Her son slept in the same room. She was not awakened during the night, and did not wake until about 6 o'clock, when she heard footsteps in the passage. She woke up her son, and told him to go and see what was the matter. He came back and said a woman had been killed in the yard. Witness did not go out. She did not hear anything during the night, but had often heard people going through the passage into the yard. She had not gone to see who they were. She did not know the deceased, and to her knowledge had never seen her.

John Richardson, of 2, John-street, stated that he acted as a porter in Spitalfields Market, and also assisted his mother in the business of packing-case making. Between a quarter and 20 minutes to 5 he went to 29, Hanbury-street. He went there to see whether the place was properly secured, as some months ago it was broken into. He only went there at that time on market mornings, and had done so for a long time past. When he got to the house he found the front door closed. He lifted the latch and went through the passage to the yard door. He did not go into the yard, but went and stood on the steps. The back door was closed when he got to it. He stood on the steps and cut a piece of leather from off one of his boots. He cut it with a table knife about 5 in. long. It was now at his house in John-street. It being market morning he put the knife into his pocket. He could not say why he put the knife into his pocket, and supposed he did so by mistake. After cutting the piece of leather off his boot he tied up the boot and went out of the house. He did not close the back door, as it closed itself. He was sure he closed the front door. He was not more than three minutes in the house. It was not light, but was getting so, and was sufficient for him to see all over the place. He could not have failed to notice the deceased had she been lying there then. He saw the body two or three minutes before the doctor came, and saw it from the adjoining yard. He went there in consequence of a man named Pearman, in the market, telling him there was a murder in Hanbury-street.

By the CORONER. – He cut the piece of leather off his boot because it hurt him. He took a piece out on the previous day, but that was not sufficient. As a matter of fact that was the only thing that he did at Hanbury-street. He did not go into the yard at all. His object principally in going to the house was to see that the cellar was all right, and he looked and found that was so.

The CORONER. – You do not seem to have taken much trouble to see that it was all right.

Witness, continuing, said he could see the padlock was on the door. He did not sit upon the top step, but rested his feet on the flags of the yard. That would be quite close to the spot where the woman was found. He had been to the house and in the passage at all hours of the night and had seen lots of strangers there. These he had seen at all hours. He had seen both men and women there, and had turned them out.

The witness was here sent to fetch the knife he had spoken about.

Amelia Richardson, recalled, said she had never lost anything, and was so confident of her neighbours that she left her door open. A long while ago she missed a saw and a hammer from the cellar. She used to lock the cellar, but on this occasion it was broken open. The cellar door was fastened with a padlock, and after the robbery was committed the door was put to. That robbery was committed in the early morning. She was aware that her son was in the habit of coming to the house to see whether the place was all right. She never had any suspicion that her yard was used for immoral purposes. Her son wore a leather apron while at work in the cellar, and on Thursday she washed it. On Saturday morning the apron was against the fence and the police took possession of it. At that time it was in the yard under the tap. The police found it in the same position in which it was put. The tap supplied the house with water, and the apron was left lying on the stones from the Thursday until Saturday. The police also took away a nail box, but there were no nails in it. On Friday night there was a pan full of water by the tap, and it was in the same position on Saturday morning. Witness had never known that women had been found on the first floor landing, and her son had never spoken to her about it.

By the jury. – The pan of water was just under the tap and the apron was not quite under it.

John Pizer, 22, Mulberry-street, Commercial-road, stated he was a bootmaker. He had been known by the nickname of "Leather Apron." He went home on Thursday night from the West-end of the town. He reached Mulberry-street about a quarter to 11 o'clock. His brother and stepmother also lived there. He remained indoors until he was arrested by Sergeant Thicke on Monday morning. Up to that time he had not left the house. His brother advised him to remain indoors as he was the object of a false suspicion. He did so in consequence of that. He was not now in custody and had cleared his character.

The CORONER. – I called you to give you an opportunity of doing so.

Witness, in answer to the Coroner, said he was in the Holloway-road on Thursday week.

The CORONER. – It is important you should say where you were and give an account of your time.

Witness said he stayed at Crossman's common lodging-house in the Holloway-road. It was called the "Round-house." He slept the night there. It was the night of the London Dock fire and he went into the lodging-house about a quarter past 2 on the Friday morning. He left there at 11 o'clock the same morning. He then saw on the placards the report of another horrible murder. At 11 o'clock the previous night he had his supper at the lodging-house. He then went out and went as far as the Seven Sisters'-road. Then he turned and went down the Holloway-road. He then saw the reflections of a fire. He went as far as the church in the Holloway-road and saw the lodging-house keeper of the "Round-House" and one or two constables talking together. He asked a constable where the fire was. He replied it was a long way off. Witness then asked him where he thought it was, and the officer replied, "Down by the Albert Docks." It was then about 1.30 as near as he could recollect. He then went as far as the Highbury railway station, then turned back, and went into the lodging-house. The night watchman did not complain of his being late, but as it was after 11 o'clock, the time when all unoccupied beds would be re-let, witness paid him 4d. for another bed. Witness then sat on a form in the kitchen for a time, smoking a clay pipe. He then went to bed. He got up at 11 o'clock, when the day attendant told him he must get up, as he wanted to make the bed. He dressed and went down into the kitchen. That was all he had to say.

By the jury. – When he spoke of the West-end of the town, he came from a lodging-house in Peter-street, Westminster.

The CORONER. – I think it only fair to say that this statement can be corroborated.

Detective-Sergeant William Thicke [*sic*] H Division, said that a man named "Leather Apron" having been suspected of the murder, on Monday morning he arrested Pizer at 22, Mulberry-street. He had known Pizer for many years, and when people in the neighbourhood spoke of "Leather Apron" they meant Pizer. He was released from custody on Tuesday night at 9.30.

John Richardson, recalled, produced the knife with which he cut the piece of leather from his boot. He found the knife on his table.

By the jury. – His mother had heard him speak of finding people acting immorally in the passage.

The CORONER said he thought the police should have the knife, and handed it to them.

Henry John Holland, 4, Aden-yard, Mile-end-road, stated that on Saturday morning he was passing along Hanbury-street on his way to his work in Chiswell-street. It was about eight minutes past 6 when he passed No. 29. He saw an elderly man come out of the house, and said "Come and look in the back yard." Witness went through the passage and saw the deceased lying in the yard just by the back door. Witness went into the yard and looked at the deceased, but did not touch her or her clothes. He did not see any one touch her. He then went for a policeman. The first one he saw was in Spitalfields Market. He said he could not come, and witness must get one from outside. He was unable to see another constable.

By the jury. – He told the policeman that it was a murder and a similar case to that which had happened in Buck's-row. The policeman was standing by himself and was not doing anything. The same afternoon witness went to the Commercial-street Police-station and reported the conduct of the constable.

The Foreman. – I think the constable ought to have gone.

An inspector stated there were certain spots which the constables were not allowed to leave under any circumstances, but they were supposed to send some one else.

The inquiry was then adjourned until to-day.

The press interest in Pizer was not restricted to his appearance in the inquest reports. *The Times* of Wednesday, 12 September 1888, carried the following report[3]:

THE WHITECHAPEL MURDER.

The latest reports as to the search for the murderer are not of a hopeful character. On Monday evening it was stated that John Pizer, the man who was detained on suspicion of being concerned in causing the death of the woman Annie Chapman, was still in custody at the Leman-street Police-station. Last night it was decided to release him.

Many reports of a startling character have been circulated respecting the acts of violence committed by a man wearing a leather apron. No doubt many of the accounts of assaults committed on women in this district have been greatly exaggerated, yet so many versions have been related that the police give credit to at least a portion of them. They have, therefore, been keeping a sharp lookout for "leather apron," but nothing has been heard of his whereabouts. The friends of Pizer stoutly denied that he was known by that name; but on the other hand Sergeant Thicke [*sic*] who has an intimate knowledge of the neighbourhood in which the murder was committed, affirms that he knew Pizer well by sight, and always knew him by the nickname spoken of. Sergeant Thicke also knew that he was in the habit of wearing a leather apron after the news of the murder was circulated. A half-Spaniard and half-Bulgarian, who gave the name of Emanuel Delbast Violenia, waited on the police with respect to this inquiry. He stated that he, his wife, and two children tramped from Manchester to London with the view of being able to emigrate to Australia, and took up their abode in one of the lodging-houses in Hanbury-street. Early last Saturday morning, walking alone along Hanbury-street, he noticed a man and woman quarrelling in a very excited manner. Violenia distinctly heard the man threaten to kill the woman by sticking a knife into her. They passed on, and Violenia went to his lodging. After the murder he communicated what he had seen to the police. At 1 o'clock yesterday afternoon Sergeant Thicke assisted by Inspector Cansby, placed about a dozen men, the greater portion of whom were Jews, in the yard of the Leman-street Police-station. Pizer was then brought out and allowed to place himself where he thought proper among the assembled men. He is a man of short stature, with black whiskers and shaven chin. Violenia, who had been accommodated in one of the lower rooms of the station-house, was then brought up into the yard. Having keenly scrutinized all the faces before him, he at once, without any hesitation or doubt whatever, went up to Pizer and identified him as the man whom he heard threaten a woman on the night of the murder. Pizer, who has not been allowed to have communication with any of his friends, was then taken back to the station-house. It was then decided, with the approval of Detective-inspector Abberline, that Violenia should be taken to the Whitechapel mortuary to see whether he could identify the deceased woman as the one he had seen in Pizer's company early on Saturday morning. The result is not announced, but it is believed that he was unable to identify her. Subsequently, cross-examination so discredited Violenia's evidence that it was wholly distrusted by the police, and Pizer was set at liberty . . .

Last evening Timothy Donovan, the deputy of the lodging-house in Dorset-street, at which the woman Chapman formerly lived, made a statement to a representative of a news agency. He says he knows "Leather Apron" well. Some months ago he ejected him from the lodging-house, and that was for offering violence to a woman who was staying there. Donovan is surprised that the police have not called on him to go to Leman-street Police-station, as he would have no difficulty in deciding whether the prisoner there is "Leather Apron". Yesterday morning two police-constables visited Donovan and showed him two rings, one a half-worn out "engaged" ring, the other appearing to be a wedding ring, which they stated had been discovered at a pawnbroker's. Donovan did not think they were the rings he had seen Mrs. Chapman wearing. The policemen then left, and Donovan heard no more of the incident. Both Donovan and a former watcher at the lodging-house named West say that when they last saw "Leather Apron" he was wearing a kind of deerstalker hat, double peaked. West describes him as a man not more than 5 ft. 4 in. in height. Mrs. Fiddyman [*sic*] the landlady of the house into which it was stated a blood-stained and wild-looking man entered shortly after the hour at which the murder was probably committed on Saturday morning, has been taken to Leman-street Station, and on seeing Pizer she expressed herself as quite certain that he was not the man who came into her house on the occasion spoken of.

Pigott, the other man arrested, whose father was well known in Gravesend for many years as an insurance agent, was first seen in Gravesend on Sunday afternoon about 4 o'clock. He then asked four young men, who were standing in the London-road, near Princes-street, where he could get a glass of beer, he having walked from Whitechapel. The young men told him. Following their directions he jumped into a tramcar going towards Northfleet. The young men noticed that he had a bad hand, and that he carried a black bag. He was without this bag when subsequently seen. He left a paper parcel at a fish shop, kept by Mrs. Beitchteller, stating he was going across the water to Tilbury. Instead of doing so he went to the Pope's Head publichouse, where his conversation about his hatred of women aroused suspicion, and led to his being detained by the police authorities. Superintendent Berry, who is making most active and exhaustive inquiries, found the paper parcel at the fish shop to contain two shirts and a pair of stockings, one of the shirts, a blue-striped one, being torn about the breast, and having marks of blood upon it. At the police-station, Pigott first said he knocked down the woman who had bitten his hand in a yard at the back of a lodging-house in Whitechapel, but he subsequently said the occurrence took place in Brick-lane. What has become of the black bag which Pigott was seen to have in Gravesend on Sunday afternoon is not known. It appears that Pigott of late years has followed the business of a publican, and that seven or eight years ago he was in a good position, giving £8,000 to go into a house at Hoxton. Some question having arisen as to Pigott's mental condition, it may be added that he appeared perfectly rational during his detention at Gravesend.

The next report of this inquest[4] appeared in *The Times* of Friday, 14 September 1888, page 4:

THE WHITECHAPEL MURDER.

Yesterday Mr. Wynne E. Baxter, Coroner for the South-Eastern Division of Middlesex, resumed his inquiry at the Working Lads' Institute, Whitechapel-road, respecting the death of Annie Chapman, who was found murdered in the back yard of 29, Hanbury-street, Spitalfields, last Saturday morning.

Detective-inspectors Abberline (Scotland-yard), Helson, Chandler, Beck, and Detective-sergeant W. Thicke, H Division, again represented the Criminal Investigation Department.

Inspector Joseph Chandler, H Division, said that about two minutes past 6 on Saturday morning he was on duty in Commercial-street. He saw several men running up Hanbury-street, and he beckoned to them. One of them said, "Another woman has been murdered." Witness at once went with him to 29, Hanbury-street, and passed through the passage into the yard. There were several people in the passage, but no one was in the yard. He saw the body of the deceased lying on the ground on her back. Her head was towards the back wall of the house, but it was some 2 ft. from the wall, and the body was not more than 6 in. or 9 in. from the steps. The face was turned on the right side, and the left hand rested on the left breast. The right hand was lying down by the left side, and the legs were drawn up. The body was lying parallel with the fencing, and was about two yards distant. Witness, remaining there, sent for the divisional surgeon, Dr. Phillips, and also to the station for the ambulance and further assistance. When the constables arrived he removed all persons from the passage, and saw that no one touched the body till the doctor arrived. He obtained some sacking from one of the neighbours to cover the body pending the arrival of the doctor. Dr. Phillips arrived about half-past 6 and examined the body. He then directed the body to be removed to the mortuary, which was done on the police ambulance. After the body had been removed a piece of coarse muslin and a small pocket haircomb case were found. A portion of an envelope was found lying near where her head had been, and a piece of paper containing two pills. He had not the pills there, as inquiries were being made about them. On the back of the envelope was the seal of the Sussex Regiment. The other portion of the writing was torn away. On the other side of the envelope was the letter "M" in a man's handwriting. There was also a post-office stamp, "London, 28 Aug., 1888," with a stamp that was indistinct. There was no postage stamp on that portion. On the front side of the envelope were the letters "Sp." in writing. He also found a leather apron lying in the yard saturated with wet and it was about 2 ft. from the water tap. A box, commonly used by packing-case makers, a piece of flat steel that had since been identified by Mrs. Richardson, and also a spring were found lying close to where the body was found.

By the CORONER. – Some portions of the yard were composed of earth and others of stones. It had not been properly paved. Some of the stones were flat while others were round. He could not detect any appearance of a struggle having taken place. The palings were only temporarily erected, although they might support the weight of a man while he was getting over them. There was no evidence of any one having recently got over them, and there was no breakage. Witness examined the adjoining yard. None of the palings had been broken, although they had since been broken. The palings near the body were stained with blood. In the wall of No. 27 marks were discovered on Tuesday last, and they had been seen by Dr. Phillips. There were no drops of blood in the passage or outside, and the bloodstains were only found in the immediate neighbourhood of the body. There were also a few spots of blood on the back wall at the head of the body and some 2 ft. or 3 ft. from the ground. The largest spot was about the size of a sixpenny piece. They were all within a small compass. Witness assisted in drawing out a plan of the place, and the plan produced was a correct one. Witness searched the clothing of the deceased after the body was removed to the mortuary. The outside jacket, which was a long black one and reached to the knees, had bloodstains round the neck, both on the inside and out, and two or three spots on the left arm. The jacket was hooked at the top and buttoned down. There did not appear to have been any struggle with the jacket. The pocket produced was found worn under the skirt. It was torn down the front and also at the side and did not contain anything. The deceased had on a black skirt, on which was a little blood at the back. There was no damage to the lower portion of the clothing. The boots were on her feet, while the stockings were bloodstained. None of the clothing was torn. Witness saw young John Richardson a little before 7 o'clock in the passage of the house. He told witness he had been to the house about a quarter to 5 that morning, that he went to the back door and looked down at the cellar to see that all was right. He then went away to his work in the market. He did not say anything to witness about cutting his boot, but said he was sure the woman was not there at the time.

By the Foreman. – The back door opened outwards into the yard, on the left-hand side. That was the side on which the body was lying. Richardson might not have seen the body if he did not go into the yard. If he went down the steps and the body was there at the time he was bound to see it. Richardson told witness he did not go down the steps, and did not mention the fact that he sat down on the steps and cut his boots.

The Foreman. – Are you going to produce the pensioner we have heard so much about?

Witness. – We have not been able to find him. No one can give us the least idea who he is. We have instructed the deputy of the lodging-house to let us know at once if he again goes there.

The CORONER. – I should think that if the pensioner knows his own business he would come forward himself.

The Foreman. – It is important he should be here, as he was in the habit of spending Saturday nights with the deceased.

Sergeant Edmund Barry, 31 H, stated that on Saturday last he conveyed the body of the deceased from 29, Hanbury-street, to the White-chapel mortuary on the police ambulance. Detective-sergeant Thicke examined the body and gave out a description of it to witness. In doing this that sergeant moved the clothing about. Two females from 35, Dorset-street, were also present, and described the clothing to witness. They did not touch the clothing or the body. Inspector Chandler then came.

Inspector Chandler, recalled, said he reached the mortuary a few minutes after 7 o'clock, and the body, which was lying on the ambulance, did not appear to have been disturbed. He did not remain until the doctor arrived, but left a constable in charge. It was Constable Barnes, 376 H.

Robert Mann an inmate of the Whitechapel Union, stated that he had charge of the mortuary. At 7 o'clock on Saturday morning he received the body of the deceased, and remained with it until the doctor arrived at 2 o'clock. Two nurses from the infirmary came and undressed the body. He was not in the shed when that was done.

The CORONER. – This is not a mortuary, but simply a shed. Bodies ought not to be taken there. In the East-end, where mortuaries are required more than anywhere else, there are no mortuaries. When bodies are thrown up from the river off Wapping they have to be put in boxes, as there is no mortuary.

The Foreman agreed that one was necessary. He added that a reward should be offered in this case by the Government. Some gentlemen were forming a fund to offer a reward, and Mr. Montagu, M.P., had offered £100.

The witness, in further examination, said he was present when Dr. Phillips made his post-mortem examination. While he was doing so witness picked up the handkerchief produced from off the clothing, which was lying in a corner of the room. He gave the handkerchief to Dr. Phillips, who told him to put it in some water. Witness did not see the handkerchief across the throat of the deceased. It had blood on it as though it had been across her throat.

Timothy Donovan, 35, Dorset-street, recalled, identified the handkerchief produced, which deceased generally wore round her throat. She bought it off another lodger at the lodging-house a week or a fortnight before she met with her death. She was wearing it when she left the lodging-house on Saturday morning and had under it a piece of black woollen scarf. It was tied in the front in one knot.

By the Foreman. – He would recognize the pensioner if he saw him again, and he knew "Harry the hawker." He had not seen the pensioner since Saturday. On that day, when he came to the lodging-house, witness sent for the police, but before they came he went away. He was a man of soldierly appearance, and at times used to come differently attired.

Mr. George Bagster Phillips, 2, Spital-square, stated he was a divisional surgeon of police, and had been for 23 years. At 6.20 on Saturday morning he was called by the police to 29, Hanbury-street, and he arrived there at 6.30. He found the dead body of a female in the possession of the police, lying in the back yard, on her back and on the left hand of the steps. The head was about 6 in. in front of the level of the bottom step, and her feet were towards a shed, which proved to contain wood, at the bottom of the yard. The left arm was placed across the left breast. The legs were drawn up, the feet resting on the ground, and the knees turned outwards. The face was swollen and turned on the right side. The tongue protruded between the front teeth, but not beyond the lips. The tongue was evidently much swollen. The front teeth were perfect, so far as the first molar, top and bottom, and very fine teeth they were. The body was terribly mutilated. He searched the yard, and in doing so found a small piece of coarse muslin and a pocket comb in a paper case lying at the feet of the woman near the paling; and they apparently had been placed there in order or arranged there. He also found and delivered to the police other articles, including the leather apron. The stiffness of the limbs was not marked, but was evidently commencing. He noticed that the throat was dissevered deeply; that the incisions through the skin were jagged, and reached right round the neck. On the back wall of the house, between the steps and the paling which bounded the yard on the left side, about 18 in. from the ground, were about six patches of blood, varying in size from a sixpenny piece to a small point. On the wooden paling, between the yard in question, and the next, smears of blood, corresponding to where the head of the deceased lay, were to be seen. These were about 14 in. from the ground, and immediately above the part where the blood lay that had flowed from the neck. Soon after 2 o'clock on Saturday he went to the labour yard of the Whitechapel Union for the purpose of further examining the body. He was surprised to find that the body had been stripped, and was lying ready on the table for his examination. It was under great difficulty he could make his examination, and, as on many occasions he had met with similar difficulties, he now raised his protest as he had previously done that members in his profession should be called upon to perform their duties in these inadequate circumstances. There were no adequate conveniences for a post-mortem examination; and at particular seasons of the year it was dangerous to the operator.

The CORONER. – As a matter of fact there is no public mortuary in the City of London up to Bow.

Witness, continuing, said, – The body had evidently been attended to since the removal to the mortuary, probably to be washed. He noticed the same protrusion of the tongue. There was a bruise over the right temple. On the upper eyelid there was a bruise, and there were two distinct bruises, each of the size of the top of a man's thumb, on the forepart of the top of the chest. The stiffness of the limbs was now well marked. There was a bruise over the middle part of the bone of the right hand. There was an old scar on the left side of the frontal bone. The stiffness was more noticeable on the left side, especially in the fingers, which were partly closed. There was an abrasion over the ring finger, with distinct markings of a ring or rings. The throat had been severed as before described. The incisions into the skin indicated that they had been made from the left side of the neck. There were two distinct, clean cuts on the left side of the spine. They were parallel from each other and separated by about half an inch. The muscular structures appeared as though an attempt had been made to separate the bones of the neck. There were various other mutilations of the body, but he was of opinion that they occurred subsequent to the death of the woman, and to the large escape of blood from the division of the neck. At this point Dr. Phillips said that, as from these injuries he was satisfied as to the cause of death, he thought that he had better not go into further details of the mutilations, which could only be painful to the feelings of the jury and the public. The Coroner decided to allow that course to be adopted. Witness, continuing, said, – The cause of death was visible from the injuries he had described. From these appearances he was of opinion that the breathing was interfered with previous to death, and that death arose from syncope, or failure of the heart's action in consequence of loss of blood caused by the severance of the throat.

By the CORONER. – He should say that the instrument used at the throat and the abdomen was the same. It must have been a very sharp knife, with a thin, narrow blade, and must have been at least 6 in. to 8 in. in length, probably longer. He should say that the injuries could not have been inflicted by a bayonet or sword bayonet. They could have been done by such an instrument as a medical man used for post-mortem purposes, but the ordinary surgical cases might not contain such an instrument. Those used by slaughter-men, well ground down, might have caused them. He thought the knives used by those in the leather trade would not be long enough in the blade. There were indications of anatomical knowledge, which were only less indicated in consequence of haste. The whole of the body was not present, the absent portions being from the abdomen. The mode in which these portions were extracted showed some anatomical knowledge. He did not think these portions were lost in the transit of the body. He should say that the deceased had been dead at least two hours, and probably more, when he first saw her; but it was right to mention that it was a fairly cool morning, and that the body would be more apt to cool rapidly from its having lost a great quantity of blood. There was no evidence about the body of the woman of a struggle having taken place. He was positive that the deceased entered the yard alive. He made a practical search of the passage and the approach to the house and he saw no trace of blood. There was no blood on the apron, which had the appearance of not having been recently unfolded. He was shown some staining on the wall of No. 25. To the eye of a novice it looked like blood, but it was not so. The deceased was far advanced in disease of the lungs and membranes of the brain, but they had nothing to do with the cause of death. The stomach contained a little food, but there was not any sign of fluid. There was no appearance of the deceased having taken alcohol, but there were signs of great deprivation, and he should say she had been badly fed. He was convinced she had not taken any strong alcohol for some hours before her death. The injuries were certainly not self-inflicted. The bruises on the face were evidently recent, especially about the chin and the sides of the jaw, but the bruises in front of the chest and temple were of longer standing – probably of days. He was of opinion that the person who cut the deceased's throat took hold of her by the chin, and then commenced the incision from left to right. He thought it was highly probable that a person could call out, but with regard to an idea that she might have been gagged he could only point to the swollen face and protruding tongue, both of which were signs of suffocation. The handkerchief produced, together with the pocket, he separated from the rest of some articles said to be taken from the body of deceased at the Whitechapel mortuary, and not then in the custody of the mortuary keeper. A handkerchief was round the throat of the deceased when he saw her early in the morning. He should say it was not tied on after the throat was cut.

Mary Elizabeth Simonds, nurse at the Whitechapel Infirmary, said on Saturday morning she and a nurse named Frances Wright were instructed to go to the mortuary. The body was lying on the ambulance. They were directed by Inspector Chandler to undress the deceased. Witness took the clothes off and placed them in a corner of the shed. They left the handkerchief round the neck of deceased. They washed the blood off the body. There was blood on the chest, as if it had run down from the throat. She found the pocket, the strings of which were not broken.

Inspector Chandler stated he did not instruct the nurses to undress and wash the body.

The Coroner's officer said it was done by order of the clerk to the guardians.

At this point the inquiry was adjourned until Wednesday next.

The Times of the same day [Friday, 14 September 1888, page 4f] also reported:

Up to the present time the police have not succeeded in connecting any person with the crime.

Dr. Phillips's positive opinion that the woman had been dead quite two hours when he first saw the body at half-past 6, throws serious doubt upon the accuracy of at least two important witnesses, and considerably adds to the prevailing confusion.

The man arrested at Holloway [Isenschmid] has for some reason been removed to the asylum at Bow. His own friends give him an indifferent character. He has been missing from home for nearly two months, and it is known that he has been in the habit of carrying several large butcher's knives about his person. Inquiries are now being made with a view to tracing his movements during the past two months.

The principal officers engaged in investigating the Whitechapel murders were summoned to Scotland-yard yesterday. Later in the day Mr. Bruce, Assistant Commissioner, and Colonel Monsell, Chief Constable, paid a private visit to the Whitechapel district without notifying the local officials of their intention to do so. They visited the scene of the Buck's-row murders as well as Hanbury-street, and made many inquiries. They spent nearly a quarter of an hour at No. 29, Hanbury-street, and minutely inspected the house and the yard in which were found the mutilated body of Mrs. Chapman.

The police have satisfied themselves that the man Piggott could have had nothing to do with the murders. His movements have been fully accounted for, and he is no longer under surveillance.

The *Lancet* says: – "The theory that the succession of murders which have lately been committed in Whitechapel are the work of a lunatic appears to us to be by no means at present well established. We can quite understand the necessity for any murderer endeavouring to obliterate by the death of his victim his future identification as a burglar. Moreover, as far as we are aware, homicidal mania is generally characterised by the one single and fatal act, although we grant this may have been led up to by a deep-rooted series of delusions. It is most unusual for a lunatic to plan any complicated crime of this kind. Neither, as a rule, does a lunatic take precautions to escape from the consequences of his act; which *data* are most conspicuous in these now too celebrated cases."

The police-courts column of the same paper carried the following reports, the first reflecting the excitement produced by the murders in the minds of some, the second concerning a murderous cut-throat attack by a disturbed father on his daughter, and the third about the detention of a prisoner by Inspector Andrews who would later convey that prisoner to Canada and then pursue enquiries for a "Ripper" suspect in New York:

At the THAMES Police-court, a Japanese, named SOPIWAJAN, 38, was charged with cutting and wounding Ellen Norton, 9, Jamaica-passage, Limehouse. Prosecutrix, whose head was bandaged, said about 12 o'clock on Wednesday night [12 September] she was in the Coach and Horses beershop, West India Dock-road, when she heard screams close by the Strangers' Home. She went out and saw the accused in the act of stabbing her friend, Emily Shepherd. Witness rushed forward and received the knife stab in her head. She then remembered no more until she was at the station, having her head dressed by a doctor. Witness had been drinking, but had not been in the prisoner's company. Emily Shepherd said the prisoner came up to her and said to her, "If you go away from me to-night I will rip you up the same as the woman was served in the Whitechapel-road." She screamed out, when the prosecutrix ran up. The accused then stabbed Norton in the head with the long-bladed knife produced. He then kicked witness, and afterwards broke a plate glass window at the Strangers' Home. Constable 448K said he heard screams of "Police" and "Murder," and on going towards the spot he saw the prisoner jump through the glass panel of the door of the Asiatic Home. He gained admission to the Home, and found prisoner in the yard washing blood off his hands. Witness took him into custody. Sergeant Brown, 2K, produced the knife, which was covered with blood. Mr. Lushington committed the prisoner for trial.

At LAMBETH, THOMAS JAMES UBERFIELD, 63, described as a tailor, living at 268, Kennington-road, was charged with attempting to murder his daughter, Jane Uberfield, by cutting her throat. Police-constable Hutchins, 18 L, stated that at 9 o'clock that morning [13 September] he was called to the house, and saw the prisoner on the first floor landing. He had only his trousers and shirt on. He was greatly excited, and upon witness asking what was the matter, he said, "I've cut my daughter's throat: I don't know what possessed me to do so." Witness had not been long there before Dr. Farr arrived and attended to the injured girl. Witness detained prisoner, and afterwards removed him to the Kennington-road Police-station. He was charged with attempting to murder his daughter. Dr. Frederick William Farr, of Kennington-road, said he knew the prisoner as a patient for nearly 18 months. He had been of unsound mind for some time. His delusion was chiefly that he had animals crawling about inside him. Instruction was given to watch him. He had never shown symptoms to suppose he would do injury to anybody. He found the injured girl seated in a chair in an upstairs room. She was bleeding very much from an incised wound on the throat about two and three-quarter inches in length and about half an inch deep in the deepest part. He thought she was likely to recover, and she was now lying at home. Mr. Chance ordered a remand, and said it was a sad affair, and no doubt the result of a sudden fit of insanity.

At WANDSWORTH, ROLAND GIDEON ISRAEL BARNETT, who described himself as a theatrical manager of Craven-street, Strand, was re-examined on the charge of obtaining a sum of £45 from Henry Charles Britton, a butcher, of Tooting, with intent to defraud, the offence having, it was alleged, been committed in 1878. Mr. Pollard appeared to prosecute on behalf of the Solicitor to the Treasury; and Mr. Poland defended the accused. Mr. Pollard asked the magistrate to deal with the case on the evidence already before him, and said the only additional witnesses he could call were the clerk of the bank on which the particular cheque in question was drawn and Inspector Andrews, of the Criminal Investigation Department, by whom the accused was arrested. Mr. Plowden said he had had an opportunity of reading the information on which the warrant was granted, and unless it could be supplemented by additional evidence he would take upon himself the responsibility of discharging the prisoner, believing that no jury would convict. Mr. Pollard thought it right to tell the magistrate that he had no additional evidence. Mr. Plowden then discharged the prisoner, observing that he would be required to clear himself of another charge of a more serious character. The prisoner then left the dock, but was re-arrested by Inspector Andrews on an extradition warrant, charging him with obtaining money from certain persons in Toronto by false representations.

The Times of Saturday, 15 September 1888 [page 6a] carried further information on the hunt for the Whitechapel murderer:

THE WHITECHAPEL MURDERS.

The police at the Commercial-street Police Station have made another arrest on suspicion in connexion with the recent murders. It appears that among the numerous statements and descriptions of suspected persons are several tallying with that of the man in custody, but beyond this the police know nothing at present against him. His apprehension was of a singular character. Throughout yesterday his movements are stated to have created suspicion among various persons, and last night he was handed over to a uniform constable doing duty in the neighbourhood of Flower and Dean-street on suspicion in connexion with the crime. On his arrival at the police station in Commercial-street the detective officers and Mr. Abberline were communicated with, and an inquiry concerning him was at once opened. On being searched perhaps one of the most extraordinary accumulation of articles were discovered – a heap of rags, comprising pieces of dress fabrics, old and dirty linen, two purses of a kind usually used by women, two or three pocket handkerchiefs, one a comparatively clean white one, and a white one with a red spotted border; two small tin boxes, a small cardboard box, a small leather strap, which might serve the purpose of a garterstring, and one spring onion. The person to whom this curious assortment belongs is slightly built, about 5 ft. 7 in. or 5 ft. 8 in. in height, and dressed shabbily. He has a very careworn look. Covering a head of hair, inclined somewhat to be sandy, with beard and moustache to match, was a cloth skull cap, which did not improve his appearance. Suspicion is the sole motive for his temporary detention, for the police, although making every possible inquiry about him, do not believe his apprehension to be of any importance.

Regarding the man Pigott, who was captured at Gravesend, nothing whatever has been discovered by the detectives in the course of their inquiries which can in any way connect him with the crime or crimes, and his release, at all events, from the custody of the police is expected shortly.

In connexion with the arrest of a lunatic at Holloway, it appears that he has been missing from his friends for some time now. The detectives have been very active in prosecuting their inquiries concerning him, and it is believed the result, so far, increases their suspicion. He is at present confined in the asylum at Grove-road, Bow.

All inquiries have failed to elicit anything as to the whereabouts of the missing pensioner who is wanted in connexion with the recent murder.

On the question as to the time when the crime was committed, concerning which there was a difference between the evidence of the man Richardson and the opinion of Dr. Phillips, a correspondent yesterday elicited that Mr. Cadoche [sic], who lives in the next house to No. 29, Hanbury-street, where the murder was committed, went to the back of the premises at half-past 5 a.m. As he passed the wooden partition he heard a woman say "No, no." On returning he heard a scuffle and then some one fell heavily against the fence. He heard no cry for help, and so he went into his house. Some surprise is felt that this statement was not made in evidence at the inquest. There is a very strong feeling in the district and large numbers of persons continue to visit the locality.

Annie Chapman, the victim of the crime, was buried early yesterday morning at Manor Park Cemetery. Some of her relatives attended the funeral.

The Times of Wednesday, 19 September 1888, page 3 f, detailed the continuing story of the investigations into the murders:

THE WHITECHAPEL MURDERS.

Several reports were current in London yesterday as to discoveries by the police in connexion with the Hanbury-street murder; but the value of the clues said to have been obtained is extremely doubtful. One statement is to the effect that on the day of the murder a man changed his clothes in the lavatory of the City News Rooms, Ludgate-circus, and left hurriedly, leaving behind him a shirt, a pair of trousers, and a pair of socks. The attendant threw the discarded clothes into the dustbin, and they were carted off in the City Sewers cart on the following Monday. The police are said to be endeavouring to trace these clothes, but decline to give information on the subject. It is obviously difficult to conceive why the murderer, having possessed himself of a change of clothes, should pass from Whitechapel to Ludgate-circus and change his dress in a *quasi*-public place such as the City News Rooms. The police, however, will thoroughly sift the matter.

Charles Ludwig, the German charged yesterday at the Thames Police-court with being drunk and threatening to stab, was at once connected by popular imagination with the murder. Our police report will show that some of the circumstances of the case seem to support such a hypothesis. The youth who was threatened early yesterday morning stated to a correspondent that the first he saw of Ludwig, as he calls him, was about a quarter to 4 o'clock. The prisoner was then at the top of Commercial-street, in company with a woman, whom he was conducting in the direction of the Minories. "I took no notice of this at the time," added the witness, "except to make a remark to a coffee-stall keeper. In about a quarter of an hour the woman ran back in a state of fright, as it seemed. At any rate she was screaming and exclaiming, 'You can't do that to me.' Again I thought little of it, as I only fancied she had had some drink, but within five minutes the prisoner came up and asked for a cup of coffee at the stall where I was standing. He, at all events, was drunk, and would only produce a halfpenny in payment for the coffee which was given him. I supposed he noticed me looking at him, for he suddenly turned round and asked in broken English, 'What are you looking at?' I replied that I was doing no harm, but he said, 'Oh, you want something,' and pulled out a long penknife, with which he made a dash at me. I eluded him and snatched from the stall a dish, which I prepared to throw at his head, but as he retreated after making the first dash I only called to a policeman who was near by and had him arrested. He is slightly built, and perhaps about 5 ft. 6 in. in height, dark complexioned, and wearing a grizzled beard and moustache. I should think he is about 40 years of age. There is something the matter with one of his legs, and he walks stiffly. I heard that at the police-court this morning he pretended not to understand English, but his English when he addressed me was plain enough, though broken; and besides, when the officer who had him in charge told me on the way to Leman-street to see that he did not throw anything away, he at once dropped the penknife – which had till then been in his possession – as if the idea of getting rid of it had only just occurred to him. I have never seen him before.'' Ludwig entered the employment of Mr. C. A. Partridge, hairdresser, the Minories, a fortnight ago last Saturday. On Monday night last he went to an hotel in Finsbury, where he had previously lodged, and remained there until about 1 o'clock in the morning. He produced a number of razors, and acted in such a manner that some of the inmates were quite frightened. The landlady of this hotel states that on the day after the last murder in Whitechapel Ludwig called early in the morning and washed his hands, stating that he had been injured. Another person has alleged that there was blood on the man's hands, but as to this the landlady cannot speak.

In the same issue of *The Times* a letter[5] from the Rev. Samuel A. Barnett, the vicar of St. Jude's, appeared. This is particularly interesting as he lived at the heart of the area in which the murders were being committed, and it gives an interesting insight into the social conditions prevailing in the area:

AT LAST.
TO THE EDITOR OF THE TIMES.

Sir, – Whitechapel horrors will not be in vain if ''at last'' the public conscience awakes to consider the life which these horrors reveal. The murders were, it may almost be said, bound to come; generation could not follow generation in lawless intercourse, children could not be familiarized with scenes of degradation, community in crime could not be the bond of society and the end of all be peace.

Some of us who, during many years, have known the life of our neighbours do not think the murders to be the worst fact in our experience, and published evidence now gives material for forming a picture of daily or nightly life such as no one has imagined.

It is for those who, like ourselves, have for years known these things to be ready with practical suggestions, and I would now put some forward as the best outcome of the thought of my wife and myself. Before doing so, it is necessary to remind the public that these criminal haunts are of limited extent. The greater part of Whitechapel is as orderly as any part of London, and the life of most of its inhabitants is more moral than that of many whose vices are hidden by greater wealth. Within the area of a quarter of a mile most of the evil may be found concentrated, and it ought not to be impossible to deal with it strongly and adequately. We would submit four practical suggestions:–

1. Efficient police supervision. In criminal haunts a licence has been allowed which would not be endured in other quarters. Rows, fights, and thefts

have been permitted, while the police have only been able to keep the main thoroughfares quiet for the passage of respectable people. The Home Office has never authorized the employment of a sufficient force to keep decent order inside the criminal quarters.

2. Adequate lighting and cleaning. It is no blame to our local authority that the back streets are gloomy and ill-cleaned. A penny rate here produces but a small sum, and the ratepayers are often poor. Without doubt, though, dark passages lend themselves to evil deeds. It would not be unwise, and it certainly would be a humane outlay, if some of the unproductive expenditure of the rich were used to make the streets of the poor as light and as clean as the streets of the City.

3. The removal of the slaughter-houses. At present animals are daily slaughtered in the midst of Whitechapel, the butchers with their blood stains are familiar among the street passengers, and sights are common which tend to brutalize ignorant natures. For the sake of both health and morals the slaughtering should be done outside the town.

4. The control of tenement houses by responsible landlords. At present there is lease under lease, and the acting landlord is probably one who encourages vice to pay his rent. Vice can afford to pay more than honesty, but its profits at last go to landlords. If rich men would come forward and buy up this bad property they might not secure great interest, but they would clear away evil not again to be suffered to accumulate. Such properties have been bought with results morally most satisfactory and economically not unsatisfactory. Some of that which remains might now be bought, some of the worst is at present in the market, and I should be glad, indeed, to hear of purchasers.

Far be it from any one to say that even such radical changes as these would do away with evil. When, however, such changes have been effected it will be more possible to develop character, and one by one lead the people to face their highest. Only personal service, the care of the individual by individual, can be powerful to keep down evil, and only the knowledge of God is sufficient to give the individual faith to work and see little result of his work. For men and women who will give such service there is a crying demand. I am, truly yours,

SAMUEL A. BARNETT.

St. Jude's Vicarage, Whitechapel, Sept. 18.

Another letter in the same column indicated the close public interest in the reports of the coroner's inquest, and the feeling by some that they were too lengthy and revealing:

TO THE EDITOR OF THE TIMES.

Sir, – Is it not time that the inquest on Annie Chapman should close, and a verdict of "Wilful Murder against some person or persons unknown" be given?

The question which the jury are soon to determine – viz., how, when, and where the deceased met with her death, and who she was – is virtually solved.

The discovery of the murderer or murderers is the duty of the police, and if it is to be accomplished it is not desirable that the information they obtain should be announced publicly in the newspapers day by day through the medium of the coroner's inquiry.

J.P.

This would seem to be a criticism of coroner Wynne Baxter's lengthy and revealing enquiries, which many thought gave away too much of the information the police were working on, and is one of the few press statements fully supporting the police viewpoint. Perhaps the initials "J.P" indicate Justice of the Peace, and that the writer was a magistrate supporting the police.

The next extract[6] from *The Times* is dated 20 September 1888, page 3, and refers to the resumed inquest:

THE WHITECHAPEL MURDER.

Yesterday Mr. Wynne E. Baxter, Coroner for the South-Eastern Division of Middlesex, resumed his inquiry, at the Working Lads' Institute, White-chapel-road, respecting the death of Annie Chapman, who was found murdered in the back yard of No. 29, Hanbury-street, Spitalfields, on the morning of the 8th inst.

Detective-inspectors Helson and Chandler and Detective-sergeant Thicke [*sic*], H Division, watched the case on behalf of the Criminal Investigation Department.

Eliza Cooper stated that she lived at 35, Dorset-street, Spitalfields, and had done so for the last five months. Witness knew the deceased, and had a quarrel with her on the Tuesday before she was murdered. On the previous Saturday deceased came in and asked the people there to give her a piece of soap. She was told to ask "Liza". Deceased then came to witness, who opened the locker and gave her a piece of soap. Deceased then handed the soap to Stanley, who went and washed himself. Deceased also went out, and when she came back witness asked her for the soap, which, however, she did not return, but said "I will see you by and by". Stanley gave deceased 2 s., and she paid for the bed for two nights. Witness saw no more of deceased that night.

By the CORONER. – Witness was treated by Stanley. On the following

Wednesday witness met deceased in the kitchen and asked her to return the piece of soap. Deceased threw a halfpenny on the table and said "Go and get a halfpennyworth of soap." They then began to quarrel, and afterwards went to the Ringers public-house, where the quarrel was continued. Deceased slapped her face and said "Think yourself lucky I did not do more." Witness believed she then struck deceased in the left eye and then on the chest. She could afterwards see that the blow had marked deceased's face.

By the jury. – That was the last time she saw deceased alive. At that time she was wearing three rings on the third finger of the left hand. Deceased bought the rings, which were brass ones, of a black man. Deceased had never possessed a gold wedding ring since witness had become acquainted with her. She had known deceased for about 15 years, and knew that she associated with "Harry the Hawker", and other men. Witness could not say whether any of these persons were missing. With the exception of Stanley, deceased used only casually to bring other men to the lodging-house.

Dr. George Bagster Phillips was recalled. Before he was examined.

The CORONER said it was necessary that all the evidence the doctor had obtained from his post-mortem examination should be on the records of the Court for various reasons which he need not then enumerate, however painful it might be.

Dr. Phillips said that had notice been given him he should have been better prepared with the evidence, but he had his original notes with him. While bowing to the Coroner's decision, he still thought it a great pity that he should have to give this evidence, as matters which had since come to light had shown the wisdom of the course pursued on the last occasion, and he could not help reiterating his regret that the Coroner had come to a different conclusion. On the last occasion he mentioned that there were reasons why he thought that the person who inflicted the cut on the woman's throat had caught hold of her chin. He came to that conclusion because on the left side, on the lower jaw, were scratches one and a half to two inches below the lobe of the ear, and going in a contrary direction to the incision in the throat. They were of recent date. The abrasions on the left side and on the right side were corresponding bruises. He washed them, when they became more distinct, whereas the bruises mentioned in his last evidence remained the same. The deceased had been seized by the throat while the incisions into the throat had been perpetrated. The witness here stated that in the interests of justice he thought it would be better not to give more details.

The CORONER. – We are here to decide the cause of death, and therefore have a right to hear all particulars. Whether that evidence is made public or not rests with the Press. I might add I have never before heard of any evidence being kept back from a coroner.

Dr. Phillips. – I am in the hands of the Court, and what I was going to detail took place after death.

The CORONER. – That is a matter of opinion. You know that medical men often differ.

Dr. Phillips repeated that he did not think the details should be given.

The court having been cleared of all women and boys, the witness proceeded to give medical and surgical evidence, totally unfit for publication, of the deliberate, successful, and apparently scientific manner in which the poor woman had been mutilated, and expressed his opinion that the length of the weapon was at least five to six inches, probably more, and the appearance of the cuts confirmed him in the opinion that the instrument, like the one which divided the neck, had been of a very sharp character. The mode in which the knife had been used seemed to indicate great anatomical knowledge.

By the CORONER. – He thought he himself could not have performed all the injuries he described, even without a struggle, under a quarter of an hour. If he had done it in a deliberate way such as would fall to the duties of a surgeon, it probably would have taken him the best part of an hour. He had not been able to discover any trace of blood on the walls of the next house.

In answer to the jury, the witness said that he had no practical opinion about a person's eyes being photographed, but his opinion would be useless; also with regard to employing bloodhounds. In the latter case they would more probably scent the blood of the murdered woman. The injuries to the body would produce at once partial insensibility.

Elizabeth Long 198, Church-row, Whitechapel, stated that she was the wife of James Long, a park-keeper. On Saturday morning the 8th inst., she was passing down Hanbury-street from home and going to Spitalfields Market. It was about 5 30. She was certain of the time, as the brewers' clock had just struck that time when she passed 29, Hanbury-street. Witness was on the right-hand side of the street – the same side as No. 29. She saw a man and woman on the pavement talking. The man's back was turned towards Brick-lane, while the woman's was towards the Spitalfields Market. They were talking together, and were close against the shutters of No. 29. Witness saw the woman's face. She had since seen the deceased in the mortuary, and was sure it was the face of the same person she saw in Hanbury-street. She did not see the man's face, except to notice that he was dark. He wore a brown deerstalker hat, and she thought he had on a dark coat, but was not quite certain of that. She could not say what the age of the man was, but he looked to be over 40, and appeared to be a little taller than deceased. he appeared to be a foreigner, and had a shabby genteel appearance. Witness could hear them talking loudly, and she overheard him say to deceased, "Will you?" She replied, "Yes." They still stood there as witness passed, and she went on to her work without looking back.

By the CORONER. – She saw nothing to indicate they were not sober. It was not an unusual thing to see men and women talking together at that hour in that locality.

The Foreman remarked that the time stated by the witness was not consistent with that stated by the doctor.

The CORONER observed that Dr. Phillips had since qualified his statement.

Edward Stanley stated that he lived at 1, Osborne-street, Whitechapel. He was a brick-layer's labourer, and was known by the name of "The Pensioner." He knew the deceased, and he sometimes visited her at 35, Dorset-street. He was not there with her more than once or twice, but had been elsewhere with her at times. He last saw her alive on Sunday, the 2d inst., between 1 and 3 o'clock in the afternoon. At that time she was wearing two rings on one of her fingers. One was a flat ring and the other oval. He should think they were brass ones. Witness did not know of any one with whom deceased was on bad terms.

By the CORONER. – When he last saw deceased her eye was slightly blackened. His memory might be confused, and it was possible he might have seen deceased after the time he had stated, for when he did see her she certainly had a black eye, and spoke to him about it.

The Foreman. – A previous witness stated that the blows were not inflicted on deceased's face until the Tuesday.

In answer to the jury, the witness denied that he was in the habit of spending Saturdays and Sundays with the deceased.

The CORONER. – Are you a pensioner?

Witness. – Am I bound to answer this question?

The CORONER. – You have to answer all questions affecting this case that are put to you.

Witness. – I am not a pensioner, and have not been in the Essex Regiment. What I say will be published all over Europe. I have lost five hours in coming here.

The deputy of 35, Dorset-street, was here called into the room and said Stanley was the person they called "The Pensioner." He was the man who used to come to the lodging-house with the deceased on Saturday and stay till the Monday. Stanley had been to the lodging-house six or seven times. The last time he was there was the Saturday before the woman's death, and he stayed till the Monday. Stanley paid for one night, and deceased afterwards paid for Sunday night.

The CORONER. – What do you think of that, Stanley?

Stanley. – The evidence given by Donovan is incorrect. When you talk to me, Sir, you talk to an honest man. I was at Gosport from the 6th of August up to the 1st of September. The deceased met me at the corner of Brushfield-street that night.

The Foreman. – Did you see any quarrel?

Witness. – I saw no quarrel, only the effects of it. I have known the deceased about two years, when she was living at Windsor. I was told by a shoeblack that deceased had been murdered, and I then went to the lodging-house and inquired whether it was correct. After I saw the Coroner's observations in the newspapers, I went to the Commercial-street Police-station.

In further examination the witness said he was told the police wanted him.

The CORONER thought the lodging-house keeper had made a mistake in the man.

Albert Cadosch a carpenter, stated that he resided at No. 27, Hanbury-street. That was next door to No. 29. On Saturday, the 8th inst. he got up at about 5.15 and went out into the yard of his house. As he returned across the yard, to the back door of his house, he heard a voice say quite close to him, "No." He believed it came from No. 29. He went into the house, and returned to the yard three or four minutes afterwards. He then heard a sort of a fall against the fence, which divided his yard from No. 29. Something seemed suddenly to touch the fence. He did not look to see what it was. He did not hear any other noise.

By the CORONER. – He did not hear the rustling of any clothes. Witness then left the house and went to his work. When he passed Spitalfields Church it was about 32 minutes past 5. He did not hear people in the yard as a rule, but had now and then heard them at that time in the morning.

By the jury. – He did not go into the yard twice out of curiosity. He had been under an operation at the hospital. He informed the police the same day of what he had heard. The palings were about 5 ft. 6 in. in height. He had not the curiosity to look over the fence, as at times the next door people were early risers. When he left the house he did not see any man or woman in Hanbury-street. He did not see Mrs. Long.

William Stevens, a painter, of 35, Dorset-street, deposed that he knew the deceased, whom he last saw alive about 12 minutes past 12 on the early morning of her death. She was then in the kitchen of the lodging-house, and was not the worse for drink. At that time she had rings on her fingers. Witness believed the piece of envelope produced was the one he saw deceased pick up by the fireplace. He noticed it was about the size of the piece produced, and he saw it had a red post mark on it. Deceased then pulled out a box containing pills from her pocket, and the box breaking she put the pills into the piece of paper, and put it into her pocket. He saw deceased leave the kitchen, and thought she was going to bed, as she said she would not be long out of bed.

By the CORONER. – He did not know of any one with whom the deceased was on bad terms.

The CORONER said that was all the evidence forthcoming. It was a question for the jury whether they would adjourn the case or return their verdict.

The Foreman stated that the reward of Mr. S. Montagu, M.P., of £100 had been posted about, but the Government did not, as the Coroner had previously stated, now offer rewards. At the same time, if the Government had offered a reward, it would have looked more official.

After some further conversation, the inquiry was adjourned until Wednesday next, when it will be completed.

No further arrest in connexion with the Whitechapel murders had been made up to last night, [19 September], and the police are still at fault.

The following letter has been sent to the secretary of the Vigilance Committee lately formed in Mile-end: –

"Whitehall, Sept. 17, 1888.

"Sir, – I am directed by the Secretary of State to acknowledge the receipt of your letter of the 16th inst. with reference to the question of the offer of a reward for the discovery of the perpetrators of the recent murders in Whitechapel, and I am to inform you that had the Secretary of State considered the case a proper one for the offer of a reward he would at once have offered one on behalf of the Government; but that the practice of offering rewards for the discovery of criminals was discontinued some years ago because experience showed that such offers of reward tended to produce more harm than good; and the Secretary of State is satisfied that there is nothing in the circumstances of the present case to justify a departure from this rule.

"I am, Sir, your obedient servant,

E. LEIGH PEMBERTON.

"Mr. B. Harris, The Crown, 74, Mile-end-road, E."

Home Secretary Matthews, apparently stung by the increasing criticism of the lack of success on the part of the police, and the two-week absence of Anderson, sent a memo[7], dated 22 September 1888, to his Principal Private Secretary, Evelyn Ruggles-Brise:

"Stimulate the Police about Whitechapel murders. *Absente* Anderson, Monro might be willing to give a hint to the C.I.D. people if needful."

This indicates Matthews's dissatisfaction with the CID and his obvious feeling that they should be under the guidance of their old chief, Monro.

The final day of the lengthy inquest on the murder of Annie Chapman was 26 September 1888. The proceedings were reported in *The Times* of Thursday, 27 September 1888 and, all the evidence having been heard, an account[8] was given of Mr Wynne Baxter's summing-up and views on the enquiry:

THE WHITECHAPEL MURDER.

Yesterday afternoon Mr. Wynne E. Baxter, the coroner for the South-Eastern Division of Middlesex, resumed his adjourned inquiry at the Working Lads' Institute, Whitechapel, respecting the death of Annie Chapman, aged 47, a widow, who was found brutally murdered in the back yard of 29, Hanbury-street, Whitechapel, on the early morning of Saturday the 8th inst.

Inspectors Helson, Chandler, and Bannister watched the case on behalf of the Commissioners of Police.

Having been informed there was no further evidence forthcoming,

The CORONER proceeded to sum up. He congratulated the jury that their labours were then nearly completed. Although up to the present they had not resulted in the detection of the criminal, he had no doubt that if the perpetrator of this foul murder were eventually discovered, their efforts would not have been useless. The evidence given was on the records of that Court, and could be used even if the witnesses were not forthcoming; while the publicity given had already elicited further information, which he would later on have to mention, and which he hoped he was not sanguine in believing might perhaps be of the utmost importance. The deceased was a widow, 47 years of age, named Annie Chapman. Her husband was a coachman living at Windsor. For three or four years before his death she had lived apart from her husband, who allowed her 10 s. a week until his death at Christmas, 1886. She had evidently lived an immoral life for some time, and her habits and surroundings had become worse since her means had failed. She no longer visited her relations, and her brother had not seen her for five months, when she borrowed a small sum from him. She lived principally in the common lodginghouses in the neighbourhood of Spitalfields, where such as she herded like cattle. She showed signs of great deprivation, as if she had been badly fed. The glimpse of life in those dens which the evidence in this case disclosed was sufficient to make them feel there was much in the 19th century civilization of which they had small reason to be proud; but the jury, who were constantly called together to hear the sad tale of starvation, or semi-starvation, of misery, immorality, and wickedness which some of the occupants of the 5,000 beds in that district had every week to relate at coroner's inquests, did not require to be reminded of what life in a Spitalfields lodginghouse meant. It was in one of those that the older bruises found on the temple and in front of the chest of the deceased were received, in a trumpery quarrel, a week before her death. It was in one of those that she was seen a few hours before her mangled remains were discovered. On the afternoon and evening of Friday, the 7th of September, she spent her time partly in such a place, at 35, Dorset- street, and partly in the Ringers publichouse, where she spent whatever money she had; so that between 1 and 2 o'clock on the morning of Saturday, when the money for her bed was demanded, she was obliged to admit that she was without means, and at once turned out into the street to find it. She left there at 1.45 a.m. She was seen off the premises by the night watchman, and was observed to turn down Little Paternoster-row into Brushfield-street, and not in the more direct direction of Hanbury-street. On her wedding finger she was wearing two or three rings, which appeared to have been palpably of base metal, and value. They now lost sight of her for about four hours, but at half-past 5 o'clock Mrs. Long was in Hanbury-street, on the way from her home in Church-street, Whitechapel, to Spitalfields Market. She walked on the northern side of the road, going westward, and remembered having seen a man and woman standing a few yards from the place where the deceased was afterwards found, and, although she did not know Annie Chapman, she was positive that the woman was the deceased. The two were talking loudly, but not sufficiently so to arouse her suspicions that there was anything wrong. The words she overheard were not calculated to do so. The laconic inquiry of the man, "Will you?" and the simple assent of the woman, viewed in the light of subsequent events, could be easily translated and explained. Mrs. Long passed on her way, and neither saw nor heard anything more of her, and that was the last time she was known to have been alive. There was some conflict in the evidence about the time at which the deceased was despatched. It was not unusual to find inaccuracy in such details, but that variation was not very great or very important. She was found dead about 6 o'clock. She was not in the yard when Richardson was there at 4.50 a.m. She was talking outside the house at half-past 5, when Mrs. Long passed them. Cadosh [sic] said it was about 5.20 when he was in the back yard of the adjoining house and heard a voice say "No," and three or four minutes afterwards a fall against the fence; but if he was out of his reckoning but a quarter of an hour the discrepancy in the evidence of fact vanished; and he might be mistaken, for he admitted that he did not get up until a quarter past 5, and that it was after the half-hour when he passed the Spitalfields clock. It was true that Dr. Phillips thought that when he saw the body at 6.30 the deceased had been dead at least two hours, but he admitted that the coldness of the morning and the great loss of blood might affect his opinion, and if the evidence of the other witnesses was correct, Dr. Phillips had miscalculated the effect of those forces. But many minutes after Mrs. Long passed them could not have elapsed before the deceased became a mutilated corpse in the yard of No. 29, Hanbury-street, close by where she was last seen by any witness. That place was a fair example of a large number of houses in the neighbourhood. It was built, like hundreds of others, for the Spitalfields weavers, and when hand looms were driven out by steam and power they were converted into dwellings for the poor. Its size was about such as a superior artisan would occupy in the country, but its condition was such as would to a certainty leave it without a tenant. In that place 17 persons were living, from a woman and her son, sleeping in a cats' meat shop on the ground floor, to Davis and his wife and their three grown up sons, all sleeping together in an attic. The street door and the yard door were never locked, and the passage and yard appeared to have been constantly used by persons who had no legitimate business there. There was little doubt that deceased knew the place, for it was only 300 or 400 yards from where she lodged. If so, it was unnecessary to assume that her companion had any knowledge – in fact, it was easier to believe that he was ignorant both of the nest of living beings by whom he was surrounded, and of their occupations and habits. Some were on the move late at night, some were up long before the sun. A carman named Thompson left the house as early as 3.50 a.m.; an hour later John Richardson was paying the house a visit of inspection; shortly after 5.15 Cadosh, who lived in the next house, was in the adjoining yard twice. Davis, the carman who occupied the third floor front, heard the church clock strike a quarter to 6, got up, had a cup of tea, and went into the back yard, and was horrified to find the mangled body of the deceased. It was then a little after 6 a.m. – a very little, for at ten minutes past the hour Inspector Chandler had been informed of the discovery while on duty in Commercial-street. There was nothing to suggest that the deceased was not fully conscious of what she was doing. It was true that she had passed through some stages of intoxication, for although she appeared perfectly sober to her friend who met her in Dorset-street at 5 o'clock the previous evening, she had been drinking afterwards; and when she left the lodginghouse shortly after 2 o'clock, the night watchman noticed that she was the worse for drink, but not badly so, while the deputy asserts that, though she had been evidently drinking, she could walk straight, and it was probably only malt liquor that she had taken, and its effects would pass off quicker than if she had taken spirits. The post-mortem examination showed that while the stomach contained a meal of food, there was no sign of fluid and no appearance of her having taken alcohol, and Dr. Phillips was convinced that she had not taken any alcohol for some time. The deceased, therefore, entered the house in full possession of her faculties, although with a very different object to her companion's. From the evidence which the condition of the yard afforded and the medical examination disclosed, it appeared that after the two had passed through the passage and opened the swing door at the end, they descended the three steps into the yard. On their left-hand side there was a recess between those steps and the palings. Here, a few feet from the house and a less distance from the palings, they must have stood. The wretch must have then seized the deceased, perhaps with Judas-like approaches. He seized her by the chin. He pressed her throat, and while thus preventing the slightest cry, he at the same time produced insensibility and suffocation. There was no evidence of any struggle. The clothes were not torn. Even in those preliminaries, the wretch seems to have known how to carry out efficiently his nefarious work. The deceased was then lowered to the ground, and laid on her back; and although in doing so she may have fallen slightly against the fence, the movement was probably effected with care. Her throat was then cut in two places with savage determination, and the injuries to the abdomen commenced. All was done with cool impudence and reckless daring; but perhaps nothing was more noticeable than the emptying of her pockets, and the arrangement of their contents with business-like precision in order near her feet. The murder seemed, like the Buck's-row case, to have been carried out without any cry. None of the occupants of the houses by which the spot was surrounded heard any thing suspicious. The brute who committed the offence did not even take the trouble to cover up his ghastly work, but left the body exposed to the view of the first comer. That accorded but little with the trouble taken with the rings, and suggested either that he had at length been disturbed, or that, as daylight broke, a sudden fear suggested the danger of detection that he was running. There were two things missing. Her rings had been wrenched from her fingers and had not since been found, and the uterus had been taken from the abdomen. The body had not been dissected, but the injuries had been made by some one who had considerable anatomical skill and knowledge. There were no meaningless cuts. The organ had been taken by one who knew where to find it, what difficulties he would have to contend against, and how he should use his knife so as to abstract the organ without injury to it. No unskilled person could have known where to find it or have recognised it when it was found. For instance, no mere slaughterer of animals could have carried out these operations. It must have been some one accustomed to the post mortem room. The conclusion that the desire was to possess the missing abdominal organ seemed overwhelming. If the object were robbery, the injuries to the viscera were meaningless, for death had previously resulted from the loss of blood at the neck. Moreover, when they found an easily accomplished theft of some paltry brass rings and an internal organ taken, after at least a quarter of an hour's work and by a skilled person, they were driven to the deduction that the abstraction of the missing portion of abdominal viscera was the object, and the theft of the rings was only a thin-veiled blind, an attempt to prevent the real intention being discovered. The amount missing would go into a breakfast cup, and had not the medical examination been of a thorough and searching character it might easily have been left unnoticed that there was any portion of the body which had been taken. The difficulty in believing that the purport of the murderer was the possession of the missing abdominal organ was natural. It was abhorrent to their feelings to conclude that a life should be taken for so slight an object; but when rightly considered the reasons for most murders were altogether out of proportion to their guilt. It had been suggested that the criminal was a lunatic with morbid feelings. That might or might not be the case, but the object of the murderer appeared palpably shown by the facts, and it was not necessary to assume lunacy, for it was clear there was a market for the missing organ. To show the jury that, he (the coroner) must mention a fact which at the same time proved the assistance which publicity and the newspaper Press afforded in the detection of crime. Within a few hours of the issue of the morning papers containing a report of the medical evidence given at the last sitting of the Court he received a communication from an officer of one of our great medical schools that they had information which might or might not have a distinct bearing on that inquiry. He attended at the first opportunity, and was informed by the sub-curator of the Pathological Museum that some months ago an American had called on him and asked him to procure a number of specimens of the organ that was missing in the deceased. He stated his willingness to give £20 apiece for each specimen. He stated that his object was to issue an actual specimen with each copy of a publication on which he was then engaged. He was told that his request was impossible to be complied with, but he still urged his request. He wished them preserved, not in spirits of wine, the usual medium, but glycerine, in order to preserve them in a flaccid condition, and he wished them sent to America direct. It was known that this request was repeated to another institution of a similar character. Now was it not possible that the knowledge of this demand might have incited some abandoned wretch to possess himself of a specimen? It seemed beyond belief that such inhuman wickedness could enter in to the mind of any man; but, unfortunately, our criminal annals proved that every crime was possible. He need hardly say that he at once communicated his information to the Detective Department at Scotland-yard. Of course he did not know what use had been made of it, but he believed that publicity might possibly further elucidate this fact, and therefore he had not withheld the information. By means of the Press some further explanation might be forthcoming from America, if not from here. He had endeavoured to suggest to the jury the object with which this crime was committed and the class of person who must have committed it. The greatest deterrent from crime was the conviction that detection and punishment would follow with rapidity and certainty, and it might be that the impunity with which Mary Anne [*sic*] Smith and Ann [*sic*] Tabram were murdered suggested the possibility of such horrid crimes as those which the jury and another jury had been considering. It was therefore a great misfortune that nearly three weeks had already elapsed without the chief actor in this awful tragedy having been discovered. Surely it was not too much even yet to hope that the ingenuity of our detective force would succeed in unearthing this monster. It was not as if there were no clue to the character of the criminal or the cause of his crime. His object was clearly divulged. His anatomical knowledge carried him out of the category of a common criminal, for that knowledge could only have been obtained by assisting at post mortems or by frequenting the post mortem room. Thus the class in which search must be made, although a large one, was limited. In addition to the former description of the man Mrs. Long saw, they should know that he was a foreigner, of dark complexion, over 40 years of age, a little taller than deceased, of shabby genteel appearance, with a brown deerstalker hat on his head and a dark coat on his back. If the jury's views accorded with his, they would be of opinion that they were confronted with a murder of no ordinary character, committed not from jealousy, revenge, or robbery, but from motives less adequate than many which still disgraced our civilization, marred our progress, and blotted the pages of our Christianity.

The jury returned a verdict of "Wilful murder against some person or persons unknown," the Foreman remarking that they were going to add a rider with respect to the mortuary accommodation, but as that had already been done by another jury they would let it stand. The Foreman then said that, as the jury had been there on five occasions, the majority thought they should be excused from further attendance for at least two years.

The CORONER said if possible that would be done.

CHAPTER 6

September 1888 – Dr Anderson on Sick Leave and the Question of a Reward

The departure of James Monro as Assistant Commissioner in charge of the CID from Scotland Yard is noted in the Metropolitan Police Entry Book[1], 1.9.1888–20.11.1888:

A5085

1 September 1888

Sir,

I am directed by the Secretary of State to inform you that upon the retirement of Mr. Monro on the 31st. ult. Mr. A. Carmichael Bruce becomes one of the Senior Assistant Commissioners of Police and will receive the same salary and allowances from the Police funds as are usually paid to the Senior Assistant Commissioner:- viz

Salary	£800
House – Rent	£300
Dockyard visits	£150
Allowance for working telegraph at home	£45.
Allowances for tolls & bailing	£ 10. 10. 0
	£1305 10. 0

with one horse, stabling, Keep &c
The Commissioner of Police
   for the Metropolis

The new (Junior) Assistant Commissioner in charge of the Criminal Investigation Department at Scotland Yard was Dr Robert Anderson. He had taken up his post on 1 September 1888, succeeding James Monro. The Home Office Police Entry Book contains a letter[2] referring to Anderson's appointment:

Pressing [1.9.1888]
   Mr. Robert Anderson will from this day's date inclusive be placed in

charge of the Criminal Investigation Department as (Junior) Assistant Commissioner, and will receive the following salary and allowances:

viz. Salary	. . . .	£800
House Rent	. . . .	£300
Allowance for telegraph at home	. . . .	£45
Allowances for tolls & bailing	. . . .	£10. 10. 0.
		£1155. 10. 0.

with one horse, stabling
                      & keep.
The whole of the salary and allowances to be paid from the Police Fund.

I am,
   Sir,
Your obedient Servant,

Anderson's pension record[3] shows that he was "appointed 3rd Assistant Commissioner of Metropolitan Police, 25 August, 1888 . . ."

There is an interesting letter[4] from Warren to Anderson, dated 28 August 1888, as follows:

Perros Gueru.
Lannion
Cotes du Nord,
France
    28 August

Dear Mr. Anderson,

I expect to return to London about 7 Sept. and I see no reason why you should not be able to go on leave a day or two after – you do not say how long you wish to be away – but this will no doubt depend upon the position of affairs.

Last year we had a good deal of disturbance in October, and if the unusual matter we have lately experienced puts men out of work we may expect a good deal of trouble this winter. – If a month will be enough to put your throat right I think we can manage it.

Truly yours
Charles Warren

Anderson took up his new post for the first week of September, but on the 8th, under doctor's orders, he left for a month's recuperative holiday in Switzerland. It was the day of Annie Chapman's murder. The CID, at this crucial time, was left without its chief.

A revealing document relevant to the Whitechapel Murders enquiry surfaced in October 1987. It belonged to James Swanson, grandson of Chief Inspector Donald Sutherland Swanson. This document, appointing Swanson to take overall charge of the enquiry and dated 15 September 1888, originated from Sir Charles Warren, but was probably mainly written by a secretary at his dictation. It reads as follows:

A.C. C.I.D.

I am convinced that the Whitechapel Murder case is one which can be successfully grappled with if it is systematically taken in hand. I go so far as to say that I could myself in a few days unravel the mystery provided I could spare the time & give individual attention to it. I feel therefore the utmost importance to be attached to putting the whole Central Office work in this case in the hands of one man who will have nothing else to concern himself with. Neither you or I or Mr. Williamson can do this, I therefore put it in the hands of Chief Inspr. Swanson who must be acquainted with every detail. I look upon him for the time being as the eyes & ears of the Commr. in this particular case.

He must have a room to himself, & every paper, every document, every report every telegram must pass through his hands. He must be consulted on every ["telegram" – *deleted*] subject. I would not send any directions anywhere on the subject of the murder without consulting him. I give him the whole responsibility. On the other hand he should consult Mr. Williamson, you, or myself on every important particular before any action unless there is some extreme urgency.

I find that a most important letter was sent to Divn. yesterday without his seeing it. This is quite an error & should not occur again. All the papers in Central Office on the subject of the murder must be kept in his room & plans of the positions &c.

I must have this matter at once put on a proper footing so as to be a guide for the future in cases of importance.

Everything depends upon a careful compliance with these directions.

[*The following paragraph in Warren's own hand*]

Every document, letter received or telegram on the subject should ["go to" – *deleted*] go to his room before being directed, & he should be responsible for its being directed when necessary. This is [*to*] avoid the possibility of documents being delayed or action retarded.

CW 15.9.88

[*There is marginal annotation at the left margin at the start of the document*: Mr. Williamson Supt Shore & Ch. Insp. Swanson to see. ACB 15.9.88 – Seen 15.9.88 John Shore Supt – Seen AFW 15/9]

The contentious question of a reward was the subject of the next communication[5] with the Home Office and appears under a file cover dated 10 September 1888:

[Stamped: – HOME OFFICE 10 SEP.88 DEPt. No.] No. A49301B/2
DATE Sept 10th/88   Commissioner of Police
REFERENCES, &c.   Encloses copy communication from
Mr. Samuel Montagu M.P. for Whitechapel expressing his desire to offer £100 reward for the discovery and conviction of the murderer or murderers of a woman in Hanbury St. on the 8th inst.

Requests earliest possible instructions.

[*There is a marginal note against the above* – A36117. First decision of Sir W. Harcourt not to grant rewards.

V1834. Second case (Middlesborough murder).

A3800R. Letter to London City Council explaining reasons for change of practice.

X6551. Sir R.Cross concurs.

A42607. Question in Hse (Sep 86)]

Very Pressing MINUTES.

The H.O. rule is against offering rewards: and, even if exceptions to the rule are to be allowed, I think this case is the last in which it should be done.

It is generally agreed that the Whitechapel murderer has no accomplices who could betray him.

Any person, other than an accomplice, who possesses information, would be certain, in the present state of public feeling, to give it without prospect of reward.

On the other hand the offer of a reward would be almost certain to produce false information.

Even if the case were a proper one for a reward, the M.P. for the district is not the proper person to offer it. Of course SofS. cannot forbid Mr. Montagu to publish the offer, but he can forbid Police to give their authority to it.

?Say that, had the case been considered [*a*] proper one for the offer of a reward, SofS. [*would*] at once have offered one on behalf of the Govt., but the practice of offering rewards was discontinued some years ago because experience showed that in their general effect such offers ["were" – *deleted*] produce more harm than good, and the SofS. ["is & does not" – *deleted*] thinks the present case one in which there is special risk that the offer of a reward might hinder rather than promote the ends of justice.

Add that the offer of a reward while any person is under arrest on suspicion, is open to special objections. and has ["never" – *deleted*] not at any time be [*sic*] allowed.

CET 11.9.88.   I agree
ELP. 11. Sept.88.

Mr. Matthews
    H.M.   Wrote accordingly
       12 Sept./88   13 Sep: 1888.

The letter[6] from the Assistant Commissioner of Police to the Home Office is annexed, dated 10 September 1888:

<u>Very Pressing</u>   [Stamped: – HOME OFFICE 10 SEP.88 DEPt. No.]
                                A49301B/2
                         4 Whitehall Place, S.W.
                         10th September, 1888

Sir,
    The Commissioner of Police of the Metropolis has to acquaint you, for the information of the Secretary of State, that he has received a communication from Mr. Samuel Montagu, M.P. for Whitechapel, expressing his desire to offer a Reward of £100 for the discovery and conviction of the murderer or murderers of a woman in Hanbury Street on the 8th inst.

The Commissioner will be glad to receive the instructions of the Secretary of State in the matter at his earliest convenience, as Mr. Montagu is anxious that no time should be lost.
<u>ELP</u>   I am,
                                 Sir,
                 Your most obedient Servant,
                      ACBruce
                 Assistant Commissioner.

The Under
    Secretary of State,
       &c. &c. &c.

The letter[7] written by Samuel Montagu, dated 10 September, is as follows:

Sept. 10th 1888

Dear Sir

Feeling keenly the slur cast upon my constabulary by the recent murders & the non discovery of the criminal or criminals I hereby authorise you to print & distribute at my expense posters offering £100 reward for the discovery & conviction of the murderer or murderers, which reward I will pay

Samuel Montagu
Member for Whitechapel

A reply[8] to the police concerning this letter, from the Home Office, is as follows:

A 49354   Pressing   WHITEHALL.
                                                 13th September 1888.

Sir,

I am directed by the Secretary of State to acknowledge the receipt of your letter of the 10th instant forwarding copy of a letter from Mr. S. Montagu M.P., in which he offers to pay a Reward of £100 for the discovery and conviction of the murderer or murderers of a woman in Hanbury Street on the 8th instant, and asking for the Secretary of States instructions, and in reply I am to say that, had the case been considered a proper one for the offer of a reward the Secretary of State would at once have offered one on behalf of the Government; but that the practice of offering rewards was discontinued some years ago because experience showed that in their general effect such offers produce more harm than good, and the Secretary of State thinks the present case one in which there is special risk that the offer of a reward might hinder rather than promote the ends of justice.

I am to add that the offer of a reward while any person is under arrest on suspicion is open to special objections and has not at any time been allowed.

I am,
Sir,

The Commissioner   Your obedient Servant,
of Metropolitan Police.   ELeighPemberton.

A letter[9] dated 18 September 1888, from Mr. Montagu to Sir Charles Warren, is worded as follows:

60. Old Broad Street,
London E.C.
Sepr. 18th 1888

Dear Sir Charles,

The letter of the 15 September signed by the Assistant Commissioner and addressed to 12 Kensington Palace Gardens reached me only last night.

The opinion of the Home Secretary that no reward should be offered for the discovery of the perpetrator of the Whitechapel murders is not in accord with the general feeling on the subject. The argument advanced by some that the expectation of a possible increase in the amount of the reward might deter a prompt disclosure could not apply in respect to my offer. Nevertheless had the decision of the Home Secretary been promptly obtained & communicated to me I should not have intervened in the matter.

On Monday the 10th inst about mid-day I made my offer to Inspector West. He stated that he would submit it to you. On the Tuesday he called here & said that the proposal had been submitted to the Home Office & he thought it would be favourably received. I regret that you did not obtain the decision of the Home Secy. at once by telegram, because on Tuesday my proposal must have transpired & was published in the daily papers on Wednesday last.

Under these circumstances it is too late to withdraw my offer & in case information is received, leading to conviction of the murderer or murderers, I must pay the £100. to the person entitled to receive it.

It remains for you to decide whether notices of the reward shall be posted up in Whitechapel by the police at my expense, otherwise I shall not take any further action but await the result of the investigation now pending. I may add that when I made the proposal I was not aware that the Government had ceased to offer rewards in cases of murder.

Col.	Yours very truly
Sir Charles Warren	Saml. Montagu
G.C.M.G.R.E.	

A letter[10] from Sir Charles Warren to Mr Montagu, dated 19 September 1888 but endorsed *Not sent by Sir C Warrens directions. [ ] 20.9.88* reads:

Sepr. 19. 88   Private

Dear Mr. Montagu.

Your letter was received on 10th Sepr. & submitted to H. Office same day, it was impossible for me to have replied to you on Wednesday 12th as I had not received the reply on that date.

My letter to you should have been received on Saturday night 15th. and if you will forward to me the envelope with the post marks on it I will ascertain how it was that you did not receive it the Monday night.

As however you say that your offer must have transpired on Tuesday 11th. ins. I do not see that any subsequent delay affects the matter.

I have no power to decide whether notices of any reward offered by you should be posted in Whitechapel by police at your expense; the police would not undertake this after the S of S expression of opinion on subject.

There is no request in your letter of 10th Sepr. for an immediate reply by telegraph, and the Acting Supt. informs me that he told you at the time that he did not think the offer of a reward should be made until result of investigation in case of man then in custody was known.

I can only regret that you should have thought fit to impute delay to me in a matter entirely outside my control and duties. It was a matter lying entirely between you and the S. of State and if you required an immediate reply you could have telegraphed the Sec of State ["himself" – *deleted*] yourself.

After the receipt of your letter of Sep. 18th I only regret that I did not reply to you requesting that you would communicate your wishes to the S of State yourself.

> truly yours
> C Warren

The question of a reward was raised again and is contained in a file cover[11] dated 16 September 1888:

[Stamped: – HOME OFFICE 17 SEP.88 RECEIVED] No. A49301B/3
DATE 16 Sept. 1888   Mr. B.Harris. (Hon. Secy.)
REFERENCES, &c.   The East <u>End</u> Murders. <u>Rewards</u>.
On behalf of a Committee, asks Secy. of State to augment the Fund, which they are about to raise for the discovery of the murderer or murderers, or that he will kindly state his reasons for declining.

> <u>Pressing</u>

MINUTES.

?Say [that, had the ["reward" – *deleted*] SofS. considered the case a proper one for the offer of a reward, he would at once have offered one on behalf of the Govt. but ["? Say" – *deleted*] that the practice of offering rewards for the discovery of criminals was discontinued some years ago, because experience showed that such offers of rewards tended to produce more harm than good] and [the S.ofS. is satisfied that there is nothing in the ["present" – *deleted*] circumstances of this present case to justify a departure from this rule.]

> CET 17.9.88.
> ELP. 17 Sept.88
> Wrote accordingly
> 17.9.88.

A copy[12] of the Home Office letter, dated 17 September 1888, is included:

(Copy)

Pressing

A 49301/3   Whitehall
                                            17th September 1888

Sir,

I am directed by the Secretary of State to acknowledge the receipt of your letter of the 16th instant with reference to the question of the offer of a Reward for the discovery of the perpetrators of the recent murders in Whitechapel, and I am to inform you that had the Secretary of State considered the case a proper one for the offer of a reward, he would at once have offered one on behalf of the Government; but that the practice of offering rewards for the discovery of criminals was discontinued some years ago, because experience showed that such offers of rewards tended to produce more harm than good, and the Secretary of State is satisfied that there is nothing in the circumstances of the present case to justify a departure from this rule.

I am,
Sir,
Your obedient Servant,
(sd) E.Leigh Pemberton.

Mr. B. Harris,
   "The Crown"
      74 Mile End Road,
         E.

The letter[13] from Mr. Harris is annexed:

   " 'The Crown'' A49301B/3
      74 Mile End Rd.
         16/9/8
To the Right Honourable
   The Home Secretary
         Whitehall.
Sir

At a meeting of ["the" – *deleted*] a Committee held at the above address, It was resolved to approach you on the subject of the Reward we are about to Issue for the Discovery of the Author, or Authors of the late atrocities in the East End of London & to ask you Sir to

The original Jack the Ripper files as stored at New Scotland Yard prior to being sent to the Public Records Office in Kew.

The Whitehall Place buildings which housed the offices of Great Scotland Yard at the time of the Ripper murders – these offices moved in 1890 to new buildings on the Embankment which became known as New Scotland Yard.

Metropolitan police officers involved in the Ripper enquiry in order of seniority: Sir Charles Warren, Chief Commissioner of the Metropolitan Police Force 1886–1888.

Assistant Commissioner James Monro, who was replaced by Dr Robert Anderson in August 1888.

Dr Robert Anderson who finally retired from the Metropolitan Police Force in 1901.

Far Left Major Henry Smith, appointed as a chief superintendent of the City of London Police Force. He was later made commissioner.

Left Sir Melville Leslie Macnaghten, Assistant Chief Constable. Appointed to Chief Constable in the Metropolitan Police Force in June 1889.

Right Frederick Adolphus Williamson, appointed Superintendent in 1870 and then Chief Constable in 1886. He was the only career police officer to attain such a high rank in the Metropolitan Police Force at this time.

Far Right John Shore, Superintendent, Central Office CID, Scotland Yard, at the time of the murders. Many of the official Scotland Yard reports on the murders are signed or minuted by Shore.

Far Left Chief Inspector Donald Sutherland Swanson, Central Office CID. He was appointed by Warren in September 1888 to head the Ripper enquiry.

Left Superintendent Thomas Arnold, head of the H (Whitechapel) Division of CID throughout the period of the murders.

Detective Inspector Frederick George Abberline of the Central Office, who headed the enquiry into the Whitechapel murders from September 1888 to early 1889, when he was succeeded by Inspector Henry Moore.

Detective Inspector Henry Moore. His last known report on the subject of the Whitechapel murders was as late as 1896.

Detective Inspector Edmund Reid, a local inspector throughout the period of the murders. He is seen here sketched at the Stride inquest.

Detective Inspector Walter Andrews, Central Office CID was the third inspector sent with Abberline to Whitechapel in connection with enquiries to the murders.

Detective Sergeant William Thick of H (Whitechapel) Division CID. He was later himself accused as a Ripper suspect.

Detective Sergeant George Godley of J (Bethnal Green) Division CID became involved in the Ripper enquiry with the murder of Mary Ann Nichols.

St Mary's Church, Whitechapel Road. It was near here that the first Whitechapel victim, Emma Smith, was attacked by a gang on 3 April 1888.

Gunthorpe Street (formerly George Yard), Whitechapel. George Yard Buildings, the spot where Martha Tabram was murdered, can be seen at the top left of the street.

George Yard Buildings as viewed from the junction with Wentworth Street.

A contemporary sketch from the *Illustrated Police News* of the body of Martha Tabram lying on the first floor landing of George Yard Buildings.

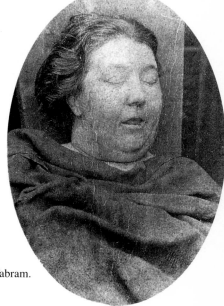

Mortuary photograph of Martha Tabram.

A contemporary sketch showing the discovery of the body of Mary Ann Nichols in Buck's Row, Whitechapel, by PC John Neil on 31 August 1888.

P.C.NIEL

PC 97J John Neil of Bethnal Green Police at the time of the murder.

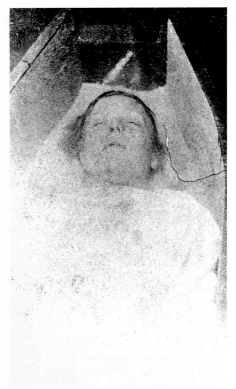

Mortuary photograph of Mary Ann Nichols.

INSP.ᴿ HELSON

Detective Inspector Joseph Henry Helson, local inspector in J (Bethnal Green) Division CID who initially took charge of the enquiries into the Nichols murder.

D.ᴿ LLEWELLYN

Dr Rees Ralph Llewellyn, called out by the Bethnal Green police to examine the body of Mary Ann Nichols.

Top Left The front of number 29 Hanbury Street, Spitalfields, scene of the murder of Annie Chapman as it appeared in 1967, shortly before demolition.

Top Right The front of number 29 Hanbury Street, as shown in a contemporary sketch. It is interesting to note it shows the house as originally having only one front door and not the two which later photographs show.

Bottom Left A contemporary sketch of the rear yard of number 29 Hanbury Street, the actual spot where the murder of Annie Chapman took place on 8 September 1888.

Bottom Right A contemporary sketch of John Richardson, who had been in the rear yard of 29 Hanbury Street on the night of the murder. Initially treated as a suspect, Richardson was later released without charge.

A sketch from the *Illustrated Police News* showing John Richardson at the murder scene prior to the discovery of the body.

A sketch from the *Illustrated Police News* showing Dr George Bagster Phillips, Whitechapel Divisional Police Surgeon, examining the body of Annie Chapman. Dr Phillips felt the murderer had some anatomical knowledge.

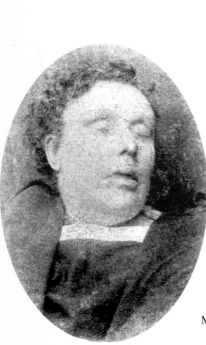

Mortuary photograph of Annie Chapman.

Augment our Fund for the <u>said purpose</u> or, kindly state your reasons for Refusing.

Waiting your Reply
I am Sir
Yours Obediently
B. Harris
<u>Hon.Secy.</u>

<u>To The</u>
    Right Hone.
      <u>H. C. Matthews</u>

Reports from the Home Office files now follow, the first a memo[14] by J.S. Sandars, assistant to E.J. Ruggles-Brise, the private secretary to the Home Secretary, Henry Matthews, and dated 19 September 1888, on "Secretary of State Home Department" headed paper:

[*A note in the top left corner of this report states:* Mr.Brise, this ought perhaps to be put with other papers re the Whitechapel Murders. H.M.]
Mr Matthews,
Mr. Ruggles Brise left town on Monday but returned this aftn. I sent on your memo to him to Sir Charles Warren this morning for observations.

Sir Charles came to see me both yesterday & today about the Whitechapel murders, and his note deals with such information as he mentioned as being in the possession of the police. But he remarked to me very strongly upon the great hindrance, which is caused to the efforts of the Police, by the activity of agents of Press Associations & Newspapers. These "touts" follow the detectives wherever they go in search of clues, and then having interviewed persons with whom the police have had conversation and from whom inquiries have made, compile the paragraphs which fill the papers. This practice impedes the usefulness of detective investigation and moreover keeps alive the excitement in the district & elsewhere.

/An irritation I had accepted for the first part of this week has been postponed and I do not leave town until Friday.

J.S.S.
19 Sep '88.

There then follows a report[15] by Sir Charles Warren, dated 19 September 1888:

Mr Ruggles Brise.
    In reply to Mr. Matthews note which I return.

No progress has as yet been made in obtaining any definite clue to the Whitechapel murderers. A great number of clues have been examined & exhausted with out finding any thing suspicious.

A large staff of men are employed and every point is being examined which seems to offer our prospect of a discovery.

There are at present three cases of suspicion.

1. The lunatic Isensmith [*sic*], a Swiss arrested at Holloway – who is now in an Asylum at Bow & arrangements are being made to ascertain whether he is the man who was seen on the morning of the murder in a public house by Mrs. Fiddymont.

2. A man called Puckeridge was released from an asylum on 4 August. He was educated as a Surgeon – has threatened to rip people up with a long knife. He is being looked for but cannot be found as yet.

3. A Brothel Keeper who will not give her address or name writes to say that a man living in her house was seen with blood on him on morning of murder. She described his appearance & said where he might be seen – when the detectives came near him he bolted, got away & there is no clue to the writer of the letter.

All these three cases are being followed up & no doubt will be exhausted in a few days – the first seems a very suspicious case, but the man is at present a violent lunatic.

I will say tomorrow if any thing turns up about him.

Moreover the reporters for the press are following our detectives about everywhere in search of news & cross examine all parties interviewed so that they impede police action greatly – they do not however as yet know of the cases 2 & 3.

CW

The response of the respectable residents and tradesmen of the area was to form the Whitechapel Vigilance Committee and a letter[16] was received by the Home Office, dated 25 September 1888, from this body, as follows (including cover):

DATE 24 Septr. 1888, The Vigilance Committee, (Whitechapel Murders) Requests S. of S. to attend a meeting of the Inhabitants (?of the Vigilance Committee) with respect to the refusal to offer a reward.

MINUTES.

Ackn & say S of S regrets he is unable to attend the Vigilance Committee as proposed by them [ ] 26 Sept 88 [ ] 25.9.88
S of S H.M. 27 Sept./88

Wrote 28/9/88.

"The Crown",
74 Mile End Rd,
24 Sepr 1888.

To The Right Honourable
    The Home Secretary.

Sir,

    The Vigilance Committee think it advisable at the receipt of the letter from the Home Secretary wherein he refuses to grant or issue a Reward for the apprehension of the author, or authors, of the Recent Murders in the East of London, to lay his letter before the public at a general meeting of the Inhabitants. Will you Sir, do us the Honour to attend at a time & place convenient to yourself, & give us the Benefit of your advice & counsel.

I am Sir,
Yours Obediently
B. Harris
Hon Sec y
To The Vigilance Committee

To The
Hona. H.C. Matthews
    Home Secretary.

CHAPTER 7

30 September 1888 – Murder of Elizabeth Stride

Three weeks later, in the early hours of Sunday, 30 September 1888, the residents of the East End of London were again terrorized by savage murder committed by an unknown killer. Two victims were to fall in the area in one night, the first being Elizabeth Stride whose throat was savagely cut in Dutfield's Yard, Berner Street, St George's-in-the-East. What is not generally known is that a third woman was murdered by having her throat cut on the same night, shortly before the murder of Stride and only about three miles away. This demonstrates the long arm of coincidence – and the prevalence of domestic murder. In this case the husband gave himself up, so this particular killing is all but forgotten and cannot be added to the Ripper's tally.

The Times of Monday, 1 October 1888, reported[1]:

MURDER IN WESTMINSTER.

A murder was committed in Westminster on Saturday. Shortly before midnight John Brown, a gardener, employed in St. James's-park, asked the police at Rochester-row Police-station to permit him to see the inspector on duty. He was brought before Inspector Fairlie, to whom he stated that he had killed his wife, and that her body would be found at their place in Regency-gardens, Regency-street, near the Horseferry-road. He handed the inspector a large, spring-backed clasp knife, which had blood on it, as also had his clothes. The man was detained, and the police went to the house, where the woman was found lying dead on the floor with her throat cut. Several wounds had been inflicted in the shape of stabs and cuts. The body was seen by a medical man, who pronounced life to be extinct. When charged with the murder Brown declared that he had committed it in consequence of the woman's unfaithfulness. He had been brooding over her misconduct since his return from a convalescent home, to which he had been sent after treatment for an acute illness in Westminster Hospital. The woman is stated to be nearly the age of her husband who is 45. When at the police-station Brown was quite calm and did not appear to have been drinking to excess. But it is said that he has of late been peculiar in his manner. He will be brought up at the Westminster Police-court this morning.

The Times of the following day reported[2] on the hearing. Brown was described as "a man of rather powerful build" and he was charged before the magistrate, Mr Partridge, with the murder of his wife, Sarah. It was stated that ". . . the deceased woman unsuccessfully invoked the assistance of the authorities to put her husband under restraint as a person who was at times unaccountable for his actions and likely to murder her, and that on Saturday night in a state of terror she went to the parochial district medical officer and also expressed her apprehensions to the police." On the arrival of Detective Sergeant Waldock at the address he had found two little boys standing at the door, crying. Brown was their stepfather. A witness, a next-door neighbour, Mr Charles Redding, of 12 Regency Gardens, stated that he had heard a scuffle shortly before eleven o'clock in the front room next door. He had heard a distressed cry from the woman of "Oh don't", followed by a dull thud on the floor. The story given by the stepchildren was that their mother was planning to leave Brown that night. He had returned from work on the Saturday afternoon and told her that he had "something in a box" for her. Six or seven weeks previously Brown had been to Westminster Hospital where he was kept for three or four weeks. He subsequently went to a convalescent home and on his return there was something the matter with him. He kept saying that their mother let men into the house and he would look for them before he went to work in the morning. When he came home at night he would light matches "to peer into corners" and on one night he had walked about and lit an entire box of matches. He had sharpened a large knife every day before the woman at both dinner and tea times, although he did not use it with his meals. When Brown returned from work on the Saturday, the mother had told her son, Robert Young, nine years, that Brown was going to kill her. All in all, it is a distressing tale and it is amazing to think that this killing occurred within two hours of the murder of Elizabeth Stride.

For an overall summary of the Stride murder we turn again to Chief Inspector Donald S. Swanson and a report[3] dated 19 October 1888 to the Home Office:

METROPOLITAN POLICE.
Criminal Investigation Department,
Scotland Yard.
19th day of October, 1888

SUBJECT Murder of
Elizabeth Stride at Duf-
fields [sic] yard Berner St.

Body found at 1am
30th Sept. 1888.

I beg to report that the following are the particulars respecting the murder of Elizabeth Stride on the morning of 30th Sept. 1888.——

1 a.m. 30th Sept.   A body of a woman was found with the throat cut, but not otherwise mutilated by Louis Diemshitz (Secretary to the Socialist Club) inside the gates of Duffield's Yard in Berner St. Commercial Road East, who gave information to the police. P.C. 252 Lamb proceeded with them to the spot & sent for Drs. Blackwell & Phillips.

1.10 a.m.   Body examined by the Doctors mentioned who pronounced life extinct, the position of the body was as follows:- lying on left side, left arm extended from elbow, cachous lying in hand, right arm over stomach back of hand & inner surface of wrist dotted with blood, legs drawn up knees fixed feet close to wall, body still warm, silk handkerchief round throat, slightly torn corresponding to the angle of right jaw, throat deeply gashed and below the right angle apparent abrasion of skin about an inch and a quarter in diameter.

Search was made in the yard but no instrument found.

From enquiries made it was found that at:-

12.35 a.m.30th   P.C. 452H Smith saw a man and woman the latter with a red rose talking in Berner Street, this P.C. on seeing the body identified it as being that of the woman whom he had seen & he thus describes the man as age about 28. ht. 5ft. 7in: comp. dark, small dark moustache, dress black diagonal coat, hard felt hat, white collar & tie.

12.45 a.m. 30th   Israel Schwartz of 22 Helen [*sic* – Ellen] Street, Backchurch Lane stated that at that hour on turning into Berner St. from Commercial Road & had got as far as the gateway where the murder was committed he saw a man stop & speak to a woman, who was standing in the gateway. The man tried to pull the woman into the street, but he turned her round & threw her down on the footway & the woman screamed three times, but not very loudly. On crossing to the opposite side of the street, he ‚saw a second man standing lighting his pipe. The man who threw the woman down called out apparently to the man on the opposite side of the road ‘‘Lipski’’ & then Schwartz walked away, but finding that he was followed by the second man he ran as far as the railway arch but the man did not follow so far. [*Here there is a marginal note. –* ‘‘The use of ‘Lipski’ increases my belief that the murderer was a Jew’’.] Schwartz cannot say whether the two men were together or known to each other. Upon being taken to the mortuary Schwartz identified the body as that of the woman he had seen & he thus describes the first man who threw the woman down:- age about 30 ht. 5 ft. 5in. comp. fair hair dark, small brown moustache, full face, broad shouldered, dress, dark jacket & trousers black cap with peak, had nothing in his hands.

second man age 35 ht. 5ft. 11in. comp. fresh, hair light brown, moustache brown, dress dark overcoat, old black hard felt hat wide brim, had a clay pipe in his hand.

about 1 a.m. 30th   Leon Goldstein of 22 Christian Street Commercial Road, called at Leman St. & stated that he was the man that passed down Berner St. with a black bag at that hour, that the bag contained empty cigarette boxes & that he had left a coffee house in Spectacle Alley a short time before. [*Here there is a marginal note. –* "Who saw this man go down Berner St. or did he come forward to clear himself in case any questions might be asked".]

The description of the man seen by the P.C. was circulated amongst Police by wire, & by authority of Commissioner it was also given to the press. On the evening of 30th the man Schwartz gave the description of the man he had seen ten minutes later than the P.C. and it was circulated by wire. It will be observed that allowing for differences of opinion between the P.C. and Schwartz as to apparent age & height of the man each saw with the woman whose body they both identified there are serious differences in the description of dress:- thus the P.C. describes the dress of the man whom he saw as black diagonal coat, hard felt hat, while Schwartz describes the dress of the man he saw as dark jacket black cap with peak, so that it is at least rendered doubtful whether they are describing the same man.

If Schwartz is to be believed, and the police report of his statement casts no doubt upon it, it follows if they are describing different men that the man Schwartz saw & described is the more probable of the two to be the murderer, for a quarter of an hour afterwards the body is found murdered. At the same time account must be taken of the fact that the throat only of the victim was cut in this instance which measured by time, considering meeting (if with a man other than Schwartz saw) the time for the agreement & the murderous action would I think be a question of so many minutes, five at least, ten at most, so that I respectfully submit it is not clearly proved that the man that Schwartz saw is the murderer, although it is clearly the more probable of the two. [*Here there is a marginal note –* "This is rather confused: If the man whom the P.C. saw is not the same as the man whom Schwartz saw at 12.45 then it is clearly more probable that the man whom Schwartz saw was the murderer, because Schwartz saw his man a quarter of an hour later than the P.C.

But I understand the Inspector to suggest that Schwartz' man need not have been the murderer. True only 15 minutes elapsed between 12.45 when Schwartz saw the man & 1.0 when the woman was found murdered on the same spot. But the suggestion is that Schwartz' man may have left her, she being a prostitute then accosted or was accosted by another man, & there was time enough for this to take place & for this other man to murder her before 1.0.

The Police apparently do not suspect the 2nd man whom Schwartz saw on the other side of the street & who followed Schwartz''.] Before concluding in dealing with the descriptions of these two men I venture to insert here for the purpose of comparison with these two descriptions, the description of a man seen with a woman in Church Passage close to Mitre Square at 1.35 a.m. 30th by two men coming out of a club close by:- age 30 ht. 5 ft. 7 or 8 in. comp. fair, fair moustache, medium build, dress pepper & salt colour loose jacket, grey cloth cap with peak of same colour, reddish handkerchief tied in a knot, round neck, appearance of a sailor. In this case I understand from City Police that Mr. Lewin [*sic* – Lawende] one of the men identified the clothes only of the murdered woman Eddowes, which is a serious drawback to the value of the description of the man. Ten minutes afterwards the body is found horribly mutilated & it is therefore reasonable to believe that the man he saw was the murderer, but for purposes of comparison, this description is much nearer to that given by Schwartz than to that given by the P.C.

The body was identified as that of Elizabeth Stride, a prostitute, & it may be shortly stated that the enquiry into her history did not disclose the slightest pretext for a motive on behalf of friends or associates or anybody who had known her. The action of police besides being continued in the directions mentioned in the report respecting the murder of Annie Chapman was as follows

a. Immediately after the police were on the spot the whole of the members who were in the Socialist Club were searched, their clothes examined and their statements taken.

b. Extended enquiries were made in Berner Street to ascertain if any person was seen with the woman.

c. Leaflets were printed & distributed in H Division asking the occupiers of houses to give information to police of any suspicious persons lodging in their houses.

d. The numerous statements made to police were enquired into and the persons (of whom there were many) were required to account for their presence at the time of the murders & every care taken as far as possible to verify the statements.

Concurrently with enquiry under head **a** the yard where the body was found was searched but no instrument was found.

Arising out of head **b**, a, Mr. Packer a fruiterer, of Berner St. stated that at 11 p.m. 29th Sept. a young man age 25 to 30 about 5 ft. 7 in. dress long black coat, buttoned up, soft felt hat, (Kind of Yankee hat) rather broad shoulders, rough voice, rather quick speaking, with a woman wearing a geranium like flower, white outside, red inside, & he sold him 1/2 lb of grapes. The man & woman went to the other side of road & stood talking till 11.30 p.m. then they went towards the Club (Socialist) apparently listening to the music. Mr. Packer when asked by the police stated that he did not see any suspicious person about, and it was not until after the publication in the newspapers of the description of man seen by the P.C. that Mr. Packer gave the foregoing particulars to two private enquiry men acting conjointly with the Vigilance Comtee. and the press, who upon searching a drain in the yard found a grape stem which was amongst the other matter swept from the yard after its examination by the police & then calling upon Mr. Packer whom they took to the mortuary where he identified the body of Elizabeth Stride as that of the woman. Packer who is an elderly man, has unfortunately made different statements so that apart from the fact of the hour at which he saw the woman (and she was seen afterwards by the P.C. & Schwartz as stated) any statement he made would be rendered almost valueless as evidence.

Under head **c.** 80,000 pamphlets to occupier were issued and a house to house enquiry made not only involving the result of enquiries from the occupiers but also a search by police & with a few exceptions – but not such as to convey suspicion – covered the area bounded by the City Police boundary on the one hand, Lamb St. Commercial St. Great Eastern Railway & Buxton St. then by Albert St. Dunk St. Chicksand St. & Great Garden St to Whitechapel Rd. and then to the City boundary, under this head also Common Lodging Houses were visited & over 2000 lodgers were examined.

Enquiry was also made by Thames Police as to sailors on board ships in Docks or river & extended enquiry as to asiatics present in London, about 80 persons have been detained at the different police stations in the Metropolis & their statements taken and verified by police & enquiry has been made into the movements of a number of persons estimated at upwards of 300 respecting whom communications were received by police & such enquiries are being continued.

Seventy six Butchers & Slaughterers have been visited & the characters of the men employed enquired into, this embraces all servants who had been employed for the past six months.

Enquiries have also been made as to the alleged presence in London of Greek Gipsies, but it was found that they had not been in London during the times of the previous murders.

Three of the persons calling themselves Cowboys who belonged to the American Exhibition were traced & satisfactorily accounted for themselves.

Up to date although the number of letters daily is considerably lessened, the other enquiries respecting alleged suspicious persons continues as numerous.

There are now 994 Dockets besides police reports.

(sd) Donald S. Swanson

Ch. Inspr.

Thus, the very extensive Metropolitan Police enquiries instigated at the time of the Stride murder are outlined by Swanson. The area designated for police house-to-house enquiries as stated above is strange in that it does not extend south of the Commercial Road to include the Berner Street area. However, it may well be that the area surrounding Berner Street was so thoroughly covered immediately after the murder that it did not require inclusion in the later house-to-house enquiries. Some strength is given to this possibility by the fact that the Berner Street house-to-house enquiries are known to have included Packer's address.

The reports concerning the Stride murder are quite extensive and cover various aspects of the case raised in the enquiry. A report[4] dated 1 November 1888, written by Inspector Abberline, refers to the witness Schwartz:

METROPOLITAN POLICE.

Criminal Investigation Department,

Scotland Yard,

1st day of November 1888

SUBJECT Whitechapel
   Murders
REFERENCE TO PAPERS
52983
1,119

With reference to the annexed copy extract from Home Office Letter.

I beg to report that since a jew named Lipski was hanged for the murder of a jewess in 1887 the name has very frequently been used by persons as mere ejaculation by way of endeavouring to insult the jew to whom it has been addressed, and as Schwartz has a strong jewish appearance I am of opinion it was addressed to him as he stopped to look at the man he saw ill-using the deceased woman.

I questioned Israel Schwartz very closely at the time he made the statement as to whom the man addressed when he called Lipski, but he was unable to say.

There was only one other person to be seen in the street, and that was a man on the opposite side of the road in the act of lighting a pipe.

Schwartz being a foreigner and unable to speak English became alarmed and ran away. The man whom he saw lighting his pipe also ran in the same direction as himself, but whether this man was running after him or not he could not tell, he might have been alarmed the same as himself and ran away.

A house to house inquiry was made in Berner Street with a view to ascertain whether any person was seen acting suspiciously or any noise heard on the night in question but without result.

Inquiries have also been made in the neighbourhood but no person named Lipski could be found.

With regard to the second question

I beg to report that searching inquiries were made by ["Sergt. Froest" – *deleted and* "an officer" *put in margin*] in Aberdeen Place St. Johns Wood the last known address of the insane medical student named "John Sanders", but the only information that could be obtained was that a lady named Sanders resided with her son at No. 20, but left there to go abroad about 2 years ago.

F.G. Abberline, Inspr.
Supt.

This report is followed in the files by a draft letter[5] from Robert Anderson to the Home Office:

[*In margin* – 3/53983/1119]
Draft letter to H.O.
With ref. to yr letter &c. I have to state that the opinion arrived at in this Dept. upon the evidence of Schwartz at the inquest in Eliz. Stride's case is that the name Lipski which he alleges was used by a man whom he saw assaulting the woman in Berner St. on the night of the murder, was not addressed to the supposed accomplice but to Schwartz himself. It appears that since the Lipski case, it has come to be used as an epithet in addressing or speaking of Jews.

With regard to the latter portion of yr letter I have to state that [copy passage in the report as written in blue]

RA
5/11/8

This is followed by three handwritten pages, unsigned, but apparently a copy of the Home Office letter[6] querying the police reports:

Extract

A statement has been made by a man named Schwartz to the effect that he had heard a person who was pulling about a woman identified as

Elizabeth Stride 15 minutes before the murder off Berner Street took place, call out "Lipski" to an individual who was on the opposite side of the road. It does not appear whether the man used the word "Lipski" as a mere ejaculation meaning in mockery I am going to "Lipski" the woman, or whether he was calling to a man across the road by his proper name. In the latter case, assuming that the man using the word was the murderer, the murderer must have an acquaintance in Whitechapel named Lipski.

Mr Matthews presumes that this clue has been one of the suggestions with regard to which searching enquiries have been made: although no tangible results have been obtained as regards the detection of the murderer; but he will be glad if he can be furnished with a report as to any investigations made to trace the man Lipski.

Another question has arisen on the reports furnished by you. Reference is made to three insane medical students and it is stated that two have been traced and that one has gone abroad. Mr Matthews would be glad to be informed of the date when the third student went abroad, and whether any further enquiry has been made about him.

What this letter reveals is the degree to which the Home Office was following the police enquiries into the series of murders and their growing impatience for results.

With regard to the witness Packer, a report[7] dated 4 October 1888 by Inspector Henry Moore states:

> METROPOLITAN POLICE.
> Criminal Investigation Department,
> Scotland Yard
> 4th day of October 1888.

SUBJECT Whitechapel
  Murders.
REFERENCE TO PAPERS.
52983.
Referring to attached Extract from 2nd. Edition, "Evening News", of this date.

I beg to report that as soon as above came under my notice I at once (in the absence of Inspr. Abberline at C.O.) directed P.S. White, "H", to see Mr. Packer, the shopkeeper referred to, and take him to the mortuary with a view to the identification of the woman Elizabeth Stride; who it is stated was with a man who purchased grapes at his shop on night of 29th Ins.

The P.S. returned at noon and acquainted me as in report attached; in consequence of which Telegram No. 1 was forwarded to Chief Inspr Swanson and the P.S. sent to C.O. to fully explain the facts.

Telegram No. 2. was received at 12.55 p.m. from Assistant Commissioner re same subject; in reply to which Telegram No. 3. was forwarded.

Henry Moore, Inspector.

Submitted – F.G. Abberline Insp.

T. Arnold, Supt.

The report[8] written by Sergeant Stephen White concerning the witness Packer is dated 4 October 1888:

METROPOLITAN POLICE.

H DIVISION.

4th day of October 1888.

SUBJECT Whitechapel
   Murders
(Berner Street)
REFERENCE TO PAPERS.
52983

With reference to attached extract from "Evening News" of 4th Inst.

I beg to report that acting under the instructions of Inspector Abberline, I in company with P.C. Dolden C.I. Dept., made inquiries at every house in Berner Street, Commercial Road, on 30th ult, with a view to obtain information respecting the murder. Any information that I could obtain I noted in a Book supplied to me for that purpose. About 9 am I called at 44 Berner Street, and saw Matthew Packer, Fruiterer in a small way of business. I asked him what time he closed his shop on the previous night. He replied Half past twelve [*Note in margin reads:-? Half past 11.*] in consequence of the rain it was no good for me to keep open. I asked him if he saw anything of a man or woman going into Dutfields Yard, or saw anyone standing about the street about the time he was closing his shop. He replied "No I saw no one standing about neither did I see anyone go up the yard. I never saw anything suspicious or heard the slightest noise. and know nothing about the murder until I heard of it in the morning.["]

I also saw Mrs. Packer, Sarah Harris[on] and Harry Douglas residing in the same house but none of them could give the slightest information respecting the matter.

On 4th Inst. I was directed by Inspr. Moore to make further inquiry & if necessary see Packer and take him to the mortuary. I then went to 44 Berner St. and saw Mrs. Packer who informed me that two Detectives had called and taken her husband to the mortuary. I then went towards the mortuary when I met Packer with a man. I asked where he had been. He said "this detective asked me to go to see if I could identify the woman.["] I said "have you done so,["] he said "Yes, I believe she bought some grapes at my shop about 12. o clock [*Note in margin:-?* 11.] on Saturday.["] Shortly afterwards they were joined by another man. I asked the men what they were doing with Packer and they both said that they were Detectives. I asked for their Authority one of the men produced a card from a pocket Book, but would not allow me to touch it. They then said that they were private detectives. They then induced Packer to go away with them. About 4 p.m. I saw Packer at his shop and while talking to him the two men drove up in a Hansom Cab, and after going into the shop. They induced Packer to enter the Cab stating that they would take him to Scotland Yard to see Sir Charles Warren.

From inquiry I have made there is no doubt that these are the two men referred to in attached Newspaper cutting, who examined the drain in Dutfields Yard on 2nd Inst. One of the men had a letter in his hand addressed to Le Grand & Co., Strand.

Stephen White Sergt.

Extract from ''Star'' newspaper attached.

Respectfully submitted.

F.G. Abberline Inspr.

T. Arnold Supt.

There then follows a two-page summary[9] in the hand of Mr Alexander Carmichael Bruce, (Senior) Assistant Commissioner, giving details of what Packer had to say:

Matthew Packer
keeps a shop in Berner St. has a few grapes in window, black & white.
On Sat night about 11.p.m. a young man from 25–30 – about 5.7. with long black coat buttoned up – soft felt hat, kind of Yankee hat rather broad shoulders – rather quick in speaking. rough voice. I sold him 1/2 pound black grapes 3d. A woman came up with him from Back Church end (the lower end of street) She was dressed in black frock & jacket, fur round bottom of jacket a black crape bonnet, she was playing with a flower like a geranium white outside & red inside. I identify the woman at the St George's mortuary as the one I saw that night—
They passed by as though they were going up Com- Road, but – instead of going up they crossed to the other side of the road to the Board School, & were there for about 1/2 an hour till I shd. say 11.30. talking to one another. I then shut up my shutters.

Before they passed over opposite to my shop, they wait[ed] near to the club for a few minutes apparently listening to the music.

I saw no more of them after I shut up my shutters.

I put the man down as a young clerk.

He had a frock coat on – no gloves.

He was about $1\frac{1}{2}$ inch or 2 or 3 inches – a little higher than she was.

ACB

4.10.88.

The Home Office records[10] are filed under a minuted cover dated 25 October 1888:

[Stamped: – HOME OFFICE 25 OCT.88 RECd.DEPt.]   No. A49301c/8a
DATE [ ] Oct 88   The Commissioner of Police
REFERENCES, &c.   Whitechapel Murders

Forwards full report as to steps taken to detect the perpetrators of these murders.

Thank Commr. for report, and ask what part if any Met. Police took in Eddowes murder. This is the murder in which writing was rubbed out, & it is essential for H.O. to know exact facts as to this.

Also ask City Commr. for report of action taken by City Police in regard to Eddowes, & other murders, also ask Commr. for a map showing locality & position of the murders,

CW

Oct 25/88

GL

25 Oct 1888

Wrote Commr. & City Commr.

25 Oct

To Mr Matthews

I enclose also Newspaper Extracts &c

as to inquests   GL

25 Oct 1888

The statement of Schwartz that a man who was in the company of Eliz. Stride 15 m. before she was found dead, & who threw her down, addressed a companion (?) as "Lipski" seems to furnish a clue and ought to be followed up. The number of "Lipskis" in Whitechapel must be limited. If one of them were identified by Schwarz [sic] it might to lead to something of importance.

[—]

27 Oct./88.

Mr. Murdoch

Please see Mr. Wortley's pencil memo. on Sir C. Warren's letter. ?Shall the Police be asked at the same time for report as to what has become of the 3rd Insane Medical Student from the London Hosp? about whom (under the name of Dr—there is a good deal of gossip in circulation

WTB

The first letter[11] enclosed is dated 29 October 1888 and is to the Commissioner of the Metropolitan Police:

Confidential   Home Office
   A49301/8a   Whitehall
                                            S.W.

Sir,

With reference to your letter of the 24th Inst. enclosing a report as to the steps taken to detect the perpetrator of the recent murders in Whitechapel, I am directed by the Secretary of State to say that he observes that a statement has been made by a man named Schwartz to the effect that he had heard a person who was ["in the company of" – *deleted*] pulling about a woman identified as Elizabeth Stride 15 minutes before the murder off Berner Street took place ["speaking" – *deleted*] call out "Lipski" to an individual who was on the opposite side of the road ["by the name of 'Lipski'" – *deleted*]

["Mr. Matthews presumes that this" – *deleted*]

It does not appear whether the man used the word "Lipski" ["was used" – *deleted*] as a mere ejaculation, meaning in mockery I am going to "Lipski" the woman, or whether he was calling to a man across the road by his proper name. In the latter case, assuming that the man using the word was the murderer, the murderer must have an acquaintance in Whitechapel named Lipski.

Mr. Matthews presumes that this clue has been one of the "suggestions with regard to which searching enquiries have been made; although no tangible results have been obtained as regards the detection of the murderer", but he will be glad if he can be furnished with a report as to any investigations made to trace the man "Lipski".

Another question has arisen on the Reports forwarded by the ["Commissioner" – *deleted*] you. Reference is made to three insane medical students, and it is stated that two have been traced and that one has gone abroad. Mr. Matthews would be glad to be informed of the date when the third student went abroad, & whether any further inquiry has been made about him.

Wrote accordingly
29/10

The next letter[12] on the file is dated 24 October 1888, to the Under-Secretary of State from Sir Charles Warren:

A49301C/8a

["Confidential" – *deleted*]   [Stamped: – HOME OFFICE 25 OCT.88 RECd.DEPt.]

[*Across the top of the page is a note* – ?Ask when the insane student, mentioned on page 6 of Annie Chapman papers, went abroad CSW Oct 24]

4 Whitehall Place,
S.W.
24th October, 1888.

A49301C/["60" – *deleted*]8

Sir,

With reference to your letter of the 13th instant asking that Mr. Secretary Matthews may be supplied with a report of all the measures which have been taken for the detection of the perpetrator of the Whitechapel Murders and of the results;-

I have to transmit, for the information of the Secretary of State, copies of a minute by Mr. Anderson on the subject, and of Reports by Chief Inspector Swanson, which I directed to be prepared on my return from abroad early in September.

Very numerous and searching enquiries have been made in all directions, and with regard to all kinds of suggestions which have been made: these have had no tangible result so far as regards the Whitechapel Murders, but information has been obtained which will no doubt be useful in future in detecting cases of crime.

I am,
Sir,
Your most obedient Servant,
CWarren

The Under Secretary
of State
&c. &c. &c.
Home Office

The next report[13] is dated 23 October 1888 and is signed by Robert Anderson:

A49301C/8a
[Stamped: – HOME OFFICE 25 OCT.88 RECd.DEPt.]

A49301/60

The Whitechapel Murders

At the present stage of the inquiry the best reply that can be made to the Secretary of State's request for a report upon these cases is to send the accompanying copy of detailed reports prepared by Chief Inspector Swanson, who has special charge of the matter at this office.

I wish to guard against its being supposed that the inquiry is now concluded. There is no reason for furnishing these reports at this moment except that they have been called for.

That a crime of this kind should have been committed without any clue being supplied by the criminal, is unusual, but that five successive murders should have been committed without our having the slightest clue of any kind is extraordinary, if not unique, in the annals of crime. The result has been to necessitate our giving attention to innumerable suggestions, such as would in any ordinary case be dismissed unnoticed, and no hint of any kind, which was not obviously absurd, has been neglected. Moreover, the activity of the Police has been to a considerable extent wasted through the exigencies of sensational journalism, and the action of unprincipled persons, who, from various motives, have endeavoured to mislead us. But on the other hand the public generally and especially the inhabitants of the East End have shown a marked desire to assist in every way, even at some sacrifice to themselves, as for example in permitting their houses to be searched as mentioned at page 10 of the last report.

The vigilance of the officers engaged on the inquiry continues unabated.

R. Anderson

Oct 23/88

At this stage there is an index[14] to the contents of the file, dated 19 October 1888:

A49301C

Copy [Stamped: – HOME OFFICE 25 OCT.88 RECd.DEPt.]

Berner Street &c Nos. 4 & 5

Murder of Elizabeth Stride, Berner Street.

Murder of Catherine Eddowes, Mitre Square.

Subject	Page	Remarks
Murder, date & hour of	1	
Diemschitz, Louis	1	Discovered the body.
Doctors' examination	1&2	Doctors Phillips & Brown
Men seen with deceased	3.4.5. 6.7	by P.C. 452H Smith & Israel Schwartz.
Descriptions compared	5.6.7.	with man seen with Mitre Square Victim

Enquiries by police

re Socialists	8	belonging to club in Berner Street.
" Berner Street	8	
" Slaughtermen	11	in Aldgate, Whitechapel & neighbourhood
" House to House	10	boundary of area given
" Common Lod: Hos:	10	2000 lodgers seen up to date
" Sailors	11	By Thames Police
" Asiatics	11	At Homes & Opium dens
" Persons detained	11	& liberated after satisfactory enquiry
" " suspected	11	upwards of 300 whose movements enquired into
Leaflets to occupier	10	80,000 issued
Detectives private	9&10	Making enquiry at instance of Vigilance Com'tee
Gipsies Greek	11	as to presence in London
Cowboys	12	Three traced & satisfactorily accounted for
Dockets	12	Number of
Mitre Sq. Murder	6&7	Within jurisdiction of City Police

19th Oct. 1888

Donald S.Swanson
Ch: Inspr.

The next file cover[15] is dated 6 November 1888:

[Stamped: – HOME OFFICE 7 NOV.88 RECd. DEPt.]
DATE 6th Nov 88   The Commissioner of Police
REFERENCES, &c.   Whitechapel Murders
Reports as to the way the name of "Lipski" was used with reference to Schwartz's evidence, the name is now used as an epithet in addressing or speaking of Jews. Enquiries were made as to "John Saunders" the medical student but without result.

MINUTES.
Confidential
The S.ofS. Nov. 7

There then follows a two-page report[16] from Sir Charles Warren:

[Stamped: – HOME OFFICE 7 NOV.88 RECd.DEPt.]
Confidential

4 Whitehall Place, S.W.
6th November, 1888.

Sir,
    With reference to your letter of the 29th ulto. I have to acquaint you, for

the information of the Secretary of State, that the opinion arrived at upon the evidence given by Schwartz at the inquest in Elizabeth Stride's case is that the name "Lipski", which he alleges was used by a man whom he saw assaulting the woman in Berners [sic] Street on the night of the murder, was not addressed to the supposed accomplice but to Schwartz himself. It appears that since the Lipski case it has come to be used as an epithet in addressing or speaking of Jews.

With regard to the latter portion of your letter I have to state that searching enquiries were made by an officer in Aberdeen Place, St. John's Wood, the last known address of the insane medical student named "John Sanders", but the only information that could be obtained was that a lady named Sanders did reside with her son at No. 20, but left that address to go abroad about two years ago.

I am,

Sir,

Your most obedient Servant,

C. Warren

The Under
    Secretary of State,
&c. &c. &c.

This concludes the main file on the Stride murder as far as the police reports are concerned. However, detailed reports on the inquest appeared in the newspapers. The best overall picture can only be obtained by reading the two sets of reports in conjunction, so the reports of the inquest that appeared in *The Times* follow.

CHAPTER 8

October 1888–The Stride Inquest

The opening of the inquest on Elizabeth Stride is not covered in the extracts contained in the official reports, but the report is to be found in *The Times* of Tuesday, 2 October 1888, page 6:

THE MURDERS AT THE EAST-END

Yesterday, Mr. Wynne E. Baxter, Coroner for the South-Eastern Division of Middlesex, opened an inquiry at the Vestry-hall, Cable-street, St. George's-in-the-East, respecting the death of Elizabeth Stride, who was found murdered in a yard in Berner-street on Sunday morning.

Detective-inspector E. Reid, H Division, watched the case on behalf of the Criminal Investigation Department.

The jury having viewed the body, the following evidence was heard:-

William West, who claimed to affirm, said he lived at 40, Berner-street, Commercial-road, and was a printer by occupation. He lived in one of the houses on the right hand side of the gateway. No. 40, Berner-street was the International Working Men's Club. On the ground floor, facing the street, was a window and a door – the latter leading into a passage. At the side of the house was a passage leading into a yard, and at the entrance to the passage were two wooden gates.

The Foreman. – Is that right?

The CORONER. – There is a passage before you get to the yard.

Witness, continuing, said the passage had two wooden gates folding backwards from the street. In the northern gate there was a little door. The gates were sometimes closed, and at other times left open all night. When the gates were closed the doorway was usually locked. They were seldom closed until late at night, when all the tenants had retired. As far as witness knew no particular person looked after the gates. In the yard on the left hand side there was only one house, which was occupied by two or three tenants. That house contained three doors leading to the yard, but there was no other exit from the yard except through the gates. Opposite the gate there was a workshop, in the occupation of Messrs. Hindley, sack manufacturers. Witness did not believe there was any exit through that workshop. The manufacturing was on the ground floor, and he believed the ground floor of the premises was unoccupied. adjoining Messrs. Hindley's premises there was a stable, which he believed was unoccupied. Passing this stable a person would come to the premises forming the club.

At this point the Coroner examined a parish map of Berner-street, which showed the yard referred to by the witness.

The witness, continuing, said he was not sure that the gardens of the houses in Batty-street faced the yard [?]. The club premises ran back a long way into the yard. The front room on the ground floor of the club was occupied as a dining room. At the middle of the passage there was a staircase leading to the first floor. At the back of the dining room was a kitchen. In this room there was a small window over the door which faced the one leading into the yard. The remainder of the passage led into the yard. Over the door in the passage was a small window, through which daylight came. At the back of the kitchen, but in no way connected with it, was a printing office. This office consisted of two rooms. The one adjoining the kitchen was used as a composing-room, and the other one was for the editor. The compositors, on Saturday last, left off work at 2 o'clock in the afternoon, but the editor was there during the day. He was also a member of the club, and was either there or in his office until he went home. Opposite the doorway of the kitchen, and in the yard, were two closets. The club consisted of from 75 to 80 members. Any working man of any nationality could be a member of the club. It was a Socialist club.

The CORONER. – Have they to agree to any special principles?

Witness. – No person is supposed to be proposed as a member unless he was known to be a supporter of the Socialist movement.

By the CORONER. – Witness worked in the printing office. He remained in the club until about 9 o'clock on Saturday night. He then went out and returned about half-past 10. He then remained in the club until the discovery of the deceased. On the first floor of the club was a large room for entertainments, and from that room three windows faced the yard. On Saturday night a discussion was held in the large room among some 90 or 100 persons. The discussion ceased between 11 30 and 12 o'clock. the bulk of the people present then left the premises by the street door entrance, while between 20 and 30 members remained behind in the large room, and about a dozen were downstairs. Some of those upstairs had a discussion among themselves, while others were singing. The windows of the hall were partly open. Witness left the club about half-past 12. He slept at 2, William-street, and gave as his address 40, Berner-street, as he worked there all day. The distance from his lodgings to Berner-street was about five minutes' walk. Before leaving the club he had occasion to go to the printing office to put some literature there, and he went into the yard by the passage door, thence to the printing office. He then returned to the club by the same way. As he passed from the printing office to the club he noticed the yard gates were open, and went towards them, but did not actually go up to them. There was no lamp or light whatever in the yard. There were no lamps in Berner-street that could light the yard. The only light that could penetrate into the yard was from the windows of the club or the house that was let out in tenements. He noticed lights in one or two windows of the latter house, and they were on the first floor. When he went into the printing office the editor was there reading. Noises from the club could be heard in the yard, but there was not much noise on Saturday night. When he went into the yard and looked towards the gates there was nothing unusual that attracted his attention.

The CORONER. – Can you say there was any object on the ground?

Witness. – I cannot say that an object might have been there, and I not have seen it. I am rather short-sighted, but believe that if anything had been there I should have seen it.

The CORONER. – What made you look towards the gates?

Witness. – Because they were open.

In further examination, witness said after he returned to the club he called his brother and they both left by the street door and went together home. Another member of the club, named Louis Stansley, left the club at the same time, and accompanied them as far as James-street. Witness did not see any one in the yard, and as far as he could remember did not see any one in Berner-street. They went by way of Fairclough-street, Grove-street, and then to James's-street. Witness generally went home from Berner-street between 12 and 1 a.m. On some occasions he had noticed low women and men together in Fairclough-street, but had not seen any in Berner-street. He had never seen any of these women against his club. About 12 months ago he happened to go into the yard and heard some conversation between a man and a woman at the gates. He went to shut the gates, and then saw a man and a woman leave the entrance. That was the only occasion he had ever noticed anything.

By the Jury. – Witness was the overseer of the printing office.

Morris Eagle, who also claimed to affirm, stated that he lived at 4, New-road, Commercial-road, and was a traveller in jewelry. He was a member of the International Working Men's Club, and was there several times during the day. In the evening he occupied the chair and opened the discussion. About a quarter to 12 he left the club for the purpose of taking his young lady home. They left by the front door. He returned to the club about 25 minutes to 1. As he found the front door closed he went through the gateway leading into the yard, and through the back door leading into the club. As he passed through the yard he did not notice anything on the ground by the gates. He believed he passed along about the middle of the gateway, which was about 9 ft. 2 in. wide.

The CORONER. – Can you say if deceased was lying there when you went in?

Witness. – It was rather dark and I cannot say for certain if anything was there or not. I do not remember whether I met any one in Berner-street when I returned to the yard, neither do I remember seeing any one in the yard.

The CORONER. – Supposing you saw a man and woman in the yard, would you have remembered it?

Witness. – I am sure I would.

The CORONER. – Did you notice if there were any lights in the house on the left-hand side?

Witness. – I do not remember.

The CORONER. – Are you often late at night at the club, and do you often go into the yard?

Witness. – I often am there until late, but have seldom gone into the yard. In fact, I have never seen a man or woman in the yard. On the same side as the club is a beershop, and I have seen men and women coming from there.

A Juryman. – That is always closed about 9 o'clock.

The CORONER. – What were you doing at the club?

Witness. – As soon as I entered the club I went to see a friend, who was in the upstairs room, and who was singing a song in the Russian language. Afterwards I joined my friend, and we sang together. I had been there about 20 minutes, when a member named Gilleman came upstairs and said, "There is a dead woman lying in the yard." I went down in a second, and struck a match. I could then see a woman lying on the ground, near the gateway, and in a pool of blood. Her feet were about six or seven feet from the gate, and she was lying by the side of the club wall, her head being towards the yard. Another member, named Isaac, was with me at the time. As soon as I saw the blood I got very excited and ran away for the police. I did not touch her.

The CORONER. – Did you see if her clothes were disturbed?

Witness. – I could not say. When I got outside I saw Jacobs and another going for the police in the direction of Fairclough-street, and I then went to the Commercial-road, all the time shouting "Police!" On getting to the corner of Grove-street I saw two constables, and told them that a woman had been murdered in Berner-street. They returned with me to the yard. I then noticed several members of the club and some strangers were there. A constable threw his light on the body, and then told the other officer to go for a doctor, and sent me to the station for the inspector.

The CORONER. – Did you see any one touch the body?

Witness. – I think the policeman touched it, but the other persons appeared afraid to go near it. When I first saw the body of deceased, I should say it was about 1 o'clock, although I did not look at the clock.

In answer to the foreman of the jury, the witness further said he could not remember how far from the wall the body was lying. On Saturday evening there were free discussions at the club for both men and women. Any one could go in. On Saturday night there were some women there, but those he knew. He should say there were not more than six or eight women present. Saturday was not a dancing night, although after the discussion was ended some dancing might have been carried on. Had a cry of "Murder" been raised he believed they would have heard it, or even any other cry of distress. Witness had never been in the stable or in Hindley's workshop, and could not say for certain whether there was any other exit from the yard except through the gateway.

Louis Diemschutz deposed that he lived at 40, Berner-street, and was steward of the club. The correct title of the club was International Working Men's Educational Club. Witness was a married man, and his wife assisted in the management of the club. Witness left home about half-past 11 on Saturday morning, and he returned home exactly at 1 o'clock on Sunday morning. He was certain about the time. Witness had with him a coster-monger's barrow, and it was drawn by a pony. The pony was not kept in the yard of the club, but in George yard, Cable-street. He drove home for the purpose of leaving his goods. He drove into the yard, and saw that both gates were wide open. It was rather dark there. He drove in as usual, and as he entered the gate his pony shied to the left. Witness looked to the ground on his right, and saw something lying there, but was unable to distinguish what it was. Witness tried to feel the object with his whip before he got down. He then jumped down and struck a match. It was rather windy, but he was able to get a light sufficient to tell it was a woman lying there. He then went into the club, and saw his wife in the front room on the ground floor. He left his pony in the yard, just outside the club door, by itself. He told his wife, and several members who were in the room, that a woman was lying in the yard, but that he was unable to say whether she was drunk or dead. He then got a candle and went out into the yard. By the candlelight he could see that there was blood. He did not touch the body, but at once went off for the police. He passed several streets without seeing a policeman, and returned without one, although he called out "Police" as loud as he could. A young man whom he had met in Grove-street and told about the murder, returned with him. This young man lifted the woman's head up, and witness for the first time saw that her throat was cut. At the same moment the last witness and the constables arrived. When he first approached the club he did not notice anything unusual, and came from the Commercial-road end of the street.

By the CORONER. – The doctor arrived about ten minutes after the police came. No one was then allowed to leave the place until their names and addresses were taken, and they had been searched. The clothes of the deceased, as far as he remembered, were in order. Deceased was lying on her side with her face towards the wall of the club. He could not say how much of the body was lying on the side. As soon as the police came witness went into the club and remained there.

The CORONER. – Did you notice her hands?

Witness. – I did not notice what position her hands were in. I only noticed that the dress buttons of her dress were undone. I saw the doctor put his hand inside and tell the police that the body was quite warm. The doctor also told one of the constables to feel the body, and he did so.

The CORONER. – Did you notice the quantity of blood about?

Witness. – The blood ran in the direction of the house from the neck of the woman. I should say there were quite two quarts of blood on the ground. The body was lying about one foot from the wall. In the yard were a few paving stones, which were very irregularly fixed.

The CORONER. – Have you ever seen men and women in the yard?

Witness. – I have not.

The CORONER. – Have you ever heard of their being found there?

Witness. – Not to my knowledge.

The Foreman. – Was there sufficient room for you to pass the body when you went into the yard?

Witness. – Yes.; and I did so. When my pony shied I was passing the body, and was right by when I got down.

The CORONER. – Did the blood run down as far as the door of the club?

Witness. – Yes.

The Foreman. – When you went for the police, who was in charge of the body?

Witness. – I cannot say. As soon as I saw the blood I ran off.

In answer to Inspector Reid, the witness said every one who was in the yard was detained. This included the strangers. Their names and addresses were taken, and they were questioned as to their presence there. They were also searched, and their hands and clothes examined by Dr. Phillips. It would have been possible for any person to have escaped while he went into the club. Had any person run up the yard witness would have seen him.

The CORONER. – Is the body identified yet?

Inspector Reid. – Not yet.

The Foreman. – I cannot understand that, as she is called Elizabeth Stride.

The CORONER. – That has not yet been sworn to, but something is known of her. It is known where she lived. You had better leave that point until tomorrow.

At this stage the inquiry was adjourned until this afternoon.

Details of the resumed inquest appeared in *The Times* of Wednesday, 3 October, 1888, page 10:

THE EAST END MURDERS.

Yesterday afternoon Mr. Wynne E. Baxter, coroner for the South-Eastern Division of Middlesex, resumed his inquiry at the Vestry-hall, Cable-street, St. George's-in-the-East, respecting the death of Elizabeth Stride, who was found murdered in Berner-street on Sunday morning last.

Detective-inspector E. Reid, H Division, watched the case on behalf of the Criminal Investigation Department.

Police-constable Henry Lamb, 252H, deposed as follows:- About 1 o'clock, as near as I can tell, on Sunday morning I was in the Commercial-road, between Christian-street and Batty-street. Two men came running towards me. I went towards them and heard them say, "Come on! There has been another murder." I said, "Where?" As they got to the corner of Berner-street they pointed down the street. Seeing people moving about some distance down Berner-street, I ran down that street followed by Constable 426H. I went into the gateway of No. 40, Berner-street and saw something dark lying on the right-hand side, close to the gates. I turned my light on and found it was a woman. I saw that her throat was cut, and she appeared to be dead. I at once sent the other constable for the nearest doctor, and I sent a young man that was standing by to the police-station to inform the inspector that a woman was lying in Berner-street with her throat cut, and apparently dead.

The CORONER. – How many people were there in the yard?

Witness. – I should think 20 or 30. Some of that number had followed me in.

The CORONER. – Was any one touching the body when you arrived?

Witness. – No. There was no one within a yard of it. As I was examining the body some crowded round. I begged them to keep back, and told them they might get some of the blood on their clothing, and by that means get themselves into trouble. I then blew my whistle. I put my hand on the face and found it slightly warm. I then felt the wrist, but could not feel the pulse.

The CORONER. – Did you do anything else to the body?

Witness. – I did not, and would not allow any one to get near the body. Deceased was lying on her side, and her left arm was lying under her.

The CORONER. – Did you examine her hands?

Witness. – I did not; but I saw that her right arm was across the breast.

The CORONER. – How near was her head to the wall?

Witness. – I should say her face was about five or six inches away.

The CORONER. – Were her clothes disturbed?

Witness. – No. I scarcely could see her boots. She looked as if she had been laid quietly down. Her clothes were not in the least rumpled.

The CORONER. – Was the blood in a liquid state?

Witness. – Some was, and some was congealed. It extended close to the door. The part nearest to her throat was congealed.

The CORONER. – Was any blood coming from the throat at that time?

Witness. – I hardly like to say that, Sir. If there was it must have been a very small quantity. Dr. Blackwell, about ten minutes after I got there, was the first doctor to arrive.

The CORONER. – Did any one say whether the body had been touched?

Witness. – No. Dr. Blackwell examined the body, and afterwards the surrounding ground. Dr. Phillips arrived about 20 minutes afterwards; but at that time I was at another part of the ground. Inspector Pinhorn arrived directly after the doctor arrived. When I got there I had the gates shut.

The CORONER. – But did not the feet of the deceased touch the gate?

Witness. – No; they went just behind it, and I was able to close the gates without disturbing the body. I put a constable at the gate and told him not to let any one in or out. I then entered the club and, starting from the front door, examined the place. I turned my light on and had a look at the different persons there, and examined a number of their hands and also their clothing to see if I could detect any marks of blood. I did not take up each one's hand. I should say there were from 15 to 20 persons in the club-room on the ground floor. I then went into every room, including the one in which there was a stage, and I went behind it. A person was there who informed me he was the steward.

The CORONER. – You did not think to put him in charge of the front door?

Witness. – No, I did not. When further assistance came a constable was put in charge of the front door. I did not see any one leave by that entrance, and could not say if it was locked. After I examined the club, I went into the yard and examined the cottages. I also went into the water-closets. The occupiers of the cottages were all in bed when I knocked. A man came down partly dressed to let me in. Every one I saw, except this one, was undressed.

The CORONER. – There is a recess in the yard, is there not? Did you go there?

Witness. – Yes; and I afterwards went there with Dr. Phillips. I examined the dust-bin and dung-heap. I noticed there was a hoarding, but I do not recollect looking over it. After that I went and examined the steps and outside of Messrs. Hindley's premises. I also looked through the windows, as the doors were fastened.

The CORONER. — How long was it before the cottage doors were opened?

Witness. — Not long. The people seemed very much frightened and wanted to know what was the matter. I told them nothing much, as I did not want to frighten them. When I returned from there Dr. Phillips and Chief Inspector West had arrived.

The CORONER. — Was there anything to prevent any one escaping while you were examining the body?

Witness. — It was quite possible, as I was then there by myself. There was a lot of confusion, and every one was looking towards the body.

The CORONER. — A person might have escaped before you arrived?

Witness. — That is quite possible. I should think he got away before I got there, and not afterwards.

Inspector Reid. — How long was it before you passed that spot?

Witness. — I was not on the beat; but I passed the Commercial-road end of the street some six or seven minutes before I was called. When I was fetched I was going in the direction of Berner-street. Constable Smith is on the Berner-street beat. The constable who followed me down is on fixed-point duty from 9 to 5 at the end of Grove-street. All the fixed-point men ceased their duty at 1 a.m., and then the men on the beats did the whole duty.

Inspector Reid. — These men are fixed at certain places, so if a person wanted a constable he would not have to go all the way to the station for one.

The CORONER. — Did you see anything suspicious?

Witness. — No, I saw lots of squabbles and rows such as one sees on Saturday nights. I think I should have seen any one running from the gate of 40, Berner-street if I had been standing at the Commercial-road end of it. I could not tell if the lamps on the plan are correct.

The CORONER. — I may mention there are four lamps between Commercial-road and Fairclough-street. Is the street as well lit as others in the neighbourhood?

Witness. — It is lit about as well as side streets generally are, but some I know are better lighted.

A Juryman. — I think that street is lighted quite as well as any other.

In further examination, witness said, — I remained in the yard the remainder of the night. I started to help convey the body to the mortuary, but I was fetched back.

Edward Spooner said, — I live at 26, Fairclough-street, and am a horse-keeper at Messrs. Meredith's. Between half-past 12 and 1 o'clock on Sunday morning I was standing outside the Bee Hive publichouse, at the corner of Christian-street and Fairclough-street, along with a young woman. I had previously been in another beershop at the top of the street, and afterwards walked down. After talking for about 25 minutes I saw two Jews come running along and shouting out "Murder" and "Police." They then ran as far as Grove-street and turned back. I stopped them and asked what was the matter. They replied, "A woman has been murdered." I then went round with them to Berner-street, and into Dutfield's yard, adjoining No. 40, Berner-street. I saw a woman lying just inside the gate. At that time there were about 15 people in the yard, and they were all standing round the body. The majority of them appeared to be Jews. No one touched the body. One of them struck a match, and I lifted up the chin of the deceased with my hand. The chin was slightly warm. Blood was still flowing from the throat. I could see that she had a piece of paper doubled up in her right hand, and a red and white flower pinned on to her jacket. The body was lying on one side, with the face turned towards the wall. I noticed that blood was running down the gutter. I stood there about five minutes before a constable came. It was the last witness who first arrived. I did not notice any one leave while I was there, but there were a lot of people there, and a person might have got away unnoticed. The only means I had of fixing the time was by the closing of the publichouses. I stood at the top of the street for about five minutes, and then 25 minutes outside the publichouse. I should say it was about 25 minutes to 1 when I first went to the yard. I could not form any opinion about the body having been moved. Several persons stood round. I noticed that the legs of the deceased were drawn up, but the clothes were not disturbed. As soon as the policeman came I stepped back, and afterwards helped to fasten the gates. When I left it was by the front door of the club. Before that I was searched, and gave my name and address. I was also examined by Dr. Phillips.

By the CORONER. – There was no blood on the chin of the deceased, and I did not get any on my hands. Directly I got inside the yard I could see that it was a woman lying on the ground.

By the jury. – As I was going to Berner-street I did not meet any one except Mr. Harris, who came out of his house in Tiger Bay (Brunswick-street). Mr. Harris told me he had heard the policeman's whistle blowing.

Mary Malcolm said, – I live at 50, Eagle-street, Red Lion-square. I am married to Andrew Malcolm, a tailor. I have seen the body in the mortuary. I saw it on Sunday and twice yesterday. It is the body of my sister, Elizabeth Watts.

The CORONER. – You have no doubt about that?

Witness. – Not the slightest.

The CORONER. – You had some doubts at first?

Witness. – I had, but not now. I last saw her alive at a quarter to 7 last

Thursday evening. She came to me where I worked at the tailoring, at 59, Red Lion-street. She came to me to ask me to give her a little assistance, which I have been in the habit of doing off and on for the last five years. I gave her 1s. and a little short jacket. The latter is not the one she had on when found in Berner-street. She only remained with me for a few moments, and she did not say where she was going. I could not say where she was living except that it was somewhere in the neighbourhood of the tailors and Jews at the East-end. I understood she was living in a lodging-house.

The CORONER. – Did you know what she was doing for a living?

Witness. – I had my doubts.

The CORONER. – Was she the worse for drink when she came to you?

Witness. – She was sober, but unfortunately drink was a failing with her.

The CORONER. – How old was she?

Witness. – 37.

The CORONER. – Was she married?

Witness. – Yes, to Mr. Watts, wine and spirit merchant, of Walton-street, Bath. I think his name is Edward Watts, and he is in partnership with his father, and they are in a large way of business. My sister left her home because she brought disgrace on her husband. Her husband left her because he caught her with a porter. Her husband sent her home to her poor mother, who is now dead. She took her two children with her, but I believe the boy has since been sent to a boarding school by his aunt, Miss Watts. The other child, a girl, was dead. I have never seen my sister in an epileptic fit – only in drunken fits. I believe she has been before the Thames Police-court magistrate on charges of drunkenness. I believe she has been let off on the ground that she was subject to epileptic fits, but I do not believe she was subject to them. I believe she lived with a man who kept a coffee house at Poplar. His name was not Stride, but I could find out by tomorrow. She had ceased to live with him for some time, for he went to sea and was wrecked on the Isle of St. Paul. That was about three years ago. Since then she had not lived with any one to my knowledge.

The CORONER. – Have you ever heard she has been in trouble with any man?

Witness. – No, but she has been locked up several times. I have never heard of any one threatening her, or that she was afraid of any one. I know of no man with whom she had any relations, and I did not know she lived in Flower and Dean-street. I knew that she was called "Long Liz".

The CORONER. – Have you ever heard the name of Stride?

Witness. – She never mentioned that name to me. If she had lived with any one of that name I am sure she would have told me. She used to come to me every Saturday, and I always gave her 2s.

The CORONER. – Did she come last Saturday?

Witness. – No; her visit on Thursday was an unusual one. Before that she had not missed a Saturday for between two and three years. She always came at 4 o'clock in the afternoon, and we used to meet at the corner of Chancery-lane. On Saturday afternoon I went there at half-past 3, and remained there until 5, but deceased did not turn up. On Sunday morning, when I read the paper, I wondered whether it was my sister. I had a presentiment that it was. I then went to Whitechapel and spoke to a policeman about my sister. I afterwards went to the St. George's mortuary. When I first saw the body I did not at first recognize it, as I only saw it by gas light; but the next day I recognized it.

The CORONER. – Did not you have some special presentiment about your sister?

Witness. – About 1.20 a.m. on Sunday morning I was lying on my bed when I felt a kind of pressure on my breast, and then I felt three kisses on my cheek. I also heard the kisses, and they were quite distinct.

A Juryman. – Did your sister have any special mark about her?

Witness. – Yes; a black mark on her leg, and I saw it there yesterday. I told the police I could recognize her by this particular mark. The mark was caused by my sister being bitten by an adder some years ago, and I was bitten on the finger at the same time. Here is the mark (showing it to the Coroner).

The CORONER. – Has your husband seen your sister?

Witness. – He has seen her once or twice some three years ago. I have another sister and a brother who are alive, but they have not seen her for years.

The CORONER. – I hear at one time you said it was your sister, and at another time you said it was not.

Witness. – I am sure it was.

The CORONER. – Have you any one that can corroborate you?

Witness. – Only my brother and my sister. This disgrace will kill my sister. The best thing will be for her brother to come up. I have kept this shame from every one. (Here the witness sobbed bitterly.)

The CORONER. – Was there any special mark on your sister's feet?

Witness. – I know she had a hollow at the bottom of one of her feet, which was the result of an accident.

The CORONER. – Did you recognize the clothes she wore?

Witness. – No, I did not. I never took notice of what she wore, for I was always grateful to get rid of her. Once she left a baby naked outside my door, and I had to keep it until she fetched it away. It was not one of the two children already mentioned, but was by some policeman or another. I do not know any one that would do her harm, for she was a girl every one liked.

The CORONER. – Would your brother recognize her?

Witness. – I am positive he could, although he has not seen her for years. I can now recognize her by the hair.

The CORONER. – I think you ought to go again to the spot where you have been in the habit of meeting your sister to see if she comes again. You say she has not missed a single Saturday for two and a half years. How about the Saturday when she was in prison?

Witness. – She has always been fined, and the money has been paid.

Mr. Frederick William Blackwell said, – I live at 100, Commercial-road, and am a surgeon. At 10 minutes past 1 on Sunday morning I was called to 40, Berner-street. I was called by a policeman, and my assistant, Mr. Johnson, went back with him. I followed immediately I had dressed. I consulted my watch on my arrival, and it was just 1.10. The deceased was lying on her left side completely across the yard. Her legs were drawn up, her feet against the wall of the right side of the yard passage. Her head was resting almost in the line of the carriage way, and her feet were about three yards from the gateway. The feet almost touched the wall, and the face was completely towards the wall. The neck and chest were quite warm; also the legs and face were slightly warm. The hands were cold. The right hand was lying on the chest, and was smeared inside and out with blood. It was quite open. The left hand was lying on the ground and was partially closed, and contained a small packet of cachous wrapped in tissue paper. There were no rings or marks of rings on the fingers. The appearance of the face was quite placid, and the mouth was slightly open. There was a check silk scarf round the neck, the bow of which was turned to the left side and pulled tightly. There was a long incision in the neck, which exactly corresponded with the lower border of the scarf. The lower edge of the scarf was slightly frayed, as if by a sharp knife. The incision in the neck commenced on the left side, $2\frac{1}{2}$ in. below the angle of the jaw, and almost in a direct line with it. It nearly severed the vessels on the left side, cut the windpipe completely in two, and terminated on the opposite side $1\frac{1}{2}$ in. below the angle of the right jaw, but without severing the vessels on that side. The post mortem appearances will be given subsequently.

By the CORONER. – I did not ascertain if the bloody hand had been moved. The blood was running down in the gutter into the drain. It was running in an opposite direction to the feet. There was a quantity of clotted blood just under the body.

The CORONER. – Were there no spots of blood anywhere?

Witness. – No. Some of the blood had been trodden about near to where the body was lying.

The CORONER. – Was there any blood on the side of the house, or splashes on the wall?

Witness. – No. It was very dark at the time, and I only examined it by the policeman's lamp. I have not since examined the place.

The CORONER. – Did you examine the clothing?

Witness. – Yes. There was no blood on any portion of it. The bonnet was lying on the ground, a few inches from the head. The dress was undone at the top. I know about what deceased had on, but could not give an accurate description of them. I noticed she had a bunch of flowers in her jacket. The injuries were beyond the possibility of self-infliction.

The CORONER. – How long had the deceased been dead when you saw her?

Witness. – From 20 minutes to half an hour when I arrived. It was a very mild night and was not raining at the time. There was no wet on deceased's clothing. Deceased would have bled to death comparatively slowly, on account of the vessels on one side only being severed, and the artery not completely severed. Deceased could not have cried out after the injuries were inflicted as the windpipe was severed. I felt the heart and found it quite warm. My assistant was present all the time. Dr. Phillips arrived from 20 minutes to half an hour after my arrival, but I did not notice the exact time.

The CORONER. – Could you see there was a woman there when you went in?

Witness. – Yes. The doors were closed when I arrived. I formed the opinion that the murderer first took hold of the silk scarf, at the back of it, and then pulled the deceased backwards, but I cannot say whether the throat was cut while the woman was standing or after she was pulled backwards. Deceased would take about a minute and a half to bleed to death. I cannot say whether the scarf would be tightened sufficiently to prevent deceased calling out.

At this stage the inquiry was adjourned until to-day.

The next report on the resumed inquest appeared in *The Times* on Thursday, 4 October 1888, page 10:

THE EAST-END MURDERS.

Yesterday afternoon Mr. Wynne E. Baxter, Coroner for the South-Eastern Division of Middlesex, resumed his inquiry at the Vestry-hall, Cable-street, St. George's-in-the- East, respecting the death of Elizabeth Stride, who was found murdered in Berner-street on Sunday morning last.

Detective-Inspector E. Reid, H Division, again watched the case on behalf of the Criminal Investigation Department.

Elizabeth Tanner stated: I live at 32, Flower and Dean-street, Spitalfields, and am a widow. I am the deputy of No. 32, which is a common lodginghouse. I have seen the body in the mortuary, and recognize the features of the deceased as a woman who had lodged off and on at the lodginghouse for six years. I knew her by the name of ' "Long Liz." ' I do not know her right name. She told me she was a Swedish woman, but never told me where she was born. She told me she was a married woman, and that her husband and children went down in the ship Princess Alice.

The CORONER. – When did you last see her alive?

Witness. – About 6.30 on Saturday afternoon. I do not know the name of her husband, or what occupation he had followed. When I last saw deceased she was in the Queen's Head publichouse, Commercial-street. I went back to the lodginghouse, and did not see any more of her. At that time deceased had no hat or coat on. I saw her in the kitchen of the lodginghouse, and then I went to another part of the building, and never saw her again until I saw her dead body in the mortuary this afternoon.

The CORONER. – Are you sure it is her? – Witness. – I am quite sure. I recognize the features, and by the fact that she had lost the roof of her mouth. She told me that happened when the Princess Alice went down.

The CORONER. – Was she on board the ship at the time? – Witness. – Yes; and it was during that time her mouth was injured.

The CORONER. – Was she at the lodginghouse on Friday night? – Witness. – Yes; on Thursday and Friday nights; but on no other night during the week. She did not pay for her bed on Saturday night.

The CORONER. – Do you know her male acquaintances? – Witness. – Only one, and I do not know his name. She left the man she was living with on Thursday to come and stay at my lodginghouse. That is what she told me.

The CORONER. – Have you seen this man? – Witness. – Yes; I saw him on Sunday evening.

The CORONER. – Do you know if she has ever been up at the Thames Police-court? – Witness. – I do not.

The CORONER. – Do you know any other place where she has lived? – Witness. – Only Fashion-street.

The CORONER. – Do you know if she had a sister living in Red Lion-square? – Witness. – I do not.

The CORONER. – What sort of woman was she? – Witness. – She was a very quiet and sober woman.

The CORONER. – Did she stop out late at night? – Witness. – Sometimes.

The CORONER. – Do you know if she had any money? – Witness. – I do not. On Saturday she cleaned the rooms for me, and I gave her 6d.

The CORONER. – Have you seen her clothes? – Witness. – Yes. I cannot say if the two handkerchiefs belonged to her. The clothes she was wearing were the ones she usually wore, and they are the same she had on Saturday. I recognized the long jacket as belonging to her.

The CORONER. — Did she ever tell you she was afraid of any one? — Witness. — No; and I never heard her say that any one had threatened to injure her.

The CORONER. — It is a common thing for people who have been lodging in your place not to come back? — Witness. — Yes; I took no notice of it. I was sent for to go to the mortuary.

A Juryman. — Do you remember the hour she came to the lodginghouse? — Witness. — I do not, although I saw her and took 4d. from her for her lodging. At that time she was wearing the long jacket I have seen in the mortuary. I did not see her bring any parcel with her.

Inspector Reid. — Have you ever heard the name of Stride mentioned in connexion with her? — Witness. — No.

A Juryman. — How long had deceased been away from your house before last Thursday? — Witness. — About three months; but I have seen her during that time — sometimes once a week and sometimes nearly every day.

The CORONER. — Did you understand what she was doing? — Witness. — She told me she worked among the Jews, and was living with a man in Fashion-street.

The CORONER. — Could she speak English well? — Witness. — Yes; and Swedish as well.

The CORONER. — When she spoke English could you tell she was a foreigner? — Witness. — No.

The CORONER. — Was there much association between her and her country people? — Witness. — No.

The CORONER. — Have you ever heard of her having in childhood broken a limb? — Witness. — I have not heard her say. I have never heard her carry on a conversation in the Swedish language; but she told me herself she was a Swede.

Catherine Lane, 32, Flower and Dean-street, said: I am a charwoman and am married to Patrick Lane, a dock-labourer. We live together at the lodginghouse and have been living there since the 11th of February of this year. I have seen the body of deceased in the mortuary and recognize it as "Long Liz," who lived in the same lodginghouse. Lately she had only been there since Thursday last. I have known her for six or seven years. During the time she was away she called at the lodginghouse, and I used frequently to see her in Fashion-street, where she was living. I spoke to the deceased on Thursday between 10 and 11 in the morning. She told me she had a few words with the man she was living with and left him. I saw her on Saturday afternoon when she was cleaning the deputy's rooms. I last saw her between 7 and 8 o'clock on Saturday evening. She was then in the kitchen, and had a long jacket and black hat on.

The CORONER. – Did she tell you where she was going? Witness. – She did not. When she left the kitchen she gave me a piece of velvet and asked me to mind it until she came back. The deputy would always mind things for the lodgers, and I do not know why she asked me to mind the velvet for her. Deceased showed me the piece of velvet on the previous day. I knew deceased had 6d. when she left, as she showed me the money, but I cannot say if she had any more money besides that. Deceased did not tell me she was coming back. I do not think she had been drinking.

The CORONER. – Do you know any one who is likely to have injured her? Witness. – No. I have heard her say she was a foreign woman, and she told me that at one time she lived in Devonshire-street, Commercial-road. I have never heard her say that at one time she lived at Poplar. She told me she had had a husband and that he was dead. Deceased never told me she had been threatened, or that she was afraid of any one. I know nothing about her history beyond what I have stated. I am satisfied it is she. I could tell by her actions that she was a foreign woman and did not bring all her words out plainly. I have heard her speaking to persons in her own language.

A juryman. – Did you ever hear her say she had a sister? Witness. – No; never.

The CORONER. – Do you know what she has been doing lately? Witness. – I do not.

Charles Preston stated: I live at 32, Flower and Dean-street, Spitalfields, and am a barber by occupation. I have been lodging there for about 18 months. I have seen the deceased there and identified her body on Sunday afternoon at the mortuary. I am quite sure the body is that of "Long Liz." I last saw her alive on Saturday evening, between 6 and 7 o'clock. At that time she was in the kitchen of the lodginghouse and was dressed ready to go out. She asked me for the loan of a clothes-brush. At that time she had on a black jacket trimmed with fur, and it is the same one I have seen in the mortuary. She wore a coloured striped silk handkerchief round her neck, and it was the same as I saw in the mortuary. I have not seen her with a pocket-handkerchief, and am unable to say if she had two. I always understood from the deceased that she was a Swede by birth and was born at Stockholm; that she came to England in the service of a foreign gentleman. I think she told me she was about 35 years of age. She told me she had been married, and that her husband was drowned at the foundering of the Princess Alice. I have some recollection that deceased told me her husband was a seafaring man. I have heard her say she had a coffeehouse at Chrisp-street, Poplar; but she did not say she had often been at the Thames Police-court. I have known her to be in custody on one Saturday afternoon for being drunk and disorderly at the Queen's Head publichouse, Commercial-road. She was let out on her own bail on the Sunday morning. That was some four or five months ago. I have never heard her say she had met with an accident. She did not tell me where she was going on Saturday evening, and never mentioned what time she was coming back. At times the lodgers did not pay for their beds until just before going to bed. When deceased was locked up it was late in the afternoon or towards the evening time. She has always given me to understand her name was Elizabeth Stride, and that her mother was still living in Sweden. I have heard her speaking fluently in a foreign language to person in the lodging-house.

Michael Kidney stated: I live at 38, Dorset-street, Spitalfields, and am a waterside labourer. I have seen the body in the mortuary and it is that of a woman whom I lived with. I have no doubt whatever about it.

The CORONER. – Do you know what her name was? Witness. – Elizabeth Stride. I have known her about three years, and she has been living with me nearly all that time.

The CORONER. – Do you know what her age was? Witness. – Between 36 and 38. She told me she was a Swede, and that she was born at Stockholm; that her father was a farmer, and that she came to England for the purpose of seeing the country. She afterwards told me she had come to England as servant to a family.

The CORONER. – Had she any relatives in England? Witness. – Only some of her mother's friends. She told me she was a widow, and that her husband had been a ship's carpenter belonging to Sheerness. She also told me her husband had kept a coffeehouse at Chrisp-street, Poplar, and that he was drowned on the Princess Alice.

The CORONER. – You had a quarrel with her on Thursday? Witness. – No. I last saw the deceased alive on Tuesday week.

The CORONER. – Did you quarrel then? Witness. – No; I left her in Commercial-street as I was going to work.

The CORONER. – Did you expect her to meet you later on? Witness. – I expected her to be at home. When I got home I found that she had been in and gone out. I did not again see her until I identified the body in the mortuary. She was perfectly sober when I last saw her. She was subject to going away whenever she thought she would. During the three years I have known her she has been away from me altogether about five months. I have cautioned her the same as I would a wife.

The CORONER. – Do you know any one she has picked up with? Witness. – I have seen the address of some one with the family she was living with at Hyde Park; but I cannot find it.

The CORONER. – That is not what I asked you. Do you think she went away with any one else? – Witness. – I do not think that, for she liked me better than any one else. It was drink that made her go away, and she always returned without my going after her. I do not believe she left me on Tuesday to go with any other man.

The CORONER. — Had she money at that time? Witness. — I do not think she was without a 1s., considering the money I gave her to keep the house.

The CORONER. — Do you know of anyone that was likely to have run foul of her? Witness. — On Monday night I went to Leman-street Police-station for a detective to act on my information, but I could not get one.

The CORONER. — It is not too late yet; can you give us any information now? Witness. — I have heard something said that leads me to believe, that had I been able to act the same as a detective I could have got a lot more information. When I went to the station I was intoxicated. I asked for a young detective. I told the inspector at the station that if the murder occurred on my beat I would shoot myself. I have been in the Army.

Inspector Reid. — Will you give me any information now? Witness. — I believe I could catch the man, if I had the proper force at my command. If I was to place the men myself I could capture the murderer. He would be caught in the act.

Inspector Reid. — Then you have no information to give? Witness. — No.

The CORONER. — Have you heard of a sister of deceased giving her money? Witness. — No, but Mrs. Malcolm, who stated she was sister to deceased, is very much like her.

The CORONER. — Had deceased ever had a child by you? Witness. — No. She told me a policeman used to see her at Hyde Park before she was married to Stride. I never heard her say she had a child by a policeman. Deceased told me she was the mother of nine children. Two were drowned on the Princess Alice with her husband, and the remainder are in a school belonging to the Swedish Church. The school is somewhere on the other side of the Thames. I have also heard her say that some friend of her husband had two of the children. I thoroughly believe the deceased was a Swede, and came from a superior class. She could also speak Yeddish [*sic*]. Both deceased and her husband were employed on board the Princess Alice.

Edward Johnston said: — I live at 100, Commercial-road, and am assistant to Drs. Kay and Blackwell. About five or ten minutes past 1 on Sunday morning, I received a call from constable 436 H. After informing Dr. Blackwell, who was in bed, of the nature of the case, I accompanied the constable to Berner-street. In a courtyard, adjoining 40, Berner-street, I was shown the figure of a woman lying on her left side. There was a crowd of people in the yard and some policemen. No one was touching the deceased, and there was very little light. What there was came from the policemen's lanterns. I examined the woman and found an incision in the throat. The wound appeared to have stopped bleeding. I also felt the body to see if it was warm, and found it was all warm with the exception of the hands, which were quite cold. The dress was not undone, and I undid it to see if the chest was warm. I did not move the head at all, and left it exactly as I found it. The body was not moved while I was there. The knees were nearer to the wall than the head. There was a stream of blood reaching down to the gutter. It was all clotted blood. There was very little blood near the neck, as nearly all of it had run away in the direction away from the legs. As soon as Dr. Blackwell arrived I handed the case over to him.

The CORONER. – Did you look at the hands? Witness. – No. I saw the left hand was lying away from the body, and the arm was bent. The right arm was also bent. The left hand might have been on the ground.

The CORONER. – Was there any mark of a footstep on the stream of blood? Witness. – No. I was looking at the body and not at those around me. As soon as Dr. Blackwell came he looked at his watch. It was then 1.16. I was there three or four minutes before Dr. Blackwell.

The CORONER. – Did you notice the bonnet of deceased? Witness. – Yes, it was lying on the ground, beyond the head of deceased to the distance of three or four inches. I did not notice the paper in the left hand. The gates were not closed when I got there, but they were shortly afterwards.

Thomas Coram said: I live at 67, Plummer's-road, Mile-end, and am employed at a cocoanut warehouse. On Sunday night I was coming away from a friends at 16, Bath-gardens, Brady-street. I was walking on the right hand side of the Whitechapel-road towards Aldgate. When opposite No. 253 I crossed over, and saw a knife lying on the doorstep. No. 252 was a laundry business, and there were two steps leading to the front door. I found the knife on the bottom step. That is the knife I found (witness being shown a long-bladed knife). The handkerchief produced was wrapped round the handle. It was folded, and then twisted round the handle. The handkerchief was blood-stained. I did not touch them. A policeman came towards me, and I called his attention to them.

The CORONER. – The blade of the knife is dagger-shaped and is sharpened on one side. The blade is about 9in. or 10in. long, I should say.

Witness. – The policeman took the knife to the Leman-street Police-station, and I went with him.

The CORONER. – Were there many people passing at the time? Witness. – I should think I passed about a dozen between Brady-street and where I found the knife.

The CORONER. – Could it easily be seen? Witness. – Yes; and it was light.

The CORONER. – Did you pass a policeman before you got to the spot? Witness. – Yes, I passed three. It was about half-past 12 at night.

Constable Joseph Drage 282 H, stated: At 12.30 on Monday morning I was on fixed-point duty in the Whitechapel-road, opposite Great Garden-street. I saw the last witness stooping down at a doorway opposite No. 253. I was going towards him when he rose up and beckoned me with his finger. He then said, "Policeman, there is a knife down here." I turned on my light and saw a long-bladed knife lying on the doorstep. I picked up the knife and found it was smothered with blood. The blood was dry. There was a handkerchief bound round the handle and tied with string. The handkerchief also had blood-stains on it. I asked the last witness how he came to see it. He said, "I was looking down, when I saw something white." I then asked him what he did out so late, and he replied, "I have been to a friend's in Bath-gardens." He then gave me his name and address, and we went to the police-station together. The knife and handkerchief produced are the same.

The CORONER. – Was the last witness sober? Witness. – Yes. His manner was natural, and he said when he saw the knife it made his blood run cold, and added that nowadays they heard of such funny things. When I passed I should have undoubtedly seen the knife. I was passing there continually. Some little time before a horse fell down opposite the place where the knife was found. I assisted in getting the horse up, and during that time a person might have laid the knife down on the step. I would not be positive that the knife was not there a quarter of an hour previously, but I think not. About an hour previously the landlady let out some woman, and the knife was not there then. I handed the knife to Dr. Phillips on the Monday afternoon. It was then sealed and secured.

Dr. George Baxter [*sic*] Phillips said: – I live at 2, Spital-square. I was called at 1.20 on Sunday morning to Leman-street Police-station, and from there sent on to Berner-street to a yard at the side of a club-house. I found Chief-Inspector West and Inspector Pinhorn in possession of a body, which had already been seen by Dr. Blackwell, who arrived some time before me. The body was lying on the near side, with the face turned towards the wall, the head up the yard and the feet towards the street. The left arm was extended, and there was a packet of cachous in the left hand. A number of these were in the gutter. I took them from her hand and handed them to Dr. Blackwell. The right arm was over the belly. The back of the hand and wrist had on it clotted blood. the legs were drawn up, with the feet close to the wall. The body and face were warm and the hand cold. The legs were quite warm. Deceased had a silk handkerchief round her neck, and it appeared to be slightly torn. I have since ascertained it was cut. This corresponded with the right angle of the jaw. The throat was deeply gashed, and there was an abrasion of the skin about $1\frac{1}{4}$. in diameter, apparently stained with blood, under her right brow. At 3 p.m. on Monday, at St. George's mortuary, in the presence of Dr. Rygate and Mr. Johnston, Dr. Blackwell and I made a post mortem examination. Dr. Blackwell kindly consented to make the dissection. Rigor Mortis was still thoroughly marked. There was mud on the left side of the face and it was matted in the head. We then removed the clothes. The body was fairly nourished. Over both shoulders, especially the right, and under the collar-bone and in front of the chest there was a blueish discolouration, which I have watched and have seen on two occasions since. There was a clean-cut incision on the neck. It was 6in. in length and commenced $2\frac{1}{2}$ in. in a straight line below the angle of the jaw, $\frac{3}{4}$ in. over an undivided muscle, and then, becoming deeper, dividing the sheath. the cut was very clean, and deviated a little downwards. The artery and other vessels contained in the sheath were all cut through. The cut through the tissues on the right side was more superficial, and tailed off to about 2 in. below the right angle of the jaw. The deep vessels on that side were uninjured. From this it was evident that the haemorrhage was caused through the partial severance of the left carotid artery. Decomposition had commenced in the skin. Dark brown spots were on the anterior surface of the left chin. There was a deformity in the bones of the right leg, which was not straight, but bowed forwards. There was no recent external injury save to the neck. The body being washed more thoroughly, I could see some healing sores. The lobe of the left ear was torn as if from the removal or wearing through of an earring, but it was thoroughly healed. On removing the scalp there was no sign of bruising or extravasation of blood. The skull was about a sixth of an inch in thickness, and the brain was fairly normal. The left lung had old adhesions to the chest wall, the right slightly. Both lungs were unusually pale. There was no fluid in the pericardium. The heart was small, the left ventricle firmly contracted, and the right slightly so. There was no clot in the pulmonary artery, but the right ventricle was full of dark clot. The left was firmly contracted so as to be absolutely empty. The stomach was large, and the mucous membrane only congested. It contained partly-digested food, apparently consisting of cheese, potato, and farinaceous powder. All the teeth on the left lower jaw were absent. On Tuesday I again went to the mortuary to observe the marks on the shoulder. I found in the pocket of the underskirt of the deceased the following articles – key as if belonging to a padlock, a small piece of lead pencil, a pocket comb, a broken piece of comb, a metal spoon, some buttons, and a hook. Examining her jacket, I found that, while there was a small amount of mud on the right side, the left was well plastered with mud. I have not seen the two pocket-handkerchiefs.

I will answer any questions put to me, but as there is another case pending I think I had better stop here.

The CORONER. – What is the cause of death? Witness. – It is undoubtedly from the loss of blood from the left carotid artery and the division of the wind-pipe.

The CORONER. – Did you examine the blood at Berner-street? Witness. – I did. The blood had run down the waterway to within a few inches of the side entrance of the club.

The CORONER. – Were there any spots of blood on the wall? Witness. – I could trace none. Roughly estimating it I should say there was an unusual flow of blood considering the stature and the nourishment of the body.

At this point the inquiry was adjourned until Friday morning.

There then follows, in this report in *The Times*, some interesting correspondence:

The following correspondence has been sent to us for publication:

"Office of the Board of Works, Whitechapel District, 15, Great Alie-street, Whitechapel, Oct. 2.

"Sir, – At a meeting of the Board of Works for the Whitechapel District a resolution was passed, of which the following is a copy –

"That this Board regards with horror and alarm the several atrocious murders recently perpetrated within the district of Whitechapel and its vicinity and calls upon Sir Charles Warren so to regulate and strengthen the police force in the neighbourhood as to guard against any repetition of such atrocities."

"And by direction of the Board the copy resolution is forwarded to you in the hope that it will receive your favourable consideration. I am, &c.,

"ALFRED TURNER, Clerk.

"Colonel Sir Charles Warren, G.C.M.G."

"POLICE NOTICE.
"TO THE OCCUPIER.

"On the mornings of Friday, 31st August, Saturday 8th, and Sunday 30th September, 1888, women were murdered in or near Whitechapel, supposed by some one residing in the immediate neighbourhood. Should you know of any person to whom suspicion is attached, you are earnestly requested to communicate at once with the nearest police-station.

"Metropolitan Police Office, 30th September, 1888."

"4 Whitehall-place, S.W., Oct. 3.

"Sir, – In reply to a letter of the 2d inst. from the Clerk of the Board of Works for the Whitechapel District transmitting a resolution of the Board with regard to the recent atrocious murders perpetrated in and about Whitechapel, I have to point out that the carrying out of your proposals as to regulating and strengthening the police force in your district cannot possibly do more than guard or take precautions against any repetition of such atrocities so long as the victims actually, but unwittingly, connive at their own destruction.

"Statistics show that London, in comparison to its population, is the safest city in the world to live in. The prevention of murder directly cannot be effected by any strength of the police force; but it is reduced and brought to a minimum by rendering it most difficult to escape detection. In the particular class of murder now confronting us, however, the unfortunate victims appear to take the murderer to some retired spot and to place themselves in such a position that they can be slaughtered without a sound being heard; the murder, therefore, takes place without any clue to the criminal being left.

"I have to request and call upon your Board, as popular representatives, to do all in your power to dissuade the unfortunate women about Whitechapel from going into lonely places in the dark with any persons — whether acquaintances or strangers.

"I have also to point out that the purlieus about Whitechapel are most imperfectly lighted, and that darkness is an important assistant to crime.

"I can assure you, for the information of your Board, that every nerve has been strained to detect the criminal or criminals, and to render more difficult further atrocities.

"You will agree with me that it is not desirable that I should enter into particulars as to what the police are doing in the matter. It is most important for good results that our proceedings should not be published, and the very fact that you may be unaware of what the Detective Department is doing is only the stronger proof that it is doing its work with secrecy and efficiency.

"A large force of police has been drafted into the Whitechapel district to assist those already there to the full extent necessary to meet the requirements; but I have to observe that the Metropolitan police have not large reserves doing nothing and ready to meet emergencies, but every man has his duty assigned to him; and I can only strengthen the Whitechapel district by drawing men from duty in other parts of the metropolis.

"You will be aware that the whole of the police work of the metropolis has to be done as usual while this extra work is going on, and that at such a time as this extra precautions have to be taken to prevent the commission of other classes of crime being facilitated through the attention of the police being diverted to one special place and object.

"I trust that your Board will assist the police by persuading the inhabitants to give them every information in their power concerning any suspicious characters in the various dwellings, for which object 10,000 handbills, a copy of which I enclose, have been distributed.

"I have read the reported proceedings of your meeting, and I regret to see that the greatest misconceptions appear to have arisen in the public mind as to the recent action in the administration of the police. I beg you will dismiss from your minds, as utterly fallacious, the numerous anonymous statements as to recent changes stated to have been made in the police force, of a character not conducive to efficiency.

"It is stated that the Rev. Daniel Greatorex announced to you that one great cause of police inefficiency was a new system of police whereby constables were constantly changed from one district to another, keeping them ignorant of their beats.

"I have seen this statement made frequently in the newspapers lately, but it is entirely without foundation. The system at present in use has existed for the last 20 years, and constables are seldom or never drafted from their districts except for promotion or from some particular cause.

"Notwithstanding the many good reasons why constables should be changed on their beats, I have considered the reasons on the other side to be more cogent, and have felt that they should be thoroughly acquainted with the districts in which they serve.

"And with regard to the Detective Department – a department relative to which reticence is always most desirable – I may say that a short time ago I made arrangements which still further reduced the necessity for transferring officers from districts which they knew thoroughly.

"I have to call attention to the statement of one of your members that in consequence of the change in the condition of Whitechapel in recent years a thorough revision of the police arrangements is necessary, and I shall be very glad to ascertain from you what changes your Board consider advisable; and I may assure you that your proposal will receive from me every consideration.

"I am, Sir, your obedient servant,

"CHARLES WARREN.

"The Chairman, Board of Works, Whitechapel District."

The next report on the Stride inquest appears in *The Times* of Saturday, 6 October 1888, page 6:

THE EAST-END MURDERS.

Yesterday afternoon Mr. Wynne E. Baxter, Coroner for the South-Eastern Division of Middlesex, resumed his inquiry at the Vestry-hall, Cable-street, St. George's-in-the-East, respecting the death of Elizabeth Stride, who was found murdered in Berner-street, St. George's, on the early morning of

Sunday last. Superintendent T. Arnold and Detective-inspector Reid, H Division, watched the case on behalf of the Criminal Investigation Department.

Dr. Phillips was re-called and said:- After the last examination, in company with Dr. Blackwell and Dr. Brown, I went to the mortuary and examined more carefully the roof of the mouth. I could not find any injury to or absence of anything from the mouth. I have also carefully examined the two handkerchiefs, and have not found any blood on them. I believe the stains on the larger one were fruit stains. I am convinced that the deceased had not swallowed either skin or seed of a grape within many hours of her death. The abrasion which I spoke of on the right side of the neck was only apparently an abrasion, for on washing it the staining was removed and the skin was found to be uninjured. The knife that was produced on the last occasion was submitted to me by Constable 282 H. On examination I found it to be such a knife as would be used in a chandler's shop, called a slicing knife. It had blood upon it, which was similar to that of a warm-blooded being. It has been recently blunted and the edge turned by apparently rubbing on a stone. It evidently was before that a very sharp knife. Such a knife could have produced the incision and injuries to the neck of the deceased, but it was not such a weapon as I would have chosen to inflict injuries in this particular place; and if my opinion as regards the position of the body is correct, the knife in question would become an improbable instrument as having caused the incision.

The CORONER. – Could you give us any idea of the position of the victim? Witness. – I have come to the conclusion that the deceased was seized by the shoulders, placed on the ground, and that the perpetrator of the deed was on her right side when he inflicted the cut. I am of opinion that the cut was made from the left to the right side of the deceased, and therefore arises the unlikelihood of such a long knife having inflicted the wound described in the neck, taking into account the position of the incision.

The CORONER. – Was there anything in the cut that showed the incision first made was done with a pointed knife? Witness. – No.

The CORONER. – Have you formed any opinion how the right hand of the deceased was covered with blood? Witness. – No; that is a mystery. I may say I am taking it as a fact that the hand always remained in the same position in which he found it – resting across the body.

The CORONER. – How long had the deceased been dead when you arrived? Witness. – Within an hour she was alive.

The CORONER. – Would the injury take long to inflict? Witness. – Only a few seconds. It might be done in two seconds.

The CORONER. – Does the presence of the cachous in her hand show that it was done suddenly, or would it simply show a muscular grasp? Witness. –

No; I cannot say. You will remember some of the cachous were found in the gutter. I have seen several self- inflicted wounds more extensive than this one, but then they have not divided the carotid artery. You will see by that, as in the other cases, there appears to have been a knowledge where to cut the throat.

The CORONER. – Was there any other similarity between this and Chapman's case? Witness. – There is a great dissimilarity. In Chapman's case the neck was severed all round down to the vertebral column, the vertical bone being marked, and there had been an evident attempt to separate the bones.

The CORONER. – Would the murderer be likely to get bloodstained? Witness. – Not necessarily, for the commencement of the wound and the injury to the vessels would be away from him, and the stream of blood, for stream it would be, would be directed away from him, and towards the waterway already mentioned. There was no perceptible sign of an anaesthetic having been used. The absence of noise is a difficult question in this case, and under the circumstances, to account for, but it must not be taken for granted that I assumed there was no noise. If there was an absence of noise, there was nothing in this case that I can account for. She might have called out and not have been heard. As I said before, if there was a noise I cannot account for it.

The Foreman. – Was the wound caused by drawing the knife across the throat? Witness. – Undoubtedly. My reason for supposing deceased was injured when on the ground was partly on account of the absence of blood anywhere but on the left side of the body, and between that side and the wall.

The CORONER. – Was there any sign of liquor in the stomach? Witness. – There was no trace of it.

Dr. Blackwell, recalled, said: – I have little to say except to confirm Dr. Phillips's statement. I removed the cachous from the left hand, which was nearly open. The packet had lodged between the thumb and fourth finger, and had become almost hidden. That accounted for its not having been seen by several of those around. I believe the hand relaxed after the injury was inflicted, as death would arise from fainting owing to the rapid loss of blood. I wish to say that, taking into consideration the absence of any instrument it was impossible that the deceased could have committed suicide. With respect to the knife which was found, I should say I concur with Dr. Phillips in his opinion that although it might have possibly inflicted the injury it was extremely unlikely that such an instrument was used. The murderer using a sharp, round-pointed instrument would severely handicap himself, as he could only use it one way. He was informed that slaughterers always used round-pointed instruments.

The CORONER. – No one suggested anything about a slaughterer. Is it your suggestion that this was done by a slaughterer? Witness. – No, I concur with Dr. Phillips as to the postmortem appearances. There were some pressure marks on the shoulders. These were not regular bruises, and there was no abrasion of the skin.

A juryman. – Do you know how these marks were likely to have been caused? Witness. – By two hands pressing on the shoulders.

Did you see any grapes in the yard? – No, I did not.

Sven Olsson said: – I live at 36, Prince's-square, and I am clerk to the Swedish Church in that square. I saw the body of the deceased in the mortuary on Tuesday morning. I have known deceased for about 17 years.

The CORONER. – Was she a Swede? – Yes.

What was her name? – Elizabeth Gustafsdotter was her maiden name. Elizabeth Stride was her married name, and she was the wife of John Thomas Stride, a ship's carpenter. She was born on the 27th of November, 1843, at Torslander, near Gottenburg, in Sweden.

The CORONER. – Was she married in your church? Witness. – No. We register those who come to this country bringing with them a certificate and desiring to be registered.

The CORONER. – When was she registered? Witness. – Our register is dated July 10, 1866. She was registered as an unmarried woman.

The CORONER. – How do you know she was the wife of John Thomas Stride? Witness. – I suppose she gave it to the clergyman, as it is written here. In the registry I find a memorandum, undated, in the handwriting of the Rev. Mr. Palmar, in abbreviated Swedish. It means "married to an Englishman, John Thomas Stride." I do not know when this entry was made.

The CORONER. – How long has Mr. Palmar been at the church? Witness. – About a year. This registry is a new one and copied from an older book. I have seen the original entry, and it was written many years ago.

The CORONER. – Would you mind looking at the entry in the older book, and see in whose handwriting it is? Witness. – I will.

Inspector Reid. – Do you know this hymn book? Witness. – Yes.

The CORONER. – Is there any name in it? Witness. – No; I gave it to the deceased last winter.

The CORONER. – Do you know when she was married to Stride? Witness. – I think it was in 1869. She told me her husband was drowned in the Princess Alice.

The CORONER. – Have you any schools connected with the Swedish Church? Witness. – No; I do not remember hearing she ever had any children. She told me her husband went down in the Princess Alice.

The CORONER. – Have you ever seen her husband? Witness. – No; I think we gave the deceased some assistance before we knew her husband was dead.

I forget where she was living at the time, but two years ago she gave her address as Devonshire-Street, Commercial-road. She said she was doing a little work – sewing. Deceased could speak English pretty well.

The CORONER. – Do you know when deceased came to England?

Witness. – I cannot say, but I think a little before the name was registered.

William Marshall said, – I live at 64, Berner-street, Commercial-road, and am a labourer. On Sunday last I saw the body of deceased in the mortuary. I recognized it as that of a woman I saw on Saturday evening about three doors off from where I am living in Berner-street. That was about a quarter to 12. She was on the pavement opposite No. 68, and between Christian-street and Boyd-street. She was standing talking to a man. I recognize her both by her face and dress.

The CORONER. – Was she wearing a flower when you saw her? – No.

The CORONER. – Were they talking quietly? – Yes.

The CORONER. – Can you describe the man? There was no lamp near, and I did not see the face of the man she was talking to. He had on a small black coat and dark trousers. He seemed to me to be a middle-aged man.

The CORONER. – What sort of cap was he wearing? – A round cap with a small peak to it; something like what a sailor would wear.

The CORONER. – What height was he? – About 5 ft. 6 in., and he was rather stout. He was decently dressed, and I should say he worked at some light business, and had more the appearance of a clerk than anything else.

The CORONER. – Did you see whether he had any whiskers? – From what I saw of his face I do not think he had. He was not wearing gloves, and he had no stick or anything in his hand.

The CORONER. – What sort of a coat was it? – A cut-away one.

The CORONER. – You are quite sure this is the woman? – Yes, I am. I did not take much notice of them. I was standing at my door, and what attracted my attention first was her standing there some time, and he was kissing her. I heard the man say to deceased, "You would say anything but your prayers." He was mild speaking, and appeared to be an educated man. They went down the street.

The CORONER. – Would they pass the club? – They had done so.

The CORONER. – How was she dressed? – In a black jacket and black skirt.

The CORONER. – Were either of them the worse for drink? – They did not appear to be so. I went in about 12 o'clock and heard nothing more until I heard "Murder" being called in the street. It had then just gone 1 o'clock.

A Juryman. – How long were you standing at the door? – From 11.30 to 12.

The Juryman. – Did it rain then? – No, it did not rain until nearly 3 o'clock.

The Foreman. – What sort of bonnet had she on? – I believe it was a small black crape one.

Inspector Reid. – When you saw them first they were standing between your house and the club? – Yes, and they remained there for about 10 minutes. They passed me once, and I could not see the man's face, as it was turned towards the deceased. There was a lamp over No. 70.

Inspector Reid. – Were they hurrying along? – No.

Was it raining at the time? – No, it was not.

Mr. Olsson, recalled, said, – I find that the original entry of the marriage of the deceased is in the handwriting of Mr. Frost, who was the pastor for about 18 years until two years ago.

James Brown stated, – I live at 35, Fairclough-street. I saw the deceased about a quarter to 1 on Sunday morning. At that time I was going from my own house to get some supper from a chandler's shop at the corner of Berner-street and Fairclough-street. As I was going across the road I saw a man and woman standing by the Board School in Fairclough-street. They were standing against the wall. As I passed them I heard the woman say, "No, not to-night, some other night." That made me turn round, and I looked at them. I am certain the woman was the deceased. I did not notice any flowers in her dress. The man had his arm up against the wall, and the woman had her back to the wall facing him. I noticed the man had a long coat on, which came very nearly down to his heels. I believe it was an overcoat. I could not say what kind of cap he had on. The place where they were standing was rather dark. I saw nothing light in colour about either of them. I then went on and went indoors. I had nearly finished my supper when I heard screams of "Police" and "Murder." That was about a quarter of an hour after I got in. I do not think it was raining at the time. I should say the man was about 5 ft. 7 in. in height. He appeared to be stoutish built. Both the man and woman appeared to be sober. I did not notice any foreign accent about the woman's voice. When I heard screams of "Police" and "Murder" I opened the window, but could not see any one and the screams ceased. The cries were those of moving persons, and appeared to be going in the direction of Grove-street. Shortly afterwards I saw a policeman standing at the corner of Christian-street. I heard a man opposite call out to the constable that he was wanted. I then saw the policeman run along to Berner-street.

By the CORONER. – I am almost certain it was the deceased.

Police-constable William Smith, 452 H, said that on Saturday night his beat was past Berner-street. It went from the corner of Jower's-walk, Commercial-road, as far as Christian-street, down Christian-street and Fairclough-street as far as Grove-street, then back along Fairclough-street as far as Backchurch-lane, up there as far as the Commercial-road, taking all the interior streets, including Berner-street, and Batley [*sic*]-street. The witness continued, – It takes me from 25 minutes to half an hour to go round my beat. I was last in Berner-street about half-past 12 or 12.35. At 1 o'clock I went to Berner-street in my ordinary round. I saw a crowd of people outside the gates of No. 40. I did not hear any cries of "Police." When I got there I saw Constables 12 H. R and 252 H. I then saw the deceased, and, on looking at her, found she was dead. I then went to the station for the ambulance. Dr. Blackwell's assistant came just as I was going away.

The CORONER. – Did you go up Berner-street into Commercial-road? – No; I turned up Fairclough-street.

Did you see any one? – No, sir.

When you were in Berner-street the previous time did you see any one? – Yes, a man and a woman.

Was the latter anything like the deceased? – Yes, I saw her face. I have seen the deceased in the mortuary, and I feel certain it is the same person.

Was she on the pavement? – Yes, a few yards up Berner-street on the opposite side to where she was found.

Did you see the man who was talking to her? – Yes; I noticed he had a newspaper parcel in his hand. It was about 18 in. in length and 6 in. or 8 in. in width. He was about 5 ft. 7 in. as near as I could say. He had on a hard felt deerstalker hat of dark colour and dark clothes.

What kind of a coat was it? – An overcoat. He wore dark trousers.

Did you overhear any conversation? – No.

Did he seem sober? – Yes. I did not see much of the face of the man except that he had no whiskers.

Can you form any idea as to his age? – About 28 years.

Can you give any idea as to what he was? – No, sir, I cannot. He was of respectable appearance. I noticed the woman had a flower in her jacket.

When you saw them talking, which way did you go? – Straight up Berner-street into the Commercial-road. In the centre of Berner-street were some courts which led into Backchurch-lane.

When did it last rain before 1 o'clock? – To the best of my recollection, it rained very little after 11 o'clock.

The Foreman. – Was the man or the woman acting in a suspicious manner? – No.

Do you see many prostitutes or people hanging about in Berner-street? – No, very few.

Inspector Reid. – Did you see these people more than once? – No. When I saw deceased lying on the ground I recognized her at once and made a report of what I had seen.

The witness Kidney was recalled, and the CORONER said, – Have you ever seen that hymn-book before? – Yes; I recognize it as one belonging to the deceased. It used to be in my place. I found it in Mrs. Smith's room, next to my own. Mrs. Smith said deceased gave it to her to take care of when she left on Tuesday.

Inspector Reid. – When you and deceased lived together I believe you had a padlock on the door? – Yes; there was only one key, which I had, but she got in and out somehow. The hymn-book was taken from the room on Wednesday week, the day after she went away. That was done during my absence.

The CORONER. – What makes you think there was anything the matter with the roof of her mouth? – She told me she was kicked when the Princess Alice went down.

Philip Krantz, who claimed to affirm, said, – I live at 40, Berner-street, and am the editor of a Hebrew paper called the *Workers' Friend*. I work in the room at the back of the printing office on the ground floor, and the entrance is from the yard. I was in the back room from 9 o'clock on Saturday night until one of the members of the club came and told me there was a woman lying in the yard.

The CORONER. – Had you heard any cry or scream? – None.

Was your window or door open? – No.

Is it a wooden structure? – No; brick.

Supposing a woman had screamed, would you have heard it? – I do not know. They were singing upstairs.

When you went out into the yard was there any one round deceased? – Yes, members of the club were near the woman, but there was no one there that I did not know.

Were you on the look out to see if there was any stranger there? – No. I went out into the street to look for a policeman.

Do you think it possible for any one to escape without being noticed after you arrived there? – I do not think it was, but he might have done so before.

Did you see the face of deceased? – No; my name and address was taken, and I was examined and searched by the police.

Constable 12 HR said, – At half-past 5 on Sunday morning I washed all traces of blood away. That was after the doctors had left. There were no traces of blood on the wall.

Detective-inspector Edmund Reid, H Division stated, – I received a telegram at 1.25 a.m. on Sunday morning at the Commercial-street police office. I at once proceeded to 40, Berner-street. I saw there Chief Inspector West, Inspector Pinhorn, several sergeants and constables, Drs. Phillips and Blackwell, a number of residents in the yard, and club members, with persons who had come into the yard and had been shut in by the police. At that time Dr. Phillips, with Dr. Blackwell, was examining the throat of the deceased woman. Superintendent Arnold followed in, as well as several other officers.

When it was found a murder had been committed a thorough search was made of the yard, houses, and buildings, but no trace could be found of any person likely to have committed the deed. As soon as the search was over the whole of the persons who had come into the yard and the members of the club were interrogated, their names and addresses taken, their pockets searched, and their clothes and hands examined. There were 28 of them. Each person was dealt with separately. They properly accounted for themselves, and were then allowed to leave. The houses were then visited a second time and the names of the people therein taken, and they were also examined and their rooms searched. The door of a loft was found locked on the inside, and it was forced. The loft was searched, but no trace of the murderer could be found. A description was taken of the body and circulated round the surrounding stations by wire. Inquiries were made in the street at the different houses, and no person could be found who heard any disturbance during the night. I minutely examined the wall near where the body was found, but could find no spots of blood. About 4.30 the body was removed to the mortuary. I then informed you (the coroner) verbally at your residence, and then returned to the yard and made another examination. It being daylight, I searched the walls thoroughly, but could find no marks of any person having scaled them. I then proceeded to the mortuary and took a correct description of the body and clothing, which is as follows:- I guessed her age as 42, length 5 ft. 2 in., complexion pale, hair dark brown and curly. I raised an eyelid and found that her eyes were light grey; I parted her lips and found that she had lost her upper teeth in front. She had an old black skirt, and an old black jacket trimmed with fur. Fastened on the right side was a small bunch of flowers, consisting of maidenhair fern and a red rose. She had two light serge petticoats, white stockings, white chemise with insertion in front, side-spring boots, and black crape bonnet. In her jacket pocket I found two pockethandkerchiefs, a thimble, and a piece of wool on a card. That description was then circulated. Since then the police engaged in the enquiry had made house to house inquiry in the immediate neighbourhood, with the result that we have been able to produce the witnesses which have appeared before you. The inquiry is still going on. Every endeavour is being made to arrest the assassin, but up to the present without success.

At this stage the inquiry was adjourned to Tuesday week.

We are requested to state that Sir Charles Warren has been making inquiries as to the practicability of employing trained bloodhounds for use in special cases in the streets of London; and having ascertained that dogs can be procured that have been accustomed to work in a town, he is making immediate arrangements for their use in London.

The police authorities of Whitehall have had reproduced in facsimile and published on the walls of London the letter and post-card sent to the Central News agency. The language of the card and letter is of a brutal character, and is full of Americanisms. The handwriting, which is clear and plain, and disguised in part, is that of a person accustomed to write a round hand like that employed by clerks in offices. The exact colour of the ink and the smears of blood are reproduced in the placard, and information is asked in identification of the handwriting. The post-card bears a tolerably clear imprint of a bloody thumb or finger mark.

The Times of Thursday, 18 October 1888, page 7, printed the thanks of Sir Charles Warren to the people of the East End for the way they had assisted the enquiries of the Metropolitan Police:

THE EAST-END MURDERS.

We are requested to publish the following —

Sir Charles Warren wishes to say that the marked desire evinced by the inhabitants of the Whitechapel district to aid the police in the pursuit of the author of the recent crimes has enabled him to direct that, subject to the consent of the occupiers, a thorough house-to-house search should be made within a defined area. With few exceptions the inhabitants of all classes and creeds have freely fallen in with the proposal, and have materially assisted the officers engaged in carrying it out.

Sir Charles Warren feels that some acknowledgement is due on all sides for the cordial cooperation of the inhabitants, and he is much gratified that the police officers have carried out so delicate a duty with the marked good will of all those with whom they have come in contact.

Sir Charles Warren takes this opportunity of acknowledging the receipt of an immense volume of correspondence of a semi-private character on the subject of the Whitechapel murders, which he has been quite unable to respond to in a great number of instances; and he trusts that the writers will accept this acknowledgement in lieu of individual replies. They may be assured that their letters have received every consideration.

The Times of Wednesday, 24 October 1888, page 3, gave a report on the final day of the inquest into the death of Elizabeth Stride:

THE EAST-END MURDERS.

Yesterday afternoon Mr. Wynne E. Baxter, Coroner for the South-Eastern Division of Middlesex, resumed his adjourned inquiry at the Vestry-hall, Cable-street, St. George's-in-the-East, respecting the death of Elizabeth

Stride, who was found murdered in Berner-street, St. George's on the 30th ult.

Detective-inspector Reid, H Division, watched on behalf of the Criminal Investigation Department.

Detective-Inspector Edmund Reid, recalled, said, – I have examined the books of the Poplar and Stepney Sick Asylum, and find therein the entry of the death of John Thomas William Stride, a carpenter, of Poplar. His death took place on the 24th day of October, 1884. Witness then said that he had found Mrs. Watts, who would give evidence.

Constable Walter Stride stated that he recognized the deceased by the photograph as the person who married his uncle, John Thomas Stride, in 1872 or 1873. His uncle was a carpenter, and the last time witness saw him he was living in the East India Dock-road, Poplar.

Elizabeth Stokes, 5, Charles-street, Tottenham said, – My husband's name is Joseph Stokes, and he is a brickmaker. My first husband's name was Watts, a wine merchant of Bath. Mrs. Mary Malcolm, of 15, Eagle-street, Red Lion-square, Holborn, is my sister. I have received an anonymous letter from Shepton Mallet, saying my first husband is alive. I want to clear my character. My sister I have not seen for years. She has given me a dreadful character. Her evidence is all false. I have five brothers and sisters.

A juryman. – Perhaps she refers to another sister.

Inspector Reid. – She identified the deceased person as her sister, and said she had a crippled foot. This witness has a crippled foot.

Witness. – This has put me to a dreadful trouble, and trial. I have only a poor crippled husband, who is now outside. It is a shame my sister should say what she has said about me, and that the innocent should suffer for the guilty.

The CORONER. – Is Mrs. Malcolm here?

Inspector Reid. – No, Sir.

The CORONER, in summing up, said the jury would probably agree with him that it would be unreasonable to adjourn this inquiry again on the chance of something further being ascertained to elucidate the mysterious case on which they had devoted so much time. The first difficulty which presented itself was the identification of the deceased. That was not an unimportant matter. Their trouble was principally occasioned by Mrs. Malcolm, who after some hesitation, and after having had two further opportunities of viewing again the body, positively swore that the deceased was her sister – Mrs. Elizabeth Watts, of Bath. It had since been clearly proved that she was mistaken, notwithstanding the visions which were simultaneously vouchsafed at the hour of the death to her and her husband. If her evidence was correct, there were points of resemblance between the deceased and Elizabeth Watts which almost reminded one of the *Comedy of Errors*. Both had been courted by policemen; they both bore the same Christian name, and were of the same age; both lived with sailors; both at one time kept coffee-houses at Poplar; both were nick-named "Long Liz;" both were said to have had children in charge of their husbands' friends; both were given to drink; both lived in East-end common lodging-houses; both had been charged at the Thames police-court; both had escaped punishment on the ground that they were subject to epileptic fits, although the friends of both were certain that this was a fraud; both had lost their front teeth, and both had been leading very questionable lives. Whatever might be the true explanation of this marvellous similarity, it appeared to be pretty satisfactorily proved that the deceased was Elizabeth Stride, and that about the year 1869 she was married to a carpenter named John Thomas Stride. Unlike the other victims in the series of crimes in this neighbourhood – a district teeming with representatives of all nations – she was not an Englishwoman. She was born in Sweden in the year 1843, but, having resided in this country for upwards of 22 years, she could speak English fluently and without much foreign accent. At one time the deceased and her husband kept a coffee-house in Poplar. At another time she was staying in Devonshire-street, Commercial-road, supporting herself, it was said, by sewing and charing. On and off for the last six years she lived in a common lodging-house in the notorious lane called Flower and Dean-street. She was there only known by the nick-name of "Long Liz," and often told a tale, which might have been apocryphal, of her husband and children having gone down with the Princess Alice. The deputy of the lodging-house stated that while with her she was a quiet and sober woman, although she used at times to stay out late at night – an offence very venial, he suspected, among those who frequented the establishment. For the last two years the deceased had been living at a common lodging-house in Dorset-street, Spitalfields, with Michael Kidney, a waterside labourer belonging to the Army Reserve. But at intervals during that period, amounting altogether to about five months, she left him without any apparent reason, except a desire to be free from the restraint even of that connexion, and to obtain greater opportunity of indulging her drinking habits. She was last seen alive by Kidney in Com-mercial-street on the evening of Tuesday, September 25. She was sober, but never returned home that night. She alleged that she had some words with her paramour, but this he denied. The next day she called during his absence, and took away some things, but, with this exception, they did not know what became of her until the following Thursday, when she made her appearance at her old quarters in Flower and Dean-street. Here she remained until Saturday, September 29. On that day she cleaned the deputy's rooms, and received a small remuneration for her trouble. Between 6 and 7 o'clock on that evening she was in the kitchen wearing the jacket, bonnet, and striped silk neckerchief which were afterwards found on her. She had at least 6d. in her possession, which was possibly spent during the evening. Before leaving she gave a piece of velvet to a friend to take care of until her return, but she said neither where she was going nor when she would return. She had not paid for her lodgings, although she was in a position to do so. They knew nothing of her movements during the next four or five hours at least – possibly not till the finding of her lifeless body. But three witnesses spoke to having seen a woman that they identified as the deceased with more or less certainty, and at times within an hour and a-quarter of the period when, and at places within 100 yards of the spot where she was ultimately found. William Marshall, who lived at 64, Berner-street, was standing at his doorway from half-past 11 till midnight. About a quarter to 12 o'clock he saw the deceased talking to a man between Fairclough-street and Boyd-street. There was every demonstration of affection by the man during the ten minutes they stood together, and when last seen, strolling down the road towards Ellen-street, his arms were round her neck. At 12.30 p.m. [*sic* a.m.] the constable on the beat (William Smith) saw the deceased in Berner-street standing on the pavement a few yards from Commercial-street, [*sic*] and he observed she was wearing a flower in her dress. A quarter of an hour afterwards James Brown, of Fairclough-street, passed the deceased close to the Board school. A man was at her side leaning against the wall, and the deceased was heard to say, "Not to-night, but some other night." Now, if this evidence was to be relied on, it would appear that the deceased was in the company of a man for upwards of an hour immediately before her death, and that within a quarter of an hour of her being found a corpse she was refusing her companion something in the immediate neighbourhood of where she met her death. But was this the deceased? And even if it were, was it one and the same man who was seen in her company on three different occasions? With regard to the identity of the woman, Marshall had the opportunity of watching her for ten minutes while standing talking in the street at a short distance from him, and she afterwards passed close to him. The constable feels certain that the woman he observed was the deceased, and when he afterwards was called to the scene of the crime he at once recognized her and made a statement; while Brown was almost certain that the deceased was the woman to whom his attention was attracted. It might be thought that the frequency of the occurrence of men and women being seen together under similar circumstances might have led to mistaken identity; but the police stated, and several of the witnesses corroborated the statement, that although many couples are to be seen at night in the Commercial-road, it was exceptional to meet them in Berner-street. With regard to the man seen, there were many points of similarity, but some of dissimilarity, in the descriptions of the three witnesses; but these discrepancies did not conclusively prove that there was more than one man in the company of the deceased, for every day's experience showed how facts were differently observed and differently described by honest and intelligent witnesses. Brown, who saw least in consequence of the darkness of the spot at which the two were standing, agreed with Smith that his clothes were dark and that his height was about 5 ft. 7 in., but he appeared to him to be wearing an overcoat nearly down to his heels; while the description of Marshall accorded with that of Smith in every respect but two. They agreed that he was respectably dressed in a black cut away coat and dark trousers, and that he was of middle age and without whiskers. On the other hand, they differed with regard to what he was wearing on his head. Smith stated he wore a hard felt deer stalker of dark colour; Marshall that he was wearing a round cap with a small peak, like a sailor's. They also differed as to whether he had anything in his hand. Marshall stated that he observed nothing. Smith was very precise, and stated that he was carrying a parcel, done up in a newspaper, about 18 in. in length and 6 in. to 8in. in width. These differences suggested either that the woman was, during the evening, in the company of more than one man – a not very improbable supposition – or that the witness had been mistaken in detail. If they were correct in assuming that the man seen in the company of deceased by the three was one and the same person it followed that he must have spent much time and trouble to induce her to place herself in his diabolical clutches. They last saw her alive at the corner of Fairclough-street and Berner-street, saying "Not to-night, but some other night." Within a quarter of an hour her lifeless body was found at a spot only a few yards from where she was last seen alive. It was late, and there were few people about, but the place to which the two repaired could not have been selected on account of its being quiet or unfrequented. It had only the merit of darkness. It was the passage-way leading into a court in which several families resided. Adjoining the passage and court there was a club of Socialists, who, having finished their debate, were singing and making merry. The deceased and her companion must have seen the lights of the clubroom and the kitchen, and of the printing office. They must have heard the music and dancing, for the windows were open. There were persons in the yard but a short time previous to their arrival. At 40 minutes past 12, one of the members of the club, named Morris Eagle, passed the spot where the deceased drew her last breath, passing through the gateway to the back door, which opened into the yard. At 1 o'clock the body was found by the manager of the club. He had been out all day, and returned at the time. He was in a two-wheeled barrow drawn by a pony, and as he entered the gateway his pony shied at some object on his right. There was no lamp in the yard, and having just come out of the street it was too dark to see what the object was and he passed on further down the yard. He returned on foot, and on searching found the body of deceased with her throat cut. If he had not actually disturbed the wretch in the very act, at least he must have been close on his heels; possibly the man was alarmed by the sound of the approaching cart, for the death had only just taken place. He did not inspect the body himself with any care, but blood was flowing from the throat, even when Spooner reached the spot some few minutes afterwards, and although the bleeding had stopped when Dr. Blackwell's assistant arrived, the whole of her body and the limbs, except her hands, were warm, and even at 10 minutes past 1 a.m. Dr. Blackwell found her face slightly warm, and her chest and legs quite warm. In this case, as in other similar cases which had occurred in this neighbourhood, no call for assistance was noticed. Although there might have been some noise in the club, it seemed very unlikely that any cry could have been raised without its being heard by some one of those near. The editor of a Socialist paper was quietly at work in a shed down the yard, which was used as a printing office. There were several families in the cottages in the court only a few yards distant, and there were 20 persons in the different rooms of the club. But if there was no cry, how did the deceased meet with her death? The appearance of the injury to her throat was not in itself inconsistent with that of a self-inflicted wound. Both Dr. Phillips and Dr. Blackwell have seen self-inflicted wounds more extensive and severe, but those have not usually involved the carotid artery. Had some sharp instrument been found near the right hand of the deceased this case might have had very much the appearance of a determined suicide. But no such instrument was found, and its absence made suicide an impossibility. The death was, therefore, one by homicide, and it seemed impossible to imagine circumstances which would fit in with the known facts of the case, and which would reduce the crime to manslaughter. There were no signs of any struggle; the clothes were neither torn nor disturbed. It was true that there were marks over both shoulders, produced by pressure of two hands, but the position of the body suggested either that she was willingly placed or placed herself where she was found. Only the soles of her boots were visible. She was still holding in her left hand a packet of cachous, and there was a bunch of flowers still pinned to her dress front. If she had been forcibly placed on the ground, as Dr. Phillips opines, it was difficult to understand how she failed to attract attention, as it was clear from the appearance of the blood on the ground that the throat was not cut until after she was actually on her back. There were no marks of gagging, no bruises on the face, and no trace of any anaesthetic or narcotic in the stomach; while the presence of the cachous in her hand showed that she did not make use of it in self-defence. Possibly the pressure marks may have had a less tragical origin, as Dr. Blackwell says it was difficult to say how recently they were produced. There was one particular which was not easy to explain. When seen by Dr. Blackwell her right hand was lying on the chest, smeared inside and out with blood. Dr. Phillips was unable to make any suggestion how the hand became soiled. There was no injury to the hand, such as they would expect if it had been raised in self-defence while her throat was being cut. Was it done intentionally by her assassin, or accidentally by those who were early on the spot? The evidence afforded no clue. Unfortunately the murderer had disappeared without leaving the slightest trace. Even the cachous were wrapped up in unmarked paper, so that there was nothing to show where they were bought. The cut in the throat might have been effected in such a manner that bloodstains on the hands and clothes of the operator were avoided, while the domestic history of the deed suggested the strong probability that her destroyer was a stranger to her. There was no one among her associates to whom any suspicion had attached. They had not heard that she had had a quarrel with any one – unless they magnified the fact that she had recently left the man with whom she generally cohabited; but this diversion was of so frequent an occurrence that neither a breach of the peace ensued, nor, so far as they knew, even hard words. There was therefore in the evidence no clue to the murderer and no suggested motive for the murder. The deceased was not in possession of any valuables. She was only known to have had a few pence in her pocket at the beginning of the evening. Those who knew her best were unaware of any one likely to injure her. She never accused any one of having threatened her. She never expressed any fear of anyone, and, although she had outbursts of drunkenness, she was generally a quiet woman. The ordinary motives of murder – revenge, jealousy, theft, and passion – appeared, therefore, to be absent from this case; while it was clear from the accounts of all who saw her that night, as well as from the post-mortem examination, that she was not otherwise than sober at the time of her death. In the absence of motive, the age and class of woman selected as victim, and the place and time of the crime, there was a similarity between this case and those mysteries which had recently occurred in that neighbour-hood. There had been no skilful mutilation as in the cases of Nichols and Chapman, and no unskilful injuries as in the case in Mitre-square – possibly the work of an imitator; but there had been the same skill exhibited in the way in which the victim had been entrapped, and the injuries inflicted, so as to cause instant death and prevent blood from soiling the operator, and the same daring defiance of immediate detection, which, unfortunately for the peace of the inhabitants and trade of the neighbourhood, had hitherto been only too successful. He himself was sorry that the time and attention which the jury had given to the case had not produced a result that would be a perceptible relief to the metropolis – the detection of the criminal; but he was sure that all had used their utmost effort to accomplish this object, and while he desired to thank the gentlemen of the jury for their kind assistance, he was bound to acknowledge the great attention which Inspector Reid and the police had given to the case. He left it to the jury to say, how, when, and by what means the deceased came by her death.

The jury, after a short deliberation, returned a verdict of "Wilful murder against some person or persons unknown."

CHAPTER 9

30 September 1888 – Murder of Catherine Eddowes

The murders committed in the early hours of Saturday, 30 September 1888 are best remembered, and usually referred to, as "The Double Event", an appellation directly originating from the "saucy Jacky" postcard of 1 October 1888, in which the two murders are referred to in this way. The murder of Catherine Eddowes was committed in Mitre Square, Aldgate, in the City of London and therefore came under the jurisdiction of the City of London Police, not the Metropolitan Police (who were investigating the other murders). However, any objective study should examine each crime as a separate event, whilst still bearing the other in mind.

The main report[1] referring to this murder is dated 27 October 1888, from Inspector James McWilliam, head of the Detective Department, City of London Police. The cover and report are as follows:

[Stamped: – HOME OFFICE 29 OCT.88 DEPT. No. 1] No. A49301C/8b.
DATE 29 Octr. 88   Commr. of the <u>City</u> Police
REFERENCES, &c.   re <u>Mitre Square Murder</u>
                 Fds a copy of Police Report containing particulars of
above.

Pre<u>ss</u>ing

[Stamped: – HOME OFFICE 29 OCT.88 DEPt.No.]   A493018b
Copy of REPORT
Detective   CITY OF LONDON POLICE.
Department   October 27th 1888.

<u>Re East End Murders.</u>

I beg to report with reference to the recent murders in Whitechapel that, acting upon stringent orders issued by the Commissioner with a view to preventing if possible a repetition of the murders which had previously been committed in Whitechapel and to keep close observation upon all Prostitutes frequenting public-houses and walking the streets, extra men in plain clothes have been employed by this department since August last to patrol the Eastern portion of the City. On the 30th September at 1.45 a.m. a woman since identified as Catherine Eddowes was found with her throat cut & disembowelled in Mitre Square, Aldgate about 300 yards from the City boundary. The Constable who found the body immediately sent for a Surgeon and also to the Police Station at Bishopsgate Street and Inspector Collard was on the spot in a few minutes. Detective Constables Halse, Marriott, & Outram who had been searching the passages of houses in the immediate neighbourhood of the spot where the murder was committed (& where the doors are left open all night) on hearing of the murder at 1.55 a.m. at once started off in various directions to look for suspected persons. The Officer Halse went in the direction of Whitechapel and passed through Goulstone [sic] Street – where part of the deceased's apron was subsequently found at 2.20 a.m.; on returning to the Square he heard that part of an apron stained with blood had been found in Goulstone Street, he then went with D.S. Lawley & D.C. Hunt to Leman Street Station and from thence to Goulstone Street where, the spot at which the apron was found was pointed out to him. On the wall above it was written in chalk "The Jewes are the men that will not be blamed for nothing." Halse remained by the writing and Lawley and Hunt returned to Mitre Square.

In the meantime I had been informed of the murder and arrived at the Detective Office at 3.45 a.m., after ascertaining from S.S. Izzard what steps he had taken in consequence of it; I wired to Scotland Yard informing the Metropolitan Police of the murder and went with D.S. Downes to Bishops-gate Station & from thence to Mitre Square. I there found Major Smith, Superintendent Foster, Inspector Collard & several Detective Officers. Lawley and Hunt informed me of the finding of the apron & the writing on the wall, the latter of which I ordered to be photographed and directed the Officers to return at once & search the "Model" dwellings & lodging houses in the neighbourhood. I then went to the Mortuary in Golden Lane, where the body had been taken by direction of Dr. Gordon-Brown and saw the piece of apron – which was found in Goulstone Street – compared with a piece the deceased was wearing & it exactly corresponded. I then returned to the Detective Office and had telegraphed to the Divisions and Metropolitan Police a description of the murdered woman and her clothing. Additional officers had then arrived and they were sent out in various directions to make enquiry. On Monday the 1st October on the recommendation of the Commissioner, the Lord Mayor authorised a reward of £500 to be offered. Printed bills were at once ordered and circulated, in response to which a great many communications have been received & are still coming in. Enquiry was also made with a view to get the deceased identified and on the 3rd. Inst. it was ascertained that her name was Catherine Eddowes & that she had been living with a man named Kelly at Cooney's lodging house Flower and Dean Street, Spitalfields. She had lived with Kelly for seven or eight years, prior to which she had lived with a man named Thomas Conway, a pensioner for about twenty years & had three children by him – two sons & a daughter, but Conway was eventually compelled to leave her on account of her drunken and immoral habits. Considerable difficulty was experienced in finding Conway in consequence of his having enlisted in the name of Thomas Quinn, he was found however, also the three children & two sisters of the deceased.

On Thursday the 4th Inst. an Inquest was held at the mortuary by F.H. Langham Esq., "Coroner" & a Jury and adjourned till the 11th Instant, when a Verdict of "Wilful murder against some person unknown" was returned. Every effort has been made to trace the murderer, but up to the present without success. Enquiry has been made respecting persons in almost every class of society & I have sent officers to all the Lunatic Asylums in London to make Enquiry respecting persons recently admitted or discharged, many persons being of opinion that these crimes are of too revolting a character to have been committed by a sane person.

The Enquiry is still being actively followed up, but the Police are at a great disadvantage in this case in consequence of the want of identity, no one having seen the deceased from the time she was discharged from Bishopsgate Station until her body was found at 1.45 a.m., except three gentlemen who were leaving the Imperial Club in Duke Street at 1.35 a.m. and who state that to the best of their belief they saw her with a man in Church Passage at that time, but took no particular notice of them. One of the gentlemen Mr. Lewend [sic] of 79 Fenchurch Street who was nearest to the man & woman & saw most of them, says he does not think he should know the man again and he did not see the woman's face. No other person can be found who saw either of them. The murderer would seem to have been only a few minutes in the City, having just come from Berners [sic] Street & returned at once to Whitechapel via Goulstone Street where the apron was found.

On the 16th Inst. Mr. Lusk, No. 1 Alderney Road, Mile End, Chairman of the East End Vigilance Committee received by post a packet containing half of a kidney and a letter – photograph copy of which I attach hereto. He did not attach any importance to it at the time, but on mentioning the matter to other members of the Committee on the 18th Inst., they advised him to shew the piece of kidney to a medical man. He accordingly took it to Mr. Reed, 56 Mile End Road, & subsequently to Dr. Openshaw of the London Hospital, both of whom expressed the opinion that it was a portion of the kidney of a human being. Mr. Lusk then took the kidney & letter to Leman Street Station. The kidney was forwarded to this office & the letter to Scotland Yard,

Chief Inspector Swanson having lent me the letter on the 20th. Inst. I had it photographed & returned it to him on the 24th. The kidney has been examined by Dr. Gordon-Brown who is of opinion that it is human. Every effort is being made to trace the sender, but it is not desirable that publicity should be given to the Doctor's opinion, or the steps that are being taken in consequence. It might turn out after all, to be the act of a Medical Student who would have no difficulty in obtaining the organ in question.

This department is co-operating with the Metropolitan Police in the matter, and Chief Inspector Swanson and I meet daily and confer on the subject.

(Sgd) Jas. McWilliam
Inspector.

This report is followed by a Home Office minute sheet[2] which makes very interesting reading, and indicates that the government officials felt that they were not being told the full facts:

A49301/8b

Mr. Murdoch

This report tells very little.

i The City Police are wholly at fault as regards the detection of the murderer.

ii The word on the wall was "Jewes", not "Juwes". [*Here there is a marginal note:-* Not so I believe GL.] This is important : unless it [*is*] a mere clerical error.

iii The $\frac{1}{2}$ kidney sent to Mr Lusk is <u>human</u>.

The printed report of the Inquest contains much more information than this. They evidently want to tell us nothing. [*Here there is a marginal note –* "I don't think so GL."]

?Shall we ask them

A. Did the writing on the wall resemble "Jack the Ripper's" : or the enclosed?

B. Could the $\frac{1}{2}$ kidney possibly be part of the victim's kidney?

WTB –   Mr Lushington Have you any private information from
30.10.88   the Met. Police on the above points or a facsimile of Jack
the Ripper's letters.   CM Oct 30.

It is I think unadvisable to ask these questions officially, but when Mr. Matthews comes to town I would advise that he should ask Sir J. Fraser to come to the H.O. He will then have full particulars.   GL 30 Oct 1888

[*Noted marginally –* "H.M. 31Oct./88."]

This is followed by Sir James Fraser's, the City of London Police Commissioner's, covering letter[3], forwarding the McWilliam report, which is dated 29 October 1888, to the Under-Secretary of State:

[Stamped – RECD. AFTER 3.P.M.] –
A49301C/8b
[Stamped: – HOME OFFICE 29 OCT.88 DEPt.No.]   26 Old Jewry EC
                                              29th October 1888.

Sir,
    I have to acknowledge your letter of the 25th Instant (A.49301C/8d.) and in reply to the enquiries contained therein, I beg to forward for the information of the Secretary of State, the copy of a Report furnished to me by the Inspector of the Detective Department at this Office, containing particulars of the recent murder of a woman in Mitre Square, within the City, and of the steps since taken by the City Police in connection therewith.

                            I am,
                              Sir
                            Your Obedient Servant
                            James Fraser

    The Under Secretary of State
         &c. &c. &c.
      Home Office
            Whitehall.

The report that follows this is a rather lengthy one[4] dated 6 November 1888 from the Metropolitan Police Commissioner, Sir Charles Warren, concerning the Mitre Square murder and an explanation why he thought it right to have the writing on the wall wiped out. It was received at the Home Office the same date and is minuted "*Confidential and Pressing*":

[Stamp: – HOME OFFICE 6 NOV.88. RECd. DEPt.] No. A49301C/8c
DATE 6 Nov 88   The Commr. of Police
REFERENCES &c.   Whitechapel Murders.   Mitre Square Murder
Report on Mitre Square murder also full explanation as to why he thought it right to have the writing on the wall wiped out –
                        MINUTES.
                Confidential & Pressing
                The S. of S. Nov6/88.

GL
6 Nov 1888

A49301C/8c

93305/28 [Stamped: – HOME OFFICE 6 NOV.88 RECd. DEPt]
<u>Confidential</u>

4 Whitehall Place,
SW,
6th November, 1888.

Sir,

In reply to your letter of the 5th instant, I enclose a report of the circumstances of the Mitre Square Murder so far as they have come under the notice of the Metropolitan Police, and I now give an account regarding the erasing the writing on the wall in Goulston Street which I have already partially explained to Mr. Matthews verbally. –

On the 30th September on hearing of the Berners [*sic*] Street murder after visiting Commercial Street Station I arrived at Leman Street Station shortly before 5 a.m. and ascertained from Superintendent Arnold all that was known there relative to the two murders.

The most pressing question at that moment was some writing on the wall in Goulston Street evidently written with the intention of inflaming the public mind against the Jews, [*marginal note* – "<u>2 Reports enclosed</u>"] and which Mr. Arnold with a view to prevent serious disorder proposed to obliterate, and had sent down an Inspector with a sponge for that purpose telling him to await his arrival. –

I considered it desirable that I should decide this matter myself, as it was one involving so great a responsibility whether any action was taken or not. I accordingly went down to Goulston Street at once before going to the scene of the murder : it was just getting light, the public would be in the streets in a few minutes, in a neighbourhood very much crowded on Sunday mornings by Jewish vendors and Christian purchasers from all parts of London. –

There were several Police around the spot when I arrived, both Metropolitan and City. –

The writing was on the jamb of the open archway or doorway visible to anybody in the street and could not be covered up without danger of the covering being torn off at once. –

A discussion took place whether the writing could be left covered up or otherwise or whether any portion of it could be left for an hour until it could be photographed, but after taking into consideration the excited state of the population in London generally at the time the strong feeling which had been excited against the Jews, and the fact that in a short time there would be a large concourse of the people in the streets and having before me the Report that if it was left there the house was likely to be wrecked (in which from my own observation I entirely concurred) I considered it desirable to obliterate the writing at once, having taken a copy of which I enclose a duplicate.

After having been to the scene of the murder, I went on to the City Police Office and informed the Chief Superintendent of the reason why the writing had been obliterated.

I may mention that so great was the feeling with regard to the Jews that on the 13th ulto. the Acting Chief Rabbi wrote to me on the subject of the spelling of the word "Juewes" on account of a newspaper asserting that this was a Jewish spelling in the Yiddish dialect. He added, "in the present state of excitement it is dangerous to the safety of the poor Jews in the East to allow such an assertion to remain uncontradicted. My community keenly appreciates your ['kindness' – *deleted*] humane and vigilant actions during this critical time."

It may be realised therefore if the safety of the Jews in Whitechapel could be considered to be jeopardised 13 days after the murder by the question of the spelling of the word Jews, what might have happened to the Jews in that quarter had that writing been left intact.

I do not hesitate myself to say that if that writing had been left there would have been an onslaught upon the Jews, property would have been wrecked, and lives would probably have been lost, and I was much gratified with the promptitude with which Superintendent Arnold was prepared to act in the matter if I had not been there.

I have no doubt myself whatever that one of the principal objects of the Reward offered by Mr. Montagu was to shew to the world that the Jews were desirous of having the Hanbury Street murder cleared up, and thus to direct from them the very strong feeling which was then growing up.

I am,

Sir,

Your most obedient Servant,

C. Warren

This report is followed by the copy of the message[5] taken by the Metropolitan Police and is as follows:

The Juwes are
The men that
Will not
be Blamed
for nothing

This is followed by another lengthy report[6], dated 6 November 1888, by Chief Inspector Donald S. Swanson:

A49301C/8c
[Stamped: – HOME OFFICE 6 NOV. 88 RECd. DEPt.]
METROPOLITAN POLICE.
Criminal Investigation Department,
Scotland Yard,
6th day of November 1888

SUBJECT Facts known to
Met:Police. respecting the
Murder in Mitresquare &
writing on wall.

I beg to report that the facts concerning the murder in Mitre Square which came to the knowledge of the Metropolitan Police are as follows:-

1.45 a.m. 30th. Septr. Police Constable Watkins of the City Police discovered in Mitre Square the body of a woman, with her face mutilated almost beyond identity, portion of the nose being cut off, the lobe of the right ear nearly severed, the face cut, the throat cut, and disembowelled. The P.C. called to his assistance Mr. Morris, a night watchman and pensioner from Metropolitan police, from premises looking on the Square, and surgical aid was subsequently called in, short details of which will be given further on in this report.

The City police having been made acquainted with the facts by P.C. Watkins the following are the results of their enquiries so far as known to Met. Police:-

1.30 a.m. The P.C. passed the spot where the body was found at 1.45 a.m. and there was nothing to be seen there at that time.

1.35 a.m. Three Jews, one of whom is named Mr. Lewin [*sic* – Lawende], left a Club in Duke Street, and Mr. Lamende [*sic*] ["Lewin" – *deleted*], saw a man talking to a woman in Church Passage which leads directly to Mitre Square. The other two took but little notice and state they could not identify [*the*] man or woman, and eve [*n*] Mr. Lamende states that he could not identify the man, but a[*lso*] the woman stood with her back to him, with her han [*d*] on the man's breast, he coul[*d*] not identify the body mutilated as it was, as that of the woman whose back he had seen, but to the best of his belief the clothing of the deceased, which was black was similar to that worn by the woman whom he had seen. and that was the full extent of his identity.

2.20 a.m. P.C. 254A. Long (the P.C. was drafted from A. Division temporarily to assist H. Division.) stated that at the hour mentioned he visited Goldston [*sic*] Street Buildings, and there was nothing there at that time, but at,

2.55 a.m. he found in the bottom of a common stairs leading to No. 108 to 119. Goldston Street Buildings a piece of a bloodstained apron, and above it written in chalk the words, ''The Juwes are the men who will not be blamed for nothing.'' which he reported, and the City Police were subsequently acquainted at the earliest moment, when it was found that beyond doubt the piece of apron found corresponded exactly with the part missing from the body of the murdered woman.

The Surgeon, Dr. Brown, called by the City Police, and Dr. Phillips who had been called by the Metropolitan Police in the cases of Hanbury Street and Berner St. having made a post-mortem examination of the body reported that there were missing the left kidney and the uterus, and that the mutilation so far gave no evidence of anatomical knowledge in the sense that it evidenced the hand of a qualified surgeon, so that the Police could narrow their enquiries into certain classes of persons. On the other hand as in the Metropolitan Police cases, the medical evidence shewed that the murder could have been committed by a person who had been a hunter, a butcher, a slaughterman, as well as a student in surgery or a properly qualified surgeon.

The results of the City Police enquiries were as follow: — beside the body were found some pawn-tickets in a tin box, but upon tracing them, they were found to relate to pledges made by the deceased, who was separated from her husband, and was living in adultery with a man named John Kelly, respecting whom enquiry was at once made by Metropolitan and City Police, the result of which was to shew clearly that he was not the murderer. Further it shewed that the deceased's name was Catherine Eddowes, or Conway, who had been locked up for drunkenness at Bishopsgate Street Police Station at 8.45 p.m. 29th, and being sober was discharged at 1 a.m. 30th. Enquiry was also made by the City and Metropolitan police conjointly into her antecedents, and it was found that there did not exist amongst her relations or friends the slightest pretext for a motive to commit the murder.

At the Goldston Street Buildings where the portion of the bloodstained apron was found the City Police made enquiry, but unsuccessfully, and their subsequent enquiries into matters affecting persons suspected by correspondence, or by statements of individuals at Police Stations, as yet without success, have been carried on with the knowledge of the Metropolitan Police, who on the other hand have daily acquainted the City Police with the subjects and natures of their enquiries.

Upon the discovery of the blurred chalk writing on the wall, written, — although mis-spelled in the second word, — in an ordinary hand in the midst of a locality principally inhabited by Jews of all nationalities as well as English, and upon the wall of a common stairs leading to a number of tenements occupied almost exclusively by Jews, and the purport of the writing as shewn at page. 3. was to throw blame upon the Jews, the Commr. deemed it adviseable to have them rubbed out. Apart from this there was the fact that during police enquiries into the Bucks Row and Hanbury Street murders a certain section of the Press cast a great amount of suspicion upon a jew named John Piser, alias, "Leather Apron", as having been the murderer whose movements at the dates and hours of those murders had been satisfactorily enquired into by Met. Police, clearing him of any connection, there was also the fact that on the same morning another murder had been committed in the immediate vicinity of a Socialist Club in Berner Street, frequented by Jews, – considerations, which, weighed in the balance with the evidence of chalk writing on the wall to bring home guilt to any person were deemed the weightier of the two. To those police officers who saw the chalk writing, the handwriting of the now notorious letters to a newspaper agency bears no resemblance at all.

Rewards were offered by the City Police and by Mr. Montagu and a Vigilance Committee formed presided over by Mr. Lusk of Alderney Road, Mile End, and it is to be regretted that the combined result has been that no information leading to the murderer has been forthcoming. On the 18th Oct. Mr. Lusk brought a parcel which had been addressed to him to Leman Street. The parcel contained what appeared to be a portion of a kidney. He received it on 15th Oct. and submitted it for examination eventually to Dr. Openshaw curator of London Hospital Museum who pronounced it to be a human kidney. The kidney was at once handed over to the City Police, and the result of the combined medical opinion they have taken upon it, is, that it is the kidney of a human adult, not charged with a fluid, as it would have been in the case of a body handed over for purposes of dissection to an hospital, but rather as it would be in a case where it was taken from the body not so destined. In other words similar kidneys might & could be obtained from any dead person upon whom a post mortem had been made from any cause by students or dissecting room porter. [*Note in margin* – "Was there any such p.mort. made within a week in the E. or E.C. districts?"] The kidney, or rather portion of the kidney, was accompanied by a letter couched as follows. –

> *From hell*
> *Mr Lusk*
> *Sir*
> *I send you half the*
> *Kidne I took from one woman*
> *prasarved it for you. tother piece I*
> *fried and ate it was very nise. I*
> *may send you the bloody knif that*

took it out if you only wate a whil
longer
    signed Catch me when
            you can
        Mishter Lusk.

The postmarks upon the parcel are so indistinct that it cannot be said whether the parcel was posted in the E. or E.C. districts, and there is no envelope to the letter, and the City Police are therefore unable to prosecute any enquiries upon it.

The remaining enquiries of the City Police are merged into those of the Metropolitan Police, each Force cordially communicating to the other daily the nature and subject of their enquiries.

The foregoing are the facts so far as known to Metropolitan Police, relating to the murder in Mitre Square.

Donald S. Swanson.
ChInspector.

As regards Mr Lusk receiving part of a human kidney and the "From hell" letter on 16 October 1888, it is worth giving at this point two press reports containing further information about the incident. The *Daily Telegraph* of Saturday, 20 October 1888, reported:

A statement which apparently gives a clue to the sender of the strange package received by Mr. Lusk was made last night by Miss Emily Marsh, whose father carries on business in the leather trade at 218, Jubilee Street, Mile-end-road. In Mr. Marsh's absence Miss Marsh was in the front shop, shortly after one o'clock on Monday last, when a stranger, dressed in clerical costume, entered, and, referring to the reward bill in the window, asked for the address of Mr. Lusk, described therein as the president of the Vigilance Committee. Miss Marsh at once referred the man to Mr. J. Aarons, the treasurer of the committee, who resides at the corner of Jubilee-street and Mile-end-road, a distance of about thirty yards. The man, however, said he did not wish to go there, and Miss Marsh thereupon produced a newspaper in which Mr. Lusk's address was given as Alderney-road, Globe-road, no number being mentioned. She requested the stranger to read the address, but he declined, saying, "Read it out," and proceeded to write something in his pocket-book, keeping his head down meanwhile. He subsequently left the shop, after thanking the young lady for the information, but not before Miss Marsh, alarmed by the man's appearance, had sent the shop-boy, John Cormack, to see that all was right. This lad, as well as Miss Marsh, give a full description of the man, while Mr. Marsh, who happened to come along at the time, also encountered him on the pavement outside. The stranger is described as a man of some forty-five years of age, fully six feet in height, and slimly built. He wore a soft felt black hat, drawn over his forehead, a stand-up collar, and a very long black single-breasted overcoat, with a Prussian or clerical collar partly turned up. His face was of a sallow type, and he had a dark beard and moustache. The man spoke with what was taken to be an Irish accent. No importance was attached to the incident until Miss Marsh read of the receipt by Mr. Lusk of a strange parcel, and then it occurred to her that the stranger might be the person who had despatched it. His inquiry was made at one o'clock on Monday afternoon, and Mr. Lusk received the package at eight p.m. the next day. The address on the package curiously enough gives no number in Alderney-road, a piece of information which Miss Marsh could not supply. It appears that on leaving the shop the man went right by Mr. Aarons house, but did not call. Mr. Lusk has been informed of the circumstances, and states that no person answering the description has called on him, nor does he know any one at all like the man in question.

The *Sunday Times* of 21 October 1888 contained the following report:

THE WHITECHAPEL TRAGEDIES.

Notwithstanding the sensational rumours which were current yesterday afternoon, there is little to chronicle from the scene of the Whitechapel tragedies. The police have now turned their attention to the Thames and Victoria Embankments, and, to quote the words of an Inspector, it would be "impossible" for them to bestow more zeal or devotion to the task on which they are engaged. Sensational sheets teem with reports of arrests, but up to the present no arrests have been made. Mr. George Lusk, Alderney Road, Mile End, E., as chairman of the Whitechapel Vigilance Committee, was the recipient of the kidney of which so much has been heard lately.

Calling on Dr. Gordon Brown, of the City Police, last night, our reporter found that he had not quite completed his examination of the kidney which had been submitted to him. He said: "So far as I can form an opinion, I do not see any substantial reason why this portion of kidney should not be the portion of the one taken from the murdered woman. I cannot say that it is the left kidney. It must have been cut previously to its being immersed in the spirit which exercised a hardening process. It certainly had not been in spirit for more than a week. As has been stated, there is no portion of the renal artery adhering to it, it having been trimmed up, so, consequently, there could be no correspondence established between the portion of the body from which it was cut. As it exhibits no trace of decomposition, when we consider the length of time that has elapsed since the commission of the murder, we come to the conclusion that the probability is slight of its being a portion of the murdered woman of Mitre Square.''

The suspicious circumstances of the tall clerical-looking individual who called at the shop of Miss Emily Marsh, 218, Jubilee Street, Mile End Road, has not been satisfactorily accounted for. He asked for the address of Mr. Lusk . . .

The official files resume with the written report[7] of Police Constable 254A, Alfred Long, of the Metropolitan Police, Westminster Division, concerning his finding of the piece of bloody apron and the graffito on the wall in Goulston Street, in the early hours of Sunday, 30 September 1888:

A49301C/8c

6th November, 1888.

[Stamped: – HOME OFFICE 6 NOV.88 RECd. DEPt.]

I was on duty in Goulston Street on the morning of 30th Sept: at about 2.55 A.M. I found a portion of an apron covered in blood lying in the passage of the door-way leading to Nos. 108 to 119 Model Dwellings in Goulston Street.

Above it on the wall was written in chalk ''The Juews are the men that will not be blamed for nothing'', I at once called the P.C. on the adjoining beat and then searched the stair-cases, but found no traces of any person or marks. I at once proceeded to the Station, telling the P.C. to see that no one entered or left the building in my absence. I arrived at the Station about 5 or 10 minutes past 3, and reported to the Inspector on duty finding the apron and the writing.

The Inspector at once proceeded to Goulston Street and inspected the writing.

From there we proceeded to Leman St., and the apron was handed by the Inspector to a gentleman whom I have since learnt is Dr. Phillips.

I then returned back on duty in Goulston Street about 5.

Alfred Long PC 254A.

The next report[8] is written by Superintendent Thomas Arnold, H Division, dated 6 November 1888, and concerns his knowledge of the Goulston Street incident:

[Stamped: – HOME OFFICE 6 NOV.88 RECd. DEPt.] A49301C/8c

H Division

6th Nov 1888

I beg to report that on the morning of 30th Sept. last my attention was called to some writing on the wall of the entrance to some dwellings No. 108 Goulston Street Whitechapel which consisted of the following words "The Juews are not [*the word 'not' being deleted*] the men that will not be blamed for nothing", and knowing that in consequence of a suspicion having fallen upon a Jew named "John Pizer" alias "Leather Apron" having committed a murder in Hanbury Street a short time previously a strong feeling ["ag" – *deleted*] existed against the Jews generally, and as the Building upon which the writing was found was situated in the midst of a locality inhabited principally by that Sect. I was apprehensive that if the writing were left it would be the means of causing a riot and therefore considered it desirable that it should be removed having in view the fact that it was in such a position that it would have been rubbed by the shoulders of persons passing in & out of the Building. Had only a portion of the writing been removed the context would have remained. An Inspector was present by my directions with a sponge for the purpose of removing the writing when Commissioner arrived on the scene.

T Arnold Supd.

On 29 September Tom Bulling, of the Central News Limited, sent to the police a letter that they had received on 27 September. His letter[9] read:

THE CENTRAL NEWS LIMITED

5, New Bridge Street,
London, 29 Sep 1888
E.C.

[Logo: – TO NEWSPAPERS, CLUBS & NEWSROOMS/TELEGRAPHIC NEWS]
The editor presents his compliments to Mr. Williamson & begs to inform him the enclosed was sent the Central News two days ago, & was treated as a joke.

The accompanying letter[10] was in an envelope addressed to *The Boss, Central News Office, London City* and was postmarked SP 27 88 and posted in London EC. It ran as follows:

25 Sept. 1888

Dear Boss.

I keep on hearing the police have caught me but they wont fix me just yet. I have laughed when they look so clever and talk about being on the right track.

That joke about Leather Apron gave me real fits. I am down on whores and I shant quit ripping them till I do get buckled. Grand work the last job was, I gave the lady no time to squeal. How can they catch me now, I love my work and want to start again. You will soon hear of me with my funny little games. I saved some of the proper red stuff in a ginger beer bottle over the last job to write with but it went thick like glue and I cant use it. Red ink is fit enough I hope ha. ha. The next job I do I shall clip the ladys ears off and send to the police officers just for jolly wouldnt you. Keep this letter back till I do a bit more work then give it out straight. My knife's so nice and sharp I want to get to work right away if I get a chance, good luck.

Yours truly
Jack the Ripper

Dont mind me giving the trade name.
Wasnt good enough to post this before I got all the red ink off my hands curse it. No luck yet. They say I'm a doctor now ha ha.

On 1 October 1888 a postcard[11] addressed to *Central News Office, London City, EC*, was received and ran as follows:

I wasn't codding dear old Boss when I gave you the tip. You'll hear about saucy Jacky's work tomorrow double event this time number one squealed a bit couldnt finish straight off. had no time to get ears for police. thanks for keeping last letter back till I got to work again.

Jack the Ripper.

On 5 October T.J. Bulling of the Central News again communicated[12] with Chief Constable Williamson:

THE CENTRAL NEWS LIMITED.

5 New Bridge Street,
London, Oct 5 1888
E.C.

[logo]

Dear Mr. Williamson,
At 5 minutes to 9 o'clock tonight we received the following letter the envelope of which I enclose by which you will see it is in the same handwriting as the previous communications.

5 Oct. 1888

Dear Friend,
In the name of God hear me I swear I did not kill the female whose body was found at Whitehall. If she was an honest woman I will hunt down and destroy her murderer. If she was a whore God will bless the hand that slew her, for

the women of Moab and Midian shall die and their blood shall mingle with the dust. I never harm any others or the Divine power that protects and helps me in my grand work would quit for ever. Do as I do and the light of glory shall shine upon you. I must get to work tomorrow treble event this time yes yes three must be ripped. will send you a bit of face by post I promise this dear old Boss. The police now reckon my work a practical joke well well Jacky's a very practical joker ha ha Keep this back till three are wiped out and you can show the cold meat.

    Yours truly

      Jack the Ripper

Yours truly

T.J. Bulling

A.F. Williamson Esqr.

Thus the nickname "Jack the Ripper" was introduced to the world, and would never be forgotten. It would pervade and influence all aspects of the case from that day on. The nickname "Leather Apron" had been lost to the sensational Press after the arrest and clearing of Pizer. Now there was a much better one to take its place. The only police officer known to have named the press man the police thought was responsible for this sensational new name was John George Littlechild, lately Chief Inspector of the Special Branch. And he named Tom "Bullen" [*sic* – Bulling] of the Central News Agency, forwarder of the correspondence to the police. In the Littlechild letter[13] he writes:

With regard to the term "Jack the Ripper" it was generally believed at the Yard that Tom Bullen of the Central News was the originator but it is probable Moore, who was his chief, was the inventor. It was a smart piece of journalistic work. No journalist of my time got such privileges from Scotland Yard as Bullen. Mr James Munro [*sic*] when Assistant Commissioner, and afterwards Commissioner, relied on his integrity.

The Times of Tuesday, 2 October 1888 reported[14]:

The excitement caused by the murders committed early on Sunday morning in Berner-street, Commercial-road, and Mitre-square, Aldgate, has in no way abated. In the East-end statements and rumours of the most extraordinary nature were in circulation yesterday respecting conversations which certain persons, male and female, had had with two or three suspicious-looking men an hour or so before the crimes were committed, the purport of the statements in question being to connect the latter individuals with the outrages. Nothing, however, can be extracted from these statements of sufficient importance to form any clue. A few arrests have been made by the Metropolitan Police, but none had been made by the City Police up to a late hour last night. The authorities are now fully on the alert in the localities of the murders, and, as stated below, it has been decided by the City Police to offer a reward for the discovery of the assassin.

It is satisfactory to announce that one discovery at least has been made which, in the hands of efficient detectives, should prove an important clue to the lurking-place of the murderer – for the belief is now generally entertained in official quarters that no one person alone is attributable the series of crimes which in the last few weeks have horrified and alarmed the public.

It appears that after perpetrating his foul work in Mitre-square the miscreant retraced his steps towards the scene of the crime which he had committed an hour or so earlier. As stated in the particulars given in *The Times* of yesterday, part of the attire of the unfortunate woman who was butchered in Mitre-square consisted of a portion of coarse white apron, which was found loosely hanging about the neck. A piece of this apron had been torn away by the villain, who, in proceeding to his destination further east after leaving the City boundary, presumably used it to wipe his hands or his knife on, then threw it away. It was picked up in Goulston-street very shortly after the second murder had been committed, and it was brought to the mortuary by Dr. Phillips soon after the body had been removed there. It was covered with blood, and was found to fit in with the portion of apron which had been left by the murderer on his victim. Goulston-street, it may be stated, is a broad thoroughfare running parallel with the Commercial-road [*sic* – Commercial Street] and is off the main White-chapel-road, and the spot where the piece of apron was picked up is about a third of a mile from Mitre-square. By the direct and open route it is 1,550 feet, but it can be approached through several small streets, making the distance about 1,600 feet. These measurements were taken yesterday.

The only other clues in the possession of the police are two pawnbrokers' tickets which were found lying close to the spot where the Mitre-square murder was discovered, and a knife which was picked up by a police-constable in the Whitechapel-road early yesterday morning. It is described as black-handled, 10 inches long, keen as a razor, and pointed like a carving knife. The pawn-tickets are believed to have belonged to the woman. They were in a small tin box and related to pledges which had been made in August of a pair of boots and a man's shirt. The tickets had been made out in two names – Emily Birrell and Anne Kelly – and the articles had been pawned for 1s. and 6d. respectively with Mr. Jones, of Church-street, Spitalfields, who, however, cannot identify the woman as having made the pledges.

Photographs of the ill-fated creature were taken at the City Mortuary in Golden-lane both before and after the post-mortem examination, after which the features – which, as already reported in *The Times*, had been brutally cut about – were rendered more life-like by the doctors. Up to a late hour last night, however, the body had not been identified, though several persons, having missed relatives or friends, have been taken to see it by the police.

Yesterday morning, shortly after 10 o'clock, an interview respecting the Mitre-Square murder took place between Mr. M'William (the inspector of the City Detective Department), Superintendent Foster, and Inspector Collard and the City Coroner, who has arranged to hold the inquest on Thursday morning, it being hoped that the woman may be identified in the meantime. The plans taken by Mr. F.W. Foster, of Old Jewry, of the scene of this outrage immediately after it was discovered were submitted to the Coroner, and Mr. Foster will be one of the witnesses at the inquest.

The Times of Wednesday, 3 October 1888, reported:

Great satisfaction was expressed yesterday throughout the City at the promptness with which the Lord Mayor, on the part of the Corporation, and at the instance of Colonel Sir James Fraser, the Commissioner of the City Police, has offered a reward for the discovery and conviction of the murderer or murderers of the woman who was found butchered in Mitre-square. There is reason to believe that the identification of the victim has been established. It appears that on Saturday night a woman – who gave the name of Mary Anne Kelly, and her address as No.6 Fashion-street, Spitalfields – was taken intoxicated to the Bishopsgate-street police-station. It is customary in such cases for a constable who may be on duty at the station to visit at frequent intervals the person detained, to see how he or she may be progressing. The woman in question was attended to in this manner on Saturday night by Reserve Constable Hutt, who noticed that she had on a pair of men's boots, and at the same time he observed the bonnet which she was wearing as well as her attire generally. Having become sufficiently sober to be discharged, the woman was liberated on Sunday morning at 1 o'clock, when she stated that she was afraid to go home, it was understood, on account of her husband. Hutt saw her leave the station, and observed that, instead of going in the direction of Spitalfields, she turned to the left, towards Houndsditch, and consequently in the direction of Mitre-square. After the examination of the body of the murdered woman in the City mortuary in Golden-lane the boots and bonnet were left there with the keeper, the rest of the clothing being taken to the police-station. On going to the mortuary Hutt saw the boots and bonnet and identified them as belonging to the woman who had been detained at the police-station. He then gave a general description of the rest of her dress, and on an examination being made afterwards at the police-station, where, as above stated, the other clothing had been taken, it was found to correspond fairly accurately with his account. Another constable, named Simmons, has also seen the body, and he believes, too, that it is the woman who was discharged at 1 o'clock on Sunday morning from the Bishopsgate-street police-station. Inquiries have been made by the City police for a Mary Anne Kelly at the address given in Fashion-street, but no person answering the description of the woman who was detained is known there. It is, however, a common practice for persons under detention to give false names and addresses.

Up to a late hour last night no arrests had been made in connexion with the murders by the City police. No clues, in addition to the very slender ones mentioned in *The Times* yesterday, have been discovered; but it is fully believed by the police that the lurking place of the murderer is not very far from the scenes of his atrocious crimes.

The same newspaper carried an additional report on the identification of Eddowes:

THE MITRE-SQUARE VICTIM IDENTIFIED.

Last night between 9 and 10 o'clock, a labouring man, giving the name of John Kelly, 55, Flower and Dean-street – a common lodginghouse – entered the Bishopsgate-street Police-station, and stated that from what he had been reading in the newspapers he believed that the woman who had been murdered in Mitre-square was his "wife." He was at once taken by Sergeant Miles to the mortuary in Golden-lane, and there identified her as the woman, to whom he subsequently admitted he was not married, but with whom he had cohabited for seven years.

Major Henry Smith, the Assistant Commissioner of the City Police, and Superintendent Foster were telegraphed for, and immediately went to the Bishopsgate-street station. Kelly, who was considerably affected, spoke quite unreservedly, and gave a full statement as to his own movements and those of the ill-fated woman, as to whose identity he was quite positive. In this statement he was borne out by the deputy of the lodginghouse, Frederick Wilkinson, who knew the poor woman quite well, and who had just seen the body. Kelly, in answer to questions, stated that the last time he saw her – referring to her as "Kate" – was on Saturday afternoon. The last meal she had with him was a breakfast which had been obtained by the pledging of his boots for 2s. 6d. Asked if he could explain how it was that she was out so late on Saturday night, he replied that he could not say. He left her in the afternoon believing that she would return to him at the lodginghouse in Flower and Dean-street. He had told her to go and see her daughter, and to try and get "the price of a bed for the night." "Who is her daughter?" he was asked, to which he replied, "A married woman. She is married to a gun-maker, and they live somewhere in Bermondsey, in King-street, I think it is called; but I never went there." He was then asked if he knew the murdered woman's name, and if he could explain the meaning of the initials "T.C." on her arm. He at once replied that Thomas Conway was the name of her husband, but he could not state whether Conway was dead or alive, or how long, in the latter case, she had been living away from him. Being asked why he had not made inquiries before relative to her absence on Saturday night and since, he replied that he thought she had got into some trouble and had been locked up, and he thought he had better wait. She was given to drinking. He had cautioned her not to stay out late at night on account of the previous murders. The reason which had induced him at length to call at the police-station was his having read about pawntickets being found near the murdered woman relating to pledges in the names of Kelly and Birrell. Further questioned on this point, he repeated the references to the pledging of his boots with a pawnbroker named Jones, of Church-street, and stated that the ticket for the other article (a flannel shirt), pledged in the name of Emily Birrell, had been given to them by the latter, who had been with them hopping, and who had slept in the same barn with them. He further stated that he and the murdered woman were "both Londoners," and that the latter was born at Bermondsey (*sic*). They had just returned from hopping at a place which he was understood to call Hunton, adding that it was about two miles from Coxheath, in Kent. To the question how he obtained his living, he replied, "I job about the markets now." He added that he had worked pretty constantly for a fruit salesman named Lander for over 12 years. He and "Kate" had, he said, gone through many hardships together, but while she was with him he "would not let her do anything bad." He was asked if he knew whether the woman had any relatives besides the daughter mentioned, to which he replied that "Kate's" sister was living in Thrawl-street, Spitalfields, with a man who sold farthing books in Liverpool-street.

An officer was despatched from the station for the ward beadle, who brought notices in blank with him, and two of them were filled up and served on Kelly and Wilkinson to attend the inquest, which, as already announced, will be held to-morrow at the City mortuary.

Kelly is a man of about 40 years of age, of medium height, and judging from his appearance is a poor, but hard-working man. He was quite sober. It will be seen from his statements that the belief which was expressed earlier in the day by the police-constables Hutt and Simmons – to which reference is made elsewhere – as to the identity of the murdered woman with the female who had been detained for drunkenness at Bishopsgate-street Station, and who was discharged about an hour before the murder was committed, is confirmed. The boots and shirt referred to by Kelly as being in pledge are now in the possession of the police, having been obtained from the pawn-broker.

While Kelly was making his statement a man entered the station and made a confession that he was the murderer. He strongly objected to being searched, but this was done with the aid of two or three constables. Major Smith, who was present at the station, attaches no importance to the confession, the man having been drinking and having nothing of an incriminating nature in his possession. He was, however, detained.

CHAPTER 10

The Eddowes Inquest

For greater detail on the Eddowes murder reference may be made to the Inquest reports[1] filed in the Corporation of London Records Office. These records include the written statements of witnesses at the Eddowes Inquest:

Eliza Gold sister of the deceased, of Thrawl Street, Spitalfields, a widow, stated on oath —

"I recognize deceased as my sister, her name was Catherine Eddowes, singlewoman, 43 years of age. She has been living for some years with Mr. Kelly. I have not seen her for 3 or 4 weeks. She used to go out hawking. Was of sober habits. She lived with a man named Conway before she lived with Kelly, she lived with Conway for some years. I do not know if Conway is living, I have not seen him for some years. He was a Pensioner, and went out hawking. I cannot tell whether they parted on good or bad terms.

By Mr. Crawford — I have not seen her since she parted from Conway. I saw deceased with Kelly about 3 or 4 weeks ago, they were on good terms. They were lodging together at 55 Flower and Dean Street, at a person's of the name of Smith. I have not seen her since."

The mark of   X   Eliza Gold.

John Kelly labourer, of 55 Flower and Dean Street, Spitalfields, gave his statement on oath —

"I have seen the body of Deceased, I knew her as Catherine Conway. I have known her for seven years and have been living with her the whole of that time. She used to sell a few things about the street. She lived with me at 55 Flower and Dean Street, a common lodging house. I was last in her company on Saturday last at 2 o'clock in the afternoon in Houndsditch. We parted on very good terms. She said she was going over to see if she could see her daughter, Annie, at Bermondsey, a daughter she had by Conway. She promised me to be back by 4 o'clock and no later. She did not return. I heard she had been locked up at Bishopsgate, I was told by two women. I made sure she would be out on Sunday morning. It was for a little drop of drink. I never suffered her to go out for immoral purposes. She was occasionally in the habit of slightly drinking to excess. She had no money about her when I left. She went over to see her Daughter with a view of getting some money. I was without money to pay for the lodging at the time. I know of no one with whom she was at variance or likely to injure her. I do not know whether she had seen Conway or whether he was living, I never saw him.

By Jury – She usually returned about 8 or 9 o'clock.

By Mr Crawford – I do not know of anyone with whom she had been drinking. She left me some months ago in consequence of a few words. She only remained away for a few hours. She told me her Daughter lived at King Street, Bermondsey. We have lived in the same house for some years. On Friday night we did not sleep together. That night she went into the Casual Ward at Mile End. We did not sleep the whole of that week at the Lodging House. We were hop picking until Thursday. We both went to the Casual Ward on Thursday night at Shoe Lane. I saw deceased on Saturday morning at 8 o'clock. She had some tea and coffee which she had bought after I pawned my boots. She was sober when we parted. She has never brought money to me in the morning that she has earned at night. My wife pawned the boots, the date is the 28th.''

John Kelly

Frederick William Wilkinson 55 Flower and Dean Street, Brick Lane, Spitalfields, Deputy of the Lodging House, was sworn and stated –

''I have known deceased and Kelly for the last 7 or 8 years, they passed as a man and wife. They lived on very good terms. They had a few words now and again when she was in drink. Deceased got her living by hawking about the streets and cleaning amongst the Jews. When they were there they were pretty regular in their rent. She did not often drink, she was a very jolly woman. I never saw Kelly drunk. I saw deceased on Friday afternoon when she returned from hopping. I did not see Kelly. She went out on Friday night. I saw her again on Saturday morning along with Kelly between 10 & 11. I did not see deceased again until I saw her in the mortuary. She was generally in bed between 9 & 10 at nights when they stopped there. I did not know her to walk the street. I never knew or heard of her being intimate with any one but Kelly. She used to say she was married to Conway and her name was bought and paid for. She was not at variance with any one that I know of. She was quite sober on Saturday when I last saw her. When Kelly came in on Saturday night between half past 7 or 8 I asked him, 'Where's Kate?' He said, 'I have heard she's been locked up', and he took a single bed. A single bed is 4d, a double bed is 8d.''

By Mr Crawford – ''I should say it was 4 or 5 weeks since they slept together at this house, they had been hopping. I am quite positive he never went out on Saturday night. On the Saturday morning she was wearing an apron, she was not dressed in anything particular. No stranger came in between 1 and 2 on Sunday morning to take a bed. I cannot recollect whether any stranger came in at 3 o'clock.''

Frederick William Wilkinson.

Edward Watkins City Police Constable 881, swore that –

''I have been in Police for 17 years. On Saturday 29th September, I went on duty a quarter to ten. My beat returns from Duke Street/Aldgate, through Heneage Lane, a portion of Bury Street, through Cree Church Lane, into Leadenhall Street, along Leadenhall Street into Mitre Street, then into Mitre Square, round the Square into Mitre Street, then into King Street, along King Street to St James Place, round St James Place thence into Duke Street. It takes about 12 or 14 minutes. I had been continuously patrolling that beat from 10 in the evening until 1.30 o'clock. Nothing excited my attention during those hours. I passed through Mitre Square about 1.30 on Sunday morning, I had my lantern freed in my belt and on. I looked into the different passages. At half past one nothing excited my attention, I saw no one about. No one could have been in any portion of the Square without my seeing. I next came in at 1.44. I turned to the right. I saw the body of the woman lying there on her back with her feet facing the Square, her clothes up above her waist. I saw her throat was cut and her bowels protruding. The stomach was ripped up, she was lying in a pool of blood. I ran across the road to Messrs. Kearley and Tonge, the door was ajar, I pushed it open and called to the Watchman who was inside. He came out. I sent him for assistance. I remained by the body until the arrival of Police Constable Holland. Dr. Sequira followed. Inspector Collard arrived about 2, and Dr. Gordon Brown, the surgeon to the Police Force. I did not hear the sound of any footsteps, at the time I entered no one was in the Square. The watchman at Messrs. Kearley and Tonge's was at work inside cleaning the offices. The watchman blew his whistle as he was going up the Street. No one comes through Mitre Street but myself.''

Edward Watkins.

Frederick William Foster 26 Old Jewry, Architect and Surveyor, being sworn saith ''I have made the plans produced – I have them in three sections one 8 feet to an inch, another 200 feet to an inch from an Ordnance map of the City – I have marked on an Ordnance Map of the same scale from Berner Street to Mitre Street – that would be 1144 yards about $\frac{3}{4}$ of a mile – It would take about 12 minutes to walk it from one to another.'' By Mr. Crawford. ''It is the nearest route that anyone unaccustomed to it would take it – There are 2 routes to Goulstone Street one from Church Passage through Duke Street crossing Houndsditch through Gravel Lane, Stoney Lane crossing Petticoat Lane and through to Goulstone Street. A person going from Mitre Square to Flower and Dean Street would go as the most direct route across Goulstone Street – It would take within $\frac{1}{4}$ of an hour to get there.''

Fredk. W. Foster.

Frederick William Wilkinson recalled, examined by Mr. Crawford – ''Kelly was at No. 52 sleeping on Friday and Saturday – I had 6 strangers sleeping there on Saturday evening. I do not remember any one coming in about 2 o'clock on Sunday morning – I remember the police coming in about 3 o'clock – no register of the time or of the persons coming in is kept by me.''

Frederick William Wilkinson.

Edward Collard Inspector, City Police, being sworn saith – ''At 5 minutes before 2 on Sunday morning I received information at Bishopsgate Street Station that a woman had been murdered in Mitre Square – Information was telegraphed to Head Quarters and I dispatched a constable to Dr. Gordon Brown and proceeded to Mitre Square arriving there at 2 or 3 minutes past 2. I found Dr. Sequira, several Police Officers and the Deceased person lying in the South West corner of the Square in the position described by Constable Watkins – the body was not touched until the arrival of Dr. Brown who arrived shortly afterwards – the body was examined and Sergeant Jones picked up on the left side of deceased 3 small black buttons generally used for women's boots small metal button, common metal thimble, a small mustard tin containing 2 pawn tickets which were handed to me. The doctors remained until the arrival of the ambulance and saw the body placed in a Conveyance. It was then conveyed to this mortuary – and the body was stripped – I produce the list of articles found on her – she had no money whatever on her – I produce a portion of the apron which deceased was apparently wearing which had been cut through and was found outside her dress – I took immediate steps to have the neighbourhood searched. Mr. MacWilliam, chief of the Detective-Department on his arrival shortly after with a number of Detectives sent to have immediate searches both in the streets and in lodging Houses. Several men were stopped and searched without any good result. I have had had a house to house enquiry in the vicinity of Mitre Square – but I failed to find anything excepting the witnesses to be produced named Lawrence and Levy.''

By Mr. Crawford. ''Her head, neck and shoulders were lying in a pool of blood on each side of her, nothing in front – no appearance of any struggle having taken place – I made an examination round to see if there was any struggle, no trace whatever – nothing to lead to suppose there had been any struggle either in the appearance of the woman or her clothes. The blood was in a liquid state not congealed – In my opinion from what I saw I should say that the body had not been there more than $\frac{1}{4}$ of an hour. I endeavoured to find footsteps but could find no footsteps. A search was made at the back of the empty houses but I could find no trace whatever.''

Edward Collard.

The official list of Eddowes's clothes and possessions is as follows:

"<u>Black straw bonnet</u> trimmed with green & black velvet and black beads, black strings. The bonnet was loosely tied, and had partially fallen from the back of her head, no blood on front, but the back was lying in a pool of blood, which had run from the neck,

"<u>Black Cloth Jacket</u>, imitation fur edging round collar, fur round sleeves, no blood on front outside, large quantity of Blood inside & outside back, outside back very dirty with Blood & dirt, 2 outside pockets, trimmed black silk braid & imitation fur,

"<u>Chintz Skirt</u> 3 flounces, brown button on waistband, Jagged cut $6\frac{1}{2}$ inches long from waistband, left side of front, Edges slightly Bloodstained, also Blood on bottom, back & front of skirt.

"<u>Brown Linsey Dress Bodice</u>, black velvet collar, brown metal buttons down front, blood inside & outside back of neck & shoulders, clean cut bottom of left side, 5 inches long from right to left.

"<u>Grey Stuff Petticoat</u>, white waist band, cut $1\frac{1}{2}$ inch long, thereon in front, Edges blood stained, blood stains on front at bottom of Petticoat.

"<u>Very Old Green Alpaca Skirt</u>, Jagged cut $10\frac{1}{2}$ inches long in front of waistband downward, blood stained inside, front under cut.

"<u>Very Old Ragged Blue Skirt</u>, red flounce, light twill lining, jagged cut $10\frac{1}{2}$ inches long, through waist band, downward, blood stained, inside & outside back and front.

"<u>White Calico Chemise</u>, very much blood stained all over, apparently torn thus in middle of front.

"<u>Mans White Vest</u>, button to match down front, 2 outside pockets, torn at back, very much Blood stained at back, Blood & other stains on front.

"<u>No Drawers or Stays.</u>

"<u>Pair of Mens lace up Boots</u>, mohair laces, right boot has been repaired with red thread, 6 Blood marks on right boot.

"<u>1 piece of red gauze Silk</u>, various cuts thereon found on neck.

"<u>1 large White Handkerchief</u>, blood stained.

"<u>2 Unbleached Calico Pockets</u>, tape strings, cut through also top left hand corners, cut off one.

"<u>1 Blue Stripe Bed ticking Pocket</u>, waist band, and strings cut through, (all 3 Pockets) Blood stained.

"<u>1 White Cotton Pocket Handkerchief</u>, red and white birds eye border.

"<u>1 Pr. Brown ribbed Stockings</u>, feet mended with white.

"<u>12 pieces of white Rag</u>, some slightly bloodstained.

"1 piece of white coarse Linen.

"1 piece of Blue & White Shirting (3 cornered).

"2 Small Blue Bed ticking Bags.

"2 Short Clay Pipes (black).

"1 Tin Box containing Tea.

"1 do do   do   Sugar.

"1 Piece of Flannel & 6 pieces of Soap.

"1 Small Tooth Comb.

"1 White Handle Table Knife & 1 Metal Tea Spoon.

"1 Red Leather Cigarette Case, white metal fittings.

"1 Tin Match Box. empty.

"1 piece of Red Flannel containing Pins & Needles.

"1 Ball of Hemp

"1 Piece of old White Apron."

Frederick Gordon Brown 17 Finsbury Circus, Surgeon of City of London Police Force, being sworn saith – "I was called shortly after 2 o'clock I reached about 18 minutes past 2 my attention was called to body of Deceased. The body was lying in position described by Watkins. The body was on its back – the head turned to left shoulder – the arms by the side of the body as if they had fallen there, both palms upwards – the fingers slightly bent, a thimble was lying off the finger on the right side. The clothes drawn up above the abdomen, the thighs were naked, left leg extended in a line with the body, the abdomen was exposed, right leg bent at the thigh and knee. The bonnet was at the back of the head – great disfigurement of face, the throat cut across, below the cut was a neckerchief. The upper part of the dress was pulled open a little way. The abdomen was all exposed. The intestines were drawn out to a large extent and placed over the right shoulder – they were smeared over with some feculent matter. A piece of about 2 feet was quite detached from the body and placed between the body and the left arm, apparently by design. The lobe and auricle of the right ear was cut obliquely through. There was a quantity of clotted blood on the pavement on the left side of the neck, round the shoulder and upper part of arm, and fluid blood coloured serum which had flowed under the neck to the right shoulder – the pavement sloping in that direction. Body was quite warm – no death stiffening had taken place. She must have been dead most likely within the half hour. We looked for superficial bruises and saw none — no blood on the skin of the abdomen or secretion of any kind on the thighs — no spurting of blood on the bricks or pavement around. No marks of blood below the middle of the body — several buttons were found in the clotted blood after the body was removed. There was no blood on the front of the clothes. There were no traces of recent connection. When the body arrived at Golden Lane some of the blood was dispersed through the removal of the body to the mortuary. The clothes were taken off carefully from the body, a piece of deceased's ear dropped from the clothing.

Made a post mortem examination at $\frac{1}{2}$ past 2 on Sunday afternoon — rigor mortis was well marked, body not quite cold — green discolouration over the abdomen. After washing the left hand carefully a bruise the size of a sixpence, recent and red, was discovered on the back of the left hand between the thumb and first finger. A few small bruises on right shin of older date. The hands and arms were bronzed — no bruises on the scalp, the back of the body, or the elbows. The face was very much mutilated. There was a cut about $\frac{1}{4}$ of an inch through the lower left eyelid dividing the structures completely through the upper eyelid on that side, there was a scratch through the skin on the left upper eyelid — near to the angle of the nose the right eyelid was cut through to about $\frac{1}{2}$ an inch. There was a deep cut over the bridge of the nose extending from the left border of the nasal bone down near to the angle of the jaw on the right side, across the cheek — this cut went into the bone and divided all the structures of the cheek except the mucous membrane of the mouth. The tip of the nose was quite detached from the nose by an oblique cut from the bottom of the nasal bone to where the wings of the nose join on to the face. A cut from this divided the upper lip and extended through the substance of the gum over the right upper lateral incizor tooth. About $\frac{1}{2}$ an inch from the top of the nose was another oblique cut. There was a cut on the right angle of the mouth as if by the cut of a point of a knife the cut extended an inch and a half parallel with lower lip. There was on each side of cheek a cut which peeled up the skin forming a triangular flap about an inch and a half. On the left cheek there were 2 abrasions of the epithelium. There was a little mud on the left cheek — 2 slight abrasions of the epithelium under the left ear. The throat was cut across to the extent of about 6 or 7 inches. A superficial cut commenced about an inch and $\frac{1}{2}$ below the lobe and about $2\frac{1}{2}$ inches behind the left ear and extended across the throat to about 3 inches below the lobe of the right ear. The big muscle across the throat was divided through on the left side — the large vessels on the left side of the neck were severed — the larynx was severed below the vocal chords. All the deep structures were severed to the bone the knife marking intervertebral cartilages — the sheath of the vessels on the right side was just opened. the carotid artery had a fine hole opening.

the internal jugular vein was opened an inch and a half not divided. The blood vessels contained clot. All these injuries were performed by a sharp instrument like a knife and pointed. The cause of death was haemorrhage from the left common carotid artery. The death was immediate and the mutilations were inflicted after death. We examined the abdomen, the front walls were laid open from the breast bone to the pubes. The cut commenced opposite the ensiform cartilage. The incision went upwards not penetrating the skin that was over the sternum. It then divided the enciform cartilage. The knife must have cut obliquely at the expense of the front surface of that cartilage. Behind this the liver was stabbed as if by the point of a sharp instrument. Below this was another incision into the liver of about $2\frac{1}{2}$ inches and below this the left lobe of the liver was slit through by a vertical cut. 2 cuts were shewn by a jagging of the skin on the left side. The abdominal walls were divided in the middle line to within $\frac{1}{4}$ of an inch of the navel, the cut then took a horizontal course for two inches and a half towards right side. It then divided round the navel on the left side and made a parallel incision to the former horizontal incision leaving the navel on a tongue of skin. Attached to the navel was $2\frac{1}{2}$ inches of the lower part of the rectus muscle on the left side of the abdomen the incision then took an oblique direction to the right and was shelving. The incision went down the right side of the vagina and rectum for half an inch behind the rectum – There was a stab of about an inch on the left groin, this was done by a pointed instrument, below this was a cut of three inches going through all tissues making a wound of the peritoneum about the same extent. An inch below the crease of the thigh was a cut extending from the anterior spine of the ilium obliquely down the inner side of the left thigh and separating the left labium forming a flap of skin up to the groin. The left rectus muscle was not detached. There was a flap of skin formed from the right thigh attaching the right labium and extending up to the spine of the ilium. The muscles on the right side inserted into the poupart's ligament were cut through. The skin was retracted through the whole of the cut in the abdomen but vessels were not clotted – nor had there been any appreciable bleeding from the vessel. I draw the conclusion that the cut was made after death and there would not be much blood on the murderer. The cut was made by some one on right side of body kneeling below the middle of the body – I removed the contents of the stomach and placed it in a jar for further examination. There seemed very little in it in the way of food or fluid but from the cut end partly digested farinaceous food escaped – The intestines had been detached to a large extent from the mesentery. About 2 feet of the colon was cut away – The sigmoid flexure was invaginated into the rectum very tightly – right kidney pale bloodless with slight congestion of the base of the pyramids. There was a cut from the upper part of the slit on the under surface of the liver to the left side and another cut at right angles to this which were about an inch and a half deep and $2\frac{1}{2}$ inches long. Liver itself was healthy – the gall bladder contained bile, the pancreas was cut but not through on the left side of the spinal column $3\frac{1}{2}$ inches of the lower border of the spleen by $\frac{1}{2}$ an inch was attached only to the peritoneum. The peritoneal lining was cut through on the left side and the left kidney carefully taken out and removed – the left renal artery was cut through – I should say that some one who knew the position of the kidney must have done it. The lining membrane over the uterus was cut through. The womb was cut through horizontally leaving a stump $\frac{3}{4}$ of an inch, the rest of the womb had been taken away with some of the ligaments. The vagina and cervix of the womb was uninjured. The bladder was healthy and uninjured and contained 3 or 4 ounces of water. There was a tongue like cut through the anterior wall of the abdominal aorta. The other organs were healthy – There were no indications of connexion – I believe the wound in the throat was first inflicted – I believe she must have been lying on the ground – They [sic] wounds on the face and abdomen prove that they were inflicted by a sharp pointed knife and that in the abdomen by one six inches long. I believe the perpetrator of the act must have had considerable knowledge of the position of the organs in the abdominal cavity and the way of removing them. The part removed would be of no use for any professional purpose. It required a great deal of ["medical" – *deleted*] knowledge to have removed the kidney and to know where it was placed, such a knowledge might be possessed by some one in the habit of cutting up animals – I think the perpetrator of this act had sufficient time or he would not have nicked the lower eyelids. It would take at least 5 minutes – I cannot assign any reason for these parts being taken away. I feel sure there was no struggle – I believe it was the act of one person – the throat had been so instantly severed that no noise could have been emitted. I should not expect much blood to have been found on the person who had inflicted these wounds. The wounds could not have been self inflicted – My attention was called to the apron – It was the corner of the apron with a string attached. The blood spots were of recent origin – I have seen a portion of an apron produced by Dr. Phillips and stated to have been found in Goulstone Street. It is impossible to say it is human blood. I fitted the piece of apron which had a new piece of material on it which had been evidently sewn on to the piece I have. The seams of the borders of the two actually corresponding – some blood and apparently faecal matter was found on the portion found in Goulstone Street. I believe the wounds on the face to have been done to disfigure the corpse."

FGordonBrown

Adjourned until Thursday next at $\frac{1}{2}$ past 10.

George William Sequeira 34 Jewry Street, Aldgate, Surgeon, being sworn – "I was called on the 30th September at 5 to 2 and was the first medical man to arrive. I saw the position of the body and I agree with Dr. Gordon Brown as to the position. I was present and heard the whole of the evidence of Dr. Gordon Brown at the last meeting. I quite agree with the Doctor in every particular."

By Mr. Crawford – "I know the locality. This is the darkest portion of the Square. There would have been sufficient light to enable the perpetrator of the deed to have committed the deed without the addition of any extra light. I formed the opinion that the perpetrator of the deed had no particular design on any particular organ. I do not think he was possessed of any great anatomical skill – I account for the absence of noise as the death must have been so instantaneous after the severance of the wind pipe and the blood vessels – I should not have expected that the person who committed the deed necessarily bespattered with blood – Life had not been extinct more than $\frac{1}{4}$ of an hour."

George William Sequeira.

William Sedgwick Saunders 13 Queen Street, Cheapside, Dr. of Medicine, Fellow of the Institute of Chemistry, Fellow of the Chemical Society, and Public Analyst for the City of London – "I received the stomach from Dr. Gordon Brown carefully sealed with his own private seal. The ends of the stomach had been carefully tied but its contents not been interfered with in any way. I carefully examined the stomach and its contents more particularly for poisons of the narcotic class with negative results, there not being the faintest trace of these or any other poison."

By Mr. Crawford – "I was present at the post mortem. I agree with Dr. Brown and Dr. Sequeira that the wounds were not inflicted by anyone possessing great anatomical skill and I agree that the perpetrator of the deed had no particular design on any particular organ."

WmSedgwickSaunders.

Annie Phillips 12 Dilstone Grove, Southwark Park Road, wife of Louis Phillips, a Lamp Black Packer, being sworn saith – "I am Daughter of Deceased who lived with my Father. I have never seen the marriage lines altho she always told me she was married. His name was Thomas Conway. I have not seen him for the last 15 or 18 months, he was living with me and my Husband at 15 Anchor Street, Southwark Park. He was a Hawker. He left suddenly without assigning any reason. We were not on good terms. I have never seen or heard of him since. He was a teatollar, my mother and he lived on bad terms because she used to drink – I have not the least idea of where he is living now. He had no ill will to my knowledge against Deceased. He left Deceased between 7 & 8 years ago entirely on account of her Drinking Habits. My mother told me he had been in the 18 Royal Irish. He has been a pensioner since I was 8 years old. I am now 23. He left my mother between 7 & 8 years ago. I have been in the habit of seeing deceased after she left my father. She has frequently applied for money. The last time I saw her was 2 years and one month. I saw nothing of her on Saturday the day previous to her death. I formerly lived in King Street Bermondsey. I left there 2 years ago. I did not leave my address when I left King Street, Bermondsey. I have 2 brothers by Conway, they live in London. My mother did not know where to find either of them, that was purposely kept from her to prevent her being applied to for money.''

By Jury – ''My father was aware she was living with Kelly.''

By Mr. Crawford – ''My father might have belonged to the Connaught Rangers – My mother waited on me in my confinement 2 years and 2 months ago. I saw Kelly and Deceased in a lodging House in Flower and Dean Street about 3 years ago. I knew they were living as man and wife. My father is living with my 2 Brothers ages between 15 and 20. I have not seen or heard from them for 18 months and I cannot give the clue to assist the police in finding them.''

Annie Phillips.

John Mitchell Detective Sergeant, City Police, being sworn saith – ''I have made every enquiry to find the Father and Brothers of the last Witness without success. I have found a Pensioner named Conway but he is not the man. I with other officers have used every endeavour and enquiry possible to be made with a view to trace the murderer.''

John Mitchell.

Baxter Hunt Detective Constable of the City of London Police, being sworn saith – ''I discovered Conway the Pensioner belonging to the 18 Royal Irish, I have confronted him with 2 of Deceased's Sisters and they have failed to recognize him as the man who used to live with Deceased. I have made every endeavour to trace the Conway mentioned by the last Witness without success.''

Baxter Hunt.

Louis Robinson City Police Constable 931 being sworn saith – ''On the 29th at 8.30 I was on duty in Aldgate High Street, I saw a crowd of persons outside No. 29 – I saw there a woman whom I have since recognized as the Deceased lying on the footway drunk. I asked if there was one that knew her or knew where she lived but I got no answer.

I picked her up and carried her to the side by the shutters and she fell sideways. I got assistance. We then took her to Bishopsgate Street Police Station. When asked her name she made the reply 'Nothing'. We then put her in the cells. No one particular appeared to be in her company when we first picked her up.''

By Mr. Crawford – ''The last time I saw her in the Police Cell was at 10 to 9. She was wearing an apron. I believe the apron produced was the one she was wearing.''

By the Jury – ''She smelt very strongly of drink.''

Louis Robinson.

James Byfield Station Sergeant, Bishopsgate Police Station being sworn saith – ''I remember deceased being brought in at ¼ to 9 on the Evening of the 29th she was very drunk having to be supported by the 2 constables who brought her in. She was taken back to the cell and detained there until one o'clock in the morning when she was sober. I discharged her after she gave her name and address which she was unable to do when brought in. She gave the name of Mary Ann Kelly, 6 Fashion Street, Spitalfields. She said she had been hopping.''

J.G. Byfield.

George Henry Hutt Police Constable 968, City Gaoler, of Bishopsgate Street Station – ''On Saturday the 29th at ¼ to 10 at night I took over the prisoners, among them the deceased woman. I visited her several times until 5 to one on Sunday. I found deceased was sober, brought from the cell into the office and after giving the name of Mary Ann Kelly she was discharged. I pushed open the swing door leading to the passage and said 'This way Misses' She passed along the passage to the outer door. I said to her please pull it to – she said 'All right Good Night Old Cock' she pulled the door within half a foot and she turned to the left leading towards Houndsditch.''

By Mr. Crawford – ''She left the Station at one o'clock and was capable of taking care of herself. When bringing her out of the cell she asked what time it was – I replied 'Too late for you to get any more drink. She said, 'Well what time is it?' I said, 'Just on one,' and 'I shall get a Damned fine hiding when I get home.' I said, 'And serve you right you have no right to get drunk.' I noticed she was wearing an apron. I believe the one produced was the one she was wearing when she left the Station. It would take 8 minutes ordinary walking to get to Mitre Square.''

George Hutt.

George James Morris Watchman to Messrs. Kearley and Tonge, Wholesale Grocers in Mitre Square — "I went on duty at 7 in the Evening of the 29th. I was occupied for the most of the time in cleaning the offices and looking about the Warehouse. At $\frac{1}{4}$ to 2 Police Constable Watkins, who was on the Mitre Square beat, knocked at my door which was slightly on the jar at the time. I was then sweeping the steps down towards the door. The door was knocked or pushed. I was then about 2 yards from the door. I turned round and opened the door wide and saw Constable Watkins.

He said, 'For God's sake mate come to my assistance.'

I said, 'Stop till I get my lamp.'

I immediately went outside. I said, 'What's the matter?'

'Oh dear,' he said, 'there's another woman cut up to pieces.'

I said, 'Where is she?'

He said, 'In the corner.'

I went over to the corner and shewed my light on the body. I immediately blew my whistle and ran up Mitre Street into Aldgate. I saw no suspicious person. About then 2 Constables came up. They asked me what was the matter. I told them to go down Mitre Square, there was another terrible murder. I then followed the constables down and took charge of my own premises again — I heard no noise in the Square before I was called by Constable Watkins. If there had been any cry of distress I must have heard it."

By the Jury — "I was in the Warehouse where the Counting House facing the Square. The door had not been ajar more than 2 minutes."

By Mr. Crawford — "I had not quitted the Warehouse between 11 and one. I had not seen Watkins before that evening."

George James Morris.

James Harvey 964, City Police, being sworn saith — "I went on my beat at $\frac{1}{4}$ to 10 on the 29th ulto. My beat is from Bevis Marks, to Duke Street, into Little Duke Street, to Houndsditch. From Houndsditch back to Duke Street, along Duke Street to Church passage, back again into Duke Street to Aldgate. From there to Mitre Street, back again to Houndsditch. Up Houndsditch to Little Duke Street, again back to Houndsditch to Goring Street, up Goring Street to Bevis Marks, to where I started. At 20 to 2 on Sunday morning I went down Duke Street and down Church Passage as far as Mitre Square. I saw no one. I heard no cry or noise. When I got to Aldgate returning to Duke Street I heard a whistle blown and saw the Witness Morris with a lamp. I went to him and asked what was the matter. He said, 'A woman has been ripped up in Mitre Square.'

I saw a Constable on the other side of the street.

I said, 'Come with me.'

We went into Mitre Square and saw Watkins there and the Deceased. Constable Holland who followed me went for Dr. Sequeira. Private individuals were sent for other Constables, arriving almost immediately. I waited there with Watkins and information was at once sent for the Inspector. I passed the post office clock between 1 and 2 minutes to the half hour.''

By the Jury — "I go as far as to the end of Church Passage. I was at the end of Church Passage about 18 or 19 minutes to 2.''

By Mr. Crawford — "I can only speak with certainty as to time with regard to the post office clock.''

James Harvey.

George Clapp No. 5 Mitre Street, Aldgate, being sworn saith — "I am carekeeper of the premises. The back of the house looks into Mitre Square. I went to bed with my wife about 11 o'clock on Saturday night. The back of the house looks into Mitre Square. I was sleeping in a back room on the 2nd floor. During the night I heard no sound or any noise of any kind. Between 5 and 6 o'clock in the morning was the first I heard of the murder.''

By Mr. Crawford — "The only other person in the house was a Mrs. Tew, a nurse in attendance on my wife. She slept on the 3rd floor.''

George Clapp.

Richard Pearce 922, City Police, being sworn saith — "I live at No. 3 Mitre Square. I went to bed at 12.30 on Sunday morning. I heard no noise or disturbance of any sort. At 20 past 2 I was called by a Constable and first heard of the murder. From my window I could see the spot where deceased was found.''

By Mr. Crawford — "I am the only tenant in the Square.''

Richard Pearce.

Joseph Lawende 45 Norfolk Road, Dalston, Commercial Traveller, being sworn saith — "On the night of the 29th I was at the Imperial Club. Mr. Joseph Levy and Mr. Harry Harris were with me. It was raining. We left there to go out at ½ past one and we left the house about 5 minutes later. I walked a little further from the others. Standing in the corner of Church Passage in Duke Street, which leads into Mitre square, I saw a woman. She was standing with her face towards a man. I only saw her back. She had her hand on his chest. The man was taller than she was. She had a black jacket and a black bonnet. I have seen the articles which it was stated belonged to her at the police station. My belief is that they were the same clothes which I had seen upon the Deceased. She appeared to me short. The man had a cloth cap on with a cloth peak. I have given a description of the man to the police. I doubt whether I should know him again.''

By Mr. Crawford – ''The number of the Club is 16 & 17 Duke Street. It is 15 or 16 feet from the Club to the passage where they were standing. I fix the time by the Club clock and my own watch at ½ past one. I did not hear a word said. They did not either of them appear to be quarrelling. They appeared conversing very quietly. I did not look back to see where they went.''

Joseph Lawende.

Joseph Hyam Levy 1 Hutchinson Street, Aldgate, Butcher, being sworn saith – ''I was with the last Witness and Harris at the Imperial Club in Duke Street. We got up to go home at ½ past one. We came out about 3 or 4 minutes after the half hour. I saw a man and woman standing at the corner of Church Passage. I passed on taking no further notice of them. The man I should say was about 3 inches taller than the woman. I cannot give any description of either of them. We went down Duke Street into Aldgate leaving the man and woman still talking behind. I fix the time by the Club clock. I said when I came out to Mr. Harris, ''Look there, I don't like going home by myself when I see those characters about.''

By Mr. Crawford – ''There was nothing that I saw about the man and woman which caused me to fear them.''

Joseph Hyam Levy.

Alfred Long 254A, Metropolitan Police Force, being sworn saith – ''I was on duty in Goulston Street, Whitechapel on the 30th September, about 2.55 AM. I found a portion of a woman's apron which I produce. There appeared blood stains on it, one portion was wet, lying in a passage leading to the staircases of 108 to 119 Model Dwelling House. Above it on the wall was written in chalk – The Jews are the men that will not be blamed for nothing. I at once searched the staircases and areas of the Building but found nothing else. I at once took the apron to Commercial Road Police Station and reported it to the Inspector on Duty. I passed that spot where the apron was found about 2.20, the apron was not there when I passed then.''

By Mr. Crawford – ''The words that were written on the wall – the Jewes are the men that will not be blamed for nothing. I copied the words from the wall into my report – I could not say whether they were recently written. I wrote down into my book and the Inspector noticed that Jews was spelt Juews. There was a difference between the spelling.

When I found the piece of apron I at once searched the staircase leading to the Buildings. I did not make any enquiries at the tenements of the Buildings. There were 6 or 7 staircases. I searched every one, found no traces of blood or recent footmarks. Having searched I at once proceeded to the Station. Before proceeding there I had heard of a murder having been committed. I had heard of the murder in Mitre Square. I left a man 190 in charge of the Beat H Division. I told him to take an observation as to any one who entered the building or left it. I next returned to the Building about 5 o'clock. When I returned the writing had not been rubbed out. It was rubbed out in my presence at $\frac{1}{2}$ past 5 or thereabouts. I did not hear any one object to its being rubbed out.''

Alfred Long.

Daniel Halse Detective Officer of the City of London Police being sworn saith — ''On Saturday the 29th September from instructions I received I directed a number of Police Officers to patrol the City all night. At about 2 minutes to 2 I was at the corner of Houndsditch by Aldgate Church in company with Detectives Outram and Marriott of the City Police. We all 3 went to Mitre Square. I had the light turned on to the body and saw it was a murder. I gave instructions to have the neighbourhood searched and every man examined. I went by Middlesex Street into Wentworth Street where I stopped 2 men who gave satisfactory account of themselves. I came through Goulston Street at 20 past 2 and then went back to Mitre Square and accompanied Inspector Collard to the mortuary. I saw deceased stripped and saw a portion of the apron was missing. I went back with Major Smith to Mitre Square when we went ['back to Goulstone' *deleted*] I then went with Detective Hunt to Leman Street Police Station. I and Detective Hunt went on to Goulstone Street and the spot was pointed out where the apron was found. I saw some chalk writing on the black facia of the wall. I remained there and sent with a view to having the writing photographed. Directions were given to have the writing photographed and during the time some of the Metropolitan Police said as it was Sunday morning it might cause a riot or an outbreak against the Jews and decided to have it rubbed out and it was rubbed out. When Hunt returned an enquiry was made at every tenement of the Building but we could gain no witness of any one going in likely to be the murderer.''

By Mr. Crawford — ''About 20 past 2 I passed over the spot where the piece of apron was found. I did not notice anything. I suggested that the top line should be taken out of the writing on the wall. I took a note of the writing before it was rubbed out. The exact words were 'The Juwes are not the men that will be blamed for nothing.' The writing had the appearance of being recently written. I protested against the writing being rubbed out. I wished it to remain there until Major Smith had seen it.''

By the Jury — "It looked as if it had been recently written.''

Daniel Halse.

Verdict Wilful Murder by some person unknown.

Despite the fairly detailed statements of the various witnesses contained in the preceding inquest papers, they would appear to be the initial evidence of these witnesses and the reports to be found in the newspapers do contain additional information. In order to get the full details of the reported evidence in the press, we again turn to *The Times*. The first report is contained in the issue of Friday, 5 October 1888, page 4:

THE EAST-END MURDERS.

Yesterday morning Mr. S. F. Langham, the City Coroner, opened the inquest at the mortuary in Golden-lane respecting the death of Catherine Eddows [*sic*], otherwise Conway or Kelly, who was found murdered in Mitre-square, City, last Sunday morning.

Dr. Sedgwick Saunders, medical officer of health for the City; Mr. Crawford, the City Solicitor; Mr. M'William, the inspector of the City Detective Department; and Mr. Superintendent Foster were present during the inquiry.

Mr. Crawford, at the opening of the proceedings, stated that he was present as representing the City Police, for the purpose of rendering the Coroner and the jury every possible assistance. If, when the witnesses were giving evidence, he thought it desirable to put any question, probably he would have the Coroner's permission to do so.

The CORONER — By all means.

Eliza Gold was the first witness. She stated that she lived at No. 6, Thrawl-street, Spitalfields, and was a widow. She recognized the deceased as her sister, whose name was Catherine Eddows. She was not married, but was living with a man named Kelly. Her sister had not been married. Her age last birthday was 43, as well as witness could remember. She had been living for some years with Kelly. Witness last saw her alive four or five months ago. She used to get her living by going out hawking. She was a woman of sober habits. Before she went to live with Kelly she had lived with a man named Conway for some years. She had had two children by him, who were married. Witness could not say whether Conway was still living; she had not seen him. Conway was a pensioner in the Army, who used to go out hawking things. Witness could not say whether her sister and Conway had parted on good or bad terms; nor could she say whether her sister had seen Conway since they had parted. Witness was quite certain that the deceased was her sister.

By Mr. Crawford. – She had not seen Conway for seven or eight years, and she could not say on what terms her sister had lived with Kelly. She had not seen them together for three or four weeks. They were then living together quite happily. Witness could not exactly fix the time when she saw them. They were living at the time at 55, Flower and Dean-street, a common lodging-house kept by a man named Smith. The last time she saw her sister alive was when the latter visited witness, who was ill at the time.

A discrepancy in her evidence was pointed out to the witness, who had stated in one part that the last time she saw her sister alive was four or five months ago, while in another portion of her evidence she had stated that it was three or four weeks ago.

John Kelly was the next witness called. He stated that he lived at 55, Flower and Dean-street, Spitalfields. He was a labourer and jobbed about the markets. He had seen and recognized the body of the deceased as Catherine Conway. Witness had known her seven years, and had lived with her the whole of that time. She used to sell things in the streets, and had lived with witness at the lodging-house in Flower and Dean-street. Witness was last with the deceased at 2 o'clock on Saturday afternoon in Houndsditch. They parted there on very good terms. She said she was going to see if she could find her daughter Annie in Bermondsey. He believed Annie was a daughter the deceased had had by Conway. She promised to be back at 4 o'clock and no later. She did not return, but witness heard that she was locked up on Saturday night at Bishopsgate. He was told by a woman that she had seen deceased in Houndsditch with two policemen. He could not say what time it was when he heard that statement. He did not make inquiries about her, feeling sure that she would return on Sunday morning. He heard that she had been locked up because she had had "a drop of drink." He did not know that she ever went out for immoral purposes; he had never allowed her to do so. She was not in the habit of drinking to excess, but occasionally she did so. She had no money about her when witness parted from her. Her object in going to Bermondsey was to see if she could find her daughter and get a little money from her, so that she need not walk the streets.

Mr. Crawford. – You were asked before if she walked the streets, and you said she did not. – Sometimes we were without money to pay for our lodging, and we were at the time I speak of. Witness did not know of anyone with whom the deceased was at variance, or who would be likely to do her an injury. He did not know whether the deceased had seen Conway of late; he had never seen Conway himself. He did not know when the deceased was discharged from custody.

By a Juryman. – She was in the habit of returning to her lodging at 8 or 9 o'clock. He had not inquired about her because he had felt sure that she would return on Sunday morning.

By Mr. Crawford. – He did not know with whom the deceased had been drinking on Saturday afternoon. She had not on any recent occasion absented herself at night time. Some time ago – a few months or weeks – she left witness; he supposed it was in consequence of their having had a few words, but she returned to him a few hours afterwards. He had had no angry words with the deceased on the Saturday afternoon. She had told him that her daughter lived in King-street, Bermondsey. They had been living together for seven years in Flower and Dean-street. On Friday night last she did not sleep with witness. She had no money, and went to the casual ward at Mile-end. He slept that night at the lodging-house mentioned. On the previous Monday night they slept in Kent, where they were hopping. They came up from Kent on Thursday, he believed. They had no money and they went to the casual ward in Shoe-lane. They were together all Friday until the afternoon, when he earned 6d. She said to him, "You take 4d. and go to the lodging-house, and give me 2d. and I will go to the casual ward." He wanted to spend the money in food and he told her that "Fred" – the deputy of the lodging-house – would not turn them away if they had no money. She said she would go to the casual ward at Mile-end, and would see him on the following morning, when he met her accidentally. She left him at 4 o'clock on Friday afternoon to go to Mile-end for a lodging. He saw her the next morning about 8 o'clock, as well as he could remember, and was surprised to see her so soon. The tea and sugar found on her had been bought out of the 2s. 6d. for which she had pawned his boots. When she left witness she was, he was sure, quite sober. They had spent the greater part of the 2s. 6d. in food and drink. They parted on good terms. He could not say why she separated from Conway. She had lived with witness for seven years. When he saw her so early on the Saturday morning she told him that there had been some bother in the casual ward, and that that was why she had been turned out so soon. He did not know the regulations of the casual ward at Mile-end, and whether she could discharge herself when she liked.

By Mr. Crawford. – The boots were pawned on Friday or Saturday by the deceased. Witness remained outside the shop. He slept at the lodging-house in Flower and Dean-street on Saturday night.

Mr. Crawford produced the pawn-ticket, and stated that the boots were pledged last Friday.

Frederick William Wilkinson, living in Brick-lane, Spitalfields, was next examined. He said he was deputy of the lodginghouse in Flower and Dean-street. He had known Kelly and the deceased for the last seven or eight years, and they passed as man and wife. They lived on very good terms, but they had a few words occasionally when "Kate was in drink." Witness believed that deceased obtained her living by hawking things in the streets, and by charing. Whenever she and Kelly were at the lodginghouse they were pretty regular in paying. She was not often in drink, and was "a very jolly woman," often singing. Witness had never seen Kelly in drink since he had known him. He saw the deceased on her return from hopping at the lodginghouse on Friday afternoon, but he did not see Kelly at the time. She went out on Friday night, and witness saw her on the following morning between 10 and 11 o'clock with Kelly. Witness did not see her again until he saw her in the mortuary. To witness's knowledge the deceased had not been in the habit of walking the streets. When she and Kelly stopped at the lodginghouse they came in generally between 9 and 10. He had never known or heard of her being intimate with any one but Kelly. She used to say that her name was Kate Conway, and that it had been "bought and paid for," meaning that she was married to Conway. So far as witness knew she was not at variance with any one. She was quite sober when he saw her with Kelly on Saturday morning between 10 and 11. He asked Kelly when the latter came to pay for his lodging on Saturday where "Kate" was, and Kelly replied that he had heard that she had been locked up. Kelly called between 7. 30 and 8 on Saturday night and took a single bed. A single bed was 4d. and a double was 8d.

A juryman. – Do you not take the names of those who sleep at the lodginghouse? – No.

By Mr. Crawford. – He believed the last time the deceased and Kelly slept together at the lodginghouse was five or six weeks ago; before they went hopping. Kelly was there on Friday and Saturday nights. Deceased was not there on Friday or Saturday. He did not ask Kelly where she was on the Friday, and the reason why he asked the question on the Saturday night was because he had seen them together on that morning. Kelly went to bed at 10 o'clock on Saturday night, and witness was quite positive that he did not go out again. He could not say at what hour Kelly went out on Saturday, but he saw him at the lodginghouse at dinner-time. So far as he was aware, Kelly had had no quarrel with any man about the deceased. He believed she was wearing an apron on Saturday morning.

Mr. Crawford. – Did any one come to your lodginghouse on the Sunday morning between 1 and 2 o'clock and take a bed; a stranger? Witness. – I had no stranger there between 1 and 2.

Mr. Crawford. – Can you tell me who entered your lodginghouse on Sunday morning between 1 and 2? Witness. – Two detectives came and asked if I had any female out.

Mr. Crawford. — Did any one come in before that, between 1 and 2, whom you did not recognize, and take a bed? Witness. — I cannot remember. I can refer to my book and tell you whether any stranger was there.

By the jury. — I saw the deceased and Kelly together on Saturday morning between 10 and 11 at breakfast.

The examination of the witness was then adjourned to enable him to obtain the book referred to from the lodginghouse.

Edward Watkins, City Police-constable 881, was the next witness, and, in answer to Mr. Crawford, he stated that he had been in the City Police force for 17 years. On the night of Saturday, September 29, he went on duty at a quarter to 10 — on his regular beat. His beat extended from Duke-street, Aldgate, through Heneage-lane, a portion of Bury-street, through Cree Church-lane, into Leadenhall-street, along Leadenhall-street, eastward into Mitre-street, into Mitre-square, round the square, and again into Mitre-street, then into and along King-street to St. James's-place, round St. James's-place, and thence into Duke-street, the starting point. The beat took 12 or 14 minutes. He had been continually patrolling that beat from 10 o'clock on Saturday night until 1.30 on Sunday morning without anything exciting his attention. He passed through Mitre-square about 1.30 on Sunday morning. He had his lantern fixed in his belt, and in accordance with his usual practice, he looked into the different corners, passages, and warehouses. Nothing excited his attention at 1.30 nor did he see any one about. No one could have been in any portion of the square at that hour without the cognizance of the witness. He next came into Mitre-square about 1.44. He fixed the time by reference to his watch after he had called the watchman. He entered the square from the right, near the corner, where something attracted his attention. [Plans of the square made by Mr. F. W. Foster, of Old Jewry, were at this point handed in and referred to by Mr. Crawford in his examination.] About 1.44 witness came into the square, at the right, and he then saw the body of a woman lying there. She was lying on her back, with her feet facing the square. He did not touch the body. The first thing he did was to go across to Messrs. Kearsley [sic] and Tonge's warehouse. The door was ajar. He pushed it open and called to the watchman, Morris. Morris came out, and witness sent him for assistance. Witness remained by the side of the body till the arrival of Police-constable Holland. No one was there with witness till Holland arrived, and he was followed by Dr. Sequeira. Inspector Collard arrived about 2, and Dr. Gordon Brown, surgeon to the City police force, followed. When witness entered the square at 1.44 he heard nothing — no sound as of the footsteps of some one running away; and to the best of his belief no one was there but the murdered woman.

By the CORONER. — The door of the warehouse of Messrs. Kearsley [sic] and

Tonge was open, as the watchman was working inside. It was not an unusual thing for the warehouse door to be open at that time.

By the Jury. – He did not sound a whistle, because they did not carry whistles. The watchman did whistle. Witness's beat was a single beat; no other policeman entered Mitre-square.

Frederick William Foster, of 26, Old Jewry, stated that he was an architect and surveyor, and he had made the plans (produced) according to scale. He had them in three scales – one to 8 ft. to an inch, another 200 ft. to an inch, from an Ordnance map of the City; and he had marked on an Ordnance map of the same scale round from Berner-street to Mitre-street. That would be a distance of about three-quarters of a mile; and it would take from 12 to 15 minutes to walk it.

By Mr. Crawford. – The route described between Berner-street and Mitre-street was the nearest way. It was a direct line.

Mr. Crawford. – Assuming that a person was in Mitre-square, I want to know what route he would probably take, assuming that he passed by way of Goulston-street? – Witness. – There are two routes. There is only 10 ft. difference between them. One route is from Church-passage through Duke-street, crossing Houndsditch, through Gravel-lane, Stoney-lane, crossing Petticoat-lane, and through to Goulston-street. I know Flower and Dean-street.

Mr. Crawford. – Would a person, to get to the lodginghouse there from Mitre-street, go by Goulston-street? – Witness. – He might do so. It is the most direct course he could take if he knew the neighbourhood. He could do the distance in a quarter of an hour; and the distance from Berner-street to Mitre-street would be within a quarter of an hour.

Mr. Crawford, to the Coroner. – You will have evidence later on that a portion of this woman's apron was found in Goulston-street.

The witness **Wilkinson** was then re-called, and in answer to Mr. Crawford stated, referring to his book, that Kelly slept at the lodginghouse on Friday and Saturday night in "No. 52, single." Witness could not say at what time any stranger entered the place. He found that there were six male strangers there on the Sunday morning. He could not tell whether any of those men came in about 2 o'clock on the Sunday morning, nor could he remember any one going out of the place soon after 12 o'clock, as that was a very busy time. He took the money and allotted the beds. Nothing excited his suspicion between the hours of 12 a.m. and 2. He recollected the police calling at 3 o'clock on Sunday morning.

By a juryman. – It was usual for the place to be open at 2 o'clock in the morning. They generally closed at 2.30 or 3. He had no means of remembering any person coming in. He would recognize a regular customer. He did not book the times they came in.

By Mr. Crawford. – There was no register kept of the names of those sleeping there.

By the jury. – We take the money of those who come. No questions are asked, and they are shown their beds. I dare say I have over 100 sleeping there now of a night.

Inspector Edward Collard (City Police) was the next witness called. He stated that at five minutes before 2 o'clock on Sunday morning last he received information at Bishopsgate-street Police-station that a woman had been murdered in Mitre-square. The information was at once telegraphed to headquarters, and he despatched a constable at once to Dr. Gordon Brown. Witness then proceeded himself to Mitre-square, arriving there at two or three minutes past 2. He there found Dr. Sequeira, several police officers, and the deceased lying in the south-west corner of the square in the position described by Constable Watkins. The body was not touched until the arrival of Dr. Brown, who came shortly afterwards. The medical gentlemen then examined the body, and remained until the arrival of the ambulance, when the body was taken to the mortuary. No money was found on the deceased. A portion of the apron produced was found on her, and the other portion, which was picked up in Goulston-street, would also be produced. When witness arrived at the square he took immediate steps to have the neighbourhood searched for the person who had committed the murder. Mr. M'William, the chief of the detectives, on his arrival shortly afterwards with a number of detectives, sent them to make search in all directions in Spitalfields, both in the streets and the lodging-houses. Several men were stopped and searched in the streets, but without any good result. Witness had a house-to-house inquiry made in the vicinity of Mitre-square, but could find nothing beyond what would be stated by two witnesses who would be called.

By Mr. Crawford. – There was no appearance of any struggle having taken place, and there was no blood anywhere except what had come from the deceased's neck. There was nothing whatever in the appearance of the deceased or her clothing to lead him to suppose that there had been any struggle. The blood flowing from her was in a liquid state, not congealed, and from his experience he should say that the body had not been there for more than a quarter of an hour. They endeavoured to find footmarks, but they could discover no trace whatever. A search was made at the back of the empty houses adjoining the square.

Dr. Frederick Gordon Brown, of 17, Finsbury-circus, examined, said he was surgeon of the City of London Police Force. He was called on Sunday morning shortly after 2 o'clock, and reached Mitre-square about 18 minutes after 2, when his attention was called to the body of the deceased. It was lying in the position described by Constable Watkins. The body was on its back, the head turned towards the left shoulder, and the arms were by the side of the body, as if they had fallen there. Both palms were upwards and the fingers were slightly bent. A thimble was lying on the ground near the right hand. The clothes were drawn up, the left leg was extended straight down, in a line with the body, and the right leg was bent at the thigh and knee. There was great disfigurement of the face. The throat was cut across, and below the cut was a neckerchief. The upper part of the dress had been pulled open a little way. The abdomen was all exposed; the intestines were drawn out to a large extent and placed over the right shoulder; a piece of the intestines was quite detached from the body and placed between the left arm and the body.

Mr. Crawford. – By "placed," do you mean put there by design? Witness. – Yes.

Examination continued. – The lobe of the right ear was cut obliquely through; there was a quantity of clotted blood on the pavement, on the left side of the neck and upper part of the arm. The body was quite warm, and no death-stiffening had taken place. The body had been there only a few minutes.

By Mr. Crawford. – Certainly within 30 or 40 minutes.

Examination continued. – We looked for superficial bruises and saw none. There were no marks of blood below the middle of the body.

By Mr. Crawford. – There was no blood on the front of the clothes. Before they removed the body he suggested that Dr. Phillips should be sent for, and that gentleman, who had seen some recent cases, came to the mortuary. A post-mortem examination was made at 2.30 on Sunday afternoon. The temperature of the room was 55deg. Rigor mortis was well marked. After careful washing of the left hand a recent bruise, the size of a sixpence, was discovered on the back of the hand between the thumb and the first finger. There were a few small bruises on the right shin of older date. The hands and arms were bronzed as if from sunburning. There were no bruises on the scalp, back of the body, or elbows. The witness then described in detail the cuts on the face, which, he stated, was very much mutilated. The throat was cut across to the extent of about 6in. or 7in. The sterno cleido mastoid muscle was divided; the cricoid cartilage below the vocal cords was severed through the middle; the large vessels on the left side of the neck were severed to the bone, the knife marking the intervertebral cartilage. The sheath of the vessels on the right side was just open; the carotid artery had a pin-hole opening; the internal jugular vein was open to the extent of an inch and a half – not divided. All the injuries were caused by some very sharp instrument, like a knife, and pointed. The cause of death was haemorrhage from the left common carotid artery. The death was immediate. The mutilations were inflicted after death. They examined the injuries to the abdomen. The walls of the abdomen were laid open, from the breast downwards. The cut commenced opposite the ensiform cartilage, in the centre of the body. The incision went upwards, not penetrating the skin that was over the sternum; it then divided the ensiform cartilage, and being gristle they could tell how the knife had made the cut. It was held so that the point was towards the left side and the handle towards the right. The cut was made obliquely. The liver was stabbed as if by the point of a sharp knife. There was another incision in the liver, about $2\frac{1}{2}$ in., and, below, the left lobe of the liver was slit through by a vertical cut. Two cuts were shown by a jag of the skin on the left side. The abdominal walls were divided vertically in the middle line to within a quarter of an inch of the navel; the cut then took a horizontal course for $2\frac{1}{2}$ in. to the right side; it then divided the navel on the left side – round it – and made an incision parallel to the former horizontal incision, leaving the navel on a tongue of skin. Attached to the navel was $2\frac{1}{2}$ in. of the lower part of the rectus muscle of the left side of the abdomen. The incision then took an oblique course to the right. There was a stab of about an inch in the left groin, penetrating the skin in superficial fashion. Below that was a cut of 3in., going through all tissues, wounding the peritoneum to about the same extent. There had not been any appreciable bleeding from the vessels.

Mr. Crawford. – What conclusion do you draw from that? – Witness. – That the cut in the abdomen was made after death, and that there would not be much blood left to escape on the hands of the murderer. The way in which the mutilation had been effected showed that the perpetrator of the crime possessed some anatomical knowledge.

Mr. Crawford. – I think I understood you to say that in your opinion the cause of death was the cut in the throat? Witness. – Loss of blood from the throat, caused by the cut. That was the first wound inflicted.

Mr. Crawford. – Have you formed any opinion that the woman was standing when that wound was inflicted? Witness. – My opinion is that she was on the ground.

Mr. Crawford. – Does the nature of the wounds lead you to any conclusion as to the kind of instrument with which they were inflicted? Witness. – With a sharp knife, and it must have been pointed; and from the cut in the abdomen I should say the knife was at least six inches long.

Mr. Crawford. – Would you consider that the person who inflicted the wounds possessed great anatomical skill? Witness. – A good deal of knowledge as to the position of the organs in the abdominal cavity and the way of removing them.

Mr. Crawford. – Could the organs removed be used for any professional purpose? Witness. – They would be of no use for a professional purpose.

Mr. Crawford. – You have spoken of the extraction of the left kidney. Would it require great skill and knowledge to remove it? Witness. – It would require a great deal of knowledge as to its position to remove it. It is easily overlooked. It is covered by a membrane.

Mr. Crawford. – Would not such a knowledge be likely to be possessed by one accustomed to cutting up animals? Witness. – Yes.

Mr. Crawford. – Have you been able to form any opinion as to whether the perpetrator of this act was disturbed when performing it? Witness. – I think he had sufficient time. My reason is that he would not have nicked the lower eyelids if he had been in a great hurry.

Mr. Crawford. – About how long do you think it would take to inflict all these wounds, and perpetrate such a deed? Witness. – At least five minutes would be required.

Mr. Crawford. – Can you as a professional man assign any reason for the removal of certain organs from the body? Witness. – I cannot.

Mr. Crawford. – Have you any doubt in your mind that there was no struggle? Witness. – I feel sure that there was no struggle.

Mr. Crawford. – Are you equally of opinion that the act would be that of one man, one person, only? Witness. – I think so; I see no reason for any other opinion.

Mr. Crawford. – Can you as a professional man account for the fact of no noise being heard by those in the immediate neighbourhood? Witness. – The throat would be so instantaneously severed that I do not suppose there would be any time for least sound being emitted.

Mr. Crawford. – Would you expect to find much blood on the person who inflicted the wounds? Witness. – No. I should not.

Mr. Crawford. – Could you say whether the blood spots on the piece of apron produced were of recent origin? Witness. – They are of recent origin. Dr. Phillips brought on a piece of apron which had been found by a policeman in Goulston-street.

Mr. Crawford. – It is impossible to assert that it is human blood? Witness. – Yes; it is blood. On the piece of apron brought on there were smears of blood on one side as if a hand or a knife had been wiped on it. It fitted the piece of apron in evidence.

Mr. Crawford. – Have you formed any opinion as to the purpose for which the face was mutilated? Witness. – Simply to disfigure the corpse, I should think.

Mr. Crawford. – Not much violence was required to inflict these injuries? Witness. – A sharp knife was used, and not very much force would be required.

By a juryman. – He did not think any drug was administered to the woman, judging from the breath; but he had not yet examined the contents of the stomach.

At this point the inquiry was adjourned for a week.

Mr. Crawford said that it might be of interest for the jury to know that the Court of Common Council had unanimously adopted the suggestion of the Lord Mayor that a reward of £500 should be offered for the detection and conviction of the murderer.

The jury expressed satisfaction at the announcement.

From *The Times* of Tuesday, 9 October 1888:

The funeral of Catherine Eddowes, the victim of the Mitre-square murder, took place yesterday at Ilford Cemetery. The body was removed shortly after 1 o'clock from the mortuary in Golden-lane, where a vast concourse of people had assembled. A strong force of the City Police, under Mr. Superintendent Foster, was present, and conducted the cortege to the City boundary. At Old-street a large number of the Metropolitan Police were present under Inspector Barnham. The cortege passed Whitechapel parish church, and along Mile-end-road, through Bow and Stratford to the cemetery. The sisters of the ill-fated woman and the man Kelly, with whom she had lived for seven years, attended the funeral. Along the whole route great sympathy was expressed for the relatives.

It is stated by a news agency that definite instructions have been issued to the police that in the event of any person being found murdered under circumstances similar to those of the recent crimes, they are not to remove the body of the victim, but to send notice immediately to a veterinary surgeon in the South-west District, who holds several trained blood-hounds in readiness to be taken to the spot where the body may be found, and to be at once put on the scent.

The Times of Thursday, 11 October 1888, page 5, carries an update on the enquiry in respect of the murder of Catherine Eddowes:

THE EAST-END MURDERS.

A good deal of fresh evidence will be given at the adjourned inquest, which will be held to-day at the City Coroner's Court, Golden-lane, upon the body of the Mitre-square victim. Since the adjournment, Shelton, the coroner's officer, has, with the assistance of the City police authorities, discovered several new witnesses, including the daughter of the deceased, who was found to be occupying a respectable situation as a domestic in the neighbourhood of Kensington. She states that she had not seen her mother for some time, and certainly did not see her on the night she met her death. Two witnesses have also been found who state that they saw the deceased standing at the corner of

Duke-street, Aldgate, a few minutes' walk from Mitre-square. This was as near as they can recollect about half-past 1 o'clock, and she was then alone. They recognized her on account of the white apron she was wearing. The contents of the deceased's stomach have been analyzed, but no trace of a narcotic can be discovered. Ten witnesses will be called to-day, and the coroner hopes to conclude the inquiry this sitting.

The Times of Friday, 12 October 1888, page 4, takes up the report on the Eddowes inquest, resumed the previous day:

THE EAST-END MURDERS.

Yesterday morning Mr. S. F. Langham, the City Coroner, resumed the inquest at the mortuary in Golden-lane respecting the death of Catherine Eddows [sic], otherwise Conway or Kelly, who was found murdered in Mitre-square on the morning of Sunday, the 30th ult.

During the inquiry Major Henry Smith, the Assistant Commissioner of the City Police, Mr. M'William, the inspector of the City Detective Department, Mr. Superintendent Foster, and Mr. F. W. Foster, architect and surveyor, of Old Jewry, who produced plans of the square were present.

The first witness examined was **Dr. George William Sequeira**, of 34, Jewry-street, Aldgate, who stated that he was called on Sunday, the 30th ult., to Mitre-square, and was the first medical man to arrive, being on the scene of the murder at five minutes to 2. He saw the position of the body, and he entirely agreed with Dr. Gordon Brown's evidence given on the opening of the inquest.

By Mr. Crawford (the City Solicitor). – He was acquainted with the locality and knew the position of the square. It would probably be the darkest corner of the square where the body was found. There would have been sufficient light to enable the murderer to commit his crime without the aid of any additional light.

Mr. Crawford. – Have you formed any opinion that the murderer had any design with respect to any particular part? – I have formed the opinion that he had no particular design on any particular organ.

Mr. Crawford. – Judging from the injuries inflicted, do you think he was possessed of great anatomical skill? – No, I do not.

Mr. Crawford. – Can you account for the absence of any noise? – The death must have been so instantaneous after the severance of the blood vessels and the wind-pipe.

By Mr. Crawford. – He did not think that the clothes of the assassin would necessarily be bespattered with blood. When witness arrived life had been extinct probably not more than a quarter of an hour, judging from the condition of the blood.

Dr. William Sedgwick Saunders of 13, Queen-street, Cheapside, examined, said he was doctor of medicine, Fellow of the Institute of Chemistry, Fellow of the Chemical Society, and public analyst of the City of London. He received the stomach of the deceased from Dr. Gordon Brown, carefully sealed, and the contents had not been interfered with in any way. He had carefully examined the stomach and its contents, more particularly for poisons of a narcotic class, with negative results, there not being the faintest trace of any of these, or any other poison.

By Mr. Crawford. – He was present during the whole of the post-mortem examination. Having had ample opportunity of seeing the wounds inflicted, he agreed with Dr. Brown and Dr. Sequeira that they were not inflicted by a person of great anatomical skill. He equally agreed that the murderer had no particular design on any particular internal organ.

Annie Phillips, living at 12, Dilston-grove, Southwark-park-road, was the next witness. She stated that she was married, and that her husband was a lamp-black packer. She was the daughter of the deceased, who had always told witness that she was married to Thomas Conway, witness's father. She had not seen him for 15 or 18 months. The last time she saw him was when he was living with witness and her husband at 15, Anchor-street, Southwark-park. Her father was a hawker. She did not know what became of him after he left. He left without giving any particular reason for going, but he did not leave witness on very good terms. He did not say that he would never see her again. He was a teetotaller. He and her mother did not live on good terms after the latter took to drink. She had not the least idea where her father was living. He had no ill-will against the deceased, so far as witness knew. She was told that her father had been in the 18th Royal Irish. He left her mother solely because of her drinking habits. He was a pensioner and had had a pension since witness was eight years old. She was now 23. It was seven or eight years ago since her father lived with her mother. Witness frequently saw her mother after they separated; her mother applied to her for money. The last time she saw her mother alive was two years and one month ago. She did not see her on the Saturday, the day previous to her death. Witness used to live in King-street, Bermondsey – that was about two years ago. On removing from there witness did not leave any address. She had two brothers, Conway being their father. Her mother did not know where to find either of them; the information was purposely kept from her. She supposed that that was in order to prevent her mother from applying to them for money.

By a juryman. – It was between 15 and 18 months ago since her father lived with witness and her husband. Her father knew at that time that her mother was living with Kelly.

By Mr. Crawford. – She was not sure that her father was a pensioner of the

18th Royal Irish. It might have been the Connaught Rangers. [Mr. Crawford observed that there was a pensioner of the 18th Royal Irish named Conway, but he was not the Conway who was wanted.] The deceased last received money from witness about two years and two months ago, when she waited upon witness in the latter's confinement. Witness had never had a letter from her mother. She had seen Kelly and her mother together in the lodging-house in Flower and Dean-street; that was about $3\frac{1}{2}$ years ago. Witness knew that they lived together. Her father was living with her two brothers, but she could not say where. She could not give the slightest clue as to their whereabouts. Her brothers were aged 15 and 20. Witness did not know that her mother had recently been intimate with any one besides Kelly in the lodging-house.

Detective-sergeant John Mitchell (City Police), the next witness, replying to Mr. Crawford, said that he had made every effort, acting under instructions, to find the father and the brothers of the last witness, but without success. He had found a pensioner named Conway belonging to the 18th Royal Irish, but he was not identified as the Thomas Conway in question.

To the Coroner. – Every endeavour possible has been made with a view to tracing the murderer.

Mr. Crawford. – Do not go into that. I am sure that the jury believe that, and that the City Police are doing everything they can with that object.

Detective Baxter Hunt (City Police), replying to Mr. Crawford, stated that acting under instructions he had discovered the pensioner Conway belonging to the 18th Royal Irish. Witness had confronted the man with two of the deceased's sisters, who had failed to recognize him as the man who used to live with the deceased. Witness had made every effort to trace the Thomas Conway and the brothers referred to, but without result.

By a juryman. – The reason the daughter had not seen the man Conway, whom witness had traced, was that she had not at the time been discovered.

Mr. Crawford intimated that the daughter should see the man.

Witness, in reply to a juryman, stated that the Conway whom he had discovered last received his pension on the 1st inst.

By Mr. Crawford. – He is quartermaster-sergeant.

Dr. Gordon Brown at this point was re-called.

Mr. Crawford. – The theory has been put forward that it is possible for the deceased to have been taken to Mitre-square after her murder. What is your opinion about that?

Dr. Brown. – I think there is no doubt on the point. The blood at the left side of the deceased was clotted, and must have flowed from her at the time of the injury to the throat. I do not believe the deceased moved in the slightest way after her throat was cut.

Mr. Crawford. – You have no doubt that the murder was committed at that spot? – I feel quite sure it was.

Police-constable Lewis Robinson stated that about half-past 8 o'clock on the night of the 29th ult. he was on duty in High-street, Aldgate, where he saw a crowd of persons. He then saw a woman, who was drunk, and who had since been recognized as the deceased. She was lying on the footway. Witness asked if any one in the crowd knew her or where she lived, but he received no answer. On the arrival of another constable they took her to Bishopsgate Police-station, where she was placed in a cell.

By Mr. Crawford. – No one in the crowd appeared to know the woman. Witness last saw her on the same evening at about 10 minutes to 9 o'clock in the police cell.

Mr. Crawford. – Do you recollect whether she was wearing an apron? – Yes, she was.

Mr. Crawford. – Could you identify it? – I could if I saw the whole of it. A brown paper parcel was produced, from which two pieces of apron were taken and shown to the witness, who said. – To the best of my knowledge and belief that is the apron.

By a juryman. – The woman smelt very strongly of drink.

James Byfield said he was station sergeant at Bishopsgate Police-station. He remembered the woman referred to by the last witness being brought to the station at a quarter to 9 on the evening of the 29th ult. She was very drunk. She was placed in a cell, and was kept there until 1 o'clock the next morning. She was then sober, and was discharged after giving her name as Mary Ann Kelly and her address at 6, Fashion-street. In answer to questions put to her by witness, she stated that she had been hopping.

By a juryman. – He believed that nothing was given to her while she was in the cell.

By Mr. Crawford. – He did not notice that she was wearing an apron.

Constable George Henry Hutt 968, said he was gaoler at Bishopsgate-street Police-station. On Saturday night, the 29th ult., at a quarter to 10 he took over the prisoners, among whom was the deceased. He visited her several times in the cell until five minutes to 1 o'clock, when he was directed by Sergeant Byfield to see whether any of the prisoners were fit to be discharged. The deceased was found to be sober, and was brought from the cell to the office; and after giving the name of Mary Ann Kelly, she was discharged. He saw her turn to the left after getting outside the station.

By a juryman. – It was left to the discretion of the inspector, or acting inspector, to decide when a person who had been drunk was in a fit condition to be discharged.

By another juryman. – He visited the woman in the cell about every half-hour from five minutes to 10 o'clock until 1 o'clock. She was sleeping when he took over the prisoners. At a quarter-past 12 o'clock she was awake, and singing a song to herself. At half-past 12, when he went to her, she asked him when she was going to be let out, and he replied, "When you are capable of taking care of yourself." She answered that she was capable of taking care of herself then.

By Mr. Crawford. – It was not witness, but Sergeant Byfield who discharged her. She left the station about 1 o'clock. In witness's opinion she was then quite capable of taking care of herself. She said nothing to witness as to where she was going. About two minutes before 1 o'clock, when bringing her out of the cell, she asked witness the time, and he replied, "Too late for you to get any more drink." She asked him again what time it was, and he replied, "Just on 1." She then said, "I shall get a d— fine hiding when I get home." Witness gathered from that that she was going home. He noticed that she was wearing an apron, and to the best of his belief the apron shown to the last witness was the one.

By Mr. Crawford. – It would take about eight minutes to walk from the police station to Mitre-square – ordinary walking.

By a juryman. – Prisoners were not searched who were brought into the station drunk. Handkerchiefs or anything with which they could injure themselves would be taken from them.

George James Morris, the next witness called, said he was watchman at Messrs. Kearley and Tonge's, tea merchants, in Mitre-square. He went on duty there at 7 o'clock in the evening.

The CORONER. – What happened at a quarter to 2 o'clock? – Police-constable Watkins, who was on the Mitre-square beat, knocked at the door of the warehouse. It was slightly "on the jar." He was then sweeping the steps down towards the door, and as he was doing so the door was pushed. He opened it wide and saw Watkins, who said, "For God's sake, mate, come to my assistance." The constable was agitated, and witness thought he was ill. He had his lamp by his side lighted, and asked Watkins what was the matter. Watkins replied, "There is another woman cut to pieces." Witness asked where she was, and Watkins replied, "In the corner." Having been a police-constable himself, he knew what assistance was required. He went over to the spot indicated and turned his lamp on the body. He immediately ran up Mitre-street into Aldgate, blowing his whistle. He saw no suspicious person about at the time. He was soon joined by two police-constables, and he told them to go into Mitre-square, where there had been another terrible murder. He followed the constables there, and took charge of his own premises again. He had heard no noise in the square before he was called by Watkins. Had there been any cry of distress he would have heard it.

By a juryman. – He had charge of the two warehouses of Messrs. Kearley and Tonge. At the time in question he was in the one where the counting-house was; it faced the square.

By Mr. Crawford. – Before being called by Watkins he had had no occasion to go out of the offices or into the square. He was sure he had not quitted the premises before Watkins called him. There was nothing unusual in his door being open or in his being at work at a quarter to 2 o'clock on Sunday morning.

By a juryman. – His door had not been on the jar more than two or three minutes before Watkins called him.

Constable James Harvey (964 City Police) stated that at a quarter to 10 o'clock on the night of the 29th ult. he went on his beat, which he described, and which took in Mitre-street. He saw no suspicious person about while on his beat, and he heard no cry or any noise. When he got into Aldgate, returning towards Duke-street, he heard a whistle, and saw the witness Morris with a lamp. The latter, in answer to witness, said that a woman had been ripped up in Mitre-square. Witness saw a constable on the other side of the street. They went to Mitre-square, where they saw Watkins with the body of the deceased. The constable who followed witness went for Dr. Sequeira, and private persons were despatched for other constables, who arrived almost immediately, having heard the whistle. Witness waited there with Watkins, and information was at once sent to the inspector. As witness passed the post-office clock at Aldgate on his beat it was between one and two minutes to half-past 1 o'clock.

By a juryman. – His beat took him down Church-passage to the end. He was there three or four minutes before he heard the whistle; it was then about 18 or 19 minutes to 2 o'clock.

George Clapp said he lived at 5, Mitre-street, Aldgate, of which he was caretaker. The back part of the house looked into Mitre-square. On the night of the 29th ult. he and his wife went to bed at 11 o'clock. They slept in a back room on the second floor. During the night he heard no disturbance or noise of any kind. The first he heard of the murder in the square was between 5 and 6 o'clock on the following morning.

By Mr. Crawford. – The only other person in the house that night was a woman, a nurse, who slept at the top of the house, on the third-floor.

Constable Richard Pearse, 922 City Police, said he lived at No. 3, Mitre-square. He went to bed on the night of the 29th ult. about 20 minutes after 12 o'clock. He heard no noise or disturbance of any kind. He first heard of the murder at 20 minutes past 2 o'clock, when he was called by a police-constable. From his window he could plainly see the spot where the murder was committed.

By Mr. Crawford. – He was the only tenant of No. 3, Mitre-square, where he lived with his wife and family.

Joseph Lawende said that he lived at 45, Norfolk-road, Dalston. He was a commercial traveller. On the night of the murder he was at the Imperial Club in Duke-street, with Joseph Levy and Harry Harris. They went out of the club at half-past 1, and left the place about five minutes later. They saw a man and a woman standing together at a corner in Church-passage, in Duke-street, which led into Mitre-square. The woman was standing with her face towards the man. Witness could not see the woman's face; the man was taller than she. She had on a black jacket and bonnet. He saw her put her hand on the man's chest. Witness had seen some clothing at the police-station, and he believed the articles were the same that the woman he referred to was wearing.

The CORONER. – Can you tell us what sort of man it was with whom she was speaking? – He had on a cloth cap with a peak.

Mr. Crawford. – Unless the jury wish it I have a special reason why no further description of this man should be given now.

The jury assented to Mr. Crawford's wish.

The CORONER. – You have given a description of the man to the police, I suppose? – Yes.

The CORONER. – Would you know him again? – I doubt it.

By Mr. Crawford. – The distance between the Imperial Club and the top of Church-passage, where he saw the man and woman standing talking together, was about nine or ten yards. He fixed the time of leaving the club at half-past 1 by reference to the club clock and to his own watch, and it would have been about 25 minutes to 2 o'clock when he saw the man and woman standing together. He heard not a word of their conversation. They did not appear to be in an angry mood. The woman did not appear to have put her hand on the man's chest as if she were pushing him away. Witness did not look back to see where they went.

Joseph Hyam Levy of 1, Hutchison-street, Aldgate, said he was a butcher. He was in the Imperial Club with the last witness, and the time when they rose to leave was half-past 1 by the club clock. It was about three or four minutes after the half-hour when they left. He noticed a man and woman standing together at the corner of Church-passage, but he passed on without taking any further notice of them. He did not look at them. From what he saw, the man might have been three inches taller than the woman. He could not give any description of either of them. He went on down Duke-street, into Aldgate, leaving the man and woman speaking together. He only fixed the time by the club clock.

By a juryman. – His suspicions were not aroused by the two persons. He thought the spot was very badly lighted. It was now much better lighted than it was on the night of the murder. He did not take much notice of the man and woman.

By Mr. Crawford. – He was on the opposite pavement to the man and woman. There was nothing that he saw to induce him to think that the man was doing any harm to her.

Police-constable Alfred Long, 254 A, stated that he was on duty in Goulston-street, Whitechapel, on the morning of the 30th ult. At about 2.55 he found a portion of an apron (produced as before). There were recent stains of blood on it. It was lying in the passage leading to a staircase of 118 and 119, ordinary model dwelling-houses. Above it on the wall was written in chalk, "The Jews are the men that will not be blamed for nothing." He at once searched the staircases and areas of the building, but he found nothing. He then took the piece of apron to the Commercial-road [*sic* – Commercial Street] Police-station, and reported to the inspector on duty. He had previously passed the spot where he found the apron at 20 minutes after 2, but it was not there then.

By Mr. Crawford. – Witness repeated as before the words which he saw written on the wall.

Mr. Crawford. – Have you not put the word "not" in the wrong place?" Is it not, "The Jews are not the men that will be blamed for nothing?" Witness repeated the words as he had previously read them.

Mr. Crawford. – How do you spell "Jews?" Witness. – J-e-w-s.

Mr. Crawford. – Now, was it not on the wall J-u-w-e-s? Is it not possible you are wrong? – It may be as to the spelling.

Mr. Crawford. – And as to the place where the word "not" was put? Witness again read the words as before.

By Mr. Crawford. – He had not noticed the wall before. He noticed the piece of apron first, and then the words on the wall. One corner of the apron was wet with blood. His light was on at the time. His attention was attracted to the writing on the wall while he was searching. He could not form an opinion as to whether the writing was recent. He went on to the staircase of the dwelling, but made no inquiries in the house itself.

By a juryman. – The pocket-book in which he entered the words written on the wall at the time he noticed them was at Westminster.

The witness's examination was postponed, and the pocket-book was ordered to be produced.

Detective Daniel Halse (City Police) stated that on Saturday, the 29th ult., from instructions received at the Detective Office, Old Jewry, he told a number of police officers in plain clothes to patrol the City all night. At about two minutes to 2 on the Sunday morning he was at the corner of

Houndsditch, by Aldgate Church, in company with Detectives Outram and Marryat, of the City Police. They heard that a woman had been murdered in Mitre-square, and they all ran there and saw the body of the murdered woman. He gave instructions to have the neighbourhood searched, and every man to be stopped and examined. He himself went by way of Middlesex-street, at the east end of the City, into Wentworth-street, where he stopped two men, who gave a satisfactory account of themselves, and he allowed them to depart. He came through Goulston-street about 20 minutes past 2, at the spot where the apron was found, and he then went back to Mitre-square and accompanied Inspector Collard to the mortuary. He there saw the deceased undressed, noticing that a portion of the apron she wore was missing. He accompanied Major Smith back to Mitre-square, where they heard that a piece of apron had been found in Goulston-street. He then went with Detective Hunt to Leman-street Police-station, where he heard that the piece of apron that had been picked up had been handed to Dr. Phillips. Witness and Hunt then went back to Goulston-street, to the spot where the apron had been discovered. He saw some chalk writing on the wall. He remained there, and Hunt went for Mr. M'William for instructions to have the writing photographed. Directions were given for that to be done. Some of the Metropolitan Police thought it might cause a riot if the writing were seen, and an outbreak against the Jews. It was decided to have the writing rubbed out. The people were at that time bringing out their stalls, which they did very early on the Sunday morning. When Hunt returned inquiry was made at every tenement in the dwelling referred to in Goulston-street, but no tidings could be obtained as to any one having gone in who was likely to be the murderer.

By Mr. Crawford. — At about 20 minutes after 2 he passed over the spot where the piece of apron was found. If it was there then he would not necessarily have seen it, for it was in the building.

Mr. Crawford. — Did any one suggest that it would be possible to take out the word "Juwes," and leave the rest of the writing there? — I suggested that the top line might be rubbed out, and the Metropolitan Police suggested the word "Juwes." The fear on the part of the Metropolitan Police of a riot was the sole cause of the writing on the wall being rubbed out.

Mr. Crawford. — Read out the exact words you took down in your book at the time. — "The Juwes are not the men that will be blamed for nothing."

By Mr. Crawford. — The writing appeared to have been recently done. — It was done with white chalk on the black facia of the wall.

By a juryman. — The spot where the writing was is the ground of the Metropolitan Police, and they insisted on having it rubbed out.

By Mr. Crawford. – Witness protested against it being rubbed out, and wanted it to be left until Major Smith had seen it.

By a juryman. – He assumed that the writing was recent, because from the number of persons living in the tenement he believed it would have been rubbed out had it been there for any time. There were about three lines of writing, which was in a good schoolboy hand.

By another juryman. – The writing was in the passage of the building itself, and was on the black dado of the wall.

A juryman. – It seems to me strange that a police-constable should have found this piece of apron, and then for no inquiries to have been made in the building. There is a clue up to that point, and then it is altogether lost.

Mr. Crawford. – I have evidence that the City Police did make a careful search in the tenement, but that was not until after the fact had come to their knowledge. I am afraid that will not meet the point raised by you (to the juryman). There is the delay that took place. The man who found the piece of apron is a member of the Metropolitan Police.

The witness **Long** having returned with the pocket-book referred to, stated, in reply to Mr. Crawford, that the book contained the entry which he made at the time as to the words written on the wall. They were "The Jews are the men that will not be blamed for nothing." The inspector made the remark that on the wall the word was "Jeuws." Witness entered in his book what he believed was an exact copy of the words.

Mr. Crawford. – At all events there was a discrepancy between what you wrote down and what was actually written on the wall, so far as regards the spelling of the word "Jews." Witness replied that the only remark the inspector made was as to the spelling of the word "Jews."

By Mr. Crawford. – The moment he found the piece of apron he searched the staircases leading to the building. He did not make any inquiry of the inmates in the tenements. There were either six or seven staircases, one leading down, and the others upstairs. He searched every staircase, and could find no trace of blood or any recent footmarks. He found the apron at five minutes to 3, and when he searched the staircases it would be about 3 o'clock. Having searched the staircases he at once proceeded to the police-station. Before proceeding to the station he had heard that a murder had been committed in Mitre-square. When he started for the police-station he left Police-constable 190 H in charge of the building. He did not know the constable's name; he was a member of the Metropolitan Police. Witness told him to keep observation on the dwelling, to see whether any one left or entered it. Witness next returned to the building at 5 o'clock. The writing was rubbed out in witness's presence at half-past 5, or thereabouts. He heard no one object to the writing being rubbed out.

A juryman. – Having heard of the murder, and having afterwards found the piece of apron with blood on it and the writing on the wall, did it not strike you that it would be well to make some examination of the rooms in the building? You say you searched all the passages, but you would not expect that the man who had committed the murder would hide himself there. Witness. – Seeing the blood there, I thought that the murder had been committed, and that the body might be placed in the building.

The juryman. – You did not search the rooms, but left a man to watch the building, and the whole clue seems to have passed away. I do not wish to say anything harsh, as I consider that the evidence of yourself and of the other members of the police redounds to the credit of all of you; but this does seem a point that requires a little investigation. You find a piece of apron wet with blood; you search all the passages, and then you leave the building in the care of a man to watch the front. Witness. – I thought the best thing I could do was to go to the station and report the matter to the inspector on duty.

The juryman. – I feel sure you did your best.

Mr. Crawford. – May we take it that you thought you would be more likely to find the body of the murdered person there than the assassin? Witness. – Yes.

By a juryman. – Witness was a stranger in the neighbourhood. No one could have gone out of the front part of the building without being seen by the constable left on the spot by witness.

The CORONER, in summing up, observed that the evidence had been of the most exhaustive character. He thought it would be far better now to leave the matter in the hands of the police, to follow it up with any further clues they might obtain, and for the jury to return a verdict of wilful murder against some person or persons unknown. It had been shown by the evidence of Dr. Gordon Brown that the murderer must taken hold of the deceased woman and cut her throat, and by severing the vocal cords, prevented her from making any cry. All the evidence showed that no sound had been heard in connection with the crime. The assassin had not only murdered the woman, defenceless as she was, but had so mangled the corpse as to render it almost impossible for the body to be identified. He thought they would agree that the evidence clearly showed that the woman was taken to the police-station for being drunk, and that she was discharged about 1 o'clock on the morning of the murder. After that two persons – a man and a woman – were seen talking together at the corner of Church-passage by the witnesses from the Imperial Club, and one of those witnesses had expressed his opinion that the articles of clothing which he had seen at the police-station were the same as those worn by the woman. She was discharged from the station at about five minutes after 1 o'clock. At half-past 1 a police-constable went round Mitre-square, and turned his lamp on to the corner, but saw nothing there. Just 14 minutes afterwards he found there the body of a woman who had been murdered, the evidence of the doctor showing that it must have taken five minutes to commit the murder and to have inflicted the injuries on the body. The murder must have been committed between 1.30 and 1.44, and, allowing five minutes for the crime to be committed, only nine minutes were left to be accounted for. The history of the case was a very painful one. It appeared that the deceased had been living first with Thomas Conway for seven or eight years. Her drinking habits had induced him to part from her, and the sister of the deceased had stated that she was not married to him. There was nothing to suggest that either Conway or Kelly had had anything to do with the murder, both of them seeming to be totally inoffensive men. It had been clearly proved that Kelly was in bed at the lodging-house at the time of the murder. He had heard that the deceased had been taken up by the police, and knowing what the custom was in the City, he assumed that she would return to him in the morning. They had, it appeared, been out hopping for some weeks, and had returned home on the Thursday (the 27th ult,), taking a lodging for that night in Shoe-lane; and on the Saturday – the last time Kelly saw anything of her – she stated that she was going to see whether she could find her daughter. Something might turn on the fact that she did not see her daughter. According to the evidence, the deceased was going to Bermondsey to see her, but the daughter had left the address there without mentioning any other address to which she was going. It was possible that the deceased had gone to Bermondsey. What became of her in the interval between that and her being taken in charge there was nothing to show, but she had evidently been drinking. There could be no doubt that a most vile murder had been committed by some person or persons unknown, and he thought he might say by some person unknown. Dr. Brown believed that only one person was implicated. Unless the jury wished him to refer to any point in the evidence, there was nothing that need detain them further as far as that inquiry was concerned, and the police could be left with a free hand to follow up the investigation. A munificent reward had been offered by the Corporation, and it might be hoped that that would set persons on the track and cause the apprehension of the murderer.

Mr. Crawford. – Dr. Brown in his evidence expressed his belief as a medical man that only one person had committed the murder.

The Foreman. – (the jury having consulted for about a couple of minutes). – Our verdict is "Wilful murder by some person unknown."

The CORONER. – That is the verdict of all of you?

The Foreman. – Yes.

The CORONER afterwards stated that the jury desired him to thank Mr.

Crawford and the police for the assistance which they had rendered in the inquiry, and he also wished to add his own thanks.

The Times of Tuesday, 16 October 1888, page 10, carried a report of the City Police locating Thomas Conway:

THE EAST-END MURDERS.

The City Police have succeeded in discovering Thomas Conway, who some years ago lived with Catherine Eddowes, the woman murdered in Mitre-square. Up to yesterday the efforts of the detectives had been at fault, owing, as was suggested by the City Solicitor at the inquest, to the fact that Conway had drawn his pension from the 18th Royal Irish Regiment under a false name, that of Thomas Quinn. Apparently he had not read the papers, for he was ignorant till the last few days that he was being sought for. Then, however, he learned that the City detectives were inquiring for him, and yesterday afternoon he and his two sons went to the detective offices of the City Police in Old Jewry and explained who they were. Conway was at once taken to see Mrs. Annie Phillips, Eddowes's daughter, who recognized him as her father. He states that he left Eddowes in 1880 in consequence of her intemperate habits. He knew that she had since been living with Kelly, and had once or twice seen her in the streets, but had, as far as possible, kept out of her way, as he did not wish to have any further communication with her.

CHAPTER 11

October 1888 – Will the Unknown Killer Strike Again?

October 1888 had opened on a nerve-racking note with the the fresh horror of the "double event", the "Jack the Ripper" missives, and the huge press coverage both matters engendered. With this "media frenzy" came a veritable flood of correspondence to the newspapers, not only hoax letters spawned in the fevered imaginations of pretender "Rippers" but also well-meaning advice from every quarter on how to lay the killer by his heels and the inevitable false claims and rumours.

The *Evening Post* of Saturday, 6 October 1888 carried the following snippet:

> The second rumour was even worse than the one cited above, for it had absolutely no foundation; but the details of the apprehension are, under the circumstances, decidely amusing as a clever concoction. It appears that a few minutes before midnight a cab containing two men and a woman was seen to pass along Brick-lane, not one of the best thoroughfares in Spitalfields, and stop in a dark portion of the lane. The two men bore the body of the "unconscious" woman from the cab and deposited it on the pavement, afterwards re-entering the vehicle and driving rapidly away.

This incident, it later transpired, was nothing more than a drunken brawl which, because of the murders, had become garbled in the telling!

Although there were no "Whitechapel Murders" in the month of October 1888, the newspapers were full of reports on the hunt for the murderer and suspects. The torso of a woman was also found in the cellar of the New Scotland Yard Building, at this time under construction on the Embankment, on 2 October 1888, and this discovery became known as the "Whitehall Mystery". There are various reports in the official files for this month and those worthy of note will be mentioned.

Many suspects were detained and questioned. Charles Ludwig, who had been detained on Tuesday, 18 September 1888, finally appeared before the Thames Magistrates' Court after the murder of Stride and Eddowes. The disposal of this case, on 2 October 1888, was reported in

The Times of Wednesday, 3 October 1888:

CHARLES LUDWIG, 40, a decently attired German, who professed not to speak English, was brought up on remand, charged with threatening to stab Elizabeth Burns, an unfortunate, of 53, Flower and Dean-street, Spitalfields, and also with threatening to stab Alexander Finlay, of 51, Leman-street, Whitechapel. Elizabeth Burns stated about half-past 3 on the early morning of Tuesday week she went with the prisoner up Butcher's-row, Whitechapel-road. Prisoner put his arm around her neck, and she saw an open knife in his hand. She screamed and two policemen came. The evidence of Finlay showed that at 3 o'clock on the morning of Tuesday fortnight he was standing at a coffee-stall in the Whitechapel-road, when Ludwig came up in a state of intoxication. He pull out a long-bladed knife, and threatened to stab witness with it. Ludwig followed witness round the stall, and made several attempts to stab him. A constable came up and prisoner was given into custody. Evidence was given that on the way to the police-station the prisoner dropped a long-bladed knife, which was open, and when he was searched a razor and a long-bladed pair of scissors were found on him. Inspector Prinley, H Division, stated the prisoner had fully accounted for his whereabouts on the nights of the recent murders. The magistrate, taking into consideration that the prisoner had been in custody a fortnight, now allowed him to be discharged.

The following[1] was contained in the Police court columns of *The Times* of Thursday, 4 October 1888:

POLICE.

At the GUILDHALL, WILLIAM BULL, 27, was charged on his own confession with having committed the murder in Mitre-square, Aldgate. Inspector George Izzard said at 20 minutes to 11 on Tuesday night the prisoner came into the charge-room at Bishopsgate Police-station and made the following statement:

"William Bull, No. 6, Stannard-road, Dalston. I am a medical student at the London Hospital. I wish to give myself up for the murder in Aldgate on Saturday night last or Sunday morning. About 2, I think, I met the woman in Aldgate. I went with her up a narrow street, not far from the main road. I gave her half-a-crown. While walking along together a second man came up, and he took the half-crown from her." The prisoner then said, "My poor head. I shall go mad. I have done it. I must put up with it." The inspector then said to him, "What has become of your clothing that you had on when you committed the murder?" He replied, "If you wish to know, they are in the Lea, and the knife I threw away." At this point he declined to say anything more. He was drunk. Inquiries had been made at the London Hospital. No such person as the prisoner was known there. He was out of employment. The prisoner's parents appeared to be most respectable people. His father stated that the accused was at home on Saturday night. The prisoner. – I said this when I was mad drunk. I never committed a murder; I could not commit such an act. The magistrate. – I shall remand you; and you have yourself to thank for the position you are in. The prisoner was then removed to the cells.

The *Morning Advertiser* of Thursday 4 October 1888, page 5 f, reported on another "suspect":

Soon after six o'clock last evening considerable excitement was caused in the neighbourhood of Ratcliff-highway by the report that a man was roaming about there in a suspicious manner with bloodstains on his coat. A crowd gathered and followed the individual referred to, uttering threatening cries. He was respectably dressed in a light suit, was apparently about 30 years of age, and had somewhat the appearance of an American. He took shelter in a public-house, in company with another man to whom he was known; but the crowd still hung about the doors. At last a policeman appeared, who advised the man to go with him to the station and wait there until the noisy crowd had dispersed. This the man readily did, accompanying the constable to the King David-place police station, where he was allowed to sit in an ante-room. The inspector on duty thought it necessary to question the man, whose replies were considered quite satisfactory. The stains on his coat were carefully scrutinised, but were caused apparently only by grease. At any rate they were not bloodstains. For a considerable time the police-station was besieged by curious spectators, who at last got tired of seeing nothing, and so dispersed. The man, who said his name was John Lock, and his age thirty-two, made the following statement to a reporter: "I am now a sailor, and belong to the Naval Reserve. I and my wife have been in Australia for some years, and we came to England on the 28th April last. I left a friend's house at 85, Balcombe-street, Dorset-square, this (Wednesday) morning, and made my way to the docks at Wapping, for the purpose of finding a ship. I was walking along Commercial-road to go down Devonshire-road to see a man whom I knew nine years ago, when all at once I met a friend. He said to me, 'Hulloa, old man, what is all this?' and he turned round to the crowd which was following me and told them to go away. I looked round and saw that I had been followed. I said we would go up Commercial-road and have a drink at a public-house, the 'Victory,' I think. While we were there the crowd stopped outside, calling 'Leather Apron' and 'Jack the Ripper,' and someone was good enough to send for a couple of policemen. When I got to the station I explained what I had been doing." "But," said the reporter, "the people outside say that you have bloodstains on your coat and collar." "Oh," replied Lock, smiling, "those stains are old paint stains, and that only shows what the public will do now." Up to this point he did not seem to understand that he was at liberty to leave the station, but the officer explained to him that he might go on his way as soon as he liked, but that it would be wise to wait until the crowd had dispersed.

Mr. Matthews was engaged for several hours yesterday at the Home Office with reference to the murders in the East-end, and had prolonged interviews with Sir Charles Warren and others on the subject, during which the course of action already taken by the police was fully considered, as well as the steps to be taken in future with a view to the discovery of the criminal. Mr. Matthews is understood to have directed that no power in the hands of the police should be left untried, and no clue, however unpromising, neglected. The under-standing between the Metropolitan and City police is most cordial.

Yesterday the large force of police and detectives drafted into Whitechapel made house-to-house visitation and left copies of the following handbill . . .

The wording of the "Police Notice to the Occupier" leaflet was then given.

The question of offering a reward for information leading to the capture of the murderer arose; a file cover[2], dated 1 October 1888:

[Stamped: – HOME OFFICE 4 OCT.88 DEPt. No.] No. A49301B/4
DATE 1 Octr. 1888   The Financial News.
REFERENCES, &c. Whitechapel Murders.
Fds. cheque for £300. Requests that the sum may be offered as a reward, in the name of the Government, for the detection of the Criminal.

                                                              Pressing
MINUTES.
Telegram from SofS. within – also Memo's by Mr. Pemberton.
Copy of Mr Pemberton's reply below.

[*There is then affixed to the minutes section a cutting from the newspaper*]:

The following correspondence has passed between the editor of the *Financial News* and the Home Office:

    "11, Abchurch-lane, London, E.C., Oct. 1,

    "Sir, – In view of your refusal to offer a reward out of Government funds for the discovery of the perpetrator or perpetrators of the recent murders in the East-end of London, I am instructed on behalf of several readers of the *Financial News*, whose names and addresses I enclose, to forward you the accompanying cheque for £300, and to request you to offer that sum for this purpose in the name of the Government.

"Awaiting the favour of your reply, – I have the honour to be your obedient servant,

"HARRY H. MARKS."

"The Right Hon. Henry Matthews M.P., Secretary
    of State for the Home Department."

"Oct. 1.

"My dear Sir, – I am directed by Mr. Matthews to acknowledge the receipt of your letter of this date, containing a cheque for £300, which you say has been contributed on behalf of several readers of the *Financial News*, and which you are desirous should be offered as a reward for the discovery of the recent murders in the East-end of London.

"If Mr. Matthews had been of opinion that the offer of a reward in these cases would have been attended by any useful result he would himself have at once made such an offer, but he is not of that opinion.

"Under these circumstances, I am directed to return you the cheque (which I enclose), and to thank you, and the gentlemen whose names you have forwarded, for the liberality of their offer which Mr. Matthews much regrets he is unable to accept.

"I am, Sir, your obedient servant,

"E. LEIGH PEMBERTON."

TIMES 2 OCT.88.

There is then annexed a memo[3], as follows:

Memoranda by Mr. Pemberton as to Whitechapel Murders and proposed offer of reward.

Mr. Matthews

You will have got my telegram saying that the Financial News had sent a cheque for £300 proposing that it shd be offered in the name of the Government as a reward for the discovery of the Whitechapel murders. as there had been two past cases since you declined to offer a reward I did not like to act without giving you the opportunity if you saw fit to change – & I have not yet answered the letter

About 3 oclock Warren came & reported that every thing was being done that they could think of and that he was sanguine of finding the man

About 3.30 the Queen telephoned to Sec ofS expressing ["her" – *deleted*] how shocked she was & asking for information. I telephoned back to Major Edwards stating what Warren had told the H.O.

At 5 oclock Sir Chas Warren sent the word that the Lord Mayor had offered £500 reward.

In the Dynamite case the City offered £5000 reward & yet Sir W. Harcourt refused to offer anything on behalf of the Government or to promise a pardon to an accomplice I send the papers for reference.

Of course if I had known that Ld. Mayor was going to offer a reward I shd have let you know when I telephoned as I have no doubt there will many more applications about A Reward & most likely the Queen will telegraph again for information perhaps you will be so good as to telegraph to me general instructions (to act as on the previous applications or otherwise).

<u>Immediate</u>

unless you think it ["better" – *deleted*] necessary to come up & have an interview with Sir Chas. Warren.

<u>ELP. 1 Oct 88.</u>

Just received yr telegram Sir Chas Warren still adheres to his opinion that a reward wd. be of no use & Mr. Monro agrees ELP.

I will come to London tomorrow (Wednesday) and be at the H:O: soon after I [ ]purpose to see Sir C Warren.

H.M.

2d Oct./88

The *Financial News* letter[4] is annexed:

The Financial News.   A49301B/4

A Daily Journal devoted to the interests of investors

11. Abchurch Lane, E.C.

London, October 1st 1888.

The Rt. Hon. Henry Matthews, Q.C. M.P.

Secretary of State

for the Home Department.

Sir,

In view of your refusal to offer a reward out of Government funds for the discovery of the perpetrator or perpetrators of the recent murders in the East-end of London. I am instructed on behalf of several readers of the *Financial News*, whose names and addresses I enclose, to forward you the accompanying cheque for £300 and to request you to offer that sum for this purpose in the name of the Government.

Awaiting the favour of your reply

I have the honour to be

Your obedient Servant

Harry H Marks

<u>Editor</u>.

There are also two Post Office telegraphs[5] annexed (the second being a continuation of the message), as follows:

POST OFFICE TELEGRAPHS.
Handed in at – Rowlands Castle Office at 4–57p
TO Mr. Pemberton Home Office
Whitehall Ldn.
Decline offer with thanks a[nd] say that if government [ ] any prospect of useful result from Reward they would at once offer one themselves. As[k] Police at once whether any / circumstances make it desirable to offer reward now or later.

The question of a reward[6] was also raised by George Lusk of the Whitechapel Vigilance Committee, dated 2 October 1888:

[Stamped: – HOME OFFICE 4 OCT.88 RECEIVED] No. A49301B/5
DATE 2nd Oct/88.   Mr. George Lusk
REFERENCES, &c. re Whitechapel Murders.
    Petition to Her Majesty from various residents in the East End of London praying that a Government reward be offered, urging the exceptional circumstances in connection with these murders.
Pressing.

MINUTES.
?Say that the petition has been laid before the Queen, but that the SofS., though ["desirous" – *deleted*] he has given directions that no effort or expense is to be spared in endeavouring the discover [*sic*] the person guilty of the murders, ["cannot" – *deleted*] has not been able to advise H.M. that in his belief the ends of justice would be promoted by any departure from the decision already announced with regard to the proposal that a reward shd. offered by Govt.
    ELP. 4 Oct 88.   CET
4.10.88

    wrote
        6.10.

There are then annexed two newspaper cuttings[7], dated 8 October 1888:

From "The Times", Monday, 8th Oct.1888.
    In answer to the petition to Her Majesty, presented by Mr. George Lusk on behalf of his Vigilance Committee, and the inhabitants of Whitechapel generally, the following letter was received late on Saturday night:

"Whitehall, Oct. 6, 1888.

"Sir, – The Secretary of State for the Home Department has had the honour to lay before the Queen the petition signed by you praying that a reward may be offered by the Government for the discovery of the perpetrator of the recent murders in Whitechapel, and he desires me to inform you that though he has given directions that no effort or expense should be spared in endeavouring to discover the person guilty of the murders, he has not been able to advise Her Majesty that in his belief the ends of justice would be promoted by any departure from the decision already announced with regard to the proposal that a reward should be offered by Government.

"I am, Sir, your obedient servant,

"E.LEIGH PEMBERTON.

"George Lusk, Esq., 1,2, and 3, Alderney-road,

Mile-end-road, E.2."

From "Daily Telegraph", Monday, 8th Oct. 1888, with reference to the above letter.

"The gentleman to whom the above reply was addressed – Mr. George Lusk, of Alderney-street [sic], Globe-street, Mile-end – has given information of a suspicious incident which befell him on Thursday afternoon last. A stranger, who called at his private residence shortly after four o'clock, and who was informed that Mr. Lusk was not at home, appeared to have traced the President of the Vigilance Committee to an adjacent tavern. Having manifested great interest in the movements of the volunteer police, he sought an interview in a private room, but owing to the forbidding appearance of the visitor Mr. Lusk seems to have preferred the comparative publicity of the bar parlour. The conversation had scarcely begun, when Mr. Lusk, who was about to pick up a pencil which had dropped from the table, says he noticed the stranger "make a swift though silent movement with his right hand towards his side pocket." Fearing that his conduct was observed, it is added, the man asked to be directed to nearest coffee-house, and forthwith proceeded to an address in the Mile End-road with which he was supplied. Although Mr. Lusk followed without loss of time, he was not quick enough for his visitor, who abstained from visiting the coffee-house, and has not been heard of since. The man is described as between thirty and forty years of age, about 5ft9in in height, of a florid complexion, with bushy brown beard, whiskers, and moustache. In the absence of further evidence it is impossible to say whether any personal injury was actually in store for the head of the "Vigilants," but the ease with which the man escaped has awakened the members of the committee and their colleagues to an increased sense of the difficulty of the task they have in hand."

This is followed by a note[8] dated 2 October 1888, as follows:

official 4/10.   Balmoral.   A49301B/:["36" – *deleted*]5
                        2, Oct 1888.

Dear Ruggles Brise

The enclosed reached us this morning and I forward it to you for ["that" – *deleted*] information of Mr. Matthews. We have of course sent no reply from here.

Yrs very truly
Fleetwood I. Edwards.

Captain (later Sir) Fleetwood Edwards was an equerry to the Queen. This is followed by the previously mentioned petition[9]:

To Her Most Gracious Majesty
The Queen

The Humble Petition of George Lusk
of Nos. 1,2 & 3 Alderney Road in the Parish of Mile End Old T[*own*] in the County of Middlesex, Builder and Contractor, a mem[*ber*] of the Metropolitan Board of Works a Vestryman of the above named Parish and the President and Chairman of the Vigilance Committee formed for the purpose hereunder mentioned; your said Petitioner acting under the authority and on behalf of the inhabitants of the East End districts of Your Majesty's metropolis
    Sheweth
    1. That Your Majesty's Secretary of State for the Home Department has for some years past discontinued the old practice of offering a Government reward for the apprehension and conviction of those offenders against Your Sovereign Majesty Your Crown and Dignity who have escaped detection for the crime of Murder.
    2. That in the course of the present year (A.D. 1888.) no less than four murders of Your Majesty's subjects have taken place within a radius of half a mile from one point in the said district.
    3. That notwithstanding the constitution of the Scotland Yard Detective Office and the efforts of the trained Detectives of such office, the perpetrator or perpetrators of these outrages against Your Majesty still remain undiscovered.
    4. That acting under the direction of Your Majesty's liege subjects your petitioner ["I" – *deleted*] caused to be sent to your Majesty's Secretary of State for the Home Department a suggestion that he should revert to the original system of a reward looking at the fact that the present series of murders was probably the work of one hand and that the third and fourth

were certainly the work of that one hand and that inasmuch as the ordinary means of detection had failed and that the murderer would in all probability commit other murders of a like nature such offer of a reward at the earliest opportunity was absolutely necessary for securing Your Majesty's subjects from death at the hands of the above one undetected assassin.

5. That in reply to such suggestion your Petitioner received from Your Majesty's Secretary of State for the Home Department a letter of which the following is a copy viz.&;

"Sir,

I am directed by the Secretary of State to acknowledge the receipt of your letter of the 16th inst. with reference to the question of the offer of a reward for the discovery of the perpetrator of the recent murders in Whitechapel and I am to inform you that had the Secretary of State considered the case a proper one for the offer of a reward he would at once have offered one on behalf of the Government but that the practice of offering rewards for the discovery of criminals was discontinued some years ago because experience shewed that such offers of reward tended to produce more harm than good and the Secretary of State is satisfied that there is nothing in the present case to justify a departure from this rule.

I am, Sir, your obedient servant,

(signed) G.[*sic*] Leigh Pemberton"

6. That the reply above quoted was submitted to the inhabitants of the East End of London in meeting assembled and provoked a considerable amount of hostile criticism and that such criticism was re-echoed throughout Your Majesty's Dominions not only by Your Majesty's subjects at large but, with one or two exceptions the entire press of Great Britain

Your Petitioner therefore

humbly prays Your

Majesty as follows:

1 That Your Majesty will graciously accede to the prayer of Your Petitioner preferred originally through Your Majesty's Secretary of State and direct that a government reward sufficient in amount to meet the peculiar exigencies of the case may immediately be offered, Your Petitioner and those loyal subjects whom he represents being convinced that without such reward the murderer or murderers of the above four victims will not only remain undetected but will sooner or later commit other crimes of a like nature.

And Your Petitioner

will ever pray etc

George Lusk

1 2 3 Alderney Rod.

Mile End Road E

Geo B Richards

Witness to the above signature of George Lusk the Petitioner. 28 Sandal Street, Shalford Essex. 27th September 1888.

There then follows a letter[10], dated 19 October 1888:

TELEGRAPHIC ADDRESS QUEEN, CHESTER.   QUEEN HOTEL,
                                                                     CHESTER.
                                                                     19 Oct. 1888.

Dear Murdoch,

There is one case of successful reward omitted from my Memo which it would be well to add.

It was a case of a burglary in Cromwell Road in which a postman was shot, but not killed.

I don't think it was in the list made by the Registry – if it was, it was not mentioned as a case where the reward was paid.

I think it would be well to have it looked but, as Sir C. Warren may mention it as a clear case of a reward producing important ["evidence" – *deleted*] information: but if I remember right, it was <u>private</u> information, not evidence at all.

The case occurred in 81, 82, or 83.

Sorry I did not think of it while I was at work on the Memo & have to trouble you with it: but in a question of this sort we must be as safe & complete as possible.

> Your Truly
> C E Troup.

There then follow lengthy memos[11], six pages, discussing rewards, which, as they are not directly relevant to the Whitechapel Murders but simply concern the merits of offering a reward, will not be reproduced. In these memos, the case of Mullins and the murder of Mrs Elmsley in Grove Road, Victoria Park, in August 1860, the case of Charles Williams and the burglary in Cromwell Road, on 5 February 1881, and the wounding of a postman, and Rev. Macdonald & others in 1746, are discussed.

A note[12] is then appended, dated 8 October 1888:

Mr. Murdoch ["Ruggles Brise" – *deleted*]

Do you know how this came here.

Did Mr. Williamson or Sir C.W. bring it. if so did they make any verbal communication or recommendation on the subject?

> CM Oct 8

I do not know
ERB

The next folio carries a Post Office telegram[13]:

[Stamped : – HOME OFFICE 8 OCT.88 DEPt. No.] A49301B/6
POST OFFICE TELEGRAPHS.
Handed in at the Cornhill Office at 3.45p Received here at 3.58p
TO Williamson
    4 Whitehall Place
Lord Mayor offered five hundred pounds apprehension Whitechapel Murderer.

Bulling.

It carries an annotation below:

Sent out by Mr. Pemberton to be made official and put up.

CM Oct 9/88.

There then follows a draft, for approval, of a reply[14] to Mr Lusk:

Immediate   Whitehall.
                                             October 1888.

Draft for Approval   Sir,
    I am directed by the Secretary of State to thank you for ["your" – *deleted*] the suggestion in your letter of the 7th Instant on the subject of the recent Whitechapel murders. and to say in reply that [*inserted* – "from the first the S. ofS. has had under consideration"] the question of granting a pardon to ["persons not actually" – *deleted*] [*inserted* – "accomplices. It is obvious that not only [make ?] to such a grant be granted to persons who have not been"] concerned in contriving or [*inserted* – "in actually"] committing the murders ["has been from the first under the consideration of the Secretary of State but that the information obtained has not been such as to appear to him to render such a course at present either expedient or justifiable" – *deleted*] [*inserted* – "but the expediency and propriety of making the offer must largely depend on the nature of the information received from day to day, which is being carefully watched with a view to determine that question"] [*insertions appear to be in Matthews's hand*].
    With regard to the offer of a reward the SofS. has under the existing circumstances nothing to add to his former reply.

I am, &c.

George Lusk Esq.
    1 Alderney Road
        Mile End
            E.

There are marginal notes to the above as follows:

Appd. GL
   10 Oct 1888.
Mr. Matthews
   H.M.
   11 Oct.1888
Wrote 12.10

The next file cover[15] also relates to Mr Lusk, dated 7 October 1888:

[Stamped: – HOME OFFICE 9 OCT.88 RECd. DEPt.] No. A49301B/7
DATE 7 Oct.1888   Mr. George Lusk.
REFERENCES, &c.   The East End Murders.
On behalf of the Committee of inhabitants of the East End, points out that
these crimes are absolutely unique, and that the murderer or murderers may
possibly continue to be more than a match for Scotland Yard and the Old
Jewry combined. Calls attention to the fact that the only means left untried
for the detection of the murderer has been the offer of a Government
Reward, with the offer of a free pardon to any person not the real assassin.
[*Marginal note to above* – ''To be copied copy made'']

                                                   Pressing.

MINUTES.
Ackn. & to the Secretary of State.   9/10.88.
Acknd. 9/10/88.
    There is no reason to suspect an accomplice, quite the reverse. I therefore
see no good in offering a pardon to any person not the real assassin.
The question of a reward has already been settled in the negative.
                                 G.L. 9 Oct. 1888
Mr. Matthews
    Before answering further – send copy to Commr. and request him to
inform the S. of S. whether any useful result would be produced in his opinion
by the offer of a pardon to accomplices.
                                     H.M.
                                     9 Oct./88
                                     Wrote
                                     9/10/88.

The letter[16] from George Lusk, dated 7 October 1888, is then
annexed:

To the Secretary of State for the
Home Department
A49301B/7

[Stamped: – HOME OFFICE 9 OCT.88 RECEIVED]

1, 2 & 3 Alderney Road,
Mile End London. E.
7th October 1888.

Right Honble. Sir,

<u>The East End Murders.</u>

I have to acknowledge the receipt of a communication from the Home Office dated the 6th instant in which it is stated that although no effort or expense should be spared in endeavouring to discover the person guilty of these atrocious murders, you are unable to advise Her Majesty that in your belief the ends the ends of Justice would be promoted by any departure from the direction already announced.

In reply to such communication I beg to thank you on behalf of my Committee for your kindness in laying my petition before Her Majesty the Queen, and to say that the inhabitants of Whitechapel and the East End districts of London generally, believe that the Police authorities are sparing neither trouble nor expense in attempting to secure the murderer. At the same time however it is my duty humbly to point out that the present series of murders is absolutely unique in the annals of crime, that the cunning, astuteness and determination of the murderer has hitherto been, and may possibly still continue to be, more than a match for Scotland Yard and the Old Jewry combined and that all ordinary means of detection have failed. This being so I venture most respectfully to call your attention to the fact that the only means left untried for the detection of the murderer has been the offer of a Government reward.

Rewards are offered from other quarters including the Corporation of the City of London but in neither of these instances can a pardon be extended to an accomplice and therefore the value of these offers is considerably less than that of a Government proclamation of a really substantial reward with the extension of a free pardon to any person not the actual assassin.

I have the honor to be,
Right Honorable Sir,
Your very obedt. humble servant
(*Signed*) George Lusk.

The next file cover[17], dated 9 October 1888, is as follows:

No. A49301B/8

DATE 9 Octr.88   Comr. of Police
REFERENCES, &c.   Whitechapel Murder
         Gives reasons for recommending offer of pardon to accomplice.

Pressing

MINUTES.

Minutes within.
    Draft for approval herewith.

10.10.88.

Wrote

12.10.88

The within decision was arrived at after conference with Sir C. Warren, and Mr. Anderson.

CM. Oct. 13.88.

There then follows a note[18] [minutes?]:

Home Office,
Whitehall,
S.W.

Say to Mr Lusk that the expediency of granting a ["reward" – *deleted*] pardon to persons not actually concerned in the commission of the murders and not implicated in the terrible guilt of contriving or abetting them, has been more than once under the consideration of the S. ofS. & that the information at present in his possn. has not so far been such as to induce him to offer one. With regard to the offer of a reward the S. ofS. has nothing to add to his former reply in the present state of the cases under investigation.

There then follows a note[19] from Godfrey Lushington to Henry Matthews, dated 10 October 1888:

Mr. Matthews,
    This letter from the Commissioner and letter from Mr. Lusk on which it is founded, give you an opportunity to offer a pardon if you are so inclined. Offering a pardon is not open to the same objections as offering a reward, nor has the S. of S. done anything to commit himself to refuse to offer a pardon. The mere lapse of time occasions no difficulty, for in a crime of this atrocious character it is desirable that if possible no person, even an accessory after the fact, should receive a pardon. A pardon, therefore, is

only offered when it is pretty clear that the efforts of the Police to detect the crime have been unavailing, and if the S. of S. does not now offer a pardon his action will of course be open to the criticism that he has declined to take a step recommended by the Commissioner. On the other hand the Commissioner's letter does not appear to me to throw any new light on the case or to suggest the probability that the offer of a pardon will lead to discovery. His recommendation is based on ["the" – *deleted*] a mere supposition, one of many suppositions which have occurred to everybody from the beginning.

Then, as to the affect on the public mind. The offer of a pardon will not allay the excitement of the public who on the contrary will wrongly infer that the view of the Home Office is that the murderer had an accomplice and this will make the outrages appear of a far more grave character. Nor will the offer of a pardon restore confidence in the Police. It will be accepted as an admission of their failure to detect the crime; it will provoke renewed attention to the action of the Home Office and hostile critics are sure to say that the step if taken ought to have been taken earlier.

In my opinion it would be better for the S. of S. not to ["grant" – *deleted*] offer a pardon taking his stand on the ground that he has held from the first that it is not a case in which the offer of a pardon is appropriate.

It is quite possible however that you may be of a different opinion.

GL

10 October, 1888.

This is followed by another note[20]:

Write to Mr. Lusk.

Thank him for his letter Say that the ["advisability" – *deleted*] question of granting a pardon to persons not actually concerned in contriving or committing the murders, has been from the first under the consideration of the S.of S., but that the information hitherto obtained has not been such as to appear to him to render such a course at present either expedient or justifiable.

With regard to the offer of a reward. the S. of S. has under the existing circumstances nothing to add to his former reply.

["Add that the Metrop. Police are using every effort" – *deleted*] 10 October 1888.

There is then annexed the letter[21], dated 9 October 1888, from Sir Charles Warren:

<u>Urgent</u> [Stamped: – HOME OFFICE 10 OCT.88 DEPt. No.] A49301B/8

4 Whitehall Place, S.W.

9th October, 1888.

Sir,

In reply to your immediate letter just received on the subject of Mr. Lusk's proposal as to a pardon to accomplices in the Whitechapel murders, I have to state, for the information of the Secretary of State, that during the last three or four days I have been coming to the conclusion that useful results would be produced by the offer of a pardon to accomplices. Among the variety of theories there is the possibility that the murderer is someone who during the day-time is sane, but who at certain periods is overbalanced in his mind; and I think it possible in that case that his relatives or neighbours may possibly be aware of his peculiarities and may have gradually unwittingly slid into the position of being accomplices, and may be hopeless of any escape without a free pardon.

On the other hand if it is the work of a gang in which only one actually commits the murder, the free pardon to the accomplice may make the difference of information being obtained.

As a striking commentary on this matter I have today received a letter from a person asserting himself to be an accomplice, and asking for a free pardon; and I am commencing a communication with him through an advertisement in a journal. This letter is probably a hoax, for we have received scores of hoaxing letters, but on the other hand it may be a bona fide letter, and if so I feel what a very great loss it would be to the discovery of the murderer by omitting to offer the pardon; and I cannot see what harm could be done in this or any future case by offering a pardon.

I am,

Sir,

Your most obedient Servant,

Charles Warren.

The Under

    Secretary of State,

       &c. &c. &c.

Under a file cover dated 2 October 1888, is the following[22]:

[Stamped: – HOME OFFICE RECEIVED 2 OCT.88],

DATE 2 Octr. 88. Clerk of the Board of Works Whitechapel District Fds Resolution passed at a meeting of the Board – asking that the Police Force in the neighbourhood of Whitechapel may be strengthened.

Ackd 2.10.88   Pressing/

MINUTES

This having been acknd.

?Put up.

[ ] 3 ack -SS.   [ ]

2.10.88.

The letter enclosed[23] reads:

Office of the Board of Works Whitechapel District
No.15. Great Alie Street.Whitechapel.
2nd October 1888.

[Stamped: – Recd after 5.p.m.]
To the Rt. Hon. Hy. Matthews
Q.C. M.P.
Secretary of State, Home Department
Whitehall.
S.W.

Sir,

At a meeting of the Board of Works for the Whitechapel District a Resolution was passed of which the following is a copy:-

"That this Board regards with horror and alarm the several atrocious murders recently perpetrated within the District of Whitechapel and its vicinity and calls upon Sir Charles Warren so to regulate and strengthen the Police Force in the neighbourhood to guard against any repetition of such atrocities."

and by direction of the Board the copy Resolution is forwarded to you in the hope that it will receive your favourable consideration.

I am Sir
Your obedient Servant
Alfred Turner [?]
Clerk

A Home Office file cover[24] is as follows:

[Stamped: – HOME OFFICE 4 OCT.88 RECEIVED]   No. A49301C/5d
DATE 4 Octr. 1888.   Whitechapel, Vestry Clerk.
REFERENCES, &c.   Whitechapel Murders.
                                        Fds. [Resolution of the Vestry expressing sorrow at the murders, and urging the Government to use their utmost endeavour to discover the Criminals.]   Pressing.

MINUTES.

? Acknowledge – & say S of S [shares the feelings of the Vestry with regard to these murders: that the Police have instructions to exercise every power in their possession in their efforts to discover the murderer: and that the SofS., after personal conference with the Commissioner, in which all the difficulties of case had been fully discussed, is satisfied that no ["available" – *deleted*] means will be spared of tracing the offender and bringing him to justice-]

[ ] 4 octr 88.

or ["simply acknowledge" – *deleted*]

[ ]
4.10.88.

see explanation by Mr. Lushington within as to difference between printed & actual letter

wrote 6/10/88.

The letter from the Vestry Clerk and the resolution appear at ff. 66–67, worded as follows[25]:

5 Gt Prescot Street
Whitechapel E
4th Octr 1888

To,
    The Right Honorable
      Henry Matthews M.P.
Sir
    I have the honor to send you on the other side Copy of a Resolution Passed at a Meeting of the Vestrymen of the Parish of St. Mary Whitechapel held on the 3rd inst.

I am Sir,
Your Humble &Obedt. Serv.
Thomas D Metcalfe
Vestry Clerk

Home Office
  Whitechapel
    SW.

At a Meeting of the Vestrymen
of the Parish of St. Mary
Whitechapel held on the 3rd day
of October 1888 the following
Resolution was passed.

It was Moved
      Second & Resolved
            That this Vestry desires to express its sorrow at the diabolical murders which have lately been committed in East London and to urge Her Majesty's Government to use their utmost efforts to discover the Criminals –
            I Certify the above to be a true Extract from the Minutes.

Thomas D. Metcalfe
Vestry Clerk

The letter[26] of 6 October 1888, referred to above, is as follows:

Pressing
A49301/37

Whitehall
6 October 1888

Sir,
      I am directed by the Secretary of State to acknowledge the receipt of your letter of the 4th instant forwarding a copy of a Resolution of the Vestry of the Parish of St Mary Whitechapel, expressing sorrow at the recent murders in the east of London and urging the Government to use their utmost endeavour to discover the criminals, and I am to state that Mr. Matthews shares the feelings of the Vestry with regard to these murders that the Police have instructions to exercise every power they possess in their efforts to discover the murderer, and that the Secretary of State after personal conference with the Commissioner in which all the difficulties of the case have been fully discussed, is satisfied that no means will be spared in tracing the offender and bringing him to justice.

The Clerk to the Vestry
of the Parish of
St Mary, Whitechapel
5 Great Prescot St
Whitechapel
      E.

I am,
      Sir,
Your obedient Servant,
(sd) E.Leigh Pemberton.

The report[27] comparing the above letter with a copy of it printed in the *Daily News* and *Pall Mall Gazette* is included as follows:

Mr Matthews,
      Please look at the Home Office letters to the Vestry Clerk of Whitechapel as set out at length in the Daily News of Friday, and partially (but with comments) in the Pall Mall Gazette of today, and compare it with the copy –

enclosed of the letter which was actually written from the H.O. You will observe various discrepancies –

	Newspaper version	H.O. version
Date	Oct 10.	Oct 6.
Address	T. Metcalfe Esq Vestry Clerk Whitechapel	The Clerk to the Vestry of the Parish of St Mary Whitechapel 5 Great Prescot St Whitechapel E.
In the body of the letter	East-end of London Criminal I am instructed to state	East of London. Criminals. I am to state
	And that he has given directions and that the Police have instructions to exercise any & every power they possess and even to use an amount of discretion with regard to suspected persons in their efforts to discover the criminal	that the Police have instructions to exercise every power they possess in their efforts to discover the murderer
	And I am further to state that S of S	And that the S of S
	Commissioners of Police at which the whole of the difficulties	Commissioners of Police in which all the difficulties
	Is satisfied that no means have been or will be spared	is satisfied that no means will be spared
	Yours obediently	Your odedient servant

We are unable to explain these variations, but suppose them due to somebody having dictated the terms of the H.O. letter to shorthand notes, who took them down incorrectly & afterwards worded up that material he had; but you will probably think it unadvisable to correct them. It would be injurious to the Commr. to do so. But it is well for you to know that you did not use the words attributed to you.

We have written today to the Commr. to remind him to send to H.O. a report of the measures taken to detect the persons who committed the murder. He has also not answered on paper the 3 questions you put to him in your private letter, & which he answered verbally to you. I have no copy of that letter, so could not remind him of it.

GL

13 Oct 1888.

[*Marginal note:* – "Copy by Mr. Brise is with the other papers – memo on rewards, Harcourt's note on there—14 Oct/88."]

There is some correspondence between Charles Warren and the Home Office. The cover page[28] is as follows:

[Stamped: – HOME OFFICE 9 OCT.88 RECd. DEPT]
DATE 4th October '88. The Commissioner of Police
REFERENCES, &c.   Whitechapel Murders
Reports on J.W. Ellis' letter stating he is prepared to take any measures possible provided H.M. government will support him, but points out the risk entailed on the men who search

[MINUTES]

See copy of letter within from S of S of the 5th Inst – as to the course he proposed

["Confidential" – *deleted*]

Lay-By [ ] Oct 9.

Mr. Lushington – See S.S. minute within. I do not know if Sir C. Warren has reported privately to S. of S. if not shall a reminder be sent? [ ] Oct 13.

Sent 13.10.88

There is then a Home Office note[29] on headed paper as follows:

[Embossed paper: – SECRETARY OF STATE – HOME DEPARTMENT], [stamped:- HOME OFFICE 9 OCT 88 RECd DEPT] Official ERB 8/10 A49301c/8
the letter of Sir J. Whittaker Ellis M.P. (which has not been returned) recommended the drawing of a cordon of police round Whitechapel & a compulsory house to house search.

ERB

It is now   8/10
herewith
    H.M.

The letter from Sir J. Whittaker Ellis appears as follows:[30]

<u>A.49301C</u>
Ackn 4/10

BUCCLEUCH HOUSE,
RICHMOND.
Oct. 3. 1888

My dear Matthews,

There is no doubt but that the Whitechapel murderer remains in the neighbourhood. – Draw a cordon of half a mile round the centre & search every house. – This would surely unearth him.

It is a strong thing to do, but I should think such occasion never before arose. –

I should say he is an American Slaughterman, an occupation largely followed in South America.

Truly Yours
J.WhittakerEllis.

The Rt. Hon. Henry Matthews
Q.C. M.P. &c &c

There is a letter[31] from Sir Charles Warren, dated 4 October 1888:

[Stamped: – HOME OFFICE 9 OCT.88 RECd. DEPt.]

4 Oct 1888

Dear Mr. Ruggles Brise,

I return Sir W Ellis letter.

I am quite prepared to take the responsibility of adopting the most drastic or arbitrary measures that the Sec of State can name which would further the securing of the murderer however illegal they may be, provided H.M. Gov. will support me. But I must observe that the Sec of State cannot authorise me to do an illegal action and that the full responsibility will always rest with me over the Police Constables for anything done.

All I want to ensure is that the Government will indemnify us for our actions which must necessarily be adapted to the circumstances of the case – the exact course of which cannot be always for seen.

I have been accustomed to work under such in circumstances in what were nearly Civil wars at the [ ] & then the Government passed acts of Indemnity for those who have gone beyond the law.

Three weeks ago I do not think the public would have acquiesced in any illegal action but now I think they would welcome any thing which shews activity & enterprise.

Of course the danger of taking such a course, as that proposed by Sir W.

Ellis is that if we did not find the murderer our action would be condemned – and there is the danger that an illegal act of such a character might bond the Social democrats together to resist the Police & [ ] might be then said to have caused a serious riot. – I think I may say without hesitation that those houses could not be searched illegally without violent resistance & blood shed and the certainty of one or more Police Officers being killed & the question is whether it is worth while losing the lives of several of the community & risking serious riot in order to search for one murderer whose whereabouts is not known.

I have ascertained from Mr Williamson that he thinks that though under certain circumstances such action might be adopted or should not be justified at present in doing so such an illegal act. We have in times past done such a thing on a very much smaller scale but then we had certain information that a person was concealed in the house [*ff. 86–87 not found – resumed on f 88*] In this matter I have not only myself to think of but the lives & protection of 12000 men, any one of whom might be hanged if a death occurred in entering a house illegally.

Truly Yours
Charles Warren

Dear Sir Charles,

R.B. has forwarded me your letter of the 4th Oct. with Sir I. Ellis' letter – the suggestion in which is open to your observations & is too sweeping.

I thought my own suggestion of last Wed. more practical – take all houses in a given area which appear suspicious upon the best inquiry your detectives can make. Search all those, which the owners or persons in charge will allow you to search. Where leave is refused, apply to a magistrate for a search warrant, on the ground that it is probable or possible the murderer may be there. If search warrants are refused, you can only keep the houses under observation.

I shd. be glad now that the week is closing of a report of all the measures that have been taken for arresting the criminal, & of the results – Have any of the doctors examined the eyes of the murdered woman.

Yrs truly
H.M.

I shall be very glad to hear whether Mr. Anderson's health has permitted him to resume his duties. –

There is then a note[32] to Charles Murdoch, from Ruggles Brise, dated 8 October 1888:

[Stamped: – HOME OFFICE 9 OCT. 88 RECd. DEPT]   A49301C/

Home Office,

Whitehall,

S.W.

Mr Murdoch.

    I showed this to Mr Lushington.

    It shd. be made official & put up.   ERB

<u>8/10</u>

On Monday, 8 October 1888 *The Times*[33] reported:

[THE EAST-END MURDERS.]

Fears were expressed among the police on Saturday that the night would not pass without some startling occurrence, and the most extraordinary precautions were taken in consequence. It must not be supposed that the precautions taken apply only to the East-end of London. It is fully understood that the murderer, finding his favourite haunts too hot for him, may transfer his operations to another district, and arrangements have been made accordingly. The parks are specially patrolled, and the police, even in the most outlying districts, are keenly alive to the necessities of the situation. Having efficiently provided for the safeguarding of other portions of the large area under his jurisdiction, Sir Charles Warren has sent every available man into the East-end district. These, together with a large body of City detectives, are now on duty, and will remain in the streets throughout the night. Most of the men were on duty all last night, and the work has been found very harassing. But every man has entered heartily into the work, and not a murmur has been heard from any of the officers. They are on their mettle, and if zeal were the one thing needed to hunt down the murderer, his capture would be assured.

    Yesterday evening all was quiet in the district, and the excitement had somewhat subsided. Nevertheless, the police and the local Vigilance Committee have by no means relaxed their watchfulness, and inhabitants of the district, disregarding the improbability of the murderer risking his freedom under these circumstances, still appear to expect the early commission of a new crime. During Saturday night and the early hours of Sunday morning several persons were arrested and detained at local police-stations until all the circumstances in connexion with their apprehension were thoroughly sifted. Several of these were given into custody on grounds which proved on inquiry to be flimsy and even foolish, and the police have in consequence been put to a good deal of trouble without any corresponding result. It seemed at times as if every person in the streets were suspicious of everyone else he met, and as if it were a race between them who should first inform against his neighbour.

Alfred Napier Blanchard, who described himself as a canvasser, residing at Handsworth, was charged at Birmingham on Saturday, on his own confession, with having committed the Whitechapel atrocities. He had been arrested in consequence of a circumstantial statement which he made in a publichouse of the manner in which he had effected the murders. He now denied all knowledge of the matter, and said he had spoken under excitement, caused by reading about the murders, and heavy drinking. The Bench declined to release him, however, till to-day, in order to allow time for inquiries.

Up to a late hour last night no important arrest had been reported in connexion with the murders at the East-end at any of the City police-stations. Many communications continue to be received at Scotland-yard and by the City police, describing persons who have been seen in various parts of the country whose conduct is suspicious or who are supposed to resemble the man seen talking to the victim of the Berner-street murder on the night of her assassination . . .

According to a *Reuter* telegram from New York, the *New York Herald* declares that the seaman named Dodge, who recently stated that a Malay, whom he met in London, threatened to murder a number of Whitechapel women for robbing him, said he knew the street where the Malay stayed, but that he would not divulge the name until he learnt what chance there was of a reward. He stated, however, that the street was not far from the East India Dock-road; but he was not certain about the house where the man lived.

Another seaman said he thought the Malay was now on a vessel plying in the North Sea.

CHAPTER 12

More on Rewards and October Precautions

There is a file[1] cover dated 6 October 1888, about rewards, and the Secretary of State's letter of 7 October 1888, about the state of the investigation:

[Stamped – HOME OFFICE 15 [*deleted*] OCT.88 RECd. DEPt.] No. A49301B/9
DATE 6th October 88   The Commr of Police
REFERENCES, &c.   Whitechapel Murder – Rewards
[*In margin* – see within memo: dated: 1 Oct–] Gives his opinion that though possibly the offer of a Reward would do no good yet it could do no harm, the question now turns on a matter of Policy as if fresh murders were committed the Public at large might make such an outcry that it might affect the stability of the Government. If a Reward is offered it should be large.
MINUTES.
[SECRET – *deleted*]
See long reply from S of S within dated 7th Oct 1888
AJ 13/10/88/10

There then follows a memo[2] dated 10 October 1888:

Home Office,
Whitehall,
S.W.

Sir C. Warren: 10 Oct/88
    Answers to Questions in my letter.
1. No – Police have hardly commenced.
2. No information – beyond an anonymous letter wh is now being dealt with.
3. This is a unique murder & not in the same category as the other crimes mentd: but no special circumstance.

This is followed by the Secretary of State's letter[3] of 7 October 1888, on Home Office embossed headed paper:

copy   Department of State
                                    Home Department
                                                      7th Oct. 1888

Dear Sir Charles.

I am obliged to you for yr. letter of the 5th. It puts your views in a somewhat different light from the impression conveyed to Mr. Pemberton & myself by the interviews, which we both had with you, & which had for their principal object to elicit your opinions on the whole subject of these terrible Whitechapel murders more fully & effectually than if you had been consulted by letter.

I had understood you on the 3rd. inst: to say that in your opinion a reward was useless for the purpose of discovering the murderer; & that as rewards had already been offered by the City authorities & others, you saw no reason for making an additional offer.

I gather from your letter, that altho' from a Police point of view you have no reason to suppose a reward wd. do any good, yet you are disposed to think the offer of a very large sum, coupled with a pardon to accomplices, might possibly produce some effect; & that at any rate you think such an offer wd. have been, & wd. still be a politic step in order to allay public feeling.

I think that in your careful review of the past history of rewards, you scarcely give sufficient prominence to the elaborate consideration, that the question has undergone. Since 1884 there have been repeated, & I believe uniform decisions by Sir W. Harcourt, by Lord Cross, & by Mr Childers, refusing to offer large rewards in serious cases on behalf of the Govt. These decisions were arrived at after careful ["consideration" – *deleted*] consultation with the Treasury Solicitors, & with the heads of the Police in Ireland, as well as in England. The late Commr. on one occasion reported to Ld. Cross that: "the offer of a reward & free pardon has never produced any information, & in one case nearly caused serious trouble. Beyond satisfying the public in some small degree, the Commr. thinks the offer of a reward is useless, & shd. only be made under some special circumstances.

This series of decisions cannot be ignored; & there is much force in the observation made by Sir W. Harcourt, in one of these cases, that "vacillation of policy in such a matter wd. be a great sign of weakness & feebleness of administration."

However, there may be exceptions to every rule, & I shd. not shrink from incurring the reproach of vacillation & feebleness, if I thought I could thereby really assist in unravelling these dreadful crimes: But before taking any new departure, I should be glad if you wd. assist me with definite information on one or two points.

(1) Is it your opinion that the Police & the C.I.D. have now exhausted all

the means within their power of discovering the criminal, & have not only failed, but have no reasonable prospect of ["discovering" – *deleted*] succeeding in any moderate time?

(2) Has any information reached you, which makes you think that there are persons, who could give information, but who are holding back either from fear of consequences, or in hope of a reward; or that any persons are harbouring the criminal, & assisting his concealment?

3. Has any special circumstance been brought to your knowledge which makes it proper to offer a reward in the case of these murders, & distinguishes them from other atrocious crimes, such as the dynamite explosions, the shooting of P.C. Chamberlain, the rape & murder of Mary Cooper, & many others, in which rewards were refused?

I concur generally in what you say as to fully consulting the Commr. of Police in matters of this kind; but I wish to add that when an application, such as Mr. Montagu's, falling within a known general rule of practise, is forwarded by the Commr. without any recommendation, or suggestion of his own, it is natural to conclude that he sees no reason for departing from the general rule.

Yrs. truly
(s.) H.M.

Also annexed is the letter[4] from Sir Charles Warren, dated 6 October 1888, to Henry Matthews, to which the above was a reply:

[Stamped: – HOME OFFICE 15 [*deleted*] OCT.88 RECd. DEPt.] A49301B/9

4 Whitehall Place S.W.
6.Oct. 1888.

Dear Mr. Matthews,

Mr. Ruggles Brise has shown me your letter in which you see no occasion for offering a reward in the case of the Whitechapel Murders, and I observe that you consider that I do not recommend any reward.

I do not know that there is really any difference of opinion as to what actually has occurred during the last few days; but still as it is a very important subject and there may be some misconception about it, I wish to put in writing what my view is.

Up to 1884 the Commissioner was in the habit of recommending Rewards in cases of murder &c.

Then occurred what is called the "German explosion case" which is supposed to have been the result of a conspiracy in order to obtain a reward.

After this on 3rd July 1884, the Commissioner recommended a reward re attempted murder of P.C. Chamberlain, which the Secretary of State declined to approve, and at this time he said "since the case of the German Explosion I have a profound distrust of rewards."

At this time the view of the Commr. and others at Scotland Yard was that although a reward might not offer inducements which are likely to be accepted with a view to giving information, the offer of a good reward assists the Police by calling attention to the subject.

On the 31st July 1884 the Commissioner said "in the face of Sir Wm. Harcourt's memo I think we had better discontinue recommending the offer of rewards except in special cases."

The first special case that occurred that I am aware of, was the murder of Mrs. Samuels in 1887, in which it was supposed that there were several persons implicated. In this case the Commissioner recommended a substantial reward for information and a pardon ["for" – *deleted*] to any one implicated, but not the actual murderer.

In reply the Secretary of State approved of the pardon but did not approve the promise of a reward.

Since then the view of the Commissioner of Police and of other Police officials has not in any way changed and it is, shortly, that in special cases rewards would undoubtedly be of service.

With regard to the Whitechapel case there is simply the general view applicable to all cases, viz:- that though there may be no reason to anticipate good results from a reward, still that it is not likely to do harm, and may possibly do good.

This is purely the Police view, apart from the question of policy which is a matter entirely dependent upon public feeling.

On the 10th Sept. after the recent Whitechapel murder Mr. Montagu M.P. made an offer of a reward of £100 which I forwarded to the Secretary of State for instructions, my opinion was not in any way asked on this subject, but I received in reply a decisive and distinct answer from the Secretary of State. This reply dated 13 Sept. was "had the Secretary of State considered the case a proper one for the offer of a reward, he would at once have offered one on behalf of the Government; but that the practice of offering rewards was discontinued some years ago because experience showed that in their general effect such offers produce more harm than good, and the Secretary of State thinks the present case one in which there is special risk that the offer of a reward might hinder rather than promote the ends of justice."

I was thus distinctly informed that the Secretary of State came to conclusions upon these special cases without consulting the Commissioner.

Subsequent to this viz: on the 14th & 17th Sept. I saw Mr. Pemberton and while discussing matters generally said that I had no reason for supposing that an offer of a reward would throw light upon the murder, at the same time I may observe that I did not consider that I was in any way consulted upon the subject, because the Secretary of State had already given his formal decision in writing, and I should have expected that my opinion, if asked, would have been asked for in writing also, and <u>before</u> the decision was given.

When I saw you three days ago I gave the same opinion, viz: that, from a Police point of view, I had no reason for supposing that a reward would do any good, but that it could do no harm and might do good; but, as a matter of policy, I ["think" – *deleted*] thought that a reward should have been offered to allay the public feeling; but that, as a reward had been offered by the City Police, it was really entirely a question of policy.

The aspect of these cases from a Police point of view changes from day to day, and seeing that the City reward of £500 has produced no effect the question naturally is – "is the offer of a reward useless or has not a large enough figure been quoted?" In pursuance of this idea it seems to me that possibly an effect might be produced by the offer of a large reward say £500, and the grant of a pardon to any accomplice not being the actual murderer.

In this particular case I think that it is in your decision entirely a matter of policy. I believe if we go on long enough we can eventually work this case out; but the British public is proverbially impatient, and if other murders of a similar nature take place shortly, and I see no reason to suppose they will not, the omission of the offer of a reward on the part of the Government may exercise a very serious effect upon the stability of the Government itself.

In conclusion I cannot help feeling that in matters of this kind the Commissioner of Police ought to be fully consulted, unless the Secretary of State is quite prepared to state in Parliament that he acted entirely on his own views without consulting the Commissioner.

I write this now in order that if it comes to a question in Parliament you may be enabled to say that from a Police point of view the Commissioner had no strong opinion as to the necessity for the offer of a reward at the time you authorised the letter to be written to Mr. Montague; but at the same time I wish it to be understood that as a question of policy, with which you may perhaps think I have nothing to do, I certainly think a reward should have been offered.

> truly yours,
> Charles Warren.

There is a file cover[5] dated 13 October 1888:

[Stamped: – HOME OFFICE 15 OCT.88 RECd. Dept.] No. A49301B/10
DATE 13 Oct 1888 The Commr of Police
REFERENCES, &c.   Whitechapel Murder Rewards
    Reports that after enquiry in the Divisions Mr Anderson & himself are of opinion that the certain hope of gain is a powerful motive with ordinary people to give information [*In margin* – "/9"]
[MINUTES.]
Confidential & Pressing
This letter does not answer categorically the three questions in S.S. letter of the 7th instant.
15/Oct 88.

Mr. Matthews.
    I cannot think this affords any sufficient reason for going back from the decision already announced by S of S.   GL
15 Oct 1888
Say to the Commr with reference to his letter of 13 Oct. that it appears to indicate that he and the Assisco Commr are not altogether satisfied with the rule adopted after much consideration by the H.O. in 1884 & since repeatedly acted upon. The S.of S. wishes it to be observed that this rule applies especially to large rewards offered by Govt. in sensational cases; and has not been held to exclude small Police rewards in minor cases, which are rather in the nature of full compensation to informers for loss of time and trouble. The rule was soundly based on the results of experience showing that in the cases in which it was meant to apply, rewards had done no good, and had in many ways done harm. The S. of S. understands the Commr. in some degree to question the accuracy of these results of experience as stated in 1884–5. The matter is so important that the S. of S. desires to give the fullest consideration to any doubts the Commr. may entertain. He will be obliged if the Commr. will furnish him with the "opinions & reports of cases" which are inconsistent with the minute of Sir E. Henderson founded upon them, and any facts which may assist in the consideration of the question.
    Add that the S. of S. will thank the Commr. to give a reply in writing to the questions contained in the S. of S.'s letter of the 7th inst. –
H.M.
16 Oct/88.
Wrote 17. Oct. 88.

There follows a letter[6], dated 13 October 1888, from Sir Charles Warren to the Under-Secretary of State:

Confidential [Stamped: – HOME OFFICE 15 OCT.88 RECd. DEPt.]
A49301B/10

> 4 Whitehall Place,
> S.W.
> 13th October, 1888.

Sir,

With reference to the general question of the expediency or otherwise of offering Rewards in cases of Murder, &c., I have to acquaint you, for the information of the Secretary of State, that it is now, and so far as I can ascertain always has been, the opinion of the Metropolitan Police that the offer of Rewards in such cases may possibly be of little use but it can do no harm and it may be productive of satisfactory results. –

The Assistant Commissioner of the Criminal Investigation Department, as well as Mr. Williamson and other officers concur in this view of the matter. – The only official record I can find in opposition to it is contained in the minute of Sir E. Henderson of the 5th August, 1885, who said that ''the offer of a reward and free pardon has never produced any information, and in one case nearly caused serious trouble. Beyond satisfying the public in some small degree, the Commissioner thinks the offer of rewards is useless, and should only be made under some special circumstances''. –

But inasmuch as this minute purports to be based on opinions and reports of cases with which it is not consistent, as many of them show that the offer of rewards has been very successful, I can only imagine that it was written in reference to largess and sensational rewards such as Secretary Sir. W. V. Harcourt had in view at that time. –

I concur with Mr. Anderson that the reports from Divisions confirm us in the opinion which we have held that the certain hope of gain by giving information and help to the Police is a powerful motive with ordinary people.

> I am,
> Sir,
> Your most obedient Servant,
> CWarren.

The Under Secretary
of State
&c. &c. &c.
Home Office.

There is a file cover[7] which is worded as follows:

93305/18

H Division

SUBJECT H.O. Special P. Organization

DATE 17th Oct 1888./Home Office A49301C/10/For Sir Charles Warren 17/2.50 2/Transmits a copy letter received from Mr. S. Montague (M.P.) in which is enclosed a Petition from Tradespeople of Whitechapel, who pray that the Police of the district may be largely increased in order to remedy the grievances complained of in the petition & also to remove the feeling of insecurity which is destroying the Trade of Whitechapel.

AC.A CW 17.10.88

Chief Constable See Report

Pressing JWR 18.10.88

Supd. H.

please report

18.X.88. B.M.

Report submitted to Ch Constable T Arnold Supd 22.10.8

A.C.A.

Considering the class of population in H.Div. the recent horrible outrages, & the fact that by the presence of 125 extra men every night, the minds of the inhabitants have been kept tolerably calm, I consider that 25 men asked for are necessary. 22.X.88. B.M.

   Sir C. Warren. I think it would be well to augment the H. Division by 25 men as recommended by the Supt. and Chief Constable. JWR 23.10.88.

   I want to augment 300 men and am about to write to S of S on subject – of [ ] CW 27.10.8

A.C.A. Col Monsell. To see – When augmentation is granted the 25 asked for will be considered. JWR 24.10.88.

A file cover[8] reads as follows:

[Stamped: – HOME OFFICE 18 OCT.88 RECd.DEPt.]

No. A49301B/12

DATE 17th Oct 88   The Commr of Police

REFERENCES, &c.   Whitechapel Murders – Rewards.

Answered S of S's questions to the effect that all means have not yet been exhausted; that they continue to receive anonymous letters, that there may be persons assisting the murderer and that the murders being unique are of an entirely different category to those referred to by S of S. [*In margin* – "/10"]

[MINUTES.]

Pressing & Confidential

The Commr. in his late letters does not allude to the point why should a Gvt

Reward have a better result than the Rewards offered by the City, and by private individuals. These amount to some £1200 and so far as H.O knows have not as yet procured any trustworthy information.

It would be well to wait reply of Commr. to S. S. further enquiries on 1/ 10 before deciding on the present letter CM.18/10.

This letter is an uncertain [ ].

The Commissioner does not positively recommend a reward from a Police point of view, at the same time he half suggests it.

Note that his letter of 13 Oct in/10 seems to condemn large & sensational rewards: but if the Commissioner has recommended any reward it is one of £5000 see/9 in addition to the City Reward.

The Commr. has yet to reply to the letter written on /10 in accordance with S of S Minute.

Put up   GL

18 Oct 1888

Mr. Matthews

I have great difficulty in drawing any conclusion from this letter, except, perhaps, that the Commr. thinks rewards may do good;– & so far, is not in accord with H.O. practice. Await his reply to the letter on /10 & I will then take the earliest opportunity of going into the whole question with him & Mr. Anderson.

H.M.

19 Oct.(88.

There then follows a memo[9] as to rewards:

Memo: as to Rewards.

Mr Lushington.

I send a copy of this historical fact of this [ ] with Sir W. Harcourt's letter to the Common Council to the Commissioner of Police for his perusal.

C.M. Oct 18/88

GL

18 Oct 1888

wrote

19 Oct 1888

The following[10] appears on the cover of the preceding:

German Embassy case & the
statements <u>in H's</u> minute

There then follows a letter[11], dated 17 October 1888, from Sir Charles Warren to the Secretary of State:

Confidential   A49301B/12
      [Stamp: – HOME OFFICE 18 OCT.88 RECd. DEPt.]
                         4 Whitehall Place,
                                 S.W.
                        17th October, 1888.

Sir,

In reference to your letter of the 7th instant asking for definite information on certain points in connection with the Whitechapel Murders I have to submit the following replies. –

Question No. 1. "Is it your opinion that the Police and the C.I.D. have now exhausted all the means within their power of discovering the criminal and have not only failed, but have no reasonable prospect of succeeding in any moderate time?"

To this I have to reply, NO. I think we have hardly begun: it often takes many months to discover a criminal. –

Question No. 2. – "Has any information reached you which makes you think that there are persons who could give information, but who are holding back either from fear of consequences or in hope of a reward: or that any persons are harbouring the criminal, and assisting his concealment?"

There have been anonymous letters to this effect, but though they may be hoaxes it shews that the offer of a reward has an effect upon the mind, [*in margin* – "?"] and one of the logical solutions as to the murders is that there may be several persons who are more or less assisting the murderer. –

Question No. 3. "Has any special circumstance been brought to your knowledge which makes it proper to offer a reward in the case of these murders, and distinguishes them from other atrocious crimes such as the dynamite explosions, the shooting of P.C. Chamberlain, the rape and murder of Mary Cooper, and many others in which rewards were refused?"

I look upon this series of murders as unique in the history of our country, and of a totally different character to those mentioned above, and so far the case is in a totally different category. –

                    I am,
                      Sir,
                Your most obedient Servant,
                    C.Warren.

The Rt. Honble.
    The Secretary of State
        &c. &c. &c.

The file **MEPO** 1/55 contains a copy of the above letter.

The question of increasing police strength during this period was another pressing matter brought before the Home Office. The file cover[12], dated 17 October 1888, reads as follows:

9335/18 / Special WR / H Division / HO. Special P. Organization/17th. Oct 1888/Home Office A49301C/10/For Sir Charles Warren/
   Transmits a copy letter received from Mr. S. Montagu (M.P.) in which is enclosed a Petition from Tradespeople of Whitechapel, who pray that the Police of the district may be largely increased, in order to remedy the grievances – complained of in the petition & also to remove the feeling of insecurity which is destroying the Trade of Whitechapel.

ACA CW 17.10.8
Chief Constable – For report/Pressing/HWR. 18.10.88/
Supt. H/Please report 18.X.88.   B.M.
Report submitted to Ch Constable TArnold Supd 22.10.8
A.C.A./Considering the class of population in H.Div. the recent horrible outrages, & the fact that by the presence of 125. extra men every night, the minds of the inhabitants have been kept tolerably calm, I consider that 25. men asked for are necessary.
                    22.X.88   B.M.
Sir C. Warren.
I think it would be well to augment the H. Division by 25 men as recommended by the Supt. and Chief Constable.
H.W.R   23.10.88.
I want to augment [300?] men & about to write to S of S on subject – [ ] CW 27.10.8
A.C.A. Col. Monsell.
To [ ] – When augmentation is granted the 25 asked for will be considered. HWR. / 24.10.88

The petition from the traders is annexed and is as follows –
Saml.Montagu
To
   The Right Honourable
       The Home Secretary.
We, the undersigned Traders in Whitechapel respectfully submit for your consideration the position in which we are placed in consequence of the recent murders in our District and its vicinity.

For some years past we have been painfully aware that the protection afforded by the Police has not kept pace with the increase of Population in Whitechapel.

Acts of violence and of robbery have been committed in this neighbourhood almost with impunity owing to the existing Police regulations and the insufficiency of the number of officers. The recent murders and the failure of the authorities in discovering the criminal or criminals have had a most disastrous effect upon the Trade of our district.

The universal feeling prevalent in our midst is that the Government no longer ensure the security of Life and Property in East London and that in consequence respectable people fear to go out shopping, thus depriving us of our means of livelihood.

We confidently appeal to your sense of Justice that the Police in this district may be largely increased in order to remove the feeling of insecurity which is destroying the Trade of Whitechapel.

Signatures	addresses
Robt. Rycroft	79 High St Whitechapel
Thomas [ ]	74 High St Whitechapel
Louis Moses	75 high Whitechapel
Rudolf Silvershore	76 High Whitechapel
Joshua Horton	80 High St Whitechapel
R.W. Heimott	82 " " "
P.Cohen	83 " " "
A Randell	84 High St Whitechapel
Henry Burgless	86 High St Whitechapel
R Goldberg	91 High St Whitechapel
Arthur Cohen	92 High Str Whitechapel
John Baker	95 High St Whitechapel
Robt. Dick	96 High St Whitechapel
Thos. Trollope	116 High St Whitechapel
John Blackwell	117 H Whitechapel John Jacobson
	145 High Street Whitechapel
GHamilton	72 Whitechapel Road
W.Wright	81 High Street Whitechapel
Morras Horman	80 High St Whitechapel
L V Jones	65 High St Whitechapel
E. Frisby	61 High St Whitechapel
A. Goodall	55 High St Whitechapel
W. Stern	54 " " "

R. Morrison	53 " " "
J. Smith	18 Osborne St Whitechapel
Sandlowiter	51 High St Whitechapel
W.Repson Son	47 High St Whitechapel
Ge Sulan	46 High St Whitechapel
A Saloman	28 High Str Whitechapel
A Saloman	115 High Str Whitechapel
J. Sawyer	
S. Franklin	1 Whitechapel Road
J. East for G N Courtney	8 Whitechapel Road
E T. Johnson	11 Whitechapel Road
John Hall	102 Whitechapel Road
Thomas J Hall	50 Leman Street
Jno Jennings [?]	229 Whitechapel Rd.
W.T. Barnes	37 Whitechapel Road
A Joseph	75 Whitechapel Road
A. Brasch	77a Whitechapel Road
[ ]	78 Whitechapel Rd
[ ]	-do-
R Cohnreich	79a Whitechapel Rd
L Cohnreich	79a Whitechapel Rd
JS Hamshere	80A Whitechapel Road
T.J. Dooley	81a Whitechapel Rd
G R.Hawkey.	82a. 83a. & 88a. Whitechapel Rd
D Harris	84a Whitechapel Rd E
WDurrand	85a Whitechapel Rd
C Harvey	86a Whitechapel Rd
Stuart Doig	81 Whitechapel Road
Mrs Pricella Levy	84 Whitechapel Road E
Thomas Cole	100 Whitechapel Road E
John Scott & Co	105 Whitechapel Rd
Elsy H Afford	110 Whitechapel Rd
Fredk. W. Palmer	114 Whitechapel Rd. E.
Barber & Co	104 Whitechapel Rd
Alfred Cohen	101 Whitechapel Rd
H.J. Freiwald	100a Whitechapel Rd
H. Charik	87 Whitechapel Rd
E.J. Farbridge	79 Whitechapel Rd
J Abrahams	Royal Pavilion Theatre E
P.Abrahams	212 Whitechapel Road
JnoHDriver [?]	265 Whitechapel Rd. E.

Robt Dinnie	104 do do
Ungar & Co	52 Commercial St. E.
L. Cleaver	1 Leman St. E.
George Cushway	9 Leman St. Whitechapel E.
JH Rutter	15 Leman St. Whitechapel
C. Ragg Barker	38 Leman St. "
H Brigham	32 Leman St.
L. Schmidt	30 Leman St E.
ERBrooke	52 Great Alie St. E
E. Roberts	261 Whitechapel Road
David Harris	51 Great Alie Street
H Mitchell	5 Great Alie Street
Max Tichborne	6 Great Alie St
J Delmonte	8 " " "
M Bambery	56 88 Leman
H Lewin	8 Leman St.
R. Puta	33, Little Alie Street E.
Abrahams & Gluckstein	26 & 120 High St. Whitechapel
George Francorn	6 Commercial Rd E.
Myer Kinna	11 Commercial Rd E.
J.A. Oxley	15 Commercial Rd. E.
S. Davis & Co	18 Commercial Road East.
F.Reugelbering	25 Church Lane
D Cohen	27 " "
Isaac Statman	29 Church Lane
Alfred Emanuel	33 Church Lane
AD[ ]&co	37 Church Lane, Commercial Road E.
Henry Hart	38 Church Lane Whitechapel
Simon Cohen	32 Church Lane Whitechapel
D. Fishtein	30 " " "
G West	28 Church Lane Whitechapel
D. Oberlander	12 Church Lane Whitechapel
Lilly graham	10 " " "
C[ ] Thomas	5 Church Lane, Whitechapel
Ray. W.	4a Church Lane Whitechapel
Mr Dutton	3 Church Lane Whitechapel
Francis Dawson	119 High Street Whitechapel
Green Arthur Green	13 Commercial St. E.
Newman Enoch	15 Commercial St. E.
N. Lampoir	19 Commercial St. E.
A. S. Solomon	8 Commercial St Whitechapel

Louis[ ]	22 Commercial St. E.
Edward Carft[?]	5 Commercial St. Whitechapel
John Marritt	3 Commercial Street. E.
HRichardson	273 Whitechapel Rd.
WAGoodwin	270 Whitechapel Rd
James Hopecraft	262 Whitechapel Rd
Sarah Halliday	263 Whitechapel Rd
J W Fryett	16 Whitechapel Road
M.A. Wilderspin	18 Whitechapel Road
A. Goldstein	20 Whitechapel Road
P [?] Phillips	21 Whitechapel Road
A Tipper	23 Whitechapel Rd
Charles Tarling	64 Commercial Street
Geo. F Brady	17. Steward Street
Geo. T. Ligg	88 Hanbury St
ThosCath[ ]	66 High St Whitechapel
ChasGorton	146 do do
E. A. Choat	137 do do
Brooke Bond	129 do do
W.T.Wall	127 do do
B. Goldsmith	125. do do
Pro Henry Ford [ ]	122 High Street Whitechapel
E Richardson	98 High St Whitechapel
M Goldsten's	26 Whitechapel Road
S.Rosenhower&Co	29 & 30 Whitechapel Rd
E Brook Teare Co	31 Whitechapel Rd
Salmon Gluckheim	34 Whitechapel Rd.
W. Barker	35 Whitechapel Rd
J A Lidstone	36 Whitechapel Rd
S Joseph	40 Whitechapel Road
Ballantyne & Co	72 Whitechapel
William Goult	24 & 25 Whitechapel Rd
Messrs. Henry & Co.	42 Whitechapel Rd
JosMatrey	43
Thomas James	52&53 Whitechapel Rd
Joseph Cohen	47 Whitechapel Road
Joseph Giblers	46 Whitechapel Road
G Worteman	45 Whitechapel Road
D Goldenbry	44 Whitechapel Road E.
R J Richards	
H.Lowell	60 Whitechapel Rd

JEAlexander [?]	61 Whitechapel Rd E
S H Brunell [?]	64 Whitechapel Rd.
JDMostin	65 Whitechapel Rd
Sidney Fuller	3 Osborn St
Mr. Isaac Isaac's	9 Osborn St. East.
JWSharp [?]	57 Brick Lane
Frederick James West [?]	18 Brick Lane Whitechapel
Richard Holley	56 Turner St Whitechapel
John Coleman A.P.S.	265 Whitechapel Road
I.S.Turner [?]	103 Whitechapel Rd
C. Dixon	110 Whitechapel Road.
W.Brandurn	99 Whitechapel Road
JS Levy	15 The Mount Whitechapel
Joseph Clark	111 Mo E.
Samuel Pipert	110 Leman Street Whitechapel
WHStarbey	112 Leman St Whitechapel
M Agar	133 Leman St Whitechapel
Myer Cohen	135 Leman St Whitechapel
J.Willett	143 Leman St E.
[ ] Lehrer	11 Osborn St. Whitechapel
W.C. Magson	17 Osborn St. Whitechapel
AMOR & Co.	17 Osborn St. Whitechapel
E. Deakins	7 Osborn St. Whitechapel
H]	NagsHead 10 Whitechapel Rd
Thomas Thompson	128 High St Whitechapel
John Bligh	71 do do
I.F. Jarrett	10 Osborn St E
E.J.Combry	16 Osborn St. E.
E. Wilson	29 Osborn St.
J Wallis	33a Osborn Street. E.
H.Shickle	6 Brick Lane E
P. Webber	12 Brick Lane E.
T. Williams	20 Brick Lane E.
G.Wildersmith	26 Brick Lane E
J.Holton	36 " " "
B.Rosenbery	15 Brick Lane
William Ince	24 Commercial St. E.
Arthur H Farrow	21 " " "
John Berlyne	20 Commercial Street
John Conley	14 Commercial Street
James Ayton	259 Whitechapel Road.

This is followed by a letter[13] from Godfrey Lushington, dated 22 October 1888, to the Commissioner of Metropolitan Police:

B 5239/2
WHITEHALL.

22nd October 1888.

Sir,

I am directed by the Secretary of State to transmit to you herewith, copy of a numerously signed petition addressed to Her Majesty the Queen by women residing in East London in reference to the murders recently committed in Whitechapel and the neighbourhood.

I am to request that full enquiry may be made, and a report be furnished to the Secretary of State as to the number both of Brothels and of Common Lodging Houses in Whitechapel, and such information as you may be able to procure as to the numbers and the condition of prostitutes living, or plying their calling, in the district.

Mr. Secretary Matthews would also be glad if you would be so good as to inform him whether you have at any time received any reports from the local authorities seeking the assistance or interference of the Police in regard to brothels or common lodging houses in Whitechapel, and whether they are used as refuges or retiring places for criminals.

I am to add that the Secretary of State would be glad to receive any suggestions which appear to you to be called for by the present state of affairs.

I am,

Sir,

Your obedient Servant,

Godfrey Lushington.

The Commissioner
  of Metropolitan Police.

A report[14] by Superintendent Thomas Arnold, dated 22 October 1888, follows:

METROPOLITAN POLICE.

H Division.

22nd October 1888

Reference to Papers No. 93305 Attached

With reference to the accompanying papers. I beg to report that the Beats in that portion of Whitechapel situated on H Division are small as compared with those in the adjoining Districts of Stepney, Shadwell & St. Georges, but it is impossible to at all times keep a Constable on each Beat as owing to the number of men absent from duty from sickness, leave, attending the Police

Court, or Sessions, or employed on special duties, which are necessary, but, for which no provision has been made, such as Winter duties, men employed regulating traffic, &c. it frequently occurs that the Reserve is insufficient to fill the vacancies arising from these causes, and as a consequence some of the Beats are necessarily lengthened, thus affording an opportunity for the commission of crime, which must be expected having in view the fact that a considerable portion of the population of Whitechapel is composed of the low and dangerous classes, who frequently indulge in rowdyism and street offences. With the exception of the recent murders crime of a serious nature is not unusually heavy in the District.

I am however of opinion that considering the circumstances and general condition of the locality it is desirable that the Beats should as far as possible be kept filled and to carry this out

I beg to recommend that the Division be augmented twenty five Constables for the duty, and any not required for that purpose to be employed in specially patrolling neighbourhoods which may be considered more dangerous than others, or where any complaint has been made upon which it is thought necessary a Constable should for a time be placed on a short Beat.

Should this be approved the men could be apportioned as follows, viz ten for Leman Street & ten for Commercial Street Sub-division which would embrace the greater part of the Whitechapel District and the remainder to Arbour Square which immediately adjoins Whitechapel, and where the Beats are somewhat long. This I consider will meet the present requirements of the District, except the special arrangements made in consequence of the circumstances in which the recent murders were committed and which it will be necessary to continue for a time to prevent if possible any further outrages but I trust that some modification may be shortly made and do not ask for an augmentation for this duty but recommend that men be furnished from other Divisions as at present.

As regards the recent murders having had a disastrous effect on trade at the East End there is no doubt that since those in Berner Street and Mitre Square were committed females have to some little extent discontinued shopping in the evening but I am of opinion this will not prevail for any lengthened period there being at present very little excitement.

T Arnold Supd.

The Home Office Permanent Under-Secretary to Henry Matthews, Godfrey Lushington, wrote to the Commissioner of Police, Sir Charles Warren, requesting information on prostitution, brothels, lodging houses and other details of the East End, on 22 October 1888. This was as a result of a petition sent by Henrietta Barnett, wife of the

Reverend Samuel Barnett of Whitechapel, to Queen Victoria on behalf of the women of Whitechapel. The police reply[15], dated 25 October 1888, is as follows:

Confidential/   25/10

In reply to yr letter of 22nd October there has been no return hitherto of the probable numbers of brothels in London, but during the last few months I have been tabulating the observations of Constables on their beats, and have come to the conclusion that there are 62 houses known to be brothels on the H or Whitechapel Divn and probably a great number of other houses which are more or less intermitently [sic] used for such purposes.

The number of C.L.Hs. is 233, accommodating 8,530 persons, we have no means of ascertaining what women are prostitutes and who are not, but there is an impression that there are about 1200 prostitutes, mostly of a very low condition.

The only request that I am aware of having rec'd from Vestries about this neighbourhood is one from Mile End when the Police supplied the infn., & convictions were obtained on the evidence of Constables.

This Vestry now helps a seasoned P.S. ["to look" – *deleted*] employed in looking up cases, Mr. Charrington has been very active in evicting the holders of Brothels, and has cleared out 6 Ford St Stepney & Lady Lake Green, the result however is not conducive to morality, the unfortunate women are driven to plying for hire among respectable people, or else exercise their calling in the streets.

The lower class of C.L.Hs. is naturally frequented by prostitutes, thieves & tramps as there is nowhere else for them to go, & no law to prevent their congregating there.

I fear that in driving the Brothel keepers away from certain neighbourhoods much is being done to demoralize London generally, it is impossible to stop the supply while the demand exists.

["I would suggest, however, if it were possible that only lodging" – *deleted*]

I think it is probable that a good number of people who are not married live together at the C.L.Hs., but this also takes place in Hotels in the West End.

I do not think there is any reason whatever for supposing that the murderer of Whitechapel ["has necessarily any connection with the condition of Whitecha" – *deleted*] is one of the ordinary denizens of that place.

["I have received a letter from" – *deleted*].

The Home Office reply[16] to this letter is dated 25 October 1888:

A49301C/8a

25th October 1888.

Sir,

I am directed by the Secretary of State to acknowledge with thanks the receipt of your letter of the 22nd. instant forwarding a Report as to the circumstances of the recent murders in the District of Whitechapel, and I am to request that Mr. Matthews may be furnished with a similar report as to the circumstances of the murder in Mitre Square, and of the steps taken in connection therewith so far as the Metropolitan Police are concerned.

Mr. Matthews would also be glad to be furnished with a sketch map showing the position of the scenes of the various murders.

<blockquote>
I am,
Sir
Your obedient Servant,
Godfrey Lushington
</blockquote>

Another file contains a letter from Sir Charles Warren to the Home Office[17] as follows:

CID 3721/7

4 Whitehall Place,
S.W.
23rd October, 1888.

Sir,

With reference to your letter of the 5th ulto. A48584/, I have to acquaint you for the information of the Secretary of State, that I have directed the necessary enquiries to be made and have ascertained the particulars as to the number of trains which will arrive at Euston daily with passengers from America, and the hours of their arrival; and as two Police Constables must be present at each examination of luggage, I find it will be necessary to have three reliefs, thus requiring an augmentation of six Police Constables. I have therefore to ask for authority for this increase. – I should explain, however, that one of the three reliefs will be required to deal with passengers arriving during the night, and until the frequency of such arrivals has been tested only four constables will be actually appointed under the authority now sought.

The Midland Railway Company will no doubt apply to have similar arrangements made at St. Pancras Station, and this will necessitate my seeking a still further increase of six constables for that duty.

The cost of the augmentation shall be chargeable to the Special Tote.

<blockquote>
I am,
Sir,
Your most obedient Servant,
CWarren.
</blockquote>

A further letter on the same subject is found on p 374, as follows:

CID   4 Whitehall Pl
3721/9   S.W.
94713   November 1888.
Sir,

    With reference to your letter of the 30th ulto, A48584/12, on the subject of the proposed Police arrangements for the examination in London of the luggage of passengers arriving from America via Liverpool, I have to acquaint you, for the information of the Secretary of State, that I fail to see how the expense so incurred can be properly charged to the Inman Company who propose the charge.

    Apart from the fact that the arrangement will be for the benefit not only of the Inman, but of the Guion and other companies whose vessels arrive at Liverpool, it is clear that the Police examination (which is quite distinct from the Customs examination though made at the same time) is made for the special purposes for which the Treasury pay at Ports, and the expense can hardly therefore be a legitimate charge upon private individuals.

    It appears to me that the cost should be borne by the Special Tote. There is no precedent for a demand such as that proposed, and the Statute only allows of private persons on their own application obtaining the services of Constables.

                         I am, Sir,
                 Your most obedient Servant,
                      C. Warren.

There is a file cover[18] dated 25 October 1888, as follows:

[Stamped: – HOME OFFICE 27 OCT.88 DEPt. No.] No. A49301B/13
DATE 25 Oct. 1888   Commr of Police
REFERENCES &c. Rewards.

    Points out that Sir E. Henderson & Mr. Monro who are quoted as against the practice of offering rewards, were once in favour of it, as is shown in copies of minutes enclosed.

    Submits copies of Divisional Reports on the subject which were obtained in 1884.

                      [MINUTES].
                               ["Confidential" – *deleted*]

To
    Mr. Matthews
            GL
            24 Oct 1888
Mr. Monro certainly appears in 1884–5 to have thought that rewards "directed attention" to a case – & "probably did no harm." And Sir E.

Henderson's statement that rewards had never produced any information is not quite in accordance with the results stated by the Superintendent. I observe that the cases ment'd. by the Supertd. do not appear in the tabular statement furnished to me from the H.O.

H.M.

28 Oct./88

Only five cases of rewards offered by Govt. are mentioned by the Super-intendent. The other cases are either foreign rewards, rewards offered by private persons, or small rewards given at the discretion of the Commr. as to none of which the H.O. has any knowledge.

Of the five cases of rewards offered by Govt. three occurred previous to the time (from 1878) covered by the tabular statement – viz Muller 1864, Galloway 1871. and Peace (Dec 1876).

There remain two cases: One of these (Lefroy's case) is included in the tabular statement and is mentioned in my Memo.

The other – Williams case, the Cromwell Road burglary – appears to have been accidentally omitted in the preparation of the table: but I happened to recollect the case immediately afterwards, and it was mentioned in a separate Memo. sent forward to S of S.   CET

31.10.88.

GL

Mr Matthews 1 Nov. 1888

H.M.

2 Nov/88.

The letter[19] from Sir Charles Warren to the Under-Secretary of State, dated 25 October 1888, then follows:

[Stamped: – HOME OFFICE 27 OCT.88 DEPt. No.] A49301B/13
94300   Confidential   4 Whitehall Place

S.W.

25th October, 1888.

Sir,

In reply to your letter of the 17th instant on the subject of Rewards in cases of Murder, &c., and enclosing an history of the question, I feel I should express my view that the Secretary of State has exceedingly strong reasons for arriving at his conclusion with regard to Rewards in general: at the same time it would appear that different views have been expressed at different times and while the Secretary of State is in possession of views against Rewards expressed by Sir Edmund Henderson and Mr. Monro at one time, I have on the other hand memoranda, copies of which I enclose, which appear to show that Sir E. Henderson, Mr.Monro and Mr. Williamson were at another time in favour of Rewards. –

I enclose copies also of the report from some of the Divisions dated 1884.

I am,

Sir,

Your obedient Servant,

CWarren.

The items[20] referred to above then follow:

[Stamped: – HOME OFFICE 27 OCT.88 DEPt. No.] A49301B/13.
H:O: paper
A.36117
3 July, 1884
Extract from minutes on docket in Commissioner's Office:-
"Mr. Williamson

"Are there any cases on record in which information has been obtained by the offer of a reward. –

(Sd:) E.Y.W.H.

10 July

"I would suggest that a memo: be sent to Supts: of Divisions asking for information on this point.   (Sd:) : F.W. 18/7/84

"Send accordingly.

"E.H.

19/7/84

"Memo: sent to each Superintendent for Report.

F.W.

20.7.84

"Result submitted"

"F. Williamson"

Chief Supt:

Sir E. Henderson.

"The information received from divisions does not form a strong case for rewards. –

"Although I do not think that a reward offers really inducements which are likely to be accepted as to giving information; there is no doubt that the offer of a good ['reward' – *deleted*] sum directs attention to a case, and in this way helps the Police"

(Sd:) J.M. 30.7

"In the face of Sir W. Harcourt's memo: I think we had better discontinue recommending the offer of rewards except in special cases.

(Sd:) E.Y.W.H. 31.7.84

"payment of small sums for information is another affair and a matter of discretion. –"

(Sd:) E.Y.W.H. 31.7.84

[Stamped: – HOME OFFICE 27 OCT.88 DEPt. No.] A49301B/13

H:O: letter

X6851

The minutes on the docket of this letter in Commissioner's Office are as follows. –

To Sir E. Henderson.

"In submitting these papers I beg to draw attention to the minutes on docket No. 29920/4 3rd July 1884, and to add that Mr. Monro on speaking to me on the subject the day before he left London, remarked that the offer of rewards satisfied the public; and if they did no good they probably did no harm". –

"I beg respectfully to say that I am of the same opinion as Mr. Monro."

(Sd:) Fredk. Williamson

Ch: Supt:

3/8/85

Sir E. Henderson's minute

"Ackge (H:O: letter) and acquaint that the offer of rewards and free pardons has never produced any information and in one case nearly produced serious trouble. –

"Beyond satisfying the public in some small degree I think the offer of rewards is useless and should only be made under some special circumstances.

(Sd:) E.Y.W.H.

The question of a reward is addressed under a cover and report[21], as follows:

[Stamped: – HOME OFFICE 2 NOV.88 RECd. DEPt.]No. A49301B/14

DATE 1st Novr. 88   The Commr of Police

REFERENCES &c. Whitechapel Murders – Rewards

Draws attention to the case of a Reward offered in 1860 in the case of the murder of Mrs. Mary Elmsley in which the murderer attempted to obtain the reward by manufacturing false evidence against an innocent person, which was the means of his own conviction – He considers the offer of a reward tended directly to the furtherance of the ends of Justice.

[MINUTES.]

A precis of the facts of this case was prepared for the S. of S. some days ago.

It was a clear case of the offer of a reward prompting the concoction of a false charge against an innocent person.

Fortunately the attempt failed; but had it been made a little more skilfully, an innocent man might have hanged, and the actual murderer would have pocketed £300.

CET

2.10.88

This case seems to me to
establish the direct contrary of
the Chf Comms's conclusion.
ELP. 3 Novr 88.

S of S.

H.M.

4 Novr./88

Confidential   A49301B/14

[Stamped: – HOME OFFICE 2 NOV. 88 RECd. DEPt.] 4 Whitehall
Place, S.W.

1st November, 1888.

94300/3

Sir,

With reference to my letter of the 25th inst. on the general subject of Rewards for the apprehension and conviction of Criminal, I have to acquaint you, for the information of the Secretary of State, that my attention has recently been called to the case of the murder of Mrs. Mary Elmsley, of 9 Grove Road, Mile End Road, on the 13th August 1860, and to the facts connected with a Reward being offered in this case. It would appear that the murderer [*Note in margin* – "(James Mullins)"] a pensioned Police Officer, attempted to obtain the reward of £300 – £100 of which was offered by the Government and £200 by Mr. Ratcliff, Solicitor – by manufacturing false evidence against an innocent person. But in this he failed; and the very fact of the false evidence which he gave to the Police was the means of his own apprehension and ultimate conviction. It appears to me therefore that the offering of a Reward in this case directly led to the furtherance of the ends of justice.

I am,
Sir,

The Under   Your most obedient servant,
  Secretary of State   CWarren
    &c. &c. &c.

The vexed question of a reward rumbled on into November 1888 leading the *Star*, on the evening after Mary Jane Kelly's murder, to publish an article which read:

We have heard the wildest stories as to the reason which popular opinion in Whitechapel assigns for Mr Matthew's obstinate refusal to offer a reward. It is believed by people who pass among their neighbours as sensible folk that the Government do not want the murderer to be convicted, that they are interested in concealing his identity, that, in fact, they know it, and will not divulge it. Of course this is rank nonsense . . .

CHAPTER 13

The Bloodhounds

The involvement of bloodhounds in an effort to track the murderer is often mentioned, and there is much official documentation on this aspect. File HO 144/221/A49301E refers to the bloodhounds and the cover of the first file, f2, reads:

No. A49301 E/1 ["22" *deleted*]
H.O.

REFERENCES, &c. re – <u>Whitechapel Murders</u>
Printed letter from the Times newspaper in which Mr. P. Lindley suggests the use of bloodhounds to trace the murderer.

<u>Pressing</u>

[MINUTES.]

In the case of William Fish at Blackburn in 1876, the use of bloodhounds brought to light evidence which led to the conviction of the murderer.

I do not know whether bloodhounds could be used in the way suggested in this letter. If they could, it would be most desirable to keep one or two ready in a Police Station near Whitechapel, and to have persons able to use them stationed there, so that they might be available in case of another murder.

At any rate the Commissioner's attention might be called to this letter.

?To Commissioner

CT

ELP 3 Oct 88   2.10.88

[There is a marginal note – "54277/12 *herewith*", a stamp "REFERRED 3 OCT 88 Ansr 5.10.88 (1/45) *Index* –", and a further stamp – REGISTRY 3-OCT-88–8]

Folio 4 is the press cutting above referred to:

TO THE EDITOR OF *THE TIMES*

Sir, – With regard to the suggestion that bloodhounds might assist in tracking the East-end murderer, as a breeder of bloodhounds, and knowing their power,

I have little doubt that, had a hound been put upon the scent of the murderer while fresh, it might have done what the police have failed in. But now, when all trace of the scene has been trodden out, it would be quite useless.

Meanwhile, as no means of detection should be left untried, it would be well if a couple or so of trained bloodhounds – unless trained they are worthless – were kept for a time at one of the police head-quarters ready for immediate use in case their services should be called for. There are, doubtless, owners of bloodhounds willing to lend them, if any of the police, which, I fear, is improbable, know how to use them.

I am, Sir, your obedient servant,
PERCY LINDLEY.

York-hill, Loughton, Essex, Oct. 1.

This is followed by another file cover[1]

[Stamped: – HOME OFFICE 6 OCT. 88 RECEIVED] No. A49301E/2
DATE 5th Oct 88   Commr of Police.
REFERENCES, &c.   Bloodhounds as Detectives
Confidential   Finds from enquiries that
Bloodhounds should be kept constantly practised in the streets if they are to be of any use in towns. Is, however, enabled for a few days to obtain the use of dogs which have been worked in a town, and is getting them down at once.

Requests authority to expend a sum not exceeding £100 per annum in keeping trained bloodhounds, the amt. Required this year being £50. This is irrespective of any expenses which may occur in the special use of Bloodhounds at the present moment.   Pressing
[MINUTES.]
Just now public opinion probably would condone any measure however extreme to discover the murderer, but if the use of bloodhounds is to be authorized I think it should be strictly limited to the present emergency; as all extraordinary proceeding for extraordinary crime, & every precaution should be observed in their use.

If an accident happened from the dogs attacking an incorrect person there would be a great outcry.

C.M.
Oct 6.

Authorise expenditure
Mr Matthews   of £50 for the present occasion, but say it wd. be

desirable to see the result of the employment of the Bloodhounds before sanctioning the payt. of any annual Amt.

ELP. 6Oct88

T.O.

Sanction expenditure of £50 for the present occasion: and say that before sanctioning permanent annual expenditure for no good purpose the S. of S. thinks it desirable to ascertain by experience whether bloodhounds can render any useful service in the streets, and whether they can be used without danger to the public. It will of course be essential to have the dogs under the control of a person accustomed to them, so as to prevent any possible mischief to innocent persons.

H.M.

7th Oct./88

Wrote

10/10

Mr Byrne says a
Letter is going to
Receiver

9/10

Letter to Receiver

10. Oct./88.

There follows a letter[2] written by the Chief Commissioner, Sir Charles Warren, to the Under-Secretary of State:

A49301E/2

[Stamped: – HOME OFFICE 6 OCT 88 RECEIVED]

4 Whitehall Place,

S.W.

5th October, 1888.

Sir,

With reference to the papers marked "pressing," returned herewith, I have to acquaint you for the information of the Secretary of State that I have made enquiries, and I found that there is a difficulty in suddenly bringing bloodhounds into a town, when they have not been trained for use in the streets, owing to the confusion of scent, – and that it is desirable that they should be kept constantly practised in the streets if they are to be of any use. –

I have therefore to request the authority of the Secretary of State to expend a sum of not over £100 per annum in keeping trained bloodhounds, the amount required this year being £50. – This is irrespective of any expenses which may occur in the special use of bloodhounds at the present moment. –

I find that I am enabled for a few days at least to obtain the use of dogs which have been worked in a town, and I am getting them down at once. —

I am,

Sir,

Your most obedient Servant,

Cwarren

The Under Secretary
    Of State
&c. &c. &c.
    Home Office

There is a deleted reply[3] to the Chief Commissioner, as follows:

A49301E/2

A49301/4   Whitehall

<u>Confidential</u>   Rewritten   10 October 1888

Sir,

    With reference to previous correspondence respecting the use of bloodhounds in tracking criminals in London, I am directed by the Secretary of State to inform you that upon your recommendation he is willing to sanction an expenditure of £50 for this purpose on the present occasion, but before giving any assent to a permanent annual expenditure for so novel a purpose he thinks it desirable to ascertain by experience whether bloodhounds can render any useful service in the streets, and whether they can be used without danger to the public.

    It will of course be essential to have the hounds under the control of a person accustomed to them, so as to prevent any possible mischief to innocent persons.

I am, Sir,

Your obedient servant,

The Commissioner of Police
    of the Metropolis

There is next a file cover[4] as follows:

[Stamped: – HOME OFFICE 24 OCT.88 DEPt. No.] No. A49301/E/3
DATE 23 Octr. 88   Comr. Of Police
REFERENCES, &c.   reBloodhounds
                        Referring to his letter of the 5th. inst, submits a
                        revised estimate for the receir. of the financial year

amounting to £100, & reqts sanction of S.of S. to expend this sum, instead of the £50 as previously applied for.

<u>Pressing</u>

[MINUTES.]

The cost to the end of the financial year will be £25 hire £5 insurance.

Sir C. Warren proposes to buy a puppy for £15 & train it with the old dog. Before authorizing further expenditure? ask Sir C. Warren what has been the results of his experiments with the hound. in what manner he has been tried. & whether he (Sir CW) is satisfied with the result. & has confidence in continuing their use.

C.M. Oct 25.

These inquiries I think will better come later. The use at present is experimental only

(Wrote Comm?& Rec?   Sanction 25 Oct 1888   GL
        26.10.88.

There then follows the Chief Commissioner's letter[5]:

[Stamped: – HOME OFFICE 24 OCT.88 DEPt. No.]   A49301E/3
93925/11
                                        4, Whitehall Place,
                                                S.W.
                                23rd October, 1888.

Sir,

With reference to my letter of the 5th instant requesting authority to expend a sum of £50 during the current financial year in keeping trained bloodhounds, irrespective of any expenses which may occur in the special use of bloodhounds at the present time, I have to acquaint you, for the information of the Secretary of State, that the amount in question was suggested when I was under the impression that the dog now placed at our disposal would be lent without charge.

I am informed that Mr. Brough the owner of the dog will charge £25 for his hire until the end of March next; and with a view to indemnify himself in the event of accidents will require the dog to be insured, this will cost an additional £5. –

It will be necessary to purchase a pup at a price of say £15; it could be trained with the hired dog and would then at the end of March be fit to take his place. –

I have therefore to submit a revised estimate for the remainder of the financial year amounting to £100, and to request the sanction of the Secretary of State to expend this sum, or as much of it as may be necessary, instead of the £50 as previously applied for. –

I am,

Sir,

Your obedient Servant,

CWarren

The Under Secretary
    of State
    &c. &c. &c.
    Home Office

The cost of the bloodhounds became something of a problem and there was an exchange of correspondence with Mr A.J. Sewell of the Veterinary Infirmary, 55 Elizabeth Street, Eaton Square, S.W. These letters are held under MEPOL 2/188.

When the financing of the bloodhounds was finally settled an agreement[6] was duly drawn up but, in the event, it was never signed and the bloodhounds had both been returned to Mr Brough by the time of the Kelly murder of 9 November 1888. The agreement, however, makes interesting reading:

An Agreement made this   day of   one thousand eight hundred and eighty eight Between Alfred Joseph Sewell of 55 Elizabeth Street Eaton Square in the County of Middlesex Veterinary Surgeon of the one part and Sir Charles Warren of Scotland Yard in the said County of Middlesex Chief Commissioner of the Metropolitan Police of the other part, Whereby it is agreed as follows:-

1. The said Alfred Joseph Sewell will as from the date hereof until the thirty first March One thousand eight hundred and eighty nine keep the bloodhound ''Barnaby'' for and at the disposal of the Metropolitan Police such bloodhound to be sent (unless it be ill injured or otherwise incapacitated from work) together with a man to be supplied by Alfred Joseph Sewell to any part of the Metropolis at the earliest possible moment on receipt of instructions from Sir Charles Warren or any Metropolitan Police Superintendent or Inspector the said bloodhound to be kept at the expense of Alfred Joseph Sewell but all travelling expenses incurred in respect of this clause to be born [sic] by the said Sir Charles Warren———

2. 2. Sir Charles Warren for himself and his successors in office for the consideration mentioned in the last preceding clause covenants with Alfred Joseph Sewell to pay to Alfred Joseph Sewell the sum of Eighty pounds in

manner following that is to say. Forty pounds on the twenty fourth day of December one thousand eight hundred and eighty eight and Forty pounds the balance thereof on the thirty first March One thousand eight hundred and eighty nine And further to pay to Alfred Joseph Sewell on the signing hereof the sum of Ten pounds being the Insurance premium to be paid by Alfred Joseph Sewell for insuring the said bloodhound in his own name and for his own benefit in the Horse Insurance Company Limited and also to pay to Alfred Joseph Sewell all travelling expenses as provided for in Clause 1 hereof.

3. If the said bloodhound shall any time during the continuance of this agreement become unwell injured or in any manner incapacitated from work Alfred Joseph Sewell shall not be called upon to furnish any other bloodhound in its place neither shall he be called upon to send the said bloodhound as provided by Clause 1 hereof nor shall his remuneration as provided by Clause 2 hereof be in any way affected thereby it being the intention of the parties hereto that although the said bloodhound is to be kept by the said Alfred Joseph Sewell at his own expense it is entirely at the risk of Sir Charles Warren————

4. The costs of and incidental to the preparation and execution of this Agreement shall be borne and paid the day and year first above written————

Signed Sealed and Delivered
by the above named

The Times of Tuesday, 13 November 1888 concluded the tale of the unsuccessful role played by the bloodhounds in the efforts to capture the Whitechapel murderer:

It will be remembered that, at Sir Charles Warren's request, Mr. Brough, the well-known bloodhound breeder of Scarborough, was communicated with shortly after the Mitre-square and Berner-street tragedies, and asked to bring a couple of trained hounds up to London for the purpose of testing their capabilities in the way of following the scent of a man. The hounds were named Burgho and Barnaby, and in one of the trials Sir Charles Warren himself acted as the quarry and expressed satisfaction at the result. Arrangements were made for the immediate conveyance of the animals to the spot in the event of another murder occurring, and in order to facilitate matters Mr. Brough, who was compelled to return to Scarborough, left the hounds in the care of Mr. Taunton, of 8 Doughty-street, who is a friend of his. Mr. Taunton, who is a high authority on matters appertaining to the larger breeds of dogs, has ample accommodation in the rear of his residence for kenneling such valuable animals, and he was accordingly entrusted with their custody pending the conclusion of the negotiations which had been opened for the ultimate purchase of the dogs. Sir Charles Warren, however, it is said, would not give any definite assurance on the point, and the result was Mr. Brough insisted on resuming possession of the animals. Mr. Taunton has made the following statement:-

After the trial in Regent's Park Burgho was sent to Brighton, where he had been entered for the show, which lasted three days. In the meantime Barnaby remained in my care. Burgho would have been sent back to me, but as Mr. Brough could not get anything definite from Sir Charles Warren, he declined to do so, and wrote asking me to return Barnaby. I did not do so at first, but, acting on my own responsibility, retained possession of the dog for some time longer. About a fortnight ago I received a telegram from Leman-street Police-station asking me to bring up the hounds. It was then shortly after noon, and I took Barnaby at once. On arriving at the station I was told by the superintendent that a burglary had been committed about 5 o'clock that morning in Commercial-street, and I was asked to attempt to track the thief by means of the dog. The police admitted that since the burglary they had been all over the premises. I pointed out the stupidity of expecting a dog to accomplish anything under such circumstances and after such a length of time had been allowed to elapse, and took the animal home. I wrote telling Mr. Brough of this, and he wired insisting that the dog should be sent back at once, as the danger of its being poisoned, if it were known that the police were trying to track burglars by its aid, was very great, and Mr. Brough had no guarantee against any pecuniary loss he might suffer in the event of the animal's being maltreated. Therefore there has not been a "police bloodhound" – that is to say, a trained hound, in London for the past fortnight. The origin of the tale regarding the hounds being lost at Tooting while being practised in tracking a man I can only account for in the following way. I had arranged to take Barnaby out to Hemel Hempstead to give the hound some practice. The same day a sheep was maliciously killed on Tooting-common, and the police wired to London asking that the hounds might be sent down. I was then some miles away from London with Barnaby, and did not get the telegram until on my return, late in the evening. Somebody doubtless remarked that the hounds were missing, meaning that they did not arrive when sent for, and this was magnified into a report that they had been lost. At that time Burgho was at Scarborough. Under the circumstances in which the body of Mary Ann [sic] Kelly was found I do not think bloodhounds would have been of any use. It was then broad daylight and the streets crowded with people. The only chance the hounds would have would be in the event of a murdered body being discovered, as the others were, in the small hours of the morning, and being put on the trail before many people were about.

CHAPTER 14

October 1888 – A Strange Story

With the increasing public concern and terror that the Whitechapel Murders caused, new allegations and alarming stories began to appear in the press. One such was the so-called "Cabmen's Shelter" incident that occurred on the day of the discovery of the bodies of Stride and Eddowes. It began in the newspapers and then found its place in the official files. The story[1] appeared in the *Newcastle Chronicle* on Tuesday, 2 October 1888:

A49301/50

A STRANGE STORY.

A strange story is told, according to a London evening paper, by Thomas Ryan, who has charge of the Cabmen's Reading Room, at 43, Pickering Place, Westbourne Grove, W. Mr. Ryan is a teetotaller, and is the secretary of the Cabmen's Branch of the Church of England Temperance Society. Ryan, who tells the story without affectation, says on Saturday afternoon, while he was in his little shelter, the street attendant brought a gentlemanly-looking man to him and said: "This 'ere gentleman wants a chop, guv'ner; can you cook one for him, he says he's 'most perished with cold.'' The gentleman in question, Ryan says, was about five feet six inches in height, and wore an Oxford cap on his head, and a light check ulster, with a tippet buttoned to his throat, which he did not loosen all the time he was in the shelter. He had a thick moustache, but no beard; was round-headed, his eyes very restless, and clean white hands. Ryan said, "Come in, I'll cook one for you with pleasure." This was about four o'clock in the afternoon. Several cabmen were in the shelter at the time, and they were talking of the new murders discovered that morning at Whitechapel. Ryan exclaimed, "I'd gladly do seven days and nights if I could only find the fellow who did them." This was said directly at the stranger, who, looking into Ryan's face, quietly said, "Do you know who committed the murders?" and then calmly went on to say, "I did them. I've had a lot of trouble lately. I came back from India and got into trouble at once. I lost my watch and chain and £10." Ryan was greatly taken aback at the man's statement, and fancied he was just recovering from a drinking bout; so he replied, "If that's correct you must consider yourself engaged.'' But he then went on to speak to him about temperance work and the evils wrought by drink. Warming to his subject, Ryan spoke of his own work amongst men to try to induce them to become teetotallers; then the stranger said ''Have a drink'' to Ryan, and produced a bottle from an inner pocket, which was nearly full of a brown liquid – either whisky or brandy. Ryan told him he had better put the bottle away, as they were all teetotallers there. Ryan reasoned with him as to the folly of drinking, and at last he expressed his willingness to sign the pledge, a book containing the pledges being shown him. This the stranger examined, and at length filled up one page, writing on the counterfoil as well as on the body of the pledge. In the hand of a gentleman he wrote the following words:- ''J.Duncan, doctor, residence, Cabman's Shelter, 30th Sept., 1888.'' After doing this he said, ''I could tell a tale if I wanted.'' Then he relapsed into silence. After a pause he went on to speak of his experiences in India; and said he knew the Rev. Mr. Gregson who was engaged in temperance work amongst the English soldiers in India, and had also been for some time in Sinila. He also stated that he was at Newcastle-on-Tyne before he went to India. Ryan called his attention to the fact that he had not filled in his proper residence, and the man replied, ''I have no fixed place of abode at present. I'm living anywhere.'' In answer to further conversation about teetotalism, Duncan accepted an invitation to go with Ryan to church that evening, and afterwards accompanying him to a temperance meeting which he was going to hold. For that purpose, he said, he would return to the shelter in an hour, but he never came back. Duncan carried a stick, and looked a sinewy fellow, just such a one as was capable of putting forth considerable energy when necessary.

The file cover[2] regarding this incident is as follows:

[Stamped: – HOME OFFICE 8 OCT.88 RECEIVED]   No. A49301C/7
DATE 8 October 88   Newcastle Prison Governor.
REFERENCES, &c. Whitechapel Murders.

> Calls attention to enclosed Newspaper Extract giving an account of a man named Duncan who confessed to having committed the Murders. Has reason to believe that Duncan was twice imprisoned in Newcastle Prison.
> Fds. His description & thinks he should be traced.
> [*Marginal note:* – ''see A49301/68'']

Pressing

MINUTES.

This is the man who told the Keeper of the Cabman's shelter he had committed the murders; & failed to keep an appointment with him.

His two convictions at Newcastle are for assaults on
women.

To Commissioner of Police.

C.M. Oct 8/88.

GL

Wrote Commr.   8 Oct 1888
8.10.88.

There then follows the descriptive details[3] of Duncan:

[Stamped: – PRISON COMMISSION RECd 6 OCT 1888]A49301/50
in 12579/1
[Stamped: – HOME OFFICE 8 OCT.88 RECEIVED]
Previous convictions recorded against John. Geo. [''Duncan'' – *deleted*]
Donkin.

Name	Date	Place	Offence	Sentence	Remarks
Geo: Donkin	6th Jan.y. 1881	Tynemouth	Assault Female	1 C.M. H.L.	
John. Geo: Donkin	22nd Decr. 1881	do.	Assault Female	2 C.M. H.L.	

Description of the above
In 1881 (Decr. 22nd)

Place of birth	Morpeth
Age	28 yrs
Married	yes
Trade or occupation –	none
Complexion	Fresh
Hair	Brown
Eyes	Blue
Build	Slender
Shape of Face	Long
Height	5 ft. 8 in.
Distinctive marks:-	Scars on left thigh – mole on Back – wound on left cheek – Red mark On right shoulder.

[FMTooley(?)]

5/10/88 Governor

The letter[4] from the Governor of the prison follows:

[Stamped: – PRISON COMMISSION RECd 5 OCT 1888]A49301C/7
Pressing   ["A49301/50" – *deleted*] 12579/1
<u>Confidential</u>   [Stamped: – HOME OFFICE 8 OCT.88 RECEIVED]
H.M. Prison,
Newcastle,

Sir,

<u>re Whitechapel Murders</u>

I have today had my attention called by a man named Murray – a Solicitor's Clerk of Newcastle – to a paragraph headed "A Strange Story", which appeared in a local Newspaper on Tuesday last (vide copy enclosed)

The person to whom the "Story" refers I have reason to believe is a man who was twice committed to this prison, particulars of whose previous convictions are enclosed, showing his description at that time. He was educated at college for the medical profession, but he turned out wild & lived more or less a dissolute life. His wife obtained a divorce from him and since then he is known to have frequented the low parts of London, being very impecunious. His manners and address are those of a gentleman, and his anatomical knowledge is said to be considerable.

It may be that the recent horrible murders committed in London are the work of the person to whom I refer, & were he found I could identify him as being the man who was twice in my custody.

I give you these particulars as it appears to me that the man to whom I refer should be traced, and the same coming forcibly before me today I have felt it my duty to put you in possession of them for the information of the Home Office if you should think it well to place them before that department.

I have the honor to be,
Sir,
Your obedient Servant
[FMTooley(?)]
<u>Governor</u>

R.S. Mitford Esq
Prison Commissioner
Whitehall
London S.W.

There is then a second[5] file cover:

[Stamped: – HOME OFFICE 12 OCT.88 RECEIVED] No. A49301/68
DATE 10 Octr. 1888.Asst. Commr. Anderson.
REFERENCES, &c.   <u>-Donkin alias J. Duncan.</u>
                 Fds. Police report from which it appears that the men are not identical.

[*Marginal note*: – "See A49301/7"]
[MINUTES.]
The man who spoke to the Keeper of the Cabman's
shelter has accounted for his movements on the dates
of the murders.

?Lay by. C.M. Oct 13.

GL

15 Oct 1888

There then follows a report[6] dated 10 October 1888 from the Assistant
Commissioner, Robert Anderson, to the Home Office:

[Reference:- 52983/598]   A49301/68

Great Scotland Yard,

[Stamped: – HOME OFFICE 12 OCT.88 RECEIVED]   London, S.W.

10th day of October 1888.

From

ASSISTANT COMMISSIONER OF POLICE,

Criminal Investigation Department.

To The Under Secretary of State
for the Home Department
&c   &c   &c

Sir,

I am directed by the Commissioner of Police of the Metropolis to
acknowledge the receipt of your letter of the 8th instant enclosing a letter
from the Governor of the Prison at Newcastle giving particulars regarding a
man named Donkin who he thought was identical with one J Duncan said to
have made a confession with regard to the recent murders in Whitechapel and
to transmit for the information of Mr. Secretary Matthews a police report
. . . received on the subject from which it will be seen that the men referred
to are not identical.

The enclosures which accompanied your letter are herewith returned.

I have the honour to be,

Sir,

Your obedient servant,

RAnderson

[*There are marginal references to the above report:* – "A 49301/50" *above* "4."]

There is then attached a report[7] by Inspector Abberline, dated 10
October 1888, giving details of the result of checking out this story:

A49301/68

[Stamped: – METROPOLITAN POLICE 10.OCT.88 CRIMINAL
INVESTIGATION DEPT]
METROPOLITAN POLICE.

[Stamped: – HOME OFFICE 12 OCT 88 RECEIVED]   Central Office
10th day of Oct. 1888.

SUBJECT Whitechapel   With reference to the
    Murders   annexed.

I beg to report that the person who made the statement in the Cabmens Shelter at Pickering Place, Bayswater, 30th Ult. Has since been seen by Police, and interrogated, and satisfactorily accounted for his movements on the dates [of] the murders. His correct na[me] is John Davidson, and there[fore] cannot be the person referre[d to] in the attached correspondence from Home Office.

F.G.Abberline Inspr.
T Arnold Supt.

[*There is the marginal reference to the above:* – "REFERENCE TO PAPERS 52983 5748"]

Thus another suspicious person was cleared by police enquiry. It is interesting to see this example of how another "suspect", mentioned in newspaper reports, was brought to the attention of the Police, and was cleared.

CHAPTER 15

A Suspect Arrested in France

October 1888 was, as we have seen, a busy time for the police, with dozens of suspects being brought to their notice. This situation was exacerbated by – if not, indeed, caused by – the extensive and sensational press coverage of the murders. Two line drawings of a suspect, described by Matthew Packer, appeared in the *Daily Telegraph* and many other newspapers.

  This publicity created even more problems for the police. File HO 144/220/A49301, f3, has a cover bearing the following details:

[Stamped: – HOME OFFICE 12 OCT. 88 RECEIVED] No. A49301/67
DATE 12 Octr. 1888.   Foreign Office
REFERENCES &c.   <u>Whitechapel Murders</u>
Fds. despatch from H.M. Consul at Boulogne enclosing copies of letters he has addressed to Comr. of Police as to a suspicious person who asked to be sent to South Wales: the appearance of the man much resembles the picture of the supposed Murderer: he is detained till to-day as a vagrant, but cannot be kept longer without definite instructions.
MINUTES.
Imme<u>diate</u>

[Stamped:- METROPOLITAN POLICE
          RECEIVED
          12. OCT. 88
CRIMINAL INVESTIGATION DEPT.]
H.M. Consul is in direct communication with the Metropolitan Police on the subject of this man.
To Comr. of Police C.M.
Oct 12. GL
12 Oct 1888

This matter has now
  been cleared up.
    CW 16.10.88

[Stamped:- HOME OFFICE 20 OCT.88 DEP. No.]
?Lay by
corrs C.M.
22/10

The reports in this file follow, thus:

[*f6*] 1888/Boulogne 11 October/Consul Bonham/No 29 Immediate/2
Inclosures/Recd Oct:12./Bypost./<u>Suspicious character</u>/Encloses copies of
letter/to Metropolitan Police/Home Office/P.L./Oct 12/88
45

[*f5*]:- <u>Immediate</u>
[Stamped:- HOME OFFICE 12 OCT.88 RECEIVED]   British Consulate
Boulogne 11 October 1888
A49301/67

No29 My Lord,
     I have the honour to transmit to your Lordship, herewith enclosed, copy of
a letter I addressed to the Commissioner of Police Scotland Yard yesterday
relative to a suspicious character [*marginal note:*- ''10 Octr 1888''] and also
copy of a further letter which I send by tonight's post: the telegram I have
received requesting me to act in my discretion places me in an awkward
position [*Marginal note:*- ''11 Octr 1888''].

I have the honor to be,
with the highest respect,
My Lord,
Your Lordships most obedient,
humble Servant,

The Right Honble   E.W. Bonham
The Marquis of Salisbury k.g.
&c   &c   &c
Foreign Office

[*f8*]:- <u>Immediate</u> [Stamped: – HOME OFFICE 12 OCT.88 RECEIVED]
A49301/67

Foreign Office,
October 12 1888.
Sir,
     I am directed by the Secretary of State for Foreign Affairs to transmit to
you, to be laid before [*Marginal note:*- ''Consul Bonham No. 29/Oct 11/88

and encls:''] Mr Secretary Matthews a despatch as marked in the margin which has been received from Mr Bonham Her Majesty's Consul at Boulogne together with copies of two letters which have been addressed by that officer to the Commissioner of Police Scotland Yard relative to a suspicious character also applies for assistance at Her Majesty's Consulate.

I have to request that the enclosed correspondence may be returned to this office.

I am,

Sir,

Your most obedient,

humble Servant,

The Under Secretary of State   P.W. Currie
    Home Office

[*f 9*]: – copy/Consul Bonham/to/Commissioner of Police/Boulogne 10 Octr 1888
1/Mr Consul Bonham's/Despatch No 29 of 11/October 1888.

[*ff. 7–8*]: – copy   A49307/67
[Stamped: – HOME OFFICE 12 OCT.88 RECEIVED] British Consulate,
Immediate.   Boulogne s-mer, 10th October,
                                            1888.

Sir,

I think it right to let you know that today a man called here asking for assistance who the Vice-Consul thought so much resembled the sketch portrait of the man wanted for the East end murders, given in the Daily Telegraph of the 6th, that he mentioned it to me; I saw the man and certainly there was a likeness, he wanted assistance and to go to South Wales to work in the Coal Mines, he produced a discharge from a British Ship at Glasgow on 10 April in which he had only shipped at New York on 30 March, as he was described as born in the United States I said I would not assist him and sent him to the American Consul.

Later I procured a copy of the Daily Telegraph and handed it to the Police: they arrested the man as a vagrant and requested me to go and see him at the Police Station; I could not ask for him to be detained as I had only the newspaper account and many men might answer to that. The description he gives of himself is that he left Mines near Glasgow last Monday week with about 50s, went by rail to Leith, Steamer to London only passed through, thence rail to Dover and crossed Saturday night, thence he says he has been to Bethune and other towns seeking work in Coal Mines, but came here to get a vessel.

I asked him if I gave him a passage to England tomorrow whether he would go, he wanted to know where I would send him as he would not like to land without money, but he would go if sent to Cardiff to work in the South Wales Mines, but would prefer getting work here.

My idea had been to send him to Folkstone and to let you know he was going, but he did not care to accept a passage.

His manner was very unsatisfactory and as I declined to take charge of him the Police have taken him into custody for having no means of subsistence and not giving a satisfactory account of himself or why he came to France: he will consequently be taken before the Procureur of the Republic tomorrow morning and if you want to make any further enquiries or to have the man detained, it will be necessary for you to communicate by telegraph.

I enclose the description of the man and of his clothes which has been handed me by the Police.

I am &c &c

The Commissioner of Police	(signed) E.W. Bonham,
Scotland Yard,	H.M. Consul
London.	

[f12]: – Copy/Consul Bonham/to/Commissioner of Police/Boulogne 11 October 1888
2/Mr Consul Bonham's/Despatch No 29 of 11/October 1888

[ff. 10–11]: –   A49301/67
Very Immediate. [Stamped: – HOME OFFICE 12 OCT.88 RECEIVED]

British Consulate,
Boulogne 11 October, 1888.

Sir,

About 4 this afternoon I received the following telegram in reply to my letter of yesterday, "Re man detained definite instructions impossible please act in your discretion Anderson Assistant Commissioner police Scotland Yard".

Shortly before receiving this telegram I had seen the Procureur of the Republic who had informed me that as the man had no means of subsistence or papers he would be treated as a vagrant and sent away, but he would detain him here till tomorrow afternoon to see whether on my letter of yesterday you could give any information about him.

The Procureur again sent for him that I might speak to him as he does not speak French. I asked him as to his statement to the Vice-Consul that he had been in South Wales he said he had been there about ten months ago and then returned to America; he had been several times in England.

At the request of the Procureur I told him he was being detained because he had no papers or means of subsistence and could give no satisfactory account of himself: he then stated that when in Wales he lodged with Mrs Davis 30 Dufferin, a village two miles from Merthyr Glamorganshire, that lately he was lodging with John Richmond 47 Castle Street Hamilton near Glasgow, and that when last in America he was employed in some ironworks.

I sent you the following telegram "Modulas London, Andersons telegram Langran [*sic*] now states he lodged John Richmond 47 Castle Street Hamilton near Glasgow can you verify. will be detained until tomorrow Bonham Consul".

You ask me to act in my discretion I can only say that I do not think either his manner or the account he gives of himself satisfactory but I cannot undertake the responsibility of acting further than reporting the circumstances: he may not be connected with the East End murders but says he does not wish to go to England but wants to go to South Wales where there are Mines.

He seems to have travelled about in a curious manner and I thought you might consider it desirable that he should be seen by some one acquainted with those who are "wanted".

The Procureur asked if I wished to take charge of him to send him to his country, I replied that as he declared himself an American I could not take charge of him as a British subject or ask for him to be sent to England.

I hope I may receive a telegram from you tomorrow morning before I see the Procureur.

I am &c &c

(signed) E.W. Bonham,

H.M. Consul.

The Commissioner of Police,
    London.

There then follows another file[1], dated 16 October 1888, details as follows:

[Stamped: – HOME OFFICE 17 OCT.88 RECd. DEPTt.] No. A49301/76
DATE 16 Oct 1888   The Foreign Office
REFERENCES, &c.   <u>Whitechapel Murders</u>
Forwards Despatch from H.M. Consul at Boulogne stating that the man detained there has been released as the London Police were satisfied he was not the man required.

[MINUTES.]

Commr. of Police to see. tho' probably fact is known to them.

C.M Oct 18. 1888.

Index. C.M.   Seen R.A. 24/10
Seen by Comr.

[ ]
26/10/88.
[Stamped: – REGISTRY 19 OCT.–88 – 4] 9335/17
[Stamped: – HOME OFFICE 29 OCT.88 DEPt. No.]

[ff. 21–22]: – A49301/76
[Stamped: – HOME OFFICE 17 OCT.88 RECd. DEPt.] British Consulate
Boulogne 12 October 1888.

<u>No 30</u>
My Lord,

With reference to my despatch No 29 of yesterday I have the honor to report that this afternoon I received a telegram from the Commissioner of the Metropolitan Police stating that the address given by the man, John Langan, had been verified, and that he has no connection with the London murders. I lost no time in seeing the Procureur of the Republic and informing him that the address given had been found to be correct, he stated that as this was the case he should order the man's release.

I have the honor to be with the highest respect,
My Lord,
Your Lordship's most obedient,
humble Servant,
E.W. <u>Bonham</u>

[f 20]:- A49301/76
[Stamped:- HOME OFFICE 17 OCT.88 RECd. DEPt.]

Foreign Office,
October 16, 1888.

Sir,

With reference to my letter of the 12th instant, I am directed by the Secretary of State for Foreign Affairs to transmit to you, to be laid before Mr. Secretary Matthews, a further despatch [*marginal note* – "Consul Bonham/ No. 30. Octr. 12."] from Her Majesty's Consul at Boulogne reporting the release of the man John Langan.

I am,
Sir,
Your most obedient,
humble Servant,
P.W. Currie

The Under Secretary
of State,
Home Office.

[*f23*] is a page covering the above letter as follows:

1888/Boulogne 12 October/Consul Bonham/No 30
Recd. Octr. 13./By post/Refr. No 29 of 11th inst
<u>Suspicious character.</u>/Address given verified and/he will be released
Home Office/p.p. [ ]/Octr. 16
46

CHAPTER 16

October 1888 – A Person "Professes to be Able to Capture the Murderer"

Another very interesting exchange of correspondence took place in October 1888 and continued for several months. The suspect, although his existence possibly had no foundation in fact, was described and the preserved files are of the greatest interest for the great insight they give into the workings of the ongoing enquiry, also for the informed comments of several of the leading officials. The file[1] commences with an annotated file cover and additional pages, dated 12 October 1888:

[Stamped: – HOME OFFICE 12 OCT. 88 RECd. DEPt.]

Recd 4.45 pm   No. A49301D/1
DATE 12 Oct. 88   Foreign Office
REFERENCES, &c   <u>Whitechapel Murders</u>

    Forwards copy of despatch from H.M. Ambassador at Vienna to the effect that there is a person there who professes to be able to capture the murderer.
MINUTES.
To Commr Police

5 pm
CM

I enclose opinion of A.C.C. Investigation. I am not inclined to go so far as he does, but at the same time I feel that his opinion on such a subject is very valuable.

    I have never   experience with foreigners and I do not think that the Informant's account must necessarily be incredible.

    In the first place he scouts the idea of the picture in Daily Telegraph being like the murderer, and thinks he would not have written the letters signed "Jack the Ripper". This is in his favour.

    As Mr. Matthews is aware I have for some time past inclined to the idea that the murders may possibly be done by a secret society, as the only logical solution of the question, but I would not understand this being done by a

Socialist because the last murders were obviously done by some one desiring to bring discredit on the Jews and Socialists or Jewish Socialists.

But in the suggestion of the informant we have a solution, viz:- that it is done by a renegade socialist to bring discredit on his former comrades.

I can see no reason why Informant should not be called upon to give name of murderer and other details as proposed with a provision of 20.000 florins if it leads to arrest of murderer, but at the same time I see no reason why the Informant should put his faith in an ambassador any more than an ambassador should put his faith in the Informant.

I should not be inclined to bother the ambassador in the matter. I have known several cases where friction has occurred owing to telegraphic communication leaving no liberty of action. I propose that Mr Anderson's views should be telegraphed to Sir A Paget as a suggestion, but specially giving him freedom to use his own discretion in the matter.

If from our straining in the matter we miss the opportunity of capturing the murderer it would be unfortunate.

C.Warren

13.10.88

To my mind the whole story is incredible. The man says nothing to show how he knows that the person whom he accuses is the murderer: nor does he even state the reason why the murder was committed or either the murders. It appears to me inconceivable that Socialists should wreak this vengeance on Society by murdering women of the town – mere outcasts.

Then as to the man. He admits that he is actuated by vindictive motives: he and his friends want to get rid once for all of the men they accuse. How likely that they may make false charges against him! He is also a member of the Secret Society: & H.M. Government is also asked not only to enter into a transaction with this Society but to pay money which is admittedly to go to the funds of the Society, and the steps taken for the detection of the man are to be so to speak official action by the 2 Chiefs of the Society. The man has given information on a previous occasion, which was not realized. He also insists on being paid beforehand, as if he could not trust H.M. Ambassador, let alone that if he is successful, he is sure of the rewards already offered. He insists also on going himself to London, no reason being given but the orders of the Society.

If the offer is accepted, I anticipate as the result not only that the Govt. will be duped, but will have helped a Secret Society to punish one of its members by bringing against him a false charge of murder.

I think a telegram should be sent to the Ambassador that no further attention need be given to the informant unless he state ["facts, capable of verification" – *deleted*] the name of the murderer with definite details which can be tested showing that these are reasonable grounds of suspicion. If the information leads to his arrest & conviction the ["amount will" – *deleted*] 2000 florins will be paid to him.

[If the matter is left to the Ambassador's discretion, it is pretty clear he will send the man over – which I think would be a most regrettable step.

I cannot at all agree with the Commr.'s idea that the only logical solution of the question is that the murders may possibly have been done by a Secret Society. He also says that he cannot understand this having been done by a Socialist, because the last murders were evidently done by some one desiring to bring discredit on the Jews and Socialists or Jewish Socialists. – It seems to me on the contrary that the last murder was done by a Jew who boasted of it.]

GL

13 Oct 1888

This is followed by a copy letter[2] dated 14 October 1888, by Lushington:

(Copy)

<u>Confidential</u>

Whitehall

14   Octr.   1888

Sir,

["I am t" – *deleted*]

In reply to your letter of the 12th instant forwarding a copy of a Despatch from Her Majesty's Ambassador at Vienna giving the details of an interview with an individual who professed himself able to effect the capture of the perpetrator of the recent murders in Whitechapel, I am directed by Mr. Secretary Matthews to acquaint you for the information of the Marquis of Salisbury that the story told by this man appears to him to be highly improbable, but that inasmuch as the Ambassador and the Consul General, who have seen him, are both inclined to believe in his good faith. Mr. Matthews is disposed to think that the Ambassador should be directed to use his own discretion in the matter, and at the same time should be requested to obtain if possible, some guarantee of the bona fides of the informant, by requiring that the name of the alleged murderer or his residence calling or nationality or some detail by which he can be identified, should be communicated to the Ambassador. ["Any money paid immediately to him should be" – *deleted*] Money should be paid to him only for "travelling expenses"; and if half could be paid in Vienna and the other half in London, that would be the best arrangement. He should be directed on his arrival in London immediately to report himself to Sir Charles Warren 4 Whitehall Place.

I am, Sir

Your obedient servant

Godfrey Lushington

The
Under Secretary of State
    Foreign Office

There is then a letter[3] on Secretary of State, Home Department headed paper, dated 13 October 1888, from Lushington to Matthews:

The H.O. answer should be sent to the F.O. tomorrow Sunday at latest.
Mr. Matthews,
    I am sorry to trouble you with this.
    I have myself no doubt whatever as to the proper course to take. But in a matter of this importance especially as the Commr. has expressed his opinion the other way, I do not like to commit you without a reference to you.

GL
13 Oct 1888

There is much force in your observations and those of Mr Anderson. This informant, if he comes, will have to be most closely & vigilantly watched. But in the face of the Ambassador's opinion I do not like to throw aside what may result in some useful clue.

H.M.

Say to F.O. that the story told by the individual who has had an interview with the Ambassador at Vienna appears to the S. of S. to be highly improbable; but that, in as much as the Ambassador & the Consul General, who have seen him, are both inclined to believe in his good faith, the S. of S. is disposed to think that the Ambassador should be directed to use his own discretion in the matter, and at the same time should be requested, if possible, to obtain some guarantee of the bona fides of the informant, by requiring that the name of the alleged murderer, or his residence calling & nationality, or some detail by which he can be identified, should be communicated to the Ambassador. ["Care" − *deleted*] Money should be ["taken to pay" − *deleted*] paid to him only for "travelling expenses", & if half could be paid in Vienna, & the other half in London, that would be the best arrangement.

H.M.
13 Oct88

I enclose a copy of the letter which in accordance with Mr. Matthews' minute I have today sent to F.O.
    Send copy to Commr.

GL
14 Oct 1888

Sent to Commr. in note
15 Oct 1888

There then follows a report[4] by Robert Anderson to the Chief Commissioner, Sir Charles Warren, dated 12 October 1888:

<u>Immediate</u>   H.O. A49301/D
                                                                        1

Sir C. Warren,

After giving this matter my most earnest & careful consideration, I cannot recommend compliance with the inft's. proposal.

The answer I shd. send to Sir A. Paget wd. be to the effect that Govt. cannot authorise compliance with Inft's. terms, unless he gives <u>the name of the murderer</u> with <u>definite details</u> wh. can be tested, or in some other way gives tangible proof of capacity & <u>bona fides</u>.

And if you have misgivings about this, it might be added: 20,000 florins [he asks for 2000] will be paid him for information leading to the criminal's arrest & conviction.

I have arrived at this conclusion not merely from considering the story on its merits – & it seems to be utterly incredible & I infer that the Austrian Police do not regard the Inft as trustworthy – but further, I dread the trouble & mischief wh. such a man, if an impostor, might cause shd. he come to London on the proposed terms.

I have had series of similar proposals, recd. thro the F.O., in cases of political crime, & have occasionally interviewed infts. who made representations of this kind, & yet I have never known one single instance where I have found reason to doubt the wisdom of refusing compliance with their terms.

I may add that I handed the dispatch to Mr. Williamson without giving him the slightest hint at my opinion of the case, & he has expressed a similar opinion in even stronger terms.

                                                                R.A.
                                                                12:10:88

A Foreign Office letter[5], dated 12 October 1888, from J. Pauncefote, to the Under-Secretary of State is included:

[Stamped: – HOME OFFICE 12 OCT. 88 RECd DEPt.] A49301D
                                                                        1

Pressing   Foreign Office
and   October 12. 1888
<u>Secret</u>

Sir,

I am directed by the Marquis of Salisbury to transmit to you, herewith, a copy of a Despatch from Her Majesty's Ambassador at Vienna, giving the details of an interview with an individual professing himself able to effect the capture of the perpetrator of the recent Whitechapel Murders.

I am to request that, in laying this Despatch before Mr. Secretary Matthews, you will move him to cause Lord Salisbury to be informed, at his earliest possible convenience, as to what answer should be returned to Sir Augustus Paget.

> I am,
> Sir,
> Your most obedient
> humble servant
> J. Pauncefote.

The Under Secretary of State
Home Office

There then follows the lengthy letter[6] of Sir Augustus Paget, Ambassador at Vienna, to the Prime Minister (Lord Salisbury) regarding the informant, dated 10 October 1888:

A 49301D
1

[Stamped: – HOME OFFICE 12 OCT. 88 RECd DEPt]
Copy
No. 354   Vienna
Secret   October 10. 1888
My Lord,

I have the honour to inform M.L. that the day before yesterday I received a letter stating that the writer would undertake within fourteen days to deliver up the man who had committed the recent murders of women in London.

Without attaching undue importance to this communicn., I thought that in a case of so much mystery & horror no possible clue was to be neglected, & I therefore requested Mr. Nathan, H.M.'s Consul General to see the writer. At the request of the Cons. Genl. the writer called on him yesterday morning & Mr. Nathan was so much impressed with what he said that he suggested I should see him myself this morning. I have accordingly done so in Mr. Nathan's presence, & I have closely cross questioned him, his answers being given in a perfectly straightforword & ready manner, & with an air of good faith.

In answer to my inquiries he stated that he was born in Poland, his grandfather having been English, as his name (which however he stipulated with me I would keep secret) would appear to indicate, but that he was now an Austrian subject domiciled near Vienna where he has a manufactory of

Drugs. He is well dressed & of very respectable appearance. He told us that he is one of the chiefs of the Internationalist Society & has the management of the affairs of that Society in Austria Hungary. Some time ago there was a split in this party with two sections, one of which pursues its object by terror & assassination, the other by less violent methods. He is one of the chiefs of the latter section. He has a colleague in Paris without whom it is impossible for him to act. The rules of the Society are absolute Secrecy, so much so, that the members are frequently not known to one another, and no one can act without the order of his superior or chief.

The man who has committed the murders was formerly a member of the Society, but he was dismissed in consequence of his having denounced some of the party, who were innocent, as being connected with the Moss affair in New York; in which city, he, the present murderer, murdered his mistress & her child.

I asked him if he knew the murderer personally; he replied that he did, & when I shewed him the portraits published in the Daily Telegraph of Saturday last the 6th October, he said that they did not bear the slightest resemblance to him. I also showed him the facsimiles of letters signed "Jack the Ripper" published in the same paper of the 4th instant. He said he did not believe that the murderer could write; at all events he was quite sure he could not have written these letters, tho. they might have been written by his accomplice (Helper) for accomplice he undoubtedly had. I asked the informer what motive he and his party had for denouncing the murderer. He said to avenge themselves for his having betrayed the party. They wanted to get rid of him once for all.

He then produced a cyphered letter from the head of the party in London. and decyphered it before me by means of a piece of cardboard with holes in it which he placed in different positions over the paper.

The part of the letter referring to this business runs in translation (the original being in German) as follows,

"There is no doubt that No. 49 E(I)? (E the informer said meant Irish) is identical with the murderer and that he has a helper unknown to the party. All orders strictly observed to prevent escape, escape impossible. Highest time (hochste Zeit) to put an end to it."

I asked what the orders referred to meant and by whom they were issued. He replied that they were to prevent the murderer escaping and that he (the informer) and his Paris colleague had given them. "Highest time to act" means that by delay the murderer may possibly escape to France.

The informer then in answer to my enquiry said that in order to effect capture he must go himself to London, taking his Paris colleague with him. If he went he would require a letter of introduction to a Detective, but that the latter would not have to act until the whereabouts of the murderer had been discovered by the associates of the party. He is perfectly certain he says of effecting the capture, but he can only do it by being on the spot with his colleague in Paris. He requires 2000 florins for their journeys and necessary expenses on arriving in London for effecting capture. None of the money except journey expenses Etc would go to him and his colleague. It would belong to the Society. He is ready to give written engagement to refund the money should capture not be accomplished, but this of course must be taken for what it is worth.

I reminded him that a large reward had been offered. Why, I asked, could he not direct his party in London to deliver up the culprit without he and his Paris colleague going over. He said the rules of the Society were such that it was impossible for action to be taken without presence of the two chiefs. He could not even divulge to me his name without his colleague's sanction.

I have caused Mr. Nathan to make enquiries of the police here respecting the informer, & they say that they know him to be a socialist, that he denounced a plot to assassinate the Emperor in 1883 but that the attempt was not made, & they therefore have not much trust in him.

On the other hand he has shewn me a certificate from the Magistrate of the district in which he resided in Galicia attesting to his good character & speaking of him as a well conducted & industrious citizen who had done much good in his neighbourhood.

It is of course possible that the whole story may be a trumped up one from beginning to end, but I am bound to say that it does not give me that impression & that I am inclined to place some trust in it. The man's manner, his appearance, the readiness with which he replied to all my enquiries tended to give me this impression, though of course I may be mistaken.

I must say that at first I was inclined to be extremely sceptical on account of his not being willing to act without himself going over, but having already heard something of the workings of these secret societies & listening to what he now said, it has occurred to me as quite possible that he may be unable to act from here & without the cooperation of his colleague.

I told him that all I could do would be to report the circumstances to London & request instructions. He is anxious for an answer as soon as possible in order, if he is to go to London, that the murderer may not have time to escape before he arrives, as the accomplishment of his task would then become much more difficult. He lays the greatest stress on gaining time, & I have promised him a reply by Friday evening or Saturday morning next by which time I hope to be furnished with Y L's instructions by telegraph. Should I be desired to send him, I beg to be informed to whom I am to give a letter in London, & on whom I am to draw for the money (2000 florins) without which he will not go.

YH&c

(Signed) <u>A Paget</u>.

Copy Sir A Paget No. 314 Oct 10./88 <u>Whitechapel Murders</u>   H.O.

The next file cover[7], dated 16 October 1888, is as follows:

[Stamped: – HOME OFFICE 16 OCT. 88 RECd DEPt] No. A49301 D

2

DATE 16 Oct 1888   Foreign Office
REFERENCES &c.   Whitechapel Murders
Forwards substance of telegram from H.M. Ambassador at Vienna from which it appears that the Informer has been advanced the 2000 Florins & is to present a letter to Sir C Warren when he has found the murderer – He stipulated that neither he himself nor his associates are to be ["watched" – *deleted*] interfered with by police

MINUTES.

<u>Secret & Urgent</u>

Copy to Commr. of Police & to S. S.

CM

Oct 16. 88

Not much new in this except the
Wrote Commr: enclosing copy.   allegation that the man was a butcher.
Oct 16. 88   When you come to town I would
                                        wish to speak to you as to the source
                                        from which the Ambassador is to be
                                        reimbursed

Any denunciation by this   GL
man must be most carefully   16 Oct 1888
sifted.

H.M.

17 Oct./88

Letter to Commr to the
above effect 18 Oct 1888

There then follows a letter[8] dated 16 October 1888 from P.W Currie to the Under-Secretary of State:

[Stamped: – HOME OFFICE 16 OCT. 88 RECd DEPt] A49301D

2   Foreign Office

16 October 1888

Secret and
pressing
Sir,
    With reference to your letter of the 14th instant, I am directed by the Marquis of Salisbury to transmit to you herewith, to be laid before the Secretary of State for the Home Department, the substance of a telegram received from Her Majesty's Ambassador at Vienna respecting the Whitechapel murders.

I am, Sir,

Your most obedient

humble servant

PWCurrie

The Under Secretary of State
    Home Office

The next file cover[9] is dated 5 November 1888:

[Stamped: – HOME OFFICE 5 NOV. 88 RECd DEPt] No. A49301D

3

DATE 5 Nov 1888   Foreign Office
REFERENCES, &c.   Whitechapel Murders Vienna Informant
Memorandum left by Mr Phipps with SofS. giving certain particulars respecting the Informant who is about to return to London – also gives name & description of Supposed Murderer – Sir A Paget is convinced the man is acting in good faith

MINUTES.

Secret – See memo in file

seen CW 6.11.88

Mr Lushington to see – & Lay By. CM
Nov 8/88.

There is a letter[10] from the Ambassador at Vienna dated October 15 1888:

[Stamped: – HOME OFFICE 16 OCT.88 RECd DEPT] A49301D

2

Vienna October 15. 1888
Secret
Have seen informant who does not know murderer's residence but states he

was employed formerly in San Francisco as a <u>butcher</u>. A further letter has been received about him saying he is being <u>watched by two of the smartest men</u> in the Society. He is confident that he will be able to inform the Police of murderer's whereabouts within 24 hours after he arrives in London. Informant cannot go without having 2000 florins, or act without being himself in London in company with his superior, the head man from Paris. I believe in his <u>bona fides</u> so much that I <u>advance the money on my personal responsibility</u>, while telling him that on the arrest of the culprit and proof of his crime, he, informant can claim offered reward out of which must be deducted the 2000 florins for repayment to me. I mention his name in a letter which I give him to Sir Charles Warren, but he will not present it until he appears to <u>denounce criminal and get necessary aid from police</u>. He has stipulated that his name is never to be divulged or the Society will not effect arrest. He departs this day and he stipulates in addition that neither himself nor those of the Society at present watching criminal are in any way <u>to be interfered with by police</u>, which has been promised by me.

It is my opinion that he should be permitted to work unwatched even by the detectives.

There is a report[11] from the Foreign Office, dated 5 November 1888, to the Under-Secretary of State:

A<u>49301</u>D
3

Secret and
Pressing
Sir,

Foreign Office
November 5, 1888

With reference to my letter of the 16th ultimo, I am directed by the Marquess of Salisbury to transmit to you herewith the substance of a further telegram from Her Majesty's Ambassador at Vienna giving details respecting the identity of the supposed perpetrator of the Whitechapel murders.

[*There is a marginal note to the above* — "<u>Sir A. Paget</u> Tel. Secret already sent (through Mr Phipps)"]

I am, Sir,
your most obedient
humble servant
J.Pauncefote

The Under Secretary of State
Home Office

There is then a copy of Sir A. Paget's letter[12] to Sir Charles Warren, dated November 4 1888:

A49301 D

3

Copy   Mr Phipps delivered this memorandum personally to Mr. Matthews, who authorised him to telegraph to Sir A Paget guaranteeing the expenses
of Jonas' journey to London (if he. be without means of his own). Mr. Phipps also
stated that he wd. remain in town to meet Jonas & to take him to Sir C. Warren

ELP. 5 Nov. 88

[Stamped: – HOME OFFICE 5 NOV.88 RECd DEPt]

Secret   From Sir A. Paget.   Vienna.   Nov 4/88

Mr. Phipps stated
that he had given
Sir C. Warren a copy of
this. ELP.   Following for Sir C. Warren and Mr Phipps. –
Have just seen informant, [*Here there is a marginal note:* – "The informant's
name is Jonas ELP"] who returned here on Friday evening, but was unwell
yesterday. His object in returning to Vienna is to procure further funds, but
from his friends and not from myself; when he has this money, he purposes
starting once more for London on Tuesday or Wednesday, and is convinced
he will catch murderer. Mr. Phipps's letter was only received by him to-day,
which is proved by the Vienna postmark. He asserts that about October 25 he
sent to Sir C. Warren's Secretary the name and complete details respecting
the criminal by means of a registered letter from Paris. The particulars are
following: – the name of the man when in San Francisco, was Johann
Stammer, when in London, John Kelly, of medium height, with broad
shoulders, aged between 35 and 38 years, strongly marked features and
extremely brilliant large white teeth; has a scar due to a stab beneath the left
eye; walks like a sailor, having been a ship's cook for 3 years; is thought to be
at Liverpool; but news is expected to-day by informant. If this news comes I
will communicate by telegraph again. Personally, I am more than ever
convinced that informant is acting in good faith. The criminal has written to
my informant's superior, declaring that he will kill both of them because he is
aware they are pursuing him.

There is a file cover[13] dated 7 November 1888:

[Stamped: – HOME OFFICE 8 NOV.88 RECd DEPt] No. A49301 D

4

DATE 7th Nov 88   Foreign Office
REFERENCES, &c.   Whitechapel Murder. Vienna Informant.
Requests instructions how to reply to Sir. A. Paget as the Informant required
£100 before he comes to England

MINUTES.

Pressing & Secret

?To Commr of Police for observations — in first instance. In another record: about this man [*here there is a marginal note*: — "See /3"] it is said that he sent from Paris to the Commr. the name & description of the man he accuses of these murders ?Ask Commr:

at same time whether he has been able to make any use of the particulars, & whether he attached any importance to them CM. Nov 8/88.   GL
Wrote 7. Nov. 88.   8 Nov 1888

There is a letter[14] attached, dated 27 December 1888, from Scotland Yard to G. R. Moran:

4 Whitehall Place,
S.W.
27 December, 1888.

Dear Moran,

I return the Confidential papers which you were good enough to lend yesterday for Mr. Monro.

Yours truly
M.M. [*signature illeg.*]

G.R. Moran,Esqre.

There is a Home Office note[15], apparently in Ruggles-Brise's hand, dated 26 December 1888:

A 49301D.
  1 to 4
All F.O. letters given to mr. Kendall p/p Mr. Monro [*illeg.*] & return
  26/12/88

There is a Foreign Office letter[16], dated 7 November 1888, to the Under-Secretary of State:

[Stamped: — HOME OFFICE 8 NOV.88 RECd DEPt]   A49301 D

4
Foreign Office.

Secret &
Immediate.

November 7. 1888.

Sir,

With reference to my letter of the 5th instant in regard to the Whitechapel Murderer, I am directed by the Marquis of Salisbury to state to you that Her Majesty's Ambassador at Vienna has reported by telegraph that the informant is unable to obtain money there and requires £100 to enable him to come to

England. Sir A. Paget desires to know whether he is authorized to advance the money.

I am to request that in laying this letter before Mr. Secretary Matthews you will move him to cause Lord Salisbury to be informed what reply should be returned to His Excellency.

I am, Sir,
                    Your most obedient
                        humble servant.
In the absence of)
the Under Secretary) Charles B. Robertson.
                    (Actg. Head of Dept.)
The Under Secretary of State
                Home Office

The next file cover[17] is dated 2 January 1889:

[Stamped: – HOME OFFICE 3 JAN.89 RECd DEPt] No. A49301
                                                    4a

DATE 2 Jany 89   The Commr. of Police
REFERENCES, &c.   Whitechapel Murders
                    The Vienna Informer
Reports as to Sir A Paget's Telegram as to other information as to dynamite outrages in contemplation, and suggests that no further money be spent on the man as he attaches no importance to his statement.
                [MINUTES.]
            Confidential and Pressing
Tele F.O. of his opinion of Mr Monro. and express concurrence in this reco.
                C.M.
                Jan 3. 89
            wrote 4.1.89   GL
                3 Jan 1889

There is a letter[18] from the Chief Commissioner of Police, James Monro, to the Under-Secretary of State, dated 2 January 1889:

[Stamped: – HOME OFFICE 3 JAN.89 RECd DEPt] A49301D.
Confidential   7
                                4 Whitehall Place S.W.
                                    2 Jany. 1889.
Sir,
    With reference to Sir A. Paget's telegram of the 29th inst. [*here there is a*

marginal note — ''copy enclosed''] giving particulars of further information offered by his informant who recently undertook to discover the Whitechapel Murderer. I have to acquaint you for the information of the Secretary of State, that I attach no importance to this persons statement, and I do not recommend any further expenditure upon him.

I am, Sir,

Your most obedient Servant,

J. Monro

The Under
   Secretary of State
   &c &c &c

There then follows the message[19] from Sir A. Paget:

[Stamped: – HOME OFFICE 3 JAN.89 RECd DEPt] A49301D

Copy   5

Decypher from Sir A. Paget Vienna

D. 29

P.. – night Dec –

Following for Mr. Nathan Hms Consul 24 Queens Gate Gardens from Acting Consul Vienna –

Informer states that there are at present in Brussels from 15 to 20 terrorists, mostly leaders, who may be shortly expected in London. One was here on Monday on his way to St Petersburgh. He is a chemist & prepares explosives &c. He returns soon to London but whether by Vienna informer is ignorant. This man is acquainted with Kelly & can identify him. Informer does not know where these Terrorists will live in London, but if on the spot could soon discover. He will furnish some names in writing tomorrow He says that a large number of dynamite outrages are contemplated in London but details can only be given personally to authorities.

He is ready to come to London for 1500 florins & remain there until favourable results respecting murder of which he is certain. He pressed for decision saying no time is to be lost.

There is a further file cover[20], dated 26 February 1889:

[Stamped: – HOME OFFICE 28 FEB.89 RECd DEPt] No. A49301D

4b

DATE 26 Feby 1889   HM Secretary to the Embassy at Vienna

REFERENCES, &c.   Vienna Informer

Suggests repayment of the advance of £165, made to this man, to Sir Augustus Paget.

MINUTES.

Confidential

Mr Lushington/.

Ask Treasury explaining case.

GL

1 March '89

(Wrote 20.3.89)

Letter withdrawn & Receiver written to pay from Police Fund. Concur
informed.

See Mr L.s minute 26/3.89

There is a letter[21], dated 26 February 1889, from the British Embassy at Vienna to Godfrey Lushington:

A49301D

4   British Embassy
[Stamped: – HOME OFFICE 28 FEB.89 RECd DEPt]   Vienna
26 Feb /89

My dear Mr Lushington,

You will perhaps remember that I called on you at the Home Office, when I was in London, about the Viennese "Informant" regarding the Whitechapel murders.

I notice that in your letter to the FO of 4th January you state that no "further" expenditure is to be incurred in his regard.

You will remember that the amount which the man Jonas received was advanced by Sir Augustus Paget.

Now Sir Augustus has compunction in making an official application for repayment, but both Mr Matthews & yourself and Sir C Warren spoke as I remember so distinctly in the sense of the repayment having to be made to Sir A Paget of the advance he was compelled to make that perhaps you would kindly take the initiative in causing the necessary instructions to be given.

The amount was 2000 florins or 165£

Yours truly.

EMPhipps

to the Secretary

of Embassy

There is a note[22] from Lushington dated 25 March 1889:

I have seen Mr. Mowatt on this.

He says the Treasury would decline to pay this Bill, but that it is inexpedient for a letter to be written stating the reasons.

I have always been of opinion that this would have to be paid out of Met. Pol Funds,

So Pay accordingly

Inform Ruling

Withdraw our letter to Treasury

GL

25 March '89

There is then a lengthy letter[23] from Lushington to The Secretary of the Treasury, dated 20 March 1889:

Confidential

A49301 D

4b

Home Office

Whitehall S.W.

20th March 1889

Sir,

I am directed by the Secretary of State to acquaint you for the information of the Lords Commissioners of Her Majesty's Treasury that in October last he received a Despatch through the Foreign Office from H.M. Ambassador at Vienna to the effect that a man named Jonas had presented himself to his Excellency & had announced his ability to lay his hand on the Whitechapel Murderer, and his willingness to come to England for that purpose on the receipt of £165 (2,000 florins)

Acting on the recommendation of the then Commissioner of Metropolitan Police and influenced also by Sir A. Paget's strong belief in the bona fides of the informant, the Secretary of State expressed to the Foreign Office the opinion that it should be left to his Excellency's discretion as to whether the man's terms should be agreed to.

The sum demanded was paid; and Jonas appears to have proceeded to Paris for the purpose, as he explained, of connecting with and obtaining the indispensable cooperation of a colleague in the International Society, of which they and the alleged murderer were alike members. He presently returned to Vienna: but declined to proceed to London with a view to carrying out what he had undertaken unless a further sum of £100 was given to him.

Hereupon Mr. Matthews again consulted the Commissioner of Police and on his recommendation wrote to the Foreign Office explaining his opinion that no more money should be spent on Jonas, whose alleged information he regarded as of no importance.

The negotiations were accordingly discontinued.

The Secretary of State would be glad if you would move the Lords

Commissioners of the Treasury to sanction the repayment of the £165 already expended by Sir A. Paget.

I am,

Sir,

Your obedient servant,

Godfrey Lushington

CHAPTER 17

15 October 1888 – A Dead Letter

During this period many leads were brought to the notice of the police for investigation before it became clear that they were false. The following example is typical and is interesting in that it proposes yet another suspect. The file cover[1] reads:

[Stamped:- HOME OFFICE 17 OCT.88 RECd DEPt]   No. A49301C/12
DATE 15 Oct 88   General Post Office
REFERENCES, &c.   Whitechapel Murders
                   Hand letter to Mr Lushington from dead letter office
                   implicating a certain person –
[*Here there is a marginal note* – ''Letter sent to Sir C Warren'']
                   MINUTES.
        See Mr Lushington's memo within and Secretary of State's decision.
                              Warrant to Postmaster General
                              15th Oct. 1888

There then follows a letter[2], dated 15 October 1888, from Godfrey Lushington to the Home Secretary Henry Matthews

[Headed paper: – SECRETARY OF STATE HOME DEPARTMENT]
A49301C/12   [Stamped: – HOME OFFICE 17 OCT.88 RECd. DEPt.]
Mr Matthews,
    This refers to a letter brought here today by the P.O. authorities. The envelope was addressed to Jane Somebody (I forget the name), the address was imperfect as she could not be found there, the [''letter'' – *deleted*] envelope was placed in the P.O. The letter inside must have put there [*sic*] by mistake. It was a letter from a gentleman in Eaton Place to his son, apparently an officer in the army, in which the writer says he cannot help suspecting General Brown is the Whitechapel murderer.
    Probably there is nothing in it, but I sent it on to the Commr.: but the P.O. would not let me do this unless I undertook to get a formal Warrant from you.

GL

15 Oct 1888

Mr. Stuart Wortley is here

There then follows a note to the letter by Henry Matthews:

I have some little doubt as to the propriety of this order I presume the letter will be dealt with in the usual manner by the Dead Letter office.

H.M.

16 Oct. /88

There is then enclosed a copy of the letter[3] to Sir Charles Warren:

Copy

Confidential   15. October 1888

Sir C. Warren,

The enclosed letter came this morning from the Post Office. You will see that the envelope contains an enclosure that was never intended to be put into it, and it is the first few lines of the letter so enclosed that relate to the Whitechapel murder. As soon as you have done with it, please return it to me, that I may send it back to the Post Office who have only given it up on a warrant from the S. of S.

G. Lushington

15. Oct. 88.

[*Here there is a note in the right margin* – "Putup CM"]

There is a Home Office memo slip[4] included:

To the REGISTRY HOME OFFICE.

From

Mr. Murdoch

Send Jane Bromley's

Letter back to P.O.

GL

19 Oct 1888

Mr Moran. [*G. Moran was the Home Office superintendent of registry 1876–98*]

What was the

Date of H.O. warrant?

CM

15th [*illegible*]

This is followed by a letter[5] from Sir Charles Warren dated 17 October 1888:

17.10.88

Confidential,

Mr. Lushington.

I return the letters from Post Office.

We have made due enquiries about General Brown & he has been seen.

It seems that he has operated on horses for "racing" and this has alarmed & horrified the lady who witnessed it, and she jumped to the conclusion that he would not shirk at anything.

CWarren.

The final memo[6] in this small file reads:

Better send
explanatory note
with this result
H.O. has got
the letter.
Can you also
ask Mr Boultbee
whether Sir C.W. has
done with it as
we ought to return to PO
CM.

There would seem to have been many communications made directly with the Home Office as well as the police. Another example from the Home Office letters file is the following copy letter[7] regarding Mr John Lock who had been detained by the police, as we have seen:

[A4]9301/77   Pressing

19 October 1888

asking for report and observations

a letter from Mr. John Lock as to his having been arrested in London on suspicion of being the perpetrator of the Whitechapel murders.

Godfrey Lushington

Commissioner
Metropolitan Police.
&c. &c. &c.

CHAPTER 18

9 November 1888 – Murder of Mary Jane Kelly

The murder of Mary Jane Kelly occurred on the morning of Friday, 9 November 1888, and is the last of what have become known as "the canonical five" Ripper murders. Again, her acceptance as a recognized "Ripper" victim is contentious. Nonetheless, most students of the crimes believe her to have been the final victim of "Jack the Ripper".

The police reports on this murder are by no means extensive, but they are supplemented by the material anonymously returned to New Scotland Yard in 1987[1] and the Kelly inquest papers held in the London Metropolitan Archives.

The Home Office File cover page[2] dated 9 November 1888 states:

Commissioner of Police. Reports that information has just been received that a mutilated dead body of a woman is reported to have been found this morning inside a room in a house (No. 26) in Dorset St., Spitalfields.
The matter has been placed in Mr. Andersons hands.

Pressing.

MINUTES

I have asked Commissioner by telephone to inform H.O. as soon as possible of any further information which may reach him in the case.

C.W. Nov 9. 88.

f. 2 states:

Sir Charles Warren
            to Mr Lushington
Mutilated dead body of woman reported to be found this morning inside room of house in Dorset Street Spitalfields
Information just received
(12.30) 9.11.88.

ff. 4–5 is a letter from Charles Warren to the Under Secretary of State, Home Office:

4 Whitehall Place,
S.W.
9th November, 1888

Sir,

I have to acquaint you, for the information of the Secretary of State, that information has just been received that a <u>mutilated</u> dead body of a woman is reported to have been found this morning inside a room in a house (No. 26) in Dorset Street, Spitalfields.

The matter has been placed in the hands of Mr. Anderson, Assistant Commissioner. –

I am,
Sir,
Your Most Obedient Servant,
Cwarren

There is in the file, a photograph of the mutilated body lying on a bed, captioned: *Marie Jeannette Kelly Murdered on 9th November. 1888.*

There is a Home Office letter as follows[3]:

Home Office,
Whitehall,
S.W.
9 November
88

Dear Mr Wortley,

Troup has only just been found – after you went.

Anderson says through the telephone that the murder was committed at Spitalfields which is in the Metropolitan Police District. It is believed that the murdered woman is a prostitute named Kelly. The Police Surgeon was when Anderson spoke still examining the body.

Yours very truly
E.S. Johnson

It is interesting to see that included with the official Home Office files on the Kelly murder is a lengthy report[4] cut from the *Daily Telegraph* of Saturday, 10 November 1888. This early press report of the murder is a fascinating account of the effects of this killing – which, in the event, was the apparent climax of the series of murders suspected to have been committed by the same killer.

THE EAST END TRAGEDIES.
A SEVENTH MURDER.
ANOTHER CASE OF HORRIBLE
MUTILATION.

Yesterday a seventh murder, the most horrible of the series of atrocities attributed to the same hand, was committed in Whitechapel. As in all the previous instances, the victim was a woman of immoral character and humble circumstances, but she was not murdered in the open street, her throat having been cut and the subsequent mutilations having taken place in a room which the deceased rented at No. 26, Dorset-street. She has been identified as Mary Jane Kelly, and is believed to be the wife of a man from whom she is separated, and the daughter, it is said, of a foreman employed at an iron foundry in Carnarvon, in Wales. The unfortunate woman was twenty-four years of age, tall, slim, fair, of fresh complexion, and of attractive appearance. The room, which she occupied at a weekly rental of 4s, was on the ground floor of a three-storeyed house in Dorset-street, which is a short thoroughfare leading off Commercial-street, and in the shadow of Spitalfields Church and Market. Kelly was last seen alive on Thursday night; but as late as one a.m. yesterday morning she was heard by some lodgers in the house singing "Sweet Violets." [*sic*] No other noise appears to have been distinguished, and it was not suspected that she was at that time accompanied by a man. Entrance to her apartment was obtained by means of an arched passage, opposite a large lodging-house, and between Nos. 26 and 28, Dorset-street, ending in a *cul-de-sac* known as Miller's-court. In this court there are six houses let out in tenements, chiefly to women, the rooms being numbered. On the right-hand side of the passage there are two doors. The first of these leads to the upper floors of the house in which Kelly was living. It has seven rooms, the first-floor front, facing Dorset-street, being over a shed or warehouse used for the storage of costers' barrows. A second door opens inwards, direct from the passage, into Kelly's apartment, which is about 15 ft square, and is placed at the rear corner of the building. It has two windows, one small, looking into a yard, which is fitted with a pump. The opposite side of the yard is formed by the side wall of houses, which have whitewashed frontages, and are provided with green shutters. From some of these premises, on the left-hand side of the court, it is possible to secure a view, in a diagonal direction, of the larger window, and also the doorway belonging to the room tenanted by the deceased. In this room there was a bed placed behind the door, and parallel with the window. The rest of the furniture consisted of a table and two chairs.

It was at a quarter to eleven o'clock yesterday morning that the discovery of the latest tragedy was made. The rents of the tenements in Miller's-court are collected by John McCarthy, the keeper of a provision and chandler's shop, which is situated on the left-hand side of the entrance to the court in Dorset-street. McCarthy instructed his man, John Bowyer, a pensioned soldier, to call for the money due, the deceased woman having been 29s in arrear. Accordingly Bowyer knocked at the door of Kelly's room, but received no answer. Having failed to open the door, he passed round the angle of the house and pulled the blind of the window, one of the panes being broken. Then he noticed blood upon the glass, and it immediately occurred to him that another murder had been committed. He fetched M'Carthy, who, looking through the window, saw upon the bed, which was against the wall, the body of a woman, without clothing, and terribly mutilated. The police at Commercial-street and at Leman-street, both stations being within five minutes' walk, were instantly informed, and in response to the summons Inspector Beck arrived. This officer despatched a message for Inspector Abberline and Inspector Reid, both of the Detective department. Nothing, however, was done until the arrival of Mr. T. Arnold, the Superintendent of the H Division of Metropolitan Police, who, shortly after eleven o'clock, gave orders for the door of the room to be broken open. The last person to have left the place must have closed the door behind him, taking with him the key from the spring lock, as it is missing. A most horrifying spectacle was presented to the officers' gaze, exceeding in ghastliness anything which the imagination can picture. The body of the woman was stretched on the bed, fearfully mutilated. Nose and ears had been cut off, and, although there had been no dismemberment, the flesh had been stripped off, leaving the skeleton. The nature of the other injuries was of a character to indicate that they had been perpetrated by the author of the antecedent crimes in the same district; and it is believed that once more there are portions of the organs missing. That the miscreant must have been some time at his work was shown by the deliberate manner in which he had excised parts, and placed them upon the table purposely to add to the horror of the scene. Intelligence was promptly conveyed to Scotland-yard, and personally to Sir Charles Warren. Meanwhile the street was as far as possible closed to traffic, a cordon of constables being drawn across each end, and the police took possession of Miller's-court, refusing access to all comers in the expectation that blood-hounds would be used. Acting upon orders, the detectives and inspectors declined to furnish any information of what had occurred, and refused permission to the press to inspect the place. Every precaution was taken to preserve any trace of evidence which might be existing. Mr. Phillips, the divisional surgeon, was called, and he shortly afterwards received the assistance of other experts, among them being Dr. Bond, who came from Westminster in obedience to special instructions, and Dr. Gordon Browne, the City Police surgeon, who conducted the post-mortem in the case of the Mitre-square murder. Dr. J.R. Gabe, who viewed the body, said he had seen a great deal in dissecting rooms, but he had never witnessed such a horrible sight as the murdered woman presented. Before anything was disturbed a photograph was taken of the interior of the room. There was comparatively little blood, death having been due to the severing of the throat, the mutilations having been subsequently performed. It was evident that a large and keen knife had been used by a hand possessed of some knowledge and practice. That the woman had had no struggle with her betrayer was shown by her position and the way in which her garments, including a velvet bodice, were arranged by the fireplace. The medical men were engaged until past four p.m. in their examination upon the spot, the police, having satisfied themselves that no weapon had been left, reserving a complete investigation of the contents of the room for a later opportunity. Mr. Anderson, the recently-appointed Assistant-Commissioner, had driven up in a cab at ten minutes to two o'clock, and he remained for some time. Detectives searched all the adjacent houses for suspicious characters, but without result. All the inmates were able satisfactorily to account for their whereabouts. Not one of them had heard any sound to point to the hour when the woman must have been attacked by her assailant. The walls are of thin match lining, which makes this circumstance the more unaccountable, and the couple in the room overhead had slept soundly without being awakened by scuffling in the room beneath them. [sic]

Elizabeth Prater, the occupant of the first floor front room, was one of those who saw the body through the window. She affirms that she spoke to the deceased on Thursday. She knew that Kelly had been living with a man, and that they had quarrelled about ten days since. It was a common thing for the women living in these tenements to bring men home with them. They could do as they pleased. She had heard nothing during the night, and was out betimes in the morning, and her attention was not attracted to any circumstances of an unusual character. Kelly was, she admitted, one of her own class, and she made no secret of her way of gaining a livelihood. During the day the police succeeded in finding John [sic] Barnett, the man with whom the deceased had cohabited until a week ago, when they separated in consequence of a quarrel, in the course of which the window was broken. Barnett is a porter at the market close by, and he was able to answer the police that on Thursday night he was at a lodging-house in New-street, Bishopsgate-street, and was playing whist there until half-past twelve, when he went to bed. Another witness states that she met the deceased near the church in Commercial-street on Thursday night about seven o'clock. As far as the statements furnished to the police go, there is no actual evidence forthcoming that a man entered the room in Miller's-court. No one was seen to go there with the deceased, and there is still no clue as to the identity of the mysterious and crafty assassin who has again become the terror of White-chapel. In Dorset-street, however, the fact of a man having been in the company of a woman would probably attract no notice from those who are accustomed to such an incident. The street is fairly lighted, and, late at night especially, is pretty well frequented. It is one of those spots where a good deal of street gambling may be detected at times. Deceased was observed in the company of a man at ten p.m. on Thursday, of whom no description can be obtained. She was last seen, as far as can be ascertained, in Commercial-street, about half-past eleven. She was then alone, and was probably making her way home. It is supposed that she met the murderer in Commercial-street. The pair would have reached Miller's-court about midnight, but they were not seen to enter the house. The street-door was closed, but the woman had a latchkey. A light was seen shining through the window of the room for some time after the couple must have entered it.

Shortly after four o'clock yesterday a covered van was driven to Miller's-court, and in a few minutes the remains were placed in a shell and quietly removed to the mortuary adjoining Shoreditch Church to await the inquest, at the Shoreditch Town Hall on Monday. The room was then closed, the window being boarded up and the door padlocked. There were at times considerable numbers of spectators in the vicinity of Dorset-street, but when the police cordon was withdrawn the bystanders grew fewer. Dorset-street is made up principally of common lodging-houses, which provide not less than 600 registered beds. In one of these establishments Annie Chapman, the Hanbury-street victim, lived. Curiously enough, the warehouse at No. 26, now closed by large doors, was until a few weeks ago the nightly resort of poor homeless creatures, who went there for shelter. One of these women was Catherine Eddowes, the woman who was murdered in Mitre-square.

From the sketch-map of the locality given it will be seen that the sites of all the seven murders, five of which are, without any hesitation or doubt, ascribed by the police to one man, are contained within a limited area. A comparison of the dates reveals remarkable coincidences. The murderer has invariably chosen the latter part of the week, and when the deed has not been committed on the last day of the month it has taken place as near the 7th or 8th as can be. The Berner-street and Mitre-square murders occurred early on Sunday, Sept. 30, and the interval of about five weeks has been unusual, but was probably to be explained by the extraordinary activity of the police after the double event, or due, as some have it, to the temporary absence of the perpetrator from the country. It was on the morning of Saturday, Sept. 8, that Annie Chapman was killed in Hanbury-street, and it was on the last day of August (a Friday) that the Buck's-row tragedy took place. The two earlier murders – the one in George-yard and the other in Osborne-street – are not believed to have been the work of the miscreant who is still at large; but it is a peculiar fact, taken in conjunction with the coincidence of dates already remarked, that the murder of Mrs. Turner, in George-yard, occurred on the 7th day of August.

Sir Charles Warren did not visit the scene of the murder, but during the afternoon Colonel Monsell, chief constable of the district, and Chief Constables Howard and Roberts inspected the interior of the house. All the constables and detectives available were distributed throughout the district, and a house-to-house visitation was commenced, and all who knew the deceased woman were interrogated as to the persons last seen in her company. There was no clue.

While it is the universal belief in the district, and for only too obvious reasons, that this series of crimes has been perpetrated by the same hand, the conviction forces itself upon the police authorities that the murderer has been terrified by the hue and cry raised in consequence of his previous deeds of blood, and has thus been led to change his plan. Maniac he may be; a coward he certainly is; and hence, when he deemed it no longer safe to butcher his victims in the street, he followed them indoors. Whether this has increased the prospect of detection in the present instance is yet premature to say.

Amongst the populace there was very widespread disappointment that bloodhounds had not been at once employed in the effort to track the criminal. The belief had prevailed throughout the district that the dogs were ready to be let loose at the first notice of a murder having been committed, and the public had come to possess greater confidence in their wonderful canine instincts and sagacity than in all Sir Charles Warren's machinery of detection. They even attributed the fact that more than a month has passed since the last revolting outrage to the fear which it was thought had been inspired by the intimation that these detectives of nature would be employed. At a late hour last night it was officially stated that the bloodhounds had not been used. They were not absolutely forgotten, but apparently were not at hand, and the conclusion was come to that the trail must inevitably have been destroyed long before they could have come upon the scene by the constant stream of persons to and from the narrow street. The validity of this objection has been called in question by experts, and it would certainly have given satisfaction to the public mind if an experiment had been made. A better opportunity than the present instance afforded could hardly have occurred. A correspondent writes: ''The Whitechapel Vigilance Committee, who have recently relaxed their efforts to find the murderer, have called a meeting for Tuesday evening next at the Paul's Head Tavern, Crispin-street, Spitalfields, to consider what steps they can take to assist the police in this latter matter.''

DESCRIPTION
OF

Name _Annie Chapman_
*
Alias _Annie Siffey_
Born at
Age _45_
Profession or Calling _Prostitute_
Wanted for
**
Height _5 feet_
Build
Hair _(wavy) dark brown_
Eyebrows
Forehead
Eyes _blue_
Nose _thick nose_
Mouth _Two teeth deficient in lower jaw_
Chin
Face
Complexion _fair_
Beard
Moustache
Marks or Peculiarities _On person portion of an envelope_
stamped, Sussex Regiment, dated 23rd Aug
_1888._
Dress _Black skirt & jacket, striped petticoat_
crape bonnet
Where likely to be found,)
known, or heard of }
Nota.

' Yard, London,
day of   18
* If a Married Woman, gives also Maiden Name.

against the fence on the side
next No 29 Hanbury Street,
but he did not take any notice.
5.30 am. 8th Sept. Mrs Long of 32 Church
Street stated that she saw a
man and woman talking near
to No 29 Hanbury Street. She
heard the man say "Will you"
and the woman replied "Yes"
and passed on. She only
saw his back, and would
be unable to know him again.
She describes him as ap-
parently, over 40 years of age.
She did not see his face
He appeared to be a little
taller than the woman and
in her opinion looked like
a foreigner. She thinks
he had a dark coat on,
but she could not recognise
him again. The woman she
positively

Detail from the police descriptive form in relation to the murder of Annie Chapman.

Detail from the police report on the murder of Annie Chapman showing the first description of a suspect for the murders as given by the witness Mrs Elizabeth Long.

A contemporary sketch of the shed used as a mortuary for the Whitechapel district. The utterly inadequate and inappropriate premises – next to a playground – were criticized by the coroner Wynne Baxter.

Internal police memo of 15 September 1888, from the Commissioner instructing Swanson to take full overall charge of police enquiries into the Whitechapel murders.

A contemporary sketch showing the entrance to Dutfield's Yard and the front of the International Working Men's Educational Society Club in Berner Street, scene of the murder of Elizabeth Stride on 30 September 1888.

Mortuary photograph of Elizabeth Stride.

Right Louis Diemschutz, witness at the Stride inquest, who discovered the body.

Above PC 452H William Smith, witness at the Stride inquest who described a possible sighting of Elizabeth Stride with her killer.

Left Morris Eagle, witness at the Stride inquest, who discovered the body.

Below A contemporary sketch of coroner Wynne Baxter presiding over the Stride inquest.

Matthew Packer, fruiterer living at 44 Berner Street, who sensationally claimed to have sold grapes to the suspected murderer of Elizabeth Stride on the night of her murder.

Dr George Bagster Phillips, police surgeon for H Division, sketched at Stride's inquest.

DR PHILLIPS.
"HANG THE PAPERS"

OUTSIDE THE MORTUARY.

A contemporary sketch showing the crowd gathering outside the mortuary in St-George's-in-the-East, where the body of Elizabeth Stride lay.

DR BLACKWELL

Dr William P Blackwell also gave evidence at the Stride inquest.

Detective Sergeant Steven White of H (Whitechapel) Division, who interviewed the witness Matthew Parker.

An inquest sketch showing the position of the body of Catherine Eddowes in the southern corner of Mitre Square, Aldgate. Her murder occurred on 30 September 1888 – on the same day as the murder of Elizabeth Stride.

An inquest sketch by city surveyor Frederick William Foster of the body of Catherine Eddowes, showing details of extensive mutilation.

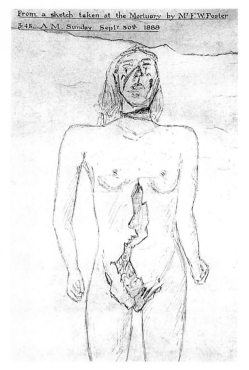

From a sketch taken at the Mortuary by Mr F.W. Foster 3.45. A.M. Sunday Sept 30th 1888

Mortuary photograph of Catherine Eddowes made before the autopsy.

Another sketch by Frederick William Foster made at the mortuary prior to the autopsy.

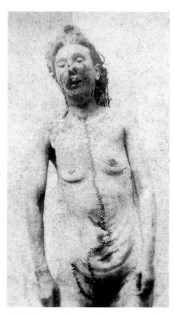

Another mortuary photograph of the body of Catherine Eddowes, propped against a wall, showing postmortem stitching.

THE POLICE CLEARING MITRE SQUARE

X THE CORNER

A contemporary sketch showing the police clearing the curious crowds that had gathered in Mitre Square after the removal of Catherine Eddowes' body.

A contemporary sketch of Dr Frederick Gordon Brown, the City of London police surgeon, who carried out the autopsy on Catherine Eddowes and later examined the piece of kidney sent to Mr Lusk of the Whitechapel Vigilance Committee.

A contemporary sketch of John Kelly, common-law husband of Catherine Eddowes.

A contemporary sketch of PC881 Edward Watkins of the City of London police, who found the body in Mitre Square at 1.45 am.

A sketch from the *Pictorial News* showing the coroner's inquest into the murder of Catherine Eddowes.

A police copy of the 'Jewes' message originally written in chalk on the entrance doorway brickwork to numbers 108–119 Wentworth Model Dwellings, Goulston Street. It was below this message that a piece of bloodstained apron was found which was later proved to have come from the apron worn by Eddowes.

The Juwes are The men That Will not Be Blamed for nothing

THE CENTRAL NEWS LIMITED

5 New Bridge Street.

London, 29 Sep 1888.
E.C.

The Editor presents
his compliments to
Mr Williamson &
begs to inform him
the Enclosed was sent
the Central News two
days ago, & was treated
as a joke.

The letter written by Tom Bulling of the
Central News Agency to Chief Constable
F A Williamson, enclosing the famous
'Dear Boss' letter.

25th Sept. 1888.
London E.C.
See 20 A + 21 + 3
Anony: Letters

The Boss
Central News
Office
London City.

The envelope in which the 'Dear
Boss' letter was delivered to the
Central News Agency.
Postmarked – 27 September 1888.

·25. Sept.· 1888.

Dear Boss.

I keep on hearing the police have caught me but they wont fix me just yet. I have laughed when they look so clever and talk about being on the right track. That joke about Leather apron gave me real fits. I am down on whores and I shant quit ripping them till I do get buckled. Grand work the last job was. I gave the lady no time to squeal. How can they catch me now. I love my work and want to start again. You will soon hear of me with my funny little games. I saved some of the proper red stuff in a ginger beer bottle over the last job to write with but it went thick like glue and I cant use it. Red ink is fit enough I hope ha. ha. The next job I do I shall clip the ladys ears off and send to the

The actual "Dear Boss" letter, dated 25 September 1888 and purporting to have come from the killer "Jack the Ripper".

police officers just for jolly wouldnt you. Keep this letter back till I do a bit more work, then give it out straight. My knife's so nice and sharp I want to get to work right away if I get a chance. Good luck.

yours truly
Jack the Ripper

Dont mind me giving the trade name

wasnt good enough to post this before I got all the red ink off my hands curse it
No luck yet. They say I'm a doctor now. ha ha

George Lusk, chairman of the Whitechapel Vigilance Committee, a local builder who received the lusk letter and parcel through the post on 16 October 1888.

The famous Lusk letter, received in a parcel which also contained a piece of human kidney.

Two press sketches of the supposed murderer as described by Matthew Packer. Published in most contemporary newspapers including the *Daily Telegraph* on 6 October 1888, they led to the detention of a suspect, John Langan, in Boulogne, France.

A typical street scene of the time showing women outside a common lodging house in Flower and Dean Street, Spitalfields.

A contemporary sketch of a Ripper suspect being taken into Leman Street police station.

A contemporary sketch of an attempt to identify the suspect in Leman Street police station.

A contemporary sketch from the *Illustrated London News* with the following legend: "Arrested on suspicion in Whitechapel. The inevitable dog inconsolable at the retirement of its owner."

A famous contemporary sketch from the *Illustrated London News* showing Vigilance Committee members watching a suspect in the East End.

Even at the height of the murders homeless women were forced to sleep on the streets.

A contemporary sketch of homeless women taken from the *Illustrated London News* in October 1888: "Outcasts sleeping in sheds in Whitechapel".

Disturbances in the street were common. Here, a police constable of H Division is seen tackling a mob in Spitalfields. Commercial Street police station can be seen in the background.

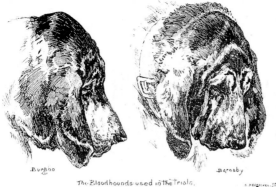

Burgho   Barnaby

The Bloodhounds used in the Trials.

Sketch of two bloodhounds –
Burgho and Barnaby – tried
out by the Metropolitan
Police for possible
employment in the tracking
of the murderer.

Sir Charles Warren puts
the bloodhounds to the
test in Hyde Park.

Dorset Street looking
east towards
Commercial Street.
A relatively short
road, it had more
than its fair share of
common lodging
houses. Miller's
Court, scene of the
Kelly murder, was
situated on the left
near the third wall
lamp.

A contemporary sketch of Mary Jane Kelly at the door of her room, number 13 Miller's Court, scene of her murder on 9 November 1888.

A contemporary sketch of the body of Mary Jane Kelly being photographed by the police at the murder scene.

Above The police crime scene photograph of Mary Jane Kelly's body as found in her bed.

Right The second police crime scene photograph of Mary Jane Kelly's body, taken from the opposite side of the bed and showing a table piled with flesh in the background.

As yet the murderer is at large, and if the police have any clue they have dissembled their knowledge with absolute success. Up to the present moment, beyond the strange coincidence of dates and the very vague and unfortunately conflicting descriptions given by witnesses at the inquests already held, scarce a vestige of evidence exists on which to base a search. It has always been the belief of East-end residents that these foul deeds were not the work of a landsman – and this mainly on account of what may be called their periodicity. "They've been done by some short-voyage man" was the expression of an opinion which is widespread. There was time, it is thought, for a sailor to have made short voyages to the Continent, and to have committed the murders either immediately on landing or just before sailing. There may be no value underlying the suggestion, and it may be next to impossible to synchronise the arrival and departure of certain ships with the dates we have given, still less to ascertain the composition of their crews, and most difficult of all to bring guilt home to any individual; but in the absence of any better trace it might be worth while to make the investigation. In this connection attention has been drawn to the following fact. It appears that the cattle boats bringing live freight to London are in the habit of coming into the Thames on Thursdays or Fridays, and leave again for the Continent on Sundays or Mondays. It has already been a matter of comment that the recent revolting crimes have been committed at the end of the week, and hence the opinion shared by some of the detectives that the murderer is a drover or butcher employed on one of these boats – of which there are many – and that he periodically appears and disappears with one of the steamers. It is thought, therefore, that the criminal may be a person either employed upon one of these boats or having occasion to travel by them. It is pointed out that at the inquests on the previous victims the coroners had expressed the opinion that the knowledge of physiology possessed by a butcher would have been sufficient to enable him to find and cut out the parts of the body which in several cases was abstracted.

Some of the reported clues must be received with caution. No end of stories are rife in the neighbourhood, told with an air of circumstantiality, which on examination prove to be utterly baseless. Almost the sole testimony which seems to have any bearing on the affair is that given by a young woman named Pannier, who sells roasted chestnuts at the corner of Widegate-street, a narrow thoroughfare about two minutes' walk from the crime. Mrs. Pannier is reported to have stated that shortly after noon yesterday a man, dressed like a gentleman, said to her, "I suppose you have heard about the murder in Dorset-street?" and that when she replied that she was aware of it he said, "I know more about it than you." He then proceeded down Sandy's-row, a narrow thoroughfare which cuts across Widegate-street, looking back as if to see whether he was watched. Mrs. Pannier described this person as a man about 5 ft 6 in high, with a black moustache, and wearing a black silk hat, dark coat, and speckled trousers. He carried a black shiny bag about eighteen inches long and a foot deep. It will be remembered that this description agrees fairly well with a personage previously described, and that the black bag has more than once figured in the evidence given. It may be worth while to recall that at the inquiry into the Berner-street murder Mrs. Mortimer said, "The only man I had seen pass through Berner-street previously was a young man who carried a black shiny bag." Similarly Arthur [sic] Bachert deposed: "On Saturday night at about seven minutes to twelve, I entered the Three Nuns Hotel, Aldgate. While in there an elderly woman, very shabbily dressed, came in and asked me to buy some matches. I refused, and she went out. A man who had been standing by me remarked that these persons were a nuisance, to which I responded 'Yes.' He then asked me to have a glass with him, but I refused, as I had just called for one myself. He then asked a number of questions about the women of the neighbourhood, and their ages, &c. He asked if I could tell him where they usually visited. He went outside and spoke to the woman, and gave her something, I believe. He was a dark man, height about 5 ft 6 in or 5 ft 7 in. He wore a black felt hat, dark clothes, morning coat, black tie, and carried a black shiny bag." But the point in Mrs. Pannier's statement which engaged the greatest amount of attention, and which, if corroborated, might unquestionably possess real significance was her further averment that she had seen the same man on the previous evening, and that he had accosted three young unfortunates in Dorset-street, who chaffed him, and asked what he had in the bag, and he replied, "Something that the ladies don't like." It remains to be seen at Monday's inquest whether this statement, and especially the latter portion of it, upon which its significance really depends, is confirmed.

The following are additional statements: A young woman named Harvey, who had slept with the woman Kelly on several occasions, said she had been on good terms with the deceased, whose education was much superior to that of most persons in her position of life. Harvey, however, took a room in New-court, off the same street, but remained friendly with the unfortunate woman, who visited her in New-court on Thursday night. After drinking together they parted at half-past seven o'clock, Kelly going off in the direction of Leman-street, which she was in the habit of frequenting. She was perfectly sober at the time. Harvey never saw her alive afterwards. Upon hearing that a murder had been committed she said, "I'll go and see if it's any one I know," and to her horror found that it was her friend.

Joseph Barnett, an Irishman, at present residing in a common lodging-house in New-street, Bishopsgate, stated that he had occupied his present lodgings since Tuesday week. Previous to that he had lived in Miller's-court, Dorset-street, for eight or nine months, with the murdered woman, Mary Jane Kelly. They were very happy and comfortable together until an unfortunate came to sleep in their room, to which he strongly objected. Finally, after the woman had been there two or three nights, he quarrelled with his "wife" and left her. The next day, however, he returned and gave Kelly money. He called several other days, and gave her money when he had it. On Thursday night he visited her, between half-past seven and eight, and told her he was sorry he had no money to give her. He saw nothing more of her. He was indoors yesterday morning when he heard that a woman had been murdered in Dorset-street, but he did not know at first who the victim was. He voluntarily went to the police, who, after questioning him, satisfied themselves that his statements were correct. Barnett believed Kelly, who was an Irishwoman, was an "unfortunate" before he made her acquaintance, and she had never had any children. She used occasionally to go to the Elephant and Castle district to visit a friend.

The poor woman who has been thus foully done to death was by no means among the lowest of her fallen class. For a considerable part of the twelve months during which she was Mr. M'Carthy's tenant she was to all appearance fairly well conducted. It was supposed that the man with whom she lived was her husband. He was employed about the fish and fruit markets, and when work was plentiful the pair seem to have paid their way honourably; but earnings were aften [sic] irregular, and then it is to be feared the woman resorted to the streets. The landlord emphatically disowns any knowledge of his tenement having been used for improper purposes. Moreover, the room which she occupied – which was on the ground floor – and for which she paid 4s a week, was part of the adjoining shop – now used as a ware-room. It was separated from the other dwellings in the narrow court, and strangers could not easily frequent it without being observed. Formerly the woman, who was of a fair complexion, with light hair, and possessing rather attractive features, dressed pretty well. Usually she wore a black silk dress, and often a black jacket, looking shabby genteel in her attire, but generally neat and clean. Latterly, it was confessed, she had been much given to drink, and had rapidly gone from bad to worse. This, it is supposed, led to the quarrel, a few days ago, between her and the man with whom she had been living, and to the arrears of 29s in the rent. Dorset-street abounds in women whose features, language, and behaviour are such that the smallest vestige of self-respect, if any remained in Mary Jane Kelly, would be sufficient to distinguish her from the more degraded of her associates. This short thoroughfare and the adjoining Paternoster-row, leading direct to the Spitalfields vegetable market, have now been given up to common lod-

ging-houses at 4d and 6d a night, or ''6d for a single bedded cabin,'' and to
women who have lost every trace of womanliness. The street and the row are
places which the police state are hardly safe for any respectable person by day
and certainly not at night. In such a neighbourhood it was impossible to rise;
to sink lower was inevitable. Evidence tends to show that when Kelly first
made its acquaintance respectable friends still looked after and wrote to her.
It is the uniform testimony of local authorities that these evil surroundings are
only remedied by wholesale demolitions, and that while they exist moral
agencies are almost hopeless. They are whirlpools, and the poor and the
wretched are dragged into them. Though the police report that Kelly's father
lives in Wales, there seems no doubt that she is Irish, and McCarthy states
that the letters for her used to come from some part of Ireland.

In the naturally intense excitement and indignation prevailing over the
whole of East London there is a danger of innocent persons becoming
suspected and suffering maltreatment. Last night a young man respectably
dressed appeared in Dorset-street, and by his anxious inquiries, especially in
regard to the possible employment of bloodhounds, drew upon himself the
unpleasant attentions of bystanders, some of whom determined to watch his
movements. On leaving the spot the young man – a clerk, it was subsequently
ascertained – found himself followed by three men. As it was quite certain
that he was the object of their regards, he became somewhat alarmed, while
his agitation only served to strengthen their suspicions. In the end he would
have suffered from the hands of the mob, but for police protection.
Fortunately Bishopsgate-street Police-station was near, and thither he was
conveyed for safety.

The Scotland-yard authorities shortly after midday telegraphed the following notification of the crime to the various police-stations: ''Found at 10.30
a.m., a woman cut to pieces in a room on the ground floor at 26, Dorset-
street, Spitalfields.''

During the course of last evening Dr. G.B. Phillips visited the House of
Commons, where he had a conference with the Under-secretary of the Home
Office, Mr. Stuart-Wortley.

The Central News states, upon what is described as indisputable authority,
that no portion of the murdered woman's body was taken away by the
murderer. The post-mortem examination was of the most exhaustive
character, and the surgeons did not quit their work until every organ had
been accounted for and placed as nearly as possible in its natural position.

Some residents in the court declare that about a quarter to two they heard
a faint cry of murder, which would seem to fix with tolerable exactitude the
time at which the crime was committed; but against this must be set the
statement of a woman residing at 26, Dorset-street, a house the backrooms of

which abut upon the court, according to which a cry of murder was heard at three o'clock. It is characteristic of the locality that no one thought anything of the incident, which, indeed, is of too common occurrence to cause interest or alarm. A man engaged as a market porter and living at 3, Miller-court, stated that, although his rooms face the scene of the murder, he heard nothing of it until he went out in the morning at half-past ten to get some milk, and was stopped by the police. A man's pilot-coat has been found in the murdered woman's room, but whether it belonged to the murderer has not been ascertained. Late last evening a man was arrested near Dorset-street on suspicion of being concerned in the murder. He was taken to Commercial-street Police-station, followed by a howling mob, and is still detained there. Another man, respectably dressed, wearing a slouch hat, and carrying a black bag, was arrested and taken to Leman-street Station. The bag was examined, but its contents were perfectly harmless, and the man was liberated.

The following report[5] relates to Dr Thomas Bond's report of his initial post-mortem examination of the body of Mary Kelly. The cover states:

16 Novr 1888
Dr. Thos: Bond
7 BroadSanctuary
S.W.
Whitechapel Murder
Result of Post Mortem
examination of body of
woman found in Dorset Street.
Mr. Anderson
Seen &noted.

This is followed by the report in Dr Bond's own hand:

Notes of examination of body of woman found murdered & mutilated in Dorset St.
Position of body,
The body was lying naked in the middle of the bed the shoulders flat, but the axis of the body inclined to the left side of the bed. The head was turned on the left cheek. The left arm was close to the body with the forearm flexed at a right angle & lying across the abdomen, the right arm was slightly abducted from the body & rested on the mattress, the elbow bent & the forearm supine with the fingers clenched. The legs were wide apart, the left thigh at right angles to the trunk & the right forming an obtuse angle with the pubes.

The whole of the surface of the abdomen & thighs was removed & the abdominal cavity emptied of its viscera. The breasts were cut off, the arms mutilated by several jagged wounds & the face hacked beyond recognition of the features. The tissues of the neck were severed all round down to the bone.

The viscera were found in various parts viz; the uterus & kidneys with one breast under the head, the other breast by the right foot, the liver between the feet, the intestines by the right side & the spleen by the left side of the body.

The flaps removed from the abdomen & thighs were on a table.

The bed clothing at the right corner was saturated with blood, & on the floor beneath was a pool of blood covering about 2 feet square. The wall by the right side of the bed & in a line with the neck was marked by blood which had struck it in a number of separate splashes.

Postmortem Examination.

The face was gashed in all directions the nose, cheeks, eyebrows & ears being partly removed. The lips were blanched & cut by several oblique incisions running obliquely down to the chin. There were also numerous cuts extending irregularly across all the features.

The neck was cut through the skin & other tissue right down to the vertebrae the 5th & 6th being deeply notched. The skin cuts in the front of the neck showed distinct ecchymosis.

The air passage was cut through at the lower part of the larynx through the cricoid cartilage.

Both breasts were removed by more or less circular incisions, the muscles down to the ribs being attached to the breasts. The intercostals between the 4 5 & 6 ribs were cut through & the contents of the thorax visible through the openings.

The skin & tissues of the abdomen from the costal arch to the pubes were removed in three large flaps. The right thigh was denuded in front to the bone, the flap of skin, including the external organs of generation & part of the right buttock. The left thigh was stripped of skin, fascia & muscles as far as the knee.

The left calf showed a long gash through skin & tissues to the deep muscles & reaching past the knee to 5 ins above the ankle.

Both arms & forearms had extensive & jagged wounds.

The right thumb showed a small superficial incision about 1 in long, with extravasation of blood in the skin & there were several abrasions on the back of the hand moreover showing the same condition.

On opening the thorax it was found that the right lung was minimally adherent by old firm adhesions. The lower part of the lung was broken & torn away.

The left lung was intact; It was adherent at the apex & there were a few adhesions over the side. In the substances of the lung were several nodules of consolidation.

The Pericardium was open below & the Heart absent.

In the abdominal cavity was some partly digested food of fish & potatoes & similar food was found in the remains of the stomach attached to the intestines.

The decision to offer a pardon to any person who was not the actual murderer and who could give information leading to the arrest of the offender is to be found under file cover A49301 B[6] as follows:

No. A49301B/15
DATE 10 Novr.88   H.O. Memo (S of S)
REFERENCES &c.   Murder of Mary Jane Kelly, Whitechapel
                            Stating that the Cabinet have decided to offer a Pardon
to any one but the actual murderer in above case. – Bills to be issued to-day
                    [MINUTES.]
To Commissioner of Police
            10 Nov 88.

Folio 300 reads as follows:

A49301B

                                                        10 Novr/'88
Dear Lushington,
    The Cabinet have decided to offer to day a Pardon to any one but the actual murderer in the case that occurred yesterday:
    No reward to be offered Let the Bills issue to day
                                    Yrs truly
                                    Henry Matthews.

The Queen, of course, had to be notified of the decision to issue this pardon and thus the following from the Prime Minister to the Queen may be found[7]:

Decypher   Novr: 10. 1888
                    Marquis of Salisbury
                            to
                        The Queen
Humble duty:
    At Cabinet today it was resolved to issue a Proclamation offering free

pardon to anyone who should give evidence as to the recent murder except the actual perpetrator of the crime.

It was resolved to delay making any recommendation on the protest of the Queensland Ministers against the appointment of Sir Henry Blake until we had seen the exact grounds of objection.

The rest of the sitting was occupied with discussing whether any measure were possible to prevent Lord Clanricarde from unreasonable conduct in the management of his property.

MEPO 3/3153 ff. 5–8 also concerns the offer of a pardon to any accomplice who shall give evidence as to the identity of the murderer(s):

The cover reads – 10th Nov 1888, Home Office,
For Sir Charles Warren
Whitechapel Murder Miller Court. Dorset Street
States that the Sec: of State will advise the grant of Her Majesty's gracious pardon to any accomplice, not being the person who contrived or actually committed the murder, who shall give such information & evidence as shall lead to the discovery and conviction of the murderer or murderers.

Notification sent to Press,copy attached. GAL 12/11/88.

The report reads:

WHITEHALL
10. November 1888

Pressing
Sir,

I am directed by the Secretary of State to inform you that, in the case of the murder committed in a house in Dorset Street, Whitechapel, on the 8th or 9th instant, he will advise the grant of Her Majesty's gracious Pardon to any accomplice, not being the person who contrived or actually committed the murder, who shall give such information and evidence as shall lead to the discovery and conviction of the murderer or murderers.

The Secretary of State desires that the enclosed notice should be issued forthwith.

I am,
Sir,
Your Obedient Servant
Godfrey Lushington

The Commissioner of Police
   Metropolitan Police'
   Murder
   Pardon

Whereas on November the 8th or 9th in Millers Court Dorset Street Spitalfields, Mary Janet Kelly was murdered by some person or persons unknown, the Secretary of State will advise the grant of Her Majesty's Gracious pardon to any accomplice not being a person who contrived or actually committed the murder who shall give such information and evidence as shall lead to the discovery and conviction of the person or persons who committed the murder.

   (Sd) Charles Warren
   Commissioner of Police
   of the Metropolis
   Metropolitan Police Office
   4 Whitehall Place
   SW
   10 November 1888

On 23 November 1888 a question was raised in the House of Commons:

CRIMINAL LAW – THE WHITECHAPEL
MURDERS – A FREE PARDON.

Mr. HUNTER (Aberdeen, N.) asked the Secretary of State for the Home Department, Whether he is prepared, in the case of the Whitechapel murders, other than that of the woman Kelly, to offer a free pardon to any person not being the actual perpetrator of the crimes?

The SECRETARY of STATE (Mr. MATTHEWS) (Birmingham, E.): I should be quite prepared to offer a pardon in the earlier Whitechapel murders if the information before me had suggested that such an offer would assist in the detection of the murderer. In the case of Kelly there were certain circumstances which were wanting in the earlier cases, and which made it more probable that there were other persons who, at any rate after the crime, had assisted the murderer.

(Hansard: 3rd Series: Volume 331: Page 16)

CHAPTER 19

November 1888 –
Sir Charles Warren Resigns and Royal Involvement

Sir Charles Warren had been Chief Commissioner of the Metropolitan Police since 1886. His tenure of the post had been marked by his clashes with officialdom at the Home Office, particularly with the Home Secretary, Henry Matthews. He earned the respect of the men under him but received much criticism from the radical press.

The Times of Wednesday, 10 October 1888, contained a statement[1] by Warren that he wished made public:

SIR CHARLES WARREN AND THE
DETECTIVE FORCE.

Sir Charles Warren requests us to publish the following statement. –

Several incorrect statements have recently been published relative to the enrolment of candidates for detective – that is to say, criminal investigation – work in the Metropolitan Police which may tend to deter candidates from applying. The following is the actual state of the case:-

For some years past the standard height in the Metropolitan Police has been 5 ft. 8½ in., and in the beginning of 1887 it was raised to 5 ft. 9 in., but the Commissioner has power from the Secretary of State to accept candidates as short as 5 ft. 7 in., and if the Criminal Investigation branch should require any particular man under 5 ft. 7 in. the Commissioner has at all times been prepared to obtain the Secretary of State's sanction to his enrolment.

The limit of age is 35, but as a rule candidates are not taken over the age of 27, in order that the police service may not lose the better part of a man's life, and also to enable him to put in sufficient service to entitle him to his full pension.

There is no rule, and never has been any rule made by the Commissioner, that candidates on joining must serve for two or three years as constables in divisions before being appointed to the Criminal Investigation branch.

The Commissioner has always been prepared to consider favourably any proposal from the Criminal Investigation branch for a candidate to join the Commissioner's office immediately on enrolment, or at any time after his enrolment, for duty in the Criminal Investigation branch.

But should a case occur that a candidate who wished to join the Criminal Investigation branch at once, and was reported favourably upon, was not physically or otherwise fit for ordinary police duties, it would be necessary, in the interests of the public, that on his enrolment a stipulation should be made that if he should subsequently be found unfit for criminal investigation work he would have to leave the police service without any compensation, should his services not entitle him to a pension or gratuity.

As a general rule it has been ascertained by the Criminal Investigation branch that the candidates who have applied to be appointed direct to detective duties have not possessed any special qualifications which would justify their being so appointed.

Sir Charles Warren tendered his resignation on 8 November 1888 and news of it appeared in *The Times* of Tuesday, 13 November 1888[2], together with reports on the murder of Mary Jane Kelly at Miller's Court, Dorset Street, Spitalfields on 9 November:

RESIGNATION OF SIR CHARLES WARREN.

As will be seen from our Parliamentary report, Sir Charles Warren tendered his resignation on Thursday last. A News Agency learns on the highest authority that the relations between Sir Charles Warren and the Home Office have for some time been strained. The action of the department in reference to the resignation of Mr. Monro caused the first serious difference of opinion. Sir Charles took exception to certain of the methods of the Assistant-Commissioner, and he intimated to Mr. Matthews that either he or Mr. Monro must resign. A few days afterwards Mr. Monro's resignation was announced. Sir Charles complains that this was accepted without consultation with him, and that prior to the Home Secretary's statement in the House of Commons last evening he was not even aware of the reason assigned by his subordinate for severing his connexion with Scotland-yard. Since Mr. Monro's transference to the Home Office matters have become worse. Sir Charles complains that, whereas he has been saddled with all the responsibility, he has had no freedom of action, and in consequence his position has become daily more unbearable. Although Mr. Monro has been no longer in evidence at Whitehall-place, he has to all intents and purposes retained control of the Criminal Investigation Department. Indeed, it was added, Mr. Matthews last evening admitted that he was deriving the benefit of the advice of Mr. Monro in matters relating to crime, and was in communication with him at the present time on the subject of the organization of the detective staff. This division of authority Sir Charles Warren has strenuously fought against. He maintains that if the Commissioner is to be responsible for the discipline of the force, instructions should be given to no department without his concurrence.

Latterly, in spite of the remonstrances of Sir Charles Warren, the control of the Criminal Investigation Department has been withdrawn more and more from Whitehall-place. Every morning for the last few weeks there has been a protracted conference at the Home Office between Mr. Monro, Mr. Anderson, and the principal detective inspectors, and the information furnished to the Commissioner in regard to these conferences has been, he states, of the scantiest character. These facts will explain how, apart from any other consideration, it was impossible for Sir Charles Warren, holding the views he did in regard to the functions of the Commissioner, to continue in command. The reproof of the Home Secretary last week in reference to the article in Murray's Magazine completed the rupture. Sir Charles thereupon took counsel with his friends and immediately tendered his resignation to the Home Secretary. Yesterday morning his books and papers were removed from the Commissioner's office, and this was the first intimation in Whitehall-place that he had relinquished the position. In the lobby last evening Mr. Monro was looked upon as the most likely person to be selected to succeed Sir C. Warren. It was pointed out that the resignation of Sir Charles Warren practically arose out of a difference of opinion with Mr. Monro, and that, inasmuch as Mr. Monro, though nominally shelved, had really gained the day, therefore it was only natural that he should assume control of the force, and develope [sic] the system of administration, the proposition of which led to his transference to the Home Office. On the other hand, it is believed in some quarters that the present opportunity will be seized to emphasize the distinction between the Criminal Investigation Department and the ordinary members of the force to which Sir Charles Warren takes exception, in which case a provincial chief constable, who has attracted much notice for his successful organization and disciplinary tact, is mentioned, as the probable head of the detective branch, as an independent branch of the force.

There is a cutting[3] on questions in the House of Commons from the *Standard* of 10 November 1888, with a Home Office date stamp of 12 Nov.88, included in the official files:

THE WHITECHAPEL MURDERS.

Mr. CONYBEARE. — I wish to ask the Home Secretary whether he has seen that another terrible murder has been committed in the East of London, and whether he does not think the time has come to replace Sir Charles Warren by some officer who would investigate these crimes.

The SPEAKER said it would be necessary to give notice of this question in the usual way.

Mr. C. GRAHAM asked whether it was true, as stated, that Sir Charles Warren was at present in St. Petersburg.

Mr. W.H. SMITH. — No, sir.

This is followed by a further cutting[4] from the *Standard*, dated 13 November 1888:

A49301C/15
RESIGNATION OF SIR C. WARREN.

Mr. CONYBEARE asked the Secretary of State for the Home Department whether he could state the exact reason why the late head of the Detective Department in the Metropolitan Police resigned his position; whether it was the fact that Sir C. Warren had now practically the direct control of the Detective Department; and whether, in view of the constant recurrence of atrocious murders, and the failure of the new organisation and methods to detect the murderer, he would consider the propriety of making some change in the arrangements of Scotland-yard. The hon. member also wished to know whether it was true, as reported in the newspapers that afternoon, that Sir C. Warren had tendered his resignation, and that it had been accepted.

The HOME SECRETARY. – I have already more than once stated the reason why Mr. Monro resigned. With regard to the remainder of the question, Mr. Anderson is now in direct control of the Criminal Investigation Department, under the superintendence and control, as provided by statute, of the Chief Commssioner. The failure of the police, so far, to detect the person guilty of the Whitechapel murders is due, not to any new reorganisation in the department, but to the extraordinary cunning and secrecy which characterise the commission of the crimes. I have for some time had the question of the whole system of the Criminal Investigation Department under my consideration, with a view to introducing any improvement that may be required. With regard to the last question, I have to inform the hon. member that the Chief Commissioner of Police did on the 8th inst. tender his resignation to Her Majesty's Government, and that his resignation has been accepted (loud opposition cheers).

The resignation of Sir Charles Warren came at a rather awkward time, coinciding as it did with another appalling and much-publicized "Whitechapel murder". Both sides in the dispute had their supporters, and the press, as always, was willing to stoke the fires of dispute. *The Times*[5] of Friday, 16 November 1888, continued the story:

SIR C. WARREN *and the* METROPOLITAN
POLICE.

A deputation representing the whole of the Metropolitan Police Force waited on Sir Charles Warren at his private residence, St. George's-road, yesterday, for the purpose of expressing their regret at his resignation. The deputation was composed of the superintendents of the various divisions. The only absentees were Superintendents Shore and Steel, who are on sick leave, and Superintendent Butt, who is out of London at present. Superintendent Draper, of the D Division, was deputed to act as spokesman. He paid a high tribute to Sir Charles Warren's thoughtfulness and care for those under his command, and, while admitting the perfection to which discipline had now been brought, repudiated the idea that such discipline was in any degree distasteful to the force so long as the regulations were administered with the fairness and equity which had characterised Sir Charles Warren's tenure of office. Speaking more especially for the superintendents, he might say that since Sir Charles Warren had been Commissioner they had been able to do their work not only much more efficiently, but with much more comfort to themselves. They felt that he was always prepared to take the responsibility for and to uphold them in what they did, and they consequently never lost that confidence without which their arduous duties could not be satisfactorily discharged. As for the men, there were only two matters which had given rise to any feeling at all since Sir Charles Warren took office. One of these was the new set of regulations in regard to drunkenness, and the other was the question of pensions for injury received while on duty. The superintendents knew perfectly well that the Commissioner was not responsible for these decisions, but the constables were not so well informed. In conclusion Mr. Draper expressed the deep regret which he and his coadjutors felt at the severance of their connection with Sir Charles Warren. Superintendent Fisher, of the A Division, having spoken.

SIR CHARLES WARREN thanked the deputation warmly for their assurances of esteem and consideration. He said it had always been his endeavour to combine discipline with justice to every member of the force, and it was gratifying to know that his efforts had not been altogether without success. With regard to the first point touched upon by Mr. Draper (the new regulations respecting drunkenness in the force), he explained that, although he had very strong views on the subject of intemperance, he was not responsible for the order which had been recently promulgated. The order emanated from the Home Secretary, who on several occasions called attention to the fact that the punishments for drunkenness were merely nominal, and ultimately instructed him to issue most stringent orders in reference to the offence. On the second point he was equally free from reproach. He had recommended several men on the chief surgeon's certificate for pensions, on the ground of injury while on duty; but the Home Secretary had taken a different view of the matter. In conclusion Sir Charles Warren said he had been greatly disappointed at having found no opportunity to visit the various divisions during his tenure of office. The work of consolidating the orders, on which he had been steadily engaged, had occupied so much of his time that he had seldom been able to leave Whitehall-place. During the past few weeks, however, he had at last succeeded in clearing the decks, and he had hoped now to see the men in their respective divisions. He again thanked them for their kindness, and assured them that their willing and cordial co-operation in such reforms as he had ventured to propose would be one of his pleasantest recollections of his Commissionership.

Another letter from Warren appeared in *The Times* of Saturday, 17 November 1888:

SIR CHARLES WARREN AND MR. MATTHEWS.
TO THE EDITOR OF THE TIMES.

Sir, — With reference to the debate last night in the House of Commons, I trust I may state that I have never to my knowledge in any way contested the lawful authority of the Secretary of State over the Metropolitan police force; and the insinuation that I have in any way contested the administration of the police being subject to Parliament through the Secretary of State seems too ridiculous for me to contradict.

In many cases, while accepting directions given me which were to all appearances contrary to the statute, I have entered a protest; and in thus protesting I have acted in accordance with the advice of the legal adviser appointed by the Secretary of State, the late Mr. J. Davis, formerly stipendiary magistrate of Sheffield.

I can only express my astonishment at the statements attributed to Mr. Matthews last night, and I venture to assert that an entirely different impression would be conveyed to the public mind about my action if the correspondence were to be made known.

I am, Sir, your obedient servant,
CHARLES WARREN.

44, St. George's-road, S.W..Nov.16.

The Times of Wednesday, 21 November 1888, carried, in its Parliamentary reports[6] columns, the following exchange:

MR. MATTHEWS AND SIR C. WARREN

In answer to questions from Mr. GRAHAM and Mr. PICKERSGILL, MR. MATTHEWS said, — I presume that Sir C. Warren's published letter refers to the voluminous correspondence on departmental matters between the Home Office and Scotland Yard. It is unusual to lay a correspondence of this kind upon the table of the House; and part of it is altogether confidential. I will, however, state generally that I know of no occasion on which I have given to Sir C. Warren directions apparently or really contrary to the statute. But if hon. members will put upon the paper a question addressed to any specific subject on which they suggest I have done so, I will inform them, as fully as public duty permits, what directions I did give, and they will be able to form their own judgment.

MR. GRAHAM asked in what manner members were to obtain information of what was known only to the Home Secretary and Sir Charles Warren.

MR. CONYBEARE asked whether, considering the circumstances of the case were altogether unusual, and that the question involved the relations that had existed for some time between the Chief Commissioner and the Home Office, it was not necessary that the House should have the whole correspondence.

MR. MATTHEWS said he did not think it was necessary that the whole correspondence should be laid before the House; but he would state fully what had occurred upon any matter that might be suggested.

A further report touching upon the Chief Commissioner appeared in questions in the House of Commons reports in *The Times* of Tuesday, 27 November 1888:

OFFICE OF COMMISSIONER OF POLICE.

MR. GRAHAM asked the Secretary of State for the Home Department why the police rules of Wednesday night last were signed by Sir Charles Warren, seeing that he was no longer Commissioner.

MR. MATTHEWS. — Although Sir Charles Warren has sent in his resignation of the office of Commissioner of Police he has not yet been relieved from the responsibility of that office, and, therefore, properly continues to discharge its functions. No successor has yet been appointed.

From these reports it will be seen that the resignation of Sir Charles Warren was not a result of the lack of police success in the investigation of the Whitechapel Murders. He was shortly thereafter replaced in office, as expected, by James Monro.

A Royal connection to the murders has always been a popular notion with theorists, writers and the public and to some extent this is justified. There can be no doubt at all that Queen Victoria herself was well aware of the murders, and that she gave them some consideration. We have already seen that in early October 1888, Mr George Lusk, Chairman of the Whitechapel Vigilance Committee, presented a petition to Her Majesty the Queen, then staying at Balmoral, to which it was deemed appropriate she should not reply. An entry in Her Majesty's Journal,[7] dated 4 October 1888, refers to the "dreadful murders of unfortunate women of a bad class, in London."

The Kelly murder marked the peak of public concern and alarm over a terrible series of crimes. A cypher telegram from the Queen at Balmoral to the Marquis of Salisbury, the Prime Minister, dated 10 November 1888, stated:

> "This new most ghastly murder shows the absolute necessity for some very decided action.
>
> All these courts must be lit, & our detectives improved. They are not what they shld be.
>
> You promised, when the 1st murders took place to consult with your colleagues about it."[8]

The Marquis of Salisbury replied, the same day, by cypher telegram:

> "Humble duty:
>
> At Cabinet to-day it was resolved to issue a Proclamation offering free pardon to anyone who should give evidence as to the recent murder except the actual perpetrator of the crime . . ."[9]

A cypher to the Queen from the Marquis of Salisbury, dated 11 November 1888, reported:

> "Humble duty:
>
> Lord Salisbury forgot to mention in previous telegram that Sir Charles Warren had resigned before the murder, because his attention had been drawn to a regulation of the Home Office forbidding writing to the newspapers on the business of the Department without leave.
>
> His resignation has been accepted.
>
> This horrid murder was committed in a room. No additional lighting could have prevented it."[10]

Both Government and Police were under harsh and unfair criticism, and it was difficult to know what to do. The Queen's continuing concern was shown in the following draft letter to Henry Matthews, the Home Secretary:

> "Nov. 13. 1888. – The Queen has received with sincere regret Mr. Matthews' letter of the 10th in which he reports the resignation of Sir Charles Warren.

It would of course be impossible to recognize Sir Charles Warren's contention that he was not under the orders of the Sec of State, but The Queen fears this resignation will have a bad effect in encouraging the lawbreaker to defy the police, who under Sir Charles Warren, have always done their duty admirably.

At the same time The Queen fears that the Detective department is not so efficient as it might be. No doubt the recent murders in Whitechapel were committed in circumstances which made Detection very difficult.

Still The Queen thinks that in the small area where these horrible crimes have been perpetrated a great number of detectives might be employed and that every possible suggestion might be carefully examined, and if practicable followed.

Have the cattle boats & passenger boats been examined?

Has any investigation been made as to the number of single men occupying rooms to themselves?

The murderer's clothes must be saturated with blood and must be kept some where.

Is there sufficient surveillance at night?

These are some of the questions that occur to The Queen on reading the accounts of this horrible crime."[11]

This letter was in the handwriting of Sir Henry Ponsonby, Private Secretary to the Queen, and he added a note at the end: "Perhaps these details might be omitted?" Mr Matthews sent the Queen a detailed explanation from Scotland Yard of all that the police were doing.

The concern evinced by the Queen and the Establishment was later to become a fertile ground for gossip and rumour. The *Referee* of 9 March 1890 hinted:

There is not the slightest "Truth" in the statement that Lord Salisbury concealed Jack the Ripper at Hatfield House on the night of the last Whitechapel murder, or that the Home Secretary has instructed Mr. Monro to discontinue all further inquiries into the atrocities in consequence of it having been discovered that Jack is a member of the House of Lords. Seriously, some such story was for a long time in circulation, especially at the East-end when I heard more than once that the police had received orders to drop the inquiry from high official quarters.

This groundswell of suspicion has pervaded and become enshrined with the facts of the case ever since.

CHAPTER 20

10 November 1888 – Dr Bond "Profiles" the Killer

Home Office files[1] contain an interesting exchange of letters regarding the murders and the efforts being made to gain any sort of clue about the perpetrator of the crimes. What resulted was a very early example of an attempt to profile a serial killer:

[Stamped:- HOME OFFICE 14 NOV.88] A49301C/21
93305/11a

4 Whitehall Place, S.W.
13th Nov. 1888.

Sir,

The Commissioner of Police of the Metropolis has to transmit to you to be laid before Mr. Secretary Matthews a copy of a letter which I have received from Mr. Thomas Bond F.R.C.S. on the subject of the Whitechapel murders.

The enclosed extract from a letter I addressed to Mr. Bond on the 25th ulto. will explain how the matter came before him, and I now propose to inform him that his report has been communicated to the Secretary of State and to thank him for the valuable assistance he has thus rendered in the investigation of the murders.

I am,
Your most obedient Servant,
RAnderson
Assistant Commissioner

The Under
Secretary of State
etc. etc. etc.

There then follows a copy of an extract from a letter to Dr Bond:

[Stamped:- HOME OFFICE 14 NOV.88] A49301C/21
Extract from a letter to Dr. Bond. –

In dealing with the Whitechapel murders the difficulties of conducting the enquiry are largely increased by reason of our having no reliable opinion for our guidance as to the amount of surgical skill and anatomical knowledge probably possessed by the murderer or murderers.

I brought this matter before Sir C. Warren some time since and he has now authorised me to ask if you will be good enough to take up the medical evidence given at the several inquests and favour him with your opinion on the matter.

He feels that your eminence as an expert in such cases – and it is entirely in that capacity that the present case is referred to you, will make your opinion specially valuable.

This is followed by Dr Bond's response[2]:

[Stamped: – HOME OFFICE 14 NOV.88]   7 The Sanctuary,
                                          Westminster Abbey,
                                          Nov: 10th. 88.

Dear Sir,   A49301C/21
                        Whitechapel Murders
I beg to report that I have read the notes of the 4 Whitechapel Murders viz:-
           1. Buck's Row.
           2. Hanbury Street.
           3. Berner's Street.
           4. Mitre Square.
I have also made a Post Mortem Examination of the mutilated remains of a woman found yesterday in a small room in Dorset Street –

1. All five murders were no doubt committed by the same hand. In the first four the throats appear to have been cut from left to right. In the last case owing to the extensive mutilation it is impossible to say in what direction the fatal cut was made, but arterial blood was found on the wall in splashes close to where the woman's head must have been lying.

2. All the circumstances surrounding the murders lead me to form the opinion that the women must have been lying down when murdered and in every case the throat was first cut.

3. In the four murders of which I have seen the notes only, I cannot form a very definite opinion as to the time that had elapsed between the murder and the discovering of the body.

In one case, that of Berner's Street, the discovery appears to have been made immediately after the deed – In Buck's Row, Hanbury Street, and Mitre Square three or four hours only could have elapsed. [sic] In the Dorset Street case the body was lying on the bed at the time of my visit, 2 o'clock, quite naked and mutilated as in the annexed report –

Rigor Mortis had set in, but increased during the progress of the examination. From this it is difficult to say with any degree of certainty the exact time that had elapsed since death as the period varies from 6 to 12 hours before rigidity sets in. The body was comparatively cold at 2 o'clock and the remains of a recently taken meal were found in the stomach and scattered about over the intestines. It is, therefore, pretty certain that the woman must have been dead about 12 hours and the partly digested food would indicate: that death took place about 3 or 4 hours after the food was taken, so one or two o'clock in the morning would be the probable time of the murder.

4. In all the cases there appears to be no evidence of struggling [*sic*] and the attacks were probably so sudden and made in such a position that the women could neither resist nor cry out. In the Dorset Street case the corner of the sheet to the right of the woman's head was much cut and saturated with blood, indicating that the face may have been covered with the sheet at the time of the attack.

5. In the four first cases the murderer must have attacked from the right side of the victim. In the Dorset Street case, he must have attacked from in front or from the left, as there would be no room for him between the wall and the part of the bed on which the woman was lying. Again, the blood had flowed down on the right side of the woman and spurted on to the wall.

6. The murderer would not necessarily be splashed or deluged with blood, but his hands and arms must have been covered and parts of his clothing must certainly have been smeared with blood.

7. The mutilations in each case excepting the Berner's Street one were all of the same character and shewed clearly that in all the murders, the object was mutilation.

8. In each case the mutilation was inflicted by a person who had no scientific nor anatomical knowledge. In my opinion he does not even possess the technical knowledge of a butcher or horse slaughterer or any person accustomed to cut up dead animals.

9. The instrument must have been a strong knife at least six inches long, very sharp, pointed at the top and about an inch in width. It may have been a clasp knife, a butcher's knife or a surgeon's knife. I think it was no doubt a straight knife.

10. The murderer must have been a man of physical strength and of great coolness and daring. There is no evidence that he had an accomplice. He must in my opinion be a man subject to periodical attacks of Homicidal and erotic mania. The character of the mutilations indicate that the man may be in a condition sexually, that may be called satyriasis. It is of course possible that the Homicidal impulse may have developed from a revengeful or brooding condition of the mind, or that Religious Mania may have been the original disease, but I do not think either hypothesis is likely. The murderer in

external appearance is quite likely to be a quiet inoffensive looking man probably middleaged and neatly and respectably dressed. I think he must be in the habit of wearing a cloak or overcoat or he could hardly have escaped notice in the streets if the blood on his hands or clothes were visible.

11. Assuming the murderer to be such a person as I have just described he would probably be solitary and eccentric in his habits, also he is most likely to be a man without regular occupation, but with some small income or pension. He is possibly living among respectable persons who have some knowledge of his character and habits and who may have grounds for suspicion that he is not quite right in his mind at times. Such persons would probably be unwilling to communicate suspicions to the Police for fear of trouble or notoriety, whereas if there were a prospect of reward it might overcome their scruples.

I am, Dear Sir,

Yours faithfully,

(Signed) Thos. Bond.

R. Anderson, Esq:

Bond's profile, however, only made part provision for "such a person". A comment carried in the Editorial column of the *Manchester Evening News* of Tuesday, 13 November 1888:

By the way, the theory is again revived that the perpetrator of the Whitechapel murders is probably a woman suffering from religious mania.

CHAPTER 21

12 November 1888 – The Kelly Inquest

The police investigating the Kelly murder took witness statements on 9 November 1888, which are held with the inquest papers[1] at the London Metropolitan Archives. These are mainly in the hand of Abberline:

Witnesses for inquest to be opened 12th <u>Nov. 88. On the body of Marie Jeanette Kelly</u>

9th November 1888

Statement of Thomas Bowyer 37 Dorset Street Spitalfields in the employ of John McCarthy, lodging house Keeper, Dorset Street.

Says that at 10.45 am 9th instant, he was sent by his employer, to number 13 room Millers Court, Dorset Street, for the rent, he knocked at the door, but not getting any answer he threw the blinds back and looked through the window which was broken and saw the body of deceased woman whom he knew as Mary Jane, seeing that there was a quantity of blood on her person and that she had been apparently murdered he immediately went and informed his employer, Mr McCarthy who also looked into the room and at once despatched Bowyer to the police Station Commercial Street, and informed the Inspector on duty. (Insp Beck) who returned with him and his employer who had also followed to the Station. He knew the deceased and also a man named Joe, who had occupied the room for some months past.

9th November 1888

Statement of John McCarthy Grocer Lodging House Keeper, 27 Dorset Street, Spitalfields.

I sent my man Thomas Bowyer to No 13 room Millers Court Dorset Street owned by me for the rent. Bowyer came back and called me, telling me what he had seen. I went with him back and looked through the broken window, where I saw the mutilated remains of deceased whom I knew as Mary Jane Kelly. I then despatched Bowyer to the Police Station Commercial Street (following myself) to acquaint the Police. The Inspector on duty returned with us to the scene at Millers Court. I let the room about ten months ago to the deceased and a man named Joe, who I believed to be her husband. It was a furnished room, at 4s/6 per week. I sent for the rent because for some time past they had not kept their payments regularly. I have since heard, the man Joe was not her husband and that he had recently left her.

Marie Jeanette Kelly.   Friday
                                                    9th <u>November 1888</u>
Statement of Joseph Barnett now residing at 24 & 25 New Street Bishopsgate ["a common" – *deleted*] labourer lodging house.

I am a porter on Billingsgate Market, but have been out of employment for the past 3 or 4 months. I have been living with Marie Jeanette Kelly who occupied No 13 Room Millers Court. I have lived lived with her altogether about 18 months, for the last eight months in Millers Court, until last Tuesday week (30 ulto) when in consequence of not Earning sufficient money to give her and her resorting to prostitution, I resolved on leaving her, but I was friendly with her and called to see her between seven and eight pm Thursday (8th) and told her I was very sorry I had no work and that I could not give her any money. I left her about 8 oclocksame evening and that was the last time I saw her alive

There was a woman in the room when I called. The deceased told me on one occasion that her father named John Kelly was a foreman of some iron works at [*sic*] lived at Carmarthen or Carnarvon, that she had a brother named Henry serving in 2nd Battn. Scots Guards, and known amongst his comrades as Johnto, and I believe the Regiment is now in Ireland. She also told me that she had obtained her livelihood as a prostitute for some considerable time before I took her from the Streets, and that she left her home about 4 years ago, and that she was married to a collier, who was killed through some explosion. I think she said her husband name was Davis or Davies.

                                                    9th November 1888
Statement of Mary Ann Cox No 5 Room Millers Court Dorset Street Spitalfields

I am a widow and an unfortunate. I have known the female occupying No 13 room Millers Court about 8 months. I knew her by the name of Mary Jane. About a quarter to twelve last night I came into Dorset Street from Commercial Street, and I saw walking in front of me Mary Jane with a man, they turned into the Court and as I entered the Court they went in doors, as they were going into her room, I said good night Mary Jane, she was very drunk and could scarcely answer me, but said good night, the man was carrying a quart can of beer. I shortly afterwards heard her singing. I went out shortly after twelve and returned about one o'clock and she was still singing in her room. I went out again shortly after one o'clock and returned at 3 o'clock, there was no light in her room then and all was quiet, and I heard no noise all night.

The man whom I saw was about 36 years old, about 5 ft 5 in high, complexion fresh and I believe he had blotches on his face, small side whiskers, and a thick carroty moustache, dressed in shabby dark clothes, dark overcoat and black felt hat.

Mary Jane was dressed I think, last night when I saw her, in a linsey frock, red knitted crossover around shoulders, had no hat or bonnet on.

9th November 1888

Elizabeth Prater wife of William Prater a boot machinist of No 20 room 27 Dorset Street states as follows:-

I went out about 9 p.m. on the 8th and returned about 1 a.m. 9th and stood at the bottom of Millers Court until about 1.30. I was speaking for a short time to a Mr. McCarthy Who keeps a chandler's shop at the corner of the court. I then went up to bed. About 3.30 or 4 a.m. I was awakened by a kitten walking across my neck, and just then I heard screams of murder about two or three times in a female voice. I did not take much notice of the cries as I frequently hear such cries from the back of the lodging-house where the windows look into Millers Court. From 1 a.m. to 1.30 a.m. no one passed up the court if they did I should have seen them. I was up again and down stairs in the court at 5.30 a.m. but saw no one except two or three carmen harnessing their horses in Dorset Street. I went to the "Ten Bells" P.H. at the corner of Church Street and had some rum. I then returned and went to bed again without undressing and slept until about 11 a.m.

9th November 1888

Statement of Caroline Maxwell, 14 Dorset Street Spitalfields, the wife of Henry Maxwell, a lodging house deputy.

I have known deceased woman during the past 4 ["'or 5'' – *deleted*] months, she was known as Mary Jane and that since Joe Barnett left her she has obtained her living as an unfortunate. I was on speaking terms with her although I had not seen her for 3 weeks until Friday morning 9th * [*here there is a marginal note* – "* about half past 8 o'clock.''] instant, she was then standing at the corner of Millers Court in Dorset Street. I said to her, what brings you up so early. she said, I have the horrors of drink upon me, as I have been drinking for some days past. I said why dont you go to Mrs. Ringers (meaning the Public House at the corner of Dorset Street called the Britannia) and have ½ pint of beer. She said I have been there and had it, but I have brought it all up again at the same time she pointed to some vomit in the roadway. I then passed on, and went to Bishopsgate on an errand, and returned to Dorset

Street about 9 am I then noticed deceased standing outside Ringers public house, she was talking to a man, age I think about 30, height about 5 ft 5 in, stout, dressed as a Market Porter, I was some distance away and am doubtful whether I could identify him. The deceased wore a dark dress black velvet body, and coloured wrapper round her neck.

9th <u>November 1888</u>

Statement of Sarah Lewis No 34 Great Pearl Street Spitalfields, a laundress

Between 2 and 3 o'clock this morning I came to stop with the Keylers, at No 2 Millers Court as I had had a few words with my husband, when I came up the Court there was a man standing over against the lodging house on the opposite side in Dorset Street ["talking to a female" – *deleted*] but I cannot describe him. Shortly before 4 o'clock I heard a scream like that of a young woman, and seemed to be not far away, she screamed out murder, I only heard it once. I did not look out at the window. I did not know the deceased. [*There is a marginal note* – "I left the Keylers at 5.30 P.M."]

Sarah Lewis further said that when in company with another female on Wednesday evening last at Bethnal Green, a suspicious man accosted her, he carried a black bag.

9 <u>November 1888</u>

Statement of Julia Venturney

I occupy No 1 room Millers Court I am a widow, charwoman but now living with a man named Harry Owen. I was awake all night and could not sleep. I have known the person occupying No 13 room opposite mine for about 4 months. I knew the man who I saw down stairs (Joe Barnett) he is called Joe, he lived with her until quite recently. I have heard him say that he did not like her ["because" – *deleted*] going out on the streets, he frequently gave her money, he was very kind to her, he said he would not live with her while she led that course of life, she used to get tipsey occasionally. She broke the windows a few weeks ago whilst she was drunk, she told me she was very fond of another man named Joe, and he had often ill-used her because she cohabited with Joe (Barnett). I saw her last about ["1.40" – *deleted*] pm yesterday. Thursday about 10 A.M.

9th <u>November 1888</u>

Statement of Maria Harvey of 3 New Court Dorset Street a laundress.

I slept two nights with Mary Jane Kelly, Monday and Tuesday last. I then took a room at the above house. I saw her last about five minutes to seven last night Thursday in her own room, when Barnett called. I then left they seemed to be on the best of terms. I left an overcoat, two dirty cotton shirts, a boy's shirt and a girls white petticoat and black crape bonnet in the room, the overcoat shewn me by police is the one I left there.

Inspector Walter Beck "H." Division who was first called together with the Constables on the beat will attend at the Inquest, also myself who will speak to contents of room &c if necessary.

F.G.Abberline Inspector.

The evidence given at the inquest into the death of Mary Jane Kelly is also included with the papers[2] held at the Greater London Record Office. It should be noted that the evidence given at the inquest is presented here as distinct from the preceding statements, taken on the day of the murder. There are some differences in the evidence given, and further differences may be found in the various newspaper reports of the inquest. These are too numerous to quote in full and would, in any case, be repetitive in the main. The inquest papers of the day of the hearing, Monday, 12 November 1888 are as follows:

MIDDLESEX,

To wit

𝔄n 𝔍nquisition taken for our Sovereign Lady the Queen, at the House known by the Name of the *Town Hall* in the Parish of *Shoreditch* in the County of MIDDLESEX, on the *Twelth [sic]* day of *November* A.D. 1888 [and by adjournment on the _____ day of _____, and the _____ day of _____].

before RODERICK MADONALD, ESQUIRE, one of the Coroners of our said Lady the Queen for the said County of MIDDLESEX, upon the Oath of good and lawful Men of the said County, duly sworn to inquire for our said Lady the Queen, on view of the Body of *Marie Jeanette Kelly otherwise Davies* as to her death, and those of the said jurors whose names are hereunto subscribed upon their Oaths duly administered do say

That on the *Ninth* day of *November* in the year aforesaid at the *1 Millers Court* in the Parish of *Shoreditch [sic]* aforesaid, the said *Marie Jeanette Kelly was found dead from the mortal effects of Severance of the right carotid artery* and so the Jurors aforesaid, upon their Oaths, do further say that *such death was due to* and the Jurors aforesaid do further say that the said *Marie Jeanette Kelly* was a *fe* male person of the age of *about twenty five* years, and a *prostitute*.

𝔍n 𝔚itness whereof as well the said Coroner as the Jurors have hereunto subscribed their Hands and Seals the Day and Year and Place first above written.

Roderick Macdonald * Coroner.   *G Gieselme* *

Joseph Gobly *   *John Lloyd* *   [illeg] *William Worf* *

George Buffery*   Samuel Jenkins*   Joseph Roberts*
E. Stevens*   Abraham Clements*   Lewis F Hunter*
John Harvey*   R Nettelfield*   George Harry Wilson*
                                                 Henry Dawkes

Middlesex, TO WIT.

The Informations of Witnesses severally taken and acknowledged on behalf of our Sovereign Lady the Queen, touching the death of *Marie Jeannette Kelly*, at the House known by the sign of the *Town Hall* in the Parish of *Shoreditch* in the County of Middlesex, on the *12* day of *November*, in the year of our Lord One thousand eight hundred and *eighty eight* before me, RODERICK MACDONALD, Esquire, one of Her Majesty's Coroners for the said County, on an Inquisition then and there taken on View of the body of the said *Marie J Kelly* then and there lying dead.

Joseph Barnett, having been sworn upon the day and year and at the place above mentioned, deposed as follows:- I reside at 24 and 25 New Street, Bishopsgate, which is a common lodging house. I am a laborer & have been a fish porter. I now live at my sisters 21 Portpool Lane, Grays Inn Road. I have lived with the deceased one year and eight months, her name was Marie Jeannette Kelly. Kelly was her maiden name and the name she always went by. I have seen the body. I identify her by the ear and the eyes. I am positive it is the same woman. I have lived with her at 13 room, Miller's Court, eight months or longer. I separated from her on the 30th of October. I left her because she had a person who was a prostitute whom she took in and I objected to her doing so, that was the only reason, not because I was out of work. I left her on the 30th October between 5 & 6 pm. I last saw her alive between 7.30 & 7.45 the night of Thursday before she was found. I was with her about one hour, we were on friendly terms. I told her when I left her I had no work and had nothing to give her of which I was very sorry, we did not drink together, she was quite sober, she was as long as she was with me of sober habits. She has got drunk several times in my presence. There was a female with us on Thursday evening when we were together, she left first and I left shortly afterwards. Deceased has often told me as to her parents, she said she was born in Limerick — that she was 25 years of age — & from there went to Wales when very young. She told me she came to London about 4 years ago. Her father's name was John Kelly, he was a Gauger at some iron works in Carnarvonshire. She told me she had one sister, who was a traveller with materials from market place to market place. She also said she had 6 brothers at home and one in the army, one was Henry Kelly. I never spoke to any of them. She told me she had been married when very young in Wales. She was married to a Collier, she told me the name was Davis or Davies, I think Davies. She told me she was lawfully married to him until he died in an explosion. She said she lived with him 2 or 3 years up to his death. She told me she was married at the age of 16 years. She came to London about 4 years ago, after her husband's death. She said she first went to Cardiff and was in an infirmary there 8 or 9 months and followed a bad life with a cousin whilst in Cardiff. When she left Cardiff she said she came to London. In London she was first in a gay house in the West End of the Town. A gentleman there asked her to go to France. She described to me she went to France. As she told me as she did not like the part she did not stay there long, she lived there about a fortnight. She did not like it and returned. She came back and lived in Ratcliffe Highway for some time, she did not tell me how long. Then she was living near Stepney Gas Works. Morganstone was the man she lived with there. She did not tell me how long she lived there. She told me that in Pennington Street she lived at one time with a Morganstone, and with Joseph Flemming, she was very fond of him. He was a mason's plasterer. He lived in Bethnal Green Rd. She told me all this, but I do not know which she lived with last, Flemming used to visit her. I picked up with her in Commercial Street, Spitalfields. The first night we had a drink together and I arranged to see her the next day, and then on the Saturday we agreed to remain together and I took lodgings in George Street where I was known, George Street, Commercial Street. I lived with her from then till I left her the other day. She had on several occasions asked me to read about the murders she seemed afraid of some one, she did not express fear of any particular individual except when she rowed with me but we always came to terms quickly.

By the jury no questions.

[The Coroner – You have given your evidence very well indeed. (To the Jury): The doctor has sent a note asking whether we shall want his attendance here to-day. I take it that it would be convenient that he should tell us roughly what the cause of death was, so as to enable the body to be buried. It will not be necessary to go into the details of the doctor's evidence, but he suggested that he might come to state roughly the cause of death.

The jury acquiesced in the proposed course.]

Thomas Bowyer
having been sworn upon the day and year and at the place above mentioned deposed as follows: I reside at 37 Dorset Street, Spitalfields. I am servant to Mr. McCarthy the owner of a chandlers shop & I serve in the shop. The shop is 27 Dorset Street. On Friday morning last at $\frac{1}{4}$ to 11 I was ordered by Mr. McCarthy to go to Mary Janes room No. 13, I only knew her as Mary Jane. I

was to go for rent. I went & knocked at the door and got no answer. I knocked again and got no answer. I went round the corner and there was a broken window in the farthest window.

Charles Ledger put in and proved plans –
Charles Ledger, inspector [*of police*], G Division. I have made plans produced and they are correct plans of the premises.

Thomas Bowyer
I refer to plan and I mean the farthest pane of the first window the small one I looked in the window there was a curtain over the window I pulled the curtain aside and looked in I saw two lumps of flesh laying on the table ["to be" – *deleted*] close against the bed, in front of the bed. The second time I looked I saw a body of some one laid on the bed, and blood on the floor. I at once went then very quietly back to my master Mr. John McCarthy. We then stood in the shop, and I told him what I had seen. We both then went directly to the police station But before doing so I and my master went and looked in the window, Then we went to the police station and told the police what we had seen. We told no one before we went to the police station we came back with the inspector, I have oven [*sic* – often] seen deceased in and out, I know Joseph Barnett and have seen him going in, I have seen deceased drunk once.
    By a juror
    I last saw deceased alive on Wednesday afternoon in the Court.
    Mr McCarthys shop is at the corner of the Court in Dorset Street.

John McCarthy having been sworn deposed as follows: I am a grocer and lodging house keeper at 27 Dorset-street. – On Friday morning last about ¼ to 11 I sent my man Bowyer to fetch rent from No 13 room Millers Court. He came back in about 5 minutes and said governor I knocked at the door and could not make any one answer. I looked through the window and saw a lot of blood. I went out with him and looked through the window and saw the body any [*sic* – and?] everything I said to my man don't tell any one let us fetch the police I knew deceased as Mary Jane Kelly I have seen the body and have no doubt as to the identity. I and Bowyer went then to the Police Court Commercial Street and saw Inspector Beck. I inquired at first for other inspectors. I told Inspector Beck what I had seen. He put on his hat and coat and came with me at once. deceased has lived in the room with Joe for 10 months both together. They lived comfortably together but once broke the two windows – the furniture and everything in the room belongs to me. I was paid 4/6d a week for the room but rent was 29s./- in arrear, the rent was paid to me weekly the room was let weekly. I very often saw deceased worse for drink she was a very quiet woman when sober but noisy when in drink she was not ever helpless when drunk. –

Mary Ann Cox having been sworn deposed as follows: I am a widow and live at No. 5 Room, Millers Court the last house top of the Court I get my living on the streets as best I can I have known the female occupying No 13 room 8 or 9 as Mary Jane I last saw her alive about midnight on Thursday very much intoxicated, in Dorset Street she went up the Court a few steps in front of me, there was a short stout man shabbily dressed with her, he had a longish coat, very shabby dark and a pot of ale in his hand, he had a hard billy cock black hat on, he had a blotchy face and a full, carrotty mustache his chin was clean.

I saw them go into her room. I said good night, Mary and the man banged the door, he had nothing in his hands but a pot of beer. She answered me I am going to have a song, I went into my room and I heard her sing "a violet I plucked from my mother's grave when a boy." I remained a quarter of an hour in my room, then went out. She was still singing, I returned about one oclock she was singing then. I warmed my hands and went out again she was still singing. I came in again at 3 o'clock, the light was out and there was no noise. I did not undress at all that night, I heard no noise, it was raining hard, I did not go to sleep at all I heard nothing whatever after one oclock – I heard men going in and out, several go in and out, I heard some one go out at a quarter to six. I do not know what house he went out of I heard no door shut. He did not pass my window –

The man had short carroty mustache all his clothes were dark, they made no sound going up the Court. Mary Jane had no hat on she had a red pellorine [*sic* – pelerine] and a dark shabby skirt – I noticed she was drunk as I said good night, the man at once closed the door

By the Jury – The [*sic*] was light in the room when she was singing I saw nothing as the blinds were down, I should know the man again.

By the Coroner I should have heard any cry of murder I heard nothing, I have very often seen deceased drunk.

Elizabeth Prater having been sworn deposed as follows: I am the wife of William Prater a Boot Machinist, he has deserted me for 5 years I live at No 20 Room in Millers Court up stairs I lived in the room over where deceased lived-

On Thursday I went into the Court about 5 oclock in the evening and returned about 1 on Friday morning. I stood at the corner by Mr McCarthys shop till about 20 minutes past 1 I spoke to no one I was waiting for a man I lived with, he did not come. I went up to my room. On the stairs I could see a glimmer through the partition if there had been a light in the deceaseds room.

I might not have noticed it. I did not take particular notice – I could have heard her moving if she had moved. I went in about 1.30 I put 2 tables against the door. I went to sleep at once I had something to drink I slept soundly till a kitten disturbed me about 3.30 to 4. I noticed the lodging house light was out, so it was after 4 probably – I heard a cry of oh! Murder! As the cat came on me and I pushed her down, ["in" – *deleted*] the voice was in a faint voice – the noise seemed to come from close by – It is nothing uncommon to hear cries of murder so I took no notice – I did not hear it a second time. I heard nothing else whatever I went to sleep again and woke at 5 oclock. I got up and went down and went across to the ten bells I was there at $\frac{1}{4}$ to 6 at the corner of Church Street – I saw several men harnessing horses in Dorset Street – Mary Ann Cox could have passed down the Court during the night without me hearing her – After having a drink at the 10 Bells I went home and slept till 11 –

I went to bed at half past one – I did not hear any singing. – I should have heard any one if singing in the deceaseds room at 1 oclock, there was no one singing

Caroline Maxwell having been sworn deposed as follows: I ["am" – *deleted*] live at 14 Dorset Street my husband's name is Henry Maxwell he is a Lodging House deputy. I knew the deceased for about 4 months as Mary Jane. I also knew Joe Barnett, I believe she was an unfortunate girl. I never spoke to her except twice – I took a deal of notice of deceased this evening seeing her standing at the corner of the Court on Friday from 8 to half past I know the time by taking the plates my husband had to take care of from the house opposite. I am positive the time was between 8 & half past I am positive I saw deceased I spoke to her I said why Mary what brings you up so early she said Oh! I do feel so bad! Oh Carry I feel so bad! She knew my name – ["she as" – *deleted*] I asked her to have a drink, she said oh no I have just had a drink of ale and have brought it all up, it was in the road I saw it – as she said this she motioned with her head and I concluded she meant she had been to the Brittania [*sic*] at the corner, I left her saying I pitied her feelings – I then went to Bishopsgate as I returned I saw her outside the Brittania talking to a man – the time was then about 20 minutes to half an hour later about a quarter to nine – I could not describe the man I did not pass them I went into my house I saw them in the distance, I am certain it was deceased, the man was not a tall man – he had on dark clothes and a sort of plaid coat – I could not say what hat he had on – Mary Jane had a dark skirt – velvet body – and morone shawl & no hat – I have seen deceased in drink but not really drunk –

By a Juror – I did not notice whether deceased had on a high silk hat – if it had been so I would have noticed it I think

Sarah Lewis having been sworn deposed as follows: I live at 24 Great Powell Street, Spitalfields. I am a Laundress. I know Mrs. Keyler in Millers Court. I was at her house at half past 2 on Friday morning she lives at No 2 in the Court on the left on the first floor I know the time by having looked at Spitalfields Church clock as I passed it – When I went in the court I saw a man opposite the Court in Dorset Street standing alone by the Lodging House. He was not tall – but stout – had on a wideawake black hat – I did not notice his clothes – another young man with a woman passed along – The man standing in the street was looking up the court as if waiting for some one to come out, I went to Mrs ["Kelseys" – *deleted*] Keylers I was awake all night in a chair I dozed I heard no noise I woke up at about half past three – I sat awake till nearly five – a little before 4 I heard a female voice shout loudly one Murder! The sound seemed to come from the direction of deceaseds room there was only one scream – I took no notice of it – I left Mrs Keylers at about half past 5 in the afternoon the police would not let us out before – About Wednesday night at 8 oclock I was going along Bethnal Green Road with another female and a Gentleman passed us he turned back & spoke to us, he asked us to follow him, and asked one of us he did not mind which we refused, he went away, and came back & said if we would follow him he would treat us – he asked us to go down a passage – he had a bag he put it down saying what are you frightened of – he then undid his coat and felt for something and we ran away – he was short, pale faced, with a black small moustache, about 40 years of age – the bag he had was about a foot or nine inches long – he had on a round high hat – a high one for a round one – he had a brownish long overcoat and a short black coat underneath – and pepper & salt ["and" – *deleted*] trousers.

On our running away we did not look after the man – On the Friday morning about half past two when I was coming to Millers Court I met the same man with a female – in Commercial Street near Mr Ringers Public House – near the market – He had then no overcoat on – but he had the bag & the same hat trousers & undercoat

I passed by them and looked back at at [*sic*] the man – I was frightened – I looked again when I got to the corner of Dorset Street. I have not seen the man since I should know him if I did –

George Bagster Phillips – M R C S Regd – having been sworn deposed as follows: I am a surgeon to H Division of Metropolitan Police and reside at 2 Spital Square – I was called by the police on Friday morning last about 11 oclock and proceeded to Millers Court which I entered at 11.15 a.m. I found a room the door of which led out of the passage near 26 Dorset Street and having two windows I produce a photograph I had taken – there are two windows in the court – 2 of the panes in the window nearest the passage were broken and finding the door locked I looked through the lower broken pane and satisfied myself that the mutilated corpse lying on the bed was not in need of any immediate attention from me and I also came to the conclusion that there was nobody else on the bed or within view to whom I could render any professional assistance – Having ascertained that probably it was advisable that no entrance should be made into the room at that time, I remained until about 1.30 when the door was broken open I think by Mr McCarthy – I think by direction of Superintendent Arnold who had arrived – When I arrived the premises were in charge of Inspector Beck

On the door being opened it knocked against a table, the table I found close to the left-hand side of the bedstead and the bedstead was close up against the wooden partition, the mutilated remains of a female were lying two thirds over towards the edge of the bedstead, nearest to the door of entry she had only her under linen garment on her, and from my subsequent examination I am sure the body had been removed subsequent to the injury which caused her death from that side of the bedstead which was nearest to the wooden partition, the large quantity of blood under the bedstead, the saturated condition of the paliasse, pillow, sheet, at that top corner nearest the partition leads me to the conclusion that the severance of the right carotid artery which was the immediate cause of her death was inflicted while the deceased was lying at the right side of the bedstead and her head and neck in the top right-hand corner.

At this point *The Times* of Tuesday, 13 November 1888 added in its coverage of the inquest:

The jury had no questions to ask at this stage, and it was understood that more detailed evidence of the medical examination would be given at a further hearing.

An adjournment for a few minutes then took place, and on the return of the jury the Coroner said, "It has come to my ears that somebody has been making a statement to some of the jury as to their right and duty of being here. Has any one during the interval spoken to the jury, saying that they should not be here today?"

Some jurymen replied in the negative.

The Coroner: Then I must have been misinformed. I should have taken good care that he would have had a quiet life for the rest of the week if anybody had interfered with my jury.

The inquest papers continue with the statements of the witnesses:

Julia Venturney having been sworn deposed as follows: I live at No 1 Room Millers Court I am a charwoman I live with Harry Owen I knew the female who occupied No 13 room she said she was a married woman and her name was Kelly. She lived with Joe Barnett she frequently got drunk Joe Barnett would not let her go on the streets – Deceased said she was fond of another man named Joe who used to come and see her and give her money I think he was a costermonger she said she was very fond of him – I last saw her alive on Thursday about 10 a m having her breakfast with another woman in her own room. I went to bed on Thursday night about 8 oclock I could not sleep all night I only dozed I heard no one in the court I heard no singing, I heard no scream – deceased often sung Irish songs –

Maria Harvey having been sworn deposed as follows: I live at No. 3 New Court, Dorset Street I knew deceased as Mary Jane Kelly I slept two nights with her on Monday & Tuesday nights last I slept with her. We were together all the afternoon on Thursday, I am a Laundress I was in the room when Joe Barnett called I went away I left my bonnet there. I knew Barnett – I left some clothes in the room 2 mens shirts, 1 boy's shirt, an overcoat a black one a mans, a black crape bonnet with black strings, a ticket for a shawl in for 2/-, one little child's white petticoat – I have seen nothing of them since except the overcoat produced to me by the police. I was a friend of deceaseds – she never told me of being afraid of any one –

Walter Beck H Division Inspector Commercial Street Station I was the first police officer called to 13 Millers Court by McCarthy. I sent for the Doctor and closed the Court to all persons. I do not know by whose order the door was forced, I was there, the doctor was the first to enter the room, it was shortly after 11 oclock when I was called

Frederick George Abberline Inspector Scotland Yard ["I am in" – *deleted*] having been sworn deposed as follows: I am in charge of this case – I was on the scene of the murder by 11.30 on Friday, I had an intimation from Inspector Beck that the dogs had been sent for Dr Phillips asked me not to force the door but to test the dogs if they were coming we remained until 1.30 when Superintendent Arnold arrived & informed me that the order as to dogs had been countermanded, and he gave directions for the door to be forced I have heard the Doctors evidence and confirm what he says. I have taken an inventory of what was in the room, there had been a large fire so large as to melt the spout off the kettle I have since gone through the ashes in the grate & found nothing of consequence except that articles of womans clothing had been burnt which I presume was for the purpose of light as there was only one piece of candle in the room – I am informed by the witness Barnett that the key has been missing for some time & that they opened the door by reaching through the window, a pipe was there & used by him.

The Times gives details of the conclusion of the inquest:

The Coroner (to the jury): The question is whether you will adjourn for further evidence. My own opinion is that it is very unnecessary for two courts to deal with these cases, and go through the same evidence time after time, which only causes expense and trouble. If the coroner's jury can come to a decision as to the cause of death, then that is all that they have to do. They have nothing to do with prosecuting a man and saying what amount of penalty he is to get. It is quite sufficient if they find out what the cause of death was. It is for the police authorities to deal with the case and satisfy themselves as to any person who may be suspected later on. I do not want to take it out of your hands. It is for you to say whether at an adjournment you will hear minutes of the evidence, or whether you will think it is a matter to be dealt with in the police-courts later on, and that this woman, having met with her death by the carotid artery having been cut, you will be satisfied to return a verdict to that effect. From what I learn the police are content to take the future conduct of the case. It is for you to say whether you will close the inquiry to-day; if not, we shall adjourn for a week or fortnight, to hear the evidence that you may desire.

The Foreman, having consulted with his colleagues, considered that the jury had had quite sufficient evidence before them upon which to give a verdict.
The Coroner: What is the verdict?
The Foreman: Wilful murder against some person or persons unknown.

An important witness contacted the police after the inquest had been closed. The three-page witness statement[3] George Hutchinson remains, as follows:

Commercial Street
METROPOLITAN POLICE
H Division
12th November 1888

At 6 pm 12th George Hutchinson of the Victoria Home Commercial Street came to this Station and made the following statement.

About 2 am 9th I was coming by Thrawl Street, Commercial Street, and saw just before I got to Flower and Dean Street I saw the murdered woman Kelly. and she said to me Hutchinson will you lend me sixpence. I said I cant I have spent all my money going down to Romford. she said Good morning I must go and find some money. she went away towards Thrawl Street. a man coming in the opposite direction to Kelly tapped her on the shoulder and said something to her. they both burst out laughing. I heard her say alright to him. and the man said you will be alright for what I have told you. he then placed his right hand around her shoulders. He also had a kind of a small parcel in his left hand with a kind of a strap round it. I stood against the lamp of the ["Ten Bell" – *deleted*] Queens Head Public House and watched him. They both then came past me and the man hid down his head with his hat over his eyes. I stooped down and looked him in the face. He looked at me stern. They both went into Dorset Street I followed them. They both stood at the corner of the Court for about 3 minutes. He said something to her. she said alright my dear come along you will be comfortable He then placed his arm on her shoulder and gave her a kiss. She said she had lost her handkerchief he then pulled his handkerchief a red one out and gave it to her. They both then went up the Court together. I then went to the Court to see if I could see them but could not. I stood there for about three quarters of an hour to see if they came out they did not so I went away.

Description age about 34 or 35. height 5ft6 complexion pale, dark eyes and eye lashes ["dark" – *deleted*] slight moustache, curled up each end, and hair dark, very surley looking dress long dark coat, collar and cuffs trimmed astracan. and a dark jacket under. light waistcoat dark trousers dark felt hat turned down in the middle. button boots and gaiters with white buttons. wore a very thick gold chain white linen collar. black tie with horse shoe pin. respectable appearance walked very sharp. Jewish appearance. can be identified.

George Hutchinson
E Badham Sergt
E. Ellisdon Insp
T Arnold Supdt.

Submitted FGAbberlineInspr

The witness Hutchinson, who did not come forward until after the Kelly inquest, was interviewed by Abberline whose report of 12 November 1888 is preserved[4]:

METROPOLITAN POLICE
Criminal Investigation Department,
Scotland Yard
12th day of November, 1888

I beg to report that an inquest was held this day at the Shoreditch Town Hall before Dr. Macdonald M.P. Coroner on the body of Marie Jeanette Kelly, found murdered at No. 13

Room, Millers Court, Dorset Street, Spitalfields. A number of witnesses were called who clearly established the identity of deceased. The Coroner remarked that in his opinion it was unnecessary to adjourn the inquiry and the jury returned a verdict of ''Wilful murder against some person or persons unknown.''

An important statement has been made by a man named George Hutchinson which I forward herewith. I have interrogated him this evening and I am of opinion his statement is true. He informed me that he had occasionally given the deceased a few shillings, and that he had known her about 3 years. Also that he was surprised to see a man so well dressed in her company which caused him to watch them. He can identify the man, and arrangement was at once made for two officers to accompany him round the district for a few hours tonight with a view of finding the man if possible.

Hutchinson is at present in no regular employment, and he has promised to go with an officer tomorrow morning at 11.30. am. to the Shoreditch mortuary to identify the deceased. Several arrests have been made on suspicion of being connected with the recent murders, but the various persons detained have been able to satisfactorily account for their movements and were released.

F.G.Abberline Inspr
T Arnold Supt.

George Hutchinson's statement was given wide coverage in the national newspapers, unlike the story about Sir George Arthur gleefully reported in the *New York World*, 18 November 1888:

SPECIAL CABLE DESPATCH TO THE WORLD.
London, Nov. 17. – The most intense amusement has been caused among all classes of the London world by the arrest last week of little Sir George Arthur on suspicion of being the Whitechapal murderer. Sir George is a young Baronet holding a captaincy in the regiment of Royal Horse Guards, and is a member of most of the leading clubs in town. He is also a well-known amateur actor, and was a great friend of the late Prince Leopold Duke of Albany. Since the past few weeks the old mania for ''slumming'' in White-chapel has become fashionable again. Every night scores of young men, who have never been the East End before in their lives prowl around the neighborhood in which the murders were committed, talking with the frightened women and pushing their way into over-crowded lodging-houses. So long as any two men keep together and do not make a nuisance of themselves the police do not interfere with them. But if a man goes alone and tries to lure a woman of the street into a secluded corner to talk with her he is

pretty sure to get into trouble. That was the case with Sir George Arthur. He put on an old shooting coat, a slouch hat and went down to Whitechapel for a little fun. He got it. It occurred to two policemen that Sir George answered very much the popular descriptive of Jack the Ripper. They watched him, and when they saw him talking with women they proceeded to collar him. He protested, expostulated and threatened them with the vengeance of royal wrath, but in vain. Finally, a chance was given to him to send to a fashionable Western Club to prove his identity, and he was released with profuse apologies for the mistake. The affair was kept out of the newspapers. But the jolly young Baronet's friends as Brook's Club considered the joke too good to be kept quiet.

CHAPTER 22

21 November 1888 – A Second Outrage?

Fears of another "Ripper" attack were raised by an incident that occurred in Spitalfields on the morning of Wednesday, 21 November 1888. *The Times* of Thursday, November 22 1888, carried a report[1] of the incident:

> MURDEROUS OUTRAGE IN WHITECHAPEL.
>
> Considerable excitement was caused throughout the East-end yesterday morning by a report that another woman had been brutally murdered and mutilated in a common lodging-house in George-street, Spitalfields, and in consequence of the reticence of the police authorities all sorts of rumours prevailed. Although it was soon ascertained that there had been no murder, it was said that an attempt had been made to murder a woman, of the class to which the other unfortunate creatures belonged, by cutting her throat, and the excitement in the neighbourhood for some time was intense. Whether the woman's assailant is the man wanted for the seven recent murders committed in the district of Whitechapel is, of course, not known, although his description tallies somewhat with that given by one of the witnesses at the last inquest; but should he be, the police are sanguine of his speedy capture, as a good and accurate description of him is now obtained, and if arrested he could be identified by more than one person. The victim of this last occurrence, fortunately, is but slightly injured, and was at once able to furnish the detectives with a full description of her assailant. Her name is Annie Farmer, and she is a woman of about 40 years of age, who lately resided with her husband, a tradesman, in Featherstone-street, City-road, but, on account of her dissolute habits, was separated from him. On Monday night the woman had no money, and, being unable to obtain any, walked the streets until about half-past 7 yesterday morning. At that time she got into conversation, in Commercial-street, with a man, whom she describes as about 36 years of age, about 5ft. 6in. in height, with a dark moustache,and wearing a shabby black diagonal suit and hard felt hat. He treated her to several drinks until she became partially intoxicated. At his suggestion they went to the common lodging-house, 19, George-street, and paid the deputy

8d. for a bed. That was about 8 o'clock, and nothing was heard to cause alarm or suspicion until half-past 9, when screams were heard proceeding from the room occupied by the man and Farmer. Some men who were in the kitchen of the house at the time rushed upstairs and met the woman coming down. She was partially undressed, and was bleeding profusely from a wound in the throat. She was asked what was the matter, and simply said ''He's done it,'' at the same time pointing to the door leading into the street. The men rushed outside, but saw no one, except a man in charge of a horse and cart. He was asked if he had noticed any person running away, and said he had seen a man, who he thought had a scar at the back of the neck, run down George-street and turn into Thrawl-street, but not thinking much of the occurrence, had not taken particular notice of the man and had made no attempt to detain him. By this time a considerable number of people had assembled, and these ran into Thrawl-street and searched the courts leading out of that thoroughfare, but without any success. While this was being done the police were communicated with and quickly arrived on the scene. In the meantime the deputy of the lodging-house had wrapped a piece of rag over the woman's wound, and, seeing that it did not appear to be a dangerous cut, got her to dress herself. Dr. George Bagster Phillips, divisional surgeon of the H Division, together with his assistant, quickly arrived, and the former gentleman stitched up the wound. Seeing that it was not a dangerous one, and in order to get the woman away from the crowd of inmates, who pressed round, he suggested that she should be removed to the Commercial-street Police-station, and that was quickly done on the ambulance. Although none but police officers were allowed to interview her with regard to the attack, and consequently nothing definite is known as to the cause, it has transpired that she had previously met her assailant some 12 months since, and owing to this fact the officers are doubtful whether the man had anything to do with the murders. Owing to the excellent description given they are sanguine of securing the man's arrest within a very short space of time. Superintendent T. Arnold, who was quickly apprised of what had happened, at once ordered Detective-officers Thicke [*sic*], New, M'Guire, and others to endeavour to capture the man, and by about 10.30 a full description of him was telegraphed to all the police-stations throughout the metropolitan police district. It is stated that Farmer is able to converse freely, and that lodgings will be found for her by the police until the person who attacked her is captured. Directly the police arrived at the house in George-street a constable was stationed at the door, and no person was allowed to leave until his or her statement and full particulars concerning each one had been written down. During the whole of the day a crowd collected in front of 19, George-street, apparently drawn thither merely out of curiosity to view the house, but none not belonging to it were allowed to enter.

A further report mentioning the attack on Farmer appeared in the *East Anglian Daily Times* of Monday, 26 November 1888:

THE EAST END MURDERS.

Upon enquiry at two o'clock on Sunday morning it was found that no positive clue to the murderer had been discovered nor was anyone detained in custody upon suspicion. As regards the assault made upon Annie Farmer in a common lodging-house at George Street, Flower and Dean Street, by a man who afterwards made his escape, nothing further of him has been seen, and the police are inclined to believe that the affair was only an ordinary brawl, and that the woman is acquainted with the man who assailed her, but will not give information which will lead to his detection. On Saturday night there were still many amateur detectives parading the streets with intent to assist the police, but in some cases their vigilance appeared to be a little over-zealous. It seems that a man of foreign appearance, who was in search of the murderer, provided himself with a revolver, and in a moment of confidence showing it to a policeman in plain clothes, he was arrested and taken to Leman Street Police Station for unlawfully having firearms in his possession. The case was investigated, and a satisfactory explanation having been given, the man was discharged.

Two of the men who described at the time the man believed to have committed the Berners [sic] Street and other murders, to-day reported that they have again seen him, but that though they followed him he disappeared suddenly down an unfrequented turning.

CHAPTER 23

Police Activity Following the Kelly Murder

The excitement caused by the Kelly murder understandably caused further criticism of the police by press and public, and resulted in yet further increases in police strength in the area. An idea of the official activity is conveyed in the reports of this period of time.

There is a report in the file[1], date-stamped 14 NOV.88, as follows:

> Home Office,
> Whitehall,
> S.W.

Mr. Murdoch.

Anderson left this with the Chief this morning. He told me that he wd. send a covering letter officially.

> CRB

13/11.

This is followed by a Home Office cover page[2] which is as follows:

[Stamped: – HOME OFFICE 14 NOV.88 RECEIVED]
DATE 14 Nov. 1888.   Dr. Forbes Winslow.
REFERENCES, &c.   East End Murders.

        Expresses his opinion that the murderer is a homicidal lunatic. Places his services at the Gov.'s disposal.

> Pressing

[MINUTES.]
Ackgd. 14.11.88

To Police.
   CW
      Nov 15. 88.
        EP 17 Nov 88
          Forwarded with other letters
            under. /107
            17th.Nov.1888.

There is no enclosure with this cover and it is followed by another cover page[3] as follows:

[Stamped: – HOME OFFICE 15 NOV.88 RECEIVED]
DATE 15 Novr.88.   Louis Solomon
REFERENCES &c.   Directors fd copies of statements recd. from Offrs of Woking Prison who think it possible that above may be the Whitechapel Murderer.

MINUTES.

For letter see A21640 (*Destroyed*)
an ordinary criminal case.

There is a letter[4] dated 29 November 1888 from Godfrey Lushington to the Commissioner of the Metropolitan Police:

B 5329/5   WHITEHALL.
                                              29th November 1888.

Sir,
    With reference to the letter from this Department of the 22nd. ultimo and your replies of the 25th. and 30th. ultimo, I am directed by the Secretary of State to request that you will be so good as to furnish him with a statement showing, (i). the area. (ii) the number of inhabited houses, and, so far as you are able to give the information, (iii) the population of the "H" or Whitechapel Division.

I am,
Sir,
Your obedient Servant,
Godfrey Lushington

The Commissioner
of the Metropolitan Police.

The reply to this letter is not included.
    A file date[5] reads as follows:

[Stamped: – HOME OFFICE 8 DEC.88 RECEIVED]
                                  No. A49301G/1
DATE 7 Decr.88.   Comr. of Police
REFERENCES &c.   Recomds. that the Offrs. employed specially in plain clothes to patrol the neighbourhood of the Whitechapel Murders be granted 1s/- per day allce.

[MINUTES.]

The original authority for payment of 1s/- a day to permanent patrols which

Mr Munro desires these men should have was accorded on the formation of the C.I.D. in 1878 – see 66692/43a.

The expense as Mr Munro admits is considerable £5 a day.

?First to Receiver for financial observations.

CM Dec. 19.

GL

19 Dec 1888

Wrote 20/12 a/21.12.88 ($\frac{1}{2}$)

The following report is included:

A49301G/1

96318

4 Whitehall Place,
S.W.
7th December, 1888.

Sir,

I have to acquaint you, for the information of the Secretary of State, that, in connection with the recent murders in Whitechapel, one Inspector 9 Sergeants and 126 Constables of the uniform branch of the Force have been employed specially in plain clothes to patrol the neighbourhood of the Murders with a view to prevent a repetition of the Crime.

These officers are entitled to the usual plain clothes allowance, viz: 1s/11d per week for Sergeants and Constables and 3s/11d for the Inspector. –

Many of them, however, come from other divisions and have to patrol at a distance from their homes, and they have continuous night duty, which will be very trying when the winter sets in. – The work is specially irksome and unpleasant, and these men are practically doing the duty of permanent patrols.

The usual allowance is inadequate to compensate a man for the wear and tear of his clothes when he is engaged for a lengthened period. –

Under the circumstances therefore I have to recommend to the favourable consideration of Mr. Secretary Matthews that the men employed on this special duty should receive the allowance of 1s/- per diem as granted to permanent patrols.

The expense will be considerable, amounting to about £5 per diem; but it is in my opinion justifiable and should be incurred. –

I am,

Sir,

Your most obedient Servant,

JMonro.

The Under Secretary
of State
Home Office.

The following letter[6] on this subject, dated 21 December 1888, is as follows:

5185/1   A49301G/2
                                          4 Whitehall Place
                                          21 Decr. 1888

Sir,

In returning Mr. Munro's letter of 7th inst. proposing the grant of an allowance of 1/- a day to officers specially employed on patrol duty in the neighbourhood of the Whitechapel murders, I have the honour to state that having regard to the nature of the duty I concur with the Commissioner's recommendation.

In view however of the great expense involved, I submit that some limit should be fixed by the Secretary of State, and having consulted with the Commissioner on the matter, I believe he would be satisfied if the allowance were granted from the date of this application and not retrospectively from the commencement of the duties.

I would therefore suggest that the total extra expenditure for this service should be limited to £300, and when that amount is expended that the subject should be re-considered.

                    I have the honour to be,
                              Sir,
                    Your obedient Servant
                    A.S. [ ].

The international interest in the now infamous series of Whitechapel crimes attracted many people who felt they could cast some light on the identity of the killer. A Spanish contender appeared in early December 1888 and the official file cover[7] reads as follows:

[Stamped: – HOME OFFICE 7 DEC.88 RECd.DEPt.] No. A49301/5
DATE   6 Decr 1888 Foreign Office
REFERENCES, &c.   Whitechapel Murderer
                    Forwards letter and translation from Mr Thomas
                    Romero giving a description of the man whom he
                    believes to be the murderer.
[*There is a marginal note* – "Copy of translation made original letter sent"]
                    MINUTES.
                    ["Confidential & Pressing" – *deleted*]
              Ackn and
                    To Police.

C.M. Decr. 7.
Ackd. & Wrote Comr.
7/12.

There follows a letter[8] from the Foreign Office:

A49301D/5
[Stamped: – HOME OFFICE 7 DEC.88 RECd. DEPt.]

Pressing   Foreign Office,
Confidential   December 6 1888.
Sir,

I am directed by the Secretary of State for Foreign Affairs to transmit to you, herewith, for the information of the Secretary of State for the Home Department the translation of a letter from a Spaniard Mr. Thomas Romero giving the description of a man whom he believes to be the Whitechapel murderer.

I am,

Sir,

Your most obedient,

humble Servant.

T.V. Lister

The

Under Secretary of State
Home Office.

There then follows the translation[9] of the said letter, addressed to the Prime Minister, Lord Salisbury, from the Foreign Office:

[Stamped: – HOME OFFICE 7 DEC.88 RECd. DEPt.]   A49301D/5
Translation   26 Nov: 1888.
My Lord,

With the fear and curiosity inspired by the monstrous crimes now being committed in Whitechapel I am following step by step the horrible tragedies which will not end so long as the miserable assassin is at liberty.

Today I see that the disemboweller of women could not finish his last crime because the cries of the victim brought the police and the public, who did not succeed, notwithstanding their generous efforts, in capturing the assassin.

The woman who thus was able miraculously to escape from what would have been certain death but for such immediate assistance, has, of course, given a detailed description of the murderer, with whom I believe I have been and whom I believe I knew when I was in London in 1885, as a refugee for political offences committed through the columns of the newspaper called

"La Coalicion" of which I was editor. The ferocious man in question told me one day, as the most natural thing in the world, of the means he employed in order to study certain functions of life; they consisted in tearing out the organs of a person who had recently died by violence, I therefore add below the description of that man in order that the victim may be questioned as to whether it agrees with that of the Whitechapel murderer.

Short; hair light chestnut rather than fair; eyes, blue, small, round and deep sunk; moustache, silky and fair; beard very light (he wore English whiskers when I was with him); age somewhere about 35 years; nose, so depressed in the middle as hardly to hold the smoke coloured spectacles which he always wore; one or two teeth were missing in the upper jaw and he spoke English, French, German, Russian and Spanish; he would so readily say he was an American as a German, for he talked of Berlin and of New York as cities that he was very well acquainted with; he once told me, whom he particularly affected among the friends that met together, that he was a German Socialist and once on going to the Natural History Museum at London (I think that is the name of the place at the entrance of which you see the skeleton of a colossal crocodile or some reptile of that family) he told me how, after abandoning himself to the pleasures of Venus, he extracted the uterus of a woman whom he killed in the year 1880 or 1881.

I thought such a man a great impostor and from the day on which he told me of that deed, I took such an aversion to him and he inspired me with extreme repugnance, that I tried to avoid his company and from that day we met but a few times more.

One day he was dining with us at Veglio's, a restaurant in Tottenham Court Road, and told us that we should dine much better and cheaper at an eating house in a little street near Oxford St. where we dined twice and did not return on account of the horrid cook of that tavern or cook-shop.

A girl leading a gay life, called "Nelis Cherinton" who lived somewhere in the City, had supper with this man & myself one night after leaving the Alhambra and as the girl was a little gay owing to her having had a good quantity of whiskey given to her at the bar of the theatre, he said he was going to take her to pay her off for an insult she had offered him, I tried to prevent it but as I did not succeed, I said to him that he should let me take the girl with me and that he could come and fetch her another day and do what he liked with her, that was in November 1885, the girl would remember if the description was given to her and when she meets him she could watch him and if he is the murderer of the women he could be captured when he tried to commit the next murder.

As is right, I wish that all these revelations should be kept absolutely secret, not because I fear the vengeance of that man but because if he did not turn out to be guilty of such barbarous acts, I should be sorry to have called the attention of the police and of the English people to an innocent man by my imprudent revelations.

Therefore if the English Govt. thinks fit to accept my information, they may send somebody and to him I will, with the map of London in my hands, show the places the man I mean used to frequent and if it is necessary in the interests of humanity I myself will go to London and, there, when I meet him I will point him out to the police so that they may watch him and capture him – when he tries to commit another outrage.

If the English Govt. asks any information concerning me of the Spanish Govt., I shall at once refuse absolutely to say one word more about the man I suppose to be the "disemboweller of women", I say I do not want them to ask anybody about me, for Spain would accuse me of want of patriotism if I contributed to the good or to the peace of a people that snatched a bit of her territory from my beloved country, for until it is given back to Spain we must hold the English people to be usurpers ["what" – *deleted*] I wish that what I do for the good of humanity and in obedience to the most noble dictates of my soul which sympathises with a people justly alarmed at harbouring in its bosom without knowing him a man without human feelings, ["I wish to be o" – *deleted*] may be kept such an impenetrable secret that, even in the event of the assassin being discovered, I wish the glory of this good work to fall not on me but on my country whose nobleness and uprightness are proverbial and well known throughout the world.

Let the last victim be asked about the description I have given and if it coincides with that of the ["assassin" – *deleted*] man I suppose to be the assassin, be sure that I myself will cut off the destroying arm which is striking terror into the heart of London.

If they think my help necessary and wish to write to me let them do so in Spanish and address as under: –

Spain

Senor don Tomas Romero

Provincia de Cirdad Real

Herencia.

where they may command your

obedient servant

(s) Tomas Romero

Lord Salisbury

Foreign office.

The final page in this section[10] is a file cover, thus:

Tomas Romero
Nov 26
Dec 6 1888
<u>Whitechapel Murder</u>
Says he knows all
about it
comm'. By the Lord
Mayor Nov. 30.88
H.O.
386   Spain

The Kelly murder had helped boost public interest in the press's reporting of the ongoing series of killings. This press interest was, as we have seen, international. A file[10] dated 14 December 1888, refers to news of another foreign suspect, as follows:

[Stamped: – HOME OFFICE 15 Dec.88 RECd DEPT] No.A49301D/6
DATE 14 Decr 1888   Foreign Office
REFERENCES, &c.   Whitechapel Murders
Forwards copy of a despatch from Dresden as to a statement made by an American German Julius. I. Lowenheim re a Polish Jew Wirtkofsky who he used to meet in a "Christian Home" in Finsbury? Square – as this man told him he was determined to kill a certain woman & the rest of her class –
MINUTES.
<u>Pressing & confidential</u>
Ackn, and to Police
          C.M. Dec. 15. 88.
Ackd & sent Despatch to Police.
          15. 12. 88

The reports under this cover commence:

[Stamped: – HOME OFFICE 15 DEC.88 RECd DEPT] A49301D/6

Foreign Office
December 14 1888.

Sir,
    I am directed by the Secretary of State for Foreign Affairs to transmit to

you, to be laid before the Secretary of State for the Home Department, copy of a Despatch, as marked in the margin, relating to the Whitechapel murders. [*Marginal note:*- Mr. Shackey / No 58. December 11.]

I am,

Sir,

Your most obedient,

humble Servant,

N. Lister

The Under-Secretary of State,

Home Office.

Copy   A49301D

Dresden

11 December 1888

My Lord,

Regarding American German, Julius I. Lowenheim, came here this morning with a statement respecting the Whitechapel murders. He said that shortly before the occurrence of the first crime he became acquainted in a "Christian Home" in Finsbury Square, with a Polish Jew one Julius Wirtkofsky, who, after consul[ting] him on a special pathological con[dition] told him that he was determined to kill the person conc[erned and] all the rest of her cl[ass] informant added, that he had recently addressed the London Police Authorities on the subject, without having received an answer.

He further said that he could throw no light on the subsequent movements of Wirtkofsky, but that he could identify him without fail.

Lowenheim stated that his address, after the next few days would be, Poste Restante Nuremburg. It of course struck me that I had heard a similar [ ] before, and that the youth's object was to accomplish a journey to London, gratis.

However, he showed no anxiety in that respect, and the impression which he made upon me was not unfavourable.

[*signature &c. illegible.*]

Another suspect, Nikaner Benelius, appeared at Worship Street Police Court in November. *The Times* of Monday, 19 November 1888, reported:

At WORSHIP-STREET, shortly before Mr. Bushby left the bench at the close of the day's business, a Swede named NIKANER A. BENELIUS, 27 years of age, and described as a traveller, living in Great Eastern-street, Shoreditch, was placed in the dock charged with entering a dwelling-house in Buxton-street, Mile-end, for an unlawful purpose and with refusing to give any account of himself. The prisoner is a man of decidedly foreign appearance, with a moustache, but otherwise cannot be said to resemble any of the published descriptions of men suspected in connexion with the Whitechapel murders. Detective-sergeant Dew attended from Commercial-street Station, and stated that the prisoner had been arrested that morning under circumstances which made it desirable to have the fullest inquiries made as to him. Before the last murder – of Mary Kelly, in Miller's-court – the prisoner had been arrested by the police and detained in connexion with the Berner-street murder, but was eventually released. He had, however, remained about the neighbourhood, lodging in a German lodging-house, but having, the officer said, no apparent means of subsistence. The landlord said that the prisoner was 25s. in debt to him. Harriet Rowe, a married woman, living in Buxton-street, Mile-end, then deposed that at about 10.30 that morning she had left the street door open, and while sitting in the parlour the prisoner, a stranger to her, opened the door and walked in. She asked him what he wanted, but he only grinned in reply. She was greatly alarmed, being alone, and ran to the window. The prisoner then opened the parlour door and left. She followed him into the street until she saw a constable; but the prisoner first stopped the officer and spoke to him. Witness ran up and told the constable what the prisoner had done, and he was thereupon taken to the station. The police-constable, Imhoff, 211H, said that the prisoner was asking him the way to Fenchurch-street when the witness Rowe ran up. After hearing her complaint he asked the prisoner what he wanted to go to Fenchurch-street for, and the prisoner said he expected some letters at the post-office. The prisoner was searched at the station, but nothing was found on him. In answer to the charge he said he only went into the house to ask his way to Fenchurch-street. Mr. Bushby said he should follow the usual course and remand the prisoner for inquiries. The prisoner was remanded till Friday. Two men, one of whom was stated to be the prisoner's landlord, subsequently called about him and said that he had been preaching in the streets at times and acting of late very strangely.

The Times of Monday, 19 November 1888, reported[12] another suspect:

THE WHITECHAPEL MURDERS.

On Saturday afternoon the police arrested at Euston Station a man who had just arrived from Birmingham, and who described himself as a doctor. Upon being questioned the suspect made certain statements as to his whereabouts at the times of the murders which the police are now investigating. The man was susequently released.

The funeral of the murdered woman Kelly will take place to-day, when her remains will be buried in the Roman Catholic Cemetery at Leytonstone. The hearse will leave the Shoreditch Mortuary at half-past 12.

The Star of the same day reported on this suspect, adding more detail:

WHITECHAPEL.
The London Police Blunder Over a Birmingham Suspect.

Considerable excitement was caused in London yesterday by the circulation of a report that a medical man had been arrested at Euston, upon arrival from Birmingham, on a charge of suspected complicity in the Whitechapel murders. It was stated that the accused had been staying at a common lodging-house in Birmingham since Monday last, and the theory was that if, as was supposed by the police, he was connected with the East-end crimes, he left the metropolis by an early train on the morning of the tragedies. The suspected man was of gentlemanly appearance and manners, and somewhat resembled the description of the person declared by witnesses at the inquest to have been

SEEN IN COMPANY WITH KELLY

Early on the morning that she was murdered. Upon being minutely questioned as to his whereabouts at the time of the murders, the suspect was able to furnish a satisfactory account of himself, and was accordingly liberated. It has since transpired that he has been watched by Birmingham police for the last five days, and when he left that town on Saturday the Metropolitan police were advised to continue to "watch" him, not to arrest him. But, in spite of this warning, the London police seem to have stupidly warned the man that he was suspected.

A *Star* man made a round of the police-stations this morning, and received everywhere the report of a very quiet night. Neither at Commercial-street nor Leman-street was anyone detained. Expectation of another murder being discovered this morning was the only cause of stir, and the detectives were mustered at the stations in readiness for any emergency. Up to twelve o'clock, however, nothing had turned up. Late last night there was some little excitement consequent on the arrest in a Flower and Dean-street tenement house of a young man named Charles Akehurst, of Canterbury-road, Ball's Pond-road, N. He accompanied a woman to her room, and there had the misfortune to make use of expressions which caused her to jump to the conclusion that

SHE WAS IN THE HANDS OF THE MURDERER.

She ran trembling to a policeman, who arrested the man. He satisfied the detective, however, and was released after a short detention. Full inquiries have been made into the movements of the Swede Nikaner A. Benelius, remanded by Mr. Bushby on a charge of being on private premises for an unlawful purpose. Inspector Reid states that the man's innocence of any hand in the murders has been fully established. The man, who has been lodging at a German lodging-house at 90, Great Eastern-street, has been preaching in the streets, and behaving in a manner which suggests that he is not so fully responsible for his actions as he might be. It was therefore thought advisable to make the fullest inquiries, which, however, have quite cleared him. He was arrested on suspicion in connection with the Berners-street [sic] murder, and is likely to be arrested every time the public attention is strained to the point of suspecting every man of odd behaviour. Dorset-street has still its knot of loungers, although it is more than a week since it achieved notoriety.

The *Northern Daily Telegraph* of Friday, 7 December 1888 reported the arrest of someone believed to be an important suspect:

THE LONDON HORRORS.
A BIG THING AT LAST.
ARREST OF A POLISH JEW.

The Metropolitan Police yesterday made a singular arrest, which was reported to be in connection with the Whitechapel murders. It appears that during the afternoon a man, described as a Polish Jew, was arrested near Drury-lane, but for what offence is not quite clear. This individual, who is of short stature, with black moustache, was taken to the Bow-street Station, where he was detained for a time. A telegraphic communication was forwarded thence to Leman-street Police Station, the headquarters of the Whitechapel division, requesting the attendance of one of the inspectors. Detective-inspector Abberline immediately proceeded to Bow-street, and subsequently brought away the prisoner in a cab, which was strongly escorted. The detectives at the East End made every inquiry in the neighbourhood concerning the suspect, who is well known in the locality, although he is stated to have been absent lately. It was subsequently ascertained that the man was apprehended for stealing a watch, with which offence he has been charged. The police, however, were led to believe that he was connected, not with the mutilations, but with the recent attempt to murder a woman in George-street, Spitalfields. Exhaustive inquiries were made, but as far as can be ascertained the man could in no way be connected with that outrage. It is further stated that the inspector was heard to say to one of his subordinates: "Keep this quiet; we have got the right man at last. This is a big thing."

The *London Evening News* of Saturday, 8 December 1888 also reported on the arrest of the suspect, Isaacs:

THE WHITECHAPEL MURDERS.

Joseph Isaacs, 30, who said he had no fixed abode, and described himself as a cigar maker, was charged at Worship-street, yesterday, with having stolen a watch, value 30s., the goods of Julius Levenson.

The prisoner, who was brought up in the custody of Detective-sergeant Record, H Division, is the man who was arrested in Drury-lane on Thursday afternoon on suspicion of being connected with the Whitechapel murders. It transpired during the hearing of this charge that it was committed at the very time the prisoner was being watched as a person "wanted." The prosecutor, Levenson, said that the prisoner entered his shop on the 5th instant, with a violin bow, and asked him to repair it. Whilst discussing the matter, the prisoner bolted out of the shop, and witness missed a gold watch belonging to a customer. The watch had been found at a pawn-shop. To prove that the prisoner was the man who entered the shop, a woman named Mary Cusins was called. She is deputy of a lodging-house in Paternoster-row, Spitalfields, and said that the prisoner had lodged in the house, as a single lodger, for three or four nights before the Dorset-street murder – the murder of Mary Janet [*sic*] Kelly, in Miller's-court. He disappeared after that murder, leaving the violin bow behind. The witness on the house to house inspection gave information to the police, and said she remembered that on the night of the murder she heard the prisoner walk about his room. After her statement a look out was kept for the prisoner, whose appearance certainly answered the published description of a man with an astrachan trimming to his coat. He visited the lodging-house on the 5th, and asked for the violin bow. It was given to him and the witness Cusins followed him to give him into custody as requested. She saw him enter Levenson's shop, and almost immediately run out, no constable being at hand.

Detective Record said that there were some matters alleged against the prisoner, which it was desired to inquire into.

Mr. Bushby remanded the prisoner.

The *Manchester Evening News* of Monday, 10 December 1888 also ran a small piece on the suspect:

THE WHITECHAPEL MURDER.
THE POLISH JEW SUSPECT.

The police are continuing their inquiries into the antecedents of Joseph Isaacs, said to be a Polish Jew, who is now in custody on a charge of watch stealing.

Mary Cusins, the deputy of a lodging-house in Paternoster Row, near Dorset-street, and Cornelius Oakes, a lodger, state that the conduct of the prisoner was frequently strange. Although he had a violin and four or five other musical instruments, he was never known to play any of them. Oakes says the prisoner used often to change his dress. He heard him threaten violence to all women above 17 years of age.

The *Sunday Times* of Sunday, 23 December 1888 reported on yet another unlikely suspect for the Whitechapel murders:

THE WHITECHAPEL MURDERS – A CONFESSION — At Dalston Police-court, yesterday, Theophil Hanhart, 24, lately a French and German master at a school near Bath; was charged with being a person of unsound mind, and with confessing to be the Whitechapel murderer. The prisoner, who, it was said, exactly corresponded in description with the man "wanted" for the Whitechapel murders, was seen on Friday afternoon on the bank of the Regent's Canal at Haggerston. He told a constable that he was the cause of the Whitechapel murders, and he was very uneasy in his mind about it. He was seen by a medical man, who had certified that he was suffering from mental derange-ment, and not fit to be at large. The Rev. W. Mathias said the prisoner had been in his care since Sept. 16, and from that date he had never been out of his sight. A few days ago, finding that he was suffering from delusions he, on medical advice, brought the man to London, but on Thurday afternoon he missed him in the Strand. The prisoner was the son of a German pastor, and the matter had been reported to the German Consul in London. Inspector Reid, from Whitechapel, said he was satisfied that the prisoner could not have committed the murders, but Mr. Bros, being satisfied that the prisoner was not fit to be at large, sent him in a cab to the Shoreditch Infirmary.

CHAPTER 24

Edward Knight Larkins – An Early "Ripper" Theorist

A very early example of an obsessive "Ripper" theorist appeared in November 1888 in the person of Edward Knight Larkins, a clerk in HM Customs Statistical Department. He had applied his intellect and imagination to the problem of the Whitechapel Murders and he was determined that the authorities should take note of – and act upon – his advice. To that end he sent copies of his theory not only to the police but to the QC and magistrate Montagu Williams (who was apparently convinced that Larkins had hit upon the solution of the mystery), and to the London Hospital.

The first of the files regarding Larkins carries a cover[1], thus:

No. A49301C/25

DATE 23 Nov 88	Foreign Office
REFERENCES, &c.	Mr Larkins Theory re arrival of cattle ships from Oporto in connection with Whitechapel murders.

MINUTES.

Pages referred to Commr of Police CID
24/11/88

Enclosures returned from Mr Anderson today and given to Mr Ruggles-Brise [*init. Illeg.*]
31/1/89

This is followed by f 231, a second cover page:

[Stamped: – HOME OFFICE 26 NOV. 88 RECd. DEPt.] No. A49301C/25a

DATE 26 Nov 88	Foreign Office
REFERENCES, &c.	<u>Whitechapel Murders</u>

Forwards copy of despatch from HM Consul at Oporto with a report addressed to the Criminal Investigation dept as to the questions of the arrival of certain ships raised by Mr Larkins

[MINUTES.]

["Secret & immediate" – *deleted*]
To Commr. of Police.
(Forces) CM. Nov 26.88
Sent
26.11

The first report, f 232, is a letter from the Foreign Office to the Under Secretary of State:

Secret.   A49301C/25a
[Stamped: – HOME OFFICE 26 NOV.88 RECd. DEPT]
Foreign Office
November 26 1888

Sir,
    With reference to my letter of the 23rd instant
                I am directed by the Secretary of State for Foreign
    Affairs to transmit to you, to be laid before Mr. Secretary Matthews,
    a copy of a Despatch from H.M. Consul at Oporto, transmitting a
    Report addressed to the Chief of the Criminal Investigation Department
    on the points raised by Mr. Larkins in reference to the Whitechapel
    murders.

I am,
Sir,
Your most obedient,
Humble Servant,
(For Sir J.)

The Under Secretary of State   HG Ber[ ]
    Home Office

There then follows a letter[2] from the Consulate in Oporto, to the Prime Minister, the Marquis of Salisbury:

A49301C

H.M. Consulate
No 8 [Stamped: – HOME OFFICE 26 NOV.88 RECEIVED DEPt.] Oporto
Consular   Nov.22.1888.
My Lord,
    In obedience to Y.L.'s instructions conveyed in telegrams received
yesterday and the day before, I have enquired into the points raised in
Mr. Larkins' letter in reference to the Whitechapel murders, and have
reported directly by telegraph to Scotland Yard. I likewise address U.F.S. to

the Chief of the Criminal Investigation Dept the enclosed full report on the subject.

I [ ]

(sd) Oswald Crawford

The Marquis of Salisbury
" —

The next file cover[3] introduces the full information regarding Mr Larkins and his theory, and is dated 10 January 1889:

[Stamped: – HOME OFFICE 11 JAN.89 RECd. DEPt.] NO. A49301C/25b
DATE 10th Jany 89   Mr. E.K. Larkins Statistics Dept Customs
REFERENCES, &c.   Whitechapel Murders
    Forwards memorandum as to his theory re Cat-
    tlemen from Oporto and states that the "City of
    Cork" is due in a day or two.
    MINUTES.
    ["Pressing & Confidential" – *deleted*]
Ackn: and to Mr Monro.
    CM. Jan 11.89
[Stamped: – REFERRED 11 JAN. 89 ANSr 11]
    If any one of the Boats named had been in
London at the date of each of the murders, this man's
theory wd. be of great practical interest, But his scheme
requires the adoption of the further theory that some
man changed from one boat to another. Hitherto he has
kept to two boats: he now introduces a third. The matter
was referred to the Consul of Oporto, who reported that
no such transfer took place, & that Larkins' theories were
untenable. The most careful inquiry here has led to the
same conclusion. I fear the man is a troublesome
"faddist", & that it is idle to continue the subject with
him. His recent letters are in a tone which renders
further correspondence with him impossible
    RA
        22/1/89
        [Stamped: – HOME OFFICE 23 JAN.89]
    ? Putup
        HBS
        23/1
        GL 23 Jan '89

I see in the newspapers that there is a scare in Spain that the man has got over there & has committed two murders. Whether there is anything in it I do not know. Perhaps the Cattle boat theory has given rise to it.

CM Jan 23.

[*Here there is a marginal note at right angles to this section:- –* "Wrote Mr. Larkins 20 Feb: 1889"]

I regret that Mr Larkins letter was, through misadventure not ackd: as directed on the other side. But see Mr. Anderson's minute above as to discontinuing correspondence.

? Express regret Mr Larkins, thro misadventure did not receive ackt of his letter which [received full consideration – as well as investigation on the part of the Police] CM

[ ] Feb 18th

There then follows the memorandum[4] referred to, from Mr Larkins:

[Stamped: – HOME OFFICE 11 JAN.89 RECd.DEPt.] Memorandum

The theory I have formed is that the murderer is a Portuguese cattle-man who comes over with the cattle, from Oporto, in the vessels belonging to Messrs. Coverley & Westray [?], in all probability he is a middle aged married man, this I judge from his victims being all verging on 50 years of age, had he been a young man I presume he would have selected younger women.

My opinion is that on a voyage previous to the 30th August, this monster contracted a certain disease by coming in contact with one of these unfortunates, being in all probability a married man he became exasperated by finding himself in that condition and with the characteristic revengefulness of the Portuguese race he determined to wage war upon these fallen women.

From inquiries I have made I find these cattle men live in the hold of the vessel, sometimes, remaining below during the whole of the voyage.

The "City of Oporto" came into the London Docks on the 30th August, on the 31st he committed his first murder returning, no doubt, at once to his safe retreat in the hold of the vessel, finding he was not suspected and to baffle any clue that might be obtained he did not return in the "City of Oporto" but shifted onto the "City of Cork" which came into Dock on the 7th Sept and committed his second murder on the 8th Sept, at once returning to his safe quarters in the hold of the "City of Cork" and returning in that vessel to Oporto, on the 27th September he again came to this country in the "City of Cork" and probably, on inquiry, finding no clue had been obtained he committed the double murder on the 30th Sept. again returning hastily to his safe quarters in the hold of the "City of Cork" and returned to Oporto in that vessel, fearing from the outcry that was raised by this double atrocity that some possible clue might have been obtained, he probably did not venture over in the "City of Cork" on the voyage which terminated here on the 19th October, but finding none had been obtained, he again came over in the "City of Cork" on the 8th November and committed another murder on the 9th of that month.

I gave information of the movements of these vessels and the suspicions which I entertained on the 10th November, from which time or soon after these vessels have been watched incessantly, whenever in the Docks, which I have no doubt has been observed by this monster, the result being that <u>no murder</u> of the kind has since taken place.

EKLarkins

There then follows a seven-page report[5] from Larkins regarding his actions and theory:

[Stamped: – HOME OFFICE 11 JAN.89 RECd. DEPt.]

On the 10th November, after considerable research with regard to the dates, I called upon Inspector Moore at Leman Street Police Station and communicated to him the result, with reference to the following vessels.

Ship	Date and time of arrival in London Docks	Date of Murder
"City of Oporto"	August 30th–7P.M.	August 31st.
"City of Cork"	September 7th 2P.M.	September 8th.
"	" 27th 4P.M.	" 30th.
"	November 8th 2.30P.M.	November 9th.

On the 12th I again saw Inspector Moore and communicated the fact that the crews of these vessels with the exception of the Officers, were all <u>Portuguese</u> and that the <u>cattle-men</u> who came over with the cattle from Oporto, were also Portuguese, this fact greatly confirmed my suspicions, knowing their revengeful character.

On the 13th November I called upon Mr. A.F. Williamson at the Criminal Investigation Department and at his special request Inspector Swanson again took down the statement I had previously made to Inspector Moore.

To my great astonishment on the 16th I found the "City of Cork" had been allowed to proceed to sea on the 15th without any arrest having been made, there was not a moment to be lost, as I knew it would take <u>three</u> days for a letter to reach Oporto and these vessels take only <u>four</u> so I hastily penned a letter to the British Consul at Oporto stating my suspicions of these cattle-men and requesting him to put himself in communication with the police at

Oporto to note these men when they arrived, on the 17th I sent him a further communication requesting information, as early as possible whether the same men were returning to London in the "City of Cork" as on the previous voyage, on the 19th I had an interview with S. Montagu, Esq, M.P. to suggest that the Under Secretary for Foreign Affairs should be asked to telegraph to the Consul at Oporto to make every inquiry with regard to my letter, I received a letter from S. Montagu, Esq, on the 20th stating the Under Secretary had acceded to my request: (I am unable to give you a copy of these letters to the Consul as Mr. Montagu left them with the Under Secretary for Foreign Affairs.)

On the 22nd I wrote to Mr. A.F. Williamson as follows,

"If the inquiries made by your Department are correct that *no man who served on board the "City of Oporto" up to the 31st August is now serving on board the "City of Cork," it shows, very clearly, that instead of one individual being engaged in these terrible atrocities there are others equally guilty: there is no getting over these facts, that upon every occasion when these tragedies have taken place either the "City of Oporto" or the "City of Cork" has been in the London Docks."

[*Here there is a note at the bottom of the page*: – "*This refers to the crew only and not to the cattle-men"]

"The revengeful character of the Portuguese is a matter of history, in fact the mutilations, which have taken place in Whitechapel, are of the same terrible character as recorded in the history of the Peninsular War where it is stated that the Spanish and Portuguese peasantry armed with the terrible knives which they are in the habit of carrying and which they use on the slightest provocation, fell upon the stragglers of the French army and after cutting their throats, disembowelled them and subjected their bodies to other indignities with the ferocity of savages.

"These ships when in London Docks should be watched incessantly, day and night, and the movements of every man connected with them, who leaves the ship should be closely watched.

"Both these vessels are due, in the London Docks next week"

On the 26th November I addressed a further letter to Mr. A.F. Willamson,

"On the arrival of any vessel in the Docks it is boarded and rummaged by Customs Officers (generally very experienced men) when every nook and corner is thoroughly examined, after an interval, at the discretion of the Officer in charge of the Station, the vessel is re-rummaged by another distinct set of Officers. I would suggest in the event of any other murder taking place, immediately it becomes known, these vessels should be thoroughly re-rummaged by the Customs rummagers who should be secretly instructed as to looking for blood stained clothes and knives. No suspicion need be excited if these men were employed as it would naturally be supposed, by those on board, they were looking for contraband goods, as the Officers are enjoined to frequently rummage vessels on their station.''

On the 3rd December I again wrote to Mr. A.F. Williamson, as follows,

''Have any steps been taken to ascertain if the same crews and cattle-men are on board the 'City of Oporto' and the 'City of Cork' as on the voyages immediately preceding this? I would suggest this information should be obtained, in future, directly these vessels arrive, any change to be specially noted''

The following letter I left with Inspector Swanson on the 8th December to be laid before the Commissioner of Police, upon the distinct understanding that I should be informed whether my suggestion would be carried out or not.

''I wish to direct attention to the probability of a change of vessels arriving from Oporto during this month and would suggest that all vessels belonging to Messrs. Coverley & Westray should be closely watched, last December, in addition to the 'City of Oporto' and the 'City of Cork', the 'City of Malaga' came from Oporto with cattle.

The next step to be taken in this matter is to obtain a list of the cattle-men who come over in these vessels, which will necessitate some rather minute inquiry being made and if carried out in the manner I propose there ought to be no difficulty in bringing the matter home to the guilty party. It is very evident whoever the murderer may be, he is no stranger to that part of London, to be able to get away from the scenes of his crimes without exciting suspicion, shews that very clearly.

I therefore propose to obtain a list of the cattle-men who were on board the following vessels.

"City of Cork"	5th December	<u>1887</u>
"City of Oporto"	14th "	"
"City of Malaga"	27th "	"

it might perhaps be necessary to go further back than that, but that will answer my purpose for the present, another list of those on board the following vessels will also be required,

"City of Oporto"	8th August	1888
"	30th "	"
"	19th September	"
"	15th October	"
"City of Cork"	6th September	"
"	27th "	"
"	19th October	"
"	9th November	"

With regard to these cattle-men it is very probable that Messrs. Coverley & Westray would not be able to give a correct list, as I have every reason to believe these cattle-men are not in their employ, nor do I think any assistance could be obtained from the Captains as from inquiries I have made, with reference to the cattle trade, I find there is a very loose supervision, <u>if any</u>, over these men and then again under the Merchant Shipping Act a written declaration of the number of Aliens on board has to be made by the Captain, under a penalty of £20, so that any lapse in that direction is not likely to be admitted by him.

The cattle by these boats are consigned to Messrs. Hope & Harrington, 60 Queen Victoria Street and Messrs. Palgrave, Murphy & Co. 155 Fenchurch Street, they would, of course, be able to give the names of the firms in Oporto who had consigned the cattle to them and I understand these men are paid when they return to Oporto, there ought to be no difficulty, <u>once the paymaster is found</u>, in tracing the names of these men. It appears to me that it will be necessary to send some astute officer to Oporto to make these inquiries, I do not think it can be satisfactorily carried out by correspondence"

Not having received any reply to the above paper, I wrote to Inspector Swanson, as follows,

"Will you please inform me if anything has been done with regard to the suggestion I made on Saturday?"

Being still without any reply, on the 7th January I addressed the following letter to the Commissioner of Police,

"On the 8th December I left a further communication with Inspector Swanson, respecting the Whitechapel tragedies, to be laid before you, on the distinct understanding that your decision was to be communicated to me, as in the event of your deciding to send an officer to Oporto I wished to furnish further particulars, on the 12th December not having received any communication with regard to my suggestion, I wrote reminding Inspector Swanson, but even to that no reply has been given.

I am quite certain that the information I have given if followed up in an <u>intelligent</u> manner would lead to its being brought home to one particular individual & if your subordinates are incapable of doing it, it will be done by others.

Had I thought it possible the police would have acted in the manner they have done, I should have taken other steps and the "City of Cork" would certainly not have sailed from this country on the 15th November without the murderer having been arrested, as the information I gave was the day following the murder of the 9th November and had that vessel been thoroughly searched, at once, it would I feel convinced have been with satisfactory results."

E.K.Larkins

There then follows a further file cover[6] dated 9 March 1889, with reference to Larkins:

[Stamped: – HOME OFFICE 9 MAR.89 DEP No.] No. A49301C/28
DATE 9 March 89   Mr. E.K. Larkins
REFERENCES, &c.   Submits copy of Memorandum which he
has forwarded to the Asst Commr. of Police
shewing the result of further investigations into
the Whitechapel Murders –
MINUTES.
?Ackn: and putup.
HBS
12.3.89
ELP. 13 March 89.
Ackd. 13/3.

This is followed by a note[7] from Larkins:

[Stamped: – HOME OFFICE 9 MAR.89DEPt No]   A49301C/28
Statistical Department,
Custom House, E.C.
March 9th 1889,
Sir,
    I beg to enclose a copy of memorandum A, which I have this day
forwarded to the Assistant Commissioner of Police, shewing the result
of further investigations I have made respecting the Whitechapel
murders,
                    I have the honour to be,
                        Sir
                Your obedient Servant,
                    EK Larkins
The Right Honble
    The Home Secretary.

There then follows the memorandum[8] referred to, which is badly
damaged at the right hand margin with resulting loss of text:

                    Memorandum   A49301[C]/28
    [Stamped: – HOME OFFICE 9 MAR.89 DEPt No]
    I have made further enquiries into the subject [of] the Whitechapel
tragedies and they confirm in ev[ery] way, the views I have already expressed

to the previous description of the voyages of the suspected vessels I have added the time of their departure from London.

Ship	Date and hour Of arrival in London Docks	Date of murder	Departure from London
"City of Oporto"	August 30th 7P.M.	August 31st	September 4th
"City of Cork"	September 7th 2 "	September 8th	" [ ]
"	" 27th 4 "	" 30th	October 2nd [ ]
	November 8th 2.30 "	November 9th	November [ ]

The conclusions at which I have arrived, as the result of my investigations are that there are two murderers concerned in these horrible tragedies but not acc[ ] the first murder I assume was committed by [a man] out of revenge, those which followed were committed [by] another man in a spirit of devilry.

The cattlemen, who were in this country on board these [ships] when these murders took place were Manuel Cruz Xavier and Jose Laurenco.

Manuel Cruz Xavier signed articles at Oporto on the [ ] August and came over in the "City of Oporto" upon the [voyage] which terminated here on 30th August, returning to Oporto in that vessel, where he was discharged on the [ ] September, so that it is impossible for him to have [been] concerned in the murders which followed the one of [the] 31st August, as, whether fearful of being found out, [he did] not rejoin the "City of Oporto" until the 8th October and [was] paid off in London on the 19th November (The "City of Op[orto"] left London on the 6th November.

With regard to Jose Laurenco he joined the "City of Cork" at Oporto on the 31st August arriving here on the 7th September, the day previous to the murder on the 8th returning in the sa[me] vessel to Oporto where he was discharged on the 20th September. Rather unusual for a cattleman he joined the same vessel for the return voyage arriving on the 27th September so was here when the double murder occurred on the 30th September returning again to Oporto in the "City of Cork." When the time arrived for the return of that vessel on the 13th October Jose Laurenco, who was engaged for the voyage, failed to join the ship, no doubt, to some extent, terror stricken, at the prospect of being discovered.

Since then he does not appear by the ship's articles, either of the "City of Cork" or the "City of Oporto" to have come to this country, but I am of opinion, notwithstanding that, he did come over in the "City of Cork" on the voyage which terminated here on the 8th November, the day previous to the murder of the 9th probably as a stowaway (as the "City of Cork" did not bring any cattle this voyage), Jose Laurenco having made two voyages in this ship, besides being an old hand in the trade, would necessarily be well acquainted with the crew of the "City of Cork" so that he would not experience any of the difficulties stowaways usually meet with

I would add with regard to Jose Laurenco that whereas <u>all</u> others on board are marked Ability V.G. Conduct V.G. he is marked as G and G. also that previous to being in the Oporto trade he appears to have served on board the "Olga" of Dublin which vessel is engaged in the cattle trade between Newcastle and Denmark. March 8th 1889   EK Larkins

The next file cover[9] concerning Larkins encloses a printed version of his theory and is as follows:

[Stamped: – HOME OFFICE 10 Feb: 92 RECEIVED] No. A49301C/31
DATE. 10 Feb 92   Mr. E.K. Larkins.
REFERENCES, &c.   Whitechapel Murders
                                Fd's print of his final papers on the subject – pointing
                                to Portuguese cattlemen as the authors of the out-
                                rages.
                                        MINUTES.
                        Ackd.
                            See /28 & /25b
                                ? Layby
                                W.P.B.   CM 12
                                11 Feby 2

The printed and final version of Larkins' theory[10] then follows:

[Stamped: – HOME OFFICE 10 FEB.92 RECEIVED]
                                        A493301C/31
WHITECHAPEL MURDERS, 1888–9.

This statement refers to what are known as the "Ripper" murders. The first of this series occurred on the 1st September, 1888, [*sic*] and the last on the 17th July, 1889. These murders are six in number.

THE CONSPIRACY TO MURDER UNMASKED.
STORMING OF OPORTO BY THE FRENCH, 1809.

"In one of the principal squares they found several of their comrades who had been made prisoners, fastened upright and living, but with their eyes burst, their tongues torn out, and their bodies mutilated and gashed.* Those who beheld the sight spared none of those who fell in their way."

*These atrocities were committed by the Portuguese.-NAPIER'S "PE-NINSULAR WAR."

The following will show that in deeds of blood their sons differ in no way from their forefathers:-

On 30th August, 1888, at 7 p.m., the "City of Oporto" entered the London Docks, having on board Manuel Cruz Xavier, age 37, a Portuguese cattleman. On the morning of the 1st September[sic], Mrs. Nicholls [sic] was found murdered; this man was again here on the 19th September, and again on the 15th October. Whether the hue and cry which was raised after the double murder acted as a deterrent, this fact is clear, he returned to Oporto, and has not been over since. He is now employed as a lighterman at Oporto.

I have traced this man's movements from the time of the first murder, and they prove conclusively that he has never been here when any of the other murders have taken place.

On the 7th September, 1888, at 2 p.m., the "City of Cork" entered the London Docks, having on board Joao de Souza Machado (aged 41), and Jose Laurenco (aged 26), both Portuguese cattlemen. On the 8th September Annie Chapman was found murdered.

On the 27th September, 1888, at 4 p.m., the "City of Cork" entered the London Docks, again having on board Joao de Souza Machado (aged 41), and Jose Laurenco (aged 26), both Portuguese cattlemen. On the 30th September Elizabeth Stride and Mrs. Eddowes were found murdered.

On the 19th October, 1888, the "City of Cork" entered the London Docks, having on board Joao de Souza Machado (aged 41), *no longer a cattleman, but as* A.B. Jose Laurenco had *disappeared*. The log book of the "City of Cork" explains this. It says: "13/10/88. Jose Laurenco, cattleman, deserted from ship, and did not appear up to the time of ship sailing." The cattleman who took his place on this voyage says he was working in a stevedore's gang and that Jose Laurenco induced him to change places with him. From that time Laurenco does not appear to have come over. No murder took place during the month of October.

On the 8th November, 1888, at 2.30 p.m., the "City of Cork" entered the London Docks, having on board Joao de Souza Machado (aged 41), now, as on the previous voyage, *an A.B.* Early the following morning Mary Jane Kelly was found murdered, with unheard of brutality. This man, Machado, is a most experienced cattleman, having made several voyages to this country in that capacity previous to these murders, and being a man of mature age, the *sang froid* displayed upon the occasion of this murder is easily accounted for.

This man's coolness seems to have stood him in good stead, as, in order to avoid any suspicion, he continued to come over until the month of March, 1889, upon one occasion as *Quartermaster*, in fact, *in any capacity but his rightful one as Cattleman.*

After this murder, I gave information to the police, on the 10th November, that *when the "City of Oporto" or the "City of Cork" were in, then, and then only, did these murders take place*, that I was certain it was the cattlemen who were on board these vessels. I informed them on the 12th November that these men were Portuguese, and that that made me more confident than ever that they were the men.

Although the police were at this time watching the arrival of cattle boats, they were not aware these vessels carried cattle until I gave them the information.

Immediately after I had given them the information, the "City of Cork" was closely watched, but allowed to proceed to sea on the 14th November without *any arrest* being made. As soon as these vessels were watched the outrages *ceased*.

Although these vessels have made many voyages since then, no outrage has taken place when either of the vessels have been here.

On the 17th July, 1889, Alice McKenzie was murdered. This was evidently an attempt at renewing these outrages. At that time there were two vessels here from Oporto, the "Petrel" and the "Grebe," each having a Portuguese cattleman on board. Joachim da Rocha (aged 23), who was on board the "Grebe," lying at Fresh Wharf, was formerly a seaman in the "City of Oporto," at the time Xavier and Laurenco were in the habit of coming over in that vessel.

Notwitstanding my urgent request that these men should be detained to be seen by the police who were on duty in the neighbourhood of the murder, they were allowed to return to Oporto. Rocha is now employed there as a stevedore.

"JACK THE RIPPER."

I felt quite satisfied when the letters, signed "Jack the Ripper," commenced to appear, that they were not the work of those who were committing these atrocities; and I formed a pretty shrewd guess as to where their author might be found.

When, in October, 1890, there was a renewal of these cowardly missives, I wended my way to——.

Having stated my errand, and the part I had taken in reference to these outrages, I was most courteously received, in marked contrast to the dog-in-the-manger policy pursued by the police; and every facility was placed at my disposal.

Having, sometime previously, been furnished with a fac-simile of the original letter of "Jack the Ripper," I compared it with the handwriting of a certain individual, and I knew at once that I had fixed my man; I asked what was known about him. The reply was, "As you have fixed upon him, I may say he is not one of the men who has been shadowed by the police." (Mr. R. Anderson and several of the police had already been there, and some of the men had been "shadowed"); "but he is capable of anything, in fact, I should not be surprised at anything he did; he has only lately returned to his duties, having been away for some time on the plea of illness." So there is this plain fact, that directly he returned to his duties, he began his old game of terrorising the inhabitants of the district.

The handwriting of these missives has been characterised as "legal." This man's father is in the legal profession.

I consulted a magistrate, and by his advice went to the authorities of Scotland Yard. What the police have done since I cannot tell; he may have been "shadowed;" he has *not* been arrested; but these cruel missives have *ceased*, and the infamous person who wrote them is still allowed to be at large.

There then follows a plan[11] of the London Docks with the "City of Cork" in her berth. See plan at [. . .]

The next page is a list[12] of the murders, descriptions circulated, and Larkins's descriptions of his suspects:

PRIVATE, CONFIDENTIAL
                    INFORMATION.

Date and locality.	Description Circulated.	Description of cattlemen who were here when the murders took place.

1888
September 1–
BUCK'S ROW.

MANUEL CRUZ XAVIER
Age 37. A short man, black
Hair. Now employed as a
Boatman at Oporto.

September 8–
HANBURY ST.

Age 37. Height 5 ft. 7 in.
Rather dark beard and
Moustache. Dress: shirt
Dark jacket, dark vest
and Trousers, black scarf
and black felt hat. Spoke
with a foreign accent.
In addition to the above
Description. He was a
foreigner of dark
complexion, over 40
years of age, a little taller
than the deceased, of
shabby genteel appearance,
with a brown deerstalker
on his head and a dark
coat on his back.

JOAO DE SOUZA MACHADO
Age 41. Middle height, black
moustache. Now a bathing man
and oarsman at Oporto.

September 30–
BERNER STREET

Age about 28. No
whiskers. Height about
5 ft. 7 in. Complexion
dark. Had on a hard felt
deerstalker hat of dark
colour and dark clothes,
had on an overcoat, dark
trousers.

JOSE LAURENCO.
Age 26. He is a dark young
fellow. Now employed as a
boatman at Oporto.

September 30–
MITRE-SQUARE.

Age 30 to 35. Height 5 ft.
7 in., with brown hair
and big moustache,
dressed respectably.
Wore a pea jacket, muffler
and a cloth cap with a peak
of the same material.

JOAO DE SOUZA MACHADO
Age 41. Middle height, black
moustache. Now a bathing man
and oarsman at Oporto.

November 9–
DORSET STREET

Age 34 or 35. Height

JOAO DE SOUZA MACHADO
Age 41. Middle height, black

about 5 ft. 6 in., dark complexion and dark moustache, turned up at the ends. He was wearing a long dark coat trimmed with astrachan. Looked like a foreigner. He had on a soft felt hat, drawn down some- what over his eyes.

moustache. Now a bathing man and oarsman at Oporto.

1889.
July 17–
CASTLE-ALLEY.

J. DA ROCHA,
Age 23. Is rather short, fair, with light beard. Now captain of a small tug at Oporto.

NOTE. –MACHADO is evidently a man whose age it is rather difficult to tell from observation, as my correspondent at Oporto states he is now (in 1891) about 40 years of age, whereas he is 44.

The following page[13] is a continuation of details on the suspects:

PRIVATE, CONFIDENTIAL
THE ORDER IN WHICH THESE MEN CAME OVER.

SIGNED ON AT OPORTO.	SHIP.	MEN. OCCUPATION.	SIGNED OFF AT OPORTO.
1888.			1888.
July 9	City of Cork	MACHADO Cattleman	July 20
" 20	City of Cork	MACHADO " and XAVIER	August 9
August 2	City of Oporto	LAURENCO " (*paid off in London*)	" 9
" 10	City of Cork	*Neither of these men came over on this voyage.*	
" 23	*City of Oporto	XAVIER "	September 13
" 31	*City of Cork	MACHADO and " LAURENCO	" 20
September 13	City of Oporto	XAVIER "	October 8
" 20	*City of Cork	MACHADO and "	" 13

		LAURENCO (LAURENCO'S last voyage. *Deserted* at Oporto, Oct. 13)	
October 8	City of Oporto	XAVIER. (*his last voyage*.)	PAID OFF IN LONDON 19
" 13	City of Cork	MACHADO	A.B. November 2
November 2	*City of Cork	MACHADO	" " 23
" 23	City of Cork	MACHADO	" December 13 1889
December 13 1889	City of Cork	MACHADO	" January 11
January 11	City of Cork	MACHADO	" February 1
February 1	City of Cork	MACHADO. (*His last voyage*) March 8	

*NOTE.-Voyages when the murders were committed.

There is a letter[14] from Larkins to the Home Secretary [out of order in the files but no doubt taken out of the earlier file for reference] dated 10 January 1889:

> Statistical Department,
> Custom House, E.C.
>
> [Stamped: – HOME OFFICE 11 JAN.89 RECd. DEPt.]   10th January, 1889,
>
> Sir,
>
> I beg to enclose a memorandum I have drawn up on the subject of the Whitechapel murders, also a "resume" of the steps I have taken.
>
> The "City of Cork" is due in a day or two, when, if the police have carried out my suggestion in obtaining a list of these cattle-men every voyage, they will be able to ascertain if the same men are on board as were on board at the date of the last murder, on the 9th November, had the "City of Cork" been searched immediately after the information I gave, on the 10th November, it is probable that the knife and blood stained garments might have been found and had these men been taken into custody on suspicion it is extremely probable that one of them might have been identified as having been seen in the neighbourhood where the murder took place.
>
> It is not too late even now for them to be taken into custody and probably one would be identified. I think it is very possible the clothes might also be found as these men belong to the poorest class and would be quite unable to be continually purchasing fresh clothing.

I have the honour to be,
                    Sir,
          Your obedient Servant,
                    EKLarkins

The Right Honble.
     The Home Secretary.

There is then a page of notes[15] with the letter, as follows:

Whitechapel Murders
Mr Darling calls see me at <u>HO</u> Feb 12–89.
& inquiries as below: A
     Larkins   Jan 10.
          Pepys Road –
          Brockley
Mr Darling says that a constituent of his, named as above, sent suggestions to
the HO on Jan 10th 89) as to the identity of "Jack the Ripper", and "has
never heard anything since."
     Was his letter even ackd.?
                    CWS:[?] Feb 12 89
Add this to official papers, as an inquiry by Mr. Darling, M.P.

There then follows an accompanying letter[16] (to the 1892 correspondence) from Larkins to the Home Secretary:

[Stamped: – HOME OFFICE 10 FEB.92 RECEIVED]   A49301C/31
                              Statistical Department,
                              Custom House, E.C.
                              Feb. 10, 1892,
Sir,
I have the honour to enclose my final paper on the subject of the Whitechapel
tragedies,
                    I am,
                         Sir,
               Your obedt. Servant,
                    EKLarkins

The Rt. Honble.
     The Home Secretary

A further file cover[17] follows:

[Stamped: – Home Office 7 FEB. 93] No. A49301C/34

DATE. 6th Feb.'93   Asst. Commr. C.I.D.

REFERENCES, &c.   Whitechapel Murders.

        States that Mr. E.K. Larkins is a troublesome busybody whose vagaries on the subject of the Whitechapel Murders have cost the C.I.D., the Public Prosecutor, & the Foreign Office, a great deal of useless trouble, & that it is a mere waste of time attempting to deal with him on the subject.

 1/33 Refers to A49301C/25b.

       MINUTES.

    See u/25, u/28, u/31

      ? Layby

       MD

See especially/25 9.2.93

Mr.L. has had an   C.M.9.

ackt.

  ELP. 10 Feby 93.

There then follows a typed letter[18] from Dr Robert Anderson, AC CID, to the Home Office:

           A49301C/34

[Reference] 57885/821 [Stamped: – HOME OFFICE 7 Feb.93 DEPt. No.]

Scotland Yard,

           London, S.W.

          6th February 1893.

From THE ASSISTANT COMMISSIONER OF POLICE,

   CRIMINAL INVESTIGATION DEPARTMENT.

To the Under Secretary of State,

    Home Office.

Sir,

 In returning the enclosures which accompanied your letter of the 1st instant I have to acquaint you for the information of the Secretary of State that Mr E.K.Larkins is a troublesome busybody whose vagaries on the subject of the Whitechapel Murders have cost this Department, the Public Prosecutor and the Foreign Office a great deal of useless trouble. His theories have been tested and they have proved untenable and worthless, and it is a mere waste of time attempting to deal with him on the subject.

 I have refused latterly to acknowledge his letters, hence his strictures upon my Department.

I beg to refer to Home Office file No.A.49301C/25. on this subject.

I am,

Sir,

Your obedient Servant,

R. Anderson

The final file cover[19] concerning Larkins is dated 26 January 1893:

[Stamped: – HOME OFFICE 28 JAN.93 RECEIVED] No. A49301C/33

DATE. 26 Jan. 1893   Mr. E.K. Larkins, of the Statistical Dept. Customs
House.

REFERENCES, &c.   Whitechapel Murders.
Fds papers on the subject of the Whitechapel
tragedies. Charges the head of the Criminal Investigation Dept. that he has connived at the escape of these
men & that he has prevented the men being brought to
justice. Requests S.ofS's attention to the matter.
MINUTES.

? ACO &
To Mr. Anderson.
F.V.O.[?]
31. Jan. 93
C.M. 31.
Ackn? & wrote)
Mr. Anderson)1/2/93
[ ]6.2.93 (1/34)

This is followed by a Larkins letter[20], dated 26 January 1893, to H.H.
Asquith, QC, MP:

[Stamped: – HOME OFFICE 28 JAN.93 RECEIVED] A49301C/33

Statistical Department,

Custom House, E.C.

January 26, 1893.

Sir,

I respectfully submit, for your consideration, the enclosed papers on the
subject of the Whitechapel tragedies.

I have consulted both the magistrates at Worship Street Police Court,
Mr. Bushby said, "It is the duty of the Commissioner of Police to follow
up these men, it is a serious matter, but I have no control over the
police."

They have not been followed up. The late Mr. Montagu Williams, Q.C,
assured me repeatedly that he had no doubt whatever as to the correctness of

my views on this subject and was most indignant at the conduct of the police authorities.

I distinctly charge the head of the Criminal Investigation Department that he has deliberately connived at the escape of these men that he has deliberately thrown every obstacle in the way of their being brought to justice.

I therefore appeal to you, Sir, in the name of our common humanity, if not upon higher grounds, that you will not suffer this official or any combination of officials, whatever their position may be, any longer to defeat the ends of justice.

I have the honour to be,
      Sir,
Your most obedient Servant,
      EKLarkins
The Right Honble
    H.H. Asquith, Q.C, M.P.

There is then included a printed extract[21] from the book *Later Leaves* by Montagu Williams, QC, page 398, outlining Williams's meeting with Larkins and his belief in his theory, stamped as received at the Home Office on 28 Jan.93. Also enclosed in this file is a further copy[22] of Larkins's printed papers (as already reproduced).

There is a printed and bound copy of Larkins's papers in the London Hospital that provides the researcher with an interesting historical insight into the sort of contemporary theorizing that was taking place.

CHAPTER 25

December 1888 – An American View

The idea that the murderer of Stride might not have been one and the same person as Eddowes's killer is not a new one. Indeed, Stride was dismissed as a "Ripper" victim by William Stewart in his 1939 book *Jack the Ripper – A New Theory*. But he most certainly was not the first to propose this idea publicly: it is possible to go back to 1888 to find such a public reference. Indeed, if the sources stated in the piece are correct, the City of London Police themselves may have held this view. Included in the MEPO 3/140 files is a press cutting[1] which is an extract from the *Philadelphia Times* of 3 December 1888:

THE WHITECHAPEL MURDERS
STARTLING THEORY OF THE CITY OF
LONDON DETECTIVES.
NOT ONE MAN'S WORK
Probably a Conspiracy to Murder
Unfortunates Conceived by Reli-
gious Monomaniacs.

SPECIAL CABLE TELEGRAM TO THE TIMES.
LONDON, December 2. – I have ascertained that the police have for some time past been working on a clue on which a more than plausible theory explanatory of the motive for the commission of the Whitechapel horrors has been built up. The city police are entitled to the credit of whatever results may eventuate from their discovery, but hitherto they have been exceedingly reticent as to the result of their investigations. To-day, however, I gathered the following details of the lines they are working on from a thoroughly reliable source.

The City of London detectives first came into the case with full authority on September 30, shortly before one o'clock in the morning of which day Elizabeth Stride was murdered outside the Socialist Club in Berners [sic] street, and Catharine Beddowes [sic] was butchered in Mitre Square. Previous to this date the pursuit of the Whitechapel fiend had been directed by the

Scotland Yard authorities, they being in control of the Metropolitan as distinct from the city police. The woman Beddowes, however, whose body was found in Mitre Square, having been slain within the city limits, the control of the investigation devolved upon the authorities in the old Jewry, the headquarters of the city detective force. The city Vidocqs are, taken as a body, a far more intellectual class of men than their bretheren of Scotland Yard.

THE POLICE AT WORK.

The ablest officers were detailed to work up the case, but the fullest investigation of the meagre facts at their disposal failed to lead to the apprehension of the murderer. They however arrived at a conclusion which, if correct, tends to explode the almost universally-held theory that these horrible crimes are all the work of a single miscreant. Carefully calculating the time it would take to cover the ground between Berners street and Mitre Square and having approximately fixed the hour at which each murder was committed they were forced to the conclusion that if the same man murdered both the women Catherine Beddowes must have met him by appointment in Mitre Square, as the supposition that he found her in this unfrequented place at the exact moment he desired was clearly untenable. It must be borne in mind that the saloons in London all close promptly at 12.30 A.M. The unhappy women of the class to which Elizabeth Stride and Catharine Beddowes belonged find the only field for obtaining their wretched means of livelihood, after the drinking places have closed, among the crowds of half-drunken men who throng the leading thoroughfares of the district.

It is obvious, then, that at 1 P.M. [*sic*] the woman Stride [*sic? – Eddowes*] would not have been parading the silent Mitre Square, wholly unfrequented after dark, unless she was waiting there for some one. On the other hand if the murderer of Elizabeth Stride in Berners street had not been interrupted in his ghastly work, judging by the mutilation practiced in the other cases, he would have spent at least another quarter of an hour at his devilish work. Admitting this, he would then have been too late to keep his appointment with Beddowes, and it is only on the supposition that such an appointment had been made, and that the woman went there to meet the murderer, that the theory of the two murders having been committed by the same hand will hold water.

TWO MURDERERS.

The city detectives then early in the first week of October came to a definite conclusion, namely, that the two women met their death at the hands of different men. It was but taking a single step to further conclude that these two men were acting in collusion. The long interval that had elapsed between this and the previous butchery, the fact that the women belonged to the same class and the coincidence that the killing was done within the same thirty-five minutes all pointed to the same conclusion – that the murders had been deliberately planned, probably to be consummated at the same moment for if even a couple of hours had elapsed between the two crimes the neighbourhood would in the discovery of the first, have become so "hot" that the perpetrator of the second outrage would have found the matter of his escape rendered doubly difficult.

The two brainy men who thus theorised, although they firmly believed they had at last opened the case, were still at a loss in what direction to look for the authors of the fearful crimes. With the utmost patience they sought out the degraded companions of the dead women, and bit by bit they learned all that probably ever will be known of their habits, tastes and mode of life.

A WOMAN'S STORY.

After a week or more of this dreary work they struck a woman whose half drunken babbling seemed to suggest a possible clue to the unraveling of the secret they were so industriously working at. This woman had known Beddowes intimately, and only about a week before the day she met her death poor Catharine had in a fit of maudlin confidence told this companion that she meditated going into a reformatory. She had, she said, on the previous night got into conversation with a stranger, who had, as she put it, tried to convert her, and earnestly begged her to discontinue her mode of life. He had worked on the woman's feelings by drawing a fearful picture of the hereafter staring her in the face if she should be suddenly cut off in her life of sin and shame. On his leaving her she pleaded poverty as an excuse for her sinful mode of life, and he thereupon gave her five shillings, telling her to meet him again in a week's time, adding that if in the meantime she would give up her evil ways and decide to go into a home he would use his influence to get her into one. The woman could not fix the exact date on which Beddowes made this statement to her, but thought it was about a week before the woman was killed. At eleven o'clock on the night of Thursday, the day before the murder, she saw Catharine and took a drink with her. Beddowes was then much the worse for liquor. She left her shortly after that hour, saying she was going to meet a friend. She was never seen again alive, but less than two hours later her mutilated body was found lying in Mitre Square.

LOOKING FOR THE MAN.

The detectives had no reason to doubt this story and every effort by advertisements and handbills was made to discover the man who had talked with Catharine Beddowes a week before the murder and given her five shillings. Up to the present the personality of the man remains shrouded in mystery. The detectives argued that if he was innocent in intent he would at once have come forward, most people would be inclined to agree with them.

Having got thus far, the detectives had a consultation with George Lewis, the great criminal lawyer, of Ely Place, Holborn. They went to him because it was well known that he had from the first held the theory that the murders were the work of a religious mono-maniac, and the slender clue they had picked up seemed to point in that direcetion. No man has had so wide a criminal experience as George Lewis. He has been in every great murder case for the last twenty years and his father before him enjoyed the largest criminal practice in England. From a careful and exhaustive consideration of the facts laid before him by the city detectives, Mr. Lewis is understood to have deduced the following conclusions:

Positive-First. That the murders of Elizabeth Stride and Catharine Beddowes were not committed by one and the same person. Second. That the two or more murderers were acting in collusion and by pre-arrangement.

Probable-First. That the series of murders have been committed by two or more men whose motive is the checking of prostitution. The unprecedented barbarities practiced on the bodies are perpetrated with the view of terrifying the women of the district into abandoning their mode of life. Second. That the murderers are religious monomaniacs.

ARE THEY ON THE RIGHT TRACK?

The city detectives have since been quietly working in this direction. For obvious reasons they decline to afford any information as to the result of their investigations. It is an open secret, however, that certain members of a quasi-religious organization whose eccentric methods have again and again encountered adverse criticism at the hands of the press and the public have been closely watched for some time past. As at present it is understood that not a tittle of direct evidence is forthcoming against these suspects no arrests have been made. The fact that so long a period elapsed between the murders of September 30 and the slaughtering of the latest victim on November 9 leads the detectives to believe that they are on the right track. The last murder, on November 9, came as a great surprise to them, but it was skilfully timed, as that being Lord Mayor's Day, on which the city is thronged with sight-seers, every available city detective and policeman was on street duty.

The mere fact that this cutting is preserved in the official police files tends to lend weight to its importance. The Metropolitan Police obviously felt it merited keeping on record.

CHAPTER 26

20 December 1888 –
Murder of Rose Mylett, alias Lizzie Davis

The discovery of the body of another prostitute, Rose Mylett, in Poplar on 20 December 1888 kept the excitement at a peak, and provided the press with even more ammunition against the police. Although not a "Ripper" killing – not even murder, according to some contemporary opinion – it resulted in further acrimonious official exchanges.

This File is dated *23 Decr. '88*, is headed *Poplar Murder* and states:

> Gives particulars respecting above & states that the Police are endeavouring to trace the identity of the woman murdered.

There is a note[1] as follows:

> This memorandum seems to show that some person able to detect marks of strangulation ought to have seen the body before it was moved. Valuable indications may have been missed.
>
> H. M.
25Dec/88.

This is followed by another note[2]

> Dec 24. 88 Dear Ruggles Brise, The enclosed note on Poplar murder case was written yesterday. Since it was written the woman has been identified & police are tracing. Please return enclosed when read. I have not had time to get it copied.
>
> Yrs sincerely
JMonro

A third note[3] reads:

Dec 26. Dear Monro, You will like to see, possibly to observe on S.S. minute on the Poplar Murder.

Yours C.M.

The reply[4] is:

Dear Murdoch/ Thanks. I shall make observation later on in the case.

26/12 JM

This is followed by a lengthy report[5] by Monro:

Poplar Murder

The facts of this case as ascertained hither to are briefly these. Early on the morning of Thursday the 20th December the body of a woman was discovered by a Sergeant & Constable on beat in a small yard or court off a street in Poplar. Life was extinct. The body was warm, showing that death had but recently taken place. The face was perfectly placid. The clothes were <u>not</u> disarranged and round the neck was a handkerchief <u>loosely folded</u>, but not tied. In the pocket of the dress was a small phial, empty. In one of the ears was an ear-ring; the other was missing. There were absolutely no signs whatever of any struggle, and no marks of violence visible. The police believed from the appearance of the body that the case was one of suicide or sudden death from natural causes. The Divisional Surgeon was called in, and his assistant saw the body. He naturally gave no opinion as to the cause of death, but he discovered no marks or signs of violence suggesting that there was any suspicion of foul play. The body was removed to await inquest by the coroner.

Whether the Divisional Surgeon saw and made a post mortem examination of the body on Thursday afternoon, or Friday morning, is not at present quite clear. This is a point to be cleared up. It is stated that on Friday morning the Divisional Surgeon saw the Inspector who was to attend the inquest, but, (so says the Inspector) did not suggest that the case was one of murder. This also requires enquiry, but I do not at present delay reporting on the case till such enquiry is completed.

At the inquest, which was held on Friday, the Divisional Surgeon gave evidence that the case was one of <u>murder</u> – That the woman had been <u>strangled</u> with a four lag cord. (equal to packing-string of very moderate thickness!) and that the <u>marks of strangulation were plainly visible on the</u> throat & neck.

This evidence was certainly a matter of surprise to the police, but accepting the medical evidence as correct, the case was clearly one of murder.

The absence of <u>all signs of violence</u> when the body was discovered & examined by the police and the assistant to the Divisional Surgeon – the fact that there were absolutely no signs of any struggle – The perfectly placid state of the features – The circumstance of a handkerchief having been found loosely folded round the neck of the corpse – all these circumstances, I am bound to say, made me rather hesitate to accept, without further confirmation the statement of the Divisional Surgeon as conclusive with reference to the cause of death. My experience in cases of strangulation led me to believe that the features of a woman so murdered would be swollen, livid, & discoloured, probably protruding – That the eyes would be staring – and that there would have been the livid <u>marks of the cord on the neck, accompanied probably with abrasion of the skin</u>.

I therefore sent off the Assist. Commissioner Mr. Anderson to make further enquiries on the spot, and directed Dr. Bond of the A Division to assist the Divisional Surgeon make a second examination. Dr. Bond was otherwise engaged, and on learning this I asked the Chief Surgeon, Mr. MacKellar, to be good enough to proceed to the spot, & give me the benefit of his opinion. This he cheerfully consented to do, and meanwhile Dr. Hibbert, who had opened the letter of Dr. Bond in that gentleman's absence, also proceeded to the spot, & made a further examination of the body. I have not yet received the detailed report of Dr. Hibbert's examination, but I saw Mr. Mackellar on his return, and that gentleman fully supports the Divisional Surgeon in his opinion that death was produced by strangulation.

There is therefore no doubt that the case was one of murder – and murder of a strange and unusual type.

At present there is absolutely no trace of the identity of the woman, and till this is ascertained, there is really nothing for Police to work upon. She is believed to be one of the unfortunate class, but in spite of all enquiries which have been made, she has not yet been identified. To this point of identification the energies of Police have been directed in the first instance, and a special officer, Inspector Swanson, from Central Office has been deputed to assist the local Police of Poplar in their enquiries.

How this murder could have been carried out, without a sign of the <u>ground being disturbed by the struggles of the victim</u>, or of her murderer, I confess is very difficult to understand. Whether she may have first been rendered insensible before being murdered is a matter for consideration. Whether she was murdered in the spot where the body was discovered is also a point to be noted – whether one or more persons were engaged in the crime – whether the missing ear-ring points to murder in some spot other than that where she was found – whether this case has any connection with the Whitechapel crimes – all these are points which must be carefully considered, but with reference to which it would be premature to theorize. The first point which may afford some light on the case, is the identity of the woman, till this is ascertained we are absolutely in the dark as to the circumstances of this murder, which at present appears to be devoid of motive, as were the outrages in Whitechapel. I need not say that the Assist. Comr. and officers of the Criminal Investigation Dept. are doing & will do, all they can to detect this mysterious crime.

Dec. 23. 88   JMonro.

The Scotland Yard file on this crime is particularly sparse and consists of two extracts[6] from the *Daily Chronicle* dated 28 and 29 December 1888. The first reads:

A CLUE TO THE POPLAR MYSTERY.

The police have succeeded in finding Mrs. Mylett, the mother of the woman found dead in Clarke's Yard, Poplar, a few days ago. The deceased woman had frequently spoken of her mother living somewhere near Baker's Row, Whitechapel, and it was near this thoroughfare, in Pelham-street, that Mrs. Mylett was found to be residing. When the detectives called at the house on Boxing Day they found the inmates indulging in Christmas festivities, and upon their stating the object of their visit one of the women in the house had a serious fit. Upon visiting the mortuary Mrs. Mylett stated that she had no doubt that the body shown her was that of her daughter, and added that she last saw the deceased alive on Sunday week, when she called at Pelham-street. The mother had frequently remonstrated with her daughter upon her mode of life, but without avail. Mrs. Mylett, who is an Irishwoman, also stated that her daughter was born in London, and some years ago married, unknown to her parents, a man named Davis, whom Mrs. Mylett believed was an upholsterer by trade. The young couple had one child, but as they often disagreed they separated. This child is now in a school at Sutton, and is about seven years of age. A curious fact in reference to the woman having had a child is that Dr. Brownfield, when at the inquest, expressed the opinion that the deceased had never been a mother.

Inspector Swanson, Inspector Wildey, and the Criminal Investigation officers under their guidance are working energetically to elucidate the mystery, and another statement has afforded the detective officers with an additional clue. It appears that Charles Ptomoley, an attendant at the Poplar Union, was proceeding to the workhouse last Wednesday night week when he saw two sailors having an altercation with the deceased woman, who was heard strenuously to decline their overtures to accompany them. They were then at the corner of England-row, within sight of Clarke's-yard. Ptomoley has given the police authorities a full description of the men's appearance, and says that, though in other respects they were dressed as seamen, one had a fur cap, drawn partly over his face, while the other wore a round black hat. This statement has been verified, for the two men described by the attendant were seen by others in the district, and it also confirms the assertion of Alice Graves, who knew the deceased well, and who states that she saw the unfortunate woman walking along early on the morning of the tragedy with two men dressed as sailors.

The second report ran as follows:

THE POPLAR MURDER.

On inquiry at the East-end police-station last night our representative was informed that despite the most strenuous exertions on the part of the police nothing in the shape of a clue to the identity of the murderer of the woman Mylett or Davies had been obtained. The detectives had been engaged throughout the day in Spitalfields with the view of discovering the persons with whom the deceased associated just prior to her death. The statements which have been furnished to the police are not regarded as of the slightest value, and have given them no assistance in their investigations. An order has been issued to the various stations to the effect that persons making statements should be required to append their names and addresses, and that statements so made should be forwarded, marked "of pressing importance," to the head divisional station at Bow. Owing to the extraordinary circumstances attending the death of the unfortunate woman various conflicting theories are held by those who have had the case in hand. Dr. Brownfield, the divisional surgeon of police, however, has not the slightest reason, it is said, to alter the opinion he expressed at the inquest – namely, that the deceased was foully murdered. The medical men who have been concerned in the inquiry are of opinion not only that the deceased was murdered, but that the deed was the work of a skilful hand. A second examination of the body was made, subsequent to the inquest, and on the skin of the neck being removed a quantity of congealed blood was found, which proved that considerable pressure must have been applied from without. It is understood that sensational medical evidence may be expected when the coroner's inquiry is resumed on Wednesday next.

Mr. Charles Ptolomey, whose name was mentioned in our columns yesterday as having seen two seamen accost the woman near where she was discovered dead, has received a visit from some officers of Scotland-yard. Mr. Ptolomey, who is a night attendant at the Poplar Union, made the following statement to a reporter yesterday:- "Last night some detectives from Scotland-yard came to see me about this mysterious affair. They asked me if I could identify the sailors? I told them I could pick the men out of a thousand. How I came to notice them in this way: It was about five minutes to eight o'clock on Wednesday night, when I was going to my work. Upon going up England-row (nearly opposite Clarke's-yard) I noticed two sailors. The shorter one was speaking to the deceased, and the tall one was walking up and down. So strange did it seem that I stopped and 'took account' of them. Then I heard the woman say several times 'No! no! no!' and the short sailor spoke in a low tone. The tall one was about 5 ft. 11 in. He looked like a Yankee. The shorter one was about 5 ft. 7 in. It struck me that they were there for no good purpose, and that was the reason I took so much notice of their movements. I shall always remember their faces, and could, as I say, pick them out of a thousand. I have been to the mortuary, and seen the deceased. She is the same woman, and she was sober when I saw her with the sailors.''

There is a second file[7] concerning the so-called "Poplar Mystery", dated 11 January 1889, which adds to the somewhat sparse material already quoted:

MEPO 3/143
No. 98122

MEPOL 3

1888 – Dec 24
1889 – Feb 14   K
Janry 11th 1889   A.C.
                                   C.I.Dept.
SUBJECT Special   "The Poplar Mystery" – Death of Catherine
                                   Millet.

[Reports that he has informed Supt. K. that he does not intend taking any further steps in the matter now withstanding [sic] ["the verdict of" – deleted] Difference of opinion as to "wilful murder" or accidental death.

Refers to the Coroner's strictures upon the action of the Police in "sending down doctor after doctor without his sanction" – (vide extract from "Morning Advertiser" of 10/1/89); and asks for an authoritative decision as to the claim of the Coroner to control the action of Police – a point of great importance which may be raised at any moment.

REFERENCES.

To previous papers:
C.I.D. No. 54710   } Attd.
"(Serious Crime) 402. }
To subsequent papers:
       /2.

MINUTES.

"Mr. Anderson."

"Before sending this to H.O. what has hitherto been the practice with regard to the Coroner being consulted when Police think it advisable to have another medical opinion? What was done in the Whitechapel case, & in the Rainham case? (sd) J.M." 14/1 "Mr. Monro"

"It wd. seem that in the other cases you name ['acted' – *deleted*] Mr. Bond acted, either with the privity of the Coroner, or else before the Coroner was seized of the case. Reports from C.C. &c attached. (sd)"R.A." 19/1.

This is followed by a report[8] from Chief Inspector Donald S. Swanson, dated 18 January 1889:

METROPOLITAN POLICE.

CRIMINAL INVESTIGATION DEPARTMENT,

SCOTLAND YARD,

18th day of January 1889.

SUBJECT Employment
of Mr Bond to Ex-
amine bodies of mur-
dered, or supposed mur-
dered persons.

I beg to submit Correspondence No. 93305/11 from General Registry which sets forth how Mr. Bond was employed as an expert to examine and report upon the surgical reports of the four murders, ending with Mitre Square, but in these cases he did not examine the bodies. The final body, which he examined was that of Mary Janet Kelly, but so far as I am aware, the examination was with the consent of Dr. Phillips, who was first called by Police, and the reports do not shew that the Coroner's consent was asked for or necessary. Mr. Bond did not give evidence before the Coroner.

Donald SSwanson

Ch Inspr.

JohnShore

Supt.

There is then annexed a report from *The Star* of 24 December 1888:

IS HE A THUG?

A STARTLING LIGHT ON THE WHITE-CHAPEL CRIMES.

THE ROPE BEFORE THE KNIFE.

The Police Surgeon Theory that the Poplar Murder was the Work of the Whitechapel Fiend Borne Out by Hitherto Inexplicable Evidence – Why the Murdered Women Never Cried Out.

The Poplar murder has developed under inquiry a startling and sensational aspect. So far, it has passed almost unnoticed. The town has supped so full of horrors that mere murder unaccompanied by revolting mutilation passes apparently for common-place, and the discovery on Thursday morning in Clarke's-yard, Poplar, of a woman's dead body with the white mark of a strangler's cord around her throat has failed to create any excitement even in the neighbourhood. The police themselves appear to have shared the general feeling of non-interest. The swift and silent method of the Thug is a new and terrifying feature in London crime, and this murder is invested with a startling significance by the discovery that it has a possible bearing upon the series of Whitechapel crimes. The suggestion is this:- "Was this Poplar murder another of the series of Whitechapel and the work of the same man? If so, has the murderer changed his methods, or is it not possible that the deed of Clarke's-yard is a new revelation of his old methods – that in the other cases partial strangulation was first of all resorted to, and that when the victims were by this means rendered helpless,

THE KNIFE WAS USED

in such a manner as to obliterate the traces of the act?"

The theory is no empty speculation of sensationalism. It derives weight from the fact that it originates with Dr. Matthew Brownfield, of 171, East India Dock-road, who, as the divisional police surgeon of Poplar, made the post-mortem examination of the body found in Clarke's-yard, and who gave evidence at the inquest on Friday. Dr. Brownfield put forward the suggestion on Saturday in an interview with a *Star* reporter.

"I have no doubt at all," said Dr. Brownfield, "that death was caused by strangulation, of which the mark round the neck of the body is the evidence."

There was a disposition on the part of the police to believe, or to affect to believe, that the mark round the which was spoken of at the inquest was

ONLY A COINCIDENCE-

that it was not caused by the act which brought about the woman's death, but that it had been previously inflicted. Our reporter, therefore, put the question,

"Is there any doubt that the mark round the neck was quite recent, and was simultaneous with death?"

"None whatever. It was a white mark, and there were no signs of "sloughing" or of inflammation coming on around it, as there must have been if it had been borne during life."

"The mark could not have been caused on the day before she died?" – "Impossible! The cord was pulled round her neck, and was kept there until she was dead. Otherwise there must have been signs of inflammation, as I have said." "And the other post-mortem appearances?"

"ALL INDICATED DEATH BY SUFFOCATION.

The left side of the heart was full of fluid black blood – particularly filled and particularly black – and the lungs were gorged with the same fluid black blood, meaning that for the space of several respirations she had not breathed before the heart ceased to pulsate. Looking at the condition of all the organs in conjunction with the mark round the throat, my opinion is that death was caused by strangulation by means of a cord being pulled tightly round the neck."

"From the appearance of the mark, you believe it was a thin cord which caused death, doctor?" – "I experimented, and have come to the conclusion that it was

A PIECE OF "FOUR-STRAND" CORD

– not thick cord by any means. With such a piece of cord I could produce a facsimile of that mark upon you. I smelt the stomach, and was unable to find any trace of alcohol at all. Neither should I say from the condition of the organs that she was a woman who was much given to drink."

"Do you think, doctor, that the woman met her death anywhere else, and that her dead body was carried to the place where it was found?" – "I think it extremely improbable, considering the great difficulty of carrying a dead body about from one place to another. At the time the body was found death had not taken place more than three-quarters of an hour. I think it very probable she was an immoral woman."

All the facts seemed to combine to one suggestion – that this was the work of the Whitechapel murderer. Our reporter put this to Dr. Brownfield, and it was then that he made the

NEW AND STARTLING SUGGESTION.

"The question is," he said, "whether there is not another and still more striking point of resemblance. If this murder was the work of the same man the question is whether strangulation is not the beginning of all his operations. Does he strangle or partially strangle them first, and then cut their throats afterwards?"

Then Dr. Brownfield went on to explain why this was likely. "If his object is mutilation," "he said, he could cut their throats so much more cleanly and deliberately. And this would explain, too, how the murderer would be able to do his work without getting covered with blood."

"But, if the other victims had been first strangled would there not be post-mortem indications?" — "If he

CUT THE THROAT ALONG THE LINE

of the cord he would obliterate the traces of partial strangulation."

"And in the present case?" — "The question is whether he did not intend to cut the throat as in the other cases, but was disturbed, and had to leave his work half finished."

The evidence given by Dr. Phillips on 18 Sept. at the Hanbury-street inquest is incontrovertible proof that Annie Chapman was partially strangled before her throat was cut. When Dr. Phillips was called to see the body he found that

THE TONGUE PROTRUDED

between the front teeth, but not beyond the lips. The face was swollen, the finger-nails and lips were turgid, and in the brain, on the head being opened, he found the membranes opaque and the veins and tissues loaded with black blood. All these appearances are the ordinary signs of suffocation. In Dr. Phillip's own words, "I am of opinion that the breathing was interfered with previous to death, but that death arose from syncope consequent on the loss of blood following the severance of the throat." Subsequently, under cross-examination, the doctor said, "I am clearly of opinion that the person who cut the deceased's throat took hold of her by the chin and then commenced the incision from right to left." The Coroner asked could that be done so instantaneously and a person

COULD NOT CRY OUT?

Dr. Phillips — By pressure on the throat no doubt it would be possible.

The Foreman — There would probably be suffocation? — Dr. Phillips was understood to express assent.

Here there is everything to support Dr. Brownfield's theory. The woman's throat was cut all round in such a manner that the mark of strangulation must have been completely obliterated.

Of the Whitechapel murders this is the only case in which there is actual proof of strangulation so severe as to leave its traces after death. But in all the other cases the facts are perfectly consistent with the supposition that the murderer first of all seized his victims in the grip of strangler's cord, and having thus effectually prevented them from crying out despatched them with the knife. For in all the cases the throat was so cut that the mark of the cord would have been obliterated and in some of the cases there are circumstances which have never been explained, but which are reconcilable with the theory of strangulation. For instance, in the evidence of Dr. Phillips given at the

BERNERS-STREET

inquest on 8 Oct., there is the following remarkable passage: -

"I have come to the conclusion, both as regards the position of the victim and that of the perpetrator of the deed, that she was seized by the shoulders and placed on the ground. The murderer was on the right side when he inflicted the cut. The absence of noise is a difficult question to account for. She could not cry out after the cut, but why did she not whilst she was being put on the ground.

I CANNOT ACCOUNT FOR THE ABSENCE OF NOISE."

Dr. Phillips qualified this statement by the suggestion that the woman might have cried out, but without her cries being heard. But, on the other hand, is it not much more likely that there was no cry, and that the reason was that the victim, before being laid down, was rendered by partial strangulation incapable of crying out. In Mitre-square Catherine Eddowes was first laid down on the ground and her throat was afterwards cut. If she had been suddenly seized as the victim of Clarke's-yard was seized, and thus forced upon the ground, there would not necessarily be post mortem indications of the fact.

WHAT DR. PHILLIPS THINKS

is a matter of direct and most important bearing upon the question because Dr. Phillips, of course, knows more of the medical bearings of the murders than any other man. So *The Star* man called upon the doctor at his surgery in Spital-square. Dr. Phillips was disinclined to express any opinion on the matter to a newspaper man, but from another source our reporter ascertained that Dr. Phillips, as soon as he knew of the Poplar discovery, expressed the opinion that it was

THE WORK OF THE SAME MAN

He also recalled at once the fact of the strangulation in the Hanbury-street case. With respect to the other murders Dr. Phillips points out that the retraction of the skin following immediately upon severance of the throat would immediately destroy the marks of the cord supposing it to have been first used. But there is also another and a most important point of resemblance which Dr. Phillips is understood to perceive. He has always maintained the opinion that the murderer was a man of considerable surgical knowledge. In this belief the Poplar case confirms him. "The murderer," he says, "must be a man who had

STUDIED THE THEORY OF STRANGULATION,

for he evidently knew where to place the cord so as to immediately bring his victim under control. It would be necessary to place the cord in the right place. It would be a very lucky stroke for a man at the first attempt to hit upon the proper place."

Here, then, we arrive at this. That in the opinion of the man who is best qualified to judge the Poplar murderer and the Whitechapel murderer are one and the same man, that the method of preliminary strangulation was certainly employed in Hanbury-street, and was possibly employed in the other cases. Does not this new theory open out a vista of probabilities which, being followed, may lead to the identification of the murderer.

One more word as to the practicability of the theory. Dr. Brownfield most distinctly asserts that by the employment of a cord arranged on the tourniquet principle the victim could be so suddenly seized as to prevent the possibility of a scream.

The following folio, D, carries another newspaper extract, this time from the *Advertiser* of 10 January 1889, its cover being worded as follows:

The Poplar Mystery. Comments on, the inquest on the body of Rose Millett.
REFERENCE TO PAPERS.
Commissioner's minute within I await report from C.I.D. about this (signed) J.M. Report submitted.
ARW
12.1.89   *Insp.*

EXTRACT
From the *Advertiser*
of 10th January 1889

It is unfortunate that there is a fundamental difference of opinion between the coroner and the jury who have been investigating what has become known as the Poplar mystery. For months past there has been a succession of abhorrent enormities forced upon public attention, and it would have been a great relief to have been assured that the death of ROSE MILLETT was due to accidental strangulation. As the matter stands additional responsibility is thrown upon the metropolitan police, who from the first have contended that the death was attributable to natural causes, and who have, in the person of DR. BOND, what the public will justly consider to be weighty authority in support of their view. MR. WYNNE BAXTER, the coroner, says "there is no evidence to show that death was the result of violence." In that he follows DR. BOND. The jury flatly disagree with him, and return a verdict of wilful murder against some person or persons unknown, being chiefly guided to that conclusion by the evidence of Doctors BROWNFIELD, HARRIS, HIBBERD [*sic*], and M'KENNA, each of whom is of opinion that the woman was murdered by means of something of the nature of a cord drawn tightly around her neck. It is impossible for the lay reader to accurately estimate the value of the medical testimony for and against the theory of murder. In arriving at their verdict the jury were probably influenced by other than expert evidence. The woman was an unfortunate, the yard in which she was found bore an ill character, and the skilful murderer of others of her class is still at large. Much might be said in favour of their verdict and much against. It is about equally open to belief that the woman fell in a drunken stupor, and that the weight of her head against the collar of her dress compressed her larynx and caused suffocation, or that she was strangled by a cord held in a similar way to that by which soap is often cut. Either conclusion is feasible. The truth may never be known with certainty until the adage that "murder will out" − if murder it be − is once more justified.

[There is a marginal note to the above cutting as follows: − "*I await report from C.I.D. about this (signed) J.M.*"
        10/1]

There is a report[9] dated 11 January 1889 by Robert Anderson, six pages long:

The Poplar Case.

Mr. Monro,

I send you herewith Supt. Steed's report of the inquest upon Catherine Millett, and also Messrs Wontner's notification of the verdict of "Wilful Murder."

The Supt. has come to this Office to ask instructions in view of this verdict. I have thought it only fair to him and his officers to tell him plainly that neither the evidence given at the inquest, nor the verdict arrived at, affects the judgment I formed when I personally investigated the case on the 22nd ult:, and that I did not intend to take any further action in the matter.

Having regard to the Coroner's strictures upon the action of the Police, it may be well to place the facts on record.

About 4 A.M. on the 20th Decbr., the woman was found by a P.S. and a P.C. lying in "Clarke's Yard", High St:, Poplar. The P.S. at once went to fetch Mr. Brownfield the Divisional Surgeon, and his assistant, Mr. Harris, a qualified practitioner, returned with him to High St:, examined the body, certified to the fact of death without any suspicion of death by violence, and left the officers to remove the remains to the mortuary.

Mr. Brownfield made a P.M: on the morning of the 21st and formed the opinion that the woman had been murdered; but this was not communicated to the Police. The first intimation I had of it was derived from the report of the inquest in the Evening Paper, which I took up after midnight on the 21st on my return from a surprise visit to Whitechapel.

Next morning I brought the matter before you, and by your desire I went to Poplar to investigate the case personally, writing to Mr. Bond to meet me there. Mr. Bond, however, was unfortunately out of town for the day.

The statements of the officers who found the body, and especially of P.S. Golding, who impressed me as being an exceptionally safe and reliable witness, seemed so incompatible with the theory of murder that I brought them to the scene of the death, and finally I undertook the distasteful task of going on to the mortuary and examining the body myself.

As the result I came to the conclusion that the death had not been caused by homicidal violence. The woman was found lying on her side in a position of natural repose, her arms at rest, her hands open, her face perfectly placid, her eyes and mouth closed, a handkerchief placed loosely round her neck – not even tied; not the slightest injury to the skin of the neck, save a few slight abrasions, admitted by all to have been caused by her own fingers, the other marks upon her neck (not injuring the skin) being such as would be caused by the stiff collar of her tight-fitting cloth jacket, and which could not have been caused in any other way save under conditions which did not exist – all this added to the fact that the slightest scream or cry would have been heard by persons who are known to have been close at hand, and that the slightest struggle would have left its marks on the soft ground of the Yard, led me, as I have said, to the conclusion, not only that there was no proof of murder, but that the facts and circumstances were inconsistent with such an hypothesis. And this is now abundantly confirmed by what has since been learned as to the woman's drunken habits, by the medical evidence of Mr. Bond, and, lastly, by the opinion of Mr. Wontner, and, I think perhaps, I may add by that of the Coroner himself.

To resume – Mr. Bond's assistant, Mr. Hibbert [sic], had opened my note to Mr. Bond, and (unfortunately I think) decided to act for him in the case. He thus arrived at Poplar soon after I left the mortuary, and made a second P:M: on the body.

In ignorance of this, I made such representations to you on my return to Whitehall that you asked the Chief Surgeon to go down himself; and he reached Poplar just after Mr. Hibbert had left. Finally Mr. Bond went down next day to verify Mr. Hibbert's notes.

All three Doctor's [sic] confirmed Mr. Brownfield's view of the case, and Mr. Bond and Mr. Hibbert called on me on the 24th with a report to that effect. After a long conference, in which I pressed my difficulties and objections, I referred them to you. But that same afternoon Mr. Bond went again to Poplar to make a more careful examination of the woman's neck, and he returned to tell me he had entirely altered his view of the case, and was satisfied that though death was due to strangulation, it was produced accidentally and not by homicidal violence.

This is the basis of the Coroner's complaint that "the Assistant Comr. sent down Doctor after Doctor without his sanction"; and this claim on the part of the Coroner to control the action of the Police in cases of supposed homicide raises a question of such great practical importance that I think an authoritative decision upon it should be obtained.

No one is more ready than I am to spare the susceptibilities (or even to humour the vanity) of any official, but my estimate of the position and duty of the Commissioner of Police is wholly inconsistent with the idea that he must obtain the sanction of the Coroner before taking steps imperatively necessary for the investigation of a crime. This question may arise again at any moment, and I submit it to you for prompt and definite solution.

RA

11 : 1 : 89

[There are two marginal references at the start of this report, as follows–
"*S.C. 402/13*
Cor. 54710/11."]

There is then annexed a report[10], dated 18 January 1889, by Inspector A. Hare on the Rainham Mystery,

METROPOLITAN POLICE.
CRIMINAL INVESTIGATION DEPARTMENT,
SCOTLAND YARD,
18th day of January, 1889.

SUBJECT Rainham
Mystery
REFERENCE TO PAPERS.
45492.

I beg to report that in the case of the Rainham Mystery Mr. Bond was requested to make an examination of the portions of the body found, by Assistant Commissioner, Mr. Monro. He did so and submitted his report. After that some other portions were found in the Regents Canal and Dr. Thomas, the Coroner, decided to hold an inquest. Mr. Bond gave evidence but it was at the instigation of Police and the Coroner was not consulted. I believe the Coroner paid Mr. Bond his fee for attending the inquest but his bill for everything else was sent to Assistant Commissioner who referred it to Receiver for payment.:

A. Hare. Inspr.
JohnShore
<u>Supt</u>

This is followed by a three-page response[11] by the Commissioner, James Monro:

Write to Chief <u>Surgeon</u>

In connection with the recent case at Poplar in which the Coroners Jury have returned a verdict of Wilful Murder, I have to bring to your notice two points in connection with the action of the Divisional Surgeon Dr. Brownfield, with refce. to which, in justice to that gentleman, some explanation it seems to me should be afforded.

It has been reported to me that no indication of the grave nature of the case, as found by the Divl. Surgeon was conveyed by him to the Police; and that the first intimation which the Police received of the case being one of murder was afforded by Dr. Brownfield's evidence at the inquest. I shall be glad to know whether this is correct? at which time the post mortem was made? and what action was taken by Dr. Brownfield in the way of communicating to the Police the conclusion at which he had arrived as to the case being one of murder.

I think it right to bring to your notice an article in the Star of 24th ulto. in which the result of an alleged interview between Dr. Brownfield and a Star reporter is given. I think you will agree with me in thinking that, in justice to Dr. Brownfield he should be asked whether the statements made are correct.

21.1.89   J.M.

[On the reverse of f N above is the annotation –
"Done G.:[. . .]
21.1.89"].
This is followed by a letter[12] from Dr Brownfield, dated 30 January 1889, to the Chief Surgeon:

Received A.O.M.K.
     1.1.89 [*sic* – 1.2.89?]

171 East India Rd.
E.
Jan 30th 89.

A.O. M'Kellar Esq F.R.C.S.
     Surgeon in Chief
          Metropolitan Police
My Dear Sir,

I have to inform you with regard to the case my lett. that I received the Coroner's order overnight and made PM examination at 9 o'clock following morning, then enquired what officer was to attend inquest and was informed an Inspector the inquest being fixed for eleven a.m. With regard to "Star reports" I hope you do not think me responsible for their reporters articles.

Yours very faithfully.
M.Brownfield
Divl. Surgeon.

There is a letter attached from the Chief Surgeon regarding his investigation, dated 3 February 1889, as follows:

Feb. 3rd 1889

Dear Mr. Staples,

    I enclose the report of Dr. Brownfield, in reply to the questions of the Commissioner respecting the Poplar case (Millett). I hope to call upon you on Monday

Yours very truly
Alexr. O. MacKellar.

There is annexed a letter, dated 9 February 1889, from the Chief Surgeon:

Feb. 9th 1889

Dear Mr. Monro,

    I forward the enclosed received last evening from Dr. Brownfield. I fear that Dr. B. has an aversion to the writing of letters.

Yours very truly
Alexr. O. MacKellar.

There is then a letter, dated 7 February 1889, from Dr. Brownfield to the Chief Surgeon:

171, East India Road,
London, E.
Feb. 7th 1889.

My Dear Sir,

    In answer to yours of the 6th inst I deny that portion marked with blue lines & shown to me in your "Star" and further was most careful not to state to anyone more than what I had said at the inquest.

    I am very sorry you should have had so much trouble and hoping this will prove satisfactory

I remain
Yours very truly
M.Brownfield

A.O. MacKellar Esqr FRCS
   Surgeon in Chief
     Metropolitan Police.

The reply[13] of the Chief Surgeon then follows, dated 14 February 1889:

In the case of any further communication on this subject, please quote the
following reference (C.S. 405)
and address:-
    The Chief Surgeon,
        Metropolitan Police Force,
            London, S.W.

Great Scotland Yard,
London, S.W.,
14th day of February 1889.

From

    The Chief Surgeon,
        Metropolitan Police Force. [Stamped: – REGISTRY 14 FEB -89–4]
    To   J. Monro Esq.
                        the Commissioner of Police
                            of the Metropolis.

Sir,

In reply to your letter 98.122/3 I have the honour to inform you that in my opinion Divisional Surgeons should not give information referring to any police question to members of the Press except with the knowledge and approval of the Police. The same rule should also be applied to private individuals. I further consider that Divisional Surgeons are bound to give Police the earliest possible information of cases of death to which suspicion of foul play attaches. I have every reason to believe that this is the opinion that obtains generally amongst the Divisional Surgeons.

I am, Sir,
Your obedient Servant.
Alexr. O. MacKellar.

This concludes the information contained in this file, and leaves singularly unresolved the questions asked by the police about the conduct of Dr Brownfield in the Poplar case.

CHAPTER 27

January 1889 onwards – Continuing Vigilance in Whitechapel

The use of additional patrols in Whitechapel, and the requests for additional finance, continued into the New Year. This fact alone indicates that the police believed that the killer, or killers, was or were still at large, and might strike again.

A report[1] dated 26 January 1889 is as follows:

[Stamped: – HOME OFFICE 28 JAN.89 RECEIVED] No. A49301G/4
DATE 26 Jan. 1889.   Commissioner of Police
REFERENCES &c.   Reports that the expenditure for special allowance to the Police employed on Special Patrol duty in Whitechapel amounted to £306.13 on the 24 inst, and asks permission to expend a further £200. He is reducing the number of men specially employed as quickly as it is safe to do so.

                              MINUTES.
?Sanction up to a further £200.
WTB.
31.1.89 Better ask Receiver for financial observations in first instance in usual course.

                    ELP 1st Feby 89.   CM. Jan 31.
                    Wrote Recr. 2/2
96318/3   4 Whitehall Place, S.W.
                                       26th January, 1889.
Sir,
    With reference to your letter of the 15th inst. sanctioning an allowance of 1/- per diem to the Police employed on special patrol duty in Whitechapel, I have to acquaint you, for the information of the Secretary of State, that the expenditure on this account up to the 24th inst. inclusive amounts to £306.13.0. I shall be glad therefore to receive the sanction of the Secretary of State to a further expenditure of not more than £200.

    I am gradually reducing the number of men employed on this duty as quickly as it is safe to do so, but such reduction cannot be effected all at once.

I am,

Sir,

Your obedient Servant,

JMonro.

There is a further report[2] on this subject, as follows:

Home Office 2 Feby / Whitechapel murders. Extra allowce.

Transmitting letter from the Commr asking for authority to expend a further sum of £200. The expenditure on account of the extra allowance up to 24th inst. being £306.13.0. The S of S asks for the Receiver's observations personally, thereon.

Say that the allowance already granted was sufficient for a period of seven weeks. I think [   ] the additional £200 [   ] be proved Should be asked to say whether having regard to the reduced number now employed be [   ] £200 will cover all expenditure as far as he can foretell up to the 31 March next.

A.S.T[?]

6.2.89

Done 6/2

A49301G/4.   Receiver Metropolitan Police District 5185/3 4 FEB.89

Home Office,

2 February 1889.

Sir,

I am directed by the Secretary of State to transmit to you, with reference to the Home Office letter of the 15th ultimo and previous correspondence on the subject of the plain clothes allowance (special) to officers patrolling Whitechapel, a further letter from the Commissioner of Police; and to request the favour of your observations financially thereon.

I am,

Sir,

Your obedient Servant,

GODFREY LUSHINGTON.

The Receiver for the
Metropolitan Police District.
&c   &c   &c.

There is a report[3], dated 2 February 1889, regarding the claims for the additional patrols as follows:

No. 5227/3   A49301/5   Office of the Receiver for the
                                   Metropolitan Police District
                                   4, Whitehall Place
                                   2. Feb.1889

Sir,

I have the honor to transmit for the information of the Secretary of State, Accounts of Expenses incurred by various Police Officers on special occasions, and to request authority for payment of the same, the Commissioner having approved thereof, vizt.

Supt W Hugo for Police specially employed patrolling Whitechapel – £12.16.10

Refreshment allowance

In /1 the Commr. states that "many" of the Whitechapel patrols come from other divisions and have to patrol at a distance from their homes. There will probably therefore be further claims of this description.
? Sanction
W.T.B.
6.2.89   see/6   I have the honor to be,
                              Sir,
                   Your obedient Servant,
The Under Secretary of State   [*signature illeg.*]
    &c   &c   &c
       Home Office.

This is followed by a file cover[4], as follows:

[Stamped: – HOME OFFICE 7 FEB.89 RECEIVED] No. A49301G/6
DATE 6 Feb.1889.   Receiver.
REFERENCES, &c. Police employed on special patrol duty in Whitechapel. Thinks that Commissioner should be asked to say whether he estimates that the £200 will cover all the expenditure as far as he can foresee up to 31 March next.
                        Pressing.
            MINUTES.
? ask this question of Mr Monro by letter. also sanction Refreshment allowances recommended in 1/5 to those Police Officers [who have come from a distance for this service, and who are, according to Police orders, entitled to such additional fees.]
              CM Feb 9. 89   GL
                      9 Feb '89

Wrote Commissioner
& Receiver
12 Feb: 1889.
Comment a/15.3.89/

The report[5] from the Receiver on the above follows:

Pressing   A49301G/6
5785/3
                                                        4 Whitehall Place,
                                                        Febr. 6th. 1889
Sir,
    I have the honour to return herewith the letter from the Commissioner dated 26th ult, asking sanction for a further expenditure up to £200 in respect of the allowance to the Police employed on Special Patrol duty in Whitechapel.
    As regards this I have to state that the sum already granted covered a period of 7 weeks, and I think Mr. Monro should be asked to say whether [having regard to the reduced numbers now employed he estimates that the £200 will cover all the expenditure as far as he can foresee, up to 31st March next.]
                I have the honour to be,
                    Sir,
              Your obedient Servant,
              [   ]

There is an interesting entry[6] for expenses in the Police Entry book, dated 14 February 1889, in respect of Inspector Abberline:

A49301/159

                                                        14th February 1889.
                  Authorising
No 5227/4   5th Instant,
    Inspector Abberline for expenses in connection with the Whitechapel murders, £39. 0. 1,

Recr.

There is another report[7], dated 15 March 1889, as follows:

No. A49301G/7
DATE. 15 March 1889.   Commissioner of Police
REFERENCES, &c. Reports [cessation of the special patrol duty in White-chapel & stating that the total expenditure thereon has been £351]; requests

sanction for the extra expenditure not covered by H.O. authority of 15 Jan. last.

MINUTES.

See 1/4

? To Receiver

     for observations.

[illeg. initials]

   8.3.89.   C.M. Mar:19

[Stamped: – Referred 19 MAR.89.]

   I think that Mr. Monro's proposal may receive the sanction of the Secretary of State, and the excess expenditure of £51, sanctioned.

A:S:S:

19.3.89.

[Stamped: – HOME OFFICE 21 MAR.89] ?Sanction

?   [PP]

22.3.89   GL

    Wrote Commissioner   23 March '89

        & Receiver   28 March 1889.

A49301G/7

96318/5

4, Whitehall Place,

S.W.

15th March, 1889.

Sir,

   In reply to your letter [*Marginal note* – "A49301G/6"] of the 12th ultimo on the subject of the Police employed on special patrol duty in Whitechapel, I have to acquaint you, for the information of the Secretary of State, that this duty has now ceased. –

   The total expense of the special allowance to the Police employed amounts to £351; and I have accordingly to request that Mr. Secretary Matthews may be pleased to sanction the extra expenditure not covered by the Home Office authority of the 15th January last.-

I am, Sir,

The Under Secretary   Your most obedient Servant,

of State   J.Monro

&c – &c – &c

Home Office

The cover sheets regarding the above report are filed under MEPO 3/ 141, as follows:

[*At top of page is stamp:* – Receiver for the Metropolitan Police]
HO a49301G/7
19 March
Whitechapel murders Extra Allowance of 1/- per day
Referring without covering letter to letter from the Commr. reporting cessation of patrol duty in Whitechapel & stating that the total expenditure has been £351, & requesting sanction for extra expenditure.

Copy of Receiver's minute "I think that Mr.Monro's proposal may receive the sanction of the Secy of State and the excep expenditure of £51 sanctioned"
ARP.

19.3.89.

This followed by a further cover:

G&A
S/Sy H.O.
28 March
Whitechapel Murders.
Forwards copy of letter to Commr., sanctioning £51 more being expended for the specl. allowances of 1/- per diem.
Pressing
Pass for payment
A[ ]
30.3.89.
[   ]
Done. ARP

The next police communication, on social conditions in the East End, is a letter[8] from James Monro, dated 5 May 1889:

Reply to H.O. 5.5.89
Any thing that Mr. Barnet writes on such a subject is entitled to respect for no one who knows the work which the vicar of St. Jude's has done, and the spirit in which he does it can entertain anything but sentiments of regard for him & sympathy with his aspirations. Practically what he says is this. Vice of a very low type exists in Whitechapel – such vice manifests itself in brawling and acts of violence which shock the feelings of respectable persons. Such acts of violence are not repressed by action taken either before the Police or magisterial authorities, clear out the slums and lodging houses to which vicious persons resort – and vice will disappear, respectability taking its place.

There is no doubt whatever that vice of a low and degraded type is only too visible in Whitechapel. The facility with which the Whitechapel murderer obtains victims has brought this prominently to notice, but to any one who will take a walk late a night in the districts where the recent atrocities have been committed, the only wonder is that his operations have been so restricted. There is no lack of victims ready to his hand, for scores of these unfortunate women may be seen any night muddled with drink in the streets & alleys, perfectly reckless as to their safety, and only anxious to meet with any one who will help them in plying their miserable trade.

There is no doubt that brawling & fighting go on, repressed as far as possible by police, but it must be remembered that these women do not care to be protected against those who assault them, very seldom have recourse to the station to complain, & still more seldom to appear at any police court to prosecute any charge which they may have laid before the police.

It is also true that common lodging houses are not all that they might be in the way of discouraging immorality, altho' I do not think that so much of the reproach in this respect which is generally levelled at them in reality is attributable to them. On this subject I have already expressed my views in my letter of [missing]. Much however of the immorality which goes on finds its place in the low lodgings which are let to prostitutes by the day or week, where they take home men, with reference to which the law is practically powerless. These are the houses from which no charges are brought before the police, & to these much more than to the common lodging houses is the violence conjoined with immorality attributable.

That respectability would be benefitted [sic] by clearing out such localities admits of little doubt. That the moral atmosphere of Whitechapel would be purified by the substitution of better lodging houses for the dens at present to be found there, is perfectly clear, but this would not remove vice, it would only delocalize it, and transfer it to some neighbouring parish at present not quite so disreputable as some parts of Whitechapel.

I do not mean to say that their might not be a gain – it certainly would be a gain to Whitechapel, and it may be said that if other parishes took similar steps, similar results would follow within their limits. But the question still remains – what is to become of the residuum of vice which is thus moved on? I do not believe in such a transfer of a vicious population as likely to remove vice generally from the metropolis, and I suspect it may be taken as a fact that wherever landlords or lodging house keepers can secure their rent, they will not hesitate in taking it from prostitutes with as much readiness as from persons of a different class.

Behind the whole question lies the larger matter of street prostitution generally, and until that is taken up, and regulated (objectionable as this may appear to a public which confuses between liberty & license) the mere multiplying of comfortable lodging houses will not have any appreciable effect in diminishing the number of & [ ] resulting from a class who do not want comfortable lodging houses, & the scene of whose operations is on the streets.

3/8 JM.

CHAPTER 28

17 July 1889 – Murder of Alice McKenzie

It was July 1889 before another murder occurred that could be linked with the 1888 series. It was the murder of a prostitute, Alice McKenzie, on 17 July 1889 that revived fears that the "Ripper" might still be at work in the East End of London.

The first papers[1] relevant to this murder are as follows:

Commercial Street Station

Metropolitan Police

H Division

17th July   1889

I beg to report that about 12.48 am 17th inst. I visited PC272H Walter Andrews in Castle Alley, Whitechapel. He being on the Beat No. 11 on the 4th Section. I said to him alright he replied alright Sergeant. I then left him and went to visit another P.C. on an adjoining beat. I had only got about 150 yards from P.C.272H when I heard a whistle blow twice. I rushed to the bottom of Castle Alley and heard P.C.272H say come on quick he ran up the alley, and I followed, and on the pavement closer to two vans on the right side of the footway I saw a woman laying on her right side with her clothes half up to her waist exposing her abdomen. I also noticed a quantity of blood under her head on the footway. The P.C. said here's another murder. I directed the P.C. not to leave the body or let anyone touch it until the Dr. arrived. The P.C. said it's quite warm as he touched her. I got the assistance of P.C. 101H here and P.C. 423 Allen. The former P.C. I directed to search the place and sent P.C. 423 for the Doctor, and Inspr. on duty, and upon his return to make search. Other Constables arrived shortly afterwards, also the Local Inspr. Mr. Reid C.I.D. I also hailed a passing cab and acquainted the Superintendent of what had taken place. Several men were drafted in different directions to make enquiries at Lodging Houses Coffee Houses &c to see if any suspicious man had recently entered them. The body was afterwards conveyed by me on the ambulance to the Whitechapel mortuary where the body was searched by Inspr. Reid who gave me a description of the body.

Description age about 40 length 5 ft 4 complexion pale hair and eyes brown top of thumb of left hand deficient also tooth deficient in upper jaw. Dress red stuff bodice patched under arms and sleeves with marone one black and one marone stockings brown stuff skirt kilted brown lindsey petticoat, white chemise and apron, paisley shawl. button boots. all old nothing found on person.

E Badham Sergt

Thos. Hawkes Insp.

An old clay pipe and a farthing were found under the body.

This statement is followed[2] by that of PC Walter Andrews:

Commercial Street Station
Metropolitan Police.
H Division
July 17th 1889

I beg to report that at 10 minutes to 1 o'clock the 17th inst. I was passing through Castle Alley Whitechapel trying the doors when I saw a woman lying on the pavement with her throat cut but I saw no one in the street at the time. I touched the body with my hand and found that she was quite warm. I at once blew my whistle when I saw Isaac Lewis Jacob of No. 12 New Castle place Whitechapel going towards Wentworth Street with a plate in his hand he said that he was going to get something for his supper. I said you had better stop here with me as there have been a woman murdered. Just at that minute Sergeant Badham heard the whistle blow and came running up to my assistance. I told the Sergeant that there was a woman laying on the foot way in Castle Alley with her throat cut. I ran back and took charge of the body until the Doctor arrived and examined the woman and stated the woman was dead. The body was afterwards conveyed to the mortuary on the ambulance.

Walter Andrews
PC 272H
Thos. Hawkes, Inspr.

These reports are followed by a lengthy report[3] by Inspector Moore, one of the team who had been sent from Scotland Yard to investigate the Whitechapel murders in September 1888:

METROPOLITAN POLICE.
Criminal Investigation Department,
Scotland Yard,
17th day of July 1889.

Referring to case of Murder at Castle Alley, Whitechapel.

I beg to report that enquiry has been continued in this case; but the following are the only facts obtained at present.

On learning that the deceased had been identified I caused enquiry to be made by P.S. Record D. and P.S. Kuhrt "G"., who ascertained from John McCormac, of 52 Gun Street, Spitalfields that he was a labourer, and had been employed by Jewish Tailors at Hanbury St. and elsewhere for about 16 years. He has been living with the deceased Alice McKenzie about 6 or 7 years. He first met her at Bishopsgate, and they have been living in Common Lodging Houses about Whitechapel ever since; but lately at 52 Gun St., as above. He came from his work at about 4 p.m. 16th Inst. when he saw her and gave her some money (1s/8d); he then went to sleep, and when he awoke between 10 and 11 p.m. she had gone out. He did not see her again until he identified her body at the Mortuary this afternoon. She has mentioned to him that she came from Peterborough; but he cannot remember that she ever said who her friends were.

The officers also saw Betsy Ryder, of 52 Gun Street, Spitalfields, the deputy of the Lodging House; who stated that the deceased woman and McCormac had been lodging there on and off for the past 12 months, and appeared to live comfortably together. She saw her go out between 8.30 and 9 pm. 16th, and noticed that she had some money in her hand, but the amount is not known. She did not return home again. At 2 p.m. this day "Ryder" was taken to the mortuary where she identified the body of deceased woman; who she had often heard mention that she had sons abroad, but the exact place is not known. She is believed to be 39 years of age and used to go out at night; but whether as a prostitute or not is not known to Mrs. Ryder; although the Police looked upon her as such. She was much addicted to drink.

At 5p.m. this day an Inquest was opened at the "Working Lads Institute", Whitechapel Road, by W.E. Baxter, Esq., Coroner for East Middlesex; and after various witnesses had been examined as to the finding of the body and identification; the further hearing was adjourned till 10a.m. tomorrow (18th). A post-mortem examination has been made by Drs. Phillips, ["Bond" – *deleted*] McKeller and others, the result of which will be given at inquest tomorrow.

Careful enquiry has been made at Coffee and Lodging Houses; but no information has been obtained at present, and the enquiry is being continued.

During the day since submitting the previous report two men have been detained in H Division both of which were at Commercial St. Station, but were liberated subsequently upon enquiry being found satisfactory.

I wish to point out that every effort is being made to obtain something tangible in regard to the perpetrator of the crime.

Henry Moore, Inspector
T Arnold Supt.

The next reference[4] to this murder is contained in a Home Office file dated 17 July 1889:

No. A49301I/1

DATE 17 July 1889   Commissioner of Police

REFERENCES, &c.   Forwards police report respecting the commission of a murder in Castle Alley, Whitechapel, this morning. States that every effort will be made to discover the murderer, who, he thinks, is identical with "Jack the Ripper," but that the assassin has not left the slightest clue to his identity.   <u>Immediate</u>

MINUTES.

The Secretary of State. The plan is from Pall Mall of today July 17.

[There is here appended a copy of the map of the area entitled "THE WHITECHAPEL MURDERS" and showing the sites of all the murders from that of Emma Smith through to that of Alice McKenzie (eight murders.)]

Returned by S.S. and Mr. S. Wortley. also seen by Mr Lushington
Lay by C.M. July 20.

This is followed by the report[5] of the Chief Commissioner of Police, James Monro:

A49301I/1

<u>Immediate.</u>   17th July 1889.

     Sir,

     I have the honour to send herewith for the information of the Secretary of State a Police report regarding the murder of a woman in Castle Alley, Whitechapel this morning.

     As soon as I received a telegram announcing the commission of the crime I started about 3 am for the spot, for the purpose of viewing the scene of the occurrence, and assisting at the inquiry.

     I need not say that every effort will be made by the Police to discover the murderer, who, I am inclined to believe is identical with the notorious "Jack the Ripper" of last year.

     It will be seen that in spite of ample Police precautions and vigilance the assassin has again succeeded in committing a murder and getting off without leaving the slightest clue to his identity.

     I have the honour to be,

Sir,
Your obedient servant,
J. Monro

The Under Secretary
    of State,
&c &c &c.

This report is followed by a more detailed summary[6] by Superintendent Arnold, H Division, dated 17 July 1889, of police action taken, as follows:

METROPOLITAN POLICE.
H Division.
17th July 1889.

SUBJECT Whitechapel
Murders.
<u>52,983</u>

I beg to report that at 12.50 am this day P.C. 272H Andrews was passing through Castle Alley, Whitechapel, when he noticed a woman lying on the pavement, and upon examination discovered that her throat was cut about two inches on left side, the body being quite warm. An alarm was at once raised by the Constable blowing his whistle when Sergeant Badham came immediately upon the scene. He found a woman, age about 40. to 45, length 5ft 4in, complexion pale, hair and eyes brown, top of thumb of left hand deficient, also tooth deficient in upper jaw, dress red stuff bodice, patched under arms, and sleeves with marone coloured material, one black and one marone coloured stockings, brown stuff skirt, kilted brown linsey petticoat, white chemise and apron, paisley shawl, button boots, all old and dirty, lying on her right side with her clothing turned up to her waist exposing her abdomen, with a deep zig-zag cut extending across same, a quantity of blood was on footway. In addition to P.C. 272H Andrews, the Sergeant obtained the assistance of other constables on adjoining beats, when information was sent to the Divisional Surgeon, Dr. Phillips and to the Inspector on duty at Commercial Street Police Station, also Local Inspector Reid.

On arrival of Dr. Phillips he examined the body which was afterwards removed to the Whitechapel Mortuary to await identification and inquest, life being extinct.

I immediately came upon the scene, and directed that a thorough search of the locality, which was done, but nothing was discovered beyond an old clay pipe besmeared with blood, and a farthing, which were found lying under the body when removed.

I also instituted inquiries in various directions, especially at common lodging houses, coffee houses &c., with a view to ascertain if any suspicious men had entered either and also with a view to deceased's identification, but at present without success. Coroner and his officer have been informed and the inquest will be opened today.

The opinion formed by Dr. Phillips after his examination of the body, was that the wounds had not been inflicted by the same hand as in the previous cases, inasmuch as the injuries in this case are not so severe and the cut on stomach is not so direct. I should have mentioned before that at the time of the discovery no person was seen in or near Castle Alley, but on the constable blowing his whistle, he saw Isaac Lewis Jacob of No. 12 Newcastle Place Whitechapel, who was going towards Wentworth Street with a plate in his hand, as he said for the purpose of fetching something for his supper, which was no doubt correct. He remained with the officer until assistance arrived.

There can be no doubt that the crime was committed as near as possible about 12.40 a.m., as P.C. 272H Andrews passed through Castle Alley at 12.20 a.m. and again at 12.50 a.m. when he found the body. P.C. 423H Allen passed through the Alley at 12.30 a.m. and remained under the lamp, exactly where the body was found, for five minutes whilst partaking of his supper, he neither saw or heard any person in the alley.

The description of deceased has been fully circulated by wire and every exertion is being made to prove her identity.

One person has been detained viz John Larkin Mills, which occurred at 2.35 a.m., but was liberated at 4.30 a.m., as after inquiry was made, his statement was found satisfactory.

I have just received information that Mrs. Smith, wife of the superintendent of the wash houses situate in Castle Alley, has identified deceased as a person who occasionally attended the wash houses for the purpose of washing her clothing and was known by the name of Kelly but whether that is her name, or where she has resided, or any of her associates, nothing is yet known.

T Arnold
Superintendent

There is a report[7] by **Dr Thomas Bond**, regarding examination of the body of the woman McKenzie:

Dear Sir,

I beg to report that in accordance with your instructions I this day inspected the dead body of a woman, who has been identified as Alice McKenzie, at Whitechapel. Before I went to the mortuary I called on Dr. Phillips & he kindly accompanied me. He informed me that the post mortem was completed yesterday & that the wounds on the throat of the woman had been so disturbed that any examination I might make, unassisted would convey no definite information as to the nature of the injuries. He pointed out to me the original wounds, their character and direction & I was able to form an opinion that there could be no doubt that the cuts were made from left to right & as far as I was able to make out, the knife appears to have been plunged deeply into the neck on the left side of the victim below the sterno mastoid muscle & brought out by a tailed incision just above the larynx on the same side. There appeared to have been two stabs, & the knife then carried forward in the same skin wound, except that a small tongue of skin remained between the two stabs. The incisions appeared to me to be in a direction from above downwards and forwards with several small superficial cuts extending upwards & tailing off into mere scratches. The two main cuts appeared to be about 3 inches long but Dr. Phillips stated that before the parts were disturbed the cuts which I saw extending down wards, really were in a direction upwards.

The cuts appeared to have been inflicted with a sharp strong knife. I could form no opinion as to the width of the blade or the length of the knife, but undoubtedly the cuts might have been done with a short knife; it must in my opinion have had a sharp point. I believe the cuts were made from the front while the woman's head was thrown back on the ground. There were two bruises high up on the chest which looked as if the murderer had made the cuts with his right hand while he held the woman down with his left. There were no bruises on the woman's face or lips.

On the right side of the abdomen extending from the chest to below the level of the umbilicus there was a jagged incision made up of several cuts which extended through the skin & subcutaneous fat & at the bottom of this cut there were 7 or 8 superficial scratches about 2 inches long parallel to each other in a longitudinal direction. There was also a small cut eighth of an inch deep, quarter inch long on the mons veneris. I think that in order to inflict the wound which I saw on the abdomen the murderer must have raised the clothes with his left hand & inflicted the injuries with his right.

Dr. Phillips showed me a small bruise on the left side of the stomach which he suggested might have been caused by the murderer pressing his right hand on the stomach while he used the knife with his left hand, but I saw no sufficient reason to entertain this opinion. The wounds could not have been self inflicted, & no doubt the wound in the throat would cause almost immediate death & I do not think the woman could call out if held down in the position she appears to have been in when the wounds were inflicted. The wounds on the abdomen could have nothing to do with the cause of death &

were in my opinion inflicted after death. I see in this murder evidence of
similar design to the former Whitechapel murders viz. sudden onslaught on
the prostrate woman, the throat skilfully & resolutely cut with subsequent
mutilation, each mutilation indicating sexual thoughts & a desire to mutilate
the abdomen & sexual organs.

　　I am of opinion that the murder was performed by the same ["hand" –
deleted] person who committed the former series of Whitechapel murders.

　　　　　　　　　　　　　　I am dear Sir,
　　　　　　　　　　　　　　　Yours faithfully,
　　　　　　　　　　　　　　Thos. Bond.

R. Anderson esq.

It seems significant that Dr Bond's report is addressed to Robert
Anderson, who had asked Dr Bond for his 10 November 1888, report
on the murders and medical aspects thereof. It is also interesting to note
that Dr Bond felt that the McKenzie murder was yet another in the
"Ripper" series, whereas Dr Phillips' feelings appeared to be the opposite as will be seen in his lengthy report[8] of 22 July 1889:

1.
Re- Alice McKenzie
　　　　　Decd.
Called 1 AM Wednesday 17th July 1889. I went to Castle Alley, White-
chapel. Arr. 1.10 AM.
It was raining sharply.
Position of body.
Found the body of a woman lying on back. face turned sharply to right. temp.
moderate.
Right arm enclosed with shawl, which extended to end of fingers. from arm
flexed over chest.
Left arm not covered with shawl was flexed & hand rested on shoulder.
Wound in neck, left.
Left side of neck is incised, wound jagged, and exposed.
Position of Dress.
Clothes turned up & exposing genitals.
Abdomen wounded in wall.
Wound of wall of abdomen apparently not opening the cavity.
Temp. of body.
Warmth still perceptible under right cheek.
Body still warm where covered. Where exposed quite cold.
Pupils.

Pupils equal dilated & eyelids open.

Haemorrhage from wound in neck.

Blood poured out from wound in neck. clotted firmly & limited on pavement to the outline of the clothes & thin contact with the ground. The clot partly broken down at margin through action of the rain & the blood so mixed ran down slanting pavement into gutter & stagnated there by various objects has run down the water way several feet. The clot probably weighed $1\frac{1}{2}$ to $1\frac{3}{4}$ the whole amount of blood lost would not amount to more than 2 pts.

No artl. spirtg.

No arterial spirting seen.

No sign of anaesthetics.

No sign of drugs or anaesthetics.

2.

Exn. of body at mortuary.

In company with Mr. Arnold & Chief Inspr. West followed the body to Pavilion Yd. WhChl. & had it placed at once on the post mortem table in the shed used as a mortuary, and without stripping the body & without displacement of any part we discussed to confirm my former note.

The wound in neck is deeper & cleaner cut than appeared at first sight.

I left the body in charge of the police and gave instructions nothing was to be touched until the body was delivered over to the coroners officer or I had again possession of it. I had witnessed the police taking a "description"

Immediate communication with police.

I communicated my conclusions to Mr. Arnold & Ch. Inspr. West & subsequently to Col. Monsell at the Leman Street Stn. so far as I was able to do so.

Instructions fr. Coroner.

Early in the morning I received instructions from the Coroner to make a P.M. section & attend an enquiry at 5 P.M.

Arrangement for P.M. Exm.

As soon as I could make arrangements I communicated them to the Ch.Surgn. and Mr. Gordon Brown who expressed a wish to be present. both attended shortly after the hour appointed 2 P.M. the former accompanied by a friend. My colleague Mr. Clark attended and a "Mr. Boswick" [?] gained admission for a short time, not with my permission.

3.

P.M. made 2P.M. same day.

At 2 P.M. at the same place, I again viewed the body it was as far as I could discover in exactly the position I had left it.

Height.

Height 5ft 5in.

Rigor Mortis.

Rigor mortis well marked most in extremities.

Fore Arms & Face freckled.

Condn. of Body.

Body well nourished.

Discovery of & subst. loss of short clay pipe.

While searching the clothing one of the attendants found a short pipe, well used, which he thoughtlessly threw onto the ground & broke it. I had the pieces put on one side meaning to preserve them but up to the time of writing this report they have not been recovered by me.

Condition of Clothing.

The clothing was fastened round the body somewhat tightly & could only be raised so as to expose about ⅓ of the abdomen. The back part of the under garment was well saturated with blood stained fluid.

Bruises upper part of chest.

Over upon & below the left collar bone there is a well defined bruise about the size of a shilling situate about the junction of the inner ⅓ & outer ⅔ of the collar bone. & on the right side an inch below the sterno clavicular articulation is another larger and more defined bruise most marked at its outer border.

Dilated veins.

Between the mammaries in middle line of sternum in a direct line downwards with the last named bruise are several congested veins seen through the skin.

Scorings & Wounds of Abdomen.

Seven inches below right nipple commences a wound 7 inches long, not quite straight in direction, inclining first inwards & then outwards, deepest at its upper part and ending below in a subcutaneous dissection possibly 3 or perhaps 4 inches. [*in whole (?)*]

4.

Abdominal cavity *not opened*. Scoring on right side.

Neither abdominal cavity opened – or muscular covering divided.

Tailing towards inner border of this wound are seven dermal marks only dividing the skin & ascending above the deeper incision, & 7 similar scorings descending lower than the major wound. & between it & pubis.

One distinct became deeper over the pubis.

Marks & blood stains left side.

There are 5 small (excoriating) marks below and between umbilicus and pubis some what transverse in direction col red one ¾ in. in length, and the smallest a [ ] in length.

Somewhat nearer to the left side there stains of blood surrounding a bruise the size of a fourpenny piece, (& corresponding with scores on right side.)

The larger marking is the lowest and the smallest nearest the right side. & all of them are 4 in. from prominence of pelvis & 4 in. below umbilicus.

Old scars & signs of injury.

There are old scars & bruisings over patella front of shins & three distinct cicatrices on Dresum of left forearm.

Loss of terminal joint of left thumb from some cutting instrument, which has left half the nail.

Genital Signs.

There is no sign of Coitus.

Syphilitic Condylomata of vagina and ulceration of mucous membrane under clitoris.

Congestion [ ] Anal

Anal external piles & excretion of a small quantity of liquid faeces.

5.

Description of wound in neck

More superficial

Two jagged wounds commence from behind the left sterno mastoid muscle leaving a triangular piece of skin attached by its base to the outside (remaining) skin about an inch long and four inches forward & upwards.

Deeper.

The deepest incision divides the Sterno M. muscle except a few posterior fibres. the vessels of the neck & sheath, the division of the Common Carotid being above the Omo hyoid muscle, down to the transverse processes of the Cervical Vertebra.

There are four jagged cuts over angle of jaw where instrument had been arrested [?] over cut under jaw.

No sign of fall backwards.

No sign of bruise back of Head or under Scalp.

Brain app. & other visceral app. *fairly normal* & healthy.

Brain healthy but meningel vessels fuller than might have been expected.

Lungs old adhesions posterior part of right. Left healthy Both well filled with air & not congested.

Heart healthy small quantity of fluid in pericardium, colour red, walls good, Valves healthy. Cavities empty & contracted. Large vessels healthy no clots.

Liver, fairly healthy rather pale.

Spleen & Kidneys fairly healthy.

Stomach large contains rather more than a pint of pultaceous matter which has a faint alcoholic smell. mucous membrane pale.

Bladder contracted and empty.

Uterus small. healthy. unimpregnated.

Ovaries contain small cysts.

6.

Conclusions.

Death was caused through Syncope arising from the division of the vessels of neck left side.

Nature of instrument & its use.

The wound was caused by sharp cutting instrument with at least two strokes. was not suicidal, was made from left to right, while the body was on the ground & effected by someone who knew the position of the vessels, at any rate where to cut with reference to causing speedy death.

No sign of struggle but of holding down.

No sign of violent struggle but of body being held down by hand as evidenced by bruises on upper chest and collar bone.

Greater Pressure – right.

There was more pressure on the right side.

Further conclusions

No physiological reason why the woman should not have uttered a cry. The wound in the throat tends to confirm the conclusion submitted as to the wounds of the abdominal wall.

That death almost immediately followed the incision of the neck.

That the woman did not move after the said incision.

The superficial marks on left side of abdomen were characteristic of pressure with a Thumb and Fingers. they compared in position to a right hand placed on the abdomen pinching up a fold of skin for at least 3 inches.

That the smearing of blood was caused in this way.

The scoring and cuts of skin on Pubis were caused through the endeavour to pass the obstruction caused by the clothing.

The long wound right side of abdomen was inflicted by a sharp pointed instrument from above downwards & (there is evidence of two thrusts of instrument before withdrawal) the instrument turned laterally while making the undermining portion of wound which was made from right to left.

Admit that the appearances observed on left side of abdomen were caused by the pressure of a right hand (possibly to facilitate the introduction of an instrument under the (tight) clothing -there-

The right wounds were produced by a left handed cut.

The abdominal injuries were caused subsequent to the throat being cut.

The instrument used was smaller than the one used in most of the cases that have come under my observation in these "White chapel Murders."

Concurrence of Dr. G. Brown.

Dr. Gordon Brown (City Police Surgeon) has been good enough to express his concurrence in the foregoing conclusions, but he has not expressed his opinion concerning the following remarks which have not formally been submitted to him.

On Thursday about 6 P.M. I accompanied Dr. Bond to view the body of Dec'd and so far as I was able explained the appearances to him.

Decomposition had fairly begun, though not very markedly.

There was great difficulty without again opening up the incisions in giving a description of the appearances – and it appeared to me that the body had been washed since the former examination.

On Saturday last at noon I again in the presence of Dr. Brown re examined the body for the purpose of demonstrating the appearances on the Abdomen.

I believe I satisfied him of the correctness of the appearances, & this must be so as he has since signified generally his assent to the report.

After careful and long deliberation I cannot satisfy myself on purely anatomical & professional grounds that the Perpetrator of all the "WhChl.murders" is one man.

I am on the contrary impelled to a contrary conclusion. This noting the mode of procedure & the character of the mutilations & judging of motive in connection with the latter.

I do not here enter into the comparison of the cases neither do I take into account what I admit may be almost conclusive evidence in favour of the one man theory if all the surrounding circumstances & other evidence are considered.

Holding it as my duty to report on the P.M. appearances and express an opinion solely on Professional Grounds, based upon my own observations. For this purpose I have ignored all evidence not coming under my own observation.

Geo.B.Phillips
2 Spital Square E
July 22nd.'89.

There is then a report[9] dated 19 July 1889 from Inspector Henry Moore regarding William W. Brodie:

METROPOLITAN POLICE.

Criminal Investigation Department,
Scotland Yard,
19th July 1889.

SUBJECT Murder of Alice McKenzie
at Whitechapel.

Reference to papers 52983.

Referring to case of murder at Castle Alley, Whitechapel, on 17th Inst., for which a man named William W. Brodie has given himself up at Leman St. Station; vide attached Report and Telegrams.

I beg to report that this morning when "Brodie" appeared sober, I saw him, and afterwards he volunteered a statement which I took down in writing and herewith submitted.

After I had taken the statement I examined his clothing; but could not discover any trace of blood.

Whilst examining his clothing he remarked that he had now committed 9 murders in Whitechapel; but none of them had troubled him except this last one; that was why he had given himself up to Police.

I find from this man's papers that on 7th May 1887 he was sentenced to 14 years P.S. for Larceny in a Dwelling House, and was liberated on 24th Augt./88.

On searching him nothing of importance was found. Directions respectfully asked.

Henry Moore, Inspr.

[*There is a marginal minute:* "Let him be charged as a lunatic. [*initialled*] 19/7."]

The next report[10], dated 19 July 1889, again refers to William Brodie:

METROPOLITAN POLICE.

Convict Supervision Office,

19th July 1889.

Lic:Holder Register No. D517 Office No. 35944 Name William Broder[?]

I beg to report that Willm. Brodie was sentenced at the Cent. Crim. Court Sess. 7th May 1877 to 14 years penal serv: for larceny in a dwelling house, (City Case).

He was released on licence 22nd August 1888 & went to reside at 2 Harveys Buildings, Strand. On the 5th Sep: 1888 he reported at this Office his intention of leaving this country for the Cape of Good Hope, via Southampton, per: S.S. Africana. Since that date and until the 16th inst. nothing more was heard of him, but on the date last mentioned he again reported at this Office stating he had returned from the Cape & would again reside at 2 Harveys Blgs., Strand.

Thos. Haines Insp.

The next report[11], dated 19 July 1889, also refers to Brodie, and was submitted by Sergeant Godley:

METROPOLITAN POLICE.

H Division.

19th day of July, 1889.

Whitechapel Murders
Reference to Papers 52983
Re William Brodie detained at Leman Street Police Station.

I beg to report that I made enquiries at Foresters Hall Place Clerkenwell Road where the above has brothers named James & Thomas Brodie who carry on Business as Printers.

I was informed by Mr. Walter Slater the Manager that Mr. James Brodie was out of town and would not return till Saturday the 20th inst. and his address is not known.

Mr. Slater saw the above in Mr. Thomas Brodie's office talking to him at about 4.45 p.m. on Tuesday the 16th and Wednesday the 17th and he is of opinion that William Brodie is a reckless character and addicted to drink.

G. Godley Sergt.

Henry Moore Insp.

There is also a report[12] of the same date by Sgt. Bradshaw, as follows:

METROPOLITAN POLICE.

H Division.

19th July 1889.

The Whitechapel Murders.

Reference to Papers 52983.

Re Licence Holder William Brodie, Office No. 35.944. I beg to report having made inquiries at 2. Harveys Buildings, Strand, and was informed by Mrs. Salvage and her daughter to whom Brodie is apparently well known that he came there between 11 & 12 on Tuesday morning last and went to bed between 10 & 11 p.m. remaining in the house till about 11. A.m. Wednesday morning, when he went out, and subsequently returned about 8 p.m. same evening in a state of drunkenness, he immediately going into the W.C. where he was subsequently discovered asleep and taken up to bed. Mrs. salvage and daughter further stated that they have known "Brodie" as being of a very quiet disposition, and when in drink he is very curious in his manners and says some quaint things.

E.C.Badham sgt.

Henry Moore, Inspr.

This is followed by the lengthy statement[13] of Brodie taken by Inspector Moore, same date:

Leman Street Station

19th July / 89.

I, William Brodie, wish to make a statement and to give myself up for committing a murder up a court way in High St. Whitechapel at about 2 a.m. on Wednesday morning last.

Last December I went to South Africa (Kimberley) on board the S.S. "Athenian" as a 3rd. class passenger which the books will show in the Mason [?] Company's office. I obtained employment in the Diamond Mines, and returned to England per the S.S. "Trojan" via Southampton, arriving at Waterloo Station at 6 p.m. on Monday 15th inst. My object in returning was to find a woman living in Whitechapel who about 2 years ago gave me the bad disorder.

On arrival at Waterloo I roamed about and eventually lodged at No. 2 Harveys Buildings, Strand, paying 6d for same. Mr. Salvage kept the house. Then on Tuesday morning I reported myself at the Convict Office, Gt. Scotland Yard; and in the afternoon I visited my brother Thomas who carries on business with my brother James, at Foresters Hall Place, Clerkenwell Road, as Lithographic Printers, etc. I then went to Lands End in Cornwall, but I only stayed there about 10 minutes. I walked there and back in half an hour or three quarters. It was before dark I got back; I think it was about 8 p.m. I returned into Whitechapel through an avenue of trees from the forest. I strolled about for 3 or 4 hours, and after the Public Houses closed and the place got dark I went into a Square where there were some coster-mongers barrows and some hundreds of people who were all smoking, both men and women. The entrance to the Square is a wide opening off the Whitechapel Road.

I remained in the Square until all the people had left, which was a very long time. I think it was 1691 or 1721 o'clock, at which time a woman came into the Square from the Whitechapel Road. I stopped her and asked her how she was going on. She was a fine woman dressed in bright red dress, boots, and hat. I gave her 1/- to have connection with her; but did not do so. She laid down under the barrow when I whipped out my knife from my outside coat pocket and cut her throat when I heard some one coming and I went away after wiping my knife on a whisp of straw which was lying near. It is a white handled knife specially made for the purpose at Sheffield. It is as sharp as a razor, and it is now with other things in charge of a man at the Baths in Lambeth Road. The knife is in a bag containing a brush and comb, pair of trousers, an old pair of boots. I had my bag (which is a red one) with me when I committed the murder, and after walking about till morning I went to Harveys Buildings and had some breakfast, which is the last meal I have had.

I think it was the York Road Baths where I left the bag and not the Lambeth Baths.

[sgd] William Wallace Brodie.

The above statement taken by and in the presence of Local Insp. Reid H. and P.S. Nearn C.O.

Henry Moore, Inspr.

The clothing which this man is wearing has been examined, and there are no signs of blood upon it, although he states he wore it at the time he committed. He appears of unsound mind and I do not think any reliance can be placed upon his statement. Inquiries are being made to find the bag he refers to.

T.Arnold Sup.

This statement is followed by a report[14] by Inspector Henry Moore, as follows:

METROPOLITAN POLICE.
Criminal Investigation Department,
Scotland Yard,
20th day of July 1889.

Whitechapel Murders
Reference to Papers
52983
Referring to attached, re arrest of William W. Brodie.

I beg to report that as directed by Assistant Commissioner I charged "Brodie" with "Being a Lunatic, wandering at large"

He was this day brought up before Mr. Lushington at the Thames Police Court, and in the end the learned Magistrate thought it advisable to re-charge the prisoner on his own confession with the wilful murder of Alice McKenzie. This I did when the prisoner was remanded till 11 am. 27th inst.

I herewith attach Extract from "Evening Standard" which give almost a verbatim report of the proceedings.

Henry Moore, Inspr.
T. Arnold Supd.

The statements taken are then appended, the first[15] being that of Margaret Franklin:

H Leman Street
22nd July 1889

Statement of Margaret Franklin, who says

I live at 56 Flower & Dean, I have known the deceased woman about 14 or 15 years in the neighbourhood I cannot say if she was married, but she used to live with a blind man, I have only known her as "Alice"

I was sitting on a door-step in Brick Lane on Tuesday 16th when I saw her passing toward Whitechapel about 20 minutes to 12. I asked her how she was getting on, she said, "All right I can't stop now" She did not appear to have been drinking She was wearing a shawl I did not see her again It commenced to rain slightly just after she left us.

Taken by A.Pearce Sergt C.I.D.

The next statement[16] is that of Elizabeth Ryder:

H Leman Street

22nd July 1889

Statement of Elizabeth Ryder who says

I am married, I am the deputy of 52 Gun Street, I saw the body of deceased at the Mortuary and identified it as Mrs. McKenzie who has been living at the house about 12 months on and off, she lived with John McCormack

I saw her about ½ past 8 on 16th passing from the kitchen to the street she had a light shawl on but no bonnet. McCormack came to me between 11 &12 p.m. and asked me if I had seen her, or whether she had paid her lodgings, I said "No" She had been drinking when she left the house. I have seen her the worse for drink before, but she rarely went out on those occasions

I have often seen her smoking she would borrow pipes from the other lodgers in the kitchen.

I have never seen her with any other man but McCormack.

Taken by A.Pearce Sergt. C.I.D.

There is a report[17] by Sergeant McCarthy on enquiries made in public houses regarding McKenzie:

METROPOLITAN POLICE

H Division.

27 day of July 1889

With reference to Asst. Commissioner's minute on attached papers. I beg to report having made careful enquiry at the "Royal Cambridge" Tavern which adjoins the Music Hall of that name, also at the public houses in the vicinity. The barman and barmaid of the "Royal Cambridge" P.H. both declared they were unable to remember a blind boy coming in there with a woman on the evening of the 16th inst. nor do they recollect any woman asking a man to treat her to a drink, although, they said, it is quite possible such a thing did occur but they didn't notice it.

At the other public-houses in the neighbourhood of the Cambridge Hall no one seemed to remember a blind boy with a woman calling on the date referred or any other day.

John McCarthy P.S. L.

Submitted

Hy. Moore, Inspr

TArnold Su.

The next report[18] is submitted by Sergeant Eugene C. Badham regarding Brodie:

METROPOLITAN POLICE

H Division

23rd day of July 1889

Re Licence Holder William Brodie Office No. 35.944- I beg to report having made enquiries at the Offices of the Union S.S. Company, 11 Leadenhall Street, E.C. and find that he/ Brodie / sailed on board the S.S. Athenian as a 3rd Class passenger on 6th September 1888 via Southampton, bound for Kimberley, South Africa, where he arrived in due course. He returned from South Africa on 15th instant per S.S. Trojan U.S. Coy. and during the voyage home he was employed as a fireman, i.e. having worked his passage. I was further informed that during the voyage home he / Brodie / performed his duty in a proper manner, and nothing out of the ordinary routine occurred on his account to arouse suspicion.

Eugene C. Bradshaw
Sergeant.

Henry Moore, Inspr.
T Arnold Supd.

The next report[19] is again by Sgt John McCarthy and is dated 24 July 1889:

METROPOLITAN POLICE.

H Division

24 day of July 1889

Referring to the attached I beg to report having seen the blind boy George Dixon at 29 Star Street Commercial Rd. He says he went with Mrs. McKenzie into a public-house near the Cambridge Music Hall at about 10 minutes past 7 on Tuesday evening 16th. He heard Mrs. McKenzie ask someone if they would stand a drink and the reply was "yes". After remaining a few minutes Mrs. McKenzie led him back to 52 Gun St. & left him there.

The boy Dixon says he would be able to recognise the voice of the person who spoke to Mrs. McKenzie in the public house.

John McCarthy P.S. 'L.

Submitted. I cannot think that the man who spoke to McKenzie at 7.10p.m. 16th had anything to do with the murder.

Henry Moore, Inspr.
T Arnold Supd.

There is then a report[20] submitted by Inspector Henry Moore, dated 27 July 1889:

METROPOLITAN POLICE.
Criminal Investigation Department,
Scotland Yard,
27th day of July, 1889.

Referring to case of William Wallace Brodie, as in attached.

I beg to report that prisoner was this morning again brought up on remand before F. Lushington, Esq., at Thames Police Court.

I acquainted the learned Magistrate with Brodie's movements since his release from Prison; also as directed by Assistant Commissioner; Vide Minutes on dockets 105 and 106, and evidence was given by Mr. Salvage, of 2 Harveys Buildings, Strand, to the effect that he assisted prisoner to bed "very drunk" about 11 p.m. 16th and that he did not go out again until about 10.20 next morning.

Mr. Lushington informed me that he had been kept under observation by the prison surgeon who had sent a certificate, stating that prisoner was now sane; although at the time he entered the prison he was suffering from acute alcoholism, causing hallucinations.

Prisoner was ultimately discharged; when I directed P.S. Bradshaw to re-arrest him upon the warrant for Fraud; which he did, and afterwards conveyed him to King's Cross Road Station where he was charged. He will be taken before Magistrate on Monday 29th.

I have submitted a report of particulars of this case with Convict Office papers for information of Chf. Inspr. Neame.

I herewith submit Newspaper Extract of proceedings at Police Court this day.

Henry Moore, Inspr.
T Arnold Sup.

There is then a report[21] from the *Kimberley Advertiser*, dated 29 June 1889, reporting Brodie confessing to the Whitechapel murders there, whilst drunk:

THE WHITECHAPEL ATROCITIES: A SELF-ACCUSED KIMBER-LEYITE:- A respectably attired man, who said his name was William Brodie, was brought before the Police Court, Capetown on Saturday last, under somewhat peculiar circumstances. Inspector Rowbotham said the man came to the Police-station and accused himself of having committed the White-chapel murders. He appeared to be suffering from a bad attack of "the horrors''. The Magistrate asked Brodie how long he had been in the Colony? – Brodie: About ten months, sir. Further asked what he had been doing during that time, Brodie said he had been up-country, and in Kimberley. The Magistrate said the man had evidently been drinking, hence his confession. Brodie said he left the Ashton Extension Railway, where he had worked, about ten days back. He had also worked at the Sultfontein Mine, Kimberley, and had come down to Capetown for a spree. He would return to Kimberley at once, if allowed to do so. The Magistrate thereupon ordered Brodie to be discharged advising him to give up drinking. – cutting out of Kimberley Advertiser, which arrived from South Africa on Monday last.

There are then two[22] minutes:

This extract has been sent by another [,] the date being given (as 29th June '89) [   ] with [   ] other papers (I have informed the Comr.) RA 26/7.

Mr Anderson/
    It wd. appear that "Brodie" has been "confessing" before now It wd be well to verify this extract by refer, to the Kimberley Advertiser as there is no date on extract, & then to officer in charge of case JM 29/7.

Returning to the employment of additional police officers as a result of the murder, a report[23] dated 17 July 1889 reads as follows:

Urgent & Confidential. A48000M/44.   WHITEHALL.
                                                        17 July 1889.
Sir,
    I am directed by the Secretary of State to acquaint you that upon the application of the Commissioner of Metropolitan Police, he has sanctioned the retention of the temporary augmentation of 1 Inspector 3 Sergeants and 30 Constables authorized for duty in Trafalgar Square, together with the addition of 2 Sergeants and 20 Constables for special duty in Whitechapel temporarily, for a period of two months.

                                I am,
The Receiver for the   Sir,
Metropolitan Police District   Your obedient Servant,
&c. &c. &c.   Godfrey Lushington.

There is a report[24] enclosing a letter by the Reverend Samuel A. Barnett which was printed in *The Times* of 23 July 1889:

[Stamped: – HOME OFFICE 25JUL.1889 DEPT N2-] No. A49301/171
DATE 23 July 1889.   H.O.
REFERENCES, &c.   Whitechapel Horrors
   Letter from the Revd. S.A. Barnett in the "Times" complaining of the
state of the streets & houses in Whitechapel.
MINUTES.
acted on – see within.
    [?JRB]
      27/7
A49301/171

Whitechapel Horrors.
"The Times". 23 July 1889.
WHITECHAPEL HORRORS.
TO THE EDITOR OF THE TIMES.
Sir, – When the series of murders occurred last year you allowed me to point
out that the act of some maniac was a less evil than the state of life shows to be
common in this neighbourhood.

At the time I was encouraged to hope that the freeholders of a large
property which is in the heart of this criminal quarter might have applied, or
have put it in the power of others to apply, some radical remedy, by closing as
leases fell in the houses in which men and women live as beasts, where crime
is protected, and where children or country people are led on to ruin, or by
employing watchmen to enforce order and make the neighbourhood distasteful to the wicked, or by getting Parliamentary powers to clear the district as
one morally insanitary.

Nothing has been done, though many were ready with time and money, if
the freeholders would have moved. The houses in the hands of the same
occupants are put to the same base uses, and the streets still offer almost every
night scenes of brutality and degradation. A body of inhabitants – residents at
Toynbee-hall and others – have patrolled the neighbourhood during the last
nine months on many nights every week between the hours of 11 p.m. and 3
a.m. Their record tells of rows in which stabbing is common, but on which
the police are able to get no charges; of fights between women stripped to the
waist, of which boys and children are spectators; of the protection afforded to
thieves, and of such things as could only occur where opinion favours vice.
The district in which all this happens is comparatively small; it forms, indeed,
a black spot, three or four acres in extent, in the midst of a neighbourhood
which in no way deserves the reputation for ill-conduct.

A district so limited might be easily dealt with, and its reform is more
important than even the capture of a murderer, who would have no victims if
they were not prepared by degradation. Its reform will be possible when

public opinion will condemn as offenders those who directly or indirectly live on the profits of vice.   I am truly yours,

SAMUEL A. BARNETT.

St. Jude's, Whitechapel, July 20.

? make official, and refer to Police for observations on [   ] of allegations.
CW. July 24.
GL
24 July '89
Wrote Commr. 27.7.89
a/5.8.89 (1/173)

Mr Lushington's letter[25] to the Chief Commissioner of the Metropolitan Police, as regards this letter, appears in the files as follows:

A49301/171   WHITEHALL.
27 July 1889.

Sir,

I am directed by the Secretary of State to refer to the letter from the Revd. S.A. Barnett, which appeared in "The Times" of the 23rd instant, headed "Whitechapel Horrors"; and to say that Mr Matthews will be glad to have your observations on the allegations therein made.

I am,
Sir,
Your obedient Servant,
Godfrey Lushington

The Commissioner of
Metropolitan Police
&c.   &c.   &c.

As a result of this request the Reverend Barnett was seen by Superintendent Arnold of H Division, who then submitted his report[26], dated 3 August 1889, for the information of the Chief Commissioner, Mr Monro:

METROPOLITAN POLICE.
H Division.
3rd August 1889

[*Marginal ref* – "No. 57885 attached"]

I beg to report that I have seen Mr. Barnett with reference to his letter in the "Times" and I find he speaks generally from reports which have been made to him by persons connected with Toynbee Hall but particularly as to the uses made of the lodgings which are known as furnished rooms, which are let to prostitutes, sometimes by the week, and in some cases by the night, and where men are taken as in the case of the murdered woman Kelly in Millers Court. He has been in communication with the Parochial Authorities on this question and was advised by the Vestry Clerk of Spitalfields that such places do not come within the meaning of the Act. Numbers of the women living in these rooms associate with men who partially if not wholly subsist on their wretched earnings, and it is surprising how quickly they submit to the brutal treatment which they receive at the hands of these fellows, and how they resent any interference for their protection, it being very seldom they can be induced to go to the Station to prefer a Charge, or if they do go so far they will not appear at the Court. It is such cases as these Mr Barnett alludes to when he writes Police can get no charges. He does not attribute any laxity on the part of Police, on the contrary praises them & considers they do all they can under the circumstances.

There can be no doubt whatever that vice in its worst forms exists in Whitechapel, and the only remedy for this is by clearing out the Lodging Houses as they at present exist, and substitute improved dwellings with better supervision which would be of immense advantage to the locality, but at the expense of other districts as there are a class of persons at present resorting to the neighbourhood who would not go to large and comfortable houses if restrictions were placed upon them, and no doubt owners or occupiers of houses would be found ready to meet their wants, although it would be a long time before such places became centralised as they at present are in Whitechapel and wherever they spring up they will depreciate the surrounding property.

That Common Lodging Houses of improved construction & with good supervision can be carried on is illustrated in the case of the Victoria Home in Commercial Street which has been established by an Association of which Lord Radstock is Chairman.

I pointed out to Mr Barnett that by clearing the neighbourhood he mentions, the persons at present there would be driven into the adjoining parishes which would naturally cause discontent, but he appears to think every one should clear his own house without regard to his neighbours.

Brawling and fighting does and will take place amongst the low class of persons to be found in Whitechapel, but not nearly to such an extent as might be expected and is generally believed by persons non resident in the district.

T Arnold Sup.

As a result of this report Mr Monro replied[27] to the Home Office, detailing these facts as follows:

[Stamped on cover: – HOME OFFICE 6 AUG. 89 RECEIVED]
No. A49301/173
DATE 5 August 1889.   The Commissioner of Police.
REFERENCES, &c.   <u>Vice in Whitechapel.</u>
     Reports on the subject of the Revd. S.A. Barnett's recent letter in the "Times." /171

MINUTES.
The Secretary of State.
                         Aug 8/89
                              CW

                              GL
                              8 Aug '89

H.M.
     9 Aug. /89.

Then follows the Chief Commissioner's report:

[Stamped: – HOME OFFICE 6 AUG. 89 RECEIVED] A49301/173
C.J.W.
          57885/1174   Whitehall Place S.W.
                                         5th August, 1889.
Sir,
     With reference to your letter of the 27th ulto., A49301/171, on the subject of the Revd. S.A. Barnett's recent letter to the "Times" respecting the condition of Whitechapel, I have to acquaint you, for the information of the Secretary of State, that anything Mr. Barnett writes on such a subject is entitled to respect, for noone who knows the work which the Vicar of St. Judes has done, and the spirit in which he does it, can entertain anything but sentiments of regard for him and sympathy with his aspirations. Practically what he says is this: Vice of a very low type exists in Whitechapel; such vice manifests itself in brawling and acts of violence which shock the feelings of respectable persons; these acts of violence are not repressed by action taken either before the Police or Magisterial authorities. Clear out the slums and lodging houses to which vicious persons resort, and vice will disappear, respectability taking its place.
     There is no doubt whatever that vice of a low and degraded type is only too visible in Whitechapel. The facility with which the Whitechapel murderer obtains victims has brought this prominently to notice, but to

anyone who will take a walk late at night in the district where the recent atrocities have been committed, the only wonder is that his operations have been so restricted. There is no lack of victims ready to his hand, for scores of these unfortunate women may be seen any night muddled with drink in the streets and alleys, perfectly reckless as to their safety, and only anxious to meet with anyone who will keep them in plying their miserable trade.

There is no doubt that brawling and fighting do go on, repressed as far as possible by the Police; but it must be remembered that these women do not care to be protected against those who assault them, very seldom have recourse to the Station to complain, and still more seldom appear at any Police Court to prosecute any charge which they may have laid before the Police.

It is also true that Common Lodging Houses are not all that they might be in the way of discouraging immorality, although I do not think that so much of the reproach in this respect which is generally levelled at them in reality is attributable to them. On this subject I have already expressed my views in my letter of the 26th December, 1888. Much however of the immorality which goes on finds its place in the low lodgings which are let to prostitutes by the day or week, where they take men home, and with reference to which the law is practically powerless. These are the houses from which no charges are brought before the Police, and to these much more than to the Common Lodging Houses is the violence conjoined with immorality attributable.

That respectability would be benefitted by clearing out such localities admits of little doubt; that the moral atmosphere of Whitechapel would be purified by the substitution of better lodging houses for the dens at present to be found there is perfectly clear; but this would not remove vice, it would only delocalise it, and transfer it to some neighbouring parish at present not quite so disreputable as some parts of Whitechapel.

I do not mean to say that this might not be a gain. It certainly would be a gain to Whitechapel, and it may be said that if other parishes took similar steps similar steps would follow within their limits. But the question still remains "What is to become of the residuum of vice which is thus moved on?" I do not believe in such a transfer of a vicious population as likely to remove vice generally from the Metropolis, and I suspect it may be taken as a fact that whenever landlords or lodging house keepers can secure their rent they will not hesitate in taking it from prostitutes with as much readiness as from persons of a different class.

Behind the whole question lies the larger matter of street prostitution generally, and until that is taken up and regulated (objectionable as this may appear to a public which confuses between liberty and licence) the mere multiplying of comfortable lodging houses will not have any appreciable effect in diminishing the number of and evils resulting from a class who do not want comfortable lodging houses, and the scene of whose operations is on the streets.

I am,

Sir,

Your most obedient Servant,

J.Monro

The Under
   Secretary of State,;

Following the McKenzie murder there follow the usual requests for sanction of allowances in respect of additional officers drafted to the Whitechapel area to assist in the enquiries.

A Home Office file[28] with such a request is dated 26 July 1889, as follows:

No. A49301G/8   5185/6

DATE 26 July 1889.   Commissioner of Police

REFERENCES, &c. Recommends grant of a special allowance of 2/- a day to the C.I. Department officers from other divisions who are employed specially in connection with the Whitechapel murders.

<u>Pressing</u>.

MINUTES.

To Receiver for financial observations.

Index 5/8   CW July 27.

29 JUL.89

I understand from the Commissioner that the total expense involved will be very small, and under these circumstances I think the special allowance may be sanctioned. [?] ARP/

29 July

?sanction

CM July 30

GL

31 July '89

Wrote Commr.
[?] 1.8.89

The Chief Commissioner's report[29] follows:

A49301G/8

96318/9

4, Whitehall Place,
26th July, 1889.

Sir,

I have to acquaint you, for the information of the Secretary of State, that the Criminal Investigation Department officers from other Divisions who are employed specially in connection with the murders in Whitechapel are engaged, on an average, for 15 hours daily making enquiries and patrolling the district to gain information respecting the outrages.-

Their authorised refreshment allowances as Sergeants is 1s/2d per diem ; but, as they are absent from their homes and divisions for so many hours, this does not cover the expense which they necessarily incur.-

Under the circumstances I strongly recommend that these officers be allowed the same rate of refreshment allowances as the Sergeants attached to the Central Office of the Criminal Investigation Department, viz: − 2s/- per diem, and I have to request that Mr. Secretary Matthews may be pleased to sanction this allowance as a special case.-

I am,
Sir,
Your obedient Servant,
J.Monro

The Under Secretary
      of State
  &c &c &c
      Home Office

There follows a similar file cover[30], relating to plain clothes allowance, dated 26 July 1889:

No. A49301G/9   5185/6
                                        1 AUG.89

DATE   26 July 1889.   Commissioner of Police.
REFERENCES, &C.   Recommends grant of a plain clothes allowance of 1s/-d a day to the men now employed on special patrol duty in connection with the Whitechapel Murder.

MINUTES.

This came to me tied up with other papers to which it did not belong [*rest illegible*] CW July 31.

First to Receiver of Police for financial observations. Index 5/9 CW July 31.

For favour of immediate reply as Commr. is pressing for an answer.

Having regard to the precedent I think this allowance must be granted it will amount to £14. 14. 0 a week. Perhaps the S. of S. will see fit to limit either the amount payable in the gross or the duration of the employment.

A.R.P.

T.O.   1 August.

?Say for two months. Report again at the end of that time.

C.M. Aug. 1. 89.

GL

2 Aug. 89

Wrote Commr. & Recd.

3.8.89.

[?comment]

a/18.9.89

(10)

The report[31] follows:

A49301G/9
96318/8

4, Whitehall Place,

S.W.

26th July, 1889.

Sir,

I have to acquaint you, for the information of the Secretary of State, that 3 Sergeants and 39 Constables are employed in plain clothes on special patrol duty in connection with the Whitechapel Murder.

As I pointed out in my letter of the 7th December last with reference to the men then similarly employed, this work is specially irksome and unpleasant and makes considerable demands on the endurance of the men. – They have continuous night duty and are practically doing the work of permanent patrols who receive a plain clothes allowance of 1s/- per day instead of 1s/11d per week. –

I have therefore to recommend that Mr. Secretary Matthews may be pleased to sanction a plain clothes allowance to these men of 1s/- per day instead of 1s/11d per week to which they are entitled, as was granted in the case of men employed during the early part of this year on similar duties. –

I am

Sir,

Your obedient Servant,

J.Monro

The Under Secretary
          of State
    &c   &c   &c
          Home Office.

The Home Office response[32] to this is noted on a file cover dated 31 July 1889:

[Stamped: – RECEIVER METROPOLITAN POLICE DISTRICT AUG 1889]
H.O. 31 July
Whitechapel Murders. 1/- a day allowance.
Refers for financial observations of Recr. recommendation of Commr. to grant a plain clothes allowance of 1/- a day to the officers employed on special patrol duty in Whitechapel.
    For favour of immediate reply as Commr. is pressing for an answer.

Copy of Receiver's minute on HO papers A49301g/9.
Having regard to the precedent I think this allowance must be granted – it will amount to £14. 14.–0 a week.
    Perhaps the S of S will see fit to limit either the amount payable in the gross or the duration of employment.

(Sgd.). A.R.P.
1 August. 89.

Papers[33] follow in a similar fashion:

A49301G/8   [Receiver's stamp dated 4 AUG.89]

1st August 1889.

<u>Pressing</u>

Sir,
    I am directed by the Secretary of State to inform you that on the Commissioner's application he has authorized the grant to the officers of the Criminal Investigation Department who are brought to Whitechapel from other Divisions in connection with the recent murders there, of the special refreshment allowance of 2/- a day ; and I am to signify to you his sanction for the payment of the same.

The Receiver	I am, Sir,
for	your obedient servant
the Metropolitan Police District	Godfrey Lushington

Notes on the file cover[34], read:

H.O.
1st Augt.
Whitechapel Murders, Special Allowance.
Sanctions grant to C.I.D. officers (brought to Whitechapel from other
Divisions) of a specl. reft. allce. of 2s/- a day.

Accountant to note
this authority
Noted Mr Wilby
[*illeg.*] A.R.P.
2 August. 2.8.89.

Then a further file cover[35] follows:

H.O.
3rd Augt.
Whitechapel Murders. Allowances.
Sanctions payment, for period of 2 months, of the plain clothes allowance of
1/- a day to 3 P.S. & 39 P.C. now employed in plain clothes in
Whitechapel.
Accountant to note.
Noted. A.R.P.
8. August 89
Mr. Wilby to note.
T.O. Done [*illeg.*] 12/8/89.
I have this day seen Mr. S Bathurst, who informs me that the Commr. in
asking for this 1/- per diem intended it as a refreshment allowance and
that it will be charged on "Black Letters" accordingly in our Cash Book
against Extraordinary Exps. instead of against clothing as originally
supposed.
                        [*illeg*] 23/8/89
Mr. [*?chance*] to note when entering these allowances that they are all to go
under Sch 5.9-

                                                    C.C.
                                                    25/8

Noted
    J.F-[?]
        22.8.89

It is interesting to note that at the time of the investigation of the
McKenzie murder, Inspector Henry Moore had taken over from In-

spector Abberline as the officer in charge of the on-the-ground investigation of the Whitechapel Murders. Moore was to remain in charge for
the remainder of the active enquiries in the case.

CHAPTER 29

10 September 1889 – Murder of an Unknown Woman

A brief survey of the facts in the case of the discovery of a female torso under a railway arch in Pinchin Street, St George's-in-the-East, in September 1889 is sufficient to indicate that this victim should not be numbered with the 1888 tally of the "Ripper". However, the circumstances of this case, and the reports written by the police of the time, are sufficiently interesting to reward the researcher with information relevant to his or her studies – the case is, indeed, included in the official files of the Whitechapel Murders.

The police file[1] is headed: *Trunk of a female – Found on 10th September 1889* and is followed by a sketch and plan of the location drawn by Inspector Charles Ledger, G Division, who would appear to have been the Metropolitan Police plan maker. From this sketch it can seen that the torso was discovered just inside the first railway arch in Pinchin Street from its junction with Backchurch Lane. This arch still exists today, AD 2000, although it is, as are the others, bricked over at the front to create garages, workshops and suchlike.

There is a lengthy report[2] by Chief Inspector Swanson, dated 10 September 1889, in the file:

METROPOLITAN POLICE.
Criminal Investigation Department,
Scotland Yard,
10th day of September, 1889.

Re – Human Remains
found at Pinchin
St. Whitechapel.

I beg to report that after an examination of the railway arch in Pinchin Street, where the trunk of a woman was found, and a close examination of the trunk, the following facts presented themselves:-

1st. Upon the spot when the trunk was found, there was no evidence of any blood, and a footmark from the nature of the ground was an impossibility; nor was there left anything in the shape of a cloth or sack to carry the trunk in.

2nd. The place of disposal must have been a selected spot; i.e. it must have been decided upon by viewing, for on all sides of it not a single inhabitant resides but it is faced by a pailing or wooden fence, and flanked by a dead wall, so that the place gained disposal was easy.

3rd. The appearance of the trunk minus head and legs, was as follows:- the head which had been cut off by clean <u>right</u> handed cuts, the vertebra being "jointed" left the neck with blood oozing from it, while both legs had also been "jointed", by right handed cuts, but the dismemberment had taken place at an earlier period than the head for the raw flesh had from continued exposure dried on the surface which presented a blackened appearance in consequence. The wound beginning at the lower part of the sternum, cutting through the skin, fatty substance, and penetrating the bowels, and uterus slightly, extended to the left side of the <u>labia major</u>. The trunk presented the undoubted appearance of having decomposition begun. Upon the chemise which was cut at the arms and down the front, I understand from Inspr Reid who examined it, there was not a single mark of any kind and the article itself of common manufacture and fabric. Beyond a small semi-circular cut on the index finger of right hand, and bruises on both arms, which the surgeons say they will be better able to describe after the post mortem examination there is absolutely nothing by which the trunk could be identified.

From Nos. 1&3 it becomes evident that death by whatever means foul or otherwise, took place, not at the spot where the trunk was found, but at some house or place, near or distant, according to Dr. Hibbert twenty four hours prior to the finding, and according to Mr. Clark, Dr. Phillips' assistant, two days, so that under any circumstances the body must have lain twenty four hours in some house or place, before removal, and disposal, so that the place of disposal (no.2) could be decided upon in the meantime. Now from the surgeons it was ascertained, firstly that as the trunk was so full of blood death did not take place from hemorrhage [*sic*], therefore death could not have taken place by cutting the throat, and the absence of the head prevents them saying that it was from violence to it, (which appears to me most probable as the trunk contains no stabs to cause death). What becomes most apparent is the absence of the attack upon the genitals as in the series of Whitechapel murders beginning at Bucks Row and ending in Miller's Court. Certainly if it ["was" – *deleted*] be a murder there was time enough for the murderer to cut off the head and limbs there was time to mutilate as in the series mentioned. It appears rather to go side by side with the Rainham, Whitehall and Chelsea murders.

The question of how conveyed is in the region of theory, for if conveyed by cart, then no limit can be fixed, but if by hand about 250 yards would be the limit; consequently enquiry has been made to find any shed house or place within that limit, so as to ascertain who what, and how the occupier was engaged, but more especially to find the missing parts.

The enquiry is being continued so far as barrows, houses sheds or places are concerned.

DonaldSSwanson
Ch Inspr
T Arnold Supd

A report[3] dated 11 September 1889 by Inspector Edmund Reid is included:

METROPOLITAN POLICE.
H Division,
11th day of September 1889.

Human remains

I beg to submit the attached reports received from P S s Thick and White and to report that on receiving information of the discovery of the Human Remains in Pinchin Street St. Georges 10th inst I at once directed P.S. White to search the adjoining Railway Arches and other likely places in the neighbourhood with a view to trace the missing parts of the body also to make inquiries with a view to gain information as to who deposited the portion of body in the arch.

I also directed P.S. Thick to make inquiries at sheds, houses, and places where barrows are kept, or lent out on hire also at butchers in the neighbourhood of Pinchin Street with a view to gain any information regarding the matter.

I directed P.S. Godley to search information with a view to trace missing persons and the identification of the remains.

I also had telegram sent to A.S asking that search be at once made with a view to find the missing portions of the body.

I have also had several officers making inquiries in the neighbourhood of Pinchin Street with a view to gain any information respecting the above matter.

I asked the Inspr. of the dust carts for the Parish of St. Georges to ask his men and direct them to report to him if any blood stained clothes were taken from any house, and let police know at once. This was done and information was received from [ ], stating that some had been found in Batty Street which is being inquired into.

Inquiries are still being made in the neighbourhood of Pinchin Street with a view to gain any information in the matter.

Edmund Reid
L.Inspector.

Submitted. Respecting the clothing found in Batty St. bearing blood stains. I have made enquiry, and although not yet quite completed I am satisfied that they are the result of a confinement. Special report will follow.

Henry Moore, Inspr.
T Arnold Supd.

A report[4] dated 11 September 1889, was submitted by Inspector Pattenden regarding enquiries made:

METROPOLITAN POLICE.
H Division,
11th September, 1889

Enquiries re murdered
remains of woman.

I beg to report having made enquiries re. Reporters met by men in Back Church Lane, on the morning of 8th. inst.

I find that the occurrence has been reported in the "New York Herald" by the reporter who met me, and that a copy of above paper is in the hands of Inspr. Moore, C.I.D.

At 12.15 am 8th. P.C. 394H Millard found a woman named Ellen Bisney of 219 Brunswick Building, Whitechapel in the High Street, and conveyed her on an ambulance to the Whitechapel Infirmary, this may have been observed by the person who gave the information to Newspaper Office, and who for the purpose of reward exaggerated the case.

I beg to ask that enquiry may be made by C.I.Department for the purpose of finding this man.

F. Pattenden Inspr.
T Arnold Sup

There is included in this file an extract[5] from the *New York Herald* as follows:

58895 <u>EXTRACT</u> From the New York Herald of 11 September 1889
Suspected Persons.

stating that a man calling himself John Cleary of 21 Whitehorse Yard had called at their offices on Sunday morning 8th. and gave particulars of an alleged murder and mutilation in Buckchurch Lane Whitechapel.
REFERENCE TO PAPERS
Chief Inspr Swanson to make full inquiry on this report by order of the Commissioner
11.9.89   J.Shore

Report submitted
12/9/89   J.Shore
                                                       Supt.

The Commissioner
<u>Supt E</u> To see and continue enquiry P.S. Partridge
                    [sgd] 12/9
E 13.9.89
Report submitted.
        CWells Act Supt.

Extract from THE NEW YORK HERALD, No. 222. LONDON EDITION,
WEDNESDAY, SEPTEMBER 11, 1889.   PRICE ONE PENNY.
                DOES HE KNOW THE RIPPER?
            WHO IS THIS MAN THAT CALLED AT
              THE "HERALD" OFFICE SUNDAY.

**He was positive a Murder Had Been Committed at Twenty
Minutes Past Eleven o'clock on Saturday Night, on the Spot
Where the Dead and Mutilated Body of a Woman was Found
Yesterday – Mystery of Mysteries.**

London in general, and Whitechapel in particular, were thrown into a
feverish state of excitement yesterday morning by the news that "Jack the
Ripper" had murdered and mutilated his ninth victim. Both the murder and
the mutilation were reported to be, and indeed proved to be, more horrible
than in any one of the eight cases preceding. The quick and close review of the
facts by the police department led to the conclusion late yesterday afternoon
that the remains found did not represent "Jack the Ripper's" handiwork, and
this may or may not be true.

There is a very extraordinary feature, however, in this case, which has
been lacking in all the others. That it is extraordinary no one will doubt who
reads the brief story of last Saturday night as detailed below. If the woman
found in archway was a victim of "Jack the Ripper," it is positively sure
either that the murderer has been seen by many people, or that another man
who knew of the murder and all the circumstances so long ago as last Saturday
night is abroad, and can be found, if the police are clever enough. On the
other hand, last Saturday night's events indicate to some extent that the body
found yesterday, be it that of a murdered woman or a body from a dissecting
room, was in the hands of more than one man who knew all about it, because
on last Saturday night a man betrayed the whole affair. The circumstances are
as follows, and will be verified in every particular by affidavit, should the
police department desire.

Last Sunday morning at five minutes past one o'clock a young man called at the HERALD office and reported that there was another "Jack the Ripper" murder. He was sent up to the editorial rooms and interviewed by the night editor. He said that a mutilated body had been found in Backchurch-lane, in Whitechapel. He said that it had been found by a policeman at twenty minutes past eleven o'clock. The map of London was immediately studied by two reporters in order to locate Backchurch-lane, while the editor cross-questioned the man. He said it had been told to him by an acquaintance of his, a police inspector whom he had met in Whitechapel High-street. He said there was no doubt about it, and that he had hurried to the HERALD office understanding that he would be rewarded for the news. He said his name was John Cleary, and that he lived at 21, White Horse-yard, Drury-lane. He was asked to write down his name and address; and he did so, the writing being preserved. His information was explicit and seemingly authentic, and two reporters were detailed to take the man with them, and go and get the story.

The two reporters went out, and one of them stopped on the landing of the stairway in going down, and asked the man some more questions. Under this examination he varied slightly, saying that the man who had told him was not a police inspector, but an ex-member of the police force. This statement has, perhaps, some significance to all who have been following the murders closely. He then went down to the street with the reporters. They called a hansom and told the man to get in with them; but he first hesitated, and then refused. His excuse was that it was too far from his home. They urged him to go, but he was firm. One of them proposed to take him back upstairs, in order to have him near at hand if necessary; but the necessity of immediate departure compelled them to start and leave the man to go his own way. He was assured that if the news proved authentic he would be handsomely rewarded, and he went away apparently contented with the arrangement.

The two reporters drove rapidly to Backchurch-lane, and found it without difficulty. They made a thorough search of the neighbourhood. They went down as far as the archway where the body was found yesterday morning, but found all quiet and no trace of any murder. They met two police officers, one an inspector, and the other a constable. They questioned both, and told them the report they had heard, and these two officers can verify the enquiry. They had heard nothing, however. The reporters again went over the ground, but found nothing. They then returned and reported. In fact, it is a certainty that on Sunday morning a murdered and mutilated body was reported as having been found in Backchurch-lane, and that exactly such a body was found yesterday morning.

The matter was passed over as unimportant on Sunday and Monday. The moment that the body was found yesterday, however, the events of Sunday morning loomed up with a significance rather colossal, and a hunt began for

John Cleary, of 21, White Horse-yard, Drury-lane. Mr. John Cleary, however, was not known at No. 21, or anywhere else in White Horse-yard, Drury-lane. The house is a four-storey one. The street floor is vacant, the first and second floors are occupied by families, and the top floor by a widow woman with two children. The widow woman was confident that no young man by the name of John Cleary either lived in the house or had ever lived there. The people in every house in White Horse-yard were questioned under circumstances which disposed them to tell all they knew, but nobody had ever heard the name of John Cleary, and everybody said that no man of that name could have lived there without their knowing it, which was quite true. It became evident, therefore, that the man had given a false address, and in all probability a false name, as such a precaution in the matter of residence would scarcely have been taken, and the precaution as to name neglected.

"Cleary's" description, however, had been carefully taken. He was a young man, apparently between twenty-five and twenty-eight years of age. He was short, his height being about 5 ft. 4in. He was of medium build, and weighed about 140 lb. He was light-complexioned, had a small fair moustache and blue eyes. On his left cheek was an inflamed spot, which looked as if a boil had lately been there and was healing. He wore a dark coat and waistcoat. His shirt was not seen, the space at the throat being covered by a dirty white handkerchief tied about his neck. His trousers were dark velveteen, so soiled at the knees as to indicate that he blacked shoes. His hat was a round, black, stiff felt. He walked with a shuffle and spoke in the usual fashion of the developing citizens of Whitechapel, whom, in all respects, he resembled.

It is thus certain that there was an intention on the part of the party or parties who had the body in keeping to place it in Backchurch-lane Saturday night, where it was found yesterday. If coincidences be of any value, it may be noted that this was the anniversary of the Hanbury-street murder. It is beyond doubt that "Cleary" got wind of the scheme, if he was not one of the principals. That the original intention was not carried out would indicate that he was an outsider acquainted with the project, who hoped to profit by it. There seems to be no reason to doubt that the body was not found by the police until yesterday morning, and that it was placed there a short time before seems reasonably sure. Nevertheless, "John Cleary," whoever he may be, must know all about the mystery, and is certainly the most valuable man in the purview of the police at the present time.

The mutilated body of "Jack the Ripper's" latest victim, if such it is, was discovered about half-past five o'clock yesterday morning beneath a railway arch on the south side of Pinchin-street, which runs eastward from Back-church-lane, a narrow thoroughfare connecting Commercial-road with Cable-street. The locality is about half a mile southward from the limited district which has been the centre of "the Ripper's" murders. It is, however, not more distant than was the Buck's-row crime, which was the third, and the point is less than three minutes from the scene of the fifth murder, the one in Berner-street. It is about the same distance from the Leman-street police-station. The south side of Pinchin-street is skirted by a long series of high brick arches, supporting the roadway of the London, Tilbury, and Great Eastern Railway. The arch beneath which the body was found is the only one which is open, the others being boarded up, or filled with huge doors, and used for storage and like purposes. This particular arch had been boarded up, as the joists stretching across it indicated, but the boards had been torn off and carried away for firewood by the people in the vicinity, a patrolman said. Anyone passing along Pinchin-street can easily see within these arches. Both officer Pennett and another patrolman say that they passed by the spot between half-past four and five o'clock, and saw nothing out of the common.

The discovery was made by Officer Pennett at half-past five o'clock. In passing along his beat, he flashed his bull's-eye into the dark arch and noticed a bundle which excited his curiosity, as it had not been there half an hour before. He went in and inspected it, and was startled to find it the trunk of a naked woman.

The remains were lying face downward. The head and legs had been removed, and the sight was so grotesque and horrible that the constable was some seconds in making out what it really was. The horrible mass was partly covered by a blood-stained chemise, much disarranged. Officer Pennett immediately whistled for assistance, and was quickly joined by several patrolmen. Word was sent to headquarters, and in a short time a group of inspectors and officials stood around the remains. When examined it appeared that the head and legs had been very neatly disjointed, and a search of the whole vicinity revealed no trace of them. There was one long cut down the centre of the body. The remains, so far as could be told by the examination, were those of a woman between thirty-five and forty years of age, rather short, and of a dark complexion. It was evident from the doctor's examination that she had never had a child. There was a mark about the waist such as would have been left by an encircling rope. There was no clothing except the chemise, which was an ordinary cotton one. There was no blood upon the ground, and all the bloodstains were dry, showing that the murder, if it had been a murder, had taken place some days before. It was evident that the body had been brought there in the condition in which it had been found. There is ample evidence that it was brought there at some time during the night. From the way in which it lay, it appeared to have been hurriedly drafted there and to have been untouched afterwards by the person who brought it. The body was discoloured in several places, and decomposition was setting in at the edge of the cuts. Everything indicated that death had taken place four or five days previously.

The remains were removed to St. George's mortuary, and were there viewed by a HERALD reporter. The body, lying on the slab in the centre of the mean little room, was a piteous and revolting spectacle. The severance of the head and legs seemed to have taken from it the fashion of humanity, and it needed a second glance to recognise the true character of the mass of inert flesh. The body there appeared to be that of a young and well-formed woman, well nourished and perfectly healthy. Except the mutilations already spoken of the only marks of violence it bore were the dark blue traces of finger marks about and below the elbow of the left arm and a shapeless bruise on the right wrist. The singularity of the mutilations was that the cuts were made with perfect cleanness and decision. There was no mangling of the flesh. The operation had been performed as neatly as if it had been done by a practical surgeon in the quiet of a dissecting-room, rather than by a brutal miscreant in the confusion and terror of committing a hideous crime. A singular circumstance, irreconcileable with the marks of putrefaction on other parts of the body, borne out also by the stench of decay, is that the flesh of the stump of the right thigh was bright and red as with a recent effusion of blood. The flesh of the other stump and of the neck was dry and caked, as were the lips of the gaping cut extending from the breastbone to the root of the thigh, exposing the intestines, which, however, have been left intact, contrary to the practice of the Whitechapel fiend, to whom so many attribute the crime. The decapitation and the cutting off of the limbs are also opposed to his practice, and help to cast doubt on that theory, and to suggest that the crime much more nearly resembles those recently committed at Rainham and Battersea. Beside the body lay the torn and bloodstained rags of the chemise, which had been flung over the body, the only scrap of material, except the body itself, yet found which may possibly assist the police in the task of identification.

THE HUNT FOR CLUES.

Scotland Yard was early astir. Before six o'clock a message was received there from Leman-street. It was only "Whitechapel again," but it sufficed to put things instantly into a ferment. Word was at once sent to Commissioner Monro and the Assistant Commissioners, and they immediately responded. Two fresh detectives were placed on the case, Inspector Abberline, who has been following it, being out of town. The hunt for clues and for information began vigorously. The first bit of evidence was a bloodstained undergarment found at half-past seven in a vacant yard in Hooper-street, 500 yards away. It had been thrust through a hole in the fence, and it was turned over to the police. The stains on this, as on the chemise, were old and dried. Then came the story of a man who said he had seen another man with a heavy bag of something on his back, about four o'clock. He was questioned, but his information was not important, the police feeling confident that the body was brought nearly to the spot in a vehicle of some kind. Chief Commissioner Monro and Colonel Monsell, Chief Constable, went all over the ground, and visited the mortuary. Three arrests were made in the shape of two sailors and a shoeblack found sleeping in an adjacent archway, but after being examined at the Lemon-street [*sic*] Station they were released, it being evident that they knew nothing of the matter. It shortly appeared that there was no more of a clue in the case than there had been in the preceding ones. Mr. Williamson, of the Criminal Investigation Department, admitted this when questioned as to whether the police had as yet formed any theory regarding the case. He replied:- ''There is not evidence enough yet on which to base any theory. As a matter of fact, the police are not nearly so fond of rushing into theorising as some of you gentlemen of the Press seem to think. One fact is worth half a dozen theories, and in this case we have to bend our energies to the discovery of facts. This case promises to be one of peculiar difficulty. The others were mysterious enough, but here the mystery is complete; the head being gone, the chances of identification are so very slight. People who are inclined to be impatient with the police should remember how enormous the difficulties of such a case as this are. Do I think it is ''Jack the Ripper'' again? As I said, I have no theories. I wait for facts.''

The remains lay all day at the Morgue, but were not identified. Identification will, in fact, be difficult, if not impossible. The only assisting fact was one revealed by Secretary Bartlett to a HERALD reporter at the Old Jewry in the afternoon. He said that a week ago a woman's hand had been picked up in Shoreditch, and all efforts to trace its owner and origin had thus far failed.

The River Police were put on the alert within twenty minutes after the finding of the body. The despatch sent to them and to all the other Metropolitan stations was as follows:-

At twenty minutes to six a.m. trunk of a woman found under the arches in Pinchin-street, E. Age about forty. Height 5 ft 3 in. Hair dark brown. No clothing except chemise, very much torn and blood-stained. Both elbows discoloured as if from habitual leaning on them. Post mortem. Marks around waist, apparently caused by a rope.

Immediately upon the circulation of this telegram, the Thames Police, under Detective-inspector Regan and Chief-inspector Moore, assisted by Sergeants Moore, Francis, Howard, Davis, and Scott, at once got their various craft on the river, and boarded all the vessels at the mouth of the Thames and in the docks. Attention was particularly directed to the cattle boats and those from Spain and America. Among those boarded in the London

Docks were the *City of Cork*, the *Cadiz*, the *Malaga*, and the *Gallicia*, and the *Lydian Monarch* in the Millwall Docks. The operation of searching these vessels had not concluded until a late hour in the evening, and so far as the investigation had gone the captains of the various vessels were able to give satisfactory accounts as to their crews.

After the removal of the remains to the mortuary. Mr. Clarke, Dr. Gordon Brown (the City Police-surgeon), and two other medical gentlemen who have had experience in previous cases of this nature, shortly after made a more careful examination of the remains. It was noticed that the trunk displayed green patches; the flesh otherwise was white. The doctors, from their investigations, concluded that the cuts had been inflicted in a left-hand manner – that is to say, the cut in the throat was evidently commenced on the left side and carried to the right with a clean sweep. The same peculiarity was observed in the other wounds, and in separating the legs more flesh had been cut from the trunk on the left side than on the other. In more than one of the previous crimes this peculiarity has been observed and commented upon. The legs are taken out clearly from the loin, showing no signs of a separating instrument. Nothing whatever was found to be missing except these members and the head. The cut severing the head from the body was skilfully done, there being no hacking or clumsy dissection noticeable. Furthermore, a saw had been used to sever the bones in such a way as to leave no doubt that the person responsible for the dismemberment possessed a good knowledge of anatomy. There were no signs about the hands which would indicate that the woman had been used to hard work, and so far as could be seen there had been no attempt to obliterate a mark on one of the fingers, apparently caused by a ring.

The body was well nourished and cared for. One of the several doctors who viewed the remains expressed the opinion that had he been asked to dissect the body in the manner in which he saw it he could not have done it more neatly and skilfully. In consequence of the similarity in the mode of dismemberment pursued in this case and those of the recent Battersea and Rainham mysteries, the officers engaged in those cases were consulted, and their general opinion is that the resemblance in all cases are so remarkable as to give grounds for the belief that the present crime is one with a different origin to that of the previous Whitechapel atrocities.

DOCTORS AND POLICE CONSULT.

A conference to which it is believed considerable importance is attached took place last evening at the Leman-street Police-station. When Dr. Phillips was telegraphed for to Bournemouth he replied that he would return to town at once; but asked the authorities to adjourn the post-mortem in the meantime. He arrived in London about five p.m. last evening, and after making some preliminary investigations attended at Leman-street Police-station soon after six o'clock. He was closeted with the Chief Constable Colonel Monsell, Mr. Arnold, and the officers from Scotland Yard. At seven p.m., Mr. Monro, the Chief Commissioner, arrived at the station in his private carriage, and joined in the deliberations which continued until nearly half-past eight o'clock. The surgeons and physicians who have examined the corpse agree that it was a living body not more than three or four days ago, the slight decomposition being due to the sudden heat of the weather. The manner in which the limbs had been severed, and the cut in the abdomen, seemed to point to the murderer or mutilator as a left-handed man, but upon this point there was some difference of opinion. The woman must have been of dark complexion, and about 35 years of age.

The inquest will open in the Vestry Hall, Cable-street, at 10 o'clock today.

Up till a late hour last evening no further arrests had been made in connection with the murder, and the police were absolutely without a clue of any kind. A circumstantial story to the effect that a suspicious-looking man was seen last night carrying a sack near where the body was found proved on investigation to be evidently valueless. As a matter of fact, no sack was found under the arch or elsewhere, and it was quite as likely as not that the murderer carried the corpse in a portmanteau or in a brown-paper parcel. In either case, unless the murderer was very impudent or unusually peculiar in appearance, he would not attract particular attention. Had there been anything suspicious in his demeanour, he could scarcely have passed through the streets of the East-end without being challenged by beat policemen or detectives, of whom the number in the district is at the present unusually large, owing to the precautions maintained by Commissioner Monro since the last murder, and to the local excitement arising out of the great strike. Special measures have been in operation for months past to maintain the vigilance and efficiency of the police at the highest point, in view of another murder by the Whitechapel fiend, the probability of which has never been questioned by the authorities. It is difficult, therefore, to see in what manner the police are to blame, or to say whence or how a clue is to be obtained.[. . .]

A DIFFERENT METHOD OF MUTILATION.

A reperusal of the circumstances of former atrocities of this nature only serves to confuse the reader's mind as to the possible origin of this last crime. It differs from the Whitechapel series in the facts that the head and lower limbs were amputated, and in the other fact that the hands were left undisturbed; but it resembles them in the infliction of the deep longitudinal cut along the lower half of the trunk. It will be remembered that last year, while the Whitechapel miscreant was in the full living of unchecked crime, a horribly mutilated human body was discovered in the basement storey of the building on the Embankment once intended for a national opera house. Here, too, the head and legs were missing, as in the case of the unfortunate woman found yesterday morning, but in this case the incomplete mutilation of the trunk had been completed in a fashion absolutely similar to that which marked the bodies of the Whitechapel victims. Nearly a month previously the right arm of a woman had been found floating in the Thames near [   ] Bridge, and several indications justified the belief that it formed part of the body found later on in the basement of the opera house. The case of the girl whose mutilated remains were enveloped in a fragment of under garment marked in black ink in a clear and clerkly hand with the name "L.E. Fisher," equally fails to offer any analogy to the other cases, as Dr. Bond, chief surgeon of the Metropolitan Police, declared death to have resulted from an operation intended to procure abortion; a motive which could not have determined any of the Whitechapel series, and certainly did not exist in the present instance, as the medical testimony declares this last victim never to have been pregnant.

It is interesting to see that the list of "Whitechapel Murders" accompanying the above article lists the following murders:

1. An unknown woman, Christmas week, 1887.
2. Martha Turner, found stabbed in 39 places on landing at George-yard-buildings, Commercial-street, Spitalfields, August 7, 1888.
3. Mrs. Mary Ann Nicholls, in Buck's-row, August 31, 1888.
4. Mrs. Annie Chapman, Hanbury-street, Sept. 7, 1888.
5. Elizabeth Stride, Berner-street, Sept. 30, 1888.
6. Catherine Eddowes, Mitre-square, Sept. 30, 1888.
7. Mary Jane Kelly, 26 Dorset-street, Spitalfields.
8. Alice Mackenzie, July 17, 1889.
9. Body of unknown woman found in Backchurch-lane, Cable-street, Sept. 10.

The file then contains a seven-page report[6] by the Chief Commissioner, James Monro, to the Home Office:

Sep. 11. 89.

Mr. Sandars.

I communicated to you yesterday the finding of the trunk of a female, minus head & legs in one of the railway arches in Pinchin Street.

This street is close to Berner Street which was the scene of one of the previous Whitechapel murders. It is not a very narrow street, but is lonely at night, & is patrolled every half hour by a constable on beat. The arch where the body was found abuts on the pavement.

The constable discovered the body some what after 20 minutes past five on the morning of Tuesday. He was in consequence of the pressure for men in Whitechapel just now, working part of two beats in addition to his own, but even so he passed & re-passed the spot every half hour. He is positive that when he passed the spot about five the body was not there. I am inclined to accept his statement thoroughly, for from another circumstance which has come to my knowledge he evidently was on the alert that night. It may therefore be assumed that the body was placed where it was found some time between 5 & 5.30 a.m. of Tuesday the 11th.

Although the body was placed in the arch on Tuesday morning, the murder – (and altho' there is not as yet before me proof of the cause of death, I assume that there has been a murder) was not committed there nor then. There was almost no blood in the arch, and the state of the body itself showed that death took place abt. 36 hours or more previously. This, then enables me to say that the woman was made away with probably on Sunday night, the 8th September. This was the date on which one of the previous Whitechapel murders was committed.

The body then must have been concealed, where the murder was committed during Sunday night, Monday, & Tuesday up till dawn. This leads to the inference that it was so concealed in some place to which the murderer had access, over which he had control, and from which he was anxious to remove the corpse. We may say then that the murder was committed probably in the house or lodging of the murderer, and that he conveyed the portion found to Pinchin Street to get rid of it from his lodging where the odour of decomposition would soon betray him.

Why did he take the trunk to Whitechapel and what does the finding of the body there show? If this is a fresh outrage by the Whitechapel murderer known by the horribly familiar nickname of Jack the Ripper the answer would not be difficult, altho' this murder, <u>committed in the murderers house</u> wd. be a new departure from the system hitherto pursued by this ruffian. I am however inclined to believe that this case is not the work of the ''Ripper'', which has characterized the previous cases has been a/. Death caused by cutting the throat, b/. Mutilation c/. Evisceration d/. Removal of certain parts of the body. e/. Murder committed in the street, except in one instance in Dorset Street. In this last case there were distinct traces of furious mania, the murderer having plenty of time at his disposal slashed and cut the body in all directions, evidently under the influence of frenzy.

In the present case, so far as the medical evidence goes there is a/. nothing to show that death was caused by cutting the throat. b/. There is no mutilation as in previous cases, altho' there is dismemberment. c/. There is no evisceration. d/. There is no removal of any portion of the organs of generation or intestines. e/. The murder was indubitably committed neither in the street, nor in the victim's house, but probably in the lodging of the murderer. Here where there was as in the previous case of murder in a house, plenty of time at the disposal of the murderer, there is no sign of frenzied mutilation of the body, but of deliberate & skilful dismemberment with a view to removal. These are all very striking departures from the practice of the Whitechapel murderer, and if the body had been found elsewhere than in Whitechapel the supposition that death had been caused by the Ripper would probably not have been entertained.

But the body has been found in Whitechapel and there is a gash on the front part extending downwards to the organs of generation – and we have to account for these facts. I place little importance on the gash; it seems to me not to have been inflicted as in the previous cases. The inner coating of the bowel is hardly touched, and the termination of the cut towards the vagina looks almost as if the knife had slipped, and as if this portion of the wound had been accidental. The whole of the wound looks as if the murderer had intended to make a cut prepatory to removing the intestines in the process of dismemberment, & had then changed his mind. Had this been the work of the previous frenzied murderer we may be tolerably sure that he would have continued his hideous work in the way which he previously adopted. It may also be that the gash was inflicted to give rise to the impression that this case was the work of the Whitechapel murderer & so divert attention from the real assassin.

As to how the body got to Whitechapel this is a great difficulty unless it be supposed that it was removed in some conveyance & placed where it was found, & unless it be supposed that the murderer, being other than the "Ripper", had good knowledge of the locality. I may get some light on this point as the case goes on – Meanwhile I am inclined to the belief that, taking one thing with another, this is not the work of the Whitechapel murderer but of the hand which was concerned in the murders which are known as the Rainham mystery, the new Police buildings case, and the recent case in which portion of a female body (afterwards identified) were found in the Thames.

Sep. 11. 89.   J.Monro
Thank Mr Monro for
this Report.
        H.M.
            12 Sept./89.

There is a doctor's report[7] on the post-mortem findings by Dr Hebbert, dated 16 September 1889:

Report

On the 11th September /89 I was present at a postmortem examination on human remains found in Whitechapel Mr. Phillips and Mr. Gordon Browne were present.

The remains consisted of the trunk and arms of a female body, the head had been cut off at the lower part of the neck and the thighs had been separated at the hip joints.

The trunk was plump and well formed, with full breasts, fair skin and dark brown hair on the pubes and axilla.

The arms well shaped, hands small and nails well kept, the weight of the trunk could not be taken, the length was 26 inches, and circumference of chest at nipple was 34 inches, below breasts $31\frac{3}{4}$.

Rigor mortis had passed off, and decomposition as shewn by green discolouration of the abdomen just beginning, the cut surfaces at the hips were black and dry, but the surface at the neck moist and red the skin and muscles of the abdomen had been cut by a vertical incision and running from 2 inches below the ensiform cartilage downwards and ending on the left side of the external genitals just opening the vagina but not opening the peritoneal cavity. There were a number of small round bruises on the forearms and arms most on the under surface of the forearms, and varying in size from a shilling to a sixpence, on the left wrist were two cuts, one just grazing the skin $\frac{3}{4}$ inch long, and the other cutting through the skin and 1 inch long. There was no ecchymosis on the edge and no gaping of the wounds. There are no lineoe albae, on the abdomen and no further scars or injuries.

The incisions separating the head were apparently two in number the first beginning behind opposite the spinal column and ending in front, on the right side and carried from left to right, the second beginning on right side in front and carried to back joining the first but leaving a tongue of skin behind there was no ecchymosis in the skin. The muscles and tissues down to the spinal column were cut on the same level, the cricoid cartilage being cut about the centre. The spinal column was divided at the junction of the fifth and sixth cervical vertebrae through the intervertebrial just a thin shaving of the body of the 5th cervical vertebra being left.

The ends of the vessels were very clean cut. There were no retraction of the muscles or other tissues.

The thighs had been separated at the hip joints the skin cut through by two or three sweeping circular incisions beginning apparently just below the hip bone, carried downward and inward around the buttock, the capsules of the hip joints were opened and the heads of the bones neatly disarticulated. There was no retraction of the muscles and tissues and the incisions both at the hip and neck and the abdomen had very clear cut edges.

The internal viscera were then examined.

Heart. The walls were flaccid, the ventricles empty and dilated, the valves healthy and competent, muscle pale and fatty, on the pericardium was a patch of old inflammation: weight $9\frac{1}{2}$ ozs. Lungs Right upper lobe adherent to pleura, by old firm adhesions. Left lung free, both lungs were apparently healthy, but were beginning to decompose.

Spleen; large, soft, decomposing, $7\frac{1}{2}$ ozs. Liver: weight 50 ozs, decomposing, substance fairly healthy.

Kidneys, Weight 7 ozs each, slight decomposition, substance fairly healthy.

Stomach, walls normal, with healthy mucous membrane about a dram or so of partly digested food, which appeared to be plums and no smell. Intestines large intestine contained faeces no abnormality.

Vulva The vulva is patent and there is no hymen the fourchette is unruptured the vagina is wide but still rugose The mucous membrane is healthy.

The uterus weighs rather less than two ozs and is 3 inches long, of which the body measures $1\frac{1}{4}$ inches & the cervix $1\frac{1}{2}$ inch the cavity of the body is triangular with a convexity downwards at the base the cervix has well marked arbor vitae, the os is small and the lips are not everted, the os just admits a large probe, there is a little whitish thick mucous oozing from the os uteri. The mucous membrane is rather thick and covered with a reddish mucous.

The ovaries are small cystic and degenerating. There is a small extravasation on the left ovary.

The measurements of the arms outstretched across the chest 64 inches, the forearm measured $16\frac{1}{2}$ inches, the hand $6\frac{1}{2}$ inches long and $6\frac{3}{4}$ inches in circumference at the palm. The stirnal epiphysis of the clavicle had united by bone.

The tissues generally were pale and bloodless.

On the first joint on the dorsal surface of the right little finger is a small round hardening not amounting to a corn, other is a similar but smaller hardening on the inner side of the first joint of the right ring finger.

Charles A. Hebbert.

M.R.C.P.

Curator of Museum of

Westm Hospl

This report is followed by the doctor's comments[8]:

Comments

The remains are those of a large well nourished woman.

Her height as calculated by the [ ] measurements and forearm about 5 ft. Her age is above 25 as shewn by the union of the epiphysis and from the condition of the ovaries approaching so that probably 35 years or so.

She had not borne children as shewn by the uterus, and absence of linese alboe and the breasts did not give the impression of having been used for suckling. She was apparently not a virgin and the vagina had been distended, though not so patent as after childbearing. The skin was fair and the hair dark brown the hands are shapely and the skin soft, there are no marks indicating any occupation, except that on the right [ ] finger is a small circular hardening, but no corn. [*Marginal note to insert* – ''This mark is such as might be made by writing. CH''] There is no mark as of a ring on the left ring finger.

The immediate cause of death was syncope as shewn by the condition of the heart and the general bloodlessness of the tissues indicating haemorrhage as the cause of death.

There was no organic disease of the viscera examined which would have caused death.

The edges of the cuts shewed that a very sharp knife had been used, all the cuts had been made after death. All the cuts were made from left to right, except those separating the right thigh, which had been carried from right to left, across the flexure of the joint, so probably done by a right handed man. The incisions were evidently made with design and were skilfully performed, as if by a man who had some knowledge of the position of joints and the readiest means of separating limbs, such knowledge as a butcher or slaughterer, they do not indicate a special anatomical knowledge of the human body.

Charles A. Hebbert

16 Sept'89   M.R.C.S.

Curator of museum

Westm. Hospl.

There is a report[9] by Chief Inspector Donald Swanson, dated 12 September 1889, concerning enquiries conducted in this case regarding John Cleary, who had called at the *New York Herald* offices:

METROPOLITAN POLICE.

Criminal Investigation Department,

Scotland Yard,

12th day of September, 1889.

Enquiries re John Cleary
who called at New York
Herald Offices at 1.5 am
Sunday 8th.

With reference to the attached article from New York Herald stating that at 1.5 am Sunday morning a young man calling himself John Cleary of 21 Whitehorse Yard, had called at their offices, and informed them that from what he had heard from an ex-member of Met: Police in Whitechapel another murder and mutilation had taken place in Back Church Lane, but had declined to accompany two reporters to the East End, I beg to report that I saw Mr. Cowen, the night editor, as well as Mr. Fletcher the reporter who had seen the man, but they were unable to give me anything additional to the contents of the extract; upon which any enquiry could be made. Upon making enquiry at No. 21 White Horse Yard, I found that the name of Cleary was unknown, but upon seeing the agent who lets the apartments, a Mr. Yates, he stated that a young man, who passed under the name of Leary, had resided there three weeks ago at 21 White Horse Yard, but had been evicted for non-payment of rent; and was now residing in Strand Buildings. Mr. Yates further said that Leary worked as odds man for a Mr. Mapley, greengrocer of Newcastle St. Enquiry at Mapley's disclosed that they had no man named Leary, or ever had, but they had a man who lived in White Horse Yard, and was now staying in Strand Buildings named Denis Lynch. Enquiry at Strand Buildings shewed that Lynch, passing as Leary who formerly resided at 21 White Horse Yard, now resided at No. 5 in the Buildings, with another man's wife and was under notice to leave for non-payment of rent. Having arranged at Mapley's to have Lynch seen at 5 p.m. I took Mr. Fletcher there, but Lynch alias Leary had had to go away with the van, and an arrangement was made for 7.30 p.m. At that hour we saw Lynch alias Leary, but Mr. Fletcher at once said he was not the man. Lynch on being questioned asserted that he did live at 21 Whitehorse Yard, but had never called at the New York Herald Office, nor did he know any person answering the description who would use his name. During the interval between 5 and 7.30 p.m. I had asked the reporters not to renew their enquiry until this man was seen, and they promised faithfully not to do so, but at the interview with Lynch the woman with whom he is living, recognised Mr. Fletcher and said, "I know you, you belong to the New York Herald, and were at my house this afternoon." This I had anticipated, and questioned them upon their enquiries, when they stated that they had been running about Drury Lane, with some loungers they had met with, who had told them lies as to a man called Stephen Cleary, and by enquiry at the alleged addresses proved it to them, at the same time reminding them that a breach of faith did not substantiate the editor's expression of a desire to assist the police in the elucidation of the matter. Lynch has been seen again, but can throw no light on the matter.

From enquiry on H. Division I find it is the fact that an Inspr. from H. named Pattenden met the reporters in Backchurch Lane on Sunday morning, and that they called at Commercial Street about 2 a.m. (Sunday) and enquired as to whether any infm. had been received respecting a murder in Back Church Lane. By the reports from H. which are attached, it appears a woman was found insensible in High St. and taken to Whitechapel Infirmary at 12 night 7th. The Inspr. thinks the occurrence may have given rise to the information but it does not account for the mention of Backchurch Lane. The New York Herald people will send here if any person should give them any information respecting Cleary, who so far as they know, had not called at any other newspaper agency.

Donald SSwanson

ChInspr.

John Shore

Supt

[*There is a marginal annotation on this report as follows*: It was stated that there was some writing on a wall abt. Cleary, and are the facts not this. I mentd this to Supt. Arnold, & he will be able to tell Ch Inspr Swanson/ I believe that the fact abt the High Street is known as Church Lane. But still this enquiry is not completed and we must try to get Cleary if possible. E.Divn. might perhaps know something abt him. JM 12/9'].

There is a statement[10] by John Arnold included, worded as follows:

Front cover:- CENTRAL OFFICE, C.I.D. Reference 58895 /6, summary of contents —

Statement of John Arnold confessing that it was he who went to the offices of the New York Herald at 1.5 am on Sunday 8th and gave infn about an alleged murder in Backchurch Lane 13/9.

John Arnold, says, I reside at No. 2 Harveys Buildings Strand. newsvendor. states. On Saturday night I had come out of the King Lud. p.h. and I had a little drop of drink. When about the middle of Fleet Street on left hand side going towards the Strand, a man dressed as a soldier, in black uniform, black cord shoulder strap lightish buttons cheese cutter cap, brass [?] ornament in front of cap like a horn cannot say whether there was a band round or not, age about 35 to 36. height 5 ft. 6 or 7. compl. fair. fair moustache, good looking. carrying a brown paper parcel about 6 or 8 in long, came up behind me and said, "Hurry up with your papers, another horrible murder", and I said. "Where". and he said "In Backchurch Lane". Immediately he told me that I ran up to the New York Herald Office, and reported to the sub editor upstairs and to two reporters, who asked me to go down to Whitechapel, but I declined as it was past one a.m. and my lodgings would have been closed for the night; and I told them so. They said if it turns out right, we'll reward you, and I said "Thank you,

I stand at Charing Cross. When before the editor I gave the name of John Kemp not Cleary of 21 Whitehorse Yard, where I had formerly lived. I gave a false name because I did not want my wife to know as I am not living with her for if she knew she would get me turned out of my lodgings. I sell the New York Herald every Sunday, and call for the papers at their offices. I do not know what became of the soldier, indeed I cannot say whether he belonged to the regulars or volunteers. The last I saw of him was in Fleet Street, as I hurried and left him. Two days afterwards I saw in the papers that a horrible murder had taken place in Back Church Lane, and I told ex.Inspr. Lansdown at Charing Cross, as I have told you. This was on Tuesday afternoon. The next I heard was that there was something about me, as John Cleary, in the New York Herald and I read it. Seeing Sergt. Froest at Charing Cross about 4.30p.m. I told him that it was I who gave the information to the New York Herald, and he took me to Whitehall Place. If I talked to the soldier for ten minutes or so, I might recognise his voice, but I am not certain that I could identify him from a number of persons. I cannot describe him further. It was not till today that I knew that police wanted to see me. and I spoke to Sergt Froest.

John Arnold

Another almost immediate effect of the discovery of the Pinchin Street torso – with the obvious implication that it had been carried to where it was found by someone who went unchallenged by any police patrol – was for Superintendent Arnold to call for a strengthening of the police patrols in the area. In a report[11] dated 11 September 1889, he stated:

METROPOLITAN POLICE
H Division
11th Sept. 18[89]
Re Whitechapel Murders

I beg to report that owing [to] the recent discovery of the body of a woman in Pinchin Street: evidently the result of a murder. no information being foun[d] to afford a clue as to how th[e] body was conveyed to the spot at which it was found, & there being no doubt it was carried there either by Barrow or by some person on his back. I beg to submit that it is desire[able] to augment. the men of this Division so as to be able to place more men on the Beats. and also to employ more in plain clothes without distressi[ng] other Divisions as is now the case. I therefore recommend an augmentation of 100 Constables which would enable me to strengthen each Subdivision, & I would ask that if approve[d] a good proportion of the men [ ] may be transferred from othe[r] Divisions as recruits wo[uld] be of but little service f[or] some months.

T Arno[ld]

This report is included in the file with another[12] of the same date by the Commissioner, James Monro, to the Home Office:

H.O.   [done GL]   11.9.89

Our experience in connection with the last Whitechapel murder shows that notwithstanding every precaution the murderer has been enabled to slip through our patrols, and dispose of the body of his victim. without being observed by police. All that I can do is to strengthen the force of police in the locality, and make it more difficult than before for these lamentable occurrences to take place. For this purpose I shall require 100 more men, both uniform &plain clothes. I cannot possibly arrange for their transfer from other Divisions, which have already furnished men for the East End, &I therefore ask for an augmentation of 100 men for a couple of months, in addition to those whom I have already have under H O letter.

As soon as I can see my way to reduce the number S of S may rely upon my doing so, but we must put a stop to these Whitechapel outrages, and for this ["men" – *deleted*] the number of men applied for ["are" – *deleted*] is absolutely necessary. I trust therefore that I may receive immediate sanction to supply the above number of men for the time mentioned.

                                                                    JM
              11/9

There is a report[13] from Inspector Henry Moore, dated 12 September 1889, with summary-of-contents cover stating:

Mr. Miller, Star Newspaper called and wished to know if it was a fact that John Cleary mentioned Back Church Lane to the Editor of the New York Herald. If so he attaches suspicion to an ex compositor of that name formerly employed on the Globe newspaper. ?Seen. Put with New York Herald papers 13/9 [sgd] pro A.C.C. 13/9

                         METROPOLITAN POLICE
                    Criminal Investigation Department,
                              Scotland Yard,
                       12th day of September, 1889.

Human remains found
in Whitechapel.
I beg to report that at 1p.m. today Mr. Miller, of the "Star Newspaper" called at Leman St. Station and was particularly anxious to know whether it was a fact that John Cleary did mention Back Church Lane, Whitechapel, in his statement to the Editor of the "New York Herald" as the place where

mutilated remains had been discovered; if so he considered it most important and he should then know what steps to take. I did not satisfy him upon the matter; but in the course of conversation learnt that if Back Church Lane was really mentioned, he attached suspicion upon an ex-compositor as the man who visited the New York Herald Office;- Viz:-

John Cleary, formerly attached to The Globe Office; age 35, ht. 6 ft., comp. fresh, hair and heavy moustache dark, bald, medium build, speaks peculiar, as though he has no roof to his mouth; who about 4 months ago was residing at 2 Savoy Buildings, Strand.

The above information I at once wired to Chf. Inspr. Swanson.

I would add that Mr. Miller is the person who found the thigh of Annie Jackson which was thrown into garden on Thames Embankment.

Henry Moore Inspr.

T Arnold Supd.

A covering report[14] by Chief Inspector Swanson, "*regarding the Man calling at New York Herald office at 1.5 am. Sunday morning*", then follows:

METROPOLITAN POLICE.

Criminal Investigation Department,

Scotland Yard.

12th day of September 1889.

I beg to report that P.S. Froest reported to me that, John Arnold, the newsvendor at Charing Cross, had told him that he was the person who had given the information to the New York Herald, and whom they were describing as John Cleary. The P.S. then went for Arnold, and I met them at Charing Cross. Attached is Arnold's statement, taken as fully as he can give it. He cannot say whether the soldier had a stripe or not round his cap, whether he wore a belt or not, or if he had any stripes on his trousers, and he cannot say whether the buttons were yellow or white, all he can remember is that they were lightish. A Commissionaire wears the uniform nearest to his description. Upon further questions he stated that he did not even know where Backchurch Lane was.

Arnold has been known for many years to officers past and present, and speaking personally, beyond that he bets in small sums, drinks occasionally, and has deserted his wife, (who is said to be intemperate and a virago), for which he was sentenced to twenty one days imprisonment, I have never heard of him being dishonest. That he could be in any way connected with others or by himself in a murder is to me improbable. He has not strength enough to have lifted the trunk which, according to the surgeons, weighed from four to five stones, (police think more), and if he knew of such a crime, he would be one of the first to inform police.

Although he is doubtful as to his power to identify, I submit that a trial might be given him in ["Fleet Street and" – *deleted*] Strand, where the head quarters of the Commissionaires are, for a few days to see at least whether the uniform is like what he saw.

Donald SSwanson,
ChInspr.
JohnShore
Supt.

The following page[15] reads as follows:

CIDCentral
12th Septr 1889

Miscellaneous

H Leman St. – Memo: Body of woman found (No. 33 Infm. and Mem. 12.30pm 10th), amended description:- Age about 35. height 5feet 3 inches; hair dark brown. skin fair; hands soft and shapely, nails well kept, small circular hardening (but no corn) on right little finger; arms small, but well shaped, body plump, and well formed, with full breasts, no marks of rings on fingers; no evidence of maternity.

The special attention of Divn. is called to the description, as to whether any woman of the unfortunate class or otherwise, answering the description has been reported, or can be ascertained to [be] missing.

Inserted in 8.30 pm Infms.

    [Sgd]   [*Sig. illegible*]
    For Supt
    13.9.89.

The following pages[16] are Dr Bagster Phillips's report, as follows:

2 Spital Square E   [Stamped: – METROPOLITAN POLICE
September 12th.   13 Sep. 89
                           Criminal Investigation Dept]

Sir

        I beg to hand you my Colleague's & my notes in the case of mutilated remains of the woman unknown now [ ] in the Mortuary St. George's East –

        I have examined them as far as practicable.

I am Sir
Your obdt. Servt.
G.M.B.Phillips

General Appearances of Body in Mortuary Septr. 10th 5p.m. –

Trunk of Female, decapitated & deprived of thighs & legs disarticulated at hip joints on both sides.

Absence of coagulated blood.

Decomposition already established and the divided tissues of neck emit air – and the veins still drain with blood.

Bust is that of a fully developed woman apparently about 35 years of age & from external appearances has not borne a child & has not suckled one.

The separation of the head has been effected with a clean sweep of some sharp instrument the spinal articulation of the bones being cleanly effected.

The section of the neck presents a particularly even surface but there is a small flap of skin at the back indicating where the incision ended. It commenced a little to the right of the middle line behind at back of neck.

Both thighs were excised by circular sweeps from level of each of hip bones.

There are several recent bruises on arms and hands.

There is a long division of external wall of abdomen, not penetrating the cavity 15 inches Commencing 2 inches below cartilage of chest and slightly penetrating the vagina below, being about 15 in. long, rather to left side.

Further appearances 10.15 am. Septr. 11th after missing the Coroners order which I had to apply for & was specially told to wait for until the Jury had viewed the remains.

The Coroner [ ] sent a message 11pm. Septr. 10th for me to make the exm. at once, but I had elected to do the exm. with other gentlm. at 10 O'c on the 11th.

Decomposition much more marked.

Length of trunk	2 ft. 2 in.
Round nipples	34 in.
Below breasts	31½ in.
Tip to tip of fingers	5 ft. 4 in.
Length of Body calculated at	5 ft. 3 in.
Length of forearm & hand elbow to tip of the fingers	16½ in.
Length of Hand	6½ in.
Breadth of Hand	6¾ in.
Weight of whole remains	67 lbs.

A small quantity of hair removed fr. Pubis & preserved.

[ ] selected notes bearing on cause of death.

Pale condition of Hands & Nails is marked

Two Vaccination marks Left arm.

Marked absence of blood in Vessels, but not so complete as in some cases of death from bleeding.

Pericardium	healthy (in fluid)
Heart	fatty & empty. Valves emptied.
Liver	signs of degeneration
Stomach	contained a little food, possibly plums.
Womb	that of a woman not having had a child, but congested at cervix.
Ovaries	of woman under 40.
Vagina	rather dilated. no sign of recent coitus.

Conclusions	That Death probably occurred within 24 to 36 hours before remains were found.

Chiefly indicated as arising from f[ ] from loss of blood. (especially indicated by empty Heart & blood vessels.

The mutilations were subsequent to death. (were effected to facilitate removal?)

The incisions & marks of separation of Head & Thighs point very strongly to their having been caused by some one accustomed to cut up animals.

That all the injuries might be made with a strong knife very sharp 8 inches or more in length of blade.

No evidence of child bearing but strong evidence of prostitution.

GM.B.Phillips.

As with other reports in the hand of Dr Bagster Phillips, this was especially difficult to transcribe. His report is followed by the report[17] of Percy J. Clark, his assistant, as follows:

A little before 6 o'clock on the morning of Sept. 10th (Tuesday) I was called by the Police to a railway arch in Pinchin Street where I saw the trunk of a woman minus the head & legs. It was lying about 18 feet from the roadway & about a foot from the right wall of the arch. The body was lying on its anterior surface [ ] with the right arm doubled beneath it & the left arm lying by the side – the arms were not severed from the body.

There was no pool of blood – no signs of any struggle – nor any reason for supposing that a murder had been committed there.

Covering over the cut surface of the neck & over the right shoulder were the remains of what had been a chemise. It was of common make & of such a size as would be worn by a woman of similar build to the trunk found. It had been torn down the front & a cut had been made from the front to the arm-hole on either side – the cuts appeared to have been made with a sharp knife & were probably for the purpose of getting it off the body.

The chemise was much blood-stained & the back of it was stained with faeces. There was no distinguishing mark on the chemise.

Rigor Mortis was not present.

The body was lifted in my presence onto the ambulance & taken to the St. George's-in-the-East mortuary by constables.

On re-examining it there I found an incision, 15 inches long, commencing 2 inches below the ensiform cartilage & running down just to the left of the middle-line, ending just below the pubes.
(The appearances of the neck & hips are described with the account of post-mortem examination by Dr. Phillips)

The body appeared to be that of a woman of about 5 ft. 3 inches in height – of stoutish build – dark complexion – & between 30 & 40 years of age.

In the middle line of the back are four bruises of recent date; the 1st being about 7 inches from the neck & the 2nd 1 inch below that – these two bruises are about the size of a 6d. Four inches below the last named bruise is another of about the size of a 2/6. On a level with the top of the sacrum & 2 inches to the left of middle line is a bruise $1\frac{1}{2}$ inches in diameter & having the appearance such as would be caused by a fall or kick.

Right Arm
There are ["two" – *deleted*] three bruises on front of the arm & one on back – they are of recent date & have the appearance as if caused by the arm being strongly grasped. The back of the forearm is bruised in a line extending from the inner condyle of the humerus to the outer side of the wrist. There are eight bruises in all.

Left Arm.
There are bruises along the inner border of the back of the forearm, there are 7 bruises in all.

Over the outer side of the forearm about the lower third are two wounds – the upper one is only an abrasion & does not penetrate thro' the skin – the lower one is an incised wound $1\frac{3}{4}$ inches long & must have been caused by a sharp knife.

There were no marks of any rings on any of the fingers.

The body was not blood-stained except where the chemise had rested upon it. The lower part of the back was stained by faeces.

The body had not the appearance of having been recently washed.

When I first saw the body decomposition was just commencing & I should think the body had been dead about 24 hours.

There was a mark round the waist caused during life probably by the clothing.

When returning from the mortuary to Leman St Police station with Inspr. Pinhorn we were called by some men to a piece of waste ground in Hooper Street; we there found near an opening at the bottom of the pailings a blood-stained petticoat, body of common make, such as would be worn by a woman of stoutish build. The blood was not very recent & appeared to be menstrual; from the manner too in which it had been folded I should think it had probably been used as a diaper. On my arrival at Leman St station I shewed it to Colonel Monsell & Supt. Arnold.
    Percy J. Clark

The next report[18] is by Inspector Henry Moore, dated 24 September 1889, and is marked, "*Daily Report re- Human Remains found at Pinchin St*":

METROPOLITAN POLICE.
Criminal Investigation Department,
Scotland Yard,
24th day of September 1889.

Re the case of Human Remains found at Pinchin Street.   "E".
    I beg to report that no information has been obtained during the past 24 hours that will assist Police in the investigation of the Crime.
    No persons have been detained or liberated on "H" Division during same period.
    This morning Mr. Wynne E. Baxter, Coroner, resumed the enquiry as to

the discovery of the trunk on 8th inst., at St. George's Vestry Hall, cable St. "E.", and in the end a verdict of Wilful murder against some person or persons unknown was returned.

I herewith submit Extract from "Evening Standard" which gives a fair account of the proceedings; as that it can be placed with papers.

Henry Moore, Inspr.
T Arnold Supd.

This is followed by f 22, which is the above-mentioned extract from the *Evening Standard* of Tuesday, 24 September 1889:

THE WHITECHAPEL
TRAGEDY.
INQUEST AND VERDICT.

Mr. Wynne E. Baxter, Coroner for South-East London, this morning resumed, at St. George's Vestry Hall, Cable-street, the inquest on the human remains found under the railway arch in Pinchin-street, on the 10th inst.

Mr. Percy John Clark, assistant to Dr. Phillips, surgeon to H division said:- A little before six a.m. on the morning of September 10 I was called by the police to Pinchin-street. Under the railway arch there, about eight feet from eight [*sic?*] from the road, and about a foot from the right wall of the arch, I saw the trunk of a woman minus the head and legs. It was lying on its chest, with the right arm doubled under the abdomen, the left arm lying at the side. The arms were not severed from the body. There was no pool of blood, and no signs of any struggle having taken place there. On moving the body I found that there was a little blood underneath where the neck had lain. It was small in quantity not clotted, and evidently had oozed from the cut surface of the neck whilst lying there. Covering the cut surface of the neck and right shoulder were the remains of what had been a chemise, of common make, and of such a size as would be worn by a woman of similar build to the trunk found. It had been torn down the front, and had been cut from the front of the armholes on each side. The cuts appeared to have been made with a knife. The chemise was bloodstained nearly all over, I think from being wrapped over the cut surface of the neck. There was no clotted blood on it, and no sign of arterial spurting. I could find no distinguishing mark on the chemise. Rigor mortis was not present, and decomposition had set in. The body was taken to the mortuary, and an examination there showed that the body was that of a woman of stoutish build, dark complexion, about five feet three inches in height, and between thirty and forty years old. I should think the body had been dead about 24 hours. Besides the wounds caused by the severance of the head and legs, there was a wound 15 inches long through the external coats of the abdomen. The body was not bloodstained, except where the chemise had rested upon it. The body seemed to have been recently washed [*sic*]. On the back were four bruises, all caused before death. One was under [?] the spine, on a level with the lower part of the shoulder blade. An inch lower down was a similar bruise. About the middle of the back also, over the spine, was a bruise about the size of half a crown. On a level with the top of the hip bone, and three inches to the left of the spine, was a bruise two and a half inches in diameter, such as might be caused by a fall or a kick. None of the bruises were of old standing. Round the waist was a pale mark and indentation such as would be caused by clothing during life. On the right arm there were eight distinct bruises, and seven on the left, all cause before death and of recent date. The backs of both forearms and hands were much bruised. On the outer side of the left forearm, about three inches above the wrist, was a cut about two inches in length, and half an inch lower down was another cut, both caused after death. The bruises on the right arm were such as would have been caused by the arm having been tightly grasped. There was an old injury on the index finger of the right hand over the last joint. Two vaccination marks were on the left arm. The arms were well formed. Both elbows were hardened and discoloured, as if they had been leant upon. The hands and nails were pallid and the former were not indicative of any particular kind of work. The breasts were well formed, and there were no signs of maternity about them.

Dr. Phillips, police surgeon of the H division, said – I first examined the body at six o'clock on the day the remains were found. I confirm, so far as I have observed, the evidence given by my colleague, Mr. Clarke [*sic*], who was present with me when I first examined the body. Decomposition of the body had been fairly established. There was an oozing of blood from the cut surface of the neck. The cut surfaces where the thighs had been removed were nearly dry. The cut surface at the neck was not so dry, but it impressed me greatly with its general even surface. The skin was beginning to peel, and the decomposition of the trunk was greater about the upper than the lower part of it. There was not a head, and the thighs had been removed from the body. Next morning, in the presence of Dr. Gordon Brown and Mr. Hibberd [*sic*], I further examined the body. Decomposition had extended greatly. The cut surface of the neck was much drier at the ends of the muscles, but more moist underneath. The neck had been severed by a clean incision commencing a little to the right side of the middle line of the neck behind, leaving a flap of skin at the end of the incision. It had severed the whole of the structures of the neck, dividing the cartilage of the neck in front, and separating the bone of the spine behind. The walls of the belly were divided from just below the cartilage of the ribs. The two small cuts upon the forearm appear to me as likely to have been caused when the sweep of the knife divided the muscles covering the upper part of the thigh. Both thighs were excised by the extensive circular sweep of the knife, or some sharp instrument, penetrating the joint from below and separating the thighs at the hip joint, but the cartilages within the joint and those which deepen the joint and surround it had not been injured. The marks upon the fingers had fairly healed, and had evidently been in the process of healing for some time previous to death. I think the pallor of the hands and the nails is an important element in enabling me to draw a conclusion as to the cause of death. I agree especially with the remarks made by Mr. Clarke as to the date. I found the length of the trunk to be 2 ft. 2 in., and the measure went round the nipple 34 in., and below the breast 31¾ in. Dr. Phillips, having given some further measurements, said that the Deceased was about 5 ft. 3 in. There was throughout the body an absence of blood in the vessels. The heart was empty; it was fatty, and the vessels coated with fat, but the bowels were healthy. The right lung was adherent, except at base, the left lung free, and, taking them both together, fairly competent, and especially considering the decomposition of the remains. The stomach was the seat of considerable post-mortem change, and contained only a small quantity of fruit, like a plum. In my opinion the woman had never been pregnant. I believe her to have been under 40 years of age. There was an absence of any particular disease or poison. I believe that death arose from loss of blood. I believe the whole of the mutilations to have been subsequent to death; that the mutilations were effected by some one accustomed to cut up animals or to see them cut up; and that the incisions were effected by a strong knife, eight inches or more long. The supposition – (and only a supposition) – which presents itself to my mind is that there had been a former incision of the neck, the signs of which had disappeared on the subsequent separation of the head. The loss of blood could not have come from the stomach, and I could not trace it coming from the lungs. I have a strong opinion that it did not.

By a Juryman. – I cannot say whether the person who severed the head from the body was a butcher or not. I merely wish to say it was a person accustomed either to see or use a knife, or some sharp instrument in cutting up animals. I have no reason for believing that he had human anatomical knowledge. In fact, it probably is known to you, and most people, that the spine is not the part to be disarticulated by a medical man.

Michael Keating, of 1 Osborne-street [*sic*], Brick-lane, a licensed shoe black, said he passed up Pinchin-street on the night of the 9th, between eleven and twelve o'clock. He saw no one about, and observed nothing under the. arch, but he was not very sober at the time. Witness went to sleep under the arch, and was not awakened during the night. The police roused him in the morning, and as he was leaving he noticed the body, which the inspector was covering up. He lent the police the sack in which he carried his blacking-box. If the body had been under the arch when he went in, he was not certain he was sober enough to have seen it. As far as he remembered, however, he went in the other side of the arch. He did not hear of anyone else coming in during the night. Witness had never slept under the arch before, but he knew it was a quiet and convenient place.

Richard Hawk, seaman, of St. Ives, Cornwall, stated that about seven or eight weeks ago he was paid off, and was in hospital till the 9th September. He walked about the streets until 20 minutes past four o'clock a.m., on the 10th, when happening to be in Pinchin-street he went under a railway arch to lie down. It was dark and he was not exactly sober.

The Coroner. – How did you know it was 20 minutes past four?

Witness. – We asked a policeman we saw close to the arch. He did not see anyone or anything in the arch when he went in. There was another man with him. His companion was in about the same condition. They met in a public-house. He neither heard nor saw anything, and went to sleep very soon.

Nehemiah Hurley, carman, said that he lived near Pinchin-street, and was called by a policeman as usual at 5 a.m. on the 10th inst. Work commenced with him occasionally at half-past five, but he left the house on the morning in question at 25 minutes to six. He went by way of Pinchin-street, where he saw a man standing at the corner, having the appearance of a tailor. The man looked as if he was waiting to go to work. Witness saw no one else until he got into Pinchin-street where he saw an inspector and other police standing by the arch where the body had been found.

Inspector Moore said he had charge of the case. There was nothing at present to show how the body was placed in the position in which it was found. He saw no reason for adjourning the inquiry. The chemise he produced had been torn and cut. It was made of common material, and was hand stitched and certainly not by an experienced needlewoman. It looked like a home-made garment, probably made by some poor person.

Police-constable Pinnett, recalled, said he was not stopped by anyone and asked the time on the night in question.

A statement was read by the Coroner from the man who was under the arch with Hawk, and confirming the latter's statement.

Dr. Phillips, recalled, said that there was not such a similarity between the manner in which the limbs were severed in this and in the Dorset-street murder, to convince him that both crimes were the work of one man, but the division of the neck,, and the attempt to disarticulate the bones of the spine were very similar in each case. The savagery shown in the mutilations

in the Dorset-street case was far worse than in that now under consideration. In the former the mutilations were most wanton, whereas in the
Pinchin-street crime he believed they were made in order to dispose of the
body. These were points that struck him *without* any comparative study of
the Dorset-street case, except such as was afforded by partial notes which he
had with him. He believed that in this case there had been greater
knowledge shown in regard to the construction of the parts composing
the spine, and on the whole their [*sic*] had been a greater knowledge shown
of how to separate a joint.

The Coroner, in summing up, pointed out that there was no evidence as to
the identity of the Deceased; but that the statements of the medical gentlemen
in the case showed clearly that the woman had died a violent death. It was a
matter of congratulation that the present case did not appear to have any
necessary connection with the previous murders in the immediate neighbourhood.

The Jury immediately returned a verdict of "Wilful Murder against some
person or persons unknown."

Hy. Moore, Inspr.

There is a report cover[19] from the CID Central Office, stating:

Inspector Moore Submitting daily report of occurrences in connection with
the human remains found in Pinchin Street on 10th inst. To Commissioner –
There will be no objection to the burial from a police point of view, if it will
not interfere with our being able to fit the head to the trunk, if we ever get it.
Till all chance of recovery of the remaining parts of the body is gone it might
be advisable to keep the trunk in spirits. HM

<u>Supn H.</u> Please ascertain from Dr. Phillips whether, in the event of the head
or legs being subsequently found, he would be in a position to say that they
belonged to the trunk if same had been buried.

[*Sgd illegible*] for ACC
27/9.

Report submitted Jno West 30/9/89 Act. Supt.

To Commissioner – for sanction. 1/10

Have the remains buried, after arranging for further preservation.
1.10   JM

Report Submitted   Jno West
5/10/89   Actg.Supt.

Mr Williamson   7/10
           JM

Seen and noted Hy Moore
Jno West
Actg Supt. 8/10/89.

The report[20] by Henry Moore, follows:

Human Remains found at Whitechapel. Reference to papers 57885
METROPOLITAN POLICE.
Criminal Investigation Department,
Scotland Yard,
24th day of September, 1889.
Re the case of "Human Remains" found at Pinchin Street.

I beg to report that during the past 24 hours no information has been obtained from the various enquiries which have been made which will assist Police in clearing up the mystery.

No persons have been detained or liberated on "H" Division during same period.

Enquiries and search has now been completed in Divisions (A. to Woolwich inclusive) for the missing portions of the "Remains", but with no good result.

Respecting the Trunk found at Pinchin Street on 10th inst., I beg to state that at the conclusion of the adjourned Inquest yesterday, the coroner, W. Baxter, Esqr. handed me the order for Burial, and remarked that he would leave it to the discretion of Police when it should be buried. I have since had Dr. Phillips seen upon the subject and he has no objection to the body being buried; but suggests that the interment should be witnessed and the lid of the tin vessel which now contains the body be secured.

I respectfully ask directions as to the burial of the body.

In conclusion I beg to add that before leaving the Coroner yesterday, he thanked me for the able assistance and attention which I had rendered him during the enquiry.

Henry Moore, Insp.

Respectfully submitted and suggest that the remains be buried as I see no reason for keeping the same any longer.

Jno. West ActgSup.

The next report[21] dated 30 September 1889, is also by Inspector Henry Moore and bears the same reference as the previous one:

METROPOLITAN POLICE.
Criminal Investigation Department,
Scotland Yard,
30th day of September 1889

Referring to attached; Vide Assistant Chief Constables Minute; dated 27th inst.

I beg to report that I was unable to see Dr. Phillips until this morning; when I consulted him as directed on the subject. He decided that the time has fully arrived for the "Remains" to be further dealt with; either by further means of preservation (more spirit) or by soldering down the mouth of tin vessel and burial. The identification probably could be made without comparison with the remains; but should the case ever be the subject of an investigation before a Judge and Jury such comparison would be absolutely necessary.

As to interment the Dr. prefers that it be effected by burying it in the tin vessel, after it has been re-charged with spirit and soldered.

I have conferred with Mr. James Wooton, Sanitary Inspector, St. George's-in-the-East; and he has promised, providing I can arrange with the Plaistow Cemetery Authorities that he will cause it to be buried as handed over to him by Police.

I will arrange if possible with the Cemetery Authorities tomorrow, and await Commissioners instructions as to the interment. Should burial be decided upon I have promised to acquaint Dr. Phillips, when he will attend at the mortuary and carry the final requirements as to preservation.

Henry Moore, Inspr.
Jno. West ActgSupt

The final report[22] regarding the disposal of the remains is dated 5 October 1889, again by Inspector Moore:

METROPOLITAN POLICE
H Division
5th day of October 1889

Referring to attached; vide Commissioners Minute dated 1st inst.

I beg to report that in accordance with directions I arranged for Dr. Phillips and Mr. John Allers, Tin Plate Worker of 2 Back Church Lane, St. George's, "E", to attend at the mortuary at 2p.m., 3rd to carry out the necessary arrangements for further preservation of the body, previous to burial; but Mr.

Allers, finding that it was a matter of impossibility to solder up the vessel which then contained the "Remains" without allowing the spirit to escape; the arrangements were postponed.

I then conferred with him and the Dr. as to what were the best steps to be taken in the course of which Mr. Allers suggested that a case, properly constructed, be supplied; which, if I thought fit he would make at reasonable cost. The Dr. having concurred in the suggestion, I directed Mr. Allers to make the case, which he did.

At 2p.m. 4th they again attended at the mortuary, when the transfer of the body was effected, spirit added, and effectually soldered down.

For making the case (2 ft. 7 in. long; 1 ft. 9 in. wide; and 1 ft. 2 in. deep; soldering etc.) Mr. Allers charged 12/-; which I have paid; and for which I respectfully ask authority.

The case was then handed over to the Sanitary Authorities; who placed it in a black painted wooden box (?) and arranged to carry out the interment at 10 a.m. today at the East London Cemetery, Grange Park, Plaistow, Essex.

I attended at the cemetery at time specified and witnessed the interment. It was placed in Grave No 16185, and upon the metal plate on box (?) was the following:

> "This case contains the
> "body of a woman (unknown)
> "found in Pinchin Street
> "St. Georges-in-the-East
> "10th Septr./89."

Henry Moore Inspr.
Jno West
ActgSupt

CHAPTER 30

Inspector Moore Interviewed
About the Whitechapel Murders

Inspector Henry Moore, as we have seen, was one of the Detective
Inspectors sent from Scotland Yard to investigate the Whitechapel
Murders. He took over as the inspector in charge of the enquiry when
Abberline moved on to other investigations in early 1889. Just before the
Pinchin Street torso case an American journalist from Philadelphia, R.
Harding Davis, visited London and researched a story on the infamous
murders. His endeavours were reported in the *Pall Mall Gazette* of 4
November 1889:

THE WHITECHAPEL TRAGEDIES.
A NIGHT SPENT WITH INSPECTOR MOORE.
REMARKABLE STATEMENTS.

Philadelphia journalist, Mr. R. Harding Davis, has been publishing in a
syndicate of American papers, an account of a night he spent upon the scene of
the Whitechapel murders, towards the end of August, in the company of
Police Inspector Moore, in the course of which some interesting statements
occur.

DR. ANDERSON ON CRIMINAL "SHOW PLACES."

Mr. Davis had taken a letter of introduction to Dr. Robert Anderson, the
head of the Criminal Investigation Department, who remarked to him, "I am
sorry to say on your account and quite satisfied on my own that we have very
few criminal 'show places' in London. Of course, there is the Scotland Yard
Museum that visitors consider one of the sights, and then there is Whitechapel. But that is all. You ought to see Whitechapel. Even if the murders had
not taken place there it would be still the show part of the city for those who
take an interest in the dangerous classes. But you mustn't expect to see
criminals walking about with handcuffs on or to find the places they live in any
different from the other dens of the district. My man can show you their
lodging houses and can tell you that this or that man is a thief or a burglar, but
he won't look any different from anyone else." The journalist suggested that
he had never found they look any different from any one else. "Well, I only

spoke of it because they say, as a rule, your people come over here expecting
to see dukes wearing their coronets and the thieves of Whitechapel in prison-
cut clothes, and they are disappointed. But I don't think you will be
disappointed in the district. After a stranger has gone over it he takes a
much more lenient view of our failure to find Jack the Ripper, as they call
him, than he did before."

INSPECTOR MOORE.

Proceeding to Leman-street police station at nine o'clock at night in fulfilment
of an engagement made by Dr. Anderson, Mr. Davis found the entrance to
the station barricaded with several crossings of red tape. It was very different
from the easy discipline of an American police station, and from the nights
when, as a police reporter, I walked unquestioned into the roll room and
woke up the sergeant in charge to ask if there was anything on the slate, and to
be told sleepily that there was "nothing but drunks" The superintendent
introduced me to a well-dressed gentleman of athletic build, whom he said
was Inspector Moore, the chief of the detective force that has since April 8,
1888, covered the notorious district of the Whitechapel murders. The
inspector has been twenty years in the force, and it was his work on the
murder committed by the American, Lamson, that brought him the
distinguished and most unwelcome work on which he is still engaged.

A TEXAN POLICE-CAPTAIN APOLOGIZES TO THE LONDON POLICE.
Inspector Moore led the journalist through the network of narrow passageways as dark and loathsome as the great network of sewers that stretches
underneath them a few feet below. "The chief of police from Austin, Texas,
came to see me," said the inspector, "and offered me a great deal of advice.
But when I showed him this place (Castle-alley) and the courts around it he
took off his hat and said: 'I apologise. I never saw anything like it before.
We've nothing like it in all America.' He said that at home an officer could
stand on a street corner and look down four different streets and see all that
went on in them for a quarter of a mile off. Now, you know, I might put two
regiments of police in this half-mile of district and half of them would be as
completely out of sight and hearing of the others as though they were in
separate cells of a prison. To give you an idea of it, my men formed a circle
around the spot where one of the murders took place, guarding they thought,
every entrance and approach, and within a few minutes they found fifty
people inside the lines. They had come in through two passageways which my
men could not find. And then, you know these people never lock their doors,
and the murderer has only to lift the latch of the nearest house and walk
through it and out the back way." In the course of their perambulations, the
inspector tells the correspondent that they call Whitechapel the "three F's
district, fried fish and fights." After they had passed through a well-known

lodging house, the correspondent asked the inspector if he did not feel nervous and he handed him his cane for an answer. It was a trivial-looking thing, painted to represent maple, but Mr. Davis found it was made of iron. "And then they wouldn't attack me," Mr. Moore said, "It's only those who don't know me that I carry the cane for."

WHITECHAPEL OVERRUN WITH SPIES.

The inspector gazed calmly up and down the street, and then remarked, apparently to a lamp across the way. "Better write; you mustn't come too often." We walked on in silence for half a block, and then I suggested that he was using amateur as well as professional detectives in his search for the murderer. "About sixty," he replied laconically. The inspector was non communicative, but I could see and hear for myself, and a dozen times during our tour women in rags, lodging-house keepers, proprietors of public-houses, and idle young men, dressed like all the other idle young men of the district, but with a straight bearing that told of discipline, and with the regulation shoe with which Scotland yard marks its men, whispered a half sentence as we passed, to which sometimes the inspector replied or to which he sometimes appeared utterly unconscious. From what he said later I learned that all Whitechapel is peopled with these spies. Sometimes they are only "plain clothes" men, but besides these he has half a hundred and at times 200 unattached detectives, who pursue their respectable or otherwise callings while they keep an alert eye and ear for the faintest clue that may lead to the discovery of the invisible murderer.

A HORRIBLE SITUATION FOR "JACK THE RIPPER."

"This was about the worst of the murders," said the inspector when they reached Dorset-street. "He cut the skeleton so clean of flesh that when I got here I could hardly tell whether it was a man or a woman. He hung the different parts of the body on nails and over the backs of chairs. It must have taken him an hour and a half in all. And when he was ready to go he found the door was jammed and had to make his escape through the larger of those two windows." Imagine how this man felt when he tried the door and found it was locked; that was before he thought of the window – believing that he was locked in with that bleeding skeleton and the strips of flesh that he had hung so fantastically about the room, that he had trapped himself beside his victim, and had helped to put the rope around his own neck. One would think the shock of the moment would have lasted for years to come, and kept him in hiding. But it apparently did not affect him that way, for he has killed five women since then. We knocked at the door and a woman opened it. She spoke to some-one inside, and then told "Mister Inspector" to come in. It was a bare whitewashed room with a bed in one corner. A man was in the bed, but he sat up and welcomed us good naturedly. The inspector apologized for the intrusion, but the occupant of the bed said it didn't matter, and obligingly traced out with his forefinger the streaks of blood upon the wall at his bedside. When he had done this he turned his face to the wall to go to sleep again, and the inspector ironically wished him pleasant dreams. I rather envied his nerve, and fancied waking up with those dark streaks a few inches from one's face.

"NOW, WHY ISN'T THAT JACK THE RIPPER?"

"What makes it so easy for him" – the inspector always referred to the murderer as "him" – "is that the women lead him, of their own free will, to the spot where they know interruption is least likely. It is not as if he had to wait for his chance; they make the chance for him. And then they are so miserable and so hopeless, so utterly lost to all that makes a person want to live, that for the sake of fourpence, enough to get drunk on, they will go in any man's company, and run the risk that it is not him. I tell many of them to go home, but they say they have no home, and when I try to frighten them and speak of the danger they run they'll laugh and say, 'Oh, I know what you mean. I ain't afraid of him. It's the Ripper or the bridge with me. What's the odds?' And it's true; that's the worst of it."

The inspector feels his work and its responsibilities keenly. He talked of nothing else, and he apparently thinks, eats, and sleeps on nothing else. Once or twice he stopped, and pointing to a man and woman standing whispering on a corner, said, "Now, why isn't that Jack the Ripper?"

Why not indeed. When I was in the Scotland-yard museum I expressed some surprise that there were no relics on exhibition of the Whitechapel murders, the most notorious series of criminal events in the history of the world when one considers the civilization of the city and of the age in which they have occurred, and the detective who was showing me about said, "We have no relics; he never leaves so much as a rag behind him. There is no more of a clue to that chap's identity than there is to the identity of some murderer who will kill some-one a hundred years from now."

WHERE SUSPICION HAS RESTED.

But they have thought they had clues. They have thought they had the murderer himself perhaps, hundreds of times. Suspicion has rested, so the inspector said, on people in every class of society – on club men, doctors and dockers, members of Parliament and members of the nobility, common sailors and learned scientists. In two squares the inspector pointed out three houses where he said he had gone to find him. He told the story to illustrate the degradation of the women of the district, but the point of interest in them to me was that in a space of 200 yards he had found three houses where the murderer was supposed to be hiding. This shows that there must have been hundreds of men suspected of whom the public have heard nothing. Inspector

Moore said his own detectives, amateur and professional, would occasionally follow each other for a week in the idea that they were tracking the murderer.

"And then we are so often misled by false clues, suggested by people who have a spite to work off. We get any number of letters throwing the most circumstantial evidence about a certain man, and when we run it out we find some woman whom he has thrown over. All this takes time and money, and from the nature of our work we can say nothing of what we are doing; we can only speak when it is done. I have received 2,000 letters of advice from America alone; you can fancy how many I get from this country.

"And then there is the practical joker who sends us letters written in blood and bottles of blood, parts of the human body or the entrails of animals which he says he took from his victim. It is not an easy piece of work, I assure you. I work seventeen and eighteen hours a day. If I get into bed I think maybe he is at it now, and I grow restless, and I finally get up and tramp the courts and alleys till morning."

It had been a five hours' walk through more misery, vice and crime than can perhaps be found in as small a space, less than a square mile, in any other great city. There had been only eight murders then. And as we neared the station I remember the inspector's pointing into the dark arches of the London, Tilbury, and Southend Railway, and saying: "Now, what a place for a murder that would be." A week later, while I was in mid-ocean on my way back, the body of the ninth victim was found just under those very arches, and not three minutes' walk from the police station. I don't know whether Jack the Ripper was lurking near us that night and had acted on the inspector's suggestion, or whether the inspector is Jack the Ripper himself, but the coincidence is certainly suspicious. As for myself, although I assented to its being a good place for murder at the time, I can prove an alibi by the ship's captain.

CHAPTER 31

An Allegation Against Sergeant Thick
– Further Allowance Claims

An extraordinary allegation that one of the Metropolitan Police's finest was none other than "Jack the Ripper" was made by a member of the public in September 1889. It was made against Sergeant William Thick of H Division who had played a prominent part in the investigations of the Whitechapel Murders in 1888.

The file cover[1] is as follows:

[Stamped: – HOME OFFICE 11 SEP.89 RECEIVED] No. A49301/177
DATE 10 Septr: 89   Mr. H. T. Haslewood.
REFERENCES, &c.   Whitechapel Murders
Believes the murderer is a Policeman. Upon hearing that his name shall not be mentioned in any way, (especially to the Police) will forward the name of the officer. Pressing

MINUTES.

This seems ridiculous and perhaps should not be encouraged, but it would do no harm to? say that if he will forward the name and any other particulars it will be kept strictly confidential.

Write as suggested   HBS
E P. 13. Sept   11.9.89
Wrote 13/9

The letter[2] received from Mr Haslewood appears, and is as follows:

Official 11/9/9. DSS Pressing [Stamped: – HOME OFFICE 11 SEP.89 RECEIVED]

[?] 3.P.M.   White Cottage A49301/177
High Rd.
Tottenham
10 Sept 1889

Sir,

    I have very good grounds to believe that the person who has committed the Whitechapel murders is a member of the police force, – upon hearing from you that my name shall not be mentioned in any way especially to the police, I will immediately forward you the name of the officer who I suspect of course it is only a suspicion, based upon very slight evidence, but with the assistance of the police records you could in a very few minutes ascertain where this person was on the respective days of the murders, you could also ascertain if he was now suffering from any complaint that might effect his mind at certain seasons,

Yours obediently,

To the Rt. Hon. HMatthews   H. T. Haslewood,
   Home Office
   Whitehall.-

There then follows a second minute cover[3] as follows:

[Stamped: – HOME OFFICE 21 OCT.89 RECEIVED] No. A49301/193
DATE 14 Oct. 1889.   Mr. H.T. Haslewood.
REFERENCES, &c.   East End Murders.
 Recommends that Sergt. T. [*sic*] Thicke be watched, as he thinks he is the murderer. Desires that his name be kept strictly secret.
[MINUTES.]
[*Marginal note – [illegible]* "Progress not having been made confidential JM[?] Ackd. 21.10.89."]
see minute on /177.
I think it is plainly rubbish – perhaps prompted by spite.
 ?shall it go to Mr. Anderson (to be treated as confidential in view of the promise given on /177.)
CT
21.10.89

The name of writer   GL
must not be given   22 Oct '89.
Sent copies (with name and address omitted).
HBS
24.10.89

A further letter[4] from Mr Haslewood follows:

A49301/177   A49301/193
  [Stamped: – HOME OFFICE 21 OCT.89 Received] White Cottage
             High Rd
             Tottenham
             14 Oct 1889.

Sir,

Referring to yours of the 13th Sept. I beg to state that through the information I have received I believe that if Sergt T.Thicke otherwise called "Johnny Upright" is watched and his whereabouts ascertained upon other dates where certain women have met their end, also to see what deceace he is troubled with, you will find the great secreate this is to be strictly private and my name is not to be mentioned.

Yours faithfully,

E.L. Pemberton Esq.   H.T. Haslewood.

A file cover[5] dated 18 September states:

H.O.
18 Sept.
Whitechapel Murders
Stating with reference to H.O. letter of 17 July (attached) that the S of S has sanctioned the 1 Inspr 5 PSs and 50 PCs being retained for special duty in Whitechapel for a further period of 1 month expiring on 16 pm
Accountant.

E.U.

19/9/89
[*illeg.*] to note – There will probably be Refreshment allowances for these men. – CC/19/9 Noted.
[*illeg*] 19.9.89

A report[6] dated 18 September 1889, from E. Leigh Pemberton to the Receiver for the Metropolitan Police District, is as follows:

Pressing A48000M/44   WHITEHALL.
                                       18 September 1889.

Sir,

With reference to the Home Office letter of the 17th July last, I am directed by the Secretary of State to acquaint you that he has signified his sanction for the augmentation of 1 Inspector 5 Sergeants and 50 Constables for special duty in Whitechapel, being retained for that work for a further period of one month expiring on the 16th proximo.

I am,
Sir,

The Receiver for the   Your obedient Servant,
Metropolitan Police District   E LeighPemberton.
&c.   &c.   &c.

The discovery of "the Pinchin Street torso" had the effect of raising fears that a killer was still abroad in the Whitechapel district, even though the police did not believe that it was another "Ripper" crime. It therefore brought further requests for allowances for additional officers drafted into the area from other Divisions.

A report[7] dated 18 September 1889 is as follows:

No. A49301G/10

DATE 18 Sept. 1889   The Commissioner of Police.

REFERENCES, &c.   Asks that the plain clothes allowances granted to the men employed in plain clothes in Whitechapel may be continued until such employment cease.

MINUTES.

? sanction for another 2 months from 17th.

       HBS

       20.9.89

       EUP. 21 Sept 89

       Wrote Comr. &Recd.

       24.9.89.

       sa(1/11)

96318   A49301G/10

           4, Whitehall Place,

             S.W.

          18th September, 1889.

[*in margin*: – A49301G/9]

Sir,

With reference to your letter of the 3rd ultimo sanctioning the payment, for a period of two months, of the plain clothes allowance of 1/- a day to the 3 Sergeants and 39 Constables employed in plain clothes in Whitechapel, I have to acquaint you, for the information of the Secretary of State, that as the duty commenced on the 17th July last that authority has now expired, – and I have accordingly to request that Mr. Secretary Matthews may be pleased to sanction a continuance of this allowance during such time as it may be deemed advisable to retain these men for special duty in Whitechapel. –

       I am,

        Sir,

    Your most obedient Servant,

       J.Monro.

The Under Secretary

    of State

  &c. &c. &c.

   Home Office.

A file cover[8] reads as follows:

H.O.
24 Sept.
Whitechapel Murders
Sanctioning the continuance of the plain clothes allowance to the 3 PSs &
39PCs employed for a further period of 2 months dating from the 17th inst.
Accountant to note
this authority
ARP
26 Sept
WWilby
      CG
Done   27/9/89.

There follows a similar cover[9] for October 1889:

H.O.
3 Oct
Whitechapel murders
Sanctioning the payment to the 2 PSs and 12 PCs, augmented for duty in
Whitechapel in consequence of the discovery of human remains in Pinchin
Street, of the usual plain clothes allowance of 1/- a day from the 11th ulto.
Accountant to note
this authority
ARP
WFesting
5 Oct 89
Noted HJW [?] 12/10/89

The report[10] appears:

5185/11   4 OCT.89
A49301/186

                                     WHITEHALL.
                                     3rd October 1889.

Sir,
    I am directed by the Secretary of State to acquaint you with reference to
the augmentation of 2 Sergeants and 12 Constables for employment in plain
clothes in Whitechapel in consequence of the discovery of human remains in
Pinchin Street on the 10th Ultimo, that he sanctions the payment to these

men of the usual plain clothes allowance of 1s/- per diem as from the 11th ultimo.

I am,
Sir,
Your obedient Servant,

The Receiver for the   E. Leigh Pemberton
Metropolitan Police District.
&c.   &c.   &c.

The next cover[11], dated 11 October 1889, is as follows:

H.O.
11 Octr.
Whitechapel Murders. Special Allce.
The grant of special plain clothes allowance of 1s/- per diem is sanctioned (as from 11th ulto.) to 3 addl. PCs; the Commr. having reported the No. to be 15 and not 12.
Accountant to note
ARP
14 Oct 89
W Wilby Done.

A further file cover[12] appears and is dated 26 October 1889, as follows:

H.O.
26. Octr.
Whitechapel Murders.
Sanctions the retention of the augmentation of 1 Inspr. 5 P.S. & 50 P.C., for specl. duty in Whitechapel, for a further period of one month from 16th inst.
Accountant to note as
augmentation of police
&[*illeg.*]
Noted CC : Noted AJW

This is not a fresh augmentation – on reference to the two letters in /9 it will be seen that 1 Insp. 3 P.S. & 30 P.C. temporarily augmented some time ago for duty in Trafalgar Square were transferred to Whitechapel, with the addition of 2 P.S. & 20 P.C. for a period of 2 months, & that subsequently by letter of 18 Sept the time was extended to 16 Oct: By this letter the period is further extended to 16 Nov:
   Mr. Wilby to note as regards the allowances – &pps Done –

CC
31/10
5185/13   28 OCT.89
A48000M/45   WHITEHALL.
                                  26th October, 1889.

Sir,

   I am directed by the Secretary of State to acquaint you with reference to previous correspondence that he has sanctioned the retention of the augmentation of 1 Inspector, 5 Sergeants and 50 Constables for special duty in Whitechapel for a further period of one month from the 16th instant.

                             I am,
                               Sir,
                        Your obedient Servant,
                           Godfrey Lushington

The Receiver
for the Metropolitan
      Police District,

The following month further reports[13] were submitted regarding the augmented officers, as follows:

[Stamped: – 14 NOV 1889 – Receiver for Metropolitan Police District]
H.O.
13th Nov.
Whitechapel, augmentation
Sanctions retention of 100 men for 1 month.
Accountant
to note
Augmentation of police
Noted CC.ARP
15.Nov Mr [ ] to note as reg [ ] allowances.
                             CC
                            15/11

[*illeg initials*]

A letter[14] follows:

5185/14   14 NOV.89
Pressing A50657/14   WHITEHALL.
                                  13 November 1889.

Sir,
   With reference to previous correspondence, I am directed by the Secretary

of State to acquaint you that he has signified to the Commissioner of Police approval of the retention for a further month of the special augmentation of 100 men for duty in Whitechapel.

I am,

Sir,

Your obedient Servant,

E. LeighPemberton.

The Receiver for the
Metropolitan Police District
&c.   &c.   &c.

The augmentation to the strength of officers in Whitechapel was the subject of further claims[15] in November, with a file cover[16] dated 16 November 1889, as follows:

[Stamped: – HOME OFFICE 18 NOV.89 RECEIVED] No. A49301G/11
DATE 16th Novr. /89   Commissioner of Police
REFERENCES, &c.   re Continuance of the Plain Clothes allow-
ance to 3 Sergeants & 39 constables employed in Whitechapel on special duty/

Requests that the S of S may be pleased to sanction a further continuance of this allowance for one month.

MINUTES.

? Sanction for a month from 16th inst.

HBS

CM 20. 20.11.89.

EUP. 21. Nov. 89./

Wrote Commr & Recd.

22/11.

This is followed by a report[17]:

[Stamped: – HOME OFFICE 18 NOV.89 RECEIVED] A49301G/11

4, Whitehall Place, S.W.

16th November 1889.

96318/15.
[*In margin* – A 49301 B./10]
Sir,

    With reference to your letter of the 24th September last sanctioning the continuance of the plain clothes allowance to 3 Sergeants and 39 constables, employed in Whitechapel on special duty, for two months dating from the 17th idem, I have to request that Mr. Secretary

Matthews may be pleased to sanction a further continuance of the allowance for a period of one month.

I am,

Sir,

Your most obedient Servant,

J.Monro

The Under
Secretary of State
&c. &c. &c.

The usual cover[18] regarding the sanction granted appears, as follows:

H.O.
19 Novr.
Whitechapel Murders
Sanctions continuance of augmentation of 1 Insp. (for special duty) 5 P.S. 50 P.C. for another month from 16th instant.
Accountant note
Noted CC ARP
20.11.89
[*illeg sig*]

The Home Office letter[19] follows:

5185/15

Pressing A48000M/46   WHITEHALL.

19 November 1889.

Sir,

    With reference to previous correspondence, I am directed by the Secretary of State to acquaint you that he has approved of the continuance for one month as from the 16th instant of the augmentation of 1 Inspector 5 Sergeants and 50 Constables for special duty in Whitechapel.

I am,

Sir,

Your obedient Servant,

E. Leigh Pemberton.

The Receiver for the
Metropolitan Police District
&c. &c. &c.

The next file cover[20] appears, as follows:

H.O. 22 Novr.
Whitechapel Murders
Sanctions continuance, for two months as from 17th inst., of plain clothes
allowance to 3 P.S. & 39 P.C. employed on special duty.
Accountant
[ ]
Noted.
Noted CC [ ]

There is a document[21] dated 5 December 1889 and marked "CLOSED
UNTIL 1990 HO144/221/A49301I", as follows:

A49301/2
No. 5227/107 & 108 [Stamped: – HOME OFFICE 6 DEC.89 RECEIVED]
Office of the
Metrop
4, Whitehall Place, S.W.
5th Decr. 1889.

Sir,
    I have the honor to transmit for the information of the Secretary of State,
Accounts of Expenses incurred by various Police Officers on special occasions,
and to request authority for payment of the same, the Commissioner having
approved thereof, vizt.

Inspector Moore	£27 : 7 : 5
– do –	£49 : 3 : 7
	Murders in Whitechapel.

Minutes
To Under Secretary
? sanction
    HBS
    16.12.89
    C.M.   Wrote to Receiver   I have the honor to be,
                18 Dec: 1889.   Sir,
                                                         Your obedient Servant,
The Under Secretary of State   A:A:[*illeg.*]
    &c.   &c.   &c.
        Home Office.

A report[22] on the conditions in the East End is included in the files, dated
27 December 1889 and signed by the Chief Commissioner, as follows:

B7590

With refce. to the article by Mr. Barnett, there is no doubt, as I have already reported that vice of the lowest type finds a refuge in the slums of Whitechapel, and that the localities to which he refer are about as bad as can be found in London. If the area containing the dens where Whitechapel vice flourishes could be cleared, there is no doubt that Whitechapel would be immensely benefitted. Where the residuum of vice thus transferred is to find a resting place is another question which must not be lost sight of.

Police do all that they can to keep violence & vice within bounds, but their duties are confined to the streets, and their efforts there can do nothing to strike at the root of the evil, which is not to be found on the streets, but in the dens to which the abandoned & criminal classes resort. This is a matter which can only be dealt with by the landlords of these houses, and if by any pressure put upon this class, better dwellings can be provided – and better dwellings mean better tenants – an improvement in the moral surroundings of Whitechapel will be effected, which will be heartily welcomed by the police.

27.12.89.   J.Monro

The augmentation of police patrols in Whitechapel continued into the new year, and the first report[23], dated 18 January 1890, is as follows:

[Stamped: – HOME OFFICE 20 JAN.90 RECEIVED] No. A49301G/12
DATE 18 Jan: 1890   Commissioner of Police
REFERENCES, &c.   Men employed on special duty in W<u>hitechapel</u>
Proposes to gradually reduce the number.

The strength at present is 3 Sergts. & 26 constables.

Requests approval of renewal of plain clothes allowance of 1s/- per diem to these men for a further period of one month.

<u>Pressing</u>
MINUTES.

? Sanction and inform Receiver
           W B
           22.1.90

Saying in such a matter as this S.S. feels that he must rely implicitly on the direction of the Commissioner that such a diminution of force may be accomplished with safety to the public.

		C.M.
Mr Matthews to see	G.L.	Jan 23.
H.M.	23 Jan '90	
27 Jan.90	Wrote Comr & Recd	
	30.1.90.	
	see (1/13)	

The report[24] follows:

A49301G/312

9618/21. [Stamped: – HOME OFFICE 20 JAN.90 RECEIVED]

4 Whitehall Place, S.W.

18th January, 1890.

Sir,

  With reference to previous correspondence [*A49301g/11*] on the subject I have to acquaint you for the information of the Secretary of State, that I propose to gradually reduce the number of men employed on special duty in Whitechapel. I have already been able to effect a considerable reduction, and the strength at present specially employed is 3 Sergeants, and 26 Constables. These I think it advisable to retain for the present, and I have to ask that the Secretary of State may be pleased to approve of the renewal of the plain clothes allowance of 1s/- per diem to these men for a further period of one month.

I am, Sir

Your most obedient Servant,

J.Monro

The Under

  Secretary of State,

    &c. &c. &c,

The next cover[25] is stamped:- RECEIVER FOR THE METROPOLITAN POLICE DISTRICT REGISTERED 5185/17:

H.O.

30 Jany.

Whitechapel Murders. Allces &c.

Forwarding copy of letter to Commr., authg continuance of plain clothes allowance to 3 P.S. and 26 P.C. for another month.

Accountant to note.

  ARP

  31 Jany 90

Noted CC

[*illeg. sgs.*]

5/2/90.

The report[26] of 30 January 1890 reads:

31/1 [Stamped: – RECEIVER FOR THE METROPOLITAN POLICE DISTRICT REGISTERED 5185/17. JAN 31 1890]   31 JAN.90

No. A49301G/12   WHITEHALL.
                                                  30th January, 1890.
Sir,

   With reference to previous correspondence, I am directed by the Secretary
of State to transmit herewith for your information and guidance a copy of a
letter which he has this day addressed to the Commissioner of Metropolitan
Police as to the renewal for another month of the plain clothes allowance to
the 3 Sergeants and 26 Police Constables who are at present specially
employed in Whitechapel.

                              I am,
                               Sir,
                         Your obedient Servant,
   The Receiver   E.Leigh Pemberton
   for the Metropolitan
       Police District.

The next file cover[27] is dated 12 February 1890, as follows:

                      No. A49301G/13
DATE   12 February 1890.
REFERENCES, &c.   Police employed in Whitechapel.
              Requests that the Plain Clothes allowance to officers
specially employed as above may be renewed for a further period of one
month.
1/12   Pressing.
                     MINUTES.
? Sanction, and inform Receiver.
                   C.M. Feb: 13.90.
                      EUP. 13 Feby 90
                  Wrote Comr &Recd 14/2/90.
                   Commr. a/17.3.90 (./14)

The report[28] follows in the usual manner, dated 12 February 1890:

Pressing 96318/23 [Stamped:- HOME OFFICE 13 FEB.90 RECEIVED]
A49301G/13.
                              4 Whitehall Place, S.W.
                              12th February, 1890.
Sir,
   With reference to your letter of the 30th ulto. on the subject of the Plain
Clothes allowance to the Police specially employed in Whitechapel, I have to

ask that the Secretary of State may be pleased to approve of the renewal of the allowance to these officers for a further period of one month.

                              I am,
                                    Sir,
                                    Your most obedient Servant,
                                    J.Monro.

The Under
Secretary of State,
       &c.   &c.   &c.

The police file cover[29] reads:

H.O.
14 Feby 90
Whitechapel Murders. &c
S of S has sanctioned the renewal for another month of the plain clothes allowance to officers specially employed.
Accountant to note
          ARP
[WF]   17 Feby 90
[ ] 20/2/90

The following month saw the continued use of a reduced number of the officers on special duty in the Whitechapel district with regard to the previous murders. File cover[30] dated 17 March 1890 refers as follows:

[Stamped:- HOME OFFICE 18 MAR.90 RECEIVED]   No. A49301G/14
DATE 17 March 1890.   Acting Commissioner of Police.
REFERENCES, &c.   Police officers specially employed in <u>Whitechapel</u>.
Requests approval of continuance of the allowance to 2 Sergeants and 11 constables for further period of one month.
1/13

                         MINUTES.
? Sanction and inform Receiver.
[ ]
19.3.90   CM 20.
                    ELP. 21st March 90.
                    Wrote 28/3/90.

The report[31] then follows:

[Stamped:- HOME OFFICE 18 MAR.90 RECEIVED]   A49301G/14
96,318   END
4, Whitehall Place,
S.W.
17th March, 1890.

Sir,

Referring to your letter of the 14th ultimo approving of the renewal for a further period of one month of the Plain Clothes' allowance to the Police officers specially employed in Whitechapel, I have now to ask that the Secretary of State may be pleased to approve of the continuation of the allowance to a portion of these officers, i.e., 2 Sergeants and 11 Constables for a further period of one month. —

I am,
Sir,
Your most obedient Servant,
A.C.Bruce
Acting Commissioner

The Under Secretary
      of State
&c.   &c.   &c.
   Home Office

CHAPTER 32

September 1889 – Dr Forbes Winslow Names a Suspect

After the publicity created by the discovery of the Pinchin Street torso the press embarked on a fresh run of stories based on the renewed "Ripper" scare. The following article appeared in the *New York Herald*, and was included in one of the now-missing files. Fortunately it is possible to include the relevant material as it was photocopied, before its loss, in the 1970s:

THE WHITECHAPEL MURDERS.

A report having been current that a man has been found who is quite convinced that "Jack the Ripper" occupied rooms in his house, and that he had communicated his suspicions in the first instance to Dr. Forbes Winslow, together with detailed particulars, a reporter had an interview with the doctor yesterday afternoon on the subject. "Here are Jack the Ripper's boots," said the doctor, at the same time taking a large pair of boots from under his table. "The tops of these boots are composed of ordinary cloth material, while the soles are made of indiarubber. The tops have great bloodstains on them." The reporter put the boots on, and found they were completely noiseless. Besides these noiseless coverings the doctor says he has the "Ripper's" ordinary walking boots, which are very dirty, and the man's coat which is also bloodstained. Proceeding, Dr. Winslow said that on the morning of Aug. 30 a woman with whom he was in communication was spoken to by a man in Worship Street, Finsbury. He asked her to come down a certain court with him, offering her £1. This she refused, and he then doubled the amount, which she also declined. He next asked her where the court led to, and shortly afterwards left. She told some neighbours, and the party followed the man for some distance. Apparently, he did not know that he was being followed, but when he and the party had reached the open street he turned round, raised his hat, and with an air of bravado said: "I know what you have been doing; good morning." The woman then watched the man into a certain house, the situation of which the doctor would not describe. She previously noticed the the man because of his strange manner, and on the morning on which the woman Mackenzie was murdered (July 17) she saw him washing his hands in the yard of the house referred to. He was in his shirt-sleeves at the time, and had a very peculiar look upon his face. This was about four o'clock in the morning. The doctor said he was now waiting for a certain telegram, which was the only obstacle to his effecting the man's arrest. The supposed assassin lived with a friend of Dr. Forbes Winslow's, and this gentleman himself told the doctor that he had noticed the man's strange behaviour. He would at times sit down and write 50 or 60 sheets of manuscript about low women, for whom he professed to have a great hatred. Shortly before the body was found in Pinchin-street last week the man disappeared, leaving behind him the articles already mentioned, together with a packet of manuscript, which the doctor said was in exactly the same handwriting as the Jack the Ripper letters which were sent to the police. He had stated previously that he was going abroad, but a very few days before the body was discovered (Sept. 10) he was seen in the neighbourhood of Pinchin-street. The doctor is certain that this man is the Whitechapel murderer, and says that two days at the utmost will see him in custody. He could give a reason for the head and legs of the last murdered woman being missing. The man, he thinks, cut the body up, and then commenced to burn it. He had consumed the head and legs when his fit of the terrible mania passed, and he was horrified to find what he had done. ''I know for a fact,'' said the doctor, ''that this man is suffering from a violent form of religious mania, which attacks him and passes off at intervals. I am certain that there is another man in it besides the one I am after, but my reasons for that I cannot state. The police will have nothing to do with the capture. I am making arrangements to station six men round the spot where I know my man is, and he will be trapped.'' The public had laughed at him, the doctor went on to say, but on the Tuesday before the last body was discovered he had received information that a murder would be committed in two or three days. In conclusion, Dr. Winslow remarked, ''I am as certain that I have the murderer as I am of being here.''

The chairman of the Whitechapel Vigilance Committee, Mr. Albert Backert [*sic*], stated yesterday that the police at Leman-street Station having received a letter stating that it has been ascertained that a tall strong woman has for some time been working at different slaughter-houses, attired as a man, searching inquiries were made yesterday morning at the slaughter-houses in Aldgate and Whitechapel by the police. It is presumed that this has something to do with the recent Whitechapel murders, and it has given rise to a theory that the victims may have been murdered by a woman. It is remarked that in each case there is no evidence of a man being seen in the vicinity at the time of the murder.

This is followed by a report by Chief Inspector Swanson dated 23 September 1889 for which no reference is given:

METROPOLITAN POLICE
Criminal Investigation Department,
Scotland Yard,
23 day of Septr   1889

SUBJECT Whitechapel
Murders

I beg to report that I saw Dr Forbes Winslow at No. 70 Wimpole Street today, and in reply to me he said first that the statement in the newspapers was a misrepresentation of a conversation with a New York Herald reporter who had called upon him in reference to an autograph book he has. Gradually the reporter drew him into a discussion about the Whitechapel Murders, and the reporter gave him to understand the discussion would not be published, but he was much surprised and annoyed to see it, especially as it so misrepresented what he said. I pointed out to him that he had not given information to police about any suspect except the foreigner at the Charing Cross Hospital, and that there was a statement in the papers to the effect that he had. He denied having said so to the Press. He produced a pair of felt galoshed boots such as are in common use in Canada, and an old coat. The felt boots were motheaten, and the slough of the moth worm remained on one of them. He then stated that the information which he relied upon was as follows:- Related by Mr. E Callaghan of 20 Gainsborough Square, Victoria Park, on Augt. 8th 1889.

"In April, 1888, my wife and myself were residing at 27 Sun Street, Finsbury Square, the upper part of our house was let off to various gentlemen. In answer to our advt: we put in Daily Telegraph a Mr. G. Wentworth Bell Smith, whose business was to raise money for the Toronto Trust Society; applied and took a large bed["room" – *deleted*] sitting room. He said that he was over here on business and that he might stay a few months or perhaps twelve. He told us that before he had come to us he had an office at Godliman Street at the back of St Pauls. Whilst at home he occupied himself in writing on religious subjects; sometimes as many as 60 sheets of foolscap were filled up with such material. Whenever he went out of doors he would wear a different suit of clothes to what he did the day before. He had many suits of clothes and quite eight or nine hats. He kept very late hours and whenever he came in it was quite noiseless. He had also a pair of India rubber boots to put over his ordinary ones to deaden any possible sound. On Augt 9th (*altered to 7th*) the date of one of the murders, Mrs Callaghan was in the country, and her sister kept house in her absence. she was however expected home that evening and we sat up for her till 4.a.m. at which hour Mr Bell Smith returned stating that he had had his watch stolen in Bishopsgate Street, which on investigation proved to be false. Shirts were found hanging on his towel horse he having washed them himself, and marks of blood on the bed. This I saw myself. Two or three days after this murder of Augt. 9th, with the stated reason of returning to Toronto. I however found that he had not done so, but he did not return to my house. He was seen getting into a tramcar in Septr. of 1888. We all regarded him as a lunatic and with delusions regarding "Women of the streets," who he frequently said ought to be all drowned. He told me that he was greatly impressed with the amount of immorality in London; and said that a number of whores walked up and down St. Pauls Cathedral during the service. He also said that women in the East End especially ought to be drowned. He also had delusions respecting his wealth stating that he had large wealth at his command. At night he would talk and moan to himself frequently. One day he said, "Physically I am a very weak man, but the amount of my willpower is so great that I am able to outwork several men." implying that he had great brain power. Frequently on his return he would throw himself down on a sofa and groan. He kept concealed in a chest of drawers in his room three loaded revolvers. He would if taken by surprise by anyone knocking at his door rush and place his back against this chest. The following post card came on[e] day for him signed "Dodger, we can't get through it. Can you give us any help." I gave this information to the police in August after the man left my house, and curiously enough the detectives came over to my house to make enquiries also about this same man, at the instigation of a lady from the Surrey side of the water. The writing of Bell Smith is in every way similar to that sent to the Police & signed Jack the Ripper. I am positive that he is the man. He is about 5 ft 10 in in height walks very peculiarly with his feet wide apart, knees weak and rather bending in, hair dark, complexion the same, moustache and beard closely cut giving the idea of being unshaven, nice looking teeth probably false, he appearede well conducted, was well dressed and resembled a foreigner speaking several languages entertains strong religious delusions about women, and stated that he had done some wonderful operations. His manner and habits were peculiar. Without doubt this man is the perpetrator of these crimes."

Sept. 9. 1889.

A woman in the East End on Sunday at 2 am told Mr Callaghan that she saw a man on 30th. inst, who accosted her in Worship Street Bishopsgate She noticed him particularly as she remembered him as being the man that she saw washing himself in a yard at the back of her house about 4 am on the morning of one of the Whitechapel murders. He was in his shirtsleeves, his coat being thrown onto a wooden fence. She drew the neighbours attention, and the neighbours watched him into Sun Street. Finsbury, where he arrived about 4 30am. He raised his hat to the man when he left him evidently knowing that he had been followed. At the meeting on

Sunday last, the man asked her to have a drink but this was refused. She knows the man perfectly well and could identify him. The description in every way coincides with the man who lodged with Mr Callaghan. She says he has a small black bag with him. At the time mentioned before when he was seen washing hands. on the morning of the murder he asked the woman where the Court went to. She often had noticed the man as a foreign looking man prowling about the neighbourhood.

The foregoing is the information he possesses. He does not know the name of the woman, but Mr Callaghan could tell. I am unable to find any such information given by Callaghan. It would be after the murder in George Yard, and before the 31st. of Augt. The matter was then in the hands of H Divn. Inspr Abberline has no record of the information. Dr Winslow desired the return tonight of the printed matter which I have copied.

Donald SSwanson

Ch Inspr

George H. Greenham

pro Supt

Donald SSwanson

Ch Inspr

Documents returned by post with thanks.

CHAPTER 33

October 1889 – Another Extraordinary Suspect

The renewed press – and consequently public – interest in the Whitechapel Murders was marked by the emergence, as we have seen, of fresh allegations about suspected persons. A suspect who emerged at the beginning of October 1889 was typical of such accusations received by the police. The point here is mainly to show the nature of such reports and how they were properly dealt with and investigated by the police. In this case the allegation was received in the form of an anonymous letter dated 1 October 1889. The initial file cover[1] is as follows:

[Stamped: – HOME OFFICE 2 OCT. 89 DEP] No. A49301/187
DATE 1 Octr. 89   Anonymous
REFERENCES, &c.   Whitechapel Murders
                          Gives particulars respecting the mysterious
             movements of a Certain Doctor.
                          MINUTES.
             ? To Police
                  W.T.B.
                    3.10.89.
                          ELP. 4 Oct.89
             Index
[Stamped: – REFERRED 5 – OCT. 89]

The letter[2] then follows:

["Private & Confidential" – *deleted*]   Octr. 1./89
[Stamped: – HOME OFFICE 2 OCT. 89 DEP] Whitechapel Murders
(Supposed important & remarkable Clue.)   A49301/187
Sir, Last Thursday night Sep 26 I had unasked for, a communication made to me respecting a gentleman & beg to forward you the particulars as made to Mr. Williamson, Criminal Investigation Office 21 Whitehall Place yesterday at 12.30 – 1PM.-

A gentleman representing himself as a Dr. in practice, took a small furnished backroom (6/6 per wk) at xxxxxxxx Rd. Kensington on the 16th inst. He stated that he came from SBG. He only goes out for short periods, does not get up till late & retires early. He is rather strange in his manners, agreeable & affable to the opposite sex but seemingly rather inquisitive concerning the occupants of the house. He has two portmanteaus (1 large & 1 smaller) also a rug or rugs. In one of his portmanteaus he has surgical instruments &c. He is a strong, well built man about 45 to 50 years of age & about 5.9 in height, rather dark complexion with short dark whiskers, beard & moustache. Wears a high hat (but has others) & check morning coat or suit. Has a curious walk (taking short steps) & his voice is rather peculiar. Stated his wife to be in a Lunatic Asylum but since, that she is lost (dead) also that he has inserted advt. In "Lancet" for situation & has had Photograph taken to send to those he is negotiating with.

Now Sir., the following very remarkable series of coincidences have occurred to me, all of which are perfectly reliable & accurate (without any exaggeration) & can be proved, –

Last Wednesday night I saw a picture in "Scraps" & asked my sister whom it resembled – she guessed.

(The following day I heard about the Dr.) On Friday I paid a visit to my sister again & related the clue I thought I had discovered. About $\frac{3}{4}$ hour later her husband came in & greeted me in a jocular manner "Jack the Ripper they will have you yet" (he had never said this before) – ordinary conversation followed. Just as we sat down to dinner ($\frac{1}{2}$ hour later) he says "There is an amusing story in 'Scraps' about a doctor sharpening his knives and a gentleman being frightened by the cook telling him that the Dr. intended cutting his 2 ears off." (Picture enclosed). I then related my story to him which until then he had not heard. Strange to say that the picture I pointed out, although older, somewhat resembles the Dr. in features . . .

I called at the Home Office yesterday morning at 12 to see you. Was referred to Whitehall Place where I made, as before stated a communication to Mr Williamson furnishing him with address & name given of Dr. & urging him to make enquiries, which he promised to do.

About 7 o'clock last night I paid another visit to my sister & she said to me "have you seen The Telegraph". I replied "No" but I had the Standard & Morning Post. She pointed out the paragraph Page 5 which to my astonishment seemed to corroborate my ideas in a remarkable manner. I immediately took train to London again & went to Whitehall Place &

Scotland Yard at 8.30. Pointed out to both Inspectors the paragraph but could not make them take any immediate measures. Then afterwards forwarded by post to Mr. Williamson the paragraph which he should get by 1st post to day. The last letter purporting to be written by Jack the R-was found at Victoria Rd. Kensington last Saturday which is within ¼ hours' walk of Dr's lodgings.

I may in conclusion state that I am the reverse of being superstitious & I have always scorned the ideas. The story however & corroboration being so remarkable I consider it to be of the utmost vital importance that immediate enquiries should be made.

Not wishing my name to appear in any way I beg to sign, as given to Mr. Williamson, should he wish to communicate with me.

Yrsobedly –

By Daily Telegraph

"H" call at Whitehall.

P.S. At present have had no communication with newspapers & others respecting the above.

The cutting of the cartoon from "Scraps" is then included. [See illustration]

A second file cover[3] concerning this allegation is then included,

[Stamped: – HOME OFFICE 10 OCT. 89 RECEIVED] No. A49301/191
DATE 9 Octr. 89   Asst. Comr. Anderson
REFERENCES, &c.   Whitechapel Murders
                                        Fds Police report respecting the
                        mysterious movements of a certain Doctor.
                                MINUTES.
                        No Police report was required about this. v/187 was
                        merely sent to the Police as are all other communications
                        respecting the Whitechapel murderer are.
                                ? Lay by
                                WTB
                                11.10.89   GL
                                        12 Oct "89

There then follows a pro-forma letter[4] from Anderson to the Under-Secretary of State, dated 9 October 1889:

[Stamped: – HOME OFFICE 10 OCT.89 RECEIVED] A49301/191
[reference – 57885/290]

Great Scotland Yard
9th day of October 1889

From

ASSISTANT COMMISSIONER OF POLICE,
Criminal Investigation Department.
To THE UNDER SECRETARY OF STATE
FOR THE HOME DEPARTMENT,
etc.   etc.   etc.

Sir,

With reference to the papers, No. A49301, herewith returned, regarding the mysterious movements of a certain doctor,

I have the honour to transmit, for the information of the Secretary of State a Report of the inquiries which I have caused to be made on the subject.

I have the honour to be,

Sir,

Your most obedient Servant
A.F.Williamson
Chief Constable
For ASSt. COMMr.

There then follows a handwritten report[5] by Chief Inspector Swanson:

[Stamped: – HOME OFFICE 10 OCT. 89 RECEIVED and METROPOLITAN POLICE RECEIVED 8-.OCT.89 CRIMINAL INVESTIGATION DEPT.] A 49301/191

METROPOLITAN POLICE.
CRIMINAL INVESTIGATION DEPARTMENT,
SCOTLAND YARD.
7th day of October 1889.

SUBJECT Anonymous
Com. To Home Office
Re a Doctor out of practice
Whom writer thinks is a
Murderer.

With reference to the attached anonymous communication, I beg to report that the writer states that a person representing himself as a Doctor out of practice took a small back room furnished at a rental of 6s/6d per week in 51 Abington Road, Kensington. The grounds of suspicion that he might be the Whitechapel murder [*sic*] being:- 1st. That he had surgical instruments in his possession. 2nd. That the Doctor was eccentric in his manner, but affable to ladies. And 3rd. that a comic sketch appeared in a paper called "Scraps". in which a Doctor invited a guest to dine off a hare but the cook having eaten the hare herself, frightened the guest by telling him that the Doctor was sharpening his knives to cut his ears off. The sketch of the Doctor in Scraps, the writer alleges to resemble the Doctor whom he suspects. 4th That a letter signed Jack the Ripper was found in the streets at Kensington.

The foregoing are the whole grounds of suspicion, no one of which affords ["affords" – *deleted*] grounds to justify that the Doctor is in any way connected with the Whitechapel murders. That a Doctor or surgeon should possess surgical instruments is perfectly natural. His manner towards ladies does not point to him as being the sexual maniac who committed the outrages in the East End. The reference to the caricature in Scraps is absurd, and the finding of a letter signed Jack the Ripper in Kensington considering that similar letters have been found in every quarter of London, does not point to the Dr. as being a murderer. The anonymous communication, I submit is the product of an excited imagination, which has jumped at a conclusion without an atom of proof.

Under these circumstances the police have not felt themselves justified in making enquiry respecting the Doctor as the Whitechapel murderer.

Donald SSwanson
ChInspr.
J.Shore Supt.

CHAPTER 34

November 1889 – Another Foreign Suspect

The continued interest in the Whitechapel murders remained truly international, and the Home Office received yet another communication from the Foreign Office with a theory from abroad. The file cover[1], much damaged, is as follows:

[Stamped: – [HOME OF]ICE [89] [RE]Cd. DEPt] No. A49301D/8
[DATE] 1889   Foreign Office
[REFERENCES,] &c.   Whitechapel Murders
                        Forwards despatch from H. M.
                        Minister in Brazil as to a statement
                        enclosed from an Italian detailing
                        a conversation he overheard of two
                        men it appeared to refer to these
                        murders.
                            MINUTES.
Seal [?] up with   ["Confidential" – *deleted*]
ordinary done with Papers
                To Commissioner of Police.
                        C.M. Nov:14.89.
                            Indexed To Commr.
                                            [*illeg.*]
        This story is altogether too vague, and the length of time (over 2
        years!) which has elapsed since these mysterious strangers seen on
        the quay at Genoa, too [ ] of any action being taken in [ ]
                                                    [ ]
        Ch: Inspr. Swanson to see.
            Seen
                Donald S.Swanson
                    ChInspr.
        [ ] F.O.
            thanks
                & Lay By C.M. 20.

There follows the letter[2] from the Foreign Office:

Translation
   [Stamped: – HOME OFFICE 14 NOV.89 RECd.DEPt.] A49301D/8
Sir,
   Y.E. will excuse the writer for communicating in Italian, as, not knowing English & having but a slight acquaintance with French, I am compelled to use my own language.
   My object in addressing this letter to Y.E. is to furnish the British authorities with some information, which tho' somewhat late, may perhaps prove useful, in regard to certain great crimes recently committed in London.
   I arrived in Brazil in November 1887, and having found employment at once in the interior of the Province, I have spent nearly two years far from any large city and consequently without news of many events in Europe. On my return to S. Paulo, towards the end of last month, many European newspapers, dating from the close of last & the early months of the present year, came into my hands, & these mentioned the mysterious crimes committed against women in London. The knowledge of these crimes brought back to my memory an occurrence which I had forgotten, which occurred on the eve of my departure from Italy & which I will now endeavour to relate to Y.E.
   On the evening of Oct. 18. 1887, at about 5 o'clock, I was standing with my wife & children on the mole of the harbour of Genoa, awaiting the arrival of the "Savoye" which was to convey us to Brazil, & while the children walked about with their mother, I leant against the parapet, watching the horizon & the ships & boats coming & going. I was so absorbed in this, that I took no notice of a small boat which came up to the steps & landed two persons of respectable appearance, when presently my attention was called towards my right by voices proceeding from the furthest angle of the battery, defending the harbour. I leaned forward & listened. At first I only heard the words. "I do not believe it I do not see clearly the object of these armies. I do not wish to have anything to do with it" & other phrases which I do not remember. Then a voice speaking with a foreign & probably English, accent said "So you do not wish to have anything to do with it, and refuse to come to ["England" – *deleted*] London. Then I must conclude that you are a coward" (This was said in bad Italian) The other voice replied with a pronounced accent of the Neapolitan provinces.
   "I said no & I repeat it. I have accompanied you this far. I have been to India, & have done all that you wished & have had more than enough of it already. I do not wish now to run my head against the English Police, for, believe me, London is not like India, as you know even better than I do, and when you have ripped up two or three women, there will be the devil of a row & who knows how it may end."

The other replied, but I could not hear what he said, except "Then this is your last word?" and after a "yes" which I heard, he continued "I shall go alone, let me have the Portmanteau & the irons by the time the steamer leaves tomorrow for Marseilles. I will write to you from Paris, & if you want me write to me to the usual address, at. . . ." (here followed a name which I forget) "Do not trust anybody, but write in Italian, since you have not yet learned English in a single year —"

I only heard indistinct words in reply.

I was seized with strong curiosity & wishing to see what the speakers were like, I took one of my children by the hand, & walked round the angle of the battery, where I found myself at three or four paces from the two men who had landed from the boat a short time before. On seeing me, they gave a sort of start, but then got up carelessly, and beginning to talk in a loud voice of the sea & of travels, & they proceeded towards the city.

But if they were surprised at seeing me, I too was greatly impressed by their appearance, for their two faces, though very different one from the other, were such as when seen once, remain impressed for a lifetime. I will give a description of them as well as I can.

The one who spoke Italian well was somewhat short of stature thin, very pale, with a low forehead, small black eyes & black moustache, & hair. He wore a long, dark, frock coat (frac) similar trousers & a black glazed hat (capello nero ingommato) The other, — the one who seemed to me to be English — was rather tall, large boned, and stout, with a high forehead, bushy eyebrows, prominent cheekbones, & a large nose. He had no moustache, but whiskers of a light brown colour, and two eyes which when half closed, seemed to flash fire. He wore a long dark grey overcoat, dark trousers & a hard hat like the other.

My first thought was to go to the nearest police station & give information of all that I had heard, but the reflection that doing so might lead to a delay in my sailing & to trouble & annoyances induced me to remain silent, tho' I did so unwillingly.

I left, came to Brazil & forgot the matter & was only reminded of it recently when I read the account of the crimes committed in London. I accordingly wrote the present letter to Y.E. in the hope that it may be of some use & declare myself ready to furnish any additional information which I may bring to mind.

> I have &c
> (sgd) P. Jose Vanzetti
> 140 Rua Comercio da Luz
> Sao Paolo. 27 August 89

The file cover[3] is as follows:

    <u>Copy</u>
Signor Vanzetti
    to
Mr. Wyndham
S. Paulo Aug. 27. 1889
<u>Whitechapel Murders:</u>

    Encl
in Mr. Wyndham's
No. 118 of October 13
    1889

There then follows a letter[4] from Mr Wyndham to Lord Salisbury:

Copy   [Stamped: – HOME OFFICE 14 NOV.89 RECd. DEPt.]
                        A49301D/8
                        Rio de Janeiro
No 118   Oct. 13. 1889
My Lord,
    I have the honour to enclose herewith to Y.L. copy & translation of a letter [*here there is a marginal note* – "Sr. Vanzetti to Mr Wyndham. Aug 27.89"] which reached me on the 3rd ult. From an Italian, P.J. Vanzetti, who is now residing at Sao Paulo, and which purports to contain information bearing upon the recent murders in Whitechapel.
    Some delay has occurred in my sending this letter to Y.L. as I begged the Italian Legation here on the 4th ult. to be so good as to make enquiries thro' the Italian Consul, at Sao Paulo as to the writer, and I have only recently received a reply, which is to the effect that Vanzetti is apparently a person to be relied on & that he is employed in giving lessons in Italian & gymnastics in the neighbourhood of the town of Sao Paulo. He stated to the consul that the appearance of the persons described in his letter is so engraved on his memory that he could perfectly recognise their photographs were they sent to him.
                   I have &c
                   (sd) Hugh Wyndham
The Marquis of Salisbury
    &c &c &c

The file cover[5] to this letter, is as follows:

Copy.
     Mr Wyndham
     No 118
<u>Whitechapel Mur</u>ders
Home Office

The covering letter[6] from the Foreign Office is included:

[Stamped:- HOME OFFICE 14 NOV.89 RECd.DEPt.]   A49301D/8
<u>Confidential</u>   Foreign Office,
Sir,
     I am directed by the Secretary of State for Foreign Affairs to transmit to
you, to be laid before Mr. Secretary Matthews the accompanying despatch
and its enclosures, as marked in the margin ["Mr. Wyndham No 118. Oct
13. '89"], from Her Majesty's Minister in Brazil, relating to the Whitechapel
murders.

                         I am,
                              Sir,
                    Your most obedient,
                         humble Servant,
                              THSanderson

The Under Secretary of State
     Home Office

CHAPTER 35

13 February 1891 – Murder of Frances Coles

The last murder included in the extant police and Home Office Files concerning the Whitechapel Murders is that of Frances Coles, which occurred on Friday, 13 February 1891 in Swallow Gardens, a passage-way running under the railway arches between Chamber Street and Royal Mint Street. An important aspect of the police enquiry into the murder of Coles is that with this killing the police immediately felt that it might be connected with the earlier series of murders.

The file commences with a report[1] by Superintendent Thomas Arnold dated 13 February 1891:

The cover states: – Report stating that James T Sadler, who was charged with the murder of Frances Coles in Swallow Gardens Whitechapel in February 1891, and who has been residing at 121 Danbrook Rd., Streatham, intends removing to 108 Faraday St., Walworth Rd.

Metropolitan Police
H DIVISION
13th February, 1891.

I beg to report that at about 2.15 A.M. this day PC240H Thompson discovered the body of a female lying in the roadway in Swallow Gardens, Royal Mint Street, Whitechapel, and upon turning on his lantern he saw blood issuing from her throat. He immediately blew his whistle when P/S 101H Hyde and 275H Hinton came to his assistance, and the former went for Dr. Oxley of Dock Street who quickly attended and pronounced life extinct. PC 275 went to the Station, and Inspector Flanagan at once proceeded to the spot, and sent for Dr. Phillips Divisional Surgeon, myself, the Chief and Local Inspector and as quickly as [ ] men arrived despatched them to carefully search the neighbourhood and make inquiries of any person who could be found likely to give any information. Dr. Phillips attended, examined the body and found two cuts in the throat, sufficient to account for death. The body was not mutilated in any other way. Immediately I arrived I ascertained that telegrams had been sent to surrounding Divisions apprising them of the occurrence and asking that careful inquiries should be made, and proceeded to direct other inquiries at Common Lodging Houses &c. The vicinity of Swallow Gardens was carefully searched, and in a space between a water pipe and some brickwork, about 18 yards from where the body was found Insp Flanagan discovered two shillings wrapped in two pieces of old newspaper apparently "Daily News" upon which however there is no date. there is nothing to connect this money with the murder nor has any instrument or article been found likely to afford a clue. The body was removed to Whitechapel Mortuary and searched, but nothing of importance was discovered.

The deceased is known to police of this Division as a Prostitute but at present has not been identified by any person, she is aged about 25, length 5feet, hair and eyes brown, dressed in old dark clothes, and appears of a low class. PC240H Thompson who is a young Constable having only joined on 29th Decr. last states that as he was passing along Chambers [sic] Street towards Swallow Gardens he heard footsteps apparently those of a man, proceeding in the opposite direction towards Mansell Street, but was not sufficiently close to discern the person. This was just immediately before he found the body and he asserts that when he first saw the deceased there was a movement of one of the eyelids. Be that as it may when the body was found it was quite warm & bleeding. The Constables on the adjoining Beats did not see any person passing about the time he mentioned.

William Friday, a Carman in the employ of the Great Northern Railway, states that at 1.45 A.M. he was passing through Royal Mint Street on his way to the stables when he saw a man and woman standing in a door way. He could not discern their faces distinctly but noticed that the woman wore a black hat. He has seen the hat worn by the deceased and identified it as that worn by the woman he saw talking in Royal Mint Street. He has also given a slight description of the man she was [with] but says he could not recognise him as he did not see his face.

Nothing further has at present been ascertained but inquiries are being prosecuted with a view to finding any person who may have been in the neighbourhood at the time the outrage was committed.

Dr. Phillips states that from the examination he has made the nature of the wound, the posture and appearances of the body &c. he does not connect this with the series of previous murders which were accompanied with mutilation.

Information has been sent to the Coroner and his officer.

T.Arnold Supt.

There is a report cover[2] from H Division CID:

Subject Murder / Body of a woman found in Swallow Gardens with her throat cut [*Stamped: – Received 13 Feb 91*] Sir E. Bradford to see. This case was reported to me in the middle of the night & I gave authority to send Supt Arnold all the aid he might require. The officers engaged in investigating the former Whitechapel murders were early on the spot, & every effort is making to trace the criminal. But as in former cases he left nothing, & carried away nothing in the nature of property, to afford a clew

RA 13/2/1

Seen & I have shown this to Mr Matthews & explained that I think it would be premature for us to venture taking opinion as to now for this case may obviously not be connected with any previous cases.

GRL/S
13/2.

As in former cases I wish to have a report each morning for the present.

RA
13/2

Memo sent
13/2/91   JS
            PS/

There is a report[3] by Sergeant Don as to the finding of the prisoner, James Thomas Sadler:

METROPOLITAN POLICE.
Criminal Investigation Department,
H Leman St.
16th day of February 1891

The Woman found murdered in Swallow Gardens.

I beg to report that about 12 noon, 14th inst in company with P.C.Gill. H. Dn. I was in Upper East Smithfield and from what I was told by a man named Samuel Harris I went to the Phoenix P.H. where I saw the prisoner. I called him outside and asked him if his name was "Sadler" he said Yes. I told him I was a Police Officer and that it was necessary he should come to Leman Street Police Station, as a woman had been found with her throat cut and it was alleged that he had been in her company the night previous. He stopped me and said, I expected this. On the way to the station he said, I am a married man and this will part me and my wife, you know what sailors are, I used her for my purpose for I have known Frances for some years. I admit I was with her, but I have a clean bill of health and can account for my time. I have not disguised myself in any way, and if you could not find me the detectives in London are no damned good. I bought the hat she was wearing and she pinned the old one under her dress. I had a row with her because she saw me knocked about and I think it was through her. He accompanied by P.C. Gill & myself came to the station & "Sadler" was handed over to Chief Inspr Swanson.

John Don P.S. R.

Henry Moore, Inspr.

There is then a statement[4] by James Thomas Sadler dated 14 February 1891, taken by Chief Inspector Donald S. Swanson, with the following on the cover sheet:

Swallow Gardens Murder/ Statement of James Thomas Saddler, Davies [?] Boarding House, East Smithfield/ Detained on suspicion of this above.

METROPOLITAN POLICE.

Criminal Investigation Department,

Scotland Yard,

14th day of February 1891.

Swallow Gardens Murder – James Thomas Saddler of Davies Boarding House, East Smithfield, says, I am a fireman and generally known as Tom Saddler. I was discharged at 7 p.m. 11th. inst. from S.S. Fez. I think I had a drink of Holland Gin at Williams Brothers at the corner of Gouldston Street. I then went at 8.30 pm to the Victoria Home. I then left the House and went into Princess Alice between 8.30 and 9 pm. I saw a woman, (whom I had previously known./ named Frances.) I had known her for eighteen months. I first met her in the Whitechapel Road and went with her to Thrawl Street, a lodging house, and I stayed with her all night; having paid for a double bed at the Lod: Ho: I don't remember the name of the Lod: Ho where I then stayed with her. I think I then took a ship the name of which I do not now remember. I did not see this woman again until I saw her in another bar of the Princess Alice, and recognising her, I beckoned her over to me. There was nobody with her. She asked me to leave the pub: ho: as when she had got a little money the customers in the pub: ho: expected her to spend it amongst them. We left the Princess Alice, and went round drinking at other pub: hos:. Among other houses I went into a house at the corner of Dorset Street, where another woman (named Annie Lawrence) joined us. This is the woman pointing to Annie Lawrence who was making a statement in the CID office. Frances stopped me from treating this woman, and we then went to Whites Row Chamber. I paid for a double bed and we stayed the night there. [*marginal note* – "Wed. night"] She had a bottle of whiskey (half pint) which I had bought at Davis, White Swan, Whitechapel. (I took the bottle back yesterday morning and the young woman (barmaid) gave me twopennyworth of drink for it.) Frances and I left Whites Row Chambers between eleven and twelve noon, and we went into a number of pub: hos: one of which was [A] the "Bell", Middlesex Street. We stayed there for about two hours drinking and laughing. When in the "Bell" she spoke to me about a hat which she had paid a shilling off. a month previously. We then went [.] [C] on the way to the bonnet shop, drinking at the pub: houses on the way. The shop is Whites Row or Bakers Row and I gave her the half a crown, which was due for the hat, and she went into the shop. She came out again and said that her hat was not ready, the woman is putting some elastic on. We then went into a pub: house in Whites or Bakers Row, and we had more drinks. Then she went for her hat, and got it. and brought it to me at the pub: ho: and I made her try it on.. I wanted her to throw the old one away, but she declined, and pinned it on to her dress. Then went to [D] the "Marlborough Head" pub: Ho: in Brick Lane. and had some more drink. I was then getting into drink and the landlady rather objected to Frances and me being in the house. I can't remember what the landlady said now. I treated some men in the house, I can't say their names. I had met them previously in the same house. From there I had an appointment to see a man Nicols in Spital Street, and I left her there to see Nicols, arranging to meet her again at a pub: ho: where I cannot say now, for I have forgotten it. We came down Thrawl Street and while going down a woman with a red shawl struck me on the head and I fell down, and when down I was kicked by some men around me. The men ran into the Lod: houses and on getting up I found my money and my watch gone. I was then penniless, and I then had a row with Frances for I thought she might have helped me when I was down. I then left her at the corner of Thrawl Street; without making any appointment that I can remember. I was downhearted at the loss of my money, because I could not pay for my bed. I then went to [F] the London Docks, and applied for admission, as I wanted to go aboard the S.S. Fez. There was a strict Sergeant inside the gate and a Constable. They refused me admission as I was too intoxicated. I cannot remember what hour this was as I was dazed and drunk. There was a Met. Police officer near the gate, a young man. I abused the Sergt. and Constable, because they refused me admission. There were some dock labourers coming out, one said something to me, and I replied abusively, and one of the labourers took it up saying, If the (Met) policeman would turn his back, he would give me a d-good hiding. The policeman walked across the road across Nightingale Lane, towards the Tower way, and as soon as he had done so, the labourers made a dead set at me, especially the one who took my abuse. This one knocked me down & kicked me, and eventually another labourer stopped him. I then turned down [H] Nightingale Lane, and the labourers went up Smithfield Way. I remained in Nightingale Lane for about a quarter of an hour feeling my injuries. I then went to the Victoria Lod: Ho: in East Smithfield and applied for a bed but was refused [G] as I was so drunk, by the night porter, a stout fat man. I begged and prayed him to let me have a bed but he refused. To the best of my belief I told him I had been knocked about. He refused to give me a bed and I left, and wandered about. I can't say what the time was. I went towards Dorset Street. I cannot say which way, but possibly Leman Street way. When I [E] got to Dorset Street I went into the Lod: Ho: where I had stopped with Frances on the previous night, and found her in the kitchen, sitting with her head on her arms. I spoke to Frances about her hat. She appeared half dazed from drink and I asked her if she had enough money to pay the double bed with. She said she had no money and I told [her] I had not a farthing but I had four pounds 15/- coming to me. I asked her if she could get trust, but she said she couldn't. I then went to the deputy, and asked for a night's lodgings on the strength of the money I was to lift next day, but was refused. I was eventually turned out by a man, and left Frances behind in the house. I then went, to the best of my belief, towards London Hospital, and [J] about the middle of Whitechapel Road a young policeman stopped me and asked where I was going, as I looked in a pretty pickle. I said that I had had two doings last night, one in Spitalfield and one at the docks. I said I had been cut or hacked about with a knife or bottle. Immediately I mentioned the word knife, he said, "Oh have you a knife about you", and he there and then searched me. I told him I did not carry a knife. My shipmates, one Mat: Curley, and another named Bowen know that I have not carried a knife for years. The policeman helped me across the road towards the Hospital gate. I spoke to the porter but he hummed and hawed about it, and I began to abuse him. However he did let me in and I went into the Accident Ward and had the cut in my head dressed. The porter asked me if I had any place to go, and I said "No," and he let me lay down on a couch in the room where the first accidents are brought in. I can give no idea of the time I called at the Hospital. When he let me out, somewhere between six and eight in the morning I went straight to the Victoria House and begged for a few halfpence but I did not succeed. I then went to the shipping office where I was paid £4.15.3. Having got my money, I went to the Victoria Upper East Smithfield and stayed there all day as I was miserable. The furthest I went out was the Phoenix about twelve doors off. I spent the night there, and I was there this morning. I had gone to the Phoenix this morning to have drink, and I was beckoned out and asked to come here (Leman Street), and I came.

As far as I can think it was between five and six that I was assaulted in Thrawl Street; at any rate it was getting dark, and it was some hours after that, that I went to the London Docks. I forgot to mention that Frances and I had some food at [B] Mrs. Shuttleworths in Wentworth Street.

My discharges are as follow –
last discharged 11.2.90 [*sic* – 91] in London ship "Fez" –
next discharge 6.9.90 London
next discharge 15.7.90 London.
next discharge 27.5.90 Barry.
Next discharge 1.10.89 London.
Next 2.10.88 London.
Engaged 17.8.88.
Next 5.5.87.
Engd. nx. 24.3.87. London.

The last I had seen of the woman Frances was when I left her in the lod: ho: when I was turned out. The lod: house deputy can give you the time.

The clothes that I am now wearing are the only clothes I have. They are the clothes I was discharged in, and I have worn them ever since. My wife resides in the country, but I would prefer no to mention it.

The Lodging House I refer to is Whites Row, not Dorset Street. It has a large lamp over it. Passing a little Hackster shop at the corner of Brick Lane and Browns Lane. I purchased a pair of earrings, or rather I gave her the money and she bought them. I think she gave a penny for them.

This statement was read over to Saddler, who said it was correct as far as he could recollect

Donald SSwanson
Ch Inspr.
T. Arnold Sup.

There can be no doubt that the police treated Sadler very seriously as a suspect for the Whitechapel Murders. This is apparent not only from the fact that he was personally interviewed by Swanson himself, but that an attempted identification of him for the City Police's Mitre Square murder was carried out. The police evidently thought that they had, at last, arrested "Jack the Ripper". The *Daily Telegraph* of Tuesday, 18 February 1891 carried the relevant report:

THE WHITECHAPEL MURDER.
EVIDENCE AT THE INQUEST.
SADLER'S ANTECEDENTS.

It was yesterday proved that the Treasury authorities attach the greatest importance to the arrest of the ship's fireman, Sadler, who is in custody for the murder of Frances Coles, in Swallow-gardens, on Friday morning last. At the resumed inquest Mr. Charles Mathews instructed by Mr. Pollard, was present to examine the witnesses, with the permission of the Coroner, Mr. Wynne Baxter, who whilst assenting to the arrangement, seemed impressed with its unprecedented character. Further, it is certain that the police are not neglecting the facts which came to light in connection with the previous murders. Probably the only trustworthy description of the assassin was that given by a gentleman who, on the night of the Mitre-square murder, noticed in Duke-street, Aldgate, a couple standing under the lamp at the corner of the passage leading into Mitre-square. The woman was identified as one victim of that night, Sept. 30, the other having been killed half an hour previously in Berner-street. The man was described as "aged from thirty to thirty-five; height 5 ft 7 in, with brown hair and big moustache; dressed respectably. Wore pea jacket, muffler, and a cloth cap with a peak of the same material." The witness has confronted Sadler and has failed to identify him.

Further enquiries into Sadler's antecedents reveals that he has a wife at Chatham, and he is believed to have been in the Hong Kong police, and also in the intervals of his voyages acted as a tram driver and conductor in the East of London. In yesterday's *Daily Telegraph* it was proved that he was in London on July 17, 1890-the date of the Castle-alley murder [sic], and left two days later in the Loch Katrine for the Mediterranean . . .

A report[5] submitted by Inspector Henry Moore concerning the identification of the murdered woman, Frances Coles, is as follows:

Swallow Gardens Murder Reference to Papers 57885-

METROPOLITAN POLICE.

Criminal Investigation Department,

H Division,

15th day of February 1891

With reference to the murder attached, I beg to report that the body of the murdered woman has now been positively identified as that of Frances Coles, an unfortunate, who has been in Whitechapel for about eight years, and is known to have lodged at various common lodging houses. She is not known to have had any kind of regular employment for many years, although she has given out that she has been in employment, and also a statement made by her that she has resided with a respectable old lady at 32 Richardson Street, Commercial Road is untrue, as that is a fictitious address.

James Williams Coles, an inmate of the Bermondsey Workhouse, Farmer Street, Bermondsey, has attended at the mortuary, and identified the body as that of his daughter Frances Coles, aged about 26 years, whom he last saw alive on the 6th instant when she visited him at the workhouse.

Mary Ann Coles, of 32 Ware Street, Kingsland Road, a single woman, of no occupation, has also attended at the mortuary, and identified the body as that of her sister Frances Coles, whom she last saw alive about 6 weeks ago, when the deceased visited her at 32 Ware Street, Kingsland Road. She was then in good health, but very poor, and according to her statement was of drunken habits.

James Murray, of 33 Old Nichol Street, Bethnal Green, labourer, has identified the body as that of Frances Coleman, an unfortunate, whom he first met casually in the streets about 8 years ago, when she was staying at Wilmots lodging house, 18 Thrawl Street, Whitechapel. This man has been on intimate terms with her until about 4 years ago, and has frequently seen her since. She has walked about the streets during the whole of the past 8 years, principally about the neighbourhood of Whitechapel; but has also walked the streets in Shoreditch and Bow. She has lodged at various lodging houses in the neighbourhood of Commercial Street, and has for several years past given way to drunken habits.

Although the deceased was known to Murray as Frances Coleman, there is no doubt that her real name is Frances Coles, because he knew her to visit her father James Williams Coles at the Bermondsey Workhouse.

F. Kuhrt, Sergt.

Submitted   Henry Moore, Insp.

T Arnold Supt.

There is a Central Office report[6] included:

Subject Miscellaneous / Swallow Gardens Murder / Supt. Arnold HL / Submits photograph of the woman Frances Coles, who was found with her throat cut on morning of 13th instant / File with papers / [*sig. illeg.*] 19/2

METROPOLITAN POLICE.
Criminal Investigation Department,
Scotland Yard,
18th day of February 1891

Swallow Gardens Murder / Reference to papers 57885 /

I beg to submit herewith a photograph of deceased woman Frances Cole, who was found with her throat cut on the morning of 13th February instant

Henry Moore
Inspector.
T Arnold Supd.

There is then a lengthy report[7] by Chief Inspector Swanson dated 21 February 1891, giving the "History of Sadler". Marginal references are shown in parentheses, thus [ ]:-

METROPOLITAN POLICE.
Criminal Investigation Department,
Scotland Yard,
21st day of February 1891

I beg to report that I proceeded to Chatham on 19th inst: and placed myself in communication with Supt: Coppinger of the local police. I learned from him, and his officers that Sadler was unknown to them as either belonging to, or working in Chatham. I then saw Mrs. Sadler at No. 3 Skinner Street; and explained to her that it was necessary to learn from her particulars as to her husband during the time she had lived with him. It was observable that a reaction had taken place in her mind, caused no doubt by the report of her interview with a reporter, which she admitted she had read in the newspapers. She refused to say more than that she had said all she would say, and it was in the papers. The reporter she said, was a tall dark man, wearing glasses, but he gave her no name, and she thinks she would recognise him again. After trying for over an hour to extract a statement from her; I got from her by question and answer a history of Sadlers employments in London during the time she resided with him. The points are shortly as follow:-

She met Sadler first in Chatham he was at that time a sailor, and after a short courtship, they were married at St Johns Church, Chatham. Beyond his mother she had never heard of any other relation. She had not seen nor heard from his mother for over six years, and she did not know her address. After marriage she went to reside with Sadler in a street near [A] the Elephant and Castle, the name of which she professes to have forgotten. At this time Sadler worked at [B] Torr's Tea warehouse in Cutler Street, Houndsditch as a labourer. Sadler did not like crossing London Bridge and they removed to a house in [C] Bucks Row, Whitechapel, the number of which she said she had forgotten, but the house was about the centre, and the people who resided in it were brush-makers working at a factory in the Minories. She had saved a little money from her savings as a servant, and from what Sadler earned by occasional work at Cutler Street, and this money, they managed to live. She doesnt recollect the date of residence. From there they removed to [D] No 77 Tetley Street Poplar, and when residing here Sadler became a conductor, which lasted only for some months. It was while residing here, that the incident of the knife took place. Reluctantly she admitted that it was time that she had taken a knife away from him, and she declined to say why she had taken it away. She said she had hidden it, but professed to be unable to say where. She was however sure that Sadler did not get it again as she never saw it with him again. She believed that a lodger, an Irishwoman, whose name she did not know took the knife. She could give no reason for her belief. This took place, she said, over eleven years ago, and all she could recollect was that it was an ordinary pocket knife, with some brass on the handle. She said she did not think she could recognise it again. She had forgotten, too, the name of the people in the house with her. From there they removed to [E] a corner shop in Hurley Road, Lower Kensington where Sadler carried on the business of a greengrocer, but it did not succeed. From there they removed to [F] Manor St., Walworth, and Sadler again went to work at the bed warehouse in Cutler Street. Their residence here was not long, and next residence was in [G] Colebrooke Terrace, Bethnal Green, in a house near the top of the Terrace, with two maiden ladies, whose name she says she has forgotten. The next residence she says she has quite forgotten, but in 1888 they resided at [H] No. 2 Johnson St., Commercial Road, where their separation took place in Augt of that year. This was caused by a slight quarrel between them and he left her without saying where he was going to, and a fortnight after, on 15th August, she left London and went to reside with her mother at Chatham where she has made her home ever since. Seven months had elapsed after leaving London before she heard from him. She is sure it was seven months, and then she got a letter from him asking her to meet him at the Fenchurch St railway Station. She was late in keeping the appointment; but met Sadler in the Street near the railway station. They then walked about the streets looking at the shops, and they stayed that night at a Coffee House opposite Mile End Gate. Sadler had work at this time in the London or St Catherines Docks. It was on a Saturday that she met him at Fenchurch Street. Sadler had to work in the docks on the Sunday, and he asked her to meet him as he came out at 4.30 or 5.30 p.m. She went to meet him, going down a Street opposite Commercial Street; as far as a railway arch, and she stood there by some steps waiting for him. She saw a number of men come from the docks, but did not see Sadler. Then after waiting $\frac{1}{2}$ an hour he came up to her from a restaurant near the arch, where he had been standing and said to her How long are you going to stay, dont you know me? She replied, "I know you, now, you speak." From there they went to a pub: ho: in Whitechapel where Sadler had some drink and began to quarrel with the customers in the compartment and she went outside the pub: ho: and waited for him. When he came out he began to "nag" her, and she said to him "You know the life I have led with you, you had better go your way and I'll go mine." Then they walked along Whitechapel Road, and he wanted to take her to a place where a woman had been murdered, but she said, "No it does not interest me." When we got as far as Whitechapel Church, she says, she ran away from him, and he ran after her and caught her and tried to make the quarrel up, saying, "Sally, you'll look over it." He did not say, "You're not afraid of me." Then she said, he asked her to go into an eelshop to have a "feed" of eels, and he did so to make up the quarrel. She went in with him and while there a woman said to him "Holloa Tom, how are you?'' and he said, ''All right.'' Mrs Sadler says she did not speak to the woman, whom she would not recognise again, and they then left the eelshop, and went to the Coffee House where they were staying and stayed with him till Monday morning, when she left and returned to Chatham. That was the only time she had stayed with him in London since August 1888. His character she said was that when he liked, he could be as good as could be, and rough when he wanted to. When he was in drink he was irritable. After he had smashed the things on one occasion, he was sorry for it. He did not stay out at nights, he used to come home sometimes at eight o'clock, and he generally had the drink before he came in.

Upon pressing her as to whether he had ever assaulted or threatened her, she declined to answer. She said that he never wrote to her besides the letter asking her to meet him. He only sent her the advance note, and she never knew where he resided in London. During her stay in Chatham he had visited her staying from a day to a week at a time, but she has no means of giving dates. The last time was in Decr. before C'mas. last.

She denied having said to the reporter that she had slept with friends on the night of Sunday, when they went into the eelshop. She denies that she said also, ''You're not afraid of me,'' as being the expression Sadler used to her, and that what Sadler said to her in reference to the place where the murder had been committed was, ''It was miraculous that any person could do such a thing and get off.''

Formerly Sadler wore whiskers when she resided with him but he cut them off as they were grey.

This was all I was able to get from her after over two hours trial. During the time I was with her there were three calls by reporters.

Donald S.Swanson
Ch Inspr.
JohnShore
Supt.

The file then contains the statement[8] of Thomas Fowles, dated 25 February 1891, witnessed by Sgt. Nearn:
The cover sheet reads:

Subject – Information / Swallow Gardens Murder / Thomas Fowles, 13 St Georges Street E / 25.2.91 / Says that between 1 and 2 a.m. 13th he was talking to his young woman Kate McCarthy at the front door of her home which is next the Seven Stars Mint Street. / Sir Edward Bradford / These are two most interesting statements, & entirely clear up the mystery of ''the man with the billy-cock hat'' who was alleged to have been seen talking to Frances

Coles near the archway, and who was believed by Mr Chas. [*Walters ?*] and the Treasury officials to be the murderer! / JWEllis [?] 26/2 / [*second sig. illegible*] / RA 27/

METROPOLITAN POLICE.
Criminal Investigation Department,
Scotland Yard,
25th February 1891

Swallow Gardens Murder / Reference to Papers 57885/
    Thomas Fowles, 13 St Georges Street, E.
        Saith

I am a labourer and am employed as Hall Porter at the "United Brothers" Club Commercial Street E. I am engaged there from 6 pm until midnight, but it is generally after 12 o'clock before I leave.

I know Kate McCarthy she is my young woman, she works opposite to me, "Stowers" the wine merchants. On the evening previous to the murder she came to me at the Club, it was between half past seven and 8 o'clock. She stayed till it closed. I think it was about a quarter to one the next morning 13th. walked with her as far as her home in Mint Street next to the "Seven Stars", public house, we stood talking together at the front door for about an hour as near as I can judge, after which I bid her good night, and went home.

During the time I stood talking to Kate McCarthy, several men belonging to the Great Northern Railway Depot Mint Street, passed on the opposite side of the way, going towards the Minories. I know some of the men by sight, but not their names, one I knew by the name of Jumbo, and I passed a remark to my young woman that Jumbo looked as if he was drunk. I do not recollect either of these men passing any remark as they went by. The time would be as near as I can remember about 2 o'clock because I did not get with my young woman to her house until about one or a little after.

Beyond the men mentioned who passed while I was in Mint Street was a Constable, and he was on the opposite side of the way to me going towards Leman Street.

My mother resides at No. 10, Split Street, Back Church Lane. I only have letters addressed there.

At the time I stated I was wearing a black pilot monkey jacket, and a black felt hat, brown cord trousers.

	Thomas Fowles
Witness	JamesWNearn
	Sergeant.

Submitted together with statement of Kate McCarthy; it will be seen that these statements will negative the evidence of Jumbo and the Knaptons', as to the man they saw being the probable murderer. Copies supplied to Treasury Solicitor.

Henry Moore, Inspr.
T Arnold Sup

The statement[9] of Kate McCarthy, with the above, is as follows:

METROPOLITAN POLICE.
Criminal Investigation Department,
Scotland Yard,
25th day of February 1891.
Kate McCarthy of No. 42 Royal Mint Street E

Saith.

I reside with my father brother and sister at 42 Royal Mint Street, and have done so all my life. I work at Messrs Stowers, wine Merchants Commercial Street E as a bottler.

I am engaged to a young man Thomas Fowles, who resides in Back Church Lane, the number of the house I do not know.

On Thursday evening 12th inst I went to the "United Brothers Club", Commercial Street, where Tom Fowles is doorman and he and I left together at about half past twelve, and walked together as far as 42 Royal Mint Street, arriving there at about 1.15 a.m. 13th inst. We stood talking together at the front door for about half an hour, until a quarter to two and Fowles then wished me goodnight or good morning, and I went straight to bed.

At about twenty minutes to two just before Fowles left me I saw the two Knaptons and another man pass on the opposite side of the Street towards the Minories, one of the Knaptons shouted out good night. Almost immediately afterwards Jumbo (who I know as well as the Knaptons) passed also on the opposite side of the Street, with a whip in his hand he was going towards the Minories.

During the time I stood at the door I saw no other person.

Kate McCarthy

Witness

James W Nearn Sergt
Sergeant

Submitted. Copy supplied to Treasury Solicitor. These are the persons who were seen by Friday alias Jumbo.

Henry Moore, Inspr
T Arnold Supd.

The next report[10] is by Inspector Henry Moore regarding the adjourned inquest, and dated 27 February 1891:

Exterior view of Miller's Court. The two panes of glass in the window nearest to the downpipe can be seen to be broken.

A contemporary sketch of the scene outside 26 Dorset Street as Mary Jane Kelly's body is removed.

DAILY TELEGRAPH, SATURDAY, NOVEMBER 10, 1888.

LOCALITY OF THE SEVEN UNDISCOVERED MURDERS.

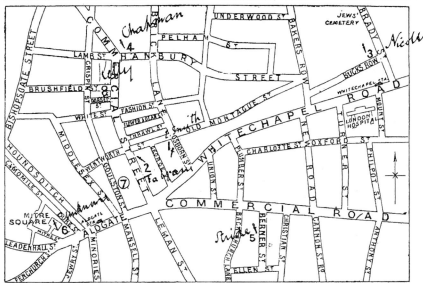

The above chart represents the locality within which, since April last, seven women of the unfortunate class have been murdered. The precise spot where each crime was committed is indicated by a dagger and a numeral.

1. April 3.—Emma Elizabeth Smith, forty-five, had a stake or iron instrument thrust through her body, near Osborn-street, Whitechapel.

2. Aug. 7.—Martha Tabram, thirty-five, stabbed in thirty-nine places, at George-yard-buildings, Commercial-street, Spitalfields.

3. Aug. 31.—Mary Ann Nicholls, forty-seven, had her throat cut and body mutilated, in Buck's-row, Whitechapel.

4. Sept. 8.—Annie Chapman, forty-seven, her throat cut and body mutilated, in Hanbury-street, Spitalfields.

5. Sept. 30.—A woman, supposed to be Elizabeth Stride, but not yet identified, discovered with her throat cut, in Berner-street, Whitechapel.

6. Sept 30.—A woman, unknown, found with her throat cut and body mutilated, in Mitre-square, Aldgate.

Figure 7 (encircled) marks the spot in Goulston-street where a portion of an apron belonging to the woman murdered in Mitre-square was picked up by a Metropolitan police-constable.

Figure 8. Nov. 9.—Mary Jane Kelly, 24, her throat cut and body terribly mutilated, in Miller's-court, Dorset-street.

A map of the murder sites which appeared in the *Daily Telegraph* on 10 November 1888.

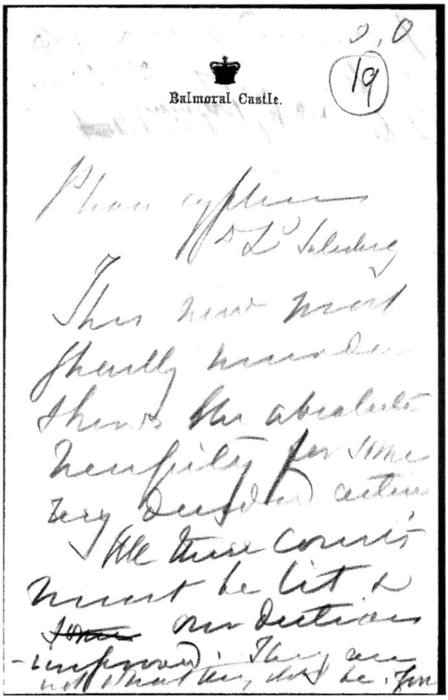

The concern of Queen Victoria over the murders is evident in this letter from Balmoral Castle dated 10 November 1888.

ease to kee~ the
Brass Fas. .ing
of the Tag out-
side.

No. A49301

3

N.B.—Please not to pin Memoranda over the Number.

c S (42,208a) 10,000 5—89

ATE 17 July 1889   Commissioner of Police.

REFERENCES, &c.

Forwards police report respecting the
commission of a murder in Castle Alley,
Whitechapel, this morning. States that every
effort will be made to discover the murderer,
who, he thinks, is identical with "Jack the Ripper",
but that the assassin has not left the slightest
clue to his identity.   Immediate

MINUTES.

The Secretary of State.
The Plan is from Pall Mall of today July 17.

SCENE of WHITECHAPEL MURDERS.

Fourth Murder,
Sept. 8, 1888,
Annie Chapman

Third Murder,
Aug. 31, 88 Buck's row
Mary Ann
Nicholls

Hanbury street

Seventh Murder,
Mary Jane Kelly,
Nov. 9

August 7. 1888
Second Murder,
Martha Tabran

London
Hospital

WHITECHAPEL ROAD

July 16, '89
Castle Alley

St. Mary's
Church

Sixth Murder,
Sept. 30, 1888
Woman unidentified
Mitre
square

HIGH STREET

Police Station

Fifth Murder,
Sept. 30, 1888
Eliz. Stride

The file cover for the murder of Alice McKenzie on 17 July 1889 has a map of
the murder sites affixed to its lower half. Importantly, the annotation shows that
initially the Chief Commissioner, James Monro, thought this to be another
Ripper murder.

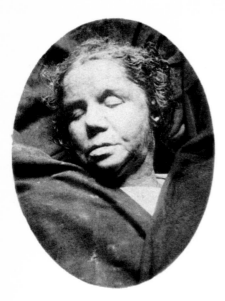

Mortuary photograph of Alice McKenzie.

Police sketch of the railway arch in Pinchin Street
where the torso of an unknown woman was found on
10 September 1889.

A contemporary sketch of Frances Coles, murdered on
13 February 1891 under a railway arch in Swallow
Gardens, Whitechapel.

Mortuary photograph of Frances Coles.

A contemporary sketch of James Thomas Sadler, arrested on suspicion of the murder of Frances Coles. The last of the Whitechapel murders, there is no doubt that initially the police believed that they had arrested Jack the Ripper.

A contemporary sketch of Sadler and Frances Coles in the doss house.

A contemporary sketch of PC 240H Ernest Thompson who discovered the body of Frances Coles.

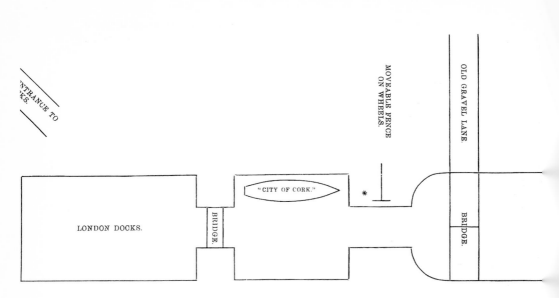

Rough Plan of the Docks, where these vessels lay, shewing there was nothing but a moveable * T fence, on wheels, to prevent these men getting on board, from Old Gravel Lane, at any time ; and, as was shewn at the time of the Sadler inquiry, that any member of the crew of a vessel in the Docks, provided he is sober, is allowed to pass into the Docks at any hour of the night.   Old Gravel Lane is within a mile of the scenes of these murders.

Plan of the London Docks and of the berthed *City of Cork*, published by early 'Ripperologist' Edward Knight Larkins in connection with his theory on the identity of the murderer.

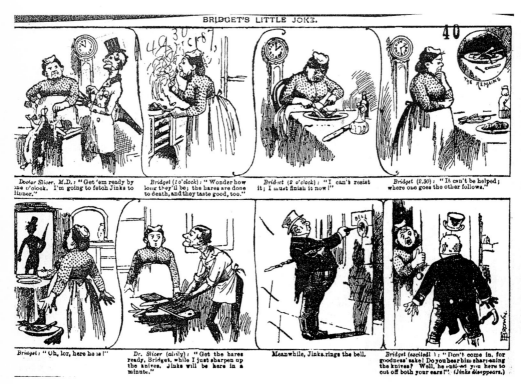

Part of a cartoon strip from a paper called *Scraps* (published in October 1889) giving support to an unfounded theory on the identity of the killer from an anonymous writer to the Home Office.

Montague John Druitt, an alleged Ripper suspect named in the Macnaghten Report of February 1894.

Michael Ostrog convicted thief and confidence trickster, named as another Ripper suspect in the Macnaghten Report of February 1894.

METROPOLITAN POLICE DISTRICT.
3.—Convict Supervision Office.—Woodcut portrait and description of Supervisee MICHAEL

OSTROG, *alias* BERTRAND ASHLEY, CLAUDE CLAYTON, and DR. GRANT, Office No. 22550, whose apprehension is sought for failing to report—age 55, height 5 ft. 11 in., complexion dark, hair dark brown, eyes grey, scars right thumb and right shin, two large moles right shoulder and one back of neck, corporal punishment marks; generally dressed in a semi-clerical suit. A Polish Jew. Was sentenced, 5th January, 1874, at Aylesbury, to 10 years' penal servitude and 7 years' police supervision for larceny. Liberated on license 25th August, 1883. Again sentenced at the Central Criminal Court, 14th September, 1887, to 6 months' hard labour for larceny. On the 10th March, 1888, he was liberated from the Surrey County Lunatic Asylum, and failed to report.
Warrant issued.
Special attention is called to this dangerous man.

Dr Francis Tumblety, an Irish-American quack doctor named by ex-Chief Inspector John George Littlechild as a Ripper suspect. He fled back to the USA in December 1888 where he was pursued by Inspector Andrews, who failed to locate him.

evidence against him.

138... because the suspect was also a Jew and also because his evidence would convict the suspect, and witness would be the means of murderer being hanged which he did not wish to be left on his mind. D.S.S.

Continuing from page 138. after the suspect had been identified at the Seaside Home where he had been sent by us with difficulty, in order to subject him to identification, and he knew he was identified. On suspect's return to his brother's house in Whitechapel he was watched by police (City CID) by day & night. In a very short time the suspect with his hands tied behind his back, he was sent to Stepney Workhouse and then to Colney Hatch and died shortly afterwards —
Kosminski was the suspect —

D.S.S.

Annotations made by ex-Chief Inspector Donald Swanson on page 138 and the end paper of Sir Robert Anderson's memoirs, regarding the Polish Jew suspect in the Ripper murders.

The cover of the report is a Central Office CID cover: Subject Inquests / Swallow Gardens Murder / Supt Arnold Submits daily report of Inspr Moore 27.2.91 / TAnld 28/2 / Mr Anderson to see / Seen RA 28/2.

METROPOLITAN POLICE.
Criminal Investigation Department,
Scotland Yard,
27th February 1891

Swallow Gardens Murder / (Daily Report)

Reference to papers 57885

With reference to the case of Frances Coles; who was found murdered at Swallow Gardens, Whitechapel, on 13th inst.

I beg to report that since yesterday no new development has taken place in connection with this case.

The adjourned inquest was resumed this morning at the Working Lads Institute, Whitechapel; before Wynne E. Baxter, Esq., coroner. Mr. Chas. Matthews appeared on behalf of Public Prosecutor; and Mr. Lawless watched the case for Sadler. At the conclusion of the evidence, which necessitated the calling of no less than 55 witnesses; the Jury retired after the summing up of the Coroner; and after an absence of 13 minutes they returned and returned a verdict of "Wilful Murder against some person or persons unknown"; and added a rider, "That the Police had done right in detaining Sadler." They also expressed satisfaction at the way P.S. Bush, C.O. had prepared the plans.

No persons have been detained on H Division during the day in relation to this case.

Henry Moore, Inspr.

T Arnold Supd.

There then follows a four-page report[11] by Inspector Moore, dated 2 March 1891, concerning enquiries made about the suspect Sadler:

METROPOLITAN POLICE.
Criminal Investigation Department,
Scotland Yard,
2nd day of March 1891.

Swallow Gardens Murder /

Reference to papers 57885.

Referring to attached and Assistant Commissioner's minute thereon.

I beg to report that enquiries have been made with reference to the points I have indicated by an initial letter in margin; and the following is the result:-

"A" – As to residence in Street near Elephant and Castle.

I find that during the time "Sadler" was a Hackney Carriage Driver he resided at three addresses near the Elephant & Castle; Viz:- 101 Penton Place, Harrington Bulds; 36 Hurley Road Kennington Lane; and 29 Manor Place, Walworth Road; this was between the years 1876 and 1877, but no person can be found now that knew him at either of the addresses. "B" – As to Tea Warehouse, Cutler St., Houndsditch.

Sadler was employed at this warehouse from 1st December 1887, till 26th July/88. He was not again heard of until 15th Octr. of same year; when he was again employed and remained till March, 1889.

In 1887 he resided at 14 Thomas St., Harding Street, Commercial Road, "E"., where he rented a room at 3/- per week; his wife joined him there and ultimately they went to reside at 2 Johnson St., Commercial Road. "C" – As to Bucks Row. –

No information can be obtained respecting Sadler; but it is alleged that he on one occasion was employed at Messrs Brown & Eagle's Wool warehouse, Bucks Row; but the Firm have no knowledge of such being the case. "D" – As to 77 Tetley St., Poplar.

It has been ascertained from Rose Moriarty, now residing at 22 Cordelia St., Poplar, that between 13 and 14 years ago; when she lived at 77 Tetley St., Sadler and his wife lodged with her. He was then a Conductor of Metropolitan Stage Carriage. She remembers one day when he came into his dinner he quarrelled with his wife, who sought protection in her (Moriarty's) room; she was followed by Sadler who had a dagger shaped knife in his hand, and threatened her.

Having heard this; although so long ago, I thought it as well that Mrs Moriarty should have an opportunity of identifying the knife sold to "Campbell", accordingly she attended at "H.D." where the knife was placed with others; but failed to identify.

"E" – As to Hurley Road; see "A."

"F" – As to Manor Place; see "A."

"G" – As to Colebrook Terrace, Bethnal Green. Sadler resided with his wife at this address; which is now 47 Entick Street, Cambridge Road; with a Miss Duffield; this was between 11 and 12 years ago; they only remained four months, and Miss Duffield saw nothing more of either until about 2 years ago when she accidentally met them outside Whitechapel Church.

"H" – As to 2 Johnson St., Commercial Road; see "B".

"I" – As to Sadler's employ at London Docks. No information can be obtained as to Sadler being actually employed at either of the Docks; but this no doubt refers to his employment at the Tea warehouse in Cutler St., which belongs to the London, India Dock Comp'y.

Henry Moore, Inspr.

T Arnold Supd.

On 3 March 1891, Sergeant Kuhrt submitted a report[12] on further enquiries about Sadler:

METROPOLITAN POLICE.
Criminal Investigation Department,
H ["Scotland Yard" – *deleted*] Division,
3rd day of March, 1891.

Swallow Gardens Murder /
Reference to papers 57885

With reference to Chief Constable's minute dated the 23rd ultimo, respecting the movements of "Sadler" between the 16th and 20th July, 1889, I beg to report that I have made enquiries, and am of opinion it may be assumed that Sadler lodged during that time at the Victoria lodging house, No. 40 Upper East Smithfield. Mr. William Dann the keeper of the lodging house has informed me that he has known him between 18 months and 2 years, and he remembers hearing that he had been discharged from the "Bilbao" on 7th July, 1889, which ship afterwards went down with all hands, which I have ascertained to be correct. Mr. Dann further stated that Sadler, when lodging there, has always paid a week in advance, but he is quite unable to say whether or not he may have been absent on one or more nights of the period in question.

The murdered woman Frances Coles was at this time lodging at no. 18 Thrawl Street, Spitalfields. I have not been able to ascertain whether she knew Sadler at that time, he has never lodged there, but he may have taken a lodging with her for a night or more at some other place, because the deceased has been absent from her lodgings for a night or two, although nothing positive can be ascertained about the time mentioned. I have made enquiries at numerous other lodging houses, I have seen Matthew Curley and Frederick Bowen; ships firemen, who have known Sadler since the 24th December last, and were his mates, whilst he was on board S.S. Fez, on her last passage, and made general enquiries, but have been unable to obtain any additional information.

I beg to add that the S.S. Loch Katrine in which Sadler embarked on the 20th July, 1889, is at present lying off the Fresh Wharf, near London Bridge. Captain Donald Cameron, who is in charge of her, has been questioned, and states that he joined the vessel on the 1st January, 1890, and that no person is now employed in her, who was on board at the time when Sadler served in her.

F Kuhrt, Sergt. G.
Submitted.   Henry Moore, Inspr
                              T Arnold Supd

Another daily report[13] on the Swallow Gardens murder, by Inspector Henry Moore, follows, dated 3 March 1891:

CENTRAL OFFICE / C.I.D. Reference SERIOUS CRIME NO. 756 55 / Submitted to A.C.,C.I.D. / Subject Results / Swallow Gardens Murder / Supt Arnold Submits daily report of Inspr Moore / 3. 3. 91. / Mr Anderson 4/3 Seen RA.

METROPOLITAN POLICE.
Criminal Investigation Department,
Scotland Yard,
3rd day of March, 1891

Swallow Gardens Murder (Daily Report) Reference to Papers 57885 /

With reference to the case of Frances Coles; who was found murdered at Swallow Gardens on 13th Ins.

I beg to report that since yesterday several statements have been taken; but no good result still had obtained from them; except to prove that the statements previously made and evidence given before the Coroner by Ellen Colanna [?] alias Calman is [ ]; especially with regard to the assault upon her which resulted in her receiving a black eye. Special report submitted.

The prisoner James Thomas Sadler was today again brought up at Thames Police Court, before F. Mead Esqr. Mr. Charles Matthews appeared on behalf of Police Prosecutor; and Mr. Lawless appeared for accused; and upon the application of the former, prisoner was discharged. Sadler on his liberation was taken away in a cab by Mr. Wallis, his solicitor, and a representative of the "Star" Newspaper. As the cab left the court yard cheers were raised by the crowd on behalf of Sadler.

No persons have been detained on this Division during the day in connection with this case.

Henry Moore, Inspr.
T Arnold Supd

There is a file cover[14] dated 6 March 1891 concerning refreshment claims for CID Sergeants working on the case:

HO 144/221

          No. A49301G/15   [Marked – "CLOSED UNTIL 1992"]
DATE. 6th Mch91.   Commissioner of Police
REFERENCES, &c.   Special <u>Refreshment Allowance Whitechapel Murder</u>

Asks for grant of special refreshment of 2/- per day to Sergeants of C.I.D. employed in connection with the recent Whitechapel Murder.

1/8

MINUTES.

See-
8

?Approve.
ET
10. 3. 1891.
CWS[?]
11.3.91
Wrote Commer. &
Receiver 11/3/91

The report[15] about the above is as follows:

A49301G/15
[Stamped: – HOME OFFICE 7 MAR.91 RECEIVED]
96318/.   New Scotland Yard, S.W.
6th March, 1891.

Sir,

With reference to your letter of the 1st August, 1889, A49301G/8, sanctioning a special Refreshment Allowance of 2/- a day to those officers of the Criminal Investigation Department who had been brought to Whitechapel from other Divisions in connection with the then recent murders there, I have the honour to acquaint you, for the information of the Secretary of State, that on the occurrence of the Swallow Gardens' murder of the 13th ult. similar arrangements for the attendance of C.I.D. officers were made; and I have to ask that the Secretary of State may be pleased to authorise the grant of a special refreshment allowance at the rate of 2/- per day, as before, to the Sergeants of the Criminal Investigation Department so employed.

I am,

Sir

Your most obedient Servant,

The Under   E. Bradford.
Secretary of State,
&c,

There is a file cover[16], dated 12 March 1891, as follows:

[Stamped: – RECEIVER FOR THE METROPOLITAN POLICE DISTRICT REGISTERED 5185/19 MAR.12 1891]
H.O.
11 Mar

Whitechapel Murders. Special allowance
Sanctions grant of special allowance of 2/- a day to P.S.'s C.I.D. employed re
late murder on same conditions as previous allowances.
Accountant to
note
       ARP
13.3.91
W[ ]
[   ] 14/3/91

The report[17] follows, dated 11 March 1891:

A49301G/15 [Stamped: – RECEIVER FOR THE METROPOLITAN PO-
LICE DISTRICT REGISTERED 5185/19 MAR 12 1891]
                               WHITEHALL.
                            11th March 1891
Sir,
    I am directed by the Secretary of State to acquaint you, that upon the
recommendation of the Commissioner of Police he sanctions the grant of a
special Refreshment Allowance at the rate of 2/- per day to those Sergeants of
the Criminal Investigation Department belonging to Divisions who have been
brought to Whitechapel from other Divisions in connection with the recent
murder in Swallow Gardens, on the same conditions as this allowance was
granted in August, 1889, to these officers when employed in connection with
the previous Whitechapel Murders.
                       I am,
                         Sir,
                 Your obedient Servant,
                     E.LeighPemberton.

The Receiver
    for the Metropolitan
        Police District.

There is a file cover sheet[18], heavily annotated, as follows:

10/3/92 / Further report / attached SLucas Supt. / Lay by MLM 11/3 /
Further Report submitted 10/5 / Report result of [ ] MLM 10/5 / [stamp] 10
MAY 92 / Report attached 17/5/92 SLucas Supt. / Seen MLM 17/5 /
Further report submd. 3/1/93 Supt Central to see. seen [ ] Inspr 4/1/93 (20
Faraday St. Walworth Rd. on "L" or "P" grd.? The Supt [ ] see this ppo
MLM 3/1 / Cent. / 57885 / 727 / Threats. / Report of an interview

between Ch. Insp. Swanson & Mrs. Sadler wife of the man Sadler who was in custody for the murder of Frances Coles at Whitechapel. Mrs. Sadler fears her husband. / [stamp:- REGISTRY received 12 DEC 91] C.I.D. MLM 12/ 12 / Mr. Anderson? Supt W. for report RA 12/12 / [stamp:- REFERRED 12 DEC.91] / Report attached 17/12/91 J Rudmore [?] actgSupt / Mr. Anderson / I think that Supt Arnold should see this report? He was speaking to me of Sadler yesterday MLM 17/12/1 / To Supt. H. to see RA 17/ / Seen T Arnold Supd 21 12 91 / P.a. JWButcher 22/12 / Further report submitted 28/12/91 Seen A. approved 28/12 ([ ] shd. like to know what Sadler is doing for a livelihood, and also if he leaves the Division, where he goes to) MLM / [stamp:- REFERRED 28 DEC.91] / Report attached 2/12/92 SLucas Supt. / By a strange coincidence I met Sadler this morning at the end of :[ ] our first meeting since he was charged with the Swallow Gardens murder. Lay by for the present. MLM 2/1. / Further report submitted 5/3/92 Mr Macnaghten MLM 5/3 / 5/3 Mr. Anderson ?Further report if, or when, anything fresh transpires. W. RA 5/

There is a report[19] dated 11 December 1891, by Chief Inspector Donald S. Swanson, about an assault by Sadler on his wife:

METROPOLITAN POLICE.
Criminal Investigation Department,
Scotland Yard,
11th day of December 1891.

Subject Mrs. Sadler assaulted by her husband.

I beg to submit the attached letter from Mrs. Sadler, of 121Danbrook Road South Streatham the wife of the man Sadler, who was charged with the murder of Frances Coles. I saw her here at 6pm today, accompanied by James Moffatt, a retired pensioner, and she said that she had been living with her husband at the above address ever since May last, and that Moffatt was a lodger. The object of the letter and her call was to ask advice, for Sadler had not only assaulted her and otherwise treated her cruelly, but he had repeatedly threatened to take her life, and she was afraid to live with him any longer. Moffatt, who is an elderly man said that although he had been at sea for many years he had never heard such horrible language as that uttered by Sadler to his wife, and he was obliged to lock his bedroom door every night for in his opinion Sadler was a treacherous and cowardly man.

The only cause that Mrs. Sadler could think of was that Sadler accused her of not assisting him in the shop, which he stocked with the money he got from some newspapers.

I advised her to apply to a magistrate stating all the facts: and that it was a matter for her own discretion how long she continued to reside with him.

I have sent a telegram (copy attached) to the W. Division.

I beg that the papers may be forwarded to Supt. W. for his information.

Donald SSwanson
Ch Inspr
JohnShore
Supt.

This is followed by a report[20] dated 16 December 1891, by Sergeant Francis Boswell of W Division:

METROPOLITAN POLICE.
W or Clapham Division,
16th day of December 1891

Subject- Mrs. Sadler's complaint of violence on the part of her husband / Reference to papers 57885 / 727

With reference to the attached report, giving particulars of a complaint made by Mrs. Sarah Sadler, residing with her husband James Sadler, at 121. Danbrook Road. Lower Streatham. of having been assaulted, threatened, and otherwise ill-treated by her husband.

I beg to report having seen both Mrs. Sadler and Mr. Moffatt, the lodger.

Mrs. Sadler informed me that her husband has not been guilty of any act of violence towards her, or threatened her since she made the complaint to Chief Inspr. Swanson, on 10th.

Both Mrs. Sadler, and Moffatt agree in describing Sadler as a most violent, subtle, and treacherous man, in the habit of using the most vile and disgusting language.

Mrs. Sadler has not applied to the magistrate for process against her husband at present but states that she shall do so should he use any further violence or threats towards her.

In accordance with Superintendent's directions a P.C. has been and is now patrolling Danbrook Road, in view of Sadler's house to render Mrs. Sadler assistance should occasion arise.

Mrs. Sadler expressed her thanks for the attention and courtesy that she has received from the Police.

Francis Boswell Sergt.
J Ludmore Actg Supt.

The next report[21] is dated 1 January 1892 and is a further report submitted by Sergeant Boswell about Sadler and his wife:

METROPOLITAN POLICE.
W or Clapham Division,
1st day of January 1892.

Re complaint against Sadler by his wife of violence &c Reference to Papers 57885 / 727.

With reference to the attached, and Chief Constable, C.I.Dept. minute thereon.

I beg to report that Sadler keeps a chandler's shop at No. 121 Danbrook Road, Lower Streatham, and does a good ready money trade, his takings averaging £2.10 per day.

Sadler opened this shop in May 1891, the man Moffatt coming to lodge with him about a fortnight later. With the exception of one occasion (a short time after he opened the shop) he has never been out, or left the house, but devoted his time to the business.

As far as I can ascertain the only person that he is in communication with or likely to visit is his mother, Mrs. Sadler, 63 or 65, Crampton Street, Newington Butts.

I am still in communication with Moffatt, who informed me that Sadler's conduct towards his wife has undergone a marked change lately he does not assault or threaten her and although he still makes use of most obscene and repulsive language he is (in Moffatt's opinion) guarded in his manner and actions.

Moffatt has promised in the event of anything of a suspicious nature arising with regard to Sadler's behaviour or movements, or should he be guilty of any further violence towards his wife to communicate with the Police.

Francis Boswell Sergt.
JBarnes Inspr.
SLucas Supt.

Sergeant Boswell's next report[22] was dated 4 March 1892, and concerned a further complaint from Mr Moffatt, the Sadlers' lodger:

METROPOLITAN POLICE.
W or Clapham Division,
4th day of March, 1892.

Subject Re James Sadler of 121 Danbrook Rd, Lower Streatham / Reference to papers 57885 / 727

I beg to report that at 6.50hrs 4th inst Mr. Moffatt, Naval pensioner, lodging at No. 121 Danbrook Road, Lower Streatham, with James Sadler, the man who was charged with the murder of Frances Coles at White-chapel, in February 1891, called at Streatham Station and stated that Sadler had refused to allow his wife to go out, or leave the house and had threatened that if she did so he would shut her out. Moffatt added that he feared that Sadler would assault her. I promised him that attention should be paid by Police, and advised him to tell Mrs. Sadler that the best plan for her to adopt would be to seek the advice of the magistrate at Lambeth Police Court.

Attention has been paid by P.C. White and myself during the evening, and P.C.'s on duty in the vicinity directed to pay attention, and act if necessary.

Francis Boswell Sergt.

Former papers at C.O., C.I.D.   J.Barnes Insp
SLucas Supt.

On 10 March 1892, Sergeant Boswell reported further[23] as follows:

METROPOLITAN POLICE.
W or Clapham Division.
10th day of March 1892.

Re James Sadler of 121 Danbrook Road Streatham / Reference to papers 57885 / 727.

With reference to the attached and Assistant Commissioner's minute thereon.

I beg to report that nothing further has transpired in connection with Sadler, and his wife.

I have seen Mrs. Sadler, who informed me that her husband who entertains strong prejudice towards persons of any religious denomination, had refused to allow her to attend Chapel, or to visit persons connected with any place of Worship.

Francis Boswell P.S.

Submitted.   J.Barnes Insp
SLucas Supt.

There is then a further report[24] by Sergeant Boswell about threats made by Sadler, dated 16 May 1892:

W Division / Subject Threats / Summary of Contents / Report giving particulars of a complaint made by Mrs. Sadler of 121 Danbrook Rd., of having been threatened by her husband, and the result of an application made by her to A Hopkins, Esqr the sitting magistrate at Lambeth Police Court for process against her husband.

METROPOLITAN POLICE.
W or Clapham Division.
16th day of May 1892.

Subject Threats to murder, result of summons for use of same / 57885 / 727.

I beg to report that James Thomas Sadler, of 121 Danbrook Road, Lower Streatham, mentioned in the attached correspondence appeared before R.I. Biron Q.C. at Lambeth Police Court on 16th inst in answer to a summons taken out against him on 9th inst, by Sarah Sadler, his wife, for threats made by him to murder her.

The learned Magistrate after hearing Mrs. Sadler's evidence (which was to the effect that her husband had threatened to cut her throat on 9th inst. and that she went in fear of him). bound defendant over in his own recognizance of £10. to keep the peace for six months.

Francis Boswell Sergt.
J.Barnes Insp
SLucas Supt

There then follows a report[25] by Sergeant Boswell, dated 2 January 1893:

W Division to the Assistant Commissioner, Criminal Investigation Department / Summary of Contents / Result of the magistrate hearing of a summons taken out by Mrs. Sadler of 121 Danbrook Rd. Streatham, against her husband James Sadler, for threats used by him against her.

METROPOLITAN POLICE.
W or Clapham Division.
2nd day of January 1893.

Subject J.T. Sadler / 57885 / 727 /

I beg to report that Mrs. Sarah Sadler, wife of James Thomas Sadler, who was charged with the murder of Frances Coles, in Swallow Gardens, Whitechapel, on 13th February, 1891, called on me at Streatham Station on 1st inst. and stated that Sadler intended removing from 121 Danbrook Road, Streatham, (where he has been residing) and has taken lodgings at No. 108, Faraday Street, Walworth Road, Camberwell.

Francis Boswell Sergt.
Respectfully submitted
Sadler was bound in his own re-

cognizances to keep the peace towards his wife, (on the 16th of May last) for 6 months and the wife appears to desire, that he should still remain under some surveillance.

ASewell Inspt.
ACConst SLucas Supt.

CHAPTER 36

May 1892 – Frederick Bailey Deeming

Most of the infamous murderers of the late-Victorian period after the Whitechapel Murders have been linked with "Jack the Ripper." They include Mary Eleanor Pearcey (1890), Frederick Bailey Deeming (1892), Dr Thomas Neill Cream (1892), and Severin Klosowski (George Chapman, 1903). There is nothing of a known substantive nature to link any one of them with the Whitechapel Murders although a file concerning one of them is to be found in the official files.

Frederick Bailey Deeming, 48 years of age, was executed for murder in Australia on 23 May 1892. In 1891, before emigrating to Australia, he had murdered his wife and four children at Rainhill, Liverpool, and had buried the bodies under the kitchen floor.

The *Pall Mall Gazette* of 8 April 1892 printed the following article:

DEEMING AND "JACK THE RIPPER."
AN INTERVIEW AT SCOTLAND YARD.

A correspondent writes:- It ought to be stated at once that, so far as the Scotland-yard authorities are concerned, they do not believe that in the capture of Deeming the mysterious fiend "Jack the Ripper" has been laid by the heels. They have arrived at this conclusion despite the scores upon scores of letters which, since Deeming's arrest, have poured in upon them from more or less imaginative persons in the East-end of London who are anxious to prove that a person like unto the Rainhill murderer was prowling around Whitechapel at the time when the crimes which terrified that neighbourhood were being committed.

An official of high rank at Scotland-yard had his attention drawn last night to the story to the effect that a girl living in London walked out with Deeming on the evening when two of the murders were committed, and saw him again on the following day, when he was strangely nervous and excited, laughed loudly and exclaimed "I have been expecting for the last week or so to see something of the kind in print." The police have been practically inundated with similar stories. One woman came to tell them that the portrait of Deeming corresponded in detail with the outline portrait which "Jack the

Ripper'' is said to have drawn of himself on the dirty wall of the house in which he hacked an unfortunate to death on the morning of Lord Mayor's Day three years ago. The female who brought this intelligence evidently did not know that the outline portrait was the work of an enterprising individual who afterwards became the tenant of the house, and showed curious visitors his handiwork and a dark stain on the floor for a trifling piece of silver. And of such as this are the stories which the police have been obliged to listen to during the last two weeks. Needless to say, they know nothing of the young girl who is alleged to have walked out with Deeming and to have been on terms of friendship with him.

But so far the police are satisfied that the man now in custody in Australia is not the perpetrator of the Whitechapel crimes; indeed they have been unable to fix his residence in London at all except on the occasion when he visited the metropolis with Miss Mather and, as the Scotland-yard official already referred to pointed out, only a creature intimately acquainted with White-chapel and knowing every court and alley in it, could have perpetrated the murders ascribed to Jack the Ripper and escaped from the scenes of his crime without being detected. It is evident from the wandering life Deeming has led, and from the fact that he is not a Londoner by birth, that he could not have possessed the knowledge of locality to enable him to do this.

The *Pall Mall Gazette* of 13 April 1892 published a further piece on this story:

DEEMING AND HIS DOCTOR – DATE OF TRIAL.
THE ''RIPPER'' ROMANCE DENIED.

The trial of Deeming is expected to begin in Melbourne, on 2[ ]th April. It is thought that the application of the defence for an adjournment in order to permit of witnesses being brought from England will not be granted. Deeming has been very orderly and industrious. He is still occupied in replying to the written inquiries of his solicitor. The doctor whom Mr. Lyle engaged in connection with the defence has withdrawn from the case. He states that he has taken this step in consequence of the impossibility of obtaining a fair hearing in a community prejudiced against the accused. He declares that Deeming belongs to the order of instinctive criminals, and is as much wanting in the moral sense as a blind man is in the sense of sight, since killing is as much a part of his nature as eating. His head measurement is 6[ ]., which is exceedingly small in comparison with his height. Deeming's whole character is one of extreme stupidity, and the jokes he makes are coarse and pointless. His escape hitherto, the doctor considers, has been due less to cunning than to accident. The statement sent from Halifax, N.S., yesterday as to a man passing under the name of "Jacobs," who in 1882 was stated to have produced a letter from a woman subsequently murdered in Whitechapel seems to be entirely romantic. The informant has now been shown the portrait of Deeming, and does not recognize a likeness between the prisoner at Melbourne and his acquaintance of former days, Jacobs. Moreover, it appears doubtful whether Deeming was in Canada in 1882.

The official file[1] concerning Deeming is dated 6 May 1892, and the file cover follows:

[Stamped: – HOME OFFICE 7 MAY.92 DEP] No. A49301C/32
DATE 6 May 1892   Mr Charles Barber
REFERENCES, &c.   Whitechapel murders & Deeming.
                    Mr Barber is of opinion that Deeming is
                    responsible for the Whitechapel murders.
                    Attention is called to P.13 of the "Spy" of Apl. 16.
                    Enclosed.
                        MINUTES.
                    His belief rests upon his "dreams", in which his vision of
                    the murderer appears to have coincided with that of
                    Deeming.
                        See marked passages on page 2.
                        ? Put up.
                        F?W
                            11 May '92
                            C.M.
                                ELP 12 May 92

The extract[2] from the *Spy*, referred to on the cover, is included, as follows:

EXTRACT.
From the   "Spy"
    of   16th April 1892
              RATHER REMARKABLE.
Just a year since Mr. Charles Barber called on us, and explained that he had constantly dreamt about the identity of the Whitechapel murderer, and so confident was he that his visions were correct that we had great difficulty in convincing him that it would be policy to allow his convictions to lie dormant for a while. In the face of recent events he again points out how true his former dreams were, and has handed us a lengthy explanation.

To begin with, we may mention that Mr. Barber wrote to Scotland Yard in 1889, and received the following acknowledgement:-
"No. 52983.

"Criminal Investigation Department,
"Gt. Scotland Yard, 1889.

"Re WHITECHAPEL MURDERS.

"Sir, – I am directed by the Commissioner of Police of the Metropolis to acknowledge, with thanks, the receipt of your letter.-I am, sir, your obedient servant,

"R. ANDERSON,
Assistant Commissioner of Police.

Mr. Barber, Ardwick."

Immediately after this Mr. Barber wrote to the secretary of the Vigilance Society in London as follows:-

5, Harriet Place, Ardwick, Manchester,
Sept. 13, 1889.

Mr. Bocker.

Dear Sir, – I cannot refrain from dropping you a line, and why I have not written before I cannot tell; but if you will only see to what I here state I verily believe that the man so called "Jack the Ripper" will soon be caught. Of course I cannot state here half of what I could say if I could see you; but suffice it to say that I have read all that has appeared in our papers from the very first, and so reading I have dreamt of the crime that this so-called "Jack the Ripper" has done. My dream of the Mitre Square murder is very clear, for I saw him on the job and afterwards take to the ship – namely, the "Alaska." Sir, you will find what I here make out – that is, the ship was in port on all the dates given: (1) April 3, 1888; (2) August 7, 1888; (3) August 31, 1888; (4) September 8, 1888; (5) September 30, 1888; (6) November 8, 1888; (7) July 17, 1889; (8) September 10, 1889. When that ship was not in port no crime was reported of this man "Jack the Ripper." Again that ship arrived at Queenstown one day last week, which I have dreamt so much about. I made this remark to my friends: "Oh, the ship 'Alaska' has arrived, and we shall soon be hearing something more of 'Jack the Ripper' again." They made but little of it, but when they saw it in the paper they wondered, and said that he must have been on the ship "Alaska." I cannot give over thinking about it. He is about 5 feet 7 inches, rather stout, a little round-shouldered or short-necked, not much hair on his face, aged 40 or over.

I saw him again in the early part of the morning of the 11th September, 1889, in my dream.

I have written to Mr. Munro [sic], and have told him about the "Alaska," and only hope that he may be caught.

You will pardon my handwriting; I know it is not good.

Believe me, yours faithfully, CHRS. BARBER.

[We shall be pleased to show the original letter to anyone who desires to see it. That the man's "visions" were remarkable is beyond doubt. – ED.]

Mr. Barber now sends us a long statement from which we extract the following:-

"While reading over the Rainhill stories and a description of this man Williams, otherwise Deeming, I cannot come to any other belief than he is none other than the so-called 'Jack the Ripper,' for I saw him on four or five different occasions in my visions. I will take it upon myself-though I don't know Whitechapel, not ever being at the place-I will mark out on a sheet of paper each one of the places where the murders have been committed, and shall be tied blindfolded, and believe me, I can give some very vivid pictures of each murder, namely, of Emma Smith, Whitechapel; of Martha Tabram, George Yard Buildings, Commercial Street, E.; of Mary Ann Nicholls [sic], Buck's Row; of Annie Chapman, Hanbury Street, Whitechapel; of Elizabeth Stride, Berners [sic] Street, Whitechapel; of Catherine Eddowes, Mitre Square; of Mary Kelly, who was murdered and mutilated in a room off Dorset Street – this was very clear; of Alice Mackenzie [sic], murdered in Castle Alley, and only partly mutilated – this was very clear; and of the mutilated remains found under a railway arch in the East End-very clear. Frances Cole [sic], murdered – I have no account of any mutilation.

I have seen this man on all the different murders, and after they were committed, for I saw him at the railway station booking to go away. He was then dressed in black clothes, with a longish coat on, a kind of billycock hat, with a black bag in his left hand. He was against the barriers getting his ticket when I saw him. After this I saw him; this was some time after in July, 1889. It was in this way I saw him: I have it that it was at some docks, where there were some large vessels. One of these vessels was ready to start off. It was a fine vessel, with its cords stretched from mast pole to bow and stern, with small flags attached, and I read the name of this vessel, 'Alaska'; and just as it was blowing off to start-for I could see the steam blowing off-this same man that I had seen times before came along the docks with a black bag in his left hand, and mounted the vessel by means of a ladder. Then off went the vessel. He seemed to me to be the last person to get on, for I saw no other person get on after him. At this I awoke, saying to myself, 'That is Jack the Ripper.' "

[Of course Mr. Barber is only dealing with what he dreamt, but his persistency in believing in the truth of those dreams struck us a year since as being most remarkable, and we have pleasure in publishing his statement in brief. He is not a myth, as he has lived for some time at 5, Harriet Place Ardwick. – ED.]

The letter[3] to the Home Secretary from Mr Barber is included:

[Stamped: – HOME OFFICE 7.MAY.92 DEPt. No.] No 5. Harriett Place
Ardwick A49301C/32
<u>May 6th 1892</u>

Rt. Hon. Hy. Matthew

Sir   I inclose you a coppy of Spy See Page 13 but in doing so you will see at once that I did give such information that I did believe at that time would have led to the aprension [*sic?*] of the East-End murderer so called Jack the Ripper otherwise Lawson, Williams, Deeming. Had they been properly carried out why they was not I cannot say.

Ask me do I still believe that he is the same man by going through the Rainhill storey I do say that he is for he unxpidetley turn up at Birkenhead as the papers today but is own Family says that he did after being away for about two years that was after the 10th September 1889 Febuy 1888 and part of 1889 for him being away that being the very time that the murders was committed at the East End for the Doctors believe that the crimes that was done afterwards was not done by the same hands and as all my information at that time was directing them to Liverpool I not only wrote to Mr. Munro him then being Chief but I wrote to the Chief at Liverpool giving to him same information not Geting a reply & also wrote my third letter to the Chairman of the Vigilant Comittee geting my own letter Returned back not finding the Adress as you will see a coppy of the letter in Page 13 of Spy along with the acknowledgement from Scotland yard singe R. Anderson.

And now Sir my intention in drawing your notice to this is seeing that Deeming as got to undergo the Justice of the Law I heavily belive that he will confess to the Whitechapel murders thereby Proveing that my information was right and at the same time Seting the Public much at Rest of one the Greatest Mysteries of the Present Century therefor if he dos confess

And I [ ] belive he will may it Please you to see that my information Has Find its just Reward as I belive that in Shuch Case's They do.

I am very sorry that he was not caught at that time for if he Deeming had been there would never have been the Rainhill Murders.

Sir the Editor of Spy or myself will only be to Pleased To give you my other information that you may wish to know

Belive me
Yours Faithfullely
Charles Barber

Rt.Hon H. Matthew

CHAPTER 37

23 February 1894 –
Suspects Named by Chief Constable M.L. Macnaghten

To assess which suspects in this case could be genuine is very difficult, even when one restricts "candidates" only to those who can be said to have any claim to be authentic. Retaining objectivity is also a problem, especially if the writer has his own preferred suspect. To make an objective and useful summary we have eliminated suspects who appear to have no basis in fact, and those already mentioned in the narrative such as Isenschmid and Pizer. The police and Home Office files contain references to non-police suspects such as those mentioned by Edward Knight Larkins, the clerk in HM Customs Statistical Department who bombarded the police with his ideas, and whom Dr Robert Anderson described as "a troublesome busybody". A further problem for the researcher is the fact that the so-called "suspects file" is now missing from the official records.

There is one report concerning suspects that has survived, dated 23 February 1894, and written by Sir Melville Macnaghten, then Assistant Chief Constable CID, second-in-command to Dr Robert Anderson. Macnaghten did not take up his post with the Metropolitan Police until June 1889, by which time the recognized "series" of "Ripper" murders had ceased.

It is interesting to note the following entry[1] in the Metropolitan Police Estimates Book, 1885–92, concerning Macnaghten and his employment as Assistant Chief Constable:

A46472D/3. Mr. Macnaghten allowed £100 in addition to salary as Asst C.C. while acting as Confidential Assistant to Asst Commr. of C.I.D. total not to exceed £600 p.a.

Chief Ins : Butcher to have rank of Sup : and salary of £350. by 10 to £400.

His report, it must be noted, names three suspects for the "Ripper" murders whose names do not appear in the extant official files prior to Macnaghten naming them in 1894. It was written by Macnaghten in response to reports that had appeared in the *Sun* newspaper [14 February *et seq.*] claiming that Thomas Hayne Cutbush, a recently detained lunatic who had stabbed and attempted to stab two women in Kennington, was "Jack the Ripper". The report[2] is as follows:

Confidential.

The case referred to in the sensational story told in "the Sun" in its issue of 13th. inst., & following dates, is that of Thomas Cutbush who was arraigned at the London County Sessions in April 1891, on a charge of maliciously wounding Florence Grace Johnson, & attempting to wound Isabella Fraser Anderson in Kennington. He was found to be insane, and sentenced to be detained during Her Majesty's pleasure.

This Cutbush, who lived with his mother and aunt at 14 Albert St. Kennington, escaped from the Lambeth Infirmary, (after he had been detained there only a few hours, as a lunatic) at noon on 5th. March 1891. He was rearrested on 9th. idem. A few weeks before this, several cases of stabbing, or "jobbing", girls behind had occurred in the vicinity, and a man named Colicott was arrested, but subsequently discharged owing to faulty identification. The cuts in the girls dresses made by Colicott were quite different to the cut made by Cutbush (when he wounded Miss Johnson) who was no doubt influenced by a wild desire of morbid imitation. Cutbush's antecedents were enquired into by Ch: Inspr. (now Supt.) Chis [holm] by Inspr. Race, and by P.S. McCarthy CID – (the last named officer had been specially employed in Whitechapel at the time of the murders there, –) and it was ascertained that he was born, & had lived, in Kennington all his life. His father died when he was quite young, and he was always a "spoilt" child. He had been employed as a clerk and traveller in the Tea trade at the Minories, & subsequently canvassed for a Directory in the East End, during which time he bore a good character. He apparently contracted syphilis about 1888, and, – since that time, – led an idle and useless life. His brain seems to have become affected, and he believed that people were trying to poison him. He wrote to Lord Grimthorpe, and others, – & also to the Treasury, complaining of a Dr. Brooks, of Westminster Bridge Rd., whom he threatened to shoot for having supplied him with bad medicines. He is said to have studied medical books by day, & to have rambled about at night, returning frequently with his clothes covered with mud; but little reliance could be placed on the statements made by his mother or his aunt, who both appear to have been of a very excitable disposition. It was found impossible to ascertain his movements on the nights of the Whitechapel murders. The knife found on him was bought in Houndsditch about a week before he was detained in the Infirmary. Cutbush was a nephew of the late Supt Executive.

Now the Whitechapel murderer had 5 victims – & 5 victims only, – his murders were

(i) 31st. Aug '88. Mary Ann Nichols, at Buck's Row, who was found with her throat cut, & with (slight) stomach mutilation.

(ii) 8th. Sept. '88. Annie Chapman – Hanbury St. throat cut, stomach & private parts badly mutilated & some of the entrails placed round the neck.

(iii) 30th. Sept '88. Elizabeth Stride, Berner's [*sic*] street, throat cut, but nothing in shape of mutilation attempted, & on same date

Catherine Eddowes. Mitre Square, throat cut, & very bad mutilation, both of face & stomach. (iv) 9th November. Mary Jane Kelly. Miller's Court throat cut, and the whole of the body mutilated in the most ghastly manner.

The last murder is the only one that took place in a room, and the murderer must have been at least 2 hours engaged. A photo was taken of the woman, as she was found lying on the bed, without seeing which it is impossible to imagine the awful mutilation.

With regard to the double murder which took place on 30th. Sept, there is no doubt but that the man was disturbed by some Jews who drove up to a club, (close to which the body of Elizabeth Stride was found) and that he then, "nondum satiatus", went in search of a further victim whom he found at Mitre Square.

It will be noticed that the fury of the mutilations increased in each case, and, seemingly, the appetite only became sharpened by indulgence. It seems, then, highly improbable that the murderer would have suddenly stopped in November '88, and been content to recommence operations by merely prodding a girl behind some 2 years & 4 months afterwards. A much more rational theory is that the murderer's brain gave way altogether after his awful glut in Miller's Court, and that he immediately committed suicide, or, as a possible alternative, was found to be so hopelessly mad by his relations, that he was by them confined in some asylum.

No one ever saw the Whitechapel murderer, many homicidal maniacs were suspected, but no shadow of proof could be thrown on any one. I may mention the cases of 3 men, any one of whom would have been more likely than Cutbush to have committed this series of murders:-

(1) A Mr. M.J. Druitt, said to be a doctor & of good family, who disappeared at the time of the Miller's Court murder, & whose body (which was said to have been upwards of a month in the water) was found in the Thames on 31st. Decr., or about 7 weeks after that murder. He was sexually insane and from private inf. I have little doubt but that his own family believed him to have been the murderer.

(2) Kosminski, a Polish Jew, & resident in Whitechapel. This man became insane owing to many years indulgence in solitary vices. He had a great hatred

of women, specially of the prostitute class, & had strong homicidal tendencies; he was removed to a lunatic asylum about March 1889. There were many circs connected with this man which made him a strong "suspect."

(3) Michael Ostrog, a Russian doctor, and a convict, who was subsequently detained in a lunatic asylum as a homicidal maniac. The man's antecedents were of the worst possible type, and his whereabouts at the time of the murders could never be ascertained.

And now with regard to a few of the inaccuracies and misleading statements made by the "Sun." In its issue of 14th Feb, it is stated that the writer has in his possession a facsimile of the knife with which the murders were committed. This knife (which for some unexplained reason has, for the last 3 years, been kept by Inspr. Race, instead of being sent to Prisoners' Property Store) was traced, & it was found to nave been purchased in Houndsditch in Feb. '91, or 2 years & 3 months after the Whitechapel murders ceased!

The statement, too, that Cutbush "spent a portion of the day in making rough drawings of the bodies of women, and of their mutilations," is based solely on the fact that 2 scribble drawings of women in indecent postures were found torn up in Cutbush's room. The head & body of one of these had been cut from some fashion plate, & legs were added to shew a woman's naked thighs & pink stockings.

In the issue of 15th inst it is said that a light overcoat was among the things found in Cutbush's house, and that a man in a light overcoat was seen talking to a woman in Backchurch Lane whose body with arms attached was found in Pinchin St. This is hopelessly incorrect! On 10th. Sept. '89 the naked body, with arms, of a woman was found wrapped in some sacking under a Railway arch in Pinchin St: the head & legs were never found nor was the woman ever identified. She had been killed at least 24 hours before the remains, (which had seemingly been brought from a distance), were discovered. The stomach was split up by a cut, and the head and legs had been severed in a manner identical with that of the woman whose remains were discovered in the Thames, in Battersea Park, & on the Chelsea Embankment on 4th June of the same year; and these murders had no connection whatever with the Whitechapel horrors. The Rainham mystery in 1887, & the Whitehall mystery (where portions of a woman's body were found under what is now New Scotland Yard) in 1888 were of a similar type to the Thames & Pinchin St crimes.

It is perfectly untrue to say that Cutbush stabbed 6 girls behind. This is confounding his case with that of Colicott.

The theory that the Whitechapel murderer was left handed, or, at any rate, "ambidexter," had its origins in the remark made by a doctor who examined the corpse of one of the earliest victims; other doctors did not agree with him.

With regard to the 4 additional murders ascribed by the writer in the Sun to the Whitechapel fiend:-

(1) The body of Martha Tabram, a prostitute, was found on a common stair case in George Yard buildings on 7th. August 1888, the body had been repeatedly pierced, probably with a bayonet. This woman had, with a fellow prostitute, been in company of 2 soldiers in the early part of the evening; these men were arrested, but the second prostitute failed, or refused, to identify, and the soldiers were accordingly discharged.

(2) Alice McKenzie was found with her throat cut (or rather stabbed) in Castle Alley on 17th. July 1889; no evidence was forthcoming and no arrests were made in connection with this case. The stab in the throat was of the same nature as in the case of the number

(3) Frances Coles, in Swallow Gardens, on 13th. February 1891, for which Thomas Sadler, a fireman, was arrested, &, after several remands, discharged. It was ascertained at the time that Sadler had sailed for the Baltic on 19th. July '89. & was in Whitechapel on the night of 17th. idem. He was a man of ungovernable temper & entirely addicted to drink, & the company of the lowest prostitutes.

(4) The case of the unidentified woman whose trunk was found in Pinchin St: on 10th. Sept. 1889 – which has already been dealt with.

MLMacnaghten
23rd. Feb. 1894

As can be seen from the above report, Macnaghten was responsible for the promulgation of several of the accepted "facts" in the case of the Whitechapel Murders, including the five above-described murders and exceptions, and the idea that the killer's mind gave way after the "awful glut" of Miller's Court. It has also been largely accepted that one of the three above-named suspects was the "most likely" to have been the killer, despite the fact that Macnaghten himself states that "no shadow of proof could be thrown on any one". He also states that "No one ever saw the Whitechapel Murderer", which seems to contradict evidence adduced at the time, especially in relation to the witnesses Mrs Long, Schwartz and Joseph Lawende. Macnaghten also firmly establishes Elizabeth Stride as a "Ripper" victim and suggests that the killer was disturbed and therefore left her body before inflicting his customary mutilation, and then searched out Catherine Eddowes to "satiate" his urges. Also that the mutilations increased in fury with each killing. An important point to note is that there are various factual errors in

Macnaghten's report, an aspect of it which should not be overlooked.

Montague John Druitt's suicide, however, was a proven fact and the following report of the inquest into his death appeared in the *Acton, Chiswick & Turnham Green Gazette* of Saturday, 5 January 1889:

FOUND DROWNED. – Shortly after mid-day on Monday, a waterman named Winslade, of Chiswick, found the body of a man, well-dressed, floating in the Thames off Thorneycroft's. He at once informed a constable, and without delay the body was conveyed on the ambulance to the mortuary. – On Wednesday afternoon, Dr. Diplock, coroner, held the inquest at the Lamb Tap, when the following evidence was adduced:- William H. Druitt said he lived at Bournemouth, and that he was a solicitor. The deceased was his brother, who was 31 last birthday. He was a barrister-at-law, and an assistant master in a school at Blackheath. He had stayed with witness at Bournemouth for a night towards the end of October. Witness heard from a friend on the 11th of December that deceased had not been heard of at his chambers for more than a week. Witness then went to London to make inquiries, and at Blackheath he found that deceased had got into serious trouble at the school, and had been dismissed. That was on the 30th of December. Witness had deceased's things searched where he resided, and found a paper addressed to him (produced). – The Coroner read the letter, which was to this effect:- "Since Friday I felt I was going to be like mother, and the best thing was for me to die."

– Witness, continuing, said deceased had never made any attempt on his life before. His mother became insane in July last. He had no other relative. – Henry Winslade was the next witness. He said he lived at No. 4, Shore-street, Paxton-road, and that he was a waterman. About one o'clock on Monday he was on the river in a boat, when he saw the body floating. The tide was at half flood, running up. He brought the body ashore, and gave information to the police.-P.C. George Moulson, 216T, said he had searched the body, which was fully dressed excepting the hat and collar. He found four large stones in each pocket in the top coat; £2 10s. in gold, 7s. in silver, 2d. in bronze, two cheques on the London and Provincial Bank (one for £50 and the other for £16), a first-class season pass from Blackheath to London (South-Western Railway), a second half return Hammersmith to Charing Cross (dated 1st December), a silver watch, gold chain with a spade guinea attached, a pair of kid gloves, and a white handkerchief. There were no papers or letters of any kind. There were no marks of injury on the body, but it was rather decomposed. – A verdict of suicide whilst in an unsound state of mind was returned.

Another report on the suicide of Druitt appeared in the *Southern Guardian* of Saturday, January 1 1889:

SAD DEATH OF A LOCAL
BARRISTER.

The *Echo* of Thursday night says : – "An inquiry was on Wednesday held by Dr. Diplock, at Chiswick, respecting the death of Montague John Druitt, 31 years of age, who was found drowned in the Thames. The deceased was identified by his brother, Mr. William Harvey Druitt, a solicitor residing at Bournemouth, who stated that the deceased was a barrister-at-law, but had lately been an assistant at a school at Blackheath. The deceased had left a letter, addressed to Mr. Valentine, of the school, in which he alluded to suicide. Evidence having been given as to discovering deceased in the Thames – upon his body were found a cheque for £60 and £16 in gold – the Jury returned a verdict of "Suicide whilst of unsound mind."

The deceased gentleman was well known and much respected in this neighbourhood. He was a barrister of bright talent, he had a promising future before him, and his untimely end is deeply deplored.

The funeral took place in Wimborne cemetery on Thursday afternoon, and the body was followed to the grave by the deceased's relatives and a few friends, including Mr. W.H. Druitt, Mr. Arthur Druitt, Rev. C. H. Druitt, Mr. J. Druitt, sen., Mr. J. Druitt, jun., Mr. J.T. Homer, and Mr. Wyke-Smith. The funeral service was read by the vicar of the Minster, Wimborne, the Rev. F.J. Huyshe, assisted by the Rev. Plater.

Other reports also appeared:

Thames Valley Times
Wednesday Evening 2nd January 1889
BODY FOUND IN THE THAMES OFF THORNEYCROFT'S
On Monday the body of a gentleman was found by Henry Winslade, waterman, in the Thames, off Thorneycroft's Wharf, and has since been identified by a season ticket and certain papers. Deceased was not a resident of the district, and the body had been in the water nearly a month. Deceased was about forty years of age, and the brother of a gentleman living at Bournemouth. The Coroner was acquainted with the fact that the remains had been removed to the mortuary, and an inquest will be held today.

Richmond & Twickenham Times
5th January 1889

SUICIDE WHILST INSANE

Dr. Diplock on Wednesday held an inquest at the "Lamb Tap" on the body of Montague John Druitt, aged 31, whose body was recovered from the Thames off Thorneycrofts' Wharf, on Monday, by a waterman named Henry Winslade. The pockets of the deceased, who was a stranger to the district were found filled with stones, and after a letter had been read in which he wrote to the effect that "what he intended to do would be the best for all parties," the jury returned a verdict of "Suicide by drowning whilst temporarily insane."

DOREST COUNTY CHRONICLE & SOMERSETSHIRE GAZETTE
January 10th 1889
[*Distressing Occurrence*]
We regret to hear of the sad death of Mr. M.J. Druitt, a barrister on this circuit, and son of Mr. Druitt, of Wimborne. An enquiry into the circumstances attending his death was held by Dr. Diplock at Chiswick on Wednesday, deceased having been found drowned in the Thames near that place. The deceased was identified by his brother, Mr. William Harvey Druitt, a solicitor, residing at Bournemouth, who stated that the deceased was a barrister-at-law, but had lately been an assistant at a school at Blackheath. The deceased had left a letter addressed to Mr. Valentine, of the school, in which he alluded to suicide. A paper had been found upon which the deceased had written,

"Since Friday I have felt as if I was going to be like mother" who for some months had been mentally afflicted. Evidence having been given as to discovering deceased in the Thames – upon his body were found a cheque for £50 and £16 in gold – the jury returned a verdict of "Suicide whilst of unsound mind".

The funeral took place at Wimborne on Thursday.

Deceased was a prominent member of the Kingston Park Cricket Club, and as such was well known in the county.

As regards the suspect Michael Ostrog, it is interesting to note that he appeared in the *Police Gazette* of 26 October 1888, as follows:

METROPOLITAN POLICE DISTRICT.

3. – Convict Supervision Office. – Woodcut portrait and description of Supervisee MICHAEL OSTROG, *alias* BERTRAND ASHLEY, CLAUDE CLAYTON, and Dr. GRANT, Office No. 22550, whose apprehension is sought for failing to report – age 55, height 5 ft. 11 in., complexion dark, hair dark brown, eyes grey, scars right thumb and right shin, two large moles

right shoulder and one back of neck, corporal punishment marks; generally dressed in a semi-clerical suit. A Polish Jew. Was sentenced, 5th January, 1874, at Aylesbury, to 10 years' penal servitude and 7 years' police supervision for larceny. Liberated on license 25th August, 1883. Again sentenced at the Central Criminal Court, 14th September, 1887, to 6 months' hard labour for larceny. On the 10th March, 1888, he was liberated from the Surrey County Lunatic Asylum, and failed to report.

Warrant issued.

Special attention is called to this dangerous man.

Index No. on Card. 9 / Michael Ostrog, *alias* . . . Bertrand Ashley (a Pole) Office No. 22550 / Last and previous Convictions. Place, Aylesbury . . . Date 5/1/74; Offence, Larceny . . . . . .

Sentence, 10 yrs. Pen. & 7 yrs. Supn. / Place, Maidstone . . . Date - /7/ 66; Offence, Robbery Three summary convictions . . . . . . Personal Description. A, 50, h. 5 ft. 11 in., c. dark, h. dark brown, e. grey; moles back of neck and on shoulders (large); scar on right thumb; corporal punishment marks / Remarks. A surgeon by profession, and stated to be a desperate man. Known on R Division.

The last mention[3] so far found of Ostrog is in the Habitual Criminals Register for 1904:

Office No. 2464–04 / Name, aliases, Prison, and Register No. John Evest, alias Matters Ostroy, Bertrand Ashley, Claude Cayton, Stanistan Sublinsky, John Sobieski and Michael Ostrog A a 1374, Parkhurst / Date and Place of Birth. 1830 at sea / Height without shoes 5 ft. 8¾ in. / Complexion, dk / Hair, bn (tg gr, thin on top) / Eyes, bn / Marks, nil / Offence (in full), place of Conviction, and Officer in Case, or Place of Committal, Lar-N.L.S. (P.S. Pullen C.I.D.-H) / Sentence and date of Conviction, 5 yrs ps 16–12–00 / Date when Penal Servitude expires or Supervision commences, 17–12–1905 / Date of Liberation, intended Address, and Occupation, 17–9–1904 29 Brooke St., Holborn Doctor / Remarks, See also office no. 47020.

CHAPTER 38

The Missing Suspects Files

Before the Scotland Yard files on the Whitechapel Murders were deposited in the Public Record Office many papers went missing during the 1970s and early 1980s. Although these missing files[1] on suspects are no longer to be found, in 1973 when Paul Bonner was carrying out research for the BBC television documentary *Jack the Ripper*, he was able to access the files and made notes with the following introduction:

> "These are reports that seem to have been called for by Scotland Yard in January 1889. They include a range of colourful suspects (mostly from outside Whitechapel)."

The missing files were also accessed in the 1970s by Donald Rumbelow and Stephen Knight when researching their own books on the case. We have extracted the recorded information from these files and have compiled the following list of these "missing" suspects:

Translation of a communication from Bremen Police, dated 27 September 1888, papers 3/52983:
289

Bremen,

27 September 1888

The police directors reply to the Police Authorities of the Criminal Investigation Department, Great Scotland Yard, London.

With reference to your communication of the 25th instant, correspondence No 52983/239, we have the honour, having regard to the letter from Leipzig, to inform you that evidently the hairdresser Mary is the person referred to. He has completed here on the 7th August last a term of seven years imprisonment and is now confined at Oslebshausen whence he will be liberated on the 7th August 1889, having been further convicted and sentenced to 12 months imprisonment for a similar offence at Strasburg.

"Translated by F. Kuhrt Sergt."

There is a second report on "Mary", as follows:

[Stamped: – Metropolitan Police Criminal Investigation Dept. 23 OCT 88
Received]
Copy
Translation   Bremen,
                                   19th October 1888

    The Hairdresser "Mary" has, in his time, been arrested by me several
times for assaulting women and young girls in the breasts and private parts.
"Mary" went, as was afterwards ascertained, at the fall of the night, to the
different promenades where he, by himself, made a sudden attack upon ladies
who were alone, striking them in the breast with some sharp instrument. The
cuts were not very deep and did not point to an attempt to kill as they were
soon healed and nobody has been killed.

    "Mary" has been found, while in his barber's shop, trying to commit a rape
upon a young girl; this young girl could give a very good description of him as she
had the opportunity of seeing him the next day and then recognized him as the
man who committed the assault, he was afterwards taken into custody.
                              (signed) Baring
                                 Detective

Translation continued
    Copy of this statement is respectfully submitted to the Chief of the
Detective Depmt in London, Great Scotland Yard, re letter No. 52983/826
                            Bremen 20 Oct 1888
                            The Chief of Police
                            Sign: Dr. Feldmann

This is followed by a report, on the same subject, from Inspector
Abberline, dated 22 October 1888:

                          METROPOLITAN POLICE
                    Criminal Investigation Department,
                             Scotland Yard
                     22nd day of October 1888

Central Officer's
Special Report
Subject Whitechapel
Murders
                   With reference to the annexed.
    I beg to report that according to letter from Bremen Police dated 27th Ult.
docket no. 289 the man called "Mary" is now undergoing 12 months'

imprisonment, and therefore could not be connected with the recent murders in Whitechapel.

With regard to the man Wetzel [*Ludwig*], it has been clearly proved that he was in no way concerned in the matter. He also was under remand at the time the Berner St. and Mitre Sq. murders were committed. See reports herewith.

F.G. Abberline, Inspr
T Arnold Supt

There is a report, dated 18 December 1888, from the Kingston Police Station, regarding a suspect:-

METROPOLITAN POLICE
Kingston
18th December 1888

Special Report
Whitechapel
Murders   Copy from O.B.

I beg to report that at 10.20 p.m. 16th November, 1888 John Hemmings 11 Youngs Buildings, Kingston, and William Shulver 201 Aspen Road, Starch Green, Middlesex, informed PC 548T, Robert Large, that at time above stated they were drinking inside the "White Hart P.H." Hampton Wick, Middlesex, and that they were talking about the "Whitechapel Murders" and another man was also inside the house, who upon hearing the conversation became very excited, and they thought his description answered that given in the daily papers of "Jack the Ripper," he was brought to this station by the PC and then stated that his name was Arthur Henry Mason 12 Portland Road, Spring Grove, Kingston, and that he was a compositor in the employ of Kelly and Co. Kingston. Enquiry was made and the man's statements found to be correct, and he was at once let go.

Description. Age 32. Height 5 ft 9 in; complexion fresh, thin face, hair whiskers and moustache, chin.

There are further reports on a suspect named "Dick Austen" forwarded from the police at Rotherham, and dated 5 October 1888:

Sir,

I have the honour to inform you that I have just had a visit from a man named James Oliver, residing at 3 Westfield View, Rotherham, a discharged soldier of the 5th Lancers, who is firmly persuaded in his own mind that he knows the perpetrator of the Whitechapel murders. He was perfectly sober and made his statement clearly and circumspectly and is of such a nature that I consider it should be laid before you without delay.

He states that there was a man named "Dick Austen" who served with him in R. Troop in the 5th Lancers, who previous to joining the Army had been a sailor, he would now be about 40 years of age – 5–8 in height, an extremely powerful and active man, but by no means heavy or stout. Hair and eyes light. Had, in service, a very long fair moustache, may have grown heavy whiskers and beard. His face was fresh, hard and healthy looking. He had a small piece bitten off the end of his nose. Although not mad, he was not right in his mind, "he was too sharp to be right." He used to be very temperate, but sometimes used to get out of bed in the night and walk about the barrack room. He never would say where he came from and often said he had no friends.

He used to sometimes brag of what he had done previously to enlisting in the way of violence but more often of what he could do, "as though qualified to do anything."

While in the Regiment he was never known to go with women and when his comrades used to talk about them in the barrack room he used to grind his teeth – he was in fact a perfect woman hater. He used to say if he had his will he would kill every whore and cut her inside out, that when he left the Regiment there would be nothing before him but the gallows.

He had gone through great hardships and rough times in various parts of the world, having been a sailor in sailing ships, he was a very sharp and witty man, and a capital scholar. Oliver believes he could recapture his handwriting. He was most plausible. His hands were long and thin.

He had 12 months for breaking into the Orderly Room and tearing up his defaulters sheets.

He is believed to have drawn his deferred pay (about 24£) and used to say he would make London his home.

He is a man who is most abstemious and will live on dry bread. He used many a day to save his money and live on what was knocking about in the Barrack Room.

Probably he would always be respectably dressed but more often the description of a sailor than a soldier –

Oliver's idea is that he would probably be working at Docks or on board ship by day-possibly, if the murderer, that he may take short voyages on some vessel and commit the murders shortly before leaving – The dates of the murders tally with this theory.

"He always had revenge against women brooding in his mind."

I have cautioned the man Oliver to say nothing about this, and he tells me that he has not as yet told anyone his suspicions excepting his own wife.

I have also promised him that unless his suspicions prove true, or of material help that his statement to me will be considered in confidence.

I have the honour to be
Sir
Your obedient Servant
L.R. Burnett Captain
C.C.

This is followed by a report from Inspector Abberline, dated 16 October 1888:

METROPOLITAN POLICE
Criminal Investigation Department
16th day of October 1888

Referring to annexed correspondence from the Chief Constable Rotherham, I beg to report that I have caused an insertion in the Informations asking if anything was known in Divisions respecting Austin giving his description and other particulars vide 25 Infn 12th inst but up to the present time with no result.

Perhaps it would be well to ask the Chief Constable of Rotherham, to cause James Oliver to be seen again and requested to furnish the date of Austin's discharge from the 5th Lancers, giving the name of the Station discharged from, and any other information.

F.G. Abberline
Inspector
T Arnold Supt.

This is followed by a reply from the Chief Constable of Rotherham, dated 19 October 1888:

[Seal of Rotherham Borough Police]   Chief Constable's Office
Rotherham
October 19 1888

52983/

[Stamped: – Received 20 OCT 88] To the Assistant Commissioner of Police

Criminal Investigation Department

Sir,

I have the honour to acknowledge the receipt of your letter of yesterday's date, relative to mine of 5th instant, and to inform you in reply that I have seen James Oliver this morning, he is unable to state the date or place of

Austin's discharge — but as stated in my former letter he is positive that Austin intended to reside in London. Application to the 5th Lancers at Aldershot would produce the date and place of discharge, and should he be entitled to draw any future deferred pay or Army Reserve pay, his whereabouts could by that means be ascertained — Oliver says several photographic groups of the Troop were taken, he has no copy, but could, if a copy was obtainable, pick out Austin — I should like a copy of some or any of the alleged letters from the murderer, as Oliver, as stated before, believes he could identify Austin's handwriting.

I have the honour to be
Sir
Your obedient Servant
L.R. Burnett Captain
C.C.

[*Pencil note*: — Make copy of letters for C.C.]

This is followed by another letter from the Chief Constable of Rotherham, dated 24 October 1888:

[Seal of the Rotherham Borough Police]   Chief Constable's Office
Rotherham
October 24 1888

52983/601
Sir,

In reply to your letter of yesterday's date enclosing Metropolitan Police Notice I have the honour to inform you that I have shown the facsimile handwriting to the man Oliver, who says that it is extremely like that of Austin, especially that of the letter (written with steel pen) that of the post card (written with quill) he does not think so like — although of course it is easy to see they are written by the same person — Austin's signature could of course be obtained from the Troop Pay Sheet of the 5th Lancers even if a large example of it could not be got from the same source.

I have the honour to be
Sir

The Assistant Commissioner   Your obedient Servant
Criminal Investigation Depart.   L.R. Burnett Captain
C.C.

Nothing more is included to indicate that any further efforts were made to trace "Austin", although the BBC researchers reported that it did seem that Abberline and Superintendent Oswald tried to find him, albeit without success.

There is a report, dated 14 January 1889, concerning another suspect:

METROPOLITAN POLICE

Criminal Investigation Department

Scotland Yard

14th day of January 1889

I beg to report that Mr. Richard Wingate, baker, 10 Church Street, Edgware Road, called and stated that about 5 weeks since he took into partnership with a man whom he now suspects of being concerned in the Whitechapel Murders. His suspicion seems to have been aroused in consequence of the man becoming suddenly reticent during a conversation about the murders and this morning a letter was received from him by a woman with whom he has been living, in which the writer expressed a fear that he would be caught today. He has also asked to sell his interest in the business to enable him to go to America.

Description, Pierce John Robinson, c/o Miss Peters, High Street, Portslade, near Brighton, age 34, height 5 ft 4 in. complexion rather dark, full beard (short) and moustache dark, thick set, dress midshipman's hat anchor on front, light jacket and vest, black trousers.

Mr. Wingate has Robinson's photo. Which he will shew to the Police but he desires that the officer making the inquiries should make an appointment with him and not call at his house.

C. Richards P.S.

[*Illegible signature*]

Superintendent

Superintendent Waghorn, Scotland Yard, went to Portslade to make enquiries. He reported that Robinson "is now a religious fanatic, claims to have had medical training and also uses the name Dr Clarke." The enquiry was taken over by Superintendent Arnold and Sergeant Thick and they found that Robinson had lived in Mile End Road. He had been convicted of bigamy for which he received four months' penal servitude. He left Mile End Road on 1 November 1888. They checked with his bigamous wife, Adelina Bird, who knew little of him but found him "inoffensive". On 9 November Robinson was at Portslade sleeping with his girlfriend, and Arnold and Thick were satisfied that he had nothing to do with the murders.

There is a report dated 18 January 1889, concerning a suspect reported by E.K. Larkins, of HM Customs:

METROPOLITAN POLICE
A Division
18th January, 1889

Ref to papers
206 information
17–1–89
Whitechapel
Murder

Persons detained in connection with
<u>Whitechapel murder at King Street Station</u>

At 12 noon 13th Novr 1887 Antoni Pricha of 11 Back Hill, Hatton Garden EC was pointed out to PC 61A Thomas Maybank in Whitehall by Edward Knight Larkins, clerk in H.M. Customs of 53 Pepys Road, New Cross who he stated that he thought answered the description of a man circulated in a newspaper as the Whitechapel murderer.

He then brought him to the station where "Precha" stated he was employed at the Royal Academy Piccadilly, as an Artist Model & known to Mr Osborn, an attendant at above. He was at his address from 6pm 8th till 8am 9th when he left for his employment. Enquiries were made by PC Hawkins C.I. Dept. A This statement found to be correct.

(sd) G. Rutt Insp
[*illegible* Supt]

[*There are marginal notes* – "<u>No des</u> Description: Age 30 height 5 feet 6½ in complexion & hair very dark long and wavy, long dark moustache. Dress, long dark brown overcoat (trimmed <u>astrachan</u>) trousers & vest in Albaman"]

This is followed by a further report dated 18 January 1889:

METROPOLITAN POLICE
A Division
18th January 1889

Ref to papers
206 information
17–1–89
Whitechapel
Murder

Persons detained in connection with
Whitechapel murder at King Street
<u>Station 9.12.88</u>

At 10.40 pm 8th inst [*insert* – "9th Decr"] Edwin Burrows of Victoria Chambers (Common Lodging House) Strutton Ground Westminster was

brought to the station by Pcs C.I.D. Bradshaw H.Division & Godley C.I.D. J Divn to be detained during enquiry at Sutton. Burrows, stating that his brother, Freeman Burrows lived there & allowed him £1 weekly. A telegram was sent to Sutton. Reply received stating that he had an allowance. The man was therefore allowed to go, the enquiry appearing satisfactory.

I might say that the man has been known to myself & a number of men of this division, as a frequenter of St. James's Park, & Mall, sleeping on seats for the past 12 months & evidently doing the best he can to subsist upon the pound per week allowed by his brother & the statement seems quite correct.

(sd) G. Rutt Insp
[*illeg.*] Supt.

[*There are marginal notes* – "No des: Description: Age 45 height 5 feet 5 in Complexion, hair, whiskers, beard & moustache dark. Dress light brown tweed jacket suit, sailor peak cap laceboots."]

The next report is of a similar nature, dated 18 January 1889:

METROPOLITAN POLICE
A Division
Rochester Row
18.1.1889

Ref to
206 Infr 17.1.89
Whitechapel
Murder

Re persons detained in connection with the Whitechapel Murders, – 206 Infr 17th inst.

I beg to report that only one case has occurred in this sub-division since 31st October 1888, and I respectfully submit the particulars of that case as entered in O. Book on 21st November 1888.

At about 12.40 pm 21st inst. Mrs Fanny Drake (Conservative Club) 15 Clerkenwell Green, came to Rochester Row Station and stated she had put the police on the Whitechapel murderer and had now called to know the result. She was walking over Westminster Bridge when a man answering the description of the murderer met her, and as he passed, gave such a grin, as she should always remember. She at once retraced her steps and followed him until opposite Westminster Abbey, when meeting a Mounted Inspector she told him of her suspicion, pointed out the man, and came to this station, the Inspector following and watching the man. About 5 minutes afterwards Inspr Walsh came in and stated that the gentleman referred to had been followed by him to the Army and Navy Stores, Victoria Street, Westminster, and had now come to the station to see the lady. I interviewed him in the charge room, when he at once produced a number of letters and business cards proving himself beyond doubt to be Mr Douglas Cow of Cow & Co., India-Rubber Merchants, 70 Cheapside, and 8 Kempshoot Road, Streatham Common. This information I imparted to the lady when she at once apologised to Mr Cow for having caused him inconvenience, and both parties then left the Station.

(sd) D.Fairey Inspr

J. Webber S.D. Inspr

[*illeg*] Supt

[*There are marginal notes:* — "<u>No des</u>. Age about 35 height 5 ft 7 or 8 in complexion and hair fair, slight moustache, shaved on chin, Dress light overcoat, dark trousers, high hat, dark gloves, carried an umbrella very respectable appearance"]

The next report, dated 18 January 1889, concerns another suspect:

METROPOLITAN POLICE

A Division

18th January 1889

I beg to report that at 9.40 pm 22nd November, 1888 James Connell of 408 New Cross Road, Draper & Clothier Age 36, Height 5 ft 9 in, complexion fresh long dark brown moustache, Dress brown check suit, ulster with cape red socks Oxford shoes, soft felt hat, an Irishman was brought to this (Hyde Park) Station by PC271A Fountain under the following circumstances. Martha Spencer of 30 Sherbourne Street Blandford Square, Married stated that he spoke to her near the Marble Arch, they walked together in the Park and he began to talk about "Jack the Ripper" and Lunatic Asylums and said that no doubt, when he was caught, he would turn out to be a lunatic, in consequence of this conversation she became alarmed and spoke to the PC who accompanied them to the Station. A telegram was then sent to Greenwich Station for enquiry as to the correctness of his address and his respectability, a satisfactory reply having been received he was then allowed to go, as nothing further suspicious transpired.

(*signed*) J. Bird Insp

[*illeg.*] Supt.

Another report, dated 19 January 1889, referring to an incident on 17 November 1888, follows:

METROPOLITAN POLICE

B Division

19th January 1889

Re No 206 Ins 17th Inst

I beg to report that at 12 mght 17th November last, Oliver Mathews of No 14 Wharton Street, Kings Cross came to this (Walton Street) Station accompanied by PC 7BR Cooper. The PC stated his attention was called to Mathews by Richard Watson, 21 Old Square, Lincoln's Inn (Barrister) who was of opinion that he, Mathews, answered the description of the White-chapel murderer. It appears that both parties were in the "Trevor" Music Hall, Knightsbridge and were sitting next to each other. Mathews had in his possession a small black bag and this aroused the suspicion of Watson who acquainted the PC. Mathews at once volunteered to come to the Station where the bag was examined and found to contain clean linen. A telegram was sent to the address given by Mathews which proved correct, he having resided there for over 12 months. His appearance did not answer that of the Whitechapel Murderer in any way with the exception of the black bag and Mathews was allowed to go away.

C.W. Sheppard

Supt

The last copy report extant in this series is dated 19 January 1889 and reads as follows:

METROPOLITAN POLICE

G Division

19 January 1889

I beg to report that on 25th Novr last Alfred Parent of 31 Rue Notre Dame, De Nazareth and 58 Rue Volka, Paris, and Bacons Hotel, Finsbury Square, age 54, height 5 feet 6 in, hair white, whiskers and moustache very grey, dress dark overcoat, do under and vest, black trousers, high hat, patent boots, was given into custody by Annie Cook, a Prostitute, who stated that Parent had offered her a sovereign to go with him for an immoral purpose, or 5 sovereigns to sleep with him for the night, and as the amount offered was rather a large one the girl thought it was done for the purpose of getting her into a house to murder her, and gave him into custody.

On 28th December Joseph Denny of 64 Myddelton Square, Clerkenwell, age 20, height 5 feet 6 in, complexion fair, hair very curly, slight moustache, no whiskers, dress long dark overcoat with black astracan collar and cuffs, dark suit under, low shoes, brown soft felt hat, came to Old Street Station accompanied by PC 177A Wraight and John Robert Hardy and Thomas

Hardy of 480 Kings Road, Chelsea, the two latter persons stated that they saw Denny accost two women in Houndsditch and thinking it suspicious, they followed him to Finsbury Pavement where they saw him accost another woman and having in mind the recent Whitechapel murders they called the PC who brought Denny to the station.

Enquiries were made respecting Denny which proved satisfactory and he was allowed to go.

At midnight 12th Novr last John Avery, a ticket writer of Southwick House, Vicarage Road, Willesden, age 43, height 5 feet 9 in, complexion hair and whiskers dark, dressed in dark clothes, high hat, respectable appearance, was brought in custody to Kings Cross Road Station by PC 208A Seymour who had been informed by Private John Carvill E Troop 11th Hussars, and Israel Hines of 5 [*illegible*] Court, Bishopsgate that Avery had informed them that he committed the recent murders at Whitechapel and that he wanted to kill some more but had lost his bag. Enquiries were made respecting his statement which proved satisfactory but as Avery was drunk he was charged with that offence and behaving in a disorderly manner, and sentenced to 14 days HL.

At 10.50 am 13th Novr last John Murphy, no fixed abode, a seaman and a native of Massachusetts, United States, age 24, height 5 feet 8 in; complexion and moustache fair, dress brown tweed jacket and trousers, blue blouse, cloth cap, with peak, lace boots, was brought to Kings Cross Rd Station by P.S. Nash CIDA from the Holborn Union Casual ward for enquiries to be made respecting a knife found in his possession on being admitted to the Casual ward, which was supposed to be connected with the Whitechapel Murders.

He was detained and a telegram sent to Inspector Abberline at H Division for enquiries to be made, which proved satisfactory, and he was released.

At 11 pm 25th Novr last PC 310A King brought to Kings Cross Road Station W. Van Burst, a Dutchman, no occupation, residing at Bacons Hotel, Fitzroy Square, age 50, height 5 feet 11 in, dark hair and moustache, dress light overcoat and trousers, lace boots, black felt flat top hat, respectable appearance accompanied by Geo Foster, 95 Bemerton Street, John Bowdell and Henry Crowley of 61 Gifford Street, and William French of No. 2a Beaconsfield Buildings Bingfield Street Caledonian Road.

Foster whose statement was corroborated by Bowdell, Crowley, and French, stated that he saw Burst opposite the Kings Cross Metropolitan Railway Station accost a female who walked away from him, after which he accosted two other females who also walked away from him. About an hour after Burst again accosted females after which he took a 2nd class ticket from Kings Cross to Farringdon Street followed by Foster and the others, and on alighting at Farringdon St. Burst entered an omnibus and Foster then thought that he was in some way connected with the Whitchapel murders and called the attention of PC King to him. The PC requested Burst to alight which he did and accompanied the PC and the others to the station.

Enquiries were made which proved satisfactory and he was allowed to go.

H Jones

Superintendent

Paul Bonner of the BBC noted:

Many men, at least 100 in the file, were taken to police stations just for carrying black bags, having foreign accents, accosting women, or talking about the "Ripper" in pubs, but then released on being able to prove their identity.

At least two suspects, one Dutch, one American, gave their addresses as Bacon's Hotel, Fitzroy Square, "which is odd".

There was no mention, in this file or anywhere else, either in the Scotland Yard files or the Home Office ones, to Macnaghten's candidates Druitt, Kosminski or Ostrog.

CHAPTER 39

December 1888 – Another Contemporary Suspect

A Dr Roslyn D'O. Stephenson [real name: Robert Donston Stephenson] wrote a letter[1] about the murders to the City Police in October 1888:

> Reply sent 17.10.88.
> The London Hospital, E.
> 16 Oct.88

Sir,

Having read Sir Charles Warren's Circular in yesterday's papers that "It is not known that there is any dialect or language in which the word Jews is spelt JUWES," I beg to inform you that the word written by the murderer <u>does</u> exist in a European language, though it was not JUWES.

Try it in script – thus,

Th<u>e</u> ["Jeu" – *deleted*] <u>J</u>uwes.&c

now place a dot over the third upstroke (which dot was naturally overlooked by lantern light) and we get, plainly,

Th<u>e</u> <u>J</u>uives

which, I need not tell you, is the French word for Jews.

The murderer unconsciously reverted, for a moment, to his native language.

Pardon my presuming to suggest that there are three points indubitably shown (& another, <u>probably</u>) by the inscription.

1. The man was a Frenchman.

2. He has resided a long time in England to write so correctly; Frenchmen being, notoriously, the worst linguists in the world.

3. He has frequented the East End for years, to have acquired, as in the sentence written, a purely East End idiom.

4. It is probable (not certain) that he is a notorious Jew-hater: though he <u>may</u> only have written it to throw a false scent.

May I request an acknowledgement that this letter has safely reached you, & that it be preserved until I am well enough to do myself the honour to ["see" – *deleted*] call upon you personally.

> I amSir
> Yr.obedt.Servant
> <u>RoslynD'O.Stephenson</u>

Please address
>   Major Stephenson
>   50, Currie Wards,
>   The London Hospital
>   E.

<u>P.S.</u> I can tell you, from a French book, a use made of the o<u>rga</u>n in question-
''d'une femme <u>prostituee</u>,'' which has not yet been suggested, if you think it
worth while. R.D'O.S

Fortunately further information on the mysterious Dr Stephenson was
copied before it, too, went missing. The first document was a letter by
Stephenson communicating his suspicions about the identity of the killer
to the police:

> Sir <u>Re – The Whitechapel Murders</u>
> 26 – Dec – 88.

I beg to draw your attention to the attitude of Dr. Morgan Davies of – Street
Houndsditch, E. with respect to these murders. But, my suspicions attach to
him principally in connexion with the last one – committed in-doors.

Three weeks ago, I was a patient in the London Hospital, in a private ward
(Davis) with a Dr. Evans, suffering from typhoid who used to be visited
almost nightly by Dr. Davies, when the murders were our usual subject of
conversation.

Dr. Davies always insisted on the fact that the murderer was a man of
sexual powers almost effete, which could only be brought into action by some
strong stimulus – such as sodomy. He was very positive on this point, that the
murderer performed on the women from behind – in fact, <u>per ano.</u>

At that time he could have had no information, any more than myself,
about the fact that the post mortem examination revealed that semen was
found up the woman's rectum, mixed with her faeces.

Many things, which would seem trivial in writing, seemed to me to
connect him with the affair – for instance – He is himself a woman-hater.
although a man of powerful frame, &, (according to the lines on his sallow
face) of strong sexual passions.

He is <u>supposed</u>, however, by his intimates, never to touch a woman.

One night, when five medicos were present, quietly discussing the subject,
& combatting his argument that the murderer did not do these things to
obtain specimens of uteri (wombs) but that – in his case – it was the lust of

murder developed from sexual lust – a thing not unknown to medicos, he acted – (in a way which <u>fairly</u> <u>terrified</u> those five doctors) the whole scene. He took a knife, "buggered" an imaginary woman, cut her throat from behind; then, when she was apparently laid prostrate, ripped & slashed her in all directions in a perfect state of frenzy.

<u>Previously</u> to this performance I had said, "['but' – *deleted*] after a man had done a thing like this, re-action would take place, & he would collapse, & be taken at once by the police, or would attract the attention of the bystanders by his exhausted condition ['?' – *deleted*]" Dr. D. said "NO! he would recover himself when the fit was over & be as calm as a lamb. I will show you!" Then he began his performance. At the end of it he stopped, buttoned up his coat, put on his hat, & walked down the room with the most perfect calmness. Certainly, his face was as pale as death, but that was all.

It was only a few days ago, ["when" – *deleted*] after I was <u>positively</u> informed by the Editor of the "Pall Mall Gazette" that the murdered woman <u>last</u> operated on had been sodomized, that I thought – "How did <u>he</u> know? His acting was the most vivid I ever saw. Henry Irving was a fool to it." Another point. He argued that the murderer did not want specimens of uteri, but grasped them, & slashed them off in his madness as being <u>the only hard</u> substances which met his grasp when his hands were madly plunging into the abdomen of his victim.

I may say that Dr. Davies was for some time House Physician at the London Hospital, Whitechapel, that he has lately taken this house in Castle St. Houndsditch; that he has lived in the locality of the murders for some years; & that he professes his intention of going to Australia shortly should he not quickly make a success in his new house.

<u>Roslyn D'O:Stephenson</u>

<u>P.S.</u> I have mentioned this matter to a pseudo-detective named George Marsh of 24, Pratt St., Camden Town N.W. with whom I have made an agreement, (enclosed herewith, to share any reward which he may derive from my information [")" – deleted].

P.P.S.   <u>R.D'O.S</u>

I can be found at any time through Mr. Iles of the "Prince Albert", St. Martin['s] Lane – in a few minutes. I live close to; but do not desire to give my address. <u>RD'S</u>

The agreement was appended:

24. Dec. 88.

I hereby agree to pay to Dr. R.D'O.Stephenson (also known as "Sudden

Death'') one half of any or all rewards or monies received by me on a/c of the conviction of Dr. Davies for wilful murder.

Roslyn D'O.Stephenson M.D.

29 Castle St.W.C.

St.Martin's Lane.

Also contained in this file, but now missing, was a statement taken by Inspector Thomas Roots of Scotland Yard from the "pseudo-detective" George Marsh, referred to by Stephenson:

Mr. George Marsh, ironmongery salesman (now, and for two months out of employment) 24, Pratt St, Camden Town, came here at 7 p.m. [*24 Dec. 1888*] and made the following statement:

"About a month ago at the Prince Albert P.H., Upper St Martin's Lane, I met a man named Stephenson and casually discussed the murders in Whitechapel with him. From that time to the present I have met him there two or three times a week and we have on each occasion discussed the murders in a confidential manner. He has tried to tell me how I could capture the man if I went his way to work. I simply told him I should go my own way about it and sooner or later I'd have him. I told him I was an amateur detective and that I had been working for weeks looking for the culprit. He explained to me how the murders were committed. he said they were committed by a woman hater after the forthcoming manner:-

"The murderer would induce a woman to go up a back street or room and to excite his passion would "bugger" her and cut her throat at the same time with his right hand, holding on by the left.

"He illustrated the action. From his manner I am of opinion he is the murderer in the first six cases, if not the last one.

"Today Stephenson told me that Dr. Davies of Houndsditch (I don't know the address although I have been there and could point it out) was the murderer and he wished me to see him. He drew up an agreement to share the reward on the conviction of Dr. Davies. I know that agreement is valueless but it secured his handwriting. I made him under the influence of drink thinking that I should get some further statement but in this I failed as he left me to see Dr. Davies and also to go to Mr. Stead of the Pall Mall Gazette with an article for which he expected £2. He wrote the article in the Pall Mall Gazette in relation to the writing on the wall about Jews. He had £4 for that. I have seen letters from Mr. Stead in his possession about it; also a letter from Mr. Stead refusing to allow him money to find out the Whitechapel Murderer.

"Stephenson has shown me a discharge as a patient from the London

Hospital. The name Stephenson is obliterated and that of Davies is marked in red ink. I do not know the date.

"Stephenson is now at the common lodging house No. 29 Castle St., St. Martin's Lane, W.C. and has been there three weeks. His description is:- Age 48, height 5 ft 10 in, full face, sallow complexion, moustache heavy – mouse coloured – waxed and turned up, hair brown turning grey, eyes sunken. When looking at a stranger generally has an eyeglass. Dress, grey suit and light brown felt hat-all well worn; military appearance: says he has been in 42 battles: well educated.

"The agreement he gave me I will leave with you and will render any assistance the Police may require. [*Marginal note by Inspector Roots that the agreement* is attached *but it was missing*].

"Stephenson is not a drunkard: he is what I call a regular soaker – can drink from 8 o'clock in the morning until closing time but keep a clear head."

There was also a report in the file by Inspector Roots, dated 26 December 1888, stating:

Whitechapel Murders, Marsh, Davies & Stephenson

With reference to the statement of Mr. George Marsh, of 24th inst., regarding the probable association of Dr. Davies and Stephenson with the murders in Whitechapel.

I beg to report that Dr. Stephenson came here this evening and wrote the attached statement of his suspicions of Dr. Morgan Davies, Castle St., Houndsditch; and also left with me his agreement with Marsh as to the reward. I attach it.

When Marsh came here on 24th I was under the impression that Stephenson was a man I had known 20 years. I now find that impression was correct. He is a travelled man of education and ability, a doctor of medicine upon diplomas of Paris & New York: a major from the Italian Army – he fought under Garibaldi: and a newspaper writer. He says that he wrote the article about Jews in the Pall Mall Gazette, that he occasionally writes for that paper, and that he offered his services to Mr. Stead to track the murderer. He showed me a letter from Mr. Stead, dated Nov. 30 1888, about this and said that the result was the proprietor declined to engage upon it. He has led a Bohemian life, drinks very heavily, and always carries drugs to sober him and stave off delirium tremens.

He was an applicant for the Orphanage Secretaryship at the last election.

The statements were forwarded to Chief Inspector Swanson.

A report in the *Pall Mall Gazette* of 31 December 1888 may well refer to Stephenson:

"UNDER OBSERVATION."

According to the Sunday Times, a gentleman who has for some time been engaged in philanthropic work in the East-end recently received a letter, the handwriting of which had previously attracted the attention of the Post-office authorities on account of its similarity to that of the writer of the letters signed "Jack the Ripper." The police made inquiries, and ascertained that the writer was known to his correspondent as a person intimately acquainted with East-end life, and that he was then a patient in a metropolitan hospital. It is stated that on an inquiry at the hospital it was discovered that the person sought had left without the consent or knowledge of the hospital authorities, but that he has been subsequently seen, and is now under observation. The police are of opinion that the last five murders were a series, and that the first two were independently perpetrated.

CHAPTER 40

The Littlechild Suspect

Until the discovery of the Littlechild letter by Stewart Evans in February 1993, the three main near-contemporary suspects were those named by Macnaghten in his report of February 1894, and Stephenson. The Littlechild letter revealed a further contemporary suspect who was amongst the police suspects in 1888. Purchased from antiquarian book-dealer Eric Barton of Richmond, the letter had been written by ex-Chief Inspector John George Littlechild (head of Special Branch at Scotland Yard 1883–93) to Macnaghten's friend, the journalist and author George R Sims. It was dated 23 September 1913, and was typed and three pages long. In 1913, by then a successful private enquiry agent, Littlechild wrote:

> 8,   The Chase,
> Clapham Common,S.W.
> 23rd September 1913.

Dear Sir.,

I was pleased to receive your letter which I shall put away in "good company" to read again, perhaps some day when old age overtakes me and when to revive memories of the past may be a solace.

Knowing the great interest you take in all matters crininal [*sic*], and abnormal, I am just going to inflict one more letter on you on the "Ripper" subject. Letters as a rule are only a nuisance when they call for a reply but this does not need one. I will try and be brief.

I never heard of a Dr. D. in connection with the Whitechapel murders but amongst the suspects, and to my mind a very likely one, was a Dr. T. (which sounds much like D.) He was an American quack named Tumblety and was at one time a frequent visitor to London and on these occasions constantly brought under the notice of police, there being a large dossier concerning him at Scotland Yard. Although a "Sycopathia [*sic*] Sexualis" subject he was not known as a "Sadist" (which the murderer unquestionably was) but his feelings towards women were remarkable and bitter in the extreme, a fact on record. Tumblety was arrested at the time of the murders in connection with unnatural offences and charged at Marlborough Street, remanded on bail, jumped his bail, and got away to Boulogne. He shortly left Boulogne and was never heard of afterwards. It was believed he committed suicide but certain it is that from this time the "Ripper" murders came to an end.

With regard to the term "Jack the Ripper" it was generally believed at the Yard that Tom Bullen [*sic* – Bulling] of the Central News was the originator but it is probable Moore, who was his chief, was the inventor. It was a smart piece of journalistic work. No journalist of my time got such privileges from Scotland Yard as Bullen. Mr James Munro [*sic* – Monro] when Assistant Commissioner, and afterwards Commissioner, relied on his integrity. Poor Bullen occasionally took too much to drink, and I fail to see how he could help it knocking about so many hours and seeking favours from so many people to procure copy. One night when Bullen "had taken a few too many" he got early information of the death of Prince Bismarck and instead of going to the office to report it sent a laconic telegram "Bloody Bismarck is dead" On this I believe Mr Charles Moore fired him out.

It is very strange how those given to "Contrary sexual instinct and degenerates" are given to cruelty, even Wilde used to like to be punched about. It may interest you if I give you an example of this cruelty in the case of the man Harry Thaw and this is authentic as I have the boys statement. Thaw was staying at the Carlton Hotel and one day laid out a lot of sovereigns on his dressing table, then rang for a call boy on pretence of sending out a telegram. He made some excuse and went out of the room and left the boy there and watched through the chink of the door. The unfortunate boy was tempted and took a sovereign from the pile and Thaw returning to the room charged him with stealing. The boy confessed when Thaw asked him whether he should send for the police or whether he should punish him himself. The boy scared to death consented to take his punishment from Thaw who then made him undress, strapped him to the foot of the bedstead, and thrashed him with a cane drawing blood. He then made the boy get into a bath in which he placed a quantity of salt. It seems incredible that such a thing could take place in any hotel but it is a fact. This was in 1906.

Now pardon me – It is finished. – Except that I knew Major Griffiths for many years. He probably got his information from Anderson who only "<u>thought he knew</u>" J.G. Littlechild

  George R. Sims Esq.,
    12, Clarence Terrace,
      Regents Park.N.W.

There are contemporary references to Tumblety in the British press. The *Monmouthshire Merlin and South Wales Advertiser*, in a piece on the Whitechapel Murders dated Friday, 7 December 1888 reported:

It is reported by cable from Europe that a certain person whose name is known, has sailed from Havre for New York, who is famous for his hatred of women, and who has repeatedly made threats against females of dissolute character.

Then, on 31 December 1888, the *Pall Mall Gazette* carried the following on page 10:

THE SEARCH FOR THE WHITECHAPEL MURDERER.
DETECTIVES ON THE OUTLOOK IN NEW YORK.

Inspector Andrews, of Scotland yard has arrived in New York from Montreal. It is generally believed that he has received orders from England to commence his search in this city for the Whitechapel murderer. Mr. Andrews is reported to have said that there are half a dozen English detectives, two clerks, and one inspector employed in America in the same chase. Ten days ago Andrews brought thither from England Roland Gideon Israel Barnet, charged with helping to wreck the Central Bank, Toronto, and since his arrival he has received orders which will keep him in America for some time. The supposed inaction of the Whitechapel murderer for a considerable period and the fact that a man suspected of knowing a good deal about this series of crimes left England for this side of the Atlantic three weeks ago, has, says the *Telegraph* correspondent, produced the impression that Jack the Ripper is in that country.

The origins of this story lie in North America and a report carried in the *St Louis Republican* of 22 December 1888 adds further clarification of Inspector Andrews's mission:

"AFTER JACK THE RIPPER."
A Scotland Yard Detective Looking for
Him in America.

Special to The Republic.

MONTREAL, Dec. 20. – Inspector Andrews of Scotland Yard arrived here to-day from Toronto and left to-night for New York. He tried to evade newspaper men, but incautiously revealed his identity at the central office, where he had an interview with Chief of Police Hughes. He refused to answer any questions regarding his mission, but said there were 23 detectives, 2 clerks and 1 inspector employed on the Whitechapel murder cases and that the police were without a jot of evidence upon which to arrest anybody.

"How many men have you working in America?"

"Half a dozen," he replied; then hesitating, continued: "American detective agencies have offered to find the murderer on salaries and payment of expenses. But we can do that ourselves, you know.''

''Are you one of the half dozen?''

''No. Don't say anything about that. I meant detective agencies.''

''But what are you here for?''

''I had rather not say just at present.''

Ten days ago Andrews brought Roland Gideon and [sic] Israel Barnet, charged with helping wreck the Central Bank of Toronto, to this country from England, and since his arrival he has received orders from England which will keep him in America for some time. It was announced at police headquarters to-day that Andrews has a commission in connection with two other Scotland Yard men to find the murderer in America. His inaction for so long a time, and the fact that a man, suspected of knowing considerable about the murders [sic] left England for this side three weeks ago, makes the London police believe ''Jack'' has left that country for this.

Tumblety's flight from England via Boulogne and Havre was reported in the New York newspapers which reported his arrival there, on 2 December, in editions of 3 December 1888. In fact, his arrest in London had been reported as early as 18 November 1888 in the *New York World*, an extract of which read:

Another arrest was that of a man who gave the name of Dr. Kumblety, of New York. The police could not hold him on suspicion of having been guilty of the Whitechapel crimes, but have succeeded in getting him held for trial at the Central Criminal Court under the special law passed soon after the ''Modern Babylon'' exposures. The police say that Kumblety is the man's right name, as is proved by letters in his possession from New York, and that he has been in the habit of crossing the ocean twice a year for several years.

The following day the same newspaper enlarged on its information on Tumblety:

THE ''ECCENTRIC'' DR. TWOMBLETY.
The American Suspected of the Whitechapel
Crimes Well Known Here.

A special London despatch to THE WORLD yesterday morning announced the arrest of a man in connection with the Whitechapel crimes, who gave his name as Dr. Kumblety of New York. He could not be held on suspicion, but the police succeeded in getting him held under the ''Modern Babylon'' exposures.

Dr. Kumblety is well known in this city. His name, however, is Twomblety, not Kumblety.

This was followed by a summary of Tumblety's known history in America.

A further report was carried in the *Quebec Daily Mercury* of 22 November 1888:

The Whitechapel Murders.

Dr. Tumblety, of New York, a notorious quack, who made himself very conspicuous in Quebec and Montreal nearly 30 years ago, and who, during his peregrinations in the Maritime Provinces, caused the death by malpractice of a locomotive engineer, for which he was indicted for manslaughter, has been arrested in London on suspicion of being connected with the Whitechapel murders. The "doctor" is a very bad quack and eccentric dresser, but is not the man for performing such terrible work as that done by the Whitechapel monster.

The interest being shown in Tumblety by the Metropolitan Police was indicated in a report that appeared in the *San Francisco Chronicle* of 23 November 1888:

DR. TUMBLETY.
THE LONDON SUSPECT'S CA-
REER IN THIS CITY.
He Disappeared From Here and
Left a Large Sum of Money in
The Hibernia Bank.

The general and world-wide interest in the Whitechapel murders is probably exhibited in no greater or less degree in this city that in other places remote from the scene of the crimes, but the fact that Dr. Tumblety, the only man that the London police seem able to connect with the dreadful affairs, formerly lived here and that certain information concerning him in the possession of the police authorities of this city may be used in clearing up his connection with the matter, may cause the public interest to be largely increased.

When the news of Tumblety's arrest reached this city, Chief of Police Crowley recollected that that the suspect man formerly lived here, and he took the necessary steps to learn all about his career in this city. He found that Tumblety arrived here in the early part of 1870 and took rooms at the Occidental Hotel. He opened an office at 20 Montgomery street, but remained in the city only a few months, leaving in September of the same year. While here he opened an account with the Hibernia Bank and left a considerable amount to his credit in that institution when he went away. The account has never been closed and the bank still has the money in its vaults. After he left Tumblety had some correspondence with the bank officials.

As soon as Chief Crowley learned these facts he cabled to the London police that specimens of Tumblety's handwriting could be secured if they wanted them. Yesterday morning the following cablegram was received:

LONDON (England), Thursday, November 22 — *P. Crowley, Chief of Police, San Francisco, Cal.:* Thanks. Send handwriting and all details you can of Tumblety.

ANDERSON, Scotland Yard.

The chief will have the correspondence photographed and will send it at once to London, together with all the information he has been able to gather concerning Tumblety.

Tumblety's flight from London went unremarked in the London papers, but not so in the American press. The *New York World* of Sunday, 2 December 1888, printed three columns, which began:

TUMBLETY IS MISSING
The American Charlatan Suspected of
The Whitechapel Murders Skips
From London.
HE WAS LAST SEEN AT HAVRE
Is He On His Way Home Over the
Ocean to New York?

HE HAD A BITTER HATRED OF WOMEN

In This City He Was Sued by a Young Man
And His True Character Was Revealed-
His Practises In Washington, Where He
Pretended to Be a Brigade Surgeon-
His Dinners to Officers and His Denun-
Ciations of Women — He Was Known
When Fifteen Years Old as a Peddler
Of Immoral Literature on Canal Boats.

Copyright 1888, by The Press Publishing Company (New York World).
SPECIAL CABLE DESPATCH TO THE WORLD.

LONDON, Dec. 1. — The last seen of Dr. Tumblety was at Havre, and it is taken for granted that he has sailed for New York. It will be remembered that the doctor, who is known in this country for his eccentricities, was arrested some time ago in London on suspicion of being concerned in the perpetration of the Whitechapel murders. The police, being unable to procure the necessary evidence against him in connection therewith, decided to hold him for trial for another offense against a statute which was passed shortly after the publication in the Pall Mall Gazette of "The Maiden Tribute," and as a direct consequence thereof Dr. Tumblety was committed for trial and liberated on bail, two gentlemen coming forward to act as bondsmen in the amount of $1,500. On being hunted up by the police to-day, they asserted that they had only known the doctor for a few days previous to his arrest.

TUMBLETY'S CAREER.

The Grounds for Suspecting Him of Com-
Mitting the Crimes.

A London detective wishing to get information about the man now under arrest for complicity in some way with the Whitechapel crimes has only to go to any large city the world over, describe the curious garb and manners of Francis Tumblety, M.D., and he can gather facts and surmises to almost any extent . . .

Tumblety's arrival in the USA was duly reported: the following appeared in the *Evening Star Sayings* for Monday, 3 December 1888:

WATCH HIM.

The American Suspected of Whitechapel
Butcheries Arrives at New York.

By Telegraph to The Star-Sayings.

NEW YORK, December 3. – Dr. Francis Tumblety, who was suspected of being concerned with the Whitechapel murders in London, arrived in this city on the French steamer "Bretagne" yesterday. A reporter called upon Inspector Byrnes this morning and asked if there was anything for which Tumblety could be arrested in this country. The Inspector replied that although Tumblety was a fugitive from justice under $1,500 bail for a nominal offense in England, he could not be arrested here. The Inspector added that in case the doctor was wanted he knew where to lay his hands on him. Two Central Office detectives were on the dock when the steamer arrived and followed Tumblety to a boarding house, the number of which will not be made public. The doctor will be kept under strict surveillance.

The *New York World* also reported on the arrival of Tumblety and the watch being kept on him:

TUMBLETY IS IN THE CITY.

A Big English Detective is Watching Him
Closely, and a Crowd of Curious People
Gaze at the House He Lives In — Inspector
Byrnes's Men Have Been On His
Track Since He Landed.

Frances Tumblety, or Twomblety, who was arrested in London for supposed complicity in the Whitechapel crimes and held under bail for other offenses, arrived in this city Sunday, and is now stopping in East Tenth Street. Two of Inspector Byrnes's men are watching him, and so is an English detective, who is making himself the laughing-stock of the whole neighborhood.

When the French steamer La Bretagne, from Havre, came up to her dock at 1.30 Sunday afternoon two keen-looking men pushed through the crowd and stood on either side of the gangplank. They glanced impatiently at the passengers until a big, fine-looking man hurried across the deck and began to descend. He had a heavy, fierce-looking mustache, waxed at the ends; his face was pale and he looked hurried and excited. He wore a dark blue ulster, with the belt buttoned. He carried under his arm two canes and an umbrella fastened together with a strap.

He hurriedly engaged a cab, gave the directions in a low voice and was driven away. The two keen-looking men jumped into another cab and followed him. The fine-looking man was the notorious Dr. Francis Twomblety, or Tumblety, and his pursuers were two of Inspector Byrnes's best men, Crowle and Hickey.

Dr. Twomblety's cab stopped at Fourth avenue and Tenth street, where the doctor got out, paid the driver and stepped briskly up the steps of No. 78 East Tenth street, the Arnold House. He pulled the bell, and, as no one came, he grew impatient and walked a little further down the street to No. 81. Here there was another delay in responding to his summons, and he became so impatient that he tried the next house, No. 79. This time there was a prompt answer to his ring and he entered. It was just 2.20 when the door closed on Dr. Twomblety and he has not been seen since.

Many people were searching for the doctor yesterday, and the bell of No. 79 was kept merrily jingling all day long. The owner of the house is Mrs. McNemara, who rents out apartments to gentlemen. She is a fat, good-natured old lady, and a firm believer in the doctor, who is an old friend. Mrs. McNemara at first said the doctor was stopping there. He had spent the night in his room, she said, and in the morning he had gone downtown to get his baggage. He would be back about 2 o'clock. The next statement was that the doctor had not been in her house for two months; that he was abroad, poor, dear gentleman, for his health; she had heard some of those awful stories about him, but, bless his kind heart, he would not hurt a chicken! Why, he never owed her a rent in his life, and once he had walked up three flights of stairs to pay her a dollar!

The revised story, to which Mrs. McNemara stuck tenaciously at last, was that she had no idea who Dr. Twomblety was. She didn't know anything about him, didn't want to know anything and could not understand why she was bothered so much.

It was just as this story was being funished to the press that a new character appeared on the scene, and it was not long before he completely absorbed the attention of everyone. He was a little man with enormous red side whiskers and a smoothly shaven chin. He was dressed in an English tweed suit and wore an enormous pair of boots with soles an inch thick. No one could be mistaken in his mission. There was an elaborate attempt at concealment and mystery which could not possibly be misunderstood. Everything about him told his business. From his little billy cock hat, alternately set jauntily on the side of his head and pulled loweringly over his eyes, down to the very bottom of his thick boots, he was the typical English detective. If he had been put on the stage just as he paraded up and down Fourth avenue and Tenth street yesterday afternoon, he would have been called a characture.

First he would assume his heavy villain appearance. Then his hat would be pulled down over his eyes and he would walk up and down in front of No. 79, staring intently into the window as he passed, to the intense dismay of Mrs. McNemara, who was peering out from behind the blinds at him with ever-increasing alarm. Then his mood changed. His hat was pushed back in a devil-may-care way and he marched by No. 79 with a swagger, whistling gayly, convinced that his disguise was complete and that no one could possibly recognize him.

His headquarters was a saloon on the corner, where he held long and mysterious conversations with the barkeeper, always ending in both of them drinking together. The barkeeper epitomized the conversations by saying: "He wanted to know about a feller named Tumblety, and I sez I didn't know nothink at all about him; and he sez he was an English detective, and then he told me all about them Whitechapel murders, and how he came over here to get the chap that did it."

When night came on the English detective became more and more enterprising. At one time he stood for fifteen minutes with his coat collar turned up and his hat pulled down, behind the lamp-post on the corner, staring fixedly at No. 79. Then he changed his base of operations to the stoop of No. 81, and looked sharply into the faces of every one who passed. He almost went into a spasm of excitement when a man went into the basement of No. 79, and when a lame servant girl limped out of No. 81 he followed her a block regarding her most suspiciously. At a late hour he was standing in front of the house directly opposite No. 79 looking over steadily and earnestly.

Everybody in the neighborhood seemed to have heard of Dr. Twomblety's arrival, and he is well known in all the stores and saloons for several blocks. One merchant who knows him very well said:

"Mrs. McNemara is a queer old lady, very religious and kind-hearted. The doctor began stopping with her years ago and he has lived there ever since when he was in New York. He used to explain his long absence at night, when he was prowling about the streets, by telling her he had to go to a monastery and pray for his dear departed wife."

Even in the saloons where he often went to drink he was spoken of with loathing and contempt.

He must have kept himself very quiet on the La Bretagne, for a number of passengers who were interviewed could not remember having seen any one answering his description. It will be remembered that he fled from London to Paris to escape being prosecuted under the new "Fall of Babylon" act.

Inspector Byrnes was asked what his object was in shadowing Twomblety.

"I simply wanted to put a tag on him," he replied, "so that we can tell where he is. Of course he cannot be arrested for there is no proof of his complicity in the Whitechapel murders, and the crime for which he was under bond in London is not extradictable."

"Do you think he is Jack the Ripper?" the Inspector was asked.

"I don't know anything about it, and therefore I don't care to be quoted. But if they think in London that they need him and he turns out to be guilty our men will probably have an idea where he can be found."

The careful watch on Dr Tumblety may not have been as good as was supposed, or perhaps the good doctor was a little too shrewd for his watchers. The *New York World* of 6 December 1888 reported:

DR. TUMBLETY HAS FLOWN.
He Gives His Watchers the Slip and Has
Probably Gone Out of Town.

It is now certain that Dr. Thomas [sic] F. Tumblety, the notorious Whitechapel suspect, who has been stopping at 79 East Tenth street since last Sunday afternoon, is no longer an inmate of the house. It is not known exactly when the doctor eluded his watchers, but a workman named Jas. Rush, living directly opposite No. 79, says that he saw a man answering the doctor's well-known description standing on the stoop of No. 79 early yesterday morning, and he noticed that he showed a great deal of nervousness, glancing over his shoulder constantly. He finally walked to Fourth avenue and took an uptown car.

A WORLD reporter last night managed to elude the vigilant Mrs. McNamara, the landlady, and visited the room formerly occupied by the doctor. No response being given to several knocks the door was opened and the room was found to be empty. The bed had not been touched and there was no evidence that the room had been entered since early morning. A half-open valise on a chair near the window and a big pair of boots of the English cavalry regulation pattern were all that remained to tell the story of Dr. Tumblety's flight.

Those who know him best think he has left New York for some quiet country town, where he expects to live until the excitement dies down.

As with all viable "Ripper" suspects there are pros and cons with Tumblety's candidacy. Research has revealed that he was arrested for the offence(s) of gross indecency on 7 November 1888, two days before the Kelly murder. The offences in question are misdemeanours and thus of a relatively minor nature, and without a court appearance within twenty-four hours Tumblety would have been bailed to reappear in seven days. The calendar of prisoners[1] for the Central Criminal Court session commencing 10 December 1888 records:

Francis Tumblety (Bailed 16th November, 1888) . . . Age 56 . . . Physician . . . Sup . . . J.L. Hannay Esq. Marlboro'-st. Police Ct . . . Date of Warrant 14th Nov . . . When received into Custody 7th Nov. . . . Offence as charged in the Indictment Committing an act of gross indecency with John Doughty, Arthur Brice, Albert Fisher, and James Crowley (1 indictment). Recognizances of Defendant Estreated.

This calendar is in tabular form and restricted to the information required in the columns, therefore any interim police bail could not be recorded on this document. It does, however, indicate that Tumblety was bailed under supervision on 7 November, and a court warrant issued on 14 November. His court bail of 16 November, after which he absconded, is shown. The papers on Tumblety's charges are held in CRIM 4/1037, 21927, and record the four offences as occurring in the County of Middlesex (London) on the following dates:

Albert Fisher, Friday, 27 July, 1888.
Arthur Brice, Friday, 31 August, 1888.
James Crowley, Sunday, 14 October, 1888.
John Doughty, Friday, 2 November, 1888.

Although a genuine contemporary suspect, as with all the others there is no hard evidence actually linking Tumblety to the murders.

CHAPTER 41

The Anderson Suspect

Dr Robert Anderson was appointed Junior Assistant Commissioner, in charge of the Criminal Investigation Department, at Scotland Yard in 1888. He was a barrister working in the Prison Department when he was appointed to his post in the Metropolitan Police on 31 August 1888, after the resignation of James Monro. After just one week, and at the time of the murder of Annie Chapman, Anderson went off to Switzerland under doctor's orders for a rest leave because he was suffering stress. This left the Senior Assistant Comissioner, Alexander Carmichael Bruce, carrying out many of Anderson's duties as head of the CID in his absence. Anderson did not return until the first week of October, after the double murder of Stride and Eddowes.

The first mention that Anderson had formulated any theory of his own about the identity of the unknown East End killer emerged in an article in the *Windsor Magazine*[1], in an article entitled "The Detective In Real Life" by Anderson's old friend Major Arthur Griffiths, the Inspector of Prisons, writing under the pen name of "Alfred Aylmer". The article stated:

> Although he has achieved greater success than any detective of his time, there will always be undiscovered crimes, and just now the tale is pretty full. Much dissatisfaction was vented upon Mr. Anderson at the utterly abortive efforts to discover the perpetrator of the Whitchapel murders. He has himself a perfectly plausible theory that Jack the Ripper was a homicidal maniac, temporarily at large, whose hideous career was cut short by committal to an asylum.

This was, of course, just a year after Macnaghten, Anderson's second-in-command, had written his famous report of February 1894, naming the three suspects Druitt, Ostrog and Kosminski. No public mention was made of these police-nominated suspects until Major Arthur Griffiths's book, *Mysteries of Police and Crime* was published in 1898. Even then no names were mentioned. Griffiths wrote:

The outside public may think that the identity of that later miscreant, "Jack the Ripper," was never revealed. So far as actual knowledge goes, this is undoubtedly true. But the police, after the last murder, had brought their investigations to the point of strongly suspecting several persons, all of them known to be homicidal lunatics, and against three of these they held very plausible and reasonable grounds of suspicion. Concerning two of them the case was weak, although it was based on certain colourable facts. One was a Polish Jew, a known lunatic, who was at large in the district of Whitechapel at the time of the murder, and who, having afterwards developed homicidal tendencies, was confined in an asylum. This man was said to resemble the murderer by the one person who got a glimpse of him – the police-constable in Mitre Court [*sic*]. The second possible criminal was a Russian doctor, also insane, who had been a convict both in England and Siberia. This man was in the habit of carrying about surgical knives and instruments in his pockets; his antecedents were of the very worst, and at the time of the Whitechapel murders he was in hiding, or, at least, his whereabouts were never exactly known. The third person was of the same type, but the suspicion in his case was stronger, and there was every reason to believe that his own friends entertained grave doubts about him. He also was a doctor in the prime of life, was believed to be insane, or on the borderland of insanity, and he disappeared immediately after the last murder, that in Miller's Court, on the 9th of November, 1888. On the last day of that year, seven weeks later, his body was found floating in the Thames and was said to have been in the water a month. The theory in this case was that after his last exploit, which was the most fiendish of all, his brain entirely gave way, and he became furiously insane and committed suicide. It is at least a strong presumption that "Jack the Ripper" died or was put under restraint after the Miller's Court affair, which ended this series of crimes. It would be interesting to know whether in this third case the man was left-handed or ambidextrous, both suggestions having been advanced by medical experts after viewing the victims. Certainly other doctors disagreed on this point, which may be said to add another to the many instances in which medical evidence has been conflicting, not to say confusing.

Anderson retired in 1901 and in *The Nineteenth Century*[2] 1901 he wrote an article, "Punishing Crime", in which he stated:

Or, again, take a notorious case of a different kind, "the Whitechapel murders" of the autumn of 1888. At that time the sensation-mongers of the newspaper press fostered the belief that life in London was no longer safe, and that no woman ought to venture abroad in the streets after nightfall. And one enterprising journalist went so far as to impersonate the cause of all this terror as "Jack the Ripper," a name by which he will probably go down to history. But all such silly hysterics could not alter the fact that these crimes were a cause of danger only to a particular section of a small and definite class of women, in a limited district of the East End; and that the inhabitants of the metropolis generally were just as secure during the weeks the fiend was on the prowl as they were before the mania seized him, or after he had been safely caged in an asylum.

Here, for the first time, Anderson himself lets slip his view on the fate of the murderer, and he later added further detail. The next comments attributable to Anderson on the identity of the killer appeared in his book *Criminals and Crime*, published in 1907, in which he repeated the above passage from his 1901 article on pages 3–4. On page 77 he added:

No one is a murderer in the sense in which many men are burglars. At least "the Whitechapel murderer" of 1888 is the only exception to this in recent years. And that case, by the way, will serve to indicate the differences I wish to enforce. In my first chapter I alluded to the fact of that fiend's detention in an asylum. Now the inquiry which leads to the discovery of a criminal of that type is different from the inquiry, for example, by which a burglar may often be detected.

The same book contains, on page 81, an interesting reference that may also refer to his thoughts on the Whitechapel murders:

When I speak of efficiency [of the CID] some people will exclaim, "But what about all the undetected crimes? I may say here that in London at least the undetected crimes are few. But English law does not permit of an arrest save on legal evidence of guilt, and legal evidence is often wholly wanting where moral proof is complete and convincing. Were I to unfold the secrets of Scotland Yard about crimes respecting which the police have been disparaged and abused in recent years, the result would be a revelation to the public. But this is not my subject here.

Anderson continued in a similar vein in an article that appeared in the *Daily Chronicle*[3] when he was interviewed about the investigation, then current, into the Luard murder case. The piece stated:

As a contribution towards the enlightenment of the public on the obstacles that Scotland Yard officers have to overcome Sir Robert Anderson has given a

representative of "The Daily Chronicle" some interesting reminiscences
. . ."Look at two notable cases that I had to deal with . . .

The Ripper Crimes

"Something of the same kind happened in the Ripper crimes. In two cases of
that terrible series there were distinct clues destroyed, wiped out absolutely –
clues that might very easily have secured for us proof of the identity of the
assassin.

"In one case it was a clay pipe. Before we could get to the scene of the
murder the doctor had taken it up, thrown it into the fire-place and smashed
it beyond recognition.

"In another case there was writing in chalk on the wall – a most valuable
clue; handwriting that might have been at once recognised as belonging to a
certain individual. But before we could secure a copy, or get it protected, it
had been entirely obliterated . . .

"I told Sir William Harcourt, who was then Home Secretary [*sic*], that I
could not accept responsibility for non-detection of the author of the Ripper
crimes for the reasons, among others, that I have given you.

Anderson serialized his reminiscences two years later in *Blackwood's
Magazine*, and in Part VI, March 1910, he wrote:

One did not need to be a Sherlock Holmes to discover that the criminal was a
sexual maniac of a virulent type; that he was living in the immediate vicinity of
the scenes of the murders; and that, if he was not living absolutely alone, his
people knew of his guilt, and refused to give him up to justice. During my
absence abroad the Police had made a house-to-house search for him,
investigating the case of every man in the district whose circumstances were
such that he could go and come and get rid of his blood-stains in secret. And
the conclusion we came to was that he and his people were low-class Jews, for
it is a remarkable fact that people of that class in the East End will not give up
one of their number to Gentile justice. And the result proved that our
diagnosis was right on every point. For I may say at once that "undiscovered
murders" are rare in London, and the "Jack-the-Ripper" crimes are not
within that category. And if the Police here had powers such as the French
Police possess, the murderer would have been brought to justice. Scotland
Yard can boast that not even the subordinate officers of the department will
tell tales out of school, and it would ill become me to violate the unwritten
rule of the service. The subject will come up again, and I will only add here
that the "Jack-the-Ripper" letter which is preserved in the Police Museum at
New Scotland Yard is the creation of an enterprising London journalist.

In a footnote he added:

> Having regard to the interest attaching to this case, I should almost be tempted to disclose the identity of the murderer and of the pressman who wrote the letter above referred to, provided that the publishers would accept all responsibility in view of a possible libel action. But no public benefit would result from such a course, and the traditions of my old department would suffer. I will only add that when the individual whom we suspected was caged in an asylum, the only person who had ever had a good view of the murderer at once identified him, but when he learned that the suspect was a fellow-Jew he declined to swear to him.

Jewish reaction to Anderson's claims appeared in the *Jewish Chronicle* of Friday, 4 March 1910 in which their columnist "Mentor" wrote:

> Sir Robert Anderson, the late head of the Criminal Investigation Department at Scotland Yard, has been contributing to *Blackwood's* a series of articles on Crime and Criminals. In the course of his last contribution, Sir Robert tells his readers that the fearful crimes committed in the East End some years ago, and known as "Jack the Ripper" crimes, were the work of a Jew. Of course, whoever was responsible for the series of foul murders was not mentally responsible, and this Sir Robert admits. But I fail to see – at least, from his article in *Blackwood's* – upon what evidence worthy of the name he ventures to cast the odium for this infamy upon one of our people. It will be recollected that the criminal, whoever he was, baffled the keenest search not alone on the part of the police, but on the part of an infuriated and panic-stricken populace. Notwithstanding the utmost vigilance, the man, repeating again his demoniacal work, again and again escaped. Scotland Yard was nonplussed, and then, according to Sir Robert Anderson, the police "formed a theory" – usually the first essential to some blundering injustice. In this case, the police came to the conclusion that "Jack the Ripper" was a "low-class" Jew, and they so decided, Sir Robert says, because they believe "it is a remarkable fact that people of that class in the East End will not give up one of their number to Gentile justice." Was anything more nonsensical in the way of a theory ever conceived even in the brain of a policeman? Here was a whole neighbourhood, largely composed of Jews, in constant terror lest their womenfolk, whom Jewish men hold in particular regard – even "low-class" Jews do that – should be slain by some murderer who was stalking the district undiscovered. So terrified were many of the people – non-Jews as well as Jews – that they hastily moved away. And yet Sir Robert would have us believe that there were Jews who knew the person who was committing the abominable crimes

and yet carefully shielded him from the police. A more wicked assertion to put into print, without the shadow of evidence, I have seldom seen. The man whom Scotland Yard "suspected," subsequently, says Sir Robert, "was caged in an asylum." He was never brought to trial – nothing except his lunacy was proved against him. This lunatic presumably was a Jew, and because he was "suspected," as a result of the police "theory" I have mentioned, Sir Robert ventures to tell the story he does, as if he were stating facts, forgetting that such a case as that of Adolph Beck was ever heard of.

But, now listen to the "proof" Sir Robert Anderson gives of his theories. When the lunatic, who presumably was a Jew and who was suspected by Scotland Yard, was seen by a Jew – "the only person who ever had a good view of the 'murderer'" – Sir Robert tells us he at once identified him, "but when he learned that the suspect was a fellow-Jew he declined to swear to him." This is Scotland Yard's idea of "proof" positive of their "theory"! What more natural than a man's hesitancy to identify another as Jack the Ripper so soon as he knew he was a Jew? What more natural than for that fact at once to cause doubts in his mind? The crimes identified with "Jack the Ripper" were of a nature that it would be difficult for any Jew – "low-class" or any class – to imagine the work of a Jew. Their callous brutality was foreign to Jewish nature, which, when it turns criminal, goes into quite a different channel. I confess that however sure I might have been of the identity of a person, when I was told he had been committing "Jack the Ripper" crimes, and was a Jew, I should hesitate about the certainty of my identification, especially as anyone – outside Scotland Yard – knows how prone to mistake the clearest-headed and most careful of people are when venturing to identify anyone else. It is a matter for regret and surprise that so able a man as Sir Robert Anderson should, upon the wholly erroneous and ridiculous "theory" that Jews would shield a raving murderer because he was a Jew, rather than yield him up to "Gentile justice," build up the series of statements that he has. There is no real proof that the lunatic who was "caged" was a Jew – there is absolutely no proof that he was responsible for the "Jack the Ripper" crimes, and hence it appears to me wholly gratuitous on the part of Sir Robert to fasten the wretched creature – whoever he was – upon our people.

As a result of this Jewish response Sir Robert Anderson was interviewed by the *Globe*, the piece appearing in the issue of Monday, 7 March 1910:

In an interview with a representative of "The Globe" on Saturday, Sir Robert said: "When I stated that the murderer was a Jew, I was stating a simple matter of fact. It is not a matter of theory. I should be the last man in the world to say anything reflecting on the Jews as a community, but what is true of Christians is equally true of Jews – that there are some people who have lapsed from all that is good and proper. We have 'lapsed masses' among Christians. We cannot talk of 'lapsed masses' among Jews, but there are cliques of them in the East-end, and it is a notorious fact that there is a stratum of Jews who will not give up their people.

"In stating what I do about the Whitechapel murders, I am not speaking as an expert in crime, but as a man who investigated the facts. Moreover, the man who identified the murderer was a Jew, but on learning that the criminal was a Jew he refused to proceed with his identification. As for the suggestion that I intended to cast any reflection on the Jews anyone who has read my books on Biblical exegesis will know the high estimate I have of Jews religiously."

Sir Robert added that one of his objects in publishing his reminiscences was to show how scares were exaggerated about "undiscovered" crimes. "As a matter of fact," he said, "there is no large city in the world where life is so safe as London. If I did not know the care and accuracy with which crimes are reported and statistics are prepared, I should not risk such a statement."

In connection with Sir Robert's assertion that the Whitechapel murderer was a Jew, it is of interest to recall that in one crime the culprit chalked up on a wall: "The Jews are not the people to be blamed for nothing." [*sic*]

In addition to the *Globe* interview, Anderson also wrote a letter to the *Jewish Chronicle* that appeared on 11 March 1910:

The "Jack the Ripper" Theory:
Reply by Sir Robert Anderson.
TO THE EDITOR OF THE "JEWISH CHRONICLE."
    Sir, – With reference to "Mentor's" comments on my statements about the "Whitechapel murders" of 1888 in this month's *Blackwood*, will you allow me to express the sincere distress I feel that my words should be construed as "an aspersion upon Jews." For much that I have written in my various books gives proof of my sympathy with, and interest in, "the people of the Covenant"; and I am happy in reckoning members of the Jewish community in London among my personal friends.
    I recognise that in this matter I said either too much or too little. But the fact is that as my words were merely a repetition of what I published several years ago without exciting comment, they flowed from my pen without any consideration.
    We have in London a stratum of the population uninfluenced by religious or even social restraints. And in this stratum Jews are to be found as well as Gentiles. And if I were to describe the condition of the maniac who

committed these murders, and the course of loathsome immorality which reduced him to that condition, it would be manifest that in his case every question of nationality and creed is lost in a ghastly study of human nature sunk to the lowest depth of degradation.

Yours obediently,
ROBERT ANDERSON.

Mentor was unappeased, and in the same paper wrote:

I have read the interview with a representative of the *Globe* which Sir Robert Anderson accorded that paper in order to reply to my observations upon what he had said in *Blackwood's Magazine* concerning the Jack the Ripper crimes. The editor of the JEWISH CHRONICLE has also been so good as to send for my perusal Sir Robert Anderson's letter to him, which appears in these columns, on the same subject. With great deference to Sir Robert, it appears to me that he misses the whole point of my complaint against what he wrote. I did not so much object to his saying that Jack the Ripper was a Jew, though so particular a friend of our people would have been well-advised, knowing the peculiar condition in which we are situated, and the prejudice that is constantly simmering against us, had he kept that fact to himself. No good purpose was served by his revealing it. It would have sufficed had he said that he was satisfied the murderer was discovered.

As I pointed out, the creature whom Sir Robert believes to have been the author of the heinous crimes was a lunatic – obviously his brain virulently diseased – so that if he *was* a Jew, however regrettable it may be that our people produced such an abnormality, in that there does not lie the aspersion. What I objected to – and *pace* Sir Robert Anderson's explanations still do – in his *Blackwood's* article, is his assertion that Jews who knew that "Jack the Ripper" had done his foul deeds, shielded him from the police, and guarded him so that he could continue his horrible career, just because he was a Jew. This was the aspersion to which I referred and about which I notice Sir Robert says nothing. Of course, when Sir Robert says that the man he means was "proved" to be the murderer, and that upon that point he spoke facts, he also ignores the somewhat important matter that the man was never put upon his trial. Knowing what I do, I would hesitate to brand even such a creature Sir Robert describes as the author of the Ripper crimes upon the very strongest evidence short of a conviction after due trial . . .

These sensational claims by Anderson did not go unnoticed in official quarters. They were the subject of comment in the House of Commons. *The Times* of 20 April 1910 reported:

Mr. MAC VEAGH asked the Secretary of State for the Home Department whether his attention had been called to the revelations published by Sir Robert Anderson with regard to what were generally known as the Jack the Ripper murders; whether he obtained the sanction of the Home Office or Scotland Yard authorities to such publication; and, if not, whether any, and if so what, steps could be taken with regard to it.

Mr. CHURCHILL. – Sir Robert Anderson neither asked for nor received any sanction to the publication, but the matter appears to me of minor importance in comparison with others that arise in connexion with the same series of articles. (Hear, hear.)

Mr. MAC VEAGH asked whether there was a Home Office minute expressly prohibiting the publication of documents of this kind.

No answer was returned.

Despite the criticism, Anderson repeated his story in his book *The Lighter Side of My Official Life* when it was published by Hodder and Stoughton later in 1910, albeit in a slightly modified form:

[Page 133 *et seq*] My last chapter brought down my story to my appointment, in September, 1888, as Assistant Commissioner of Police and head of the Criminal Investigation Department. Mr. Monro was not "an easy man to follow," and my difficulties in succeeding to the post were increased by the foolish ways of the Home Office, as well a by the circumstances of the times. As I have already said, Sir Charles Warren had then secured the loyal support of the Force generally. But the officers of the Criminal Investigation Department were demoralised by the treatment accorded to their late chief; and during the interval since his practical retirement sinister rumours were in circulation as to the appointment of his successor. If the announcement had been made that, on his official retirement on the 31st August, I should succeed to the office, things might have settled down. For all the principal officers knew and trusted me. But for some occult reason the matter was kept secret, and I was enjoined not to make my appointment known. I had been in the habit of frequenting Mr. Monro's room, as we were working together in political crime matters; but when I did so now, and Sir Charles Warren took advantage of my visit to come over to see me, it was at once inferred that he was spying on me because I was Mr. Monro's friend. The indignation felt by the officers was great, and I had some difficulty in preventing Chief-Superintendent Williamson from sending in his resignation.

Then, again, I was at that time physically unfit to enter on the duties of my new post. For some time past I had not had an adequate holiday, and the strain of long and anxious work was telling on me. "A man is as old as he feels," and by this test I was older at that time than when I left office a dozen years later. Dr. Gilbart Smith, of Harley Street, insisted that I must have two months' rest, and he added that he would probably give me a certificate for a further two months' ''sick leave.'' This, of course, was out of the question. But I told Mr. Matthews, greatly to his distress, that I could not take up my new duties until I had had a month's holiday in Switzerland. And so, after one week at Scotland Yard, I crossed the Channel.

But this was not all. The second of the crimes known as the Whitechapel murders was committed the night before I took office, and the third occurred the night of the day on which I left London. The newspapers soon began to comment on my absence. And letters from Whitehall decided me to spend the last week of my holiday in Paris, that I might be in touch with my office. On the night of my arrival in the French capital two more victims fell to the knife of the murder-fiend; and next day's post brought me an urgent appeal from Mr. Matthews to return to London; and of course I complied.

On my return I found the Jack-the-Ripper scare in full swing. When the stolid English go in for a scare they take leave of all moderation and common sense. If nonsense were solid, the nonsense that was talked and written about those murders would sink a *Dreadnought*. The subject is an unsavoury one, and I must write about it with reserve. But it is enough to say that the wretched victims belonged to a very small class of degraded women who frequent the East End streets after midnight, in hope of inveigling belated drunkards, or men as degraded as themselves. I spent the day of my return to town, and half the following night, in reinvestigating the whole case, and next day I had a long conference on the subject with the Secretary of State and the Chief Commissioner of Police. ''We hold you responsible to find the murderer,'' was Mr. Matthews' greeting to me. My answer was to decline the responsibility. ''I hold myself responsible,'' I said, ''to take all legitimate means to find him.'' But I went on to say that the measures I found in operation were, in my opinion, wholly indefensible and scandalous; for these wretched women were plying their trade under definite Police protection. Let the Police of that district, I urged, receive orders to arrest every known ''street woman'' found on the prowl after midnight, or else let us warn them that the Police will not protect them. Though the former course would have been merciful to the very small class of women affected by it, it was deemed too drastic and I fell back on the second.

However the fact may be explained, it is a fact that no other street murder occurred in the ''Jack-the-Ripper'' series. [A footnote here adds: – I am assuming that the murder of Alice M'Kenzie on the 17th of July, 1889, was by another hand. I was absent from London when it occurred, but the Chief

Commissioner investigated the case on the spot and decided that it was an ordinary murder, and not the work of a sexual maniac. And the Poplar case of December, 1888, was a death from natural causes, and but for the ''Jack the Ripper'' scare, no one would have thought of suggesting that it was a homicide.] The last and most horrible of that maniac's crimes was committed in a house in Miller's Court on the 9th of November. And the circumstances of that crime disposed of all the theories of the amateur ''Sherlock Holmses'' of that date.

One did not need to be a Sherlock Holmes to discover that the criminal was a sexual maniac of a virulent type; that he was living in the immediate vicinity of the scenes of the murders; and that, if he was not living absolutely alone, his people knew of his guilt, and refused to give him up to justice. During my absence abroad the Police had made a house-to-house search for him, investigating the case of every man in the district whose circumstances were such that he could go and come and get rid of his blood-stains in secret. And the conclusion we came to was that he and his people were certain low-class Polish Jews; for it is a remarkable fact that people of that class in the East End will not give up one of their number to Gentile justice.

And the result proved that our diagnosis was right on every point. For I may say at once that ''undiscovered murders'' are rare in London, and the ''Jack-the-Ripper'' crimes are not within that category. And if the Police here had powers such as the French Police possess, the murderer would have been brought to justice. Scotland Yard can boast that not even the subordinate officers of the department will tell tales out of school, and it would ill become me to violate the unwritten rule of the service. So I will only add here that the ''Jack-the-Ripper'' letter which is preserved in the Police Museum at New Scotland Yard is the creation of an enterprising London journalist.

Having regard to the interest attaching to this case, I am almost tempted to disclose the identity of the murderer and of the pressman who wrote the letter above referred to. But no public benefit would result from such a course, and the traditions of my old department would suffer. I will merely add that the only person who had ever had a good view of the murderer unhesitatingly identified the suspect the instant he was confronted with him; but he refused to give evidence against him.

In saying that he was a Polish Jew I am merely stating a definitely ascertained fact. And my words are meant to specify race, not religion. For it would outrage all religious sentiment to talk of the religion of a loathsome creature whose utterly unmentionable vices reduced him to a lower level than that of the brute.

The next mention of Anderson's theories appeared in *The People* of Sunday, 9 June 1912, in a series of articles entitled "Scotland Yard and its Secrets" by Hargrave L. Adam:

Who Was Jack the Ripper?

As to what was really known of the assassin we have two very good authorities – Sir Robt. Anderson and Lieut.-col. Sir Hy. Smith. The former was at the time, head of the Criminal Investigation Department, Scotland Yard, and the latter Assistant Commissioner of the City Police. I add some further particulars to those already given. The murders, which were committed during the year 1888, were, with one exception, committed outside the City Police area, the exception being the one in Mitre-sq. Sir Robt. Anderson has assured the writer that the assassin was well known to the police, but unfortunately, in the absence of sufficient legal evidence to justify an arrest, they were unable to take him. It was a case of moral versus legal proof. The only chance the police had, apparently, was to take the miscreant red-handed, and that Sir Hy. Smith declares they very nearly accomplished. Jack the Ripper, however, "had all the luck," and just managed to escape. This occurred upon the night when he committed two murders – one in Berner-st., off the Commercial-rd, and the other in Mitre-sq. Sir Hy. Smith, with several of his men, was soon at the latter place. When the body came to be examined it was discovered that one-half the apron the woman was wearing at the time she was murdered was cut clean away and was missing.

Murderer's Narrow Escape.

One of the police, a man named Halse, happened luckily to get upon the track of the murderer. He ran his best pace in the direction of Whitechapel, and, when he came to Goulston-st., he noticed a light at the door of one of the Peabody dwellings. He pulled up, and discovered that the light was that of the lantern of a member of the Metropolitan Force, who was inspecting a piece of linen on the ground. It was bloodstained, and proved to be the missing half of the murdered woman's apron. On the wall above in chalk was written: "The Jews are the men that won't be blamed for nothing." Subsequently this inscription was wiped off by order of Sir Chas. Warren, who, as has already been stated, was at Scotland Yard at the time. This, Sir Hy. Smith maintains, was a fatal mistake, as the writing might have afforded a valuable clue. Sir Charles had it done as he feared a rising against the Jews. The assassin had wiped his hands on the missing half of the apron, and, it was further discovered, had, with remarkable audacity, washed his hands at a sink up a close in Dorset-st., only a few yards from the street . . . [*sic*]

But the question still remains, who and what was "Jack the Ripper"? Sir

Robt. Anderson states confidently that he was a low-class Jew, being shielded by his fraternity. Sir Hy. Smith pooh-poohs this, declaring with equal confidence that he was a Gentile. He further states that the writing on the wall was probably a mere "blind," although the writing itself might have afforded a valuable clue. One thing is certain, namely, the elusive assassin, whoever he was, possessed anatomical knowledge. This, therefore, leads one pretty surely to the conclusion that he was a medical man, or one who had formerly been a medical student.

There can be little doubt that Anderson's suspect is the one named by Macnaghten in his February 1894 report as "Kosminski", although no first name is given. Apparent confirmation of this is contained in a copy of Anderson's memoirs, *The Lighter Side of My Official Life*, which was owned by the retired ex-Superintendent Donald S. Swanson, who maintained contact with Anderson after both men had retired. Swanson's copy of the book contains pencilled annotations in the familiar handwriting of Swanson himself. These notes received wide publicity for the first time in 1987 in the *Daily Telegraph*.

The relevant annotations appear in Swanson's copy of Anderson's book as follows. At the bottom of page 138 (the passage where Anderson had claimed that the murderer had been identified but that the witness refused to swear to it), Swanson wrote:

because the suspect was also a Jew and also because his evidence would convict the suspect, and witness would be the means of murderer being hanged which he did not wish to be left on his mind.

In the margin the annotations continue: *And after this identification which suspect knew, no other murder of this kind took place in London.*

On the rear free endpaper Swanson noted: *Continuing from page 138, after the suspect had been identified at the Seaside Home where he had been sent by us with difficulty in order to subject him to identification, and he knew he was identified. On suspect's return to his brother's house in Whitechapel he was watched by police (City CID) by day & night. In a very short time the suspect with his hands tied behind his back, he was sent to Stepney Workhouse and then to Colney Hatch and died shortly afterwards – Kosminski was the suspect – DSS*

This would seem to lead naturally on to the following chapter, which looks at all we know of the only known serious City Police suspect who was kept under observation by their Detective Department. Whether or not it is one and the same person referred to by Anderson and Swanson is not certain. But there are similarities, such as the fact that he was a Jew, and Swanson's note that the suspect was "watched by police (City CID) which seem to indicate strongly that he was. Frustratingly for modern historians, contradictions and anomalies in the various stories exist.

CHAPTER 42

A City Police Suspect

The mystery and controversy over the actual identity of the murderer has been compounded by the fact that the City of London Police records on the case have not survived. The report by Inspector McWilliam, head of the City Detective Department, on the Eddowes murder, sent to the Home Office, is the only detailed report by the City Police to survive.

To find more information on the so-called "City Police Suspect" mentioned by Anderson and Swanson we are lucky to have a few newspaper references from City sources. The best known of these is that which appeared in *Reynolds News* of 15 September 1946, in an article written by Justin Atholl:

> Inspector Robert Sagar, who died in 1924, played a leading part in the "Ripper" investigations. In his memoirs he said: "We had good reason to suspect a man who worked in Butchers' Row, Aldgate. We watched him carefully. There was no doubt that this man was insane, and after a time his friends thought it advisable to have him removed to a private asylum. After he was removed, there were no more Ripper atrocities."

However, a rather better account of Sagar's reminiscences on the "Ripper" murders is to be found in *The City Press* of Saturday, 7 January 1905, on the occasion of his retirement. It was, of course, written whilst he was still alive:

> His professional association with the terrible atrocities which were perpetrated some years ago in the East End by the so-styled "Jack the Ripper" was a very close one. Indeed, Mr. Sagar knows as much about those crimes, which terrified the Metropolis, as any detective in London. He was deputed to represent the City police force in conference with the detective heads of the Metropolitan force nightly at Leman Street Police Station during the period covered by those ghastly murders. Much has been said and written – and even more conjectured – upon the subject of the "Jack-the-Ripper" murders. It has been asserted that the murderer fled to the Continent, where he

perpetrated similar hideous crimes; but that is not the case. The police realised, as also did the public, that the crimes were those of a madman, and suspicion fell upon a man, who, without a doubt, was the murderer. Identification being impossible, he could not be charged. He was, however, placed in a lunatic asylum, and the series of atrocities came to an end. There was a peculiar incident in connection with those tragedies which may have been forgotten. The apron belonging to the woman who was murdered in Mitre Square was thrown under a staircase in a common lodging house in Dorset Street [*sic*], and someone – presumably the murderer – had written on the wall above it, "The Jewes are not the people that will be blamed for nothing." A police officer engaged in the case, fearing that the writing might lead to an onslaught upon the Jews in the neighbourhood, rubbed the writing from the wall, and all record of the implied accusation was lost; but the fact that such an ambiguous message was left is recorded among the archives at the Guildhall.

Further information on the "City suspect" is contained in an article in *Thomson's Weekly News*[1] on the occasion of the retirement of another City officer, Detective Inspector Henry Cox:

THE TRUTH ABOUT THE WHITE-
CHAPEL MYSTERIES.
TOLD BY HARRY COX,
Ex-Detective Inspector, London City Police.
Specially Written for "Thomson's Weekly News."

It is only upon certain conditions that I have agreed to deal with the great Whitechapel crimes of fifteen years ago. Much has been written regarding the identity of the man who planned and successfully carried out the outrage. Many writers gifted with a vivid imagination have drawn pictures for the public of the criminal whom the police suspected. All have been woefully wrong. In not a single case has one succeeded in discovering the persons who while the trail of blood lay thick and hot was looked upon as a man not unlikely to be connected with the crimes.

It is my intention to relate several of my experiences while keeping this fellow under observation. I may give a theory as to the cause of the crimes, but on no account can I enter into the theories of my brother officers or indicate whether or not the last has been heard of the crimes.

There are those who claim that the perpetrator was well known to the police; that at the present moment he is incarcerated in one of His Majesty's penal settlements. Others hold that he was known to have jumped over London Bridge or Blackfriars Bridge; while a third party claims that he is the inmate of a private asylum. These theories I have no hesitation in dispelling at once.

I can well remember the sensation which the first of the horrible crimes caused among those whose duty it was to investigate the untoward happenings of the East End.

The murder of Martha Turner was an amazing puzzle to each of us. Never in the course of our experience had such a case occurred. It was clearly no ordinary East End crime. Most of the bodies which are found at the riverside or in the dark squalid streets bear the marks of struggles or of blows given in anger.

But this one bore neither. It appeared rather that the woman had been quietly throttled to death, and after death mutilated in the most horrible fashion. There were almost

Forty Wounds on the Body

Nine were in the throat, seventeen in the breast, and the others in the lower parts of the body.

The woman was well known to the police, and it was a comparatively easy matter to find out the companions she had visited in the early part of the night.

The movements of all were traced and the fact established beyond doubt that none of them had been responsible for her death.

One of the suspected persons was a soldier, but he had no difficulty in proving his innocence.

There was not a clue to help us in our work, and we were stumbling along very much in the dark, when suddenly we were startled by the news of another crime of a similar nature.

It was committed in Buck's Row, a dead-and-alive street in Whitechapel made up of warehouses and slum dwellings. The murder was discovered by a young constable named John Neil. On the morning of Friday, Aug 31, of the year 1888, he was patrolling his beat when a young man obviously labouring under great excitement rushed up to him and said – " 'Ere, mister, there's been a terrible murder down at Mullin's stable."

"A murder!" said the policeman. "Are you sure?"

"Sure! Why look 'ere," spoke the young fellow, pointing to the knee of his trousers. "I was that 'urried to get to my work, 'avin slept in, that I fell over 'er afore I knew where I was. At first I thought it was a drunk woman, but in bendin' down to rouse 'er I put my 'and on my knee an' was 'orrified to find it all red with blood. Swelp me, mister, it did give me such a fright."

The body was moved to the mortuary at the instigation of Dr Henry Llewellen [sic], who was brought to the scene of the outrage by the constable. An examination speedily proved that here again was a crime the elucidation of which would be baffling in the extreme.

The woman had been mutilated beyond description, but everything pointed to the work having been done not in anger, but in a quiet, methodical manner. There was a dwelling-house adjoining the gateway, beside which the body had been found, and in it a woman and her son and daughter had been sitting at the time the murder must have taken place. All stated emphatically that although the night was quiet they

Heard Never a Sound

outside the house.

The news of the murder soon spread, and before long many amateur detectives were connecting it with the murder of Martha Turner, and advancing strange theories as to the murders.

Many believe several of them to this day, specially one to the effect that the murders were committed by some mad medical specialist, and the bodies conveyed in his own conveyance to the East End. An absurd piece of nonsense!

In nearly every case the murders were committed on the actual spot where the bodies were found, or very close to it.

We proved beyond doubt that the second victim met her unknown murderer near the scene of the crime, and was discovered dead about two hours afterwards [sic].

The woman was an inmate of a common lodging house who was forced to spend her last night on the street because she had not the few coppers necessary for her "doss."

She was seen in Whitechapel at nearly three o'clock on the Friday morning. At that time she was standing alone at the corner of Osborne [sic] Street.

A story got abroad that the body had been dragged along the roadway, but this is easily seen to be utter fiction when the evidence of Dr Llewellen at the inquest is glanced at. He stated clearly – "There were no marks of any struggle or blood as if the body had been dragged."

When the full details of the crime were gathered it speedily became apparent to us that we had no ordinary cut-throat assassin to deal with. The man was evidently a mono-maniac, and one who possessed certain anatomical knowledge.

The greatest terror reigned among women of the lowest class. Many of them came to implore me to safeguard them, and stated that they were terrified to stir beyond their lodgings at nightfall.

Each of them fixed upon a certain man as the perpetrator, and it was due to the remarkable manner in which their stories agreed that an arrest was made.

Not a scrap of evidence could be proved against the suspect, however, and he was dismissed.

About a week after the second murder another occurred. The scene of the tragedy was Hanbury Street, and the victim was another fallen woman named Annie Chapman.

The greatest sensation of all, however, occurred on the last day of the month, when two of the ghastly crimes were committed.

One took place in Berner Street, the other in Mitre Square, the victims being Elizabeth Watts [*sic*] and Catherine Eddowes respectively.

The next and the final crime of the series did not take place till the 9th of November, when Mary Kelly was done to death in Dorset Street, and this leads me to point out a fact which, of course, could scarcely be grasped at the time of the murders, and which up till the present time has been pointed out by none.

That is, that the mysterious criminal had a carefully-thought-out system under which he carried out the outrages. The first crime took place on August 6 [*sic*], the second on the last day of the month. The third occurred in the beginning of the following month, this time two days later, and the fourth and fifth were once again on the last day of the month. The final murder was again on the opening days of the month.

This, as I say, seems to point to the murderer having a system, but it also considerably strengthens the theory that the man was a sailor, and timed his murders so that he could board his vessel just as it was on the point of sailing.

We had many people under observations while the murders were being perpetrated, but it was not until the discovery of the body of Mary Kelly had been made that we seemed

To Get Upon the Trail.

Certain investigations made by several of our cleverest detectives made it apparent to us that a man living in the East End of London was not unlikely to have been connected with the crimes.

To understand the reason we must first of all understand the motive of the Whitechapel crimes. The motive was, there can be not the slightest doubt, revenge. Not merely revenge on the few poor unfortunate victims of the knife, but revenge on womankind. It was not a lust for blood, as many people have imagined.

The murderer was a misogynist, who at some time or another had been wronged by a woman. And the fact that his victims were of the lowest class proves, I think, that he was not, as has been stated, and educated man who had suddenly gone mad. He belonged to their own class.

Had he been wronged by a woman occupying a higher stage in society the murders would in all probability have taken place in the West End, the victims have been members of the fashionable demi-monde.

The man we suspected was about five feet six inches in height, with short, black, curly hair, and he had a habit of taking late walks abroad. He occupied several shops in the East End, but from time to time he became insane, and was forced to spend a portion of his time in an asylum in Surrey.

While the Whitechapel murders were being perpetrated his place of business was in a certain street, and after the last murder I was on duty in this street for nearly three months.

There were several other officers with me, and I think there can be no harm in stating that the opinion of most of them was that the man they were watching had something to do with the crimes. You can imagine that never once did we allow him to quit our sight. The least slip and another brutal crime might have been perpetrated under our very noses. It was not easy to forget that already one of them had taken place at the very moment when one of our smartest colleagues was passing the top of the dimly lit street.

The Jews in the street soon became

Aware of Our Presence

It was impossible for us to hide ourselves. They became suddenly alarmed, panic-stricken, and I can tell you that at nights we ran a considerable risk. We carried our lives in our hands so to speak, and at last we had to partly take the alarmed inhabitants into our confidence, and so throw them off the scent. We told them we were factory inspectors looking for tailors and capmakers who employed boys and girls under age, and pointing out the evils accruing from the sweaters' system asked them to co-operate with us in destroying it.

They readily promised so to do, although we knew well that they had no intention of helping us. Every man was as bad as another. Day after day we used to sit and chat with them, drinking their coffee, smoking their excellent cigarettes, and partaking of Kosher rum. Before many weeks had passed we were quite friendly with them, and knew that we could carry out our observations unmolested. I am sure they never once suspected that we were police detectives on the trail of the mysterious murderer; otherwise they would not have discussed the crimes with us as openly as they did.

We had the use of a house opposite the shop of the man we suspected, and, disguised, of course, we frequently stopped across in the role of customers.

Every newspaper loudly demanded that we should arouse from our slumber, and the public had lashed themselves into a state of fury and fear. The terror soon spread to the provinces too. Whenever a small crime was committed it was asserted that the Ripper had shifted his ground, and warning letters were received by many a terror-stricken woman. The latter were of course the work of cruel practical jokers. The fact, by the way, that the murderer

Never Shifted His Ground

rather inclines one to the belief that he was a mad, poverty-stricken inhabitant of some slum in the East End.

I shall never forget one occasion when I had to shadow our man during one of his late walks. As I watched him from the house opposite one night, it suddenly struck me that there was a wilder look than usual on his evil countenance, and I felt that something was about to happen. When darkness set in I saw him come forth from the door of his little shop and glance furtively around to see if he were being watched. I allowed him to get right out of the street before I left the house, and then I set off after him. I followed him to Lehman [*sic*] Street, and there I saw him enter a shop which I knew was the abode of a number of criminals well known to the police.

He did not stay long. For about a quarter of an hour I hung about keeping my eye on the door, and at last I was rewarded by seeing him emerging alone.

He made his way down to St George's in the East End, and there to my astonishment I saw him stop and speak to a drunken woman.

I crouched in a doorway and held my breath. Was he going to throw himself right into my waiting arms? He passed on after a moment or two, and on I slunk after him.

As I passed the woman she laughed and shouted something after me, which, however, I did not catch.

My man was evidently of opinion that he might be followed every minute. Now and again he turned his head and glanced over his shoulder, and consequently I had the greatest difficulty in keeping behind him.

I had to work my way along, now with my back to the wall, now pausing and making little runs for a sheltering doorway. Not far from where the model lodging-house stands he met another woman, and for a considerable distance he walked along with her.

Just as I was beginning to prepare myself for a terrible ordeal, however, he pushed her away from him and set off at a rapid pace.

In the end he brought me, tired, weary, and nerve-strung,

Back to the Street He Had Left

where he disappeared into his own house.

Next morning I beheld him busy as usual. It is indeed very strange that as soon as this madman was put under observation the mysterious crimes ceased, and that very soon he removed from his usual haunts and gave up his nightly prowls. He was never arrested for the reason that not the slightest scrap of evidence could be found to connect him with the crimes.

Long after the public had ceased to talk about the murders we continued to investigate them.

We had no clue to go upon, but every point suggested by the imagination was seized upon and worked bare. There was not a criminal in London capable of committing the crimes but was looked up and shadowed.

The mystery is as much a mystery as it was fifteen years ago. It is all very well for amateur detectives to fix the crime upon this or that suspect, and advance theories in the public press to prove his guilt. They are working upon surmise, nothing more.

The mystery can never be cleared up until someone comes forward and himself proves conclusively that he was the bloodthirsty demon who terrorised the country, or unless he returns to his crimes and is caught red-handed. He is still alive then? you ask. I do not know. For all I know he may be dead. I have personally no evidence either way.

And so Henry Cox concluded his reminiscences on a "City suspect", an essay which, even if it does not clearly identify the subject of the City Police observations, does give a valuable insight into the working methods of the police. Although not named by Henry Cox, there may be sufficient details given of the City suspect for him to be identified by the diligent researcher. Detective Inspector Henry Cox was to achieve a moment of fame on 18 March 1903. He was then on duty at the Bank of England when, after a desperate struggle, he arrested Samuel Herbert Dougal, the notorious "Moat Farm Murderer"

CHAPTER 43

Chief Inspector Abberline and the Chapman Theory

It cannot be doubted that in 1888 Inspector Frederick George Abberline was one of the key investigators of the mystery of the Whitechapel Murders. He led the grass-roots investigation in Whitechapel, from the time of the involvement of Scotland Yard in September 1888 until some time around March 1889. Charge of the case was then taken on by Abberline's colleague Detective Inspector Henry Moore, who had gone to Whitechapel with Abberline from the start of the investigation. Meanwhile, Abberline moved on to other investigations, notably the Cleveland Street scandal of that year. In 1890 Abberline was promoted to the rank of Chief Inspector and he retired in 1892. Abberline's retirement and a few of his reminiscences were reported in *Cassell's Saturday Journal* of 28 May 1892. The subject of the Whitechapel Murders was touched upon in this piece:

A man of such intimate acquaintance with the East End as Mr. Abberline naturally found himself recalled to the scene of his former labours when the series of Whitechapel murders horrified all the world. His knowledge of crime, and the people who commit it, is "extensive and peculiar." There is no exaggeration in the statement that, whenever a robbery or offence against the law had been committed in the district, the detective knew where to find his man and the missing property too. His friendly relations with the shady folk who crowd into the common lodging houses enabled him to pursue his investigations connected with the murders with the greatest certainty, and the facilities afforded him made it clear to his mind that the miscreant was not to be found lurking in a "dossers" kitchen. In fact, the desire of the East Enders to assist the police was so keen that the number of statements made – all of them requiring to be recorded and searched into – was so great that the officer almost broke down under the pressure. Yet his anxiety to bring the murderer to justice led him, after occupying the whole day in directing his staff, to pass his time in the streets until early morning, driving home, fagged and weary, at 5 a.m. And it happened frequently, too, that, just as he was going to bed, he would be summoned back to the East End by a telegraph, there to interrogate some lunatic or suspected person whom the inspector in charge would not take the responsibility of questioning.

"Theories!" exclaims the inspector, when conversing about the murders— "we were lost almost in theories; there were so many of them." Nevertheless, he has one which is new. He believes, from the evidence of his own eyesight, that the Miller's Court atrocity was the last of the real series, the others having been imitations, and that in Miller's Court the murderer reached the culminating point of the gratification of his morbid ideas.

The final mention of Abberline's ideas about the Whitechapel Murders appeared in news reports in March 1903 that were prompted by the stories of the recently arrested "Borough poisoner", George Chapman, whose real name was Severin Klosowski. The *Pall Mall Gazette* reported on Tuesday, 24 March 1903:

> THE CHAPMAN-RIPPER THEORY.
> INSPECTOR ABBERLINE INTERVIEWED.
> A REMARKABLE STORY.
> (Special to the "Pall Mall Gazette.")
>
> Should Klosowski, the wretched man now lying under sentence of death for wife-poisoning, go to the scaffold without a "last dying speech and confession," a great mystery may forever remain unsolved, but the conviction that "Chapman" and "Jack the Ripper" were one and the same person will not in the least be weakened in the mind of the man who is, perhaps, better qualified than anyone else in this country to express an opinion in the matter. We allude to Mr. F.G. Abberline, formerly Chief Detective-inspector of Scotland Yard, the official who had full charge of the criminal investigations at the time of the terrible murders in Whitechapel.
>
> When a representative of the *Pall Mall Gazette* called on Mr. Abberline yesterday and asked for his views on the startling theory set up by one of the morning papers, the retired detective said: "What an extraordinary thing it is that you should just have called upon me now. I had just commenced, not knowing anything about the report in the newspaper, to write to the Assistant Commissioner of Police, Mr. Macnaghten, to say how strongly I was impressed with the opinion that "Chapman" was also the author of the Whitechapel murders. Your appearance saves me the trouble. I intended to write on Friday, but a fall in the garden, injuring my hand and shoulder, prevented my doing so until to-day.
>
> Mr. Abberline had already covered a page and a half of foolscap, and was surrounded with a sheaf of documents and newspaper cuttings dealing with the ghastly outrages of 1888.

Coincidences

"I have been so struck with the remarkable coincidences in the two series of murders," he continued, "that I have not been able to think of anything else for several days past – not, in fact, since the Attorney-General made his opening statement at the recent trial, and traced the antecedents of Chapman before he came to this country in 1888. Since then the idea has taken full possession of me, and everything fits in and dovetails so well that I cannot help feeling that this is the man we struggled so hard to capture fifteen years ago.

"My interest in the Ripper case was especially deep. I had for fourteen years previously been an inspector of police in Whitechapel, but when the murders began I was at the central office at Scotland Yard. On the application of Superintendent Arnold I went back to the East End just before Annie Chapman was found mutilated, and as chief of the detective corps I gave myself up to the study of the cases. Many a time, even after we had carried our inquiries as far as we could – and we made out no fewer than 1,600 sets of papers respecting our investigations – instead of going home when I was off duty, I used to patrol the district until four or five o'clock in the morning, and, while keeping my eyes wide open for clues of any kind, have many and many a time given those wretched and homeless women, who were Jack the Ripper's special prey, fourpence or sixpence for a shelter to get them away from the streets and out of harm's way."

Chapman's Movements.

"As I say," went on the criminal expert, "there are a score of things which make one believe that Chapman is the man; and you must understand that we have never believed all those stories about Jack the Ripper being dead, or that he was a lunatic, or anything of that kind. For instance, the date of the arrival in England coincides with the beginning of the series of murders in White-chapel; there is a coincidence also in the fact that the murders ceased in London when "Chapman" went to America, while similar murders began to be perpetrated in America after he landed there. The fact that he studied medicine and surgery in Russia before he came over here is well established, and it is curious to note that the first series of murders was the work of an expert surgeon, while the recent poisoning cases were proved to be done by a man with more than an elementary knowledge of medicine. The story told by "Chapman's" wife of the attempt to murder her with a long knife while in America is not to be ignored, but something else with regard to America is still more remarkable.

A Significant Story.

"While the coroner was investigating one of the Whitechapel murders he told the jury a very queer story. You will remember that Dr. Philips, the divisional surgeon, who made the post-mortem examination, not only spoke of the skilfulness with which the knife had been used, but stated that there was overwhelming evidence to show that the criminal had so mutilated the body that he could possess himself of one of the organs. The coroner, in commenting on this, said that he had been told by the sub-curator of the pathological museum connected with one of the great medical schools that some few months before an American had called upon him and asked him to procure a number of specimens. He stated his willingness to give £20 for each. Although the strange visitor was told that his wish was impossible of fulfilment, he still urged his request. It was known that the request was repeated at another institution of a similar character in London. The coroner at the time said 'Is it not possible that a knowledge of this demand may have inspired some abandoned wretch to possess himself of the specimens? It seems beyond belief that such inhuman wickedness could enter into the mind of any man; but, unfortunately, our criminal annals prove that every crime is possible!'

"It is a remarkable thing," Mr. Abberline pointed out, "that after the Whitechapel horrors America should have been the place where a similar kind of murder began, as though the miscreant had not fully supplied the demand of the American agent.

One Discrepancy.

"There are many other things extremely remarkable. The fact that Klosowski when he came to reside in this country occupied a lodging in George-yard, Whitechapel-road, where the first murder was committed, is very curious, and the height of the man and the peaked cap he is said to have worn quite tallies with the descriptions I got of him. All agree, too, that he was a foreign-looking man, but that, of course, helped us little in a district so full of foreigners as Whitechapel. One discrepancy only have I noted, and this is that the people who alleged that they saw Jack the Ripper at one time or another, state that he was a man about thirty-five or forty years of age. They, however, state that they only saw his back, and it is easy to misjudge age from a back view."

Altogether Mr. Abberline considers that the matter is quite beyond abstract speculation and coincidence, and believes the present situation affords an opportunity of unravelling a web of crime such as no man living can appreciate in its extent and hideousness.

The following day the *Morning Advertiser* recounted the interview of the *Pall Mall Gazette* correspondent with Abberline, and added some words of their own, disagreeing with the retired detective's ideas:

Against this theory are to be set the facts that Chapman's crimes were quite unlike those of "Jack the Ripper." Chapman went about his deadly work with method and patience, taking as little risk as he could. He got rid of his "wives" merely because he was tired of them. "Jack the Ripper," on the other hand, evidently had a violent feeling against women of the class whom he killed, unless he committed his murders in order to secure and sell certain parts of their bodies, as one theory suggested.

Further, it is pretty well known, as is pointed out in our correspondence column to-day, that the police have good reason to believe that the White-chapel murders were committed by one of three men, all of whom are either dead or in confinement.

Students of modern crime are not likely to pay much heed to Inspector Abberline's theory.

The *Pall Mall Gazette* responded to criticisms of the first piece with a further report in their issue of Tuesday, 31 March 1903:

THE CHAPMAN-RIPPER THEORY.
FRESH STATEMENT FROM AN AUTHORITY.
[Special to the "Pall Mall Gazette".]

Since the *Pall Mall Gazette* a few days ago gave a series of coincidences supporting the theory that Klosowski, or Chapman, as he was for some time called, was the perpetrator of the "Jack the Ripper" murders in Whitechapel fifteen years ago, it has been interesting to note how many amateur criminologists have come forward with statements to the effect that it is useless to attempt to link Chapman with the Whitechapel atrocities. This cannot possibly be the same man, it is said, because, first of all, Chapman is not the miscreant who could have done the previous deeds, and, secondly, it is contended that the Whitechapel murderer has long been known to be beyond the reach of earthly justice.

In order, if possible, to clear the ground with respect to the latter statement particularly, a representative of the *Pall Mall Gazette* again called on Mr. F.G. Abberline, formerly Chief Detective Inspector of Scotland Yard, yesterday, and elicited the following statement from him:-

"You can state most emphatically," said Mr. Abberline, "that Scotland Yard is really no wiser on the subject than it was fifteen years ago. It is simple nonsense to talk of the police having proof that the man is dead. I am, and always have been, in the closest touch with Scotland Yard, and it would have been next to impossible for me not to have known all about it. Besides, the authorities would have been only too glad to make an end of such a mystery, if only for their own credit."

To convince those who have any doubts on the point, Mr. Abberline produced recent documentary evidence which put the ignorance of Scotland Yard as to the perpetrator beyond the shadow of a doubt.

"I know," continued the well-known detective, "that it has been stated in several quarters that "Jack the Ripper" was a man who died in a lunatic asylum a few years ago, but there is nothing at all of a tangible nature to support such a theory."

Stories Repudiated.

Our representative called Mr. Abberline's attention to a statement made in a well-known Sunday paper, in which it was made out that the author was a young medical student who was found drowned in the Thames.

"Yes," said Mr. Abberline, "I know all about that story. But what does it amount to? Simply this. Soon after the last murder in Whitechapel the body of a young doctor was found in the Thames, but there is nothing beyond the fact that he was found at that time to incriminate him. A report was made to the Home Office about the matter, but that it was 'considered final and conclusive' is going altogether beyond the truth. Seeing that the same kind of murders began in America afterwards, there is much more reason to think the man emigrated. Then again, the fact that several months after December, 1888, when the student's body was found, the detectives were told still to hold themselves in readiness for further investigations seems to point to the conclusion that Scotland Yard did not in any way consider the evidence as final."

"But what about Dr. Neil Cream? A circumstantial story is told of how he confessed on the scaffold – at least, he is said to have got as far as 'I am Jack ————' when the jerk of the rope cut short his remarks."

"That is also another idle story," replied Mr. Abberline. "Neil Cream was not even in this country when the Whitechapel murders took place. No; the identity of the diabolical individual has yet to be established, notwithstanding the people who have produced these rumours and who pretend to know the state of the official mind."

Further Criticisms Rebutted.

"As to the question of the dissimilarity of character in the crimes which one hears so much about," continued the expert, "I cannot see why one man should not have done both, provided he had the professional knowledge, and this is admitted in Chapman's case. A man who could watch his wives being slowly tortured to death by poison, as he did, was capable of anything; and the fact that he should have attempted, in such a cold-blooded manner, to murder his first wife with a knife in New Jersey, makes one more inclined to believe in the theory that he was mixed up in the two series of crimes. What, indeed, is more likely than that a man to some extent skilled in medicine and surgery should discontinue the use of the knife when his commission – and I still believe Chapman had a commission from America – came to an end, and then for the remainder of his ghastly deeds put into practice his knowledge of poisons? Indeed, if the theory be accepted that a man who takes life on a wholesale scale never ceases his accursed habit until he is either arrested or dies, there is much to be said for Chapman's consistency. You see, incentive changes; but the fiendishness is not eradicated. The victims, too, you will notice, continue to be women; but they are of different classes, and obviously call for different methods of despatch.''

With this well-publicised theory another name, that of an established murderer, was added to the long list of Ripper "suspects".

CHAPTER 44

14 October 1896 – A Letter From "Jack the Ripper"

Although the police, other agencies and individuals received literally hundreds of letters purporting to be from the murderer from September 1888 onwards, we have included here only those which are generally agreed by serious scholars of the Whitechapel Murders to be of most significance in our understanding of the case. As early as 11 October 1888, *Truth* had noted a spate of hoax letters from the lunatic fringe:

> No sooner was a letter signed "Jack the Ripper" published, than hundreds of ghastly jokers at once addressed similar letters to the authorities . . . On the doctrine of probabilities, it is long odds against the murderer having written the "Jack the Ripper" letters. He may have, and so may thousands of others.

The name "Jack the Ripper" was appended to dozens of letters in as many different hands. Although the original "Dear Boss" correspondence of 1888 was imitated many times, the last recorded communication[1] of that sort was received by the police as late as 14 October 1896. Written in red ink, it read as follows:

> *Dear Boss,*
>   *You will be surprised to*
> *find that this comes from yours*
> *as of old Jack-the-Ripper. Ha. Ha*
> *If my old friend Mr Warren is dead*
> *you can read it. you might*
> *remember me if you try and*
> *think a little Ha Ha. The last job*
> *was a bad one and no mistake nearly*
> *buckled, and meant it to*
> *be best of the lot &what curse it,*
> *Ha Ha Im alive yet and you'll*
> *soon find it out. I mean to go*
> *on again when I get the chance*
> *wont it be nice dear old Boss to*
> *have the good old times once*

again. you never caught me
and you never will. Ha Ha
   You police are a smart lot, the lot
of you could nt catch one man
Where have I been Dear Boss
you d like to know. abroad, if
you would like to know, and
just come back. ready to go on
with my work and stop when
you catch me. Well good bye
Boss wish me luck. Winters coming
"The Jewes are people that are
blamed for nothing" Ha Ha
have you heard this before

Yours truly

Jack the Ripper

The combination of the red ink, references to the famous "Dear Boss" correspondence, the Goulston Street graffito, clerkly hand, correct spelling, signature "Jack the Ripper" and threat to begin "work" again resulted in some interesting police comment on it.

The file cover on this correspondence[2] states:

Submitted through CI Dept.
      H Division
Submitting a letter signed Jack the Ripper
[Stamped: – 15 OCT 96]
Supt Central
This is not, I think, the handwriting of our <u>original</u> correspondent, but it is not a bad imitation Will you get out the old letter & compare?

[*Init. illeg.*]
15/10

Report Submitted
18/10 DSSwanson
<u>Sir E. Bradford</u> to see
   I do not think that these cases shd. be circld. to surrounding stns, but that all such letters should be sent to C.O. as soon as possible for instructions as to action, if any, to be taken.
H to see.   [*Init. illeg.*]

19/10/96

H 19.10.96 seen
      [LC?] Actg.Supt.

Central to see & lay by.
        [*Init. illeg.*]
              20/10
Seen.   D.S. Swanson.

The first report[3] by Detective Inspector Payne, dated 14 October 1896, is as follows:

METROPOLITAN POLICE.

Commercial St Station.   H DIVISION.

[Stamped: – Metropolitan Police Received 15 OCT 96 Criminal Investigation Dept.]

                                        14th Octr. 1896.

Reference to Papers.
Attached.

   I beg to submit attached letter received per post 14th inst. signed Jack the Ripper, stating that writer has just returned from abroad and means to go on again when he gets the chance. The letter appears similar to those received by police during the series of murders in this district in 1888 and 1889.

   Police have been instructed to keep a sharp lookout.

                              Geo. Payne, SDInsp

   Submitted. I caused a telegram to be sent to surrounding Divisions, upon receipt of letter 14th ins. asking that directions be given to police to keep a sharp look out, but at the same time to keep the information quiet. Writer in sending the letter no doubt considers it a great joke at the expense of police.

                              L Cross ActgSup. [?]

The final report on this subject, dated 18 October 1896, is written by Henry Moore, by now promoted to Detective Chief Inspector, who, as we have seen, was put in charge of the overall "on the ground" enquiries into the Whitechapel Murders in 1889 in place of Inspector Abberline. The report[4] reads:

METROPOLITAN POLICE.
CRIMINAL INVESTIGATION DEPARTMENT,
NEW SCOTLAND YARD,
                18th day of October 1896

SUBJECT Letter received
signed Jack the
   Ripper.

   With reference to attached anonymous letter, signed "Jack the Ripper";

wherein the writer states that he has returned from abroad; and is now ready to commence work again; vide Chief Constable's minute re same.

I beg to report having carefully perused all the old "Jack the Ripper" letters, and fail to find any similarity of handwriting in any of them, with the exception of the two well remembered communications which were sent to the "Central News" office; one a letter, dated 25th Septr./88 and the other a post-card bearing the post-mark 1st Oct./88., vide copies herewith.

On comparing the handwriting of the present letter with handwriting of that document, I find many similarities in the formation of letters. For instance the y's, t's, and w's are very much the same. Then there are several words which appear in both documents; Viz:-Dear Boss; ha ha (although in the present letter the capital H. is used instead of the small one); and in speaking of the murders he describes them as his "work" or the last "job"; and if I get a (or the) chance; then there are the words "Yours truly" and the Ripper (the latter on post-card) are very much alike. Besides there are the finger smears.

Considering the lapse of time, it would be interesting to know how the present writer was able to use the words – "The Jewes are people that are blamed for nothing" [*here there is a marginal note* – "Were not the exact words 'The Jewes are not the men to be blamed for nothing'? DSS?"]; as it will be remembered that they are practically the same words that were written in chalk, undoubtedly by the murderer, on the wall at Goulston St., Whitechapel, on the night of 30th. Sept., 1888, after the murders of Mrs. Stride and Mrs. Eddows; and the word Jews was spelt on that occasion precisely as it is now.

Although these similarities strangely exist between the documents, I am of opinion that the present writer is not the original correspondent who prepared the letters to the Central News; as if it had been I should have thought he would have again addressed it to the same Press Agency; and not to Commercial Street Police Station.

In conclusion I beg to observe that I do not attach any importance to this communication. [*This comment has the marginal marking* "A"].

Henry Moore, Chf Inspr.

In my opinion the handwritings are not the same. I agree as at A. I beg that the letter may be put with other similar letters. Its circulation is to be regretted.

Donald S.Swanson
Supt.

As far as the official police reports are concerned, the documents in this chapter are the last to appear in the official Whitechapel Murders files. It is, perhaps, appropriate that the official record ends here, on a speculative note about an anonymous letter signed "Jack the Ripper".

Sources

The Metropolitan Police (MEPO) FIles and Home Office (HO) Files are held on microfilm at the Public Record Office.

CHAPTER 1: 3 April 1888 – Murder of Emma Smith (pp. 3–7)

1 St. B.G./Wh/123/19. (London Metropolitan Archives)

CHAPTER 2: 7 August 1888 – Murder of Martha Tabram (pp. 8–20

1 Ref. MEPO 3/140, f 34
2 Ref. MEPO 3/140, ff. 44–8
3 ACB = Alexander Carmichael Bruce, Assistant Commissioner (CID)
4 Ref. MEPO 3/140, ff. 49–51
5 Ref. MEPO 3/140, ff. 52–9
6 Ref. MEPO 3/140, ff. 36–42
7 Ref. MEPO 3/140, f 43

CHAPTER 3: 31 August 1888 – Murder of Mary Ann Nichols (pp. 21–48)

1 Ref. MEPO 3/140, f 238
2 Ref. MEPO 3/140, ff. 239–41
3 Ref. MEPO 3/140, ff. 235–8
4 Ref. HO 144/220/A49301B, f177
5 Ref. HO 144/220/A49301B, f 178
6 Ref. HO 144/220/A49301B, f 179
7 Ref. HO 144/220/A49301, f 16
8 Ref. HO 144/221/A49301C, ff. 129–34
9 Ref. HO 144/221/A49301C, f 128
10 Ref. HO 144/221/A49301C, ff. 6–7
11 Ref. HO 144/221/A49301C, f 8
12 Ref. HO 144/221/A49301C, ff. 9–10
13 Ref. HO 144/221/A49301C, f 11

CHAPTER 4: 8 September 1888 – Murder of Annie Chapman (pp. 49–69)

 1 Ref. MEPO 3/140, ff. 9–11
 2 Ref. MEPO 3/140, f 11
 3 Ref. MEPO 3/140, ff. 12–13
 4 Ref. MEPO 3/140, ff. 13–15
 5 Ref. MEPO 3/140, ff. 16–17
 6 Ref. MEPO 3/140, ff. 15–16
 7 Ref. MEPO 3/140, ff. 17–20
 8 Ref. MEPO 3/140, f 20
 9 Ref. MEPO 3/140, ff. 21–3
10 Ref. MEPO 3/140, ff. 24–5
11 Ref. MEPO 3/140, ff. 26–8
12 Ref. MEPO 3/140, ff. 29–31
13 Ref. MEPO 3/140, ff. 242–56
14 Ref. HO 144/221/A49301C, f 136
15 Ref. HO 144/221/A49301C, ff. 137–45

CHAPTER 5: September 1888 – The Chapman Inquest and Police Enquiries (pp. 70–107)

 1 Ref. HO 144/221/A49301C, f 13
 2 Ref. HO 144/221/A49301C, ff. 14–15
 3 Ref. HO 144/221/A49301C, page 6 e-f
 4 Ref. HO 144/221/A49301C, ff. 16–17
 5 Ref. HO 144/221/A49301C, page 3f
 6 Ref. HO 144/221/A49301C, ff. 18–19
 7 Ref. *Sir Evelyn Ruggles-Brise* by Shane Leslie, London, 1938
 8 Ref. HO 144/221/A49301C, ff. 20–1

CHAPTER 6: September 1888 – Dr Anderson on Sick Leave and the Question of a Reward (pp. 108–19)

 1 Ref. HO 65/62, p 1
 2 Ref. HO 65/62, p 4
 3 Ref. HO 144/588/B5005
 4 In private collection
 5 Ref. HO 144/220/A49301B, ff. 180–1
 6 Ref. HO 144/220/A49301B, ff. 184–5
 7 Ref. MEPO 3/140, ff. 170–176, also copy filed under HO 144/220/A49301B, f 185
 8 Ref. MEPO 3/140, ff. 174–175 and HO 144/220/A49301B, ff. 182–3
 9 Ref. HO 144/220/A49301B, ff. 172–3
10 Ref. HO 144/220/A49301B, ff. 170–1
11 Ref. HO 144/220/A49301B, f 187

12 Ref. HO 144/220/A49301B, ff. 188–9
13 Ref. HO 144/220/A49301B, ff. 190–1
14 Ref. HO 144/221/A49301C, f 89
15 Ref. HO 144/221/A49301C, ff. 90–2
16 Ref. HO 144/221/A49301C, ff. 304–6

CHAPTER 7: 30 September 1888 – Murder of Elizabeth Stride (pp. 120–36)

 1 Ref. *The Times*, 1 October, p. 6f
 2 Ref. *The Times*, 2 October, p. 3f
 3 Ref. HO 144/221/A49301C, ff. 148–59
 4 Ref. MEPO 3/140/221/A49301C, ff. 204–6
 5 Ref. MEPO 3/140/221/A49301C, f 207
 6 Ref. MEPO 3/140/221/A49301C, ff. 208–210
 7 Ref. MEPO 3/140/221/A49301C, f 211
 8 Ref. MEPO 3/140/221/A49301C, ff. 212–14
 9 Ref. MEPO 3/140/221/A49301C, ff. 215–16
10 Ref. HO 144/221/A49301C, ff. 110–11
11 Ref. HO 144/221/A49301C, ff. 112–13
12 Ref. HO 144/221/A49301C, ff. 114–15
13 Ref. HO 144/221/A49301C, ff. 116–18
14 Ref. HO 144/221/A49301C, f 147
15 Ref. HO 144/221/A49301C, f 199
16 Ref. HO 144/221/A49301C, ff. 200–01

CHAPTER 8: October 1888 – The Stride Inquest (pp. 137–77)

All ref to *The Times*, 2 October 1888, page 6

CHAPTER 9: 30 September 1888 – Murder of Catherine Eddowes (pp. 178–98)

 1 Ref. HO 144/221/A49301C, ff. 162–70
 2 Ref. HO 144/221/A49301C, f 171
 3 Ref. HO 144/221/A49301C, f 172
 4 Ref. HO 144/221/A49301C, ff. 173–81
 5 Ref. HO 144/221/A49301C, f 183
 6 Ref. HO 144/221/A49301C, ff. 184–94
 7 Ref. HO 144/221/A49301C, ff. 195–6
 8 Ref. HO 144/221/A49301C, ff. 197–8
 9 Ref. MEPO 3/3153, f 1
10 Ref. MEPO 3/3153, ff. 2–4
11 1888 colour Police facsimile ref. MEPO 3/142, ff. 2–3
12 Ref. MEPO 3/142, ff. 491–2

13 Ref. the Littlechild letter, S.P. Evans private collection
14 Ref. p. 6b

CHAPTER 10: October 1888 – The Eddowes Inquest (pp. 199–238)

1 Ref. Coroner's inquest (L), 1888, No. 135, Catherine Eddowes inquest, 1888 (Corporation of London Record Office)

CHAPTER 11: October 1888 – Will the Unknown Killer Strike Again? (pp. 239–64)

1 Ref. page 3c
2 Ref. HO 144/220/A49301B, f 192
3 Ref. HO 144/220/A49301B, ff. 193–6
4 Ref. HO 144/220/A49301B, ff.197–8
5 Ref. HO 144/220/A49301B, ff. 199–200
6 Ref. HO 144/220/A49301B, f 201
7 Ref. HO 144/220/A49301B, f 202
8 Ref. HO 144/220/A49301B, f 203
9 Ref. HO 144/220/A49301B, ff. 204–11
10 Ref. HO 144/220/A49301B, ff. 212–13
11 Ref. HO 144/220/A49301B, ff. 214–19
12 Ref. HO 144/220/A49301B, f 220
13 Ref. HO 144/220/A49301B, f 221
14 Ref. HO 144/220/A49301B, ff. 222–3
15 Ref. HO 144/220/A49301B, f 224
16 Ref. HO 144/220/A49301B, ff. 225–7
17 Ref. HO 144/220/A49301B, f 228
18 Ref. HO 144/220/A49301B, ff. 229–30
19 Ref. HO 144/220/A49301B, ff. 231–2
20 Ref. HO 144/220/A49301B, f 233
21 Ref. HO 144/220/A49301B, ff. 234–6
22 Ref. HO 144/221/A49301C, f 64
23 Ref. HO 144/221/A49301C, f 65
24 Ref. HO 144/221/A49301C, f 52
25 Ref. HO 144/221/A49301C, ff 66–7
26 Ref. HO 144/221/A49301C, ff. 53–4
27 Ref. Ref. HO 144/221/A49301C, ff. 62–3
28 Ref. HO 144/221/A49301C, f 76
29 Ref. HO 144/221/A49301C, f 77
30 Ref. HO 144/221/A49301C, f 87–7
31 Ref. HO 144/221/A49301C, ff. 83–5
32 Ref. HO 144/221/A49301C, f 93
33 Ref. page 6e

CHAPTER 12: More on Rewards and October Precautions (pp. 265–90)

1 Ref. HO 144/220/A49301B, f 237
2 Ref. HO 144/220/A49301B, f 238
3 Ref. HO 144/220/A49301B, ff 239–45
4 Ref. HO 144/220/A49301B, ff. 246–52
5 Ref. HO/144/220/A49301B, f 253
6 Ref. HO 144/220/A49301B, ff. 255–7
7 Ref. MEPO 3/143
8 Ref. HO 144/220/A49301B, ff. 271–2
9 Ref. HO 144/220/A49301B, f 273
10 Ref. HO 144/220/A49301B, f 275
11 Ref. HO 144/220/A49301B, ff. 276–8
12 Ref. MEPO 3/141
13 Ref. MEPO 3/141, ff. 167–9
14 Ref. MEPO 3/141, ff. 164–6
15 Ref. MEPO 3/141, ff. 158–63
16 Ref. HO 65/62 pp. 355–6
17 Ref. MEPO 1/55, p 343
18 Ref. HO 144/220/A49301B, ff. 279–80
19 Ref. HO 144/220/A49301B, ff. 281–2
20 Ref. HO 144/220/A49301B, ff. 283–6
21 Ref. HO 144/220/A49301B, ff. 296–8

CHAPTER 13: The Bloodhounds (pp. 291–9)

1 Ref. HO 144/A49301E, ff. 8–9
2 Ref. HO 144/A49301E, ff. 11–12
3 Ref. HO 144/A49301E, f 10
4 Ref. HO 144/A49301E, f 13
5 Ref. HO 144/A49301E, ff. 14–16
6 Ref. MEPO 2, 188

CHAPTER 14: October 1888 – A Strange Story (pp. 300–5)

1 Ref. HO 144/221/A49301C f. 75
2 Ref. HO 144/221/A49301C, f. 71
3 Ref. HO 144/221/A49301C, f. 72
4 Ref. HO 144/221/A49301C, ff. 73–4
5 Ref. HO 144/221/A49301C, f. 13
6 Ref. HO 144/221/A49301C, f. 14
7 Ref. HO 144/221/A49301C, f. 15

CHAPTER 15: A Suspect Arrested in France (pp306–12)

1 Ref. HO 144/220/A49301, f 19

CHAPTER 16: October 1888 – A Person "Professes to be Able to Capture the Murderer" (pp 313–30)

1 Ref. HO 144/221/A49301D, ff. 23–6
2 Ref. HO 144/221/A49301D, ff. 27–8
3 Ref. HO 144/221/A49301D, ff. 29–31
4 Ref. HO 144/221/A49301D, ff. 32–3
5 Ref. HO 144/221/A49301D, f 34
6 Ref. HO 144/221/A49301D, ff. 36–47
7 Ref. HO 144/221/A49301D, f 48
8 Ref. HO 144/221/A49301D, f 49
9 Ref. HO 144/221/A49301D, f 56
10 Ref. HO 144/221/A49301D, f 54
11 Ref. HO 144/221/A49301D, f 57
12 Ref. HO 144/221/A49301D, ff. 58–61
13 Ref. HO 144/221/A49301D, f 62
14 Ref. HO 144/221/A49301D, f 63
15 Ref. HO 144/221/A49301D, f 64
16 Ref. HO 144/221/A49301D, ff. 65–6
17 Ref. HO 144/221/A49301D, f 67
18 Ref. HO 144/221/A49301D, f 71
19 Ref. HO 144/221/A49301D, ff. 72–3
20 Ref. HO 144/221/A49301D, f 74
21 Ref. HO 144/221/A49301D, ff. 75–6
22 Ref. HO 144/221/A49301D, f 77
23 Ref. HO 144/221/A49301D, ff. 78–80

CHAPTER 17: 15 October 1888 – A Dead Letter (pp. 331–3)

1 Ref. HO 144/221/A49301C, f 103
2 Ref. HO 144/221/A49301C, ff. 100–1
3 Ref. HO 144/221/A49301C, ff. 104–5
4 Ref. HO 144/221/A49301C, f 97
5 Ref. HO 144/221/A49301C, f 98
6 Ref. HO 144/221/A49301C, f 99
7 Ref. HO 65/62

CHAPTER 18: 9 November 1888 – Murder of Mary Jane Kelly (pp. 334–49)

1 Ref. MEPO 3/3153
2 Ref. HO 144/221/A49301F

3 Ref. HO 144/221/A49301C, ff. 78–9
4 Ref. HO 144/221/A49301C, ff. 42–6
5 Ref. MEPO 3/3153, ff. 10–18
6 Ref. HO 144/220/A49301B, f 299
7 Ref CAB 41, 21/17 (Public Record Office)

CHAPTER 19: November 1888 – Sir Charles Warren Resigns and Royal Involvement (pp. 350–8)

1 Ref. *The Times*, 10 October 1888, p. 5e
2 Ref. *The Times*, 13 November 1888, p. 10c
3 Ref. HO 144/221/A49301C, f 108
4 Ref. HO 144/221/A49301C, f 109
5 Ref. *The Times*, 16 November 1888, p.10f:
6 Ref. *The Times*, 21 November 1888, p. 6e
7 *The Letters of Queen Victoria* (3rd series, Vol. 1) ed. George Earle Buckle, pub. Murray, 1930
8 Ref. RA VIC/A67/19 (Royal Archives)
9 Ref. RA VIC/A67/18 (Royal Archives)
10 Ref. RA VIC/A67/20 (Royal Archives)
11 Ref. RA VIC/B40/82 (Royal Archives)

CHAPTER 20: 10 November 1888 – Dr Bond "Profiles" the Killer (pp. 359–62)

1 Ref. HO 144/221/A49301C, ff. 217–23
2 Ref. HO 144/221/A49301C, ff. 220–3

CHAPTER 21: 12 November 1888 – The Kelly Inquest (pp. 363–79)

1 Ref. MJ/SPC, NE1888, Box 3, Case Paper 19 (London Metropolitan Archives)
2 Ref. MJ/SPC, NE1888, Box 3, Case Paper 19 (London Metropolitan Archives)
3 Ref. MEPO 3/140, ff. 227–9
4 Ref. MEPO 3/140, ff. 230–2

CHAPTER 22: 21 November 1888 – A Second Outrage? (pp. 380–2)

1 Ref. *The Times*, 22 November 1888 p. 5e

CHAPTER 23: Police Activity Following the Kelly Murder (pp. 383–96)

1 Ref. HO144/221/A49310C, f 224
2 Ref. HO144/221/A49310C, f 225
3 Ref. HO144/221/A49301C, f 226
4 Ref. MEPO 3/141, f 149
5 Ref. HO144/221/A49301G, ff. 4–7
6 Ref. HO144/221/A49301G, ff. 10–11
7 Ref. HO144/221/A49301D, f 81
8 Ref. HO144/221/A49301D, f 82
9 Ref. HO144/221/A49301D, ff. 83–96
10 Ref HO144/221/A49301D, f 97
11 Ref. HO 144/221/A49301D, ff. 98–102
12 Ref. *The Times*, 19 November 1888 p. 6e

CHAPTER 24: Edward Knight Larkins – An Early "Ripper" Theorist (pp. 397–417)

1 Ref. HO 144/221/A49301C, f 230
2 Ref. HO 144/221/A49301C, f 233
3 Ref. HO 144/221/A49301C, ff. 235–6
4 Ref. HO 144/221/A49301C, ff. 237–8
5 Ref. HO 144/221/A49301C, ff. 239–45
6 Ref. HO 144/221/A49301C, f 247
7 Ref. HO 144/221/A49301C, f 248
8 Ref. HO 144/221/A49301C, ff. 249–50
9 Ref. HO 144/221/A49301C, f 259
10 Ref. HO 144/221/A49301C, ff. 260–4
11 Ref. HO 144/221/A49301C, f 262
12 Ref. HO 144/221/A49301C, f 263
13 Ref. HO 144/221/A49301C, f 264
14 Ref. HO 144/221/A49301C, ff. 68–70
15 Ref. HO 144/221/A49301C, f 70
16 Ref. HO 144/221/A49301C, f 265
17 Ref. HO 144/221/A49301C, f 279
18 Ref. HO 144/221/A49301C, f 280
19 Ref. HO 144/221/A49301C, f 270
20 Ref. HO 144/221/A49301C, f 271
21 Ref. HO 144/221/A49301C, f 273
22 Ref. HO 144/221/A49301C, ff. 274–8

CHAPTER 25: December 1888 – An American View (pp. 418–21)

1 folio ref 7–, [*illegible*]

CHAPTER 26: 20 December 1888 – Murder of Rose Mylett, alias Lizzie Davis (pp. 422–39)

1 Ref HO 144/221/A49301H, f 2
2 Ref HO 144/221/A49301H, ff. 3–4
3 Ref HO 144/221/A49301H, f 5
4 Ref HO 144/221/A49301H, f 6
5 Ref HO 144/221/A49301H, ff 7–14
6 Ref MEPO 3/140, ff. 1–2
7 Ref. MEPO 3/143
8 Ref. MEPO 3/143, f B
9 Ref. MEPO 3/143, ff. E-J
10 Ref. MEPO 3/143, f K
11 Ref. MEPO 3/143, ff. L-N
12 Ref. MEPO 3/143, f O
13 Ref. MEPO 3/143, ff. P-Q

CHAPTER 27: January 1889 Onwards – Continuing Vigilance in Whitechapel (pp. 440–7)

1 Ref. HO144/221/A49301G ff. 14–16
2 MEPO 3/141, ff. 4–5
3 Ref. HO144/221/A49301G f 17
4 Ref. HO144/221/A49301G f 18
5 Ref. HO144/221/A49301G ff. 19–20
6 Ref. HO 149/3, p 208
7 Ref. HO144/221/A49301G ff. 21–2
8 Ref. MEPO 3/141, ff. 139–44

CHAPTER 28: 17 July 1889 – Murder of Alice McKenzie (pp. 448–79)

1 Ref. MEPO 3/140, ff. 272–3
2 Ref. MEPO 3/140, f 274
3 Ref. MEPO 3/140 ff. 294–7
4 Ref. HO144/221/A49301I
5 Ref. HO144/221/A49301I ff. 5–6
6 Ref. HO144/221/A49301I Ref. ff. 7–10
7 Ref. MEPO 3/140, ff. 259–62
8 Ref. MEPO 3/140, ff. 263–71
9 Ref. MEPO 3/140, ff. 280–1
10 Ref. MEPO 3/140 ff. 279
11 Ref. MEPO 3/140 f 282
12 Ref. MEPO 3/140 f 283
13 Ref. MEPO 3/140 ff. 284–87
14 Ref. MEPO 3/140 f 288

15 Ref. MEPO 3/140, f 275
16 Ref. MEPO 3/140, f 276
17 Ref. MEPO 3/140, f 277
18 Ref. MEPO 3/140, f 289
19 Ref. MEPO 3/140, f 278
20 Ref. MEPO 3/140, ff. 290–1
21 Ref. MEPO 3/140, f 292
22 Ref. MEPO 3/140, f 293
23 Ref. MEPO 3/141, f 14
24 Ref. HO 144/220/A49301, ff. 17–18
25 Ref. MEPO 3/141, f 148
26 Ref. MEPO 3/141, ff
27 Ref. HO 144/220/A49301, ff. 24–31
28 Ref. HO144/221/A49301G, f 23
29 Ref. HO144/221/A49301G, ff. 24–5
30 Ref. HO144/221/A49301G, ff. 26–7
31 Ref. HO144/221/A49301G, ff. 28–9
32 Ref. MEPO 3/141, f 9
33 Ref. MEPO 3/141, ff. 10–12
34 Ref. MEPO 3/141, f 11
35 Ref. MEPO 3/141, f 12

CHAPTER 29: 10 September 1889 – Murder of an Unknown Woman (pp. 480–515)

 1 Ref. MEPO 3/140, f 123
 2 Ref. MEPO 3/140, ff. 136–40
 3 Ref. MEPO 3/140, ff. 148–50
 4 Ref. MEPO 3/140, f 151
 5 Ref. MEPO 3/140, ff. 134–5
 6 Ref. HO 144/221/A49301K, ff. 1–8
 7 Ref. MEPO 3/140, ff. 141–7
 8 Ref. MEPO 3/140, ff. 146–7
 9 Ref. MEPO 3/140, ff. 153–7
10 Ref. MEPO 3/140, ff. 162–4
11 Ref. MEPO 2/227, f 9 (document damaged)
12 Ref. HO 144/221/A49301K, ff 7–8
13 Ref. MEPO 3/140, ff. 158–9
14 Ref. MEPO 3/140, ff. 160–1
15 Ref. MEPO 3/140, f 165
16 Ref. MEPO 3/140, ff. 166–9
17 Ref. MEPO 3/140, ff. 170–3
18 Ref. MEPO 3/3153, f 20
19 Ref. MEPO 3/140, f 175
20 Ref. MEPO 3/140, ff. 174–5
21 Ref. MEPO 3/140, ff 176–7
22 Ref. MEPO 3/140, ff. 178–80

CHAPTER 30: Inspector Moore Interviewed About the Whitechapel Murders (pp. 516–20)

All taken from *Pall Mall Gazette*, 4 November 1889

CHAPTER 31: An Allegation Against Sergeant Thick – Further Allowance Claims (pp. 521–35)

 1 Ref. HO 144/220/A49301, f 35
 2 Ref. HO 144/220/A49301, f 36
 3 Ref. HO 144/220/A49301, f 46
 4 Ref. HO 144/220/A49301, f 47
 5 Ref. MEPO 3/141, f 15
 6 Ref. MEPO 3/141, f 13
 7 Ref. HO144/221/A49301G, ff. 30–2
 8 Ref. MEPO 3/141, f 16
 9 Ref. MEPO 3/141, f 18
10 Ref. MEPO 3/141, f 18
11 Ref. MEPO 3/141, f 19
12 Ref. MEPO 3/141, f 21
13 Ref. MEPO 3/141, the first being f 23
14 Ref. MEPO 3/141, f 22
15 Ref. HO144/221/A49301G
16 Ref. HO144/221/A49301G, f 33
17 Ref. HO144/221/A49301G, f 34
18 Ref. MEPO 3/141, f 25
19 Ref. MEPO 3/141, f 24
20 Ref. MEPO 3/141, f 26
21 Ref. HO144/221/A49301I f1
22 Ref. HO 144/220/A49301, ff. 32–4
23 Ref. HO144/221/A49301G, f 35
24 Ref. HO144/221/A49301G, f 36
25 Ref. MEPO 3/141, f 29
26 Ref. MEPO 3/141, f 27
27 Ref. HO/144/221/A49301G, f 37
28 Ref. HO144/221/A49301G, f 38
29 Ref. MEPO 3/141, f 30
30 Ref. HO/144/221/A49301G, f 39
31 Ref. HO144/221/A49301G, f 40

CHAPTER 32: September 1889 – Dr Forbes Winslow Names a Suspect (pp. 536–40)

Ref. photocopies of now-missing files

CHAPTER 33: October 1889 – Another Extraordinary Suspect (pp. 541–5)

1 Ref. HO 144/220/A49301, f 37
2 Ref. HO 144/220/A49301, ff. 38–9
3 Ref. HO 144/220/A49301, f 42
4 Ref. HO 144/220/A49301, f 43
5 Ref. HO 144/220/A49301, ff. 44–5

CHAPTER 34: November 1889 – Another Foreign Suspect (pp. 546–51)

1 Ref. HO 144/221/A49301D, f 1
2 Ref. HO 144/221/A49301D, ff. 2–13
3 Ref. HO 144/221/A49301D, f 22
4 Ref. HO 144/221/A49301D, ff. 51–3
5 Ref. HO 144/221/A49301D, f 53A
6 Ref. HO 144/221/A49301D, f 50

CHAPTER 35: 13 February 1891 – Murder of Frances Coles (pp. 552–76)

1 Ref. MEPO 3/140, ff. 112–4
2 Ref. MEPO 3/140, f 116
3 Ref. MEPO 3/140, ff. 117–8
4 Ref. MEPO 3/140, ff. 97–108
5 Ref. MEPO 3/140, ff. 119–21
6 Ref. MEPO 3/140, ff. 64–5
7 Ref. MEPO 3/140, ff 65–74
8 Ref. MEPO 3/140, ff. 83–5
9 Ref. MEPO 3/140, ff. 81–2
10 Ref. MEPO 3/140, ff. 88–90
11 Ref. MEPO 3/140 ff. 75–8
12 Ref. MEPO 3/140, ff. 79–80
13 Ref. MEPO 3/140 ff. 86–8
14 Ref. HO144/221/A49301G, f 1
15 Ref. HO144/221/A49301G, ff. 2–3
16 Ref. MEPO 3/141, f 32
17 Ref. MEPO 3/141, f 31
18 Ref. MEPO 3/140, f 91
19 Ref. MEPO 3/140, ff. 89–90
20 Ref. MEPO 3/140, ff. 92–3
21 Ref. MEPO 3/140, ff. 94–5
22 Ref. MEPO 3/140, ff. 96–7
23 Ref. MEPO 3/140, f 109
24 Ref. MEPO 3/140, f 110
25 Ref. MEPO 3/140, f 111

CHAPTER 36: May 1892 – Frederick Bailey Deeming (pp. 577-82)

1 Ref. HO 144/221/A49301C, f 266
2 Ref. HO 144/221/A49301C, f 269
3 Ref. HO 144/221/A49301C, ff. 267–8

CHAPTER 37: 23 February 1894 – Suspects Named By Chief Constable M.L. Macnaghten (pp. 583–91)

1 Ref. HO 395/1
2 Ref. MEPO 3/140, ff. 177–83
3 Ref. MEPO 6/15

CHAPTER 38: The Missing Suspects Files (pp. 592–604)

1 Under MEPO 3/141, ff. 32–135

CHAPTER 39: December 1888 – Another Contemporary Suspect (pp. 605–10)

1 Ref. CLRO Police Box 3.23 No. 390 (Corporation of London Record Office)

CHAPTER 40: The Littlechild Suspect (pp. 611–22)

1 Ref. CRIM 10/34 (Public Record Office)

CHAPTER 41: The Anderson Suspect (pp. 623–36)

1 Ref. *Windsor Magazine*, Vol. 1, January–June 1895, p. 507
2 Ref. *The Nineteenth Century*, February 1901
3 Ref. *Daily Chronicle*, 1 September 1908

CHAPTER 42: A City Police Suspect (pp. 637–44)

1 Ref. *Thomson's Weekly News*, Saturday, 1 December 1906

CHAPTER 43: Chief Inspector Abberline and the Chapman Theory (pp. 645–51)

Refs to *Pall Mall Gazette*

CHAPTER 44: 14 October 1896 – A Letter From "Jack the Ripper" (pp. 652–5)

1 Ref. MEPO 3/142, ff. 234–5
2 Ref. MEPO 3/142, f 211
3 Ref. MEPO 3/142, f 116
4 Ref. MEPO 3/142, ff. 157–9

Appendix 1

Chronicle of Events 1888–96

1888

3 April: Emma Elizabeth Smith, a 45-year-old widow, lodging at 18 George Street, Spitalfields, assaulted and robbed in Whitechapel Road/Osborn Street, by three men, one of them aged only about 19 years. Her head was bruised and a blunt instrument was thrust up her vagina, rupturing the peritoneum.

4 April: 9.00 a.m. – Emma Smith died of peritonitis at the London Hospital.

4 August: John Pizer appears before Thames Magistrates charged with indecent assault, but the case is dismissed.

7 August: Martha Tabram (Turner) murdered on first-floor landing of George Yard Buildings, Whitechapel.

31 August: Friday: Mary Ann "Polly" Nichols, murdered in Buck's Row, Whitechapel, her throat cut and abdomen mutilated. Dr Robert Anderson takes up position as Assistant Commissioner CID at Scotland Yard.

1 September: Saturday: Inquest into the death of Nichols opened by coroner Wynne Baxter, adjourned to 3 September.

3 September: Monday: inquest resumed into the death of Nichols, adjourned to 17 September.

4 September: Tuesday: press reports refer to a suspect, "Leather Apron," being sought by the police in connection with the murders.

6 September: Thursday: funeral of Mary Ann Nichols, interred at Little Ilford Cemetery.

7 September: Friday: Dr Anderson begins sick leave, and sets off for a holiday in Switzerland.

8 September: Saturday: Annie Chapman is murdered in rear yard of 29 Hanbury Street, Spitalfields, her throat cut, body mutilated and uterus and two brass rings taken by killer.

10 September: Monday: MP Samuel Montagu offers a £100 reward for the capture of the murderer. George Lusk is elected as chairman of the newly formed Whitechapel Vigilance Committee. John Pizer is arrested by Sgt Thick on suspicion of the Whitechapel murders.

11 September: Tuesday: Doctors Cowan and Crabb inform the police of their suspicion that a Holloway butcher, Joseph Isenschmid, is insane and is the murderer.

12 September: Wednesday: the Chapman inquest is opened by coroner Wynne Baxter, adjourned until 13 September.

13 September: Thursday: Chapman inquest reconvened, adjourned until 19 September.

14 September: Friday: Edward McKenna, an itinerant pedlar, arrested on suspicion of being concerned in the murders but subsequently released. Chapman inquest reconvened and adjourned until 19 September. Funeral of Annie Chapman, interred at Manor Park Cemetery.

17 September: Monday: Nichols's inquest reconvened and adjourned to 23 September. Isenschmid confined in Fairfield Row Asylum, Bow.

18 September: Tuesday: Charles Ludwig threatens a prostitute, Elizabeth Burns, with a knife and subsequently threatens Alexander Freinburg with a knife, at a coffee stall, resulting in his arrest.

19 September: Wednesday: Chapman inquest reconvened, adjourned to 26 September.

23 September: Saturday: final day of Nichols inquest.

25 September: Monday: date on the "Dear Boss" letter purporting to come from "Jack the Ripper".

26 September: Tuesday: final day of Chapman inquest.

27 September: Wednesday: date of postmark on the "Dear Boss" letter, which is received at the offices of the Central News Agency, New Bridge Street, Ludgate Circus.

29 September: Saturday: Tom Bulling of the Central News Agency sends the "Dear Boss" letter to Chief Constable Williamson at Scotland Yard. Catherine Eddowes is arrested for drunkenness in Aldgate High Street and taken to Bishopsgate Street Police Station.

30 September: Sunday: the body of Elizabeth Stride found with throat cut at approximately 1.00 a.m. in entrance to Dutfield's Yard, Berner Street, St George's-in-the-East. At this time Catherine Eddowes was released from custody at Bishopsgate Street Police Station and walked off in direction of Houndsditch. At 1.35 a.m. three Jews leaving the Imperial Club in Duke Street, Aldgate see a man and a woman talking at the end of Church Passage (leading into Mitre Square). At 1.45 a.m. body of Catherine Eddowes found in southernmost corner of Mitre Square by City PC Watkins on patrol. Her throat is cut, face and abdomen badly mutilated and the uterus and left kidney are missing.

1 October: Monday: inquest into the death of Elizabeth Stride opened by coroner Wynne Baxter, adjourned to following day. Text of the "Dear Boss" letter published in the *Daily News*. A postcard, postmarked this day, is again addressed to the Central News and signed "Jack the Ripper." Bulling sends this to the police.

2 October: Tuesday: Stride inquest resumed, adjourned to the next day.

4 October: Thursday: inquest into the death of Catherine Eddowes is opened by coroner Langham, adjourned to 5 October. Matthew Packer is taken by private detectives to view the body of Stride as he believes he sold grapes to her killer. Facsimiles of the "Dear Boss" letter and the postcard are published in the *Evening Standard*.

5 October: Friday: inquest resumed into the death of Elizabeth Stride, adjourned to 23 October. Bulling forwards a third communication to the police.

6 October: Saturday: funeral of Elizabeth Stride, interred at the East London Cemetery.

8 October: Monday: funeral of Catherine Eddowes, interred at Little Ilford Cemetery.

9 October: Tuesday: bloodhounds tried out by police at Regent's Park.

10 October: Wednesday: further test of bloodhounds in Hyde Park.

11 October: Thursday: final day of the Eddowes inquest.

12 October: Friday: Consul E.W. Bonham at Boulogne contacts police with information on suspect John Langan, an American detained at Boulogne. Suspected because he resembled a drawing of the supposed killer published in the *Daily Telegraph*.

15 October: Monday: shortly after 1.00 p.m. a suspicious male enters a shop at 218 Jubilee Street, Mile End Road, and asks Emily Marsh for George Lusk's address. She gives him the address from a newspaper.

16 October: Tuesday: Langan cleared of suspicion. George Lusk of the White-chapel Vigilance Committee receives a small package through the post containing half a human kidney and a letter addressed "From hell".

23 October: Tuesday: final day of the Stride inquest.

30 October: Tuesday: row between Joseph Barnett and Mary Jane Kelly at 13 Miller's Court, 26 Dorset Street, results in Barnett leaving Kelly.

8 November: Thursday: Sir Charles Warren, Chief Commissioner of the Metropolitan Police, tenders his resignation after disputes with the Home Office and an article he published, without permission, in *Murray's Magazine*.

9 November: Friday: murder of Mary Jane Kelly at Room 13, Miller's Court, 26 Dorset Street, Spitalfields. Her throat is cut and the body and face fearfully mutilated. Evidence suggests her heart is missing. Resignation of Sir Charles Warren accepted and announced.

10 November: Saturday: Dr Thomas Bond, Police Surgeon for A Division, submits a lengthy report to the Commissioner of Police regarding the murders and possible description of the unknown murderer. Pardon offered to "anyone other than the murderer who has information . . ." by the Home Office.

12 November: Monday: inquest, one day only, into the death of Mary Jane Kelly held in Shoreditch by coroner Dr Roderick Macdonald. Labourer George Hutchinson goes into Commercial Street Police Station to report that he saw Kelly with a stranger shortly before she was murdered. He makes a witness statement and is interrogated by Inspector Abberline.

17 November: Saturday: Nikaner Benelius, a Swede, is arrested by PC Imhoff for burglary at Harriet Rowe's house. Briefly suspected of the murders, he is later cleared of all charges.

19 November: Monday: funeral of Mary Jane Kelly, interred at Leytonstone Roman Catholic Cemetery.

20 November: Tuesday: Annie Farmer attacked in lodgings in George Street. Suspected "Ripper" attack, but later found not to be the case.

6 December: Thursday: Joseph Isaacs arrested and charged with stealing a watch. Press speculation was that he was the "Ripper".

20 December: Thursday: murder of Rose Mylett in Clarke's Yard, High Street, Poplar.

21 December: Friday: inquest opens into death of Rose Mylett.

24 December: Monday: George Marsh makes statement to police at instigation of Robert Stephenson to the effect that a Dr Morgan Davies at the London Hospital is "Jack the Ripper".

26 December: Wednesday: Robert Stephenson makes a statement at Scotland Yard accusing Dr Morgan Davies of being the murderer.

1889

3 January: Friday: second day of Mylett inquest, adjourned to 9 January.

9 January: Thursday: final day of Mylett inquest.

17 July: Murder of Alice McKenzie in Castle Alley, Whitechapel, her throat cut and superficial mutilation to abdomen. Inquest into her death opened and adjourned to 19 July.

19 July: McKenzie inquest resumed and adjourned to 14 August.

23 July: Revd. Samuel Barnett's letter about degradation in Whitechapel is published in *The Times*.

14 August: Final day of the McKenzie inquest.

10 September: Torso of a woman, minus head and legs, is found under a railway arch in Pinchin Street, St Georges-in-the-East.

1891

11 February: Wednesday: Frances Coles is met by Thomas Sadler.

13 February: Friday: Frances Coles is murdered in Swallow Gardens, Whitechapel, under a railway arch.

14 February: Saturday: Thomas Sadler is arrested on suspicion of murder. It is believed that he may be "Jack the Ripper". Inquest into the death of Frances Coles is opened by coroner Wynne Baxter at the Working Lads' Institute, Whitechapel, and adjourned to 16 February.

14–17 February: Sadler is put up for identification by Lawende, witness of the City Police in the Eddowes murder case, but Lawende is unable to identify him.

17 February: Tuesday: Coles inquest resumed into the death of Frances Coles, adjourned to 20 February.

20 February: Friday: Coles inquest resumed, adjourned to 23 February.

23 February: Monday: Coles inquest resumed and adjourned to 27 February.

27 February: Friday: final day of Coles inquest.

1894

23 February: Sir Melville Macnaghten writes his report naming Druitt, Ostrog and Kosminski as Ripper suspects.

1896

14 October: Police receive anonymous letter signed "Jack the Ripper". Comparison is made with letter dated 25 September 1888 and postcard bearing postmark 1 October 1888.

Appendix 2

Notes on Senior Police and Home Office Officials

(Appearing in the official files on the Whitechapel Murders)

Police Officials

ABBERLINE, Inspector Frederick George (1843–1929)
Born in Blandford, Dorset, 8 January 1843. Scotland Yard Central Office Detective Inspector (first-class) involved in, and in charge of, enquiries in the East End into the Whitechapel murders from September 1888 until c. March 1889. Worked as a clocksmith before joining the Metropolitan Police on 5 January 1863. Promoted to Sergeant 19 August 1865, and to Inspector 10 March 1873, and transferred to H Whitechapel Division on 13 March 1873. On 8 April 1878 appointed Local Inspector in charge of the H Division CID. On 26 February 1887 he transferred to A Division and then to Central Office at Scotland Yard on 19 November 1887. Promoted to Inspector first-class on 9 February 1888, and to Chief Inspector on 22 December 1890. He retired in this rank on 8 February 1892, on a full pension. Worked as a private enquiry agent and in 1898 took on the European Agency of the Pinkerton Detective Company of America. In 1904 he retired to Bournemouth.

He married Martha Mackness in March 1868, and she died in May 1868 of TB. He married Emma Beament in 1876. He died in 1929, and Emma died the following year.

ANDERSON, Dr (later Sir) Robert (1841–1918)
Appointed Assistant Commissioner CID at Scotland Yard on 31 August 1888. Went on sick leave to Switzerland on 7 September 1888, not returning to Scotland Yard until the first week of October. In overall charge of the CID at the time of the Whitchapel Murders but did not take an active part in the investigation. Born in Dublin, Ireland, he took his BA in 1862 and was called to the Bar in Dublin the following year. In 1867 he moved to London and worked as deputy head of the anti-Fenian intelligence department. He remained as Home Office Adviser on political crime, and also remained active in intelligence work. In 1873 he married Lady Agnes Moore, sister of the ninth Earl of Drogheda. They had three sons and a daughter. He was called to the Bar in London in 1875, LLD, and was relieved of political duties in 1886. From 1887 to 1888 he was Secretary to the Prison Commissioners. He retired in 1901 and was knighted. He died on 15 November 1918, in his seventy-seventh year, of heart failure.

ANDREWS, Inspector Walter Simon (1847–99)
Born in Boulge, Suffolk, on 27 April 1847. He married Jane Carr on 4 August 1867 and joined the Metropolitan Police Force on 15 November 1869 and was promoted to Detective Sergeant on 18 November 1875. He was promoted to the rank of Inspector on 6 July 1878. He is recorded by ex-Chief Inspector Walter Dew in his book *I Caught Crippen*, as one of three inspectors (the others being Abberline and Moore) sent from Scotland Yard in September 1888 to conduct enquiries into the Whitechapel Murders. He was the officer who was sent to New York in December 1888 in an effort to trace the suspect Francis Tumblety who had "jumped" his bail in London in November 1888. He retired in 1889 and died by hanging himself on 26 August 1899 at Horndean in Hampshire.

ARNOLD, Superintendent Thomas (b. 1835)
Joined the Metropolitan Police Force in 1855, but resigned to volunteer for service in the Crimea. Returned to England in 1856 and rejoined the Force. Was head of H Whitechapel Division at the time of the murders.

BECK, Inspector Walter (b. 1852)
Joined Metropolitan Police Force in 1871. Was duty Inspector at time of the Kelly murder and attended the scene. Resigned 1896.

BRADFORD, Colonel Sir Edward Ridley Colborne, Bt (1836–1911)
Educated Marlborough. Madras Cavalry 1853; served in Persia 1856–57. In 1860 Colonel in command of 1st Indian Horse, and Political Assistant in West Malwa. Lost his left arm in 1867 to a tigress in a hunting incident. 1874–78, general supervisor of operations against thugees and dacoiti. In 1878 Governor-General's Agent, Rajputana, and Chief Commissioner, Ajmir. KCSI, 1885. In 1887 Secretary to Secret and Political Department, India Office, London. 1889–90 conducted Prince Albert Victor on Indian tour. From 1890–1903 Chief Commissioner of Metropolitan Police Force.

BRUCE, Sir Alexander Carmichael (1850–1926)
Born 1850, the fourth son of Canon David Bruce of Ferry Hill, Durham. Assistant Commissioner, Metropolitan Police, 1884–1914. Educated Brasenose College, Oxford. Took his degree in 1873. Called to the Bar, Lincoln's Inn, 1875, practising on the North-Eastern Circuit. Married Helen, daughter of Mr John Fletcher, DL of Bolton. Knighted 1908. Promoted to Senior Assistant Commissioner in August 1888, on appointment of Robert Anderson as Junior Assistant Commissioner. Bruce appears to have performed Anderson's duty as head of the Criminal Investigation Department whilst Anderson was on sick leave from 7 September to early October 1888. Recorded as attending the scenes of the murders at Buck's Row and Hanbury Street. Died 26 October 1926 at his residence in Egerton Terrace, London, SW.

CHANDLER, Inspector Joseph Luniss (b. 1850)
Joined Metropolitan Police in 1873. Was duty Inspector, H Division at time of Chapman murder. Demoted to Sergeant for being drunk on duty in 1892. Retired in 1898.

COLLARD, Inspector Edward (1846–92)
Joined City of London Police Force in 1868. Died in 1892 while Chief Inspector, Bishopsgate Division. Actively involved in the investigation of the murder of Catherine Eddowes in Mitre Square.

CUTBUSH, Superintendent Charles Henry (1844–96)
Executive Superintendent, Scotland Yard, at the time of the murders. In charge of Supplies and Pay. Committed suicide in his own kitchen as a result of chronic depression.

ELLISDON, Inspector Ernest (b. 1846)
Joined Metropolitan Police Force in 1868. Left and rejoined in 1872. Resigned in 1894.

FOSTER, Superintendent Alfred Lawrence (1826–97)
Educated King Edward's Grammar School, Warwick. Worked in a solicitor's office prior to joining the Prison Service, eventually becoming Deputy Governor at Clerkenwell House of Detention. In 1864 was invited by Colonel Fraser to serve in the City Police Force as Superintendent. Promoted to Chief Superintendent and resigned in 1892. Attended the scene of the murder in Mitre Square. Married with two daughters and five sons.

FRASER, Colonel Sir James (1814–92)
Entered the Army, attaining the rank of Colonel of the 54th Foot. In 1854 resigned his commission and became Chief Constable of Berkshire. Aspired to be Chief Commissioner of the Metropolitan Police Force but Sir Edward Henderson was appointed to that post. In 1863 became Commissioner of the City of London Police Force. Retired in 1890.

HELSON, Inspector Joseph Henry (b. 1845)
Born at Buckland Monachorum, Devon, on 11 April 1845. Joined the Metropolitan Police Force on 4 January 1869. Promoted to Sergeant and transferred to L Division on 29 May 1872. Promoted to Local Inspector J Division Bethnal Green 24 October 1887, replacing Inspector Reid in that post. Took charge of the Divisional investigation into the murder of Mary Ann Nichols in Buck's Row on 31 August 1888. Married, wife Mary. Retired 14 January 1895, at that time living at 41 Rutland Road, South Hackney.

LITTLECHILD, Chief Inspector John George (1847–1923)
Born on 21 December 1847, at Bassingbourne. Joined the Metropolitan Police Force on 18 February 1867. He married Susan Annie Brewer at Kensington on 12 July 1870. Their first daughter was born the same year. On 11 January 1871 he was transferred to Central Office CID and was promoted to Sergeant on 23 March 1871. He had two more daughters, born in 1871 and 1877, and a fourth in 1884. He was promoted to Inspector on 8 April 1878, and to Chief Inspector on 3 February 1882. In 1883 he was put in charge of the Special Branch at Scotland Yard, a post he held until his retirement on 10 April 1893. He then began work as a private enquiry agent,

at which he was very successful, working on the cases of Oscar Wilde and Harry Thaw. His wife died in 1909, and he himself died 2 January 1923 at Matlock of chronic Bright's disease.

MACNAGHTEN, Sir Melville Leslie (1853–1921)
Educated at Eton. From 1873–87 was overseer of the family tea plantations. Joined the Metropolitan Police Force as Assistant Chief Constable, CID, in June 1889. Promoted to Chief Constable in 1890 and was deputy to Anderson until Anderson's retirement in 1901. Promoted to Assistant Commissioner CID in 1903, a post he held until his retirement in 1913.

MCWILLIAM, Inspector James (unknown)
Head of the City Police Detective Department at the time of the Eddowes murder.

MONRO, James (1838–1920)
Educated Edinburgh High School, and Edinburgh and Berlin Universities. Entered ICS by examination in 1857. Was Assistant Magistrate, Collector, District Judge, and Inspector-General of Police, Bombay. Resigned 1884. Joined Metropolitan Police Force in 1884 as Assistant Commissioner and was head of the CID. Resigned in August 1888 and was replaced by Anderson. Became Chief Commissioner of the Metropolitan Police on the resignation of Warren in November 1888. Resigned in 1890 and founded and ran the Ranaghat Christian Medical Mission until 1903. He then returned to Scotland and subsequently to England.

MONSELL, Colonel Bolton James Alfred (1840–1917)
Was Chief Constable in the Metropolitan Police Force from 1886 to 1910. Head of the policing of the East End area at the time of the Whitechapel Murders. Died 2 February 1919, while resident at 1 Tedworth Square, Chelsea.

MOORE, Inspector Henry (1848–1918)
Born 2 June 1848 in Northamptonshire. Joined the Metropolitan Police Force 26 April 1869. Promoted to Sergeant 29 August 1872 and to Inspector 25 August 1878. Moved to Central Office CID on 30 April 1888. Advanced to Inspector 1st class on 22 December 1890, and appointed Chief Inspector 27 September 1895. Retired on 9 October 1899. Then joined the Great Eastern Railway Police as a Superintendent and retired in 1913. With Abberline and Andrews was one of the three Detective Inspectors sent from Central Office to the East End on the Whitechapel Murders investigation.

REID, Inspector Edmund John James (1846–1917)
Born in Canterbury, Kent on 21 March 1846. Married Emily Jane Wilson in 1868. Eventually had two children, a daughter and a son. After several different jobs joined the Metropolitan Police Force on 4 November 1872. Joined the Detective Department in 1874. Promoted to Sergeant in 1878 and to Detective Inspector in 1885 and transferred to Scotland Yard. Moved to

the new J, Bethnal Green, Division on 31 July 1886 and to H, Whitechapel Division in July 1887. He was thus the Local Inspector in charge of the H Division CID throughout the time of the Whitechapel Murders. He moved to L, Lambeth, Division on 9 December 1895 and retired on 27 February 1896. He moved back to Kent and worked as a private investigator and a publican. His wife Emily died in 1900 and he remarried in May 1917, to Lydia Rhoda Halling. He died on 5 December 1917 at Herne Bay, of chronic interstitial nephritis and a brain haemorrhage.

SHORE, Superintendent John (b. 1839)
Born at Farmborough, near Bath, Somersetshire on 11 November 1839. Joined Metropolitan Police Force 10 January 1859, having previously served as a police constable in Bristol. Promoted to Sergeant-temporary 9 April 1862. Made Detective Sergeant 17 September 1864. Promoted to Inspector 16 July 1869. Appointed Chief Inspector 3 December 1877. Promoted to Superintendent CID 15 July 1886. Moved to Central Office (CID) 19 November 1887. Superintendent at Scotland Yard at the time of the Ripper murders. He had replaced Williamson when the latter was promoted to Chief Constable. Retired 1 May 1896, at that time residing at 260 Kennington Park Road, London.

SMITH, Major Henry (1835–1921)
Acting Commissioner of the City of London Police at the time of the Whitechapel Murders. Educated Edinburgh Academy and University. Worked as bookkeeper in Glasgow and in 1869 was commissioned in the Suffolk Artillery Militia. Later became Lieutenant Colonel. In 1885 he was appointed Chief Superintendent in the City of London Police Force. Promoted to Commissioner of that Force in 1890, and retired in 1901. KCB in 1910.

SPRATLING, Inspector John (1840–1938)
Joined the Metropolitan Police in 1870. Was a uniformed Inspector in J, Bethnal Green, Division at the time of the Nichols murder.

SWANSON, Chief Inspector Donald Sutherland (1848–1924)
Born in Thurso, Scotland. Joined the Metropolitan Police Force in 1868. By November 1887 he was a Chief Inspector in the CID. Promoted to Superintendent in 1896, and retired in 1903. Was placed in charge of the overall supervision of the Whitechapel Murders enquiry in September 1888 by Warren.

WARREN, General Sir Charles (1840–1927)
Chief Commissioner of the Metropolitan Police Force at the time of the outbreak of the Whitechapel Murders. Educated Cheltenham, Sandhurst and Woolwich. Joined the Royal Engineers in 1857. In 1867 served in Palestine and there carried out some notable archaeological work. Returned to England in 1870 and was posted to Africa as Special Commissioner for the Colonial Office 1876–87, for which he received the CMG. Commanded

Diamond Fields Horse in Kaffir War of 1877–8, and was badly wounded. Promoted to Lieutenant-Colonel and returned to England in 1880, as Chief Instructor, School of Military Engineering, Chatham. In 1882 led a search in Egypt for the missing expedition of Professor Edward Palmer, the members of which had been murdered. Warren ensured the punishment of the culprits. Awarded KCMG, and in 1884 participated in an expedition to relieve General Gordon at Khartoum. He was then sent to restore order in Bechuanaland and was awarded the GCMG. Commanded troops in Suakim, before recall to England. In 1886 he succeeded Sir Edward Henderson as Chief Commissioner of the Metropolitan Police Force. Resigned in November 1888 and returned to his Army career. He played a controversial role in the Battle of Spion Kop during the Boer War. In the latter years of his life he was involved in the Boy Scout movement.

WEST, Chief Inspector John (b. 1842)
Born Woodford, Essex, on 17 July 1842. Joined Metropolitan Police Force 6 February 1865. Joined N Division, promoted to Sergeant 19 January 1869. Transferred to V Division on 26 January 1869. Appointed to station Sergeant on 19 May 1873, and promoted to Inspector and transferred to G Division on 21 February 1877. Transferred to K Division on 14 July 1877. Promoted to Chief Inspector on 1 April 1884, and transferred to H, Whitechapel Division. Retired on 8 June 1891, at which time he was living at 7 Alfred Buildings, Cartwright Street, London.

WILLIAMSON, Chief Constable Adolphus Frederick (1830–89)
Joined the Metropolitan Police Force in 1850. Promoted to Sergeant in the Detective Department in 1852 and to Inspector in 1863. Promoted to Chief Inspector in 1867, and Superintendent in 1870. In 1886 he became Chief Constable in the CID, at a time that it was unheard of for a career officer to achieve such a high rank. He was enormously experienced, and was prominently involved in the investigation of the Kent murder case in the 1860s. Anderson relied heavily on Williamson's advice and experience. Williamson suffered from a bad heart and died, still in harness, on 9 December 1889.

Home Office Officials

BYRNE, William Patrick, KCVO (1859–1935)
Born 12 February 1859, the fourth son of Mr John Byrne of Withington. Educated St. Cuthbert's College, Ushaw, London, and St Bede's College, Manchester. Entered Civil Service (Post Office) 1881 as a clerk. Transferred to the Home Office as a junior clerk 1884. In 1886 was called to the Bar by Gray's Inn, of which he became a Bencher in 1908 and Treasurer in 1915 and 1916. He was made a CB in 1902, and KCVO in 1911. In 1891 he was appointed as Permanent Under-Secretary of State, and as Secretary of State in 1895. In 1896 he was promoted to be a Senior Clerk, and to be Assistant Under-Secretary 1908. Chairman of the Board of Control, 1913. In 1916 he was called to Dublin as a member of the Committee of Inquiry into the

connection of certain Civil Servants with the Easter Rising. In February of the same year he was appointed Under-Secretary to the Lord Lieutenant of Ireland (Lord Wimborne). He resigned in July 1918. He returned to the post of chairman of the Board of Control for Lunacy and Mental Deficiency, to which he had been appointed in 1913. He held the post until he retired on 24 June 1921. He was twice married but left no issue. He had a villa in Monaco and was a member of the Reform Club. He died 11 June 1935, and a requiem Mass was celebrated at the Brompton Oratory on 14 June 1935. He was buried at Brompton Cemetery.

DELVIGNE, Malcolm, KCVO (1868–1950)
Educated City of London School, Oxford (*literae humaniores* 1st); Civil Service Local Government Board 1892; Home Office junior clerk 1892; Assistant Under-Secretary 1913; retired Deputy Under-Secretary 1932.

LUSHINGTON, Godfrey, KCB, GCMG (1832–1907)
Born 8 March 1832, the fifth and youngest son of Dr Lushington. Educated Rugby and Balliol College, Oxford (classical moderations 1st; maths 4th). He was in the Cricket Eleven and was good at all games, especially tennis, which he played until he was well past fifty. Called to the Bar by the Inner Temple. In 1865 he married Beatrice Anne Shore, daughter of Mr Samuel Smith, of Combs Hurst, Surrey. In 1869, being then a barrister of eleven years' standing, he was nominated as counsel to the Home Office. Assistant Under-Secretary 1875, Permanent Under-Secretary 1885–95. He retired in 1895. He died 5 February 1907 at his residence at 34 Old Queen Street, London, S.W. The death was sudden and unexpected as he appeared to have been in good health. The funeral took place at St Katharine's, Savernake.

MATTHEWS, Henry MP, PC, Viscount Llandaff 1895 (1826–1913)
Educated abroad (France), he took his Doctorate in Paris. A devout Roman Catholic. Home Secretary 1886–92. Was advised and aided by his private secretary, Ruggles-Brise. At one stage Matthews wished to promote Ruggles to be Assistant Commissioner of Police under Monro at Scotland Yard, when an Assistant Commissionership was vacant in 1889.

MURDOCH, Charles S., CB (1838–1900)
Home Office 3rd class clerk 1856. Assistant Under-Secretary 1896, retired at same level in 1903.

PEMBERTON, Edward Leigh, KCB (1823–1910)
Born 14 May 1823, son of Edward Leigh Pemberton of Torry Hill, Kent. Educated Eton and Oxford (BA), barrister and Member of Parliament. Graduated in 1845, and was called to the Bar by Lincoln's Inn in 1847. Married the elder daughter of the Rev. the Hon. Francis James Noel in August 1849. In 1869 he was returned as a Conservative to represent East Kent in the House of Commons. He was a Major in the East Kent Yeomanry Cavalry and a deputy lieutenant and magistrate for Kent. Home Office Legal Assistant to the Under-Secretary 1885. Retired as same in 1894. Made a CB

in 1896 and KCB in 1898. Died on 1 February 1910 at his residence in Warwick Square, London, SW.

RUGGLES-BRISE, Evelyn, KCB (1857–1935)
Father was a country gentleman. Educated Eton and Oxford (*literae humaniores* 1st). Succeeded in the Civil Service Commission exam of 1881. Home Office Junior Clerk 1881. Private Secretary to the Home Secretary (Matthews) at the time of the Whitechapel Murders. Prison Commissioner 1891, Chairman same 1895. Married Jessie Philippa Carew in 1914. She died in 1928 and he remarried in 1933, to Sheela Maud Emily Chichester.

SIMPSON, Harry Butler, CB (1861–1940)
Educated Winchester and Magdalen College, Oxford (*lit. hum.* 1st). Married Eva, daughter of Colonel C.B. LeMesurier. A barrister-at-law, he became a Home Office junior clerk in 1884. Retired as Assistant Secretary 1925. His publications included *Cross Lights* and magazine articles. Died 12 August 1940, at which time his address was Colts, Kingwood, Henley-on-Thames.

STUART-WORTLEY, Charles Beilby, (Lord Stuart of Wortley) (1851–1926)
Born 15 September 1851, and sent to Eton in 1864, then transferred to Rugby. Went to Balliol in 1870, obtained Honours in classics and the law. Took degree in 1875 and called to the Bar, Inner Temple, in 1876. In 1880 married Beatrice Trollope, who died in 1881, then married Alice Millais in 1886. Went to the North-Eastern Circuit and took silk in 1892. In 1880 became Conservative Member for Sheffield, and in 1885 was returned for the Hallam Division. In 1885 appointed Under-Secretary at the Home Office under Sir R.A. Cross, and in 1886 returned to the post under Henry Matthews until the fall of that Government in 1892. Raised to the peerage as Lord Stuart of Wortley of the City of Sheffield in 1916. Died at his London residence, 7 Cheyne Walk, S.W. on Saturday, 24 April 1926.

TROUP, Charles Edward, KCB, KCVO (1857–1941)
Born in 1857, the son of the Rev. R. Troup of Huntley, Aberdeen. Educated Scottish parish school, Aberdeen (mental philosophy 1st), Balliol College, Oxford (BA). Later called to the Bar by the Middle Temple. He was editor of the "Judicial Statistics for England and Wales" for many years. Home Office junior clerk 1880. Married in 1897 to Winifred Louise, youngest daughter of Dr George MacDonald, poet and novelist. They had no children. Assistant Under-Secretary 1903. Permanent Under-Secretary 1908–22. He was an astute and talented Civil Servant of exceptional ability. He died at Addison Road, London, W., on 8 July 1941.

Index

The names and locations of murder victims are indicated in bold type.

11/07 ⑦ 06/07 ⑤
9/14 ⑬